GUIDE

TO COUNTY RECORDS

IN THE NORTH CAROLINA

STATE ARCHIVES

Twelfth Revised Edition

Department of Cultural Resources
Office of Archives and History
2009

ISBN 978-0-86526-342-0

Background document on front cover: Deed from Robert Blackburn and his wife to Thomas Welsh, July 20, 1769, from Tryon County Miscellaneous Records, 1765–1783, State Archives, N.C. Office of Archives and History, Raleigh, N.C.

Printed by Edwards Brothers

CONTENTS

County Records

INTRODUCTION

Since 1963, the North Carolina State Archives has been publishing guides to its holdings, including state agency records, county records, private manuscript collections, and Civil War material. Each edition has been expanded and improved, and this twelfth revised edition has been renamed the *Guide to County Records in the North Carolina State Archives*. It is the responsibility of the head of the Local Records Unit to update and revise this *Guide* periodically as county and municipal records are added to the collection. This edition describes more than 13,000 bound volumes and 22,000 boxes of loose records, as well as over 24,000 reels of microfilm, all of which are available to researchers in the State Archives, as of March 1, 2009.

The North Carolina State Archives began systematically seeking and accepting noncurrent local records from the counties in 1916 under authority of a 1907 statute permitting their transfer to the Archives. Thanks in large measure to the tactful determination of Col. Fred A. Olds, director of the Hall of History, seven counties—Carteret, Chowan, Edgecombe, Halifax, Orange, Perquimans, and Wilkes—took advantage of the act and transferred some of their oldest records to the Archives. Forty additional counties had followed suit by 1924, and the handbook issued that year describing the county records in the Archives included approximately 500 volumes, 90 boxes of loose papers, and 414 boxes of marriage bonds. By the time the Historical Records Survey of the Works Progress Administration inventoried the county records in the Archives in 1938, the counties had transferred another 950 volumes, 100 boxes of papers, and 160,000 documents. In 1941 the Archives, with the assistance of the Genealogical Society of Utah, commenced a program of microfilming many of the records that were generally retained in the counties, such as will books and deed books. World War II interrupted this program, and the Archives did not fully resume it until ten years thereafter.

In 1957, the General Assembly authorized the creation of an "inspector of county records," whose task it would be to visit all the courthouses in the state and, with his staff, inventory the records he found, microfilm volumes of permanent value for purposes of security, determine which of the records were not worth permanent preservation, set up schedules for the orderly transfer of permanently valuable noncurrent records to the Archives, and arrange and describe them for public use once they were there. This officer and his staff provided a solid foundation for an effective local records program. By 1970, the local records staff had completed records inventories and disposition schedules for all one hundred counties, and many county officials had taken advantage of the opportunity to free up storage space in their offices.

In 1981, an internal reorganization of the Archives and Records Section divided the functions of the local records program between the Records Services Branch, which helped counties and municipalities manage their records through scheduling, microfilming, and records-keeping consultations, and the Archival Services Branch, which appraised, arranged, described, and referenced the permanently valuable county records that had been sent to the State Archives in accordance with the disposition schedules. By the time of the reorganization, the local records staff had produced more than 46,000 reels of microfilm, many for security purposes only; supervised the restoration and rebinding of over 2,800 volumes in the Archives and in the counties; and encouraged the voluntary transfer of some 5,900 volumes and 6,000 cubic feet of loose records.

In October 2000, the Archives and Records Section was again realigned, creating a five-branch structure. The Records Services Branch was reorganized and renamed the Government Records Branch. The reorganized branch gained control of the arrangement and description function for the section (both state and local records), creating the Records Description Unit. Because of budget cuts and the loss of a position, the Records Description Unit was reorganized again on November 1, 2003. The functions of the Local Records Unit and the Records Description Unit (county records portion) were merged to form a reorganized Local Records Unit. The Local Records Unit provides services to local officials throughout the life cycle of the records created and used within their parent agencies. These services include consulting with local agencies on records management issues; analyzing records and writing retention schedules; providing advice on records preservation at the local level; transferring records to the State Archives for permanent preservation; and arranging and describing those records for access by researchers in the State Archives Search Room.

The vast majority of the records listed in this guide have been transferred to the State Archives from the offices of clerks of superior court and registers of deeds. Others have originated in the offices of tax supervisors, boards of county commissioners, boards of education, health departments, and social services directors. The Archives maintains a precise registration of the provenance of the county records in its custody, although there is some confusion as to the office of origin and date of transfer of certain records received in the early years of the program. Researchers needing such information are encouraged to contact the registrar of the Archives and Records Section.

Microfilm of county records has been produced either from originals that have been transferred to the State Archives or from volumes retained by the counties. Much of this film is stored in the Archives vault for security purposes and may not be accessed for general reference. However, for the convenience of researchers, reading copies have been made of older records with considerable reference value.

Records listed in the *Guide* are categorized as either original records or microfilm copies, and grouped within each category by series: bonds, census (county copies), corporations and partnerships, courts, elections, estates, land, marriage and vital statistics, military and pension, officials, roads and bridges, schools, tax and fiscal, and wills. Many very interesting and valuable records remain hidden under the heading of "Miscellaneous Records," so the less common designations have been indexed. Records are usually arranged alphabetically or chronologically within each series. The brief descriptions included in this guide are not intended to replace the more detailed finding aids available to researchers in the Archives Search Room.

The archival holdings of original and microfilmed records change constantly, as the Local Records Unit staff continue to appraise and transfer records from the counties, and as reading copies of microfilm are added to the Search Room. This edition represents county records holdings as of March 1, 2009.

This edition differs from previous ones in that it includes what are called CRX records, or records that were out of the county's custody prior to being transferred to the State Archives for permanent preservation. Cross referencing to these and other records, through the use of *See* and *See also*, has been included to help researchers. In addition, a table of contents, a glossary, and an index have been added. Headers have been provided on all pages to direct the researcher to a particular county. A map showing which counties experienced record losses is also provided courtesy of Mary Barnes and Ron Vestal.

Becky McGee-Lankford, head of the Local Records Unit, supervised this revision of the *Guide*. Doug Brown, an archivist in the Public Services Branch, and Elizabeth Preston, an archivist in the Local Records Unit, compared descriptions in the previous edition with the card catalogues for original and microfilm records, examined the original records and microfilm in cases of discrepancies, and made corrections or additions where necessary. Donna Kelly and Kenrick N. Simpson, editors in the Historical Publications Section and former Archives staff members, checked for consistency, standardized where possible, and provided cross referencing. Ms. Kelly prepared the glossary and index. I am confident that this revised edition of the guide will provide a comprehensive snapshot of the county records housed at the North Carolina State Archives.

Jesse R. Lankford
State Archivist

This revised edition is dedicated to the memory of

George Stevenson
(1937–2009)

The "Indispensable Archivist"

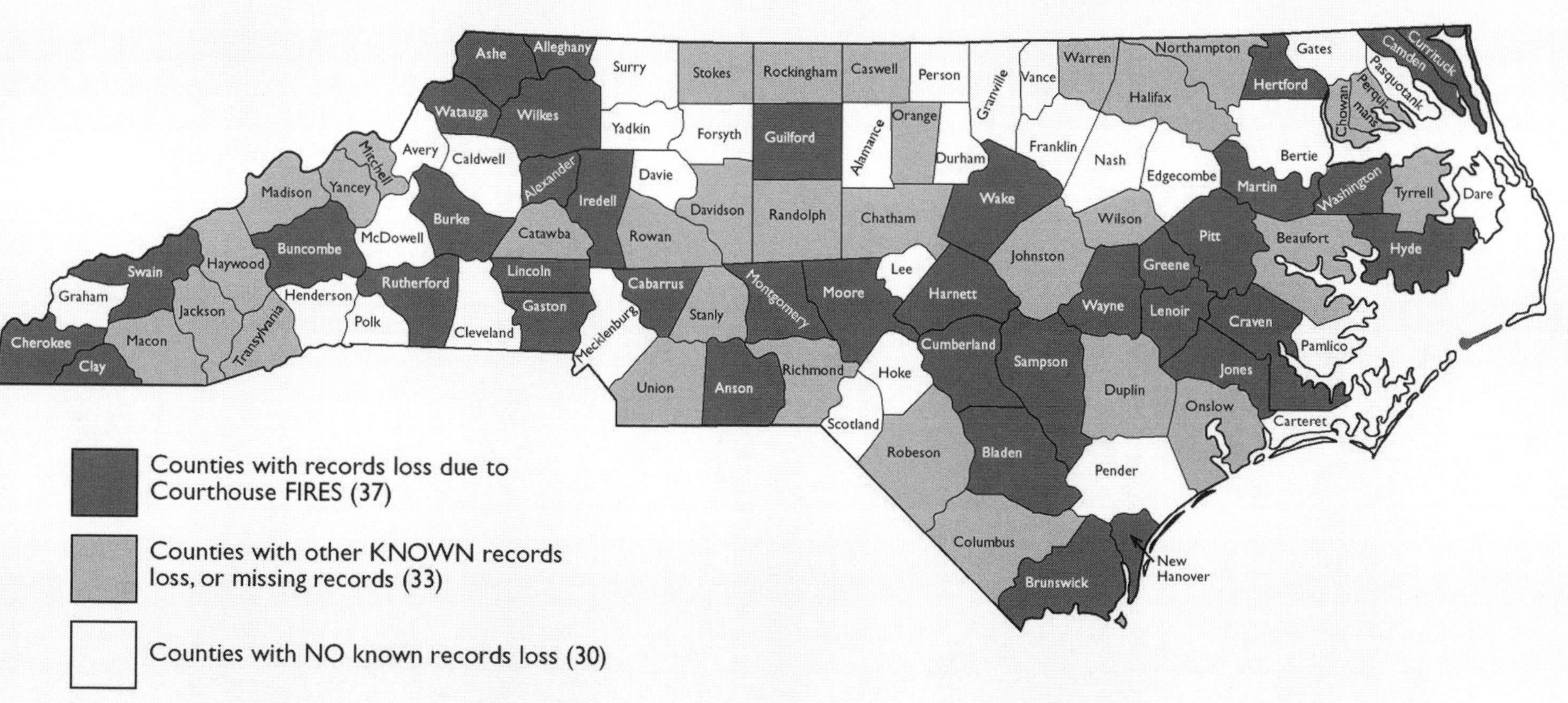

COUNTIES WITH RECORDS LOSS DUE TO FIRES, ETC.

(REVISED, 2009, BASED ON RESEARCH BY RON VESTAL)

ALAMANCE COUNTY

Established in 1849 from Orange County.

ORIGINAL RECORDS

BONDS

Apprentice Bonds, 1878-1918; 1 volume.
Bastardy Bonds and Records, 1877-1917; 1 Fibredex box.

COURT RECORDS

County Court of Pleas and Quarter Sessions
- Minutes, 1849-1860, 1866-1868; 3 volumes.
- State Docket, 1849-1868; 1 volume.

Inferior Court
- Minutes, 1877-1879; 1 volume.

Superior Court
- Civil Action Papers, 1870-1939; 2 Fibredex boxes.
- Civil Action Papers Concerning Land, 1877-1915; 2 Fibredex boxes.
- Criminal Action Papers, 1878-1917; 3 Fibredex boxes.
- Equity Minutes, 1849-1860; Clerk's Receipt Book (Land Sales), 1869-1872; 1 volume.
- Minutes, 1849-1920; 24 volumes.

ELECTION RECORDS

Elections, Record of, 1897-1968; 6 volumes.

ESTATES RECORDS [*See also* **CRX RECORDS**]

Accounts, Record of, 1869-1929; 3 volumes.
Administrators' Bonds, 1882-1902; 3 volumes.
Appointment of Administrators, Executors, and Guardians, 1869-1902; 1 volume.
Dowers, Record of (Widows' Year's Support), 1878-1968; 3 volumes.
Estates Records, 1856-1949; 21 Fibredex boxes.
Guardians' Bonds, 1882-1909; 2 volumes.
Guardians' Records, 1878-1949; 6 Fibredex boxes.
Guardians' Returns, 1849-1868; 1 volume.
Inventories and Accounts of Sales, 1849-1863, 1884-1932; 7 volumes.
Settlements, Record of, 1870-1918; 3 volumes.

LAND RECORDS

Deeds, 1793-1905; 2 Fibredex boxes.

MARRIAGE, DIVORCE, AND VITAL STATISTICS

Disinterment/Reinterment Permits, 1978; 1 manuscript box.
Divorce Records, 1889-1917; 1 Fibredex box.
Marriage Bonds, 1853-1867; 1 Fibredex box.
Marriage Certificates, Record of, 1854-1868; 1 volume.

MILITARY AND PENSION RECORDS [*See* **MISCELLANEOUS RECORDS**]

MISCELLANEOUS RECORDS

Alien Registration, 1931-1940; 1 volume.
Assignees, Receivers, and Trustees, Records of, 1884-1933; 1 Fibredex box.
Miscellaneous Records, 1822-1939; 1 Fibredex box.
Pensions, Record of, 1921-1945; 2 volumes.

Railroad Records, 1898-1919; 2 Fibredex boxes.
Trustees and Assignees, Record of Accounts of, 1895-1933; 2 volumes.

ROADS AND BRIDGES [*See* **MISCELLANEOUS RECORDS**]

WILLS
Wills, 1832-1900; 8 Fibredex boxes.

CRX RECORDS
Estate and Other Records, 1861-1903; 1 folder.

MICROFILM RECORDS

BONDS
Apprentice Bonds, 1878-1918; 1 reel.

CORPORATIONS AND PARTNERSHIPS
Corporations, Index to, 1883-1978; 1 reel.
Corporations, Record of, 1879-1946; 3 reels.
Partnerships, Index to, various years; 1 reel.

COURT RECORDS
County Court of Pleas and Quarter Sessions
Minutes, 1849-1868; 1 reel.
General County Court
Minutes, 1958-1962; 1 reel.
Superior Court
Equity Minutes, 1849-1860; Clerk's Receipt Book (Land Sales), 1869-1872; 1 reel.
Judgments, Index to, 1868-1939; 1 reel.
Judgments, Index to, Defendant, 1928-1968; 1 reel.
Minutes, 1849-1944, 1961-1963; 12 reels.

ELECTION RECORDS
Elections, Record of, 1897-1962; 1 reel.

ESTATES RECORDS
Accounts, Record of, 1869-1951; 3 reels.
Administrators' Bonds, 1882-1902; 1 reel.
Administrators, Record of, 1902-1963; 6 reels.
Appointment of Executors, 1869-1902; 1 reel.
Dowers, Record of (Widows' Year's Support), 1878-1951; 2 reels.
Estates, Index to, 1900-1968; 2 reels.
Estates, Record of, 1849-1858, 1916-1951; 4 reels.
Guardians' Bonds, 1882-1909; 1 reel.
Guardians, Record of, 1910-1963; 2 reels.
Guardians' Returns, 1849-1868, 1879-1951; 3 reels.
Inheritance Tax Records, 1924-1963; 2 reels.
Inventories of Estates, 1929-1951; 2 reels.
Inventory Book, 1859-1863; 1 reel.
Sales and Inventories, Record of, 1916-1931; 1 reel.
Settlements, Record of, 1867-1951; 5 reels.
Trustees and Guardians, Record of, 1941-1962; 1 reel.
Widows' Year's Support, Record of, 1928-1963; 1 reel.

LAND RECORDS

Deeds, Record of, 1849-1945; 69 reels.
Plat Books, 1911-1976; 5 reels.
Plats, Index to, 1911-1977; 1 reel.
Real Estate Conveyances, Index to, 1849-1941; 8 reels.
Sales and Resales of Land, Record of, 1926-1968; 4 reels.

MARRIAGE, DIVORCE, AND VITAL STATISTICS

Births, Index to, 1913-1961; 1 reel.
Deaths, Index to, 1913-1962; 1 reel.
Delayed Births, Index to, various years; 1 reel.
Maiden Names of Divorced Women, 1938-1963; 1 reel.
Marriage Bonds, 1849-1868; 3 reels.
Marriage Certificates, 1854-1946; 12 reels.
Marriage Registers, 1870-1961; 2 reels.
Marriages, Index to, 1962; 1 reel.

MILITARY AND PENSION RECORDS

Widows' and Soldiers' Pensions, 1938-1945; 1 reel.

MISCELLANEOUS RECORDS

Orders and Decrees, 1869-1951; 1 reel.
Receivership, Record of, 1925-1955; 1 reel.
Special Proceedings, 1881-1946; 4 reels.
Special Proceedings, Index to, 1877-1963; 3 reels.
Trustees and Assignees, Record of Accounts of, 1895-1933; 1 reel.

OFFICIALS, COUNTY

Board of County Commissioners, Minutes, 1868-1956; 7 reels.

SCHOOL RECORDS

County Board of Education, Minutes, 1877-1948; 1 reel.

WILLS

Wills, Cross Index to, 1850-1963; 1 reel.
Wills, Record of, 1849-1963; 8 reels.

ALBEMARLE COUNTY

Established in 1663; abolished in 1738.

MICROFILM RECORDS

MISCELLANEOUS RECORDS

Miscellaneous Records, 1678-1737; 1 reel.

ALEXANDER COUNTY

Established in 1847 from Caldwell, Iredell, and Wilkes counties.
Many court records burned by Federal troops in 1865.

ORIGINAL RECORDS

BONDS

Apprentice Bonds, 1875-1878. [*See* **COURT RECORDS**, Superior Court, Appearance Docket, Superior Court]
Bastardy Bonds and Records, 1865-1900; 2 Fibredex boxes.
Officials' Bonds and Records, 1855-1908; 2 Fibredex boxes.

COURT RECORDS

County Court of Pleas and Quarter Sessions
- Appearance Docket, 1865-1868; Summons Docket, Special Proceedings, 1870-1877; Amounts Paid Indigent Children, 1899-1913; 1 volume.
- Execution Docket, 1861-1868; 1 volume.
- State Docket, 1865-1868; 1 volume.

Superior Court
- Appearance Docket, 1866-1868; Apprentice Bonds, 1875-1878; 1 volume.
- Civil Action Papers, 1853-1927; 5 Fibredex boxes.
- Civil Action Papers Concerning Land, 1860-1952; 4 Fibredex boxes.
- Criminal Action Papers, 1861-1909; 9 Fibredex boxes.
- Equity Minutes, 1866-1868; Record of Probate of Deeds, 1866-1875; 1 volume.
- Minutes, 1866-1900; 3 volumes.

ELECTION RECORDS

Elections, Record of, 1869-1926; 5 volumes.

ESTATES RECORDS

Accounts, Record of, 1869-1894; 2 volumes.
Amounts Paid Indigent Children, 1899-1913. [*See* **COURT RECORDS**, Court of Pleas and Quarter Sessions, Appearance Docket]
Appointment of Administrators, Executors, Guardians, and Masters, 1868-1914; 1 volume.
Estates, Record of, 1861-1868; 1 volume.
Estates Records, 1839, 1858-1939; 32 Fibredex boxes.
Guardians' Records, 1866-1909; 2 Fibredex boxes.

LAND RECORDS

Deeds, Cross Index to, 1847-1928; 3 volumes.
Deeds of Sale, 1848-1953; 8 Fibredex boxes.
Land Entries, 1847-1911; 1 volume, 1 Fibredex box.
- Miscellaneous Deeds, 1850-1963; 1 Fibredex box.

Miscellaneous Land Records, 1833-1958; 2 Fibredex boxes.
Mortgage Deeds, 1872-1956; 2 Fibredex boxes.
Petitions for Partition and Sale of Land, 1863-1942; 1 Fibredex box.
Probate of Deeds, Record of, 1866-1875. [*See* **COURT RECORDS**, Superior Court, Equity Minutes.]

MARRIAGE, DIVORCE, AND VITAL STATISTICS

Divorce Records, 1867-1905; 1 Fibredex box.
Marriage Bonds, 1861; 1 Fibredex box.

MISCELLANEOUS RECORDS

Assignees and Trustees, Records of, 1869-1910, 1941, 1945; 1 Fibredex box.
Minutes and Accounts, Wardens of the Poor, 1847-1868; 1 volume.
Miscellaneous Records, 1852-1957; 3 Fibredex boxes.
Railroad Records, 1869-1903; 1 Fibredex box.
Road Records, 1863-1916; 1 Fibredex box.
Summons Docket, Special Proceedings, 1870-1877. [*See* **COURT RECORDS**, Court of Pleas and Quarter Sessions, Appearance Docket]

ROADS AND BRIDGES [*See* **MISCELLANEOUS RECORDS**]

WILLS

Wills, 1847-1949; 4 Fibredex boxes.

MICROFILM RECORDS

BONDS

Apprentice Bonds, 1875-1878; 1 reel.

CORPORATIONS AND PARTNERSHIPS

Incorporations, Record of, 1892-1968; 1 reel.
Partnerships, Record of, 1913-1970; 1 reel.

COURT RECORDS

County Court of Pleas and Quarter Sessions
- Minutes, 1865-1868. [*See* **MISCELLANEOUS RECORDS**, Special Proceedings]

Superior Court
- Civil Judgments, Cross Index to, 1867-1963; 1 reel.
- Equity Minutes, 1866-1868; 1 reel.
- Judgments, Index to, 1871-1948; 2 reels.
- Minutes, 1866-1956; 4 reels.

ELECTION RECORDS

Elections, Record of, 1869-1968; 2 reels.

ESTATES RECORDS

Accounts of Indigent Children, Record of, 1913-1946; 1 reel.
Accounts, Record of, 1869-1968; 6 reels.
Administrators and Executors, Index to, 1906-1945; 1 reel.
Administrators, Record of, 1930-1968; 2 reels.
Appointment of Administrators, Executors, and Guardians, 1868-1933; 2 reels.
Estates, Administrators, Executors, Guardians, and Trustees, Index to, 1963-1968; 1 reel.
Estates, Record of, 1861-1868; 1 reel.
Estates and Wards, Index to, 1963-1968; 1 reel.
Executors, Record of, 1930-1968; 1 reel.
Guardians, Index to, 1907-1914; 1 reel.
Guardians, Record of, 1929-1968; 1 reel.
Inheritance Tax Records, 1923-1968; 1 reel.
Settlements, Record of, 1869-1968; 2 reels.

LAND RECORDS

Deeds, Index to, Grantee, 1847-1968; 2 reels.
Deeds, Index to, Grantor, 1847-1953; 1 reel.
Deeds, Record of, 1847-1955; 34 reels.

Land Entries, 1847-1941; 1 reel.
Resale of Land by Trustees and Mortgagees, Record of, 1921-1968; 1 reel.

MARRIAGE, DIVORCE, AND VITAL STATISTICS

Births, Index to, 1913-1966; 1 reel.
Deaths, Index to, 1913-1960; 1 reel.
Delayed Births, Index to, various years; 1 reel.
Maiden Names of Divorced Women, 1940-1968; 1 reel.
Marriage Bonds, 1865-1868; 1 reel.
Marriage Licenses, 1866-1973; 13 reels.
Marriage Registers, 1867-1996; 3 reels.

MISCELLANEOUS RECORDS

Lunacy Dockets, 1907-1970; 1 reel.
Special Proceedings, 1870-1933; Court of Pleas and Quarter Sessions, Minutes, 1865-1868; 1 reel.
Special Proceedings, 1898-1960; 5 reels.
Special Proceedings, Index to, 1870-1981; 3 reels.
Wardens of the Poor, Record of, 1847-1868; 1 reel.

OFFICIALS, COUNTY

Board of County Commissioners, Minutes, 1868-1963; 4 reels.

SCHOOL RECORDS

County Board of Education, Minutes, 1885-1980; 2 reels.

TAX AND FISCAL RECORDS

Tax Lists, 1915, 1935, 1965; 1 reel.

WILLS

Wills, Cross Index to, 1865-1967; 1 reel.
Wills, Record of, 1865-1968; 2 reels.

ALLEGHANY COUNTY

Established in 1859 from Ashe County.
Courthouse fire in 1932 destroyed a few permanently valuable records.

ORIGINAL RECORDS

BONDS

Apprentice Bonds, 1869-1909; 1 volume.
Apprentice Bonds, 1863-1872; Bastardy Bonds, 1863-1910; Officials' Bonds and Records, 1859-1927; 1 Fibredex box.
Bastardy Bonds, 1872-1879; 1 volume.

COURT RECORDS

County Court of Pleas and Quarter Sessions
Execution Docket, 1863-1868; Execution Docket, Superior Court, 1869-1872; Minutes, Inferior Court, 1877-1883; Appointments of Commissioners of Affidavits, 1899-1905; Witness Docket, Superior Court, 1912-1914; 1 volume.
Minutes, 1862-1868; Witness Docket, Inferior Court, 1877-1883; Witness Docket, Superior Court, 1895-1912; List of Commissioners of Affidavits, 1866; 1 volume.
Inferior Court [*See* Court of Pleas and Quarter Sessions, Execution Docket and Minutes]
Superior Court
Civil Action Papers, 1862-1928; 5 Fibredex boxes.
Civil Action Papers Concerning Land, 1867-1920; 4 Fibredex boxes.
Criminal Action Papers, 1862-1925; 5 Fibredex boxes.
Execution Docket, 1869-1872. [*See* Court of Pleas and Quarter Sessions
Minutes, 1869-1907; 5 volumes.
Witness Dockets, 1895-1914. [*See* Court of Pleas and Quarter Sessions, Execution Docket and Minutes]

ELECTION RECORDS

Elections, Record of, 1878-1944; 5 volumes.

ESTATES RECORDS

Administrators' Bonds, 1911-1918; 1 volume.
Estates Records, 1859-1928; 30 Fibredex boxes.
Guardians' Bonds, 1869-1940; 3 volumes.
Guardians' Records, 1864-1917; 3 Fibredex boxes.
Inventories, Marriages, and Wills, Record of, 1862-1869; 1 volume.

LAND RECORDS

Deeds and Grants, 1837-1908; 1 Fibredex box.
Miscellaneous Land Records, 1874-1908; 1 Fibredex box.

MARRIAGE, DIVORCE, AND VITAL STATISTICS [*See also* ESTATES RECORDS]

Divorce Records, 1862-1932; 2 Fibredex boxes.

MISCELLANEOUS RECORDS

Appointments of Commissioners of Affidavits, 1899-1905. [*See* **COURT RECORDS**, Court of Pleas and Quarter Sessions, Execution Docket,]
Commissioners of Affidavits, List of, 1866. [*See* **COURT RECORDS**, Court of Pleas and Quarter Sessions]

Licenses to Trades, Registry of, 1874-1906; Record of Strays, 1895, 1914; 1 volume.
Miscellaneous Records, 1848-1929; 2 Fibredex boxes.
Road Records, 1861-1910; 1 Fibredex box.

ROADS AND BRIDGES [*See* **MISCELLANEOUS RECORDS**]

WILLS [*See also* **ESTATES RECORDS**]
Wills, 1859-1912; 3 Fibredex boxes.

MICROFILM RECORDS

BONDS
Apprentice Bonds, 1869-1909; 1 reel.
Bastardy Bonds, 1872-1879; 1 reel.

CORPORATIONS AND PARTNERSHIPS
Corporations, Record of, 1903-1971; 1 reel.

COURT RECORDS
County Court of Pleas and Quarter Sessions
Minutes, 1862-1868; 1 reel.
Superior Court
Judgment Docket, Tax Foreclosures, 1950-1957; 1 reel.
Judgments, Cross Index to, 1869-1970; 1 reel.
Minutes, 1869-1955; 5 reels.
Tax Judgments, 1882-1889, 1950-1957; 21 reels.

ELECTION RECORDS
Elections, Record of, 1878-1944; 1 reel.

ESTATES RECORDS
Accounts, Record of, 1870-1970; 4 reels.
Administrators' Bonds, 1911-1918; 1 reel.
Administrators, Executors, and Guardians, Cross Index to, 1911-1934, 1943-1970; 2 reels.
Administrators, Executors, and Guardians, Record of, 1919-1951; 1 reel.
Administrators, Record of, 1939-1970; 1 reel.
Estates, Index to, 1970-1971; 1 reel.
Executors, Record of, 1948-1970; 1 reel.
Final Settlements, Cross Index to, 1922-1970; 1 reel.
Guardians' Bonds, 1869-1940; 1 reel.
Guardians, Record of, 1951-1970; 1 reel.
Inheritance Tax Records, 1920-1971; 1 reel.
Inventories, Marriages, and Wills, Record of, 1862-1869; 1 reel.
Sales and Resales, Record of, 1937-1965; 1 reel.
Settlements, Record of, 1866-1970; 4 reels.

LAND RECORDS
Deeds, Record of, 1859-1961; 34 reels.
Deeds for Schools, Record of, 1884-1965; 1 reel.
Federal Tax Lien Index, 1931-1970; 1 reel.
Land Entries, Record of, 1870-1962; 1 reel.
Real Estate Conveyances, Index to, Grantee, 1859-1971; 3 reels.
Real Estate Conveyances, Index to, Grantor, 1859-1971; 3 reels.
Surveys, Record of, 1905-1933; 1 reel.
Taxes for Mortgagees, Record of, 1931-1935; 1 reel.

MARRIAGE, DIVORCE, AND VITAL STATISTICS [*See also* **ESTATES RECORDS**]
Maiden Names of Divorced Women, 1966-1970; 1 reel.
Marriage Licenses, 1861-1961; 11 reels.
Marriage Registers, 1867-1971; 2 reels.
Vital Statistics, Index to, various years; 1 reel.

MILITARY AND PENSION RECORDS
Organizational Minutes, Ex-Confederate Soldiers of Alleghany County, 1890-1920; 1 reel.

MISCELLANEOUS RECORDS
Homestead Returns, 1870-1916; 1 reel.
Lunacy, Record of, 1901-1970; 1 reel.
Official Reports, Record of, 1876-1970; 1 reel.
Orders and Decrees, 1870-1948; 1 reel.
Special Proceedings, 1884-1964; 5 reels.
Special Proceedings, Cross Index to, 1939-1970; 1 reel.

OFFICIALS, COUNTY
Board of County Commissioners, Minutes, 1868-1971; 4 reels.

SCHOOL RECORDS [*See* **LAND RECORDS**]

TAX AND FISCAL RECORDS
Tax Lists, 1915-1955; 2 reels.
Tax Scrolls, 1920-1980; 3 reels.

WILLS [*See also* **ESTATES RECORDS**]
Wills, Cross Index to, 1864-1933; 1 reel.
Wills, Record of, 1870-1970; 3 reels.

ANSON COUNTY

Established in 1750 from Bladen County.
Courthouse fire of 1868 destroyed many court records.

ORIGINAL RECORDS

BONDS

Apprentice Bonds and Records, 1873-1891; 1 Fibredex box.
Bastardy Bonds and Records, 1870-1903; 1 Fibredex box.
Officials' Bonds, 1889-1895; 1 volume.

COURT RECORDS

County Court of Pleas and Quarter Sessions
- Appearance Dockets, 1837-1845, 1856-1868; 2 volumes.
- Execution Docket, 1861-1868; 1 volume.
- Minutes, 1771-1777, 1848-1858, 1868; 4 volumes.
- Recognizance Docket, 1843-1845; Sheriffs' Settlements, 1846-1861; 1 volume.
- Trial Docket, 1852-1868; 1 volume.

Superior Court
- Civil Action Papers, 1864-1908; 12 Fibredex boxes.
- Civil Action Papers Concerning Land, 1870-1910; 2 Fibredex boxes.
- Criminal Action Papers, 1868-1904; 25 Fibredex boxes.
- Equity Minutes, 1847-1868; Equity Trial Docket, 1861-1868; 2 volumes.
- Minutes, 1868-1909; Trial Docket, 1847-1850; 11 volumes.

ELECTION RECORDS

Elections, Record of, 1878-1910; 3 volumes.

ESTATES RECORDS

Accounts, Record of, 1868-1915; 4 volumes.
Administrators' Bonds, 1873-1903; 3 volumes.
Estates, Record of, 1849-1855, 1868; 2 volumes.
Estates Records, 1805-1953; 54 Fibredex boxes. [*See also* **CRX RECORDS**]
Guardians' Bonds, 1873-1902; 1 volume.
Guardians' Records, 1848-1924; 7 Fibredex boxes.
Probate Court Minutes, 1869-1872; 1 volume.
Settlements, Record of, 1875-1910; 2 volumes.

LAND RECORDS

Deeds, 1786-1909; 1 Fibredex box.
Deeds, Index to, 1749-1916; 5 volumes.
Deeds, Record of, 1749-1838; 30 volumes.
Deeds of Trust, 1863-1910; 4 Fibredex boxes.
Miscellaneous Land Records, 1829-1909; 1 Fibredex box.

MARRIAGE, DIVORCE, AND VITAL STATISTICS

Disinterment/Reinterment Permits, 1967-1976; 1 manuscript box.
Divorce Records, 1872-1925; 2 Fibredex boxes.
Marriage Bonds, 1762; 1 folder in Fibredex box.
Vital Statistics, Index to, 1922-1932; 1 volume.

MILITARY AND PENSION RECORDS [*See* **MISCELLANEOUS RECORDS**; **CRX RECORDS**]

MISCELLANEOUS RECORDS

Declaration of Intent (to Become a Citizen), 1911-1920; 1 volume.
Miscellaneous Records, 1759-1960; 3 Fibredex boxes. [*See also* **CRX RECORDS**]
Naturalization Record, 1913, 1924; 1 volume.
Orders and Decrees, 1868-1932; 1 volume.
Pensions, Record of, 1885-1960; 5 volumes.
Road Records, 1855, 1871-1903; 1 Fibredex box.
Sheriffs' Settlements, 1846-1861. [*See* **COURT OF PLEAS AND QUARTER SESSIONS**, Recognizance Docket]
Special Proceedings, 1874-1911; 6 volumes.

ROADS AND BRIDGES [*See* **MISCELLANEOUS RECORDS**]

TAX AND FISCAL RECORDS

Tax Records, 1887; 1 Fibredex box.

WILLS

Wills, 1754-1946; 16 Fibredex boxes.
Wills, Cross Index to, 1751-1929; 1 volume.
Wills, Record of, 1751-1848; 3 volumes.

CRX RECORDS

Estates Records, 1866-1907; 1 Fibredex box.
Miscellaneous Records, 1859-1936, n.d.; 1 Fibredex box.
Pension Records, 1923-1941, n.d.; 1 Fibredex box.

MICROFILM RECORDS

CORPORATIONS AND PARTNERSHIPS

Incorporations, Record of, 1888-1960; 1 reel.
Partnerships, Record of, 1913-1973; 1 reel.

COURT RECORDS

County Court of Pleas and Quarter Sessions
  Minutes, 1771-1777, 1848-1858, 1868; 1 reel.
Superior Court
  Equity Minutes, 1847-1868; 1 reel.
  Judgment Docket, 1902-1913; 1 reel.
  Judgments, Cross Index to, 1868-1956; 1 reel.
  Minutes, 1868-1927; 9 reels.

ELECTION RECORDS

Elections, Record of, 1880-1962; 1 reel.

ESTATES RECORDS

Accounts, Record of, 1868-1944; 5 reels.
Accounts of Sales, 1868; 1 reel.
Administrators' Bonds, 1873-1954; 2 reels.
Administrators, Executors, and Guardians, Record of, 1868-1948; 3 reels.
Executors, Record of, 1948-1960; 1 reel.
Guardians' Bonds, 1873-1953; 1 reel.
Guardians, Record of, 1945-1962; 1 reel.

Indigent Orphans, Record of Accounts of, 1908-1948; 1 reel.
Inheritance Tax Records, 1920-1962; 1 reel.
Inventories and Accounts [of Sales], 1849-1855; 1 reel.
Settlements, Record of, 1875-1945; 3 reels.

LAND RECORDS

Deeds, Index to, Grantee, 1749-1973; 9 reels.
Deeds, Index to, Grantor, 1749-1973; 11 reels.
Deeds, Record of, 1749-1950; 53 reels.
Land Entries, 1851-1927; 1 reel.
Map Books, 1913-1967; 2 reels.
Map Books, Index to, 1913-1961; 1 reel.
Resale of Land by Trustees, Record of, 1920-1962; 1 reel.

MARRIAGE, DIVORCE, AND VITAL STATISTICS

Births, Index to, 1913-1982; 2 reels.
Deaths, Index to, 1913-1973; 1 reel.
Delayed Births, Index to, various years; 1 reel.
Marriage Bonds, 1749-1868; 2 reels.
Marriage Licenses, 1869-1962; 7 reels.
Marriage Registers, 1870-1962; 1 reel.

MILITARY AND PENSION RECORDS

Pensions, Record of, 1885-1960; 1 reel.

MISCELLANEOUS RECORDS

Appointment of Receivers, 1911-1938; 1 reel.
Declaration of Intent (to Become a Citizen), 1911-1920; 1 reel.
Lunacy, Record of, 1899-1968; 1 reel.
Naturalization Record, 1913-1924; 1 reel.
Orders and Decrees, 1868-1968; 1 reel.
Special Proceedings, 1874-1946, 1961-1962; 10 reels.
Special Proceedings, Index to, 1886-1920; 1 reel.

OFFICIALS, COUNTY

Board of County Commissioners, Minutes, 1868-1931; 4 reels.

SCHOOL RECORDS

County Board of Education, Minutes, 1873-1919; 1 reel.

WILLS

Wills, Cross Index to, 1751-1968; 1 reel.
Wills, Record of, 1751-1955; 4 reels.

ASHE COUNTY

Established in 1799 from Wilkes County.
Courthouse fire of 1865 destroyed many court records.

ORIGINAL RECORDS

BONDS

Apprentice Bonds, 1876-1923; 2 volumes.
Bastardy Bonds, 1828-1910; 1 volume, 1 Fibredex box.
Officials' Bonds and Records, 1821-1907; 2 Fibredex boxes.

CENSUS RECORDS (County Copy)

Census, 1880; 1 manuscript box.

COURT RECORDS

County Court of Pleas and Quarter Sessions
- Execution Dockets, 1829-1868; 2 volumes.
- Minutes, 1806-1866; 6 volumes.
- State Dockets, 1829-1868; 2 volumes.
- Trial and Appearance Dockets, 1829-1868; 2 volumes.

Inferior Court
- Minutes, 1877-1885; 1 volume.

Superior Court
- Civil Action Papers, 1807-1934; 19 Fibredex boxes.
- Civil Action Papers Concerning Land, 1827-1911; 13 Fibredex boxes.
- Criminal Action Papers, 1805-1930; 11 Fibredex boxes.
- Equity Minutes and Equity Trial Dockets, 1824-1868; 2 volumes.
- Execution Dockets, 1826-1871; 6 volumes.
- Minutes, 1807-1938; 19 volumes.
- State Dockets, 1840-1867; 2 volumes.
- Trial and Appearance Dockets, 1807-1868; 3 volumes.
- Witness Fee Book, 1845-1850; 1 volume.

ELECTION RECORDS

Election Registration Books, 1950-1970; 23 volumes.
Elections, Record of, 1878-1930; 4 volumes.
Permanent Registration of Voters, 1902-1908; 1 volume.

ESTATES RECORDS

Accounts, Record of, 1869-1936; 6 volumes.
Administrators' Bonds, 1876-1920, 1925; 4 volumes.
Administrators, Executors, and Guardians, Record of, 1920-1943; 1 volume.
Administrators, Record of, 1924-1936; 1 volume.
Appointment of Administrators, Executors, and Guardians, 1868-1920; 1 volume.
Estates, Record of, 1828-1842, 1853-1873; 2 volumes.
Estates Records, 1819-1935; 34 Fibredex boxes.
Guardians' Bonds, 1876-1941; 4 volumes.
Guardians' Records, 1829-1918; 5 Fibredex boxes.
Settlements, Record of, 1869-1938; 4 volumes.

LAND RECORDS

Deeds, 1802-1954; 8 Fibredex boxes.
Deeds and Grants, 1778-1849; 13 volumes.

Ejectments, 1827-1911; 1 Fibredex box.
Land Entries, 1803-1906; 6 volumes.
Miscellaneous Land Records, 1826-1911; 1 Fibredex box.
Mortgage Deeds, Deeds of Trust, and Miscellaneous Land Records, 1828-1949; 1 Fibredex box.
Processioners' Record, 1879-1883; 1 volume.
Tax Liens, Record of, 1933-1934; 1 volume.

MARRIAGE, DIVORCE, AND VITAL STATISTICS

Marriage Bonds, 1828-1868; 4 Fibredex boxes.
Marriage Certificates, Record of, 1851-1881; 1 volume.
Divorce Records, 1822-1912; 5 Fibredex boxes.

MILTARY AND PENSION RECORDS [*See* **MISCELLANEOUS RECORDS**]

MISCELLANEOUS RECORDS

Assignees, Receivers and Trustees, Records of, 1811-1933; 1 Fibredex box.
Clerk's Minute Docket (Special Proceedings), 1895-1922; 1 volume.
Commissioners of Affidavits, Record of, 1897-1899; 1 volume.
Committee of Finance, Settlement of County Accounts, 1839-1847; 1 volume.
Good Roads Commission, Minutes, 1919; 1 volume.
Homestead and Personal Property Exemptions, 1857-1938; 1 Fibredex box.
Homestead Returns and Personal Property Exemptions, Record of, 1869-1941; Record of Wills, 1865-1868; 1 volume.
Lunacy, Record of, 1900-1934; 1 volume.
Magistrates, Record of, 1893-1922; 3 volumes.
Miscellaneous Records, 1801-1954; 2 Fibredex boxes.
Pension Records, 1885-1919; 1 Fibredex box.
Physicians and Surgeons, Register of, 1905-1965; 1 volume.
Railroad Records, 1885-1911; 1 Fibredex box.
Receivers, Record of, 1883, 1889, 1907; 1 volume.
Road and Bridge Records, 1827-1931; 2 Fibredex boxes.
School Census, 1883-1903; 3 Fibredex boxes.
School Teachers' Vouchers, 1881-1903; 3 Fibredex boxes.
Special Proceedings [*See* Clerk's Minute Docket]
Wardens of the Poor, Minutes and Accounts, 1832-1855; 1 volume.

OFFICIALS, COUNTY [*See* **MISCELLANEOUS RECORDS**]

ROADS AND BRIDGES [*See* **MISCELLANEOUS RECORDS**]

SCHOOL RECORDS [*See* **MISCELLANEOUS RECORDS**]

WILLS

Wills, 1801-1912; 5 Fibredex boxes.
Wills, Record of, 1865-1868. [*See* **MISCELLANEOUS RECORDS**]

MICROFILM RECORDS

BONDS

Apprentice Bonds, 1876-1923; 1 reel.
Bastardy Bonds, 1876-1880, 1883; 1 reel.

CORPORATIONS AND PARTNERSHIPS

Incorporations, Record of, 1910-1966; 1 reel.
Partnerships, Record of, 1933-1966; 1 reel.

COURT RECORDS

County Court of Pleas and Quarter Sessions
Minutes, 1806-1866; 2 reels.
Superior Court
Equity Minutes, 1824-1868; Land Entries, 1870-1872; Tax Judgments, 1872-1874; 1 reel.
Judgments, Cross Index to, 1869-1970; 3 reels.
Minutes, 1807-1818, 1834-1970; 11 reels.
Witness Fee Docket, 1826-1841; 1 reel.

ELECTION RECORDS

Elections, Record of, 1878-1956; 1 reel.

ESTATES RECORDS

Accounts of Indigent Orphans, Record of, 1939-1966; 1 reel.
Accounts, Record of, 1869-1966; 6 reels.
Administrators' Bonds, 1876-1925; 1 reel.
Administrators, Executors, and Guardians, Cross Index to, 1906-1966; 1 reel.
Administrators, Executors, and Guardians, Record of, 1920-1927; 1 reel.
Administrators, Record of, 1924-1966; 2 reels.
Estates, Record of, 1853-1873; 1 reel.
Executors, Record of, 1869-1919, 1943-1970; 2 reels.
Guardians' Bonds, 1876-1941; 1 reel.
Guardians, Record of, 1927-1966; 2 reels.
Settlements, Record of, 1869-1966; 5 reels.

LAND RECORDS

Deeds, Cross Index to, 1799-1935; 4 reels.
Deeds, Record of, 1800-1955; 57 reels.
Land Entries, 1803-1906; 1 reel.
Plats, Index to, no date; 1 reel.
Plats, various years, 1966-1979; 2 reels.
Real Estate Conveyances, Index to, Grantee, 1935-1966; 4 reels.
Real Estate Conveyances, Index to, Grantor, 1935-1966; 4 reels.
Sale and Resale of Land by Trustees and Mortgagees, Record of, 1924-1966; 2 reels.
Surveys, Record of, 1905-1918; 1 reel.

MARRIAGE, DIVORCE, AND VITAL STATISTICS

Births, Index to, 1913-1979; 1 reel.
Deaths, Index to, 1913-1979; 1 reel.
Delayed Births, Index to, various years; 1 reel.
Maiden Names of Divorced Women, 1944-1966; 1 reel.
Marriage Bonds, 1799-1868; 5 reels.
Marriage Certificates, 1853-1881; 1 reel.
Marriage Registers, 1853-1966; 1 reel.

MISCELLANEOUS RECORDS

Clerk's Minute Docket, 1895-1922; 1 reel. [*See also* Special Proceedings]
Committee of Finance, Minutes, 1839-1847; 1 reel.
Lunacy, Inquisition of, 1900-1961; 1 reel.

Orders and Decrees, 1868-1956; 9 reels.
Special Proceedings, 1896-1970; 2 reels. [*See also* Clerk's Minute Docket]
Special Proceedings, Index to, 1892-1966, 1970-1979; 2 reels.
Wardens of the Poor, 1832-1855; 1 reel.

OFFICIALS, COUNTY

Board of County Commissioners, Minutes, 1870-1955; 3 reels.

SCHOOL RECORDS

County Board of Education, Minutes, 1885-1966; 1 reel.

TAX AND FISCAL RECORDS

County Tax Book, 1915-1916; 1 reel.
Tax Ledgers, 1915-1945; 1 reel.
Tax Lists, 1925, 1935; 1 reel.
Tax Scrolls, 1955; 1 reel.

WILLS

Wills, Cross Index to, 1816-1966; 1 reel.
Wills, Record of, 1816-1966; 3 reels.

AVERY COUNTY

Established in 1911 from Caldwell, Mitchell, and Watauga counties.

ORIGINAL RECORDS

COURT RECORDS
Superior Court
Criminal Action Papers, 1911-1968, 1977; 13 Fibredex boxes.

ELECTION RECORDS
Elections, Record of, 1912-1938; 3 volumes.

ESTATES RECORDS
Estates Records, 1916-1955; 2 Fibredex boxes.
Guardians' Records, 1916-1956; 1 Fibredex box.

MARRIAGE, DIVORCE, AND VITAL STATISTICS
Disinterment/Reinterment Permits, 1976-1986; 1 manuscript box.

MILITARY AND PENSION RECORDS [*See* MISCELLANEOUS RECORDS]

MISCELLANEOUS RECORDS
Abandonment and Non-Support, 1916-1968; 1 Fibredex box.
Alien Registration, 1940; 1 volume.
Miscellaneous Records, 1911-1967; 1 Fibredex box.
Pensions, Record of, 1914-1940; 1 volume.

WILLS
Wills, 1911-1961; 4 Fibredex boxes.

MICROFILM RECORDS

CORPORATIONS AND PARTNERSHIPS
Corporations, Record of, 1911-1969; 1 reel.
Partnerships, Record of, 1946-1964; 1 reel.

COURT RECORDS
Superior Court
Judgment Dockets, Land Tax Sales, 1930-1958; 2 reels.
Judgments, Cross Index to, 1911-1963; 1 reel.
Minutes, 1911-1957; 5 reels.
Tax Judgment Docket, 1947-1950; 1 reel.

ELECTION RECORDS
Elections, Record of, 1912-1970; 1 reel.

ESTATES RECORDS
Accounts of Indigent Orphans, Record of, 1924-1931; 1 reel.
Accounts, Record of, 1912-1968; 3 reels.
Administrators and Executors, Cross Index to, 1911-1968; 1 reel.
Administrators, Executors, and Guardians, Record of, 1911-1955; 1 reel.
Administrators, Record of, 1939-1968; 1 reel.
Dowers, Record of (Widows' Year's Support), 1913-1925; 1 reel.
Executors, Record of, 1955-1968; 1 reel.
Guardians, Cross Index to, 1911-1964; 1 reel.

Guardians, Record of, 1937-1968; 1 reel.
Inheritance Tax Records, 1923-1969; 1 reel.
Settlements, Record of, 1912-1968; 1 reel.

LAND RECORDS

Deeds, Record of, 1911-1966; 28 reels.
Federal Tax Lien Index, 1928-1968; 1 reel.
Land Entries, 1912-1957; 1 reel.
Land Title Guaranty Proceedings, 1914-1915; 1 reel.
Plat Books, 1914-1977; 4 reels.
Real Estate Conveyances, Index to, Grantee, 1944-1970; 2 reels.
Real Estate Conveyances, Index to, Grantor, 1944-1970; 2 reels.
Real Estate Conveyances, Index to, Grantor and Grantee, 1911-1944; 1 reel.
Registration of Titles (Torrens Act), 1925; 1 reel.
Right of Way and Easements, 1962-1969; 1 reel.
Taxes for Mortgages, Record of, 1931-1932; 1 reel.

MARRIAGE, DIVORCE, AND VITAL STATISTICS

Births and Deaths, Index to, 1914-1970; 1 reel.
Delayed Births, Index to, various years; 1 reel.
Maiden Names of Divorced Women, 1939-1961; 1 reel.
Marriage Licenses, 1913-1977; 15 reels.
Marriage Registers, 1911-1970; 1 reel.

MILITARY AND PENSION RECORDS

Pensions, Record of, 1914-1940; 1 reel.

MISCELLANEOUS RECORDS

Appointment of Receivers, 1924-1931; 1 reel.
Clerk's Minute Dockets, 1923-1968; 1 reel.
County Finance Committee, Minutes, 1917-1918; 1 reel.
Lunacy Docket, 1911-1968; 1 reel.
Orders and Decrees, 1911-1968; 1 reel.
Special Proceedings, 1911-1968; 3 reels.
Special Proceedings, Cross Index to, 1911-1977; 2 reels.

OFFICIALS, COUNTY

Board of County Commissioners, Minutes, 1911-1970; 2 reels.

SCHOOL RECORDS

County Board of Education, Minutes, 1911-1970; 1 reel.

WILLS

Wills, Cross Index to, 1911-1968; 1 reel.
Wills, Record of, 1911-1968; 1 reel.

BATH COUNTY

Established in 1696 from Albemarle County. Divided into Archdale, Pamptecough, and Wickham precincts in 1705. Abolished in 1738.

No records exist except a few which may be found in those of Beaufort County.

BEAUFORT COUNTY

Established in 1705 as Pamptecough Precinct of Bath County.
Name changed to Beaufort in 1712.

ORIGINAL RECORDS

BONDS

Bastardy Books, 1846-1860, 1866-1875; 1 manuscript box. [*See also* **CRX RECORDS**]
Officials' Bonds, Record of, 1868-1931; 2 volumes.
Officials' Bonds and Records, 1758, 1777, 1801-1871; 1 Fibredex box.

COURT RECORDS [*See also* **CRX RECORDS**]

County Court of Pleas and Quarter Sessions
- Appearance Dockets, 1828-1868; 3 volumes.
- Execution Dockets, 1808-1868; 7 volumes.
- Minutes, 1756-1868; 10 volumes.
- State Dockets, 1846-1868; 2 volumes.
- Trial and Appearance Dockets, 1744-1745, 1794-1828; 4 volumes.
- Trial Dockets, 1838-1868; 10 volumes.

Inferior Court
- Minutes, 1878-1886; 1 volume.

Superior Court
- Appearance Docket, 1811-1817; 1 volume.
- Civil Action Papers, 1785-1915; 8 Fibredex boxes. [*See also* **CRX RECORDS**]
- Civil Action Papers Concerning Land, 1855-1938; 8 Fibredex boxes.
- Civil Issues Dockets, 1868-1910; 3 volumes, 2 manuscript boxes.
- Clerk's Minute Docket, 1855-1868; 2 volumes.
- Criminal Action Papers, 1818-1935. [*See* **CRX RECORDS**]
- Criminal Issues Dockets, 1868-1966; 3 volumes, 2 manuscript boxes.
- Equity Execution Docket, 1835-1868; 1 volume.
- Equity Minutes, 1807-1868; 3 volumes.
- Equity Trial Docket, 1834-1868; 1 volume.
- Execution Dockets, 1855-1881; 2 volumes.
- Minutes, 1817-1968; 41 volumes.
- State Docket, 1855-1868; 1 volume.
- Trial Dockets, 1835-1845, 1855-1868; 6 volumes.

ELECTION RECORDS [*See also* **CRX RECORDS**]

Election Records, 1866-1932. [*See* **CRX RECORDS**]
Elections, Record of, 1878-1920, 1930-1968; 7 volumes.
Voter Registration Books, 1868, 1872-1898; 9 manuscript boxes.

ESTATES RECORDS

Accounts, Record of, 1868-1904; 3 volumes.
Administrators, Record of, 1897-1911; 1 volume.
Clerk's Account Book (Estates), 1849-1873; 1 volume.
Estates, Record of (Orphan Books), 1808-1868; 13 volumes.
Estates Records, 1760-1949; 28 Fibredex boxes. [*See also* **CRX RECORDS**]
Guardians' Bonds, 1867-1925; 2 volumes.
Guardians, Record of, 1842-1870; 1 volume.
Guardians' Records, 1794-1918, 1948; 2 Fibredex boxes. [*See also* **CRX RECORDS**]
Partitions and Divisions, 1794-1909; 1 volume.

Reports on Devised Estates, 1908-1913; 2 pamphlets.
Settlements, Record of, 1869-1914; 2 volumes.

LAND RECORDS

Attachments, Executions, Liens and Levies on Land, 1791-1904; 2 Fibredex boxes.
Corrections to Transcribed Records of Deeds, Record of, 1835-1836; 1 volume.
Deeds, 1720, 1750-1918; 3 Fibredex boxes.
Deeds, Cross Index to, 1854-1888; 3 volumes.
Deeds, Index to, Grantee, 1701-1877; 3 volumes.
Deeds, Index to, Grantor, 1701-1877; 3 volumes.
Deeds, Record of, 1695-1881; 43 volumes.
Land Entries, 1867-1926; 1 volume.
Land Records, 1835-1930. [*See* **CRX RECORDS**]
Levies, Executions, and Attachments, 1836-1913. [*See* **CRX RECORDS**]
Miscellaneous Deeds, 1803-1937; 1 Fibredex box.
Miscellaneous Land Records, 1773-1947; 2 Fibredex boxes. [*See also* **CRX RECORDS**]
Patent Record, 1798-1816; 1 volume.
Sales under Mortgage and Deeds of Trust, Record of, 1915-1968; 10 volumes.

MARRIAGE, DIVORCE, AND VITAL STATISTICS [*See also* **CRX RECORDS**]

Cohabitation, Record of, 1866-1867. [*See* Marriages, Record of]
Disinterment/Reinterment Permits, 1979; 1 manuscript box.
Divorce Records, 1868-1902, 1923; 2 Fibredex boxes.
Marriage Bonds, 1850-1851; 1 folder in Fibredex box.
Marriage and Divorce Records, 1836-1928. [*See* **CRX RECORDS**]
Marriage Registers, 1867-1930; 7 volumes.
Marriages, Record of, 1851-1866; Record of Cohabitation, 1866-1867; 1 volume.

MILITARY AND PENSION RECORDS [*See* **MISCELLANEOUS RECORDS**]

MISCELLANEOUS RECORDS

Account Book, Deputy Register of Deeds, 1850-1860; 1 volume.
Aliens, Record of, various dates; 1 volume.
Allowances to Outside Poor, Record of, 1868-1874. [*See* **TAX AND FISCAL RECORDS**]
Appointment of Receivers, 1908-1932; 1 volume.
Appointment of Road Overseers, Record of, 1843-1869; 1 volume.
Assignees, Receivers, and Trustees Record, 1859; 1 volume.
Assignees, Receivers, and Trustees, Records of, 1869-1913; 2 Fibredex boxes.
Board of Magistrates, Minutes, 1878-1895; 1 volume.
Homestead and Personal Property Exemptions, 1868-1906; 2 Fibredex boxes.
Miscellaneous Records, 1755-1942; 2 Fibredex boxes. [*See also* **CRX RECORDS**]
Nurses' Certificates of Registration, 1909-1960; 1 manuscript box.
Official Reports, Record of, 1880-1944; 3 volumes.
Optometrists' Certificates of Registration, 1909-1957; 1 manuscript box.
Pensions, Record of, 1912-1931; 1 volume.
Physicians' Certificates of Registration, 1889-1950; 1 manuscript box.
Railroad Records, 1878-1903; 2 Fibredex boxes.
Stock Marks, Record of, 1878-1921; 1 manuscript box.
Wardens of the Poor, Minutes, 1847-1868; 1 volume.

OFFICIALS, COUNTY [*See* **MISCELLANEOUS RECORDS; CRX RECORDS**]

ROADS AND BRIDGES [*See* **MISCELLANEOUS RECORDS; CRX RECORDS**]

SCHOOL RECORDS [*See* **MISCELLANEOUS RECORDS**]

TAX AND FISCAL RECORDS

Assessment of Land for Taxation, 1860; 1 volume.
Oyster Tax Receipts, 1895-1904; 1 volume.
Tax Abstract, 1879-1896; Record of Allowances to Outside Poor, 1868-1874; 1 volume.
Tax Records, 1832-1852, 1878-1905; 1 manuscript box. [*See also* **CRX RECORDS**]
Taxables, Lists of, 1841-1860, 1866; 6 volumes.

WILLS

Wills, 1720-1903; 6 volumes, 1 Fibredex box.

CRX RECORDS

Bastardy Bonds and Records, 1814-1907; 1 Fibredex box.
Civil Action Papers, 1828-1928; 11 Fibredex boxes.
Constables' Bonds and Records, 1788-1905; 2 Fibredex boxes.
County Accounts, 1863-1931; 1 Fibredex box.
Criminal Action Papers, 1818-1935; 22 Fibredex boxes.
Election Records, 1866-1932; 2 Fibredex boxes.
Estates Records, 1735-1933; 50 Fibredex boxes, 1 folder.
Guardians' Records, 1734-1926; 17 Fibredex boxes.
Land Records, 1835-1930; 1 Fibredex box.
Levies, Executions, and Attachments, 1836-1913; 4 Fibredex boxes.
Marriage and Divorce Records, 1836-1928; 1 Fibredex box.
Miscellaneous Court, Land, and Estates Records, 1838-1873; 1 Fibredex box.
Miscellaneous Records, 1741-1931; 7 Fibredex boxes.
Road Records, 1840-1931; 1 Fibredex box.
School Records, 1850-1936; 2 Fibredex boxes.
Slave Records, 1830-1867; 1 Fibredex box.
Tax Records, 1853-1937; 2 Fibredex boxes.

MICROFILM RECORDS

CORPORATIONS AND PARTNERSHIPS

Corporations, Index to, 1886-1982; 1 reel.
Corporations, Record of, 1886-1960; 2 reels.
Partnership Record, 1918-1960; 1 reel.

COURT RECORDS

County Court of Pleas and Quarter Sessions
- Minutes, 1785-1868; 3 reels.
- Minutes, Appearance, Prosecution, and Trial Dockets, 1756-1761; 1 reel.

Inferior Court
- Minutes, 1878-1886; 1 reel.

Superior Court
- Equity Minutes, 1807-1868; 2 reels.
- Judgments, Index to, Defendant, 1868-1968; 3 reels.
- Judgments, Index to, Plaintiff, 1868-1968; 3 reels.
- Judgments and Summons, Index to, Defendant, 1931-1949; 1 reel.
- Judgments and Summons, Index to, Plaintiff, 1931-1949; 1 reel.
- Minutes, 1817-1960; 18 reels.

ELECTION RECORDS

Elections, Record of, 1878-1960; 1 reel.

ESTATES RECORDS

Accounts, Record of, 1868-1960; 7 reels.
Administrators' Bonds, 1867-1898; 1 reel.
Administrators, Executors, and Guardians, Index to, 1868-1968; 1 reel.
Administrators, Index to, 1897-1940; 1 reel.
Administrators, Record of, 1897-1960; 8 reels.
Appointment of Executors, 1868-1960; 2 reels.
Clerk's Account Book (Estates), 1849-1873; 1 reel.
Clerk's Receiver Accounts, 1908-1932; 1 reel.
Estates, Index to Record of (Orphan Books), 1808-1868; 1 reel.
Estates, Record of (Orphan Books), 1808-1868; 5 reels.
Executors, Index to, 1869-1940; 1 reel.
Guardians' Bonds, 1867-1899; 1 reel.
Guardians, Index to, 1899-1940; 1 reel.
Guardians, Record of, 1845-1968; 3 reels.
Inheritance Tax Records, 1920-1960; 1 reel.
Settlements, Record of, 1869-1960; 5 reels.

LAND RECORDS

Deeds, Mortgages, and Bills of Sale, 1784, 1803-1807; 1 reel.
Deeds Proved in Court, 1802-1805; 1 reel.
Deeds, Record of, 1701-1946; 181 reels.
Land Entries, 1778-1795; 1 reel.
Land Entries and Claims Journal, 1882-1926; 1 reel.
Land Sold for Taxes, Record of, 1876-1905; 1 reel.
Partitions and Divisions, 1736-1878; 1 reel.
Patent Book (Grants), 1798-1816; 2 reels.
Plat Books, 1913-1982; 8 reels.
Plats, Index to, 1913-1982; 1 reel.
Real Estate Conveyances, Index to, Grantee, 1701-1959; 11 reels.
Real Estate Conveyances, Index to, Grantor, 1701-1959; 11 reels.
Real Estate Conveyances, Record of, 1946-1960; 75 reels.
Registration of Titles, 1915-1959; 4 reels.
Sale and Resale under Mortgages and Deeds of Trust, Record of, 1915-1960; 5 reels.

MARRIAGE, DIVORCE, AND VITAL STATISTICS

Births, Index to, 1913-1980; 7 reels.
Cohabitation, Record of, 1866. [*See* Marriages, Record of]
Deaths, Index to, 1913-1963; 2 reels.
Delayed Births, Index to, various years; 1 reel.
Delayed Births, Record of, various years; 5 reels.
Maiden Names of Divorced Women, 1926-1960; 1 reel.
Marriage Registers, 1847-1958; 9 reels.
Marriage Registers, Index to, no date; 1 reel.
Marriages, Record of, 1851-1868; Record of Cohabitation, 1866; 1 reel.

MILITARY AND PENSION RECORDS

Pensions, Record of, 1912-1930; 1 reel.

Miscellaneous Records

Alien Registration, various years; 1 reel.
Clerk's Minute Docket, 1908; 1 reel.
Inquisition of Lunacy, 1900-1968; 2 reels.
Orders and Decrees, 1869-1963; 15 reels.
Special Proceedings, 1874-1960; 4 reels.
Special Proceedings, Index to, Defendant, 1874-1960; 2 reels.
Special Proceedings, Index to, Plaintiff, 1874-1968; 2 reels.
Wardens of the Poor, Minutes, 1839-1868; 1 reel.

Officials, County

Board of County Commissioners, Minutes, Index to, 1919-1972; 1 reel.
Board of County Commissioners, Minutes, 1868-1976; 13 reels.
Board of Magistrates, Minutes, 1875-1895; 1 reel.
County Board of Health, Minutes, 1960-1975; 1 reel.

Roads and Bridges

Overseers, Record of, 1845-1868; 1 reel.

School Records

Annual Reports, Public Schools of Washington, 1898-1913; 1 reel.
County Board of Education, Minutes, 1909-1960; 2 reels.

Tax and Fiscal Records

Tax Lists and Scrolls, 1779-1927; 24 reels.

Wills

Wills, 1720-1867; 4 reels.
Wills, Cross Index to, 1720-1949; 1 reel.
Wills, Index to, Devisor, 1950-1968; 1 reel.
Wills, Record of, 1868-1968; 6 reels.

BERTIE COUNTY

Established in 1722 from Chowan Precinct as a precinct of Albemarle County.

ORIGINAL RECORDS

BONDS

Apprentice Bonds and Records, 1750-1889; 5 volumes, 4 Fibredex boxes, 1 manuscript box.
Bastardy Bonds and Records, 1739-1880; 1 volume, 2 Fibredex boxes.
Constables' Bonds, 1812-1869; 3 volumes.
County Bonds, 1872. [*See* **COURT RECORDS**, Court of Pleas and Quarter Sessions, Minutes, 1842-1843]
Officials' Bonds, 1755-1889; 2 Fibredex boxes.

COURT RECORDS [*See also* **CRX RECORDS**]

County Court of Pleas and Quarter Sessions
Appearance Dockets, 1838-1861, 1866-1868; 2 volumes.
Clerk's Account Book, 1755-1761; 1 volume.
Clerk's Receipt Book, 1824-1828; 1 volume.
Costs Docket, 1760-1763; 1 pamphlet. [*See also* Minutes, 1725, 1740-1741]
Crown Dockets, 1748-1775; 2 volumes. [*See also* Trial, Appearance, and Reference Dockets, 1739-1764, 1760-1779]
Execution Dockets, 1748-1868; 16 volumes.
Minutes, 1724-1868; 21 volumes, 1 pamphlet.
State Dockets, 1778-1868; 5 volumes.
Trial and Appearance Dockets, 1798-1868; 8 volumes.
Trial, Appearance, and Reference Dockets, 1725-1797; 11 volumes.
Trial Dockets (Rough), 1761-1862; 1 Fibredex box.

Inferior Court
Minutes, 1877-1887; 1 volume.

Superior Court
Appearance Docket, 1868-1895. [*See* Court of Pleas and Quarter Sessions, Appearance Docket, 1866-1868]
Argument Docket, 1807. [*See* Trial and Appearance Dockets]
Civil Action Papers, 1737-1905; 28 Fibredex boxes.
Civil Issues Dockets, 1870-1900; 1 Fibredex box.
Criminal Action Papers, 1734-1868; 6 Fibredex boxes.
Criminal Issues Dockets, 1871-1900; 1 Fibredex box.
Equity Execution Docket, 1824-1835; 1 volume.
Equity Trial Dockets, 1808, 1818, 1820-1833; 2 volumes.
Execution Dockets, 1808-1868; 3 volumes, 1 manuscript box. [*See also* Court of Pleas and Quarter Sessions, Execution Docket, 1861-1868]
Minutes, 1807-1915; 11 volumes, 1 manuscript box.
Miscellaneous Dockets, 1814-1875; 1 manuscript box.
Reference Docket. [*See* Trial and Appearance Dockets]
State Dockets, 1817-1868; 2 volumes. [*See also* Trial and Appearance Dockets, 1807-1813, 1807-1816]
Trial and Appearance Dockets, 1807-1871; 5 volumes.

ELECTION RECORDS

Election Returns, 1769, 1790-1914; 4 Fibredex boxes.
Elections, Record of, 1878-1926; 2 volumes.

ESTATES RECORDS

Accounts, Record of, 1868-1915; 7 volumes.
Administrators' Bonds, 1762-1769, 1848-1909; 6 volumes.
Estates, Record of, 1728-1868; 27 volumes.
Estates Records, 1730-1920; 114 Fibredex boxes. [*See also* **CRX RECORDS**]
Guardians' Accounts, 1817-1868; 5 volumes.
Guardians' Bonds, 1848-1894; 2 volumes.
Guardians' Records, 1730-1920; 16 Fibredex boxes.
Orphan Docket, 1773. [*See* **COURT RECORDS**, Court of Pleas and Quarter Sessions, State Docket, 1778-1798]
Settlements, Record of, 1869-1916; 2 volumes.

LAND RECORDS

Deeds, 1723-1890; 12 Fibredex boxes.
Deeds, Record of, 1765-1772; 1 volume.
Land Records, 1736-1861; 2 Fibredex boxes.
Miscellaneous Land Records, 1720-1861; 1 Fibredex box.
Mortgage Deeds and Deeds of Trust, 1723-1890; 2 Fibredex boxes.

MARRIAGE, DIVORCE, AND VITAL STATISTICS

Disinterment/Reinterment Permits, 1980-1986; 1 manuscript box.
Marriage Bonds, 1762-1868; 5 Fibredex boxes.
Marriage Licenses, 1870-1903; 5 Fibredex boxes. [*See also* **CRX RECORDS**]
Miscellaneous Marriage Records, 1749-1914; 1 Fibredex box.

MILITARY AND PENSION RECORDS [*See* **MISCELLANEOUS RECORDS**]

MISCELLANEOUS RECORDS

Alien Registration, 1940, 1954; 1 volume.
Board of Superintendents of Common Schools and County Board of Education, Minutes and Accounts, 1847-1878; 1 volume.
Cotton Reports, 1889-1890; 2 manuscript boxes.
County Accounts, 1741-1903; 2 Fibredex boxes.
Court Martial Minutes, 1842; 1 manuscript box.
Merchants' Accounts, 1800-1900; 1 Fibredex box.
Miscellaneous Records, 1723-1914; 5 Fibredex boxes. [*See also* **CRX RECORDS**]
Pension Board Minutes, 1903-1965; 1 volume.
Personal Accounts, 1718-1860; 2 Fibredex boxes.
Promissory Notes, 1746-1800; 1 Fibredex box.
Road, Bridge, and Ferry Records, 1734-1903; 2 Fibredex boxes.
School Records, 1850-1878, 1895; 3 manuscript boxes.
Slave Records, 1744-1865; 3 Fibredex boxes.
Special Proceedings, 1902, 1904. [*See* **COURT RECORDS**, Superior Court, Minute Docket, 1898-1902]
Stock Marks, 1722-1741; 1 pamphlet. [*See also* **COURT RECORDS**, Court of Pleas and Quarter Sessions, Minutes]
Wardens of the Poor, Minutes,1838-1851; 1 volume.

ROADS AND BRIDGES [*See* **MISCELLANEOUS RECORDS**]

SCHOOL RECORDS [*See* **MISCELLANEOUS RECORDS**]

TAX AND FISCAL RECORDS [*See also* **CRX RECORDS**]
Merchants' Purchase Returns, 1880-1887, 1898; 1 Fibredex box.
Miscellaneous Tax Records, 1843-1903; 1 manuscript box.
Taxables, Lists of, 1755-1860; 13 Fibredex boxes.

WILLS
Wills, 1749-1897; 18 Fibredex boxes. [*See also* **CRX RECORDS**]

CRX RECORDS
Bills of Cost for Criminal Actions, Inferior Court, 1885; 1 folder.
Civil Actions, 1793-1812; 2 folders.
Coroner's Inquest, 1796; 1 folder.
Estates Records, 1803-1812; 12 folders.
Insolvent Tax Lists, 1893, 1895, 1896; 1 folder.
Marriage Licenses, 1876-1877, 1881, 1889, 1904; 2 folders.
Minutes, Court of Pleas and Quarter Sessions, 1749-1750; 5 folders.
Miscellaneous Records, 1885-1898; 5 folders.
Petition for Liquor License (James Rayner), n.d.; 1 folder.
Tax Lists, 1761; 1 volume.
Trial Docket, Court of Pleas and Quarter Sessions, 1867; 1 folder.
Will (James Parker), 1761; 1 folder.

MICROFILM RECORDS

BONDS
Apprentice Bonds, 1811-1889; 2 reels.
Bastardy Bonds, 1875-1877; 1 reel.

CORPORATIONS AND PARTNERSHIPS
Corporations, Record of, 1907-1957; 1 reel.

COURT RECORDS [*See also* **MISCELLANEOUS RECORDS**]
County Court of Pleas and Quarter Sessions
Minutes, 1724-1743, 1758-1868; 7 reels.
Inferior Court
Minutes, 1877-1887; 1 reel.
Superior Court
Judgments, Index to, Defendant, 1941-1968; 1 reel.
Judgments, Index to, Plaintiff, 1941-1968; 1 reel.
Judgments, Cross Index to, 1868-1940; 4 reels.
Minutes, 1807-1955; 11 reels.

ELECTION RECORDS
Elections, Record of, 1878-1968; 2 reels.

ESTATES RECORDS
Accounts, Cross Index to, 1868-1942; 1 reel.
Accounts, Record of, 1868-1954; 7 reels.
Administrators' Bonds, 1762-1769, 1848-1903; 5 reels.
Amounts Paid to Indigent Children, 1929-1942; 1 reel.
Appointment of Administrators, Executors, and Guardians, 1909-1948; 6 reels.
Appointment of Executors, 1868-1917; 1 reel.
Clerk's Receiver Accounts, 1906-1921; 1 reel.
Estates, Record of, 1728-1871; 11 reels.

Executors and Administrators, Index to, 1905-1968; 1 reel.
Executors, Record of, 1940-1968; 1 reel.
Guardians' Accounts, 1817-1868; 1 reel.
Guardians and Administrators, Cross Index to, 1858-1907; 1 reel.
Guardians' Bonds, 1848-1931; 2 reels.
Guardians, Cross Index to, 1905-1960; 1 reel.
Guardians, Record of, 1935-1968; 1 reel.
Inheritance Tax Records, 1923-1959; 1 reel.
Settlements, Record of, 1866-1968; 4 reels.

LAND RECORDS

Land Entries, 1778-1794; 1 reel.
Map Books, 1915-1957, 1973-1985; 3 reels.
Map Books, Index to, 1771-1976; 1 reel.
Processions, Record of, 1851-1869; 1 reel.
Real Estate Conveyances, Index to, Grantee, 1722-1959; 4 reels.
Real Estate Conveyances, Index to, Grantor, 1722-1959; 4 reels.
Real Estate Conveyances, Record of, 1721-1948; 147 reels.
Resale of Land, Record of, 1925-1968; 4 reels.

MARRIAGE, DIVORCE, AND VITAL STATISTICS

Births and Deaths, Index to, 1914-1921; 1 reel.
Births, Index to, 1916-1975; 2 reels.
Cohabitation, Record of, 1866; 1 reel.
Deaths, Index to, 1917-1975; 1 reel.
Delayed Births, Index to, various years; 1 reel.
Maiden Names of Divorced Women, 1938-1968; 1 reel.
Marriage Bonds, 1741-1868; 4 reels.
Marriage Certificates, 1851-1868; 1 reel.
Marriage Registers, 1851-1945; 2 reels.
Marriage Registers, Cross Index to, 1872-1900; 1 reel.

MILITARY AND PENSION RECORDS

Confederate Veterans Association Roster, 1919-1935; 1 reel.
Court Martial Minutes, 1842; 1 reel.
Pension Board, Minutes, 1903-1960; 1 reel.

MISCELLANEOUS RECORDS

Alien Registration, 1940, 1954; 1 reel.
Lunacy, Record of, 1899-1968; 1 reel.
Orders and Decrees, 1868-1959; 17 reels.
Special Proceedings, 1868-1955; 2 reels.
Special Proceedings and Civil Actions, Index to, 1923-1968; 2 reels.
Wardens of the Poor, Minutes, 1838-1847; 1 reel.

OFFICIALS, COUNTY

Board of County Commissioners, Minutes, 1868-1947; 5 reels.

School Records

Board of Superintendents of Common Schools and County Board of Education, Minutes, 1847-1878; 1 reel.

Tax and Fiscal Records

Tax Lists, 1755-1860, 1877, 1906, 1908-1909; 7 reels.

Wills

Wills, Index to, 1761-1970; 1 reel.
Wills, Record of, 1761-1968; 7 reels.

BLADEN COUNTY

Established in 1734 from New Hanover Precinct as a precinct of Bath County.
Courthouse fires of ca. 1770, 1800, and 1893 destroyed most of the
court records and several land records.

ORIGINAL RECORDS

COURT RECORDS

County Court of Pleas and Quarter Sessions
- Execution Docket, 1761-1762. [*See* **MISCELLANEOUS RECORDS**, Miscellaneous Records, 1761-1958]
- Minutes, 1866-1867; 1 volume.

Recorder's Court
- Minutes, 1921-1968; 11 volumes.

Superior Court
- Civil Action Papers, 1893-1956; 14 Fibredex boxes.
- Civil Action Papers Concerning Land, 1893-1955; 13 Fibredex boxes.
- Civil Issues Dockets, 1885-1894, 1931; 2 volumes.
- Criminal Action Papers, 1893-1956; 1 Fibredex box.
- Criminal Issues Docket, 1899-1907; 1 volume.
- Judgment Dockets, 1871-1882; 2 volumes.
- Minutes, 1869-1890, 1893-1970; 15 volumes.
- Minutes, Index to, Defendants, 1869-1968; 4 volumes.
- Summons Docket, 1869. [*See* **MISCELLANEOUS RECORDS**, Special Proceedings Dockets]

ELECTION RECORDS

- Election Records, 1898, 1920, 1931-1952; 1 Fibredex box.
- Elections, Record of, 1896-1972; 7 volumes.
- Permanent Registration of Voters, 1902-1908; 1 volume.
- Voter Registration Book, Elizabethtown Precinct, 1950-1954; 1 volume.

ESTATES RECORDS

- Accounts, Record of, 1868-1885, 1893-1917; 2 volumes.
- Administrators' Bonds, 1909-1912; 1 volume.
- Administrators, Record of, 1917-1939; 2 volumes.
- Division of Estates, Record of, 1899-1941; 3 volumes.
- Estates Records, 1761, 1862, 1882-1956; 34 Fibredex boxes.
- Executors, Record of, 1946-1968; 1 volume.
- Guardians' Bonds, 1893-1912; 2 volumes.
- Guardians, Record of, 1922-1968; 2 volumes.
- Guardians' Records, 1894-1955; 3 Fibredex boxes.
- Inheritance Tax Record, 1924-1970. [*See* **LAND RECORDS**]
- Settlements, Record of, 1885-1923; 2 volumes.

LAND RECORDS [*See also* COURT RECORDS, Superior Court]

- Attachments, Executions, Levies, and Liens on Land and Personal Property, 1893-1956, 1961; 2 Fibredex boxes.
- Deeds and Grants, 1738-1804; 2 volumes.
- Ejectments, 1915-1955; 1 Fibredex box.
- Federal Tax Lien Index, 1919-1969; 1 volume.

Foreclosures, 1893-1955; 8 Fibredex boxes.
Inheritance Tax Record, 1924-1970; 3 volumes.
Land Condemnations, 1935-1954; 1 Fibredex box.
Land Entry Books, 1893-1920; 2 volumes.
Land Sold for Taxes, 1927-1949; 26 Fibredex boxes.
Miscellaneous Land Records, 1770-1944; 1 Fibredex box.
Petitions to Partition Land, 1898-1952; 2 Fibredex boxes.
Petitions to Sell Land, 1893-1954; 3 Fibredex boxes.
Petitions to Settle Boundary, 1904-1955; 2 Fibredex boxes.
Registration of Titles (Torrens Act), 1916-1954; 1 Fibredex box.

MARRIAGE, DIVORCE, AND VITAL STATISTICS
Divorce Records, 1893-1955; 11 Fibredex boxes.
Marriage Register, 1892-1904; 1 volume.

MISCELLANEOUS RECORDS
Alien Registration, 1940; 1 volume.
Assignee, Receiver, and Trustee Records, 1896-1955; 2 Fibredex boxes.
Canal and Drainage Records, 1897-1955; 2 Fibredex boxes.
Drainage Record, 1919-1921; 1 volume.
Homestead and Personal Property Exemptions, 1893-1955, 1965; 2 Fibredex boxes.
Inquisition of Lunacy, 1899-1965; 3 volumes.
Lunacy Records, 1895-1955; 1 Fibredex box.
Miscellaneous Records, 1761-1958; 2 Fibredex boxes.
Notary Public Record, 1946-1968; 1 volume.
Officials' Oaths, 1944-1970; 1 volume.
Physicians and Surgeons, Register of, 1895-1972; 3 volumes.
Poll Tax Book, 1902-1908; 1 volume.
Railroad Records, 1893-1944; 4 Fibredex boxes.
Road, Bridge, and Ferry Records, 1901-1955; 1 Fibredex box.
School Records, 1893-1948; 1 Fibredex box.
Special Proceedings, 1907-1922; 1 volume.
Special Proceedings Dockets, 1869-1924; 2 volumes.
Timber Records, 1910-1955; 4 Fibredex boxes.

OFFICIALS, COUNTY [*See* **MISCELLANEOUS RECORDS**]

ROADS AND BRIDGES [*See* **MISCELLANEOUS RECORDS**]

SCHOOL RECORDS [*See* **MISCELLANEOUS RECORDS**]

TAX AND FISCAL RECORDS [*See also* **LAND RECORDS; MISCELLANEOUS RECORDS**]
Reliefs to be Credited to the Sheriff, 1893-1894, 1899-1901; 1 volume.

MICROFILM RECORDS

CORPORATIONS AND PARTNERSHIPS
Corporations, Record of, 1899-1973; 2 reels.
Partners, Assumed Names, and Corporations, Index to, 1899-1984; 1 reel.
Partnership Record, 1913-1929; 1 reel.

COURT RECORDS
County Court of Pleas and Quarter Sessions
Minutes, 1866-1867; 1 reel.

Superior Court
Judgment Docket, 1930-1939; 1 reel.
Judgments, Index to, Defendant, 1869-1968; 1 reel.
Judgments, Index to, Plaintiff, 1869-1968; 1 reel.
Minutes, 1869-1968; 8 reels.
Minutes, Index to, Defendant, 1869-1968; 2 reels.
Minutes, Index to, Plaintiff, 1869-1968; 2 reels.

ELECTION RECORDS

Elections, Record of, 1896-1960; 1 reel.

ESTATES RECORDS

Accounts of Administrators, Executors, and Guardians, Record of, 1918-1968; 3 reels.
Accounts, Record of, 1868-1917; 1 reel.
Administrators' Bonds, 1909-1912; 1 reel.
Administrators, Executors, Guardians, and Trustees, Record of, 1911-1926; 1 reel.
Administrators, Record of, 1917-1968; 3 reels.
Division of Estates, Record of, 1899-1936; 1 reel.
Executors, Record of, 1946-1968; 1 reel.
Final Accounts: Executors, Administrators, and Guardians, Index to, 1869-1968; 1 reel.
Final Accounts: Wards, Index to, 1872-1968; 1 reel.
Guardians' Bonds, 1893-1912; 1 reel.
Guardians, Record of, 1922-1968; 2 reels.
Inheritance Tax Records, 1924-1970; 2 reels.
Settlements, Record of, 1885-1919; 1 reel.

LAND RECORDS

Deeds and Grants, 1738-1804; 1 reel.
Deeds, Record of, 1774-1961; 79 reels.
Entry Takers, Record of, 1893-1917, 1923-1940; 1 reel.
Map Books, 1877-1973; 5 reels.
Maps, Index to, 1877-1973; 1 reel.
Real Estate Conveyances, Index to, Grantee, 1784-1961; 12 reels.
Real Estate Conveyances, Index to, Grantor, 1784-1961; 14 reels.
Resale of Land by Mortgagees and Trustees, Record of, 1923-1966; 2 reels.

MARRIAGE, DIVORCE, AND VITAL STATISTICS

Births, Index to, 1913-1972; 1 reel.
Deaths, Index to, 1914-1972; 1 reel.
Delayed Births, Index to, various years, 1873-1966; 2 reels.
Marriage Licenses, 1909-1961; 3 reels.
Marriage Registers, 1892-1971; 2 reels.

MILITARY AND PENSION RECORDS

Roll Book, Bladen Guards (Co. K, 8th Regt. N. C. V., Artillery), 1861-1862; 1 reel.

MISCELLANEOUS RECORDS

Alien Registration, 1940; 1 reel.
Clerk's Minute Dockets, 1933-1968; 2 reels.
Inquisition of Lunacy, Record of, 1899-1959; 1 reel.
Orders and Decrees, 1868-1968; 9 reels.
Special Proceedings, 1868-1924; 1 reel.

Special Proceedings, Index to, Defendant, 1868-1968; 1 reel.
Special Proceedings, Index to, Plaintiff, 1868-1968; 1 reel.

OFFICIALS, COUNTY

Board of County Commissioners, Minutes, 1893-1905; 1 reel.

SCHOOL RECORDS

County Board of Education, Minutes, 1881-1933; 1 reel.

TAX AND FISCAL RECORDS

Tax Lists, 1883, 1895, 1898-1900, 1905, 1915, 1925-1926; 3 reels.

WILLS

Wills, Index to, Devisee, 1766-1968; 1 reel.
Wills, Index to, Devisor, 1766-1968; 1 reel.
Wills, Record of, 1766-1968; 3 reels.

BRUNSWICK COUNTY

Established in 1764 from Bladen and New Hanover counties.
Many court records were destroyed by Federal troops in 1865.

ORIGINAL RECORDS

BONDS

Apprentice Bonds and Records, 1810-1907; 1 Fibredex box.
Bastardy Bonds and Records, 1810-1930; 1 Fibredex box.
Officials' Bonds and Records, 1794-1904; 3 volumes, 1 Fibredex box.
Sheriffs' Bonds and Records, 1818-1901; 1 Fibredex box.

COURT RECORDS

County Court of Pleas and Quarter Sessions
- Minutes, 1782-1868; 11 volumes.
- Trial Dockets, 1792, 1820-1868; 2 volumes, 1 manuscript box.

Superior Court
- Civil Action Papers, 1790-1926; 11 Fibredex boxes.
- Civil Action Papers Concerning Land, 1807-1911; 3 Fibredex boxes.
- Criminal Action Papers, 1800-1920; 3 Fibredex boxes. [*See also* **CRX RECORDS**]
- Minutes, 1845-1912; 5 volumes.

ELECTION RECORDS

Election Records, 1809-1916; 1 Fibredex box.
Elections, Record of, 1898-1920; 3 volumes.

ESTATES RECORDS [*See also* **CRX RECORDS**]

Accounts, Record of, 1868-1915; 1 volume.
Appointment of Administrators, Executors, Guardians, and Masters, 1868-1914; 1 volume.
Estates Records, 1783-1920; 14 Fibredex boxes.
Guardians' Records, 1819-1909; 2 Fibredex boxes.

LAND RECORDS [*See also* **COURT RECORDS**, Superior Court; **CRX RECORDS**]

Deeds, Index to, 1764-1900; 1 volume.
Deeds, Record of, 1790-1796, 1809-1814; 2 volumes.
Deeds of Sale, 1821-1926; 2 Fibredex boxes.
Entry Books, 1853-1958; 2 volumes.
Miscellaneous Land Records, 1808-1924; 1 Fibredex box.
Mortgage Deeds and Warranty Deeds, 1798-1929; 1 Fibredex box.
Surveys, Record of, 1905-1920; 1 volume.

MARRIAGE, DIVORCE, AND VITAL STATISTICS

Disinterment/Reinterment Permits, 1963-1981; 1 manuscript box.
Divorce and Marriage Records, 1844, 1866, 1869-1905; 1 Fibredex box.
Marriage Bonds, 1804-1868; 2 Fibredex boxes.
Marriage Registers, 1870-1877, 1893-1904; 2 volumes.

MILITARY AND PENSION RECORDS [*See* **MISCELLANEOUS RECORDS**]

MISCELLANEOUS RECORDS

Alien Registration, 1940; 1 volume.
Assignees, Receivers and Trustees, Records of, 1893-1907; 1 Fibredex box.

Board of Superintendents of Common Schools, Minutes, 1841-1854; 1 pamphlet.
Miscellaneous Records, 1786-1925; 2 Fibredex boxes. [*See also* **CRX RECORDS**]
Pensions, Record of, 1927-1954; 1 volume.
Railroad Records, 1868-1908; 1 Fibredex box.
Stock Marks, 1869-1941, 1947; 2 volumes.

ROADS AND BRIDGES [*See* **MISCELLANEOUS RECORDS**]

SCHOOL RECORDS [*See* **MISCELLANEOUS RECORDS; CRX RECORDS**]

WILLS

Wills, 1765-1912; 6 Fibredex boxes.
Wills, Record of, 1781-1847; 3 volumes.

CRX RECORDS

Accounts, Record of, 1912-1928; 1 volume.
Board of County Commissioners, Minutes, 1930-1931; 1 volume.
Criminal Actions and Road Records, 1925-1938; 2 folders.
Deeds, Grants, and Will, 1784-1917; 1 folder.
Deeds for School House Sites, Index to, n.d.; 1 volume.
Miscellaneous Records, 1920-1924; 1 Fibredex box.

MICROFILM RECORDS

BONDS

Officials' Bonds, 1794-1829, 1868-1904; 1 reel.

CORPORATIONS AND PARTNERSHIPS

Corporations, Record of, 1889-1963; 1 reel.
Partnerships, Record of, 1917-1959; 1 reel.

COURT RECORDS

County Court of Pleas and Quarter Sessions
  Minutes, 1782-1786, 1789-1801, 1805-1868; 2 reels.
Superior Court
  Judgments, Index to, 1868-1963; 2 reels.
  Minutes, 1845-1954; 6 reels.

ELECTION RECORDS

Elections, Record of, 1898-1972; 1 reel.

ESTATES RECORDS

Accounts, Record of, 1868-1963; 2 reels.
Administrators, Executors, and Guardians, Index to, 1929-1963; 1 reel.
Administrators, Record of, 1929-1955; 2 reels.
Appointment of Administrators, Executors, and Guardians, 1868-1929; 1 reel.
Division of Land and Dowers, 1894-1917; 1 reel.
Executors, Record of, 1929-1963; 1 reel.
Guardians, Record of, 1930-1968; 1 reel.
Inheritance Tax Records, 1923-1963; 1 reel.
Settlements, Record of, 1868-1963; 1 reel.

LAND RECORDS

Certificate Record of Land Sold for Taxes, 1931; 1 reel.
Deeds and Land Grants, Record of, 1788-1815; 1 reel.
Federal Tax Liens, Index to, 1933-1972; 1 reel.
Land Entries, 1853-1953; 1 reel.
Maps, Index to, 1914-1974; 1 reel.
Plat Books, 1915-1973; 4 reels.
Real Estate Conveyances, Index to, Grantee, 1764-1963; 6 reels.
Real Estate Conveyances, Index to, Grantor, 1764-1963; 6 reels.
Real Estate Conveyances, Record of, 1764-1946; 50 reels.
Registration of Land Titles, 1914-1940; 1 reel.
Resale of Land by Mortgagees and Trustees, Record of, 1920-1963; 2 reels.
Surveys, Record of, 1905-1920; 1 reel.

MARRIAGE, DIVORCE, AND VITAL STATISTICS

Births, Index to, 1914-1974; 1 reel.
Births, Record of, 1913-1985; 17 reels.
Deaths, Index to, 1914-1974; 1 reel.
Deaths, Record of, 1913-1991; 13 reels.
Delayed Births, Index to, various years; 1 reel.
Delayed Births, Record of, various years; 3 reels.
Marriage Bonds, 1804-1868; 3 reels.
Marriage Registers, 1850-1974; 2 reels.

MILITARY AND PENSION RECORDS

Pensions, Record of, 1927-1953; 1 reel.

MISCELLANEOUS RECORDS

Alien Registration, 1940; 1 reel.
Lunacy, Record of, 1914-1961; 1 reel.
Special Proceedings, Cross Index to, 1938-1963; 1 reel.
Special Proceedings Dockets, 1890-1963; 5 reels.

OFFICIALS, COUNTY

Board of County Commissioners, Minutes, 1868-1963; 5 reels.

SCHOOL RECORDS

Board of Superintendents of Common Schools, Minutes, 1841-1854; 1 reel.
County Board of Education, Minutes, 1872-1963; 2 reels.

TAX AND FISCAL RECORDS

Tax Scrolls, 1873-1945; 4 reels.

WILLS

Wills, Cross Index to, 1764-1963; 1 reel.
Wills, Record of, 1764-1954; 1 reel.

BUNCOMBE COUNTY

Established in 1791 from Burke and Rutherford counties.
Courthouse fires of 1830 and 1865 destroyed many court records.

ORIGINAL RECORDS

BONDS

Apprentice Bonds, 1794-1919; 4 volumes. [*See also* **MISCELLANEOUS RECORDS**, Miscellaneous Records, 1841-1924]
Bastardy Bonds and Records, 1824-1928; 1 volume, 2 Fibredex boxes.
Officials' Bonds and Records, 1854-1909. [*See* **MISCELLANEOUS RECORDS**, Miscellaneous Records, 1841-1924]

CORPORATIONS AND PARTNERSHIPS [*See* **MISCELLANEOUS RECORDS**]

COURT RECORDS [*See also* **CRX RECORDS**]

County Court of Pleas and Quarter Sessions
- Appearance Docket, 1852-1868; 1 volume.
- Execution Dockets, 1807-1868; 10 volumes.
- Minutes, 1792-1868; 7 volumes.
- State Dockets, 1826-1868; 3 volumes.
- Trial and Appearance Dockets, 1796-1851; 4 volumes.
- Trial Dockets, 1851-1868; 2 volumes. [*See also* Superior Court, Trial Docket]

Criminal Court of Buncombe County/Circuit Criminal Court/Western District

Criminal Court
- Minutes, 1893-1900; 3 volumes.

General County Court
- Dockets. [*See* Superior Court, Judgment Dockets]
- Minutes, 1929-1930; 2 volumes.

Inferior Court
- Execution Docket, 1883-1888; 1 volume.
- Minutes, 1883-1889; 1 volume.

Superior Court [*See also* **CRX RECORDS**]
- Appearance Docket, 1866-1869; 1 volume.
- Civil Action Papers, 1812-1918; 31 Fibredex boxes.
- Civil Action Papers Concerning Land, 1808-1925; 46 Fibredex boxes.
- Criminal Action Papers, 1832-1944; 20 Fibredex boxes.
- Equity Trial and Appearance Docket, 1808-1845; 1 volume.
- Execution Dockets, 1850-1868; 4 volumes. [*See also* **MISCELLANEOUS RECORDS**, Special Proceedings Docket, 1869-1878]
- Judgment Dockets (includes Tax Suits and General County Court Dockets), 1897-1970; 150 volumes. [*See also* **LAND RECORDS**, Tax Suit Judgment Dockets]
- Minutes, 1812-1815, 1857-1892; 12 volumes.
- Minutes (Civil), 1892-1970; 90 volumes.
- Minutes (Criminal), 1900-1970; 40 volumes.
- Miscellaneous Dockets (Abstracts), 1808-1862; 1 volume.
- State Docket, 1833-1869; 1 volume.
- Trial Docket, 1853-1866; 1 volume. [*See also* Court of Pleas and Quarter Sessions, Trial Docket, 1867-1868]

ELECTION RECORDS

Election Records, 1871-1900; 1 Fibredex box.

ESTATES RECORDS

Accounts, Record of, 1868-1970; 64 volumes.
Administrators' Bonds, 1870-1897; 5 volumes.
Administrators, Record of, 1896-1907; 2 volumes.
Appointment of Administrators, Executors, Guardians, and Masters, 1868-1890; 1 volume.
Clerks's Receipt Book, Tax Refunds to Estates without Administrators, 1953-1956; 1 volume.
Estates, Record of, 1845-1868; 2 volumes.
Estates Records, 1801, 1815-1924; 122 Fibredex boxes.
Guardians' Bonds, 1870-1900; 4 volumes.
Guardians, Record of, 1899-1907; 1 volume.
Guardians' Records, 1829-1915, 1933; 15 Fibredex boxes.
Inventories, Record of, 1899-1944; 4 volumes.
Settlements, Cross Index to, 1869-1970; 3 volumes.
Settlements, Record of, 1864-1970; 67 volumes.

LAND RECORDS

Attachments, Executions, Levies, and Liens on Land, 1814-1915; 4 Fibredex boxes.
Deeds, 1807-1919; 1 Fibredex box.
Deeds, Index to, 1794-1924; 5 volumes.
Deeds, Record of, 1789-1875; 52 volumes.
Ejectments, 1818-1905; 1 Fibredex box.
Land Entries, 1794-1919; 16 volumes, 1 manuscript box.
Miscellaneous Deeds, 1841-1924; 2 Fibredex boxes.
Miscellaneous Land Records, 1798-1920; 3 Fibredex boxes.
Probate of Deeds, 1798-1804, 1820-1825, 1899; 3 volumes.
Tax Suit Judgment Dockets, 1936-1962; 35 volumes. [*See also* **COURT RECORDS**, Superior Court, Judgment Dockets]
Tax Suits, Index to, 1900-1965; 6 volumes.

MARRIAGE, DIVORCE, AND VITAL STATISTICS

Cohabitation, Record of, 1866. [*See also* **MISCELLANEOUS RECORDS**, Road Docket, 1849-1868]
Disinterment/Reinterment Permits, 1972-1986; 1 manuscript box.
Divorce Records, 1830-1918; 26 Fibredex boxes.
Marriage Bonds, 1842-1867; 1 Fibredex box.

MILITARY AND PENSION RECORDS. [*See* **MISCELLANEOUS RECORDS**]

MISCELLANEOUS RECORDS

Alien Registration, 1927-1941; 1 Fibredex box.
Assignees, Receivers, and Trustees, Records of, 1837-1911; 13 Fibredex boxes.
Board of County Commissioners, Minutes, 1868-1912; 12 volumes.
Clerk's Minute Dockets (Special Proceedings), 1873-1884; 2 volumes.
Coroners' Inquests, 1875-1929; 2 Fibredex boxes.
Homestead and Personal Property Exemptions, 1866-1906; 2 Fibredex boxes.
Incorporations, Records of, 1885-1909; 1 Fibredex box.
Lunacy, Record of, 1899-1921; 2 volumes.
Military Petitions for Naturalization, 1919-1920; 1 volume.

Miscellaneous Records, 1786-1946; 7 Fibredex boxes.
Naturalization Records, 1906, 1909-1910; 2 volumes.
Orders and Decrees, 1868-1899; 1 volume.
Pensions, Record of, 1893, 1903-1959; 6 volumes.
Railroad Records, 1857-1912; 9 Fibredex boxes.
Road and Bridge Records, 1838-1916; 2 Fibredex boxes.
Road Dockets, 1812-1816, 1849-1868; 2 volumes.
Special Proceedings, Cross Index to, [1869-1911], 1954-1966; 3 volumes.
Special Proceedings Dockets, 1869-1878, 1882-1970; 113 volumes. [*See also* Minutes, 1868-1879]

OFFICIALS, COUNTY [*See* **MISCELLANEOUS RECORDS**]

ROADS AND BRIDGES [*See* **MISCELLANEOUS RECORDS**]

WILLS

Wills, 1826-1961; 158 Fibredex boxes.
Wills, Record of, 1831-1868; 1 volume.

CRX RECORDS

Equity Enrolling Dockets, Superior Court, 1808-1832; 2 volumes.
Minutes, Court of Pleas and Quarter Sessions, 1810-1812; 1 volume.
School Records, 1859-1860; 1 folder.

MICROFILM RECORDS

BONDS

Apprentice Indentures, 1794-1874; 1 reel.
Bastardy Bonds, 1875-1879; 1 reel.

CORPORATIONS AND PARTNERSHIPS

Corporations, Index to, 1884-1964; 1 reel.
Corporations, Record of, 1884-1947; 8 reels.
Partnerships, Record of, 1913-1974; 2 reels.

COURT RECORDS

County Court of Pleas and Quarter Sessions
- Abstract of Court Minutes, Court of Pleas and Quarter Sessions, 1792-1796, 1822-1824, 1832; Superior Court, 1865-1866; 1 reel.
- Appearance Docket, 1852-1868; 1 reel.
- Execution Dockets, 1807-1814, 1823-1843, 1858-1868; 2 reels.
- Minutes, 1792-1812, 1819-1825, 1832-1868; 3 reels.
- Trial and Appearance Docket, 1796-1805; 1 reel.
- Criminal Court of Buncombe County/ Circuit Criminal Court/Western District

Criminal Court
- Minutes, 1893-1900; 2 reels.

General County Court
- Civil Actions, Cross Index to, 1929-1941; 1 reel.
- Minutes, 1929-1941; 4 reels.

Inferior Court
- Criminal Issues Docket, 1883-1889; 1 reel.
- Judgment Docket, 1887-1897; 1 reel.

Superior Court

Bills and Answers in Equity, 1809-1832; 1 reel.
Civil Actions, Cross Index to, 1858-1879, 1896-1955; 5 reels.
Civil Issues Docket, Cross Index to, no date; 1 reel.
Equity Minutes, 1854-1857; Special Proceedings, 1870-1877; 1 reel.
Execution Dockets, 1869-1870, 1883-1884; 1 reel.
Judgment Docket, Justice of the Peace Transcripts, 1930-1960; 1 reel.
Judgments, Cross Index to, Defendant, 1915-1970; 3 reels.
Judgments, Cross Index to, Plaintiff, 1868-1970; 3 reels.
Minutes, 1812-1815, 1857-1909 (includes Special Proceedings, 1868-1885); 9 reels.
Minutes (Civil), 1909-1948; 12 reels.
Minutes (Criminal), 1883-1953; 6 reels.
Motion Docket, 1868-1869; 1 reel.
Summons Docket, 1868-1893; 1 reel.
Trial Docket, 1867-1870; 1 reel.

ESTATES RECORDS

Accounts, Record of, 1868-1964; 13 reels.
Administrators' Bonds, 1870-1897; 2 reels.
Administrators, Cross Index to, 1896-1960; 1 reel.
Administrators, Record of, 1896-1963; 12 reels.
Amounts Paid for Indigent Children, Record of, 1916-1920; 1 reel.
Appointment of Administrators, Executors, and Guardians, 1868-1890; 1 reel.
Appointment and Record of Guardians, 1855-1867; 1 reel.
Commitment of Indigent Children to County Home, 1890-1911; 1 reel.
Guardians' Bonds, 1870-1900; 1 reel.
Guardians, Index to, 1899-1918; 1 reel.
Guardians, Record of, 1899-1962; 6 reels.
Inheritance Tax Records, 1919-1953; 2 reels.
Inventories, Record of, 1845-1868, 1899-1961; 4 reels.
Qualification of Trustees for Guardians and Administrators, Record of, 1936-1967; 1 reel.
Settlements, Cross Index to, 1869-1970; 1 reel.
Settlements, Record of, 1864-1964; 13 reels.
Trusts for Minors and Incompetents, Record of, 1935-1953; 1 reel.

LAND RECORDS

Deeds, Index to, Grantee, 1798-1962; 30 reels.
Deeds, Index to, Grantor, 1791-1962; 31 reels.
Deeds, Record of, 1789-1964; 294 reels.
Land Entries, 1794, 1795, 1832-1837; 1 reel.
Land Grants, 1794-1832; 1 reel.
Mountain Retreat Leases, Record of, 1898-1914; 1 reel.
Plat Books, 1912-1969; 15 reels.
Plats, Index to, 1919-1965; 2 reels.

MARRIAGE, DIVORCE, AND VITAL STATISTICS

Births and Deaths, City of Asheville, 1887-1904, 1914-1915; 1 reel.
Births, Index to, 1913-1974; 5 reels.
Deaths, City of Asheville, 1887-1904, 1914-1915; 1 reel.
Deaths, Index to, 1913-1968; 3 reels.

Marriage Bonds, 1791-1868; 1 reel.
Marriage Registers, Female, 1851-1969; 3 reels.
Marriage Registers, Male, 1851-1969; 3 reels.

MILITARY AND PENSION RECORDS

Pensions, Record of, 1893, 1903-1959; 2 reels.
War of 1812 Claims of Service, 1855; 1 reel.

MISCELLANEOUS RECORDS

Alien Registration, 1927-1941; 1 reel.
Lunacy, Record of, 1899-1949; 3 reels.
Naturalization, Record of, 1906, 1909-1910; 1 reel.
Orders and Decrees, 1868-1899; 1 reel.
Orders and Decrees, Minute Docket, and Liquidation Book, 1933-1936; 1 reel.
Special Proceedings, 1869-1953; 20 reels. [*See also* **COURT RECORDS**, Superior Court, Minutes]
Special Proceedings, Cross Index to, 1869-1954; 2 reels.
Special Proceedings, Unrecorded, Cross Index to, 1874-1957; 1 reel.

OFFICIALS, COUNTY

Board of County Commissioners, Minutes, 1872-1962; 12 reels.
Board of Trustees, Minutes; Magistrates' and Commissioners' Bonds, 1878-1917; 1 reel.

ROADS AND BRIDGES

Road Docket, 1812-1816; 1 reel.

TAX AND FISCAL RECORDS

Tax List, 1915; 1 reel.

WILLS

Wills, Cross Index to, 1831-1970; 1 reel.
Wills, Record of, 1831-1964; 18 reels.

BURKE COUNTY

Established in 1777 from Rowan County.
Many court records and most land records burned by Federal troops in 1865.

ORIGINAL RECORDS

BONDS

Apprentice Bonds and Records, 1784-1908; 1 volume, 1 Fibredex box.
Bastardy Bonds and Records, 1777-1899; 1 volume, 3 Fibredex boxes.
Constables' Bonds and Records, 1782-1875, 1892; 2 Fibredex boxes.
Officials' Bonds and Records, 1778-1949; 1 Fibredex box.

COURT RECORDS

County Court of Pleas and Quarter Sessions
- Execution Dockets, 1837-1840, 1843-1855; 3 volumes.
- Minutes, 1791-1868; 13 volumes.
- Trial and Appearance Dockets, 1792-1857; 5 volumes.

Superior Court
- Civil Action Papers, 1755-1905; 14 Fibredex boxes.
- Civil Action Papers Concerning Land, 1779-1927; 5 Fibredex boxes.
- Criminal Action Papers, 1779-1921; 21 Fibredex boxes.
- Equity Trial and Appearance Docket, 1866-1868. [*See* **MISCELLANEOUS RECORDS**, Special Proceedings, 1870-1876]
- Execution Dockets, 1824-1856; 8 volumes.
- Judgment Dockets, 1878-1895, 1917-1926; 4 volumes.
- Minutes, 1830-1857, 1866-1907; 15 volumes.
- Presentment Dockets, 1879-1912; 3 volumes.
- State Dockets, 1830-1851, 1866-1879; 3 volumes.
- Supplementary Proceedings, 1871-1876; 1 volume.
- Trial, Appearance, and Reference Dockets, 1830-1859; 4 volumes.

Western District Criminal Court
- Criminal Issues Docket, 1899-1900; 1 volume.
- Half Fee Docket, 1899-1900; 1 volume.
- Judgment Docket, 1899-1900; 1 volume.
- Minutes, 1899-1900; 1 volume.

ELECTION RECORDS

Election Records, 1806-1931; 3 Fibredex boxes.
Elections, Record of, 1896-1908; 1 volume.

ESTATES RECORDS

Accounts, Record of, 1868-1900; 2 volumes.
Administrators' Bonds, 1868-1896; 3 volumes.
Appointment of Administrators, Executors, Guardians, and Masters, 1868-1898; 1 volume.
Clerk's Receipt Docket (Estates), 1896-1916; 1 volume.
Estates, Index to, 1868-1887; 1 volume.
Estates, Record of, 1832-1845, 1865-1868; 3 volumes.
Estates Records, 1776-1934; 62 Fibredex boxes. [*See also* **CRX RECORDS**]

Guardians' Bonds, 1870-1896; 2 volumes.
Guardians' Records, 1785-1933; 6 Fibredex boxes.
Inventories and Accounts of Sale, 1880-1899; 1 volume.
Settlements, Record of, 1869-1899; 1 volume.

LAND RECORDS [*See also* **CRX RECORDS**]
Deeds of Sale, 1805-1928; 1 Fibredex box.
Ejectments, 1784-1868; 1 Fibredex box.
Land Entries, 1770-1909; 1 volume, 1 Fibredex box.
Levies on Land for Taxes, 1875-1888; 1 volume.
Miscellaneous Deeds, 1772-1919; 1 Fibredex box.
Petitions for Partition, 1870-1910; 1 Fibredex box.

MARRIAGE, DIVORCE, AND VITAL STATISTICS
Divorce Records, 1828-1911; 3 Fibredex boxes.
Marriage Bonds, 1780-1868; 4 Fibredex boxes.
Marriage Certificates, 1865-1867. [*See* **COURT RECORDS**, Court of Pleas and Quarter Sessions, Minutes, 1865]

MILITARY AND PENSION RECORDS [*See* **MISCELLANEOUS RECORDS**]

MISCELLANEOUS RECORDS
Alien Registration, 1927-1940; 1 volume.
Assignees and Trustees, Records of, 1783-1905; 1 Fibredex box.
Confederate Oaths, 1865; 1 volume.
Confederate Pensions, Record of, 1885-1901; 2 volumes.
Declarations of Citizenship, 1911-1928; 1 volume.
Justices of the Peace, Magistrates, and Notaries Public, Record of, 1923-1953; 3 volumes.
Lunacy Records, 1899-1917; 1 volume.
Miscellaneous Records, 1776-1949; 4 Fibredex boxes. [*See also* **CRX RECORDS**]
Orders and Decrees, 1868-1923; 2 volumes.
Petitions for Naturalization, 1919-1930; 2 volumes.
Road Records, 1787-1897; 5 Fibredex boxes.
Special Proceedings, 1870-1901; 7 volumes.

OFFICIALS, COUNTY [*See* **MISCELLANEOUS RECORDS**]

ROADS AND BRIDGES [*See* **MISCELLANEOUS RECORDS**]

TAX AND FISCAL RECORDS
Tax Records, 1782-1894; 3 Fibredex boxes.

WILLS
Wills, 1790-1905; 1 Fibredex box. [*See also* **CRX RECORDS**]

CRX RECORDS
Deed, 1800; 1 folder.
Estate, 1853; 1 folder.
Land Grant, 1801, 1885; 1 folder.
Miscellaneous Records, 1777-1917; 1 Fibredex box.
Will, n.d.; 1 folder.

MICROFILM RECORDS

BONDS

Apprentice Bonds, 1868-1907; 1 reel.
Bastardy Bonds, 1868-1879; 1 reel.

CORPORATIONS AND PARTNERSHIPS

Corporations, Record of, 1886-1963; 2 reels.
Partnerships, Record of, 1944-1963; 1 reel.

COURT RECORDS

County Court of Pleas and Quarter Sessions
- Execution Dockets, 1837-1855; 1 reel.
- Minutes, 1791-1834, 1841-1849, 1865-1868; 4 reels.
- Trial and Appearance Docket, 1866-1868. [*See* **MISCELLANEOUS RECORDS,** Special Proceedings, 1870-1885]

Superior Court
- Judgment Dockets, 1885-1895; 1 reel.
- Judgments, Cross Index to, 1897-1966; 3 reels.
- Minutes, 1830-1857, 1866-1966; 18 reels.
- Minutes, Criminal, 1938-1943; Papers of Frances Silver Trial, 1832; 1 reel.
- State Dockets, 1830-1851; 1 reel.

Western District Criminal Court
- Judgment Dockets, 1899-1900; 2 reels.
- Minutes, 1899-1900; 1 reel.

ELECTION RECORDS

Elections, Record of, 1880-1970; 1 reel.

ESTATES RECORDS

Accounts, Record of, 1896-1916; 1 reel.
Administrators' Bonds, 1868-1896; 1 reel.
Administrators, Record of, 1897-1963; 6 reels.
Annual Accounts, Record of, 1868-1963; 6 reels.
Appointment of Administrators, Executors, and Guardians, 1868-1898; 1 reel.
Executors and Guardians, Record of, 1897-1916; 1 reel.
Executors, Record of, 1915-1959; 1 reel.
Guardians, Record of, 1913-1963; 3 reels.
Inheritance Tax Records, 1924-1963; 1 reel.
Inventories and Sales of Estates, Record of, 1832-1963; 5 reels.
Money Paid by Administrators, Executors, and Guardians, Record of, 1916-1962; 1 reel.
Settlements, Record of, 1869-1963; 6 reels.

LAND RECORDS

Deeds, Record of, 1860-1960; 142 reels.
Land Entries, 1778-1795, 1833-1900, 1913-1945; 3 reels.
Land Sold for Taxes, Record of, 1931-1941; 1 reel.
Levies on Land for Taxes, 1867-1888; 1 reel.
Plat Books, 1922-1980; 4 reels.
Real Estate Conveyances, Index to, Grantee, 1865-1965; 8 reels.
Real Estate Conveyances, Index to, Grantor, 1865-1965; 9 reels.
Resale by Trustees and Mortgagees, Record of, 1932-1952; 1 reel.
Surveys, Record of, 1905-1935; 1 reel.

Marriage, Divorce, and Vital Statistics

Births, Index to, 1913-1978; 4 reels.
Deaths, Index to, 1913-1978; 2 reels.
Marriage Bonds, 1777-1868; 3 reels.
Marriage Registers, 1867-1980; 2 reels.

Miscellaneous Records

Inquisition of Lunacy, Record of, 1899-1959; 2 reels.
Orders and Decrees, 1868-1923, 1935; 1 reel.
Special Proceedings, 1870-1885; Trial and Appearance Docket, Court of Pleas and Quarter Sessions, 1866-1868; 1 reel.
Special Proceedings, 1884-1954; 11 reels.
Special Proceedings, Index to, 1870-1980; 4 reels.

Officials, County

Board of County Commissioners, Minutes, 1871-1882, 1892-1959; 5 reels.
County Board of Health, Minutes, 1937-1949; 1 reel.

School Records

County Board of Education, Minutes, 1885-1948; 1 reel.

Wills

Wills, Index to, 1863-1954; 1 reel.
Wills, Record of, 1793-1963; 5 reels.

BUTE COUNTY

Established in 1764 from Granville County.
Divided into Franklin and Warren counties in 1779; additional records of Bute County may be found in the records of those counties.

ORIGINAL RECORDS

COURT RECORDS [*See also* **FRANKLIN COUNTY**, **COURT RECORDS**, Superior Court]
- County Court of Pleas and Quarter Sessions
  - Execution Docket, 1765-1768; 1 volume.
  - Minutes, 1767-1779; 2 volumes.
  - Recording Docket (Clerk of the Pleas), 1764-1787; 1 volume.
  - State Docket, 1777-1778. [*See* Trial, Appearance, and Petitions Docket]
  - Trial and Appearance Docket, 1766-1767; 1 volume.
  - Trial, Appearance, and Petitions Docket, 1772-1778; 1 volume.
- Superior Court Civil Action Paper. [*See* **CRX RECORDS**]

ESTATES RECORDS
- Estates Records, 1764-1779; 2 Fibredex boxes. [*See also* **WARREN COUNTY, ESTATES RECORDS**]
- Guardians, Record of, 1770-1779. [*See* **WARREN COUNTY, ESTATES RECORDS**, Guardians, Record of , 1770-1795]

LAND RECORDS [*See also* **FRANKLIN COUNTY** and **WARREN COUNTY, LAND RECORDS**]
- Land Entries, 1778-1785; 1 volume.

MARRIAGE, DIVORCE, AND VITAL STATISTICS
- Marriage Bonds, 1764-1779; 1 Fibredex box.

MISCELLANEOUS RECORDS
- Miscellaneous Records, 1762-1779; 1 Fibredex box. [*See also* **CRX RECORDS**]

TAX AND FISCAL RECORDS [*See also* **CRX RECORDS**]
- Miscellaneous Tax Records, 1765-1778; 1 manuscript box.

WILLS
- Wills, 1764-1779; 1 Fibredex box.
- Wills, Deeds, and Inventories, Record of, 1764-1767; 1 volume.

CRX RECORDS
- Civil Action Paper, 1769; 1 folder.
- Miscellaneous Records, 1745-1779; 3 Fibredex boxes.
- Taxables, 1766; 1 folder.
- Taxables, List of, 1777-1780; 1 volume.

MICROFILM RECORDS

COURT RECORDS
- County Court of Pleas and Quarter Sessions
  - Minutes, 1767-1779; Reference, Trial, and New Action Docket, 1766-1767; Execution Docket, 1765-1768; 1 reel.
  - Recording Docket, 1764-1787; Reference Docket, 1772-1778; 1 reel.

ESTATES RECORDS [*See* **WILLS**]

LAND RECORDS [*See* **WILLS**]

MARRIAGE, DIVORCE, AND VITAL STATISTICS

Marriage Bonds, 1764-1779; 1 reel.

MISCELLANEOUS RECORDS

Miscellaneous Unbound Records, 1764-1779; 1 reel.

TAX AND FISCAL RECORDS

List of Taxables, 1771; 1 reel.

WILLS [*See also* **WARREN COUNTY, WILLS**]

Record Book I (wills, deeds, and inventories), 1764-1767; 1 reel.
Record of Wills, 1764-1774; 1 reel.
Wills and Inventories, 1760-1800; Guardians' Accounts, 1770-1778; 1 reel.

CABARRUS COUNTY

Established in 1792 from Mecklenburg County.
Courthouse fire of 1874 resulted in the loss of a few court records.

ORIGINAL RECORDS

BONDS

Apprentice Bonds, 1875-1901; 2 volumes.
Bastardy Bonds and Records, 1869-1918; 1 Fibredex box.

COURT RECORDS

County Court of Pleas and Quarter Sessions
- Appearance Dockets, 1821-1829, 1843-1868; 2 volumes.
- Execution Dockets, 1821-1868; 8 volumes.
- Minutes, 1793-1817, 1821-1867; 9 volumes.
- State Docket, 1797-1819; 1 volume.
- Trial and Appearance Docket, 1793-1808; 1 volume.
- Trial Dockets, 1821-1829, 1843-1868; 3 volumes.

Domestic Relations Court
- Clerk's Ledger, 1957-1960; 1 volume.

Superior Court
- Appearance Docket, 1843-1869; 1 volume.
- Civil Action Papers, 1824-1935; 12 Fibredex boxes.
- Civil Action Papers Concerning Land, 1856-1944; 4 Fibredex boxes.
- Civil Issues Dockets, 1869-1930; 9 volumes.
- Criminal Action Papers, 1873-1923; 8 Fibredex boxes.
- Criminal Issues Dockets, 1869-1930; 7 volumes.
- Equity Minutes, 1846-1868; 1 volume.
- Execution Dockets, 1848-1868; 2 volumes.
- Fines, Penalties, and Forfeitures, Record of, 1879-1912; 2 volumes.
- Judgment Dockets, 1869-1890; 5 volumes.
- Minutes, 1819-1943; 24 volumes.
- Nol. Pros. Docket, 1874-1888; 1 volume.
- Trial Docket, 1843-1868; 1 volume.

ELECTION RECORDS

Elections, Record of, 1878-1920; 4 volumes.
Permanent Registration of Voters, 1902-1908; 1 volume.

ESTATES RECORDS

Accounts, Record of, 1875-1946; 9 volumes.
Administrators' Bonds, 1875-1881; 1 volume.
Administrators and Guardians, Record of, 1881-1898; 1 volume.
Administrators, Record of, 1891-1939; 7 volumes.
Appointment of Administrators, Executors, Guardians, and Masters, 1868-1911; 1 volume.
Clerk's Receipt Book (Land Sales), 1861-1919; 1 volume.
Clerk's Receiver Accounts, 1915-1942; 2 volumes.
Estates Records, 1793-1953; 48 Fibredex boxes.
Guardians' Bonds, 1853-1882; 2 volumes.
Guardians, Record of, 1899-1943; 2 volumes.

Guardians' Records, 1847-1932, 1940, 1945; 6 Fibredex boxes.
Inventories and Accounts of Sale, Record of, 1869-1943; 6 volumes.
Inventories, Accounts, and Settlements, Record of, 1846-1868; 3 volumes.
Settlements, Record of, 1869-1936; 9 volumes.

LAND RECORDS
Attachments, Executions, Liens, and Levies on Land, 1844-1925; 1 Fibredex box.
Deeds, 1821, 1869-1945; 4 Fibredex boxes.
Miscellaneous Land Records, 1818-1945; 1 Fibredex box.
Probate of Deeds, Record of, 1878-1891; 2 volumes.
Sale and Resale of Land, Record of, 1921-1940; 4 volumes.

MARRIAGE, DIVORCE, AND VITAL STATISTICS
Disinterment/Reinterment Permits, 1977-1979; 1 manuscript box.
Divorce Records, 1866, 1868, 1873-1930; 4 Fibredex boxes.
Maiden Names of Divorced Women, 1938-1970; 1 volume.
Marriage Bonds, 1792-1868; 10 Fibredex boxes.
Marriage Register, 1867-1905; 1 volume.

MILTARY AND PENSION RECORDS [*See* **MISCELLANEOUS RECORDS**]

MISCELLANEOUS RECORDS
Alien Registration, 1927, 1940-1941; 1 volume.
Appointment of Road Overseers, Record of, 1837; 1 volume.
Assignees, Trustees, and Receivers, Records of, 1854-1928; 3 Fibredex boxes.
Certificates of Registration, 1916-1966; 1 manuscript box.
Clerk's Minute Docket (Special Proceedings), 1884-1893; 1 volume. [*See also* Special Proceedings]
Confederate Veterans Association of Cabarrus County, Minutes and Roster, 1895, 1897; 1 volume.
County Accounts and Claims, 1850-1853. [See Record of Appointment of Road Overseers, 1837]
Declaration of Intent (to Become a Citizen), 1909-1921; 1 volume.
Drainage Record, 1911-1939; 1 volume.
Lunacy, Record of, 1900-1941; 2 volumes.
Magistrates and Notaries Public, Record of, 1902-1927; 2 volumes.
Miscellaneous Records, 1794-1945; 2 Fibredex boxes.
Orders and Decrees, 1868-1899; 4 volumes.
Pensions, Record of, 1919-1940; 1 volume.
Petitions for Naturalization, 1909-1921; 1 volume.
Railroad Records, 1869-1924; 3 Fibredex boxes.
Receivers, Record of, 1915-1917; 1 volume.
Soldiers in World War I, Record of, 1917-1919; 1 volume.
Special Proceedings Dockets, 1875-1914; 2 volumes. [*See also* Clerk's Minute Docket]

OFFICIALS, COUNTY [*See* **MISCELLANEOUS RECORDS**]

ROADS AND BRIDGES [*See* **MISCELLANEOUS RECORDS**]

TAX AND FISCAL RECORDS
Miscellaneous Tax Records, 1860-1921; 1 Fibredex box.
Poll Tax, Record of, 1902-1918; 1 volume.

WILLS

Wills, 1794-1921; 12 Fibredex boxes.

MICROFILM RECORDS

BONDS

Apprentice Bonds, 1875-1901; 1 reel.

CORPORATIONS AND PARTNERSHIPS

Corporations, Record of, 1885-1965; 2 reels.
Partnerships, Corporations, and Assumed Names, Index to, 1899-1982; 1 reel.
Partnerships, Record of, 1917-1965; 1 reel.

COURT RECORDS

County Court of Pleas and Quarter Sessions
    Minutes, 1793-1817, 1828-1867; 6 reels.
Superior Court
    Equity Minutes, 1846-1868; 1 reel.
    Judgments, Index to, Defendant, 1898-1970; 2 reels.
    Judgments, Index to, Plaintiff, 1898-1970; 2 reels.
    Minutes, 1819-1954; 16 reels.
    Minutes, Civil and Criminal, Index to, Defendant, 1819-1970; 3 reels.
    Minutes, Civil, Index to, Plaintiff, 1819-1970; 2 reels.

ELECTION RECORDS

Elections, Record of, 1878-1972; 1 reel.
Voter Registration Lists (by Township), 1902-1908; 1 reel.

ESTATES RECORDS

Accounts, Record of, 1875-1965; 8 reels.
Accounts of Sale of Estates, 1869-1894; 1 reel.
Administrator and Guardian Proceedings, 1881-1899; 1 reel.
Administrators' Bonds, 1875-1881; 1 reel.
Administrators, Record of, 1891-1966; 8 reels.
Appointment of Executors, 1868-1911; 1 reel.
Estates Not Exceeding $300, Record of, 1929-1966; 1 reel.
Estates, Record of, 1846-1869; 1 reel.
Executors, Record of, 1926-1966; 2 reels.
Final Accounts, Index to Administrators, Executors, and Guardians, 1846-1970; 2 reels.
Final Accounts, Index to Wards, 1846-1970; 3 reels.
Guardians' Bonds, 1853-1867, 1875-1882, 1899-1924; 1 reel.
Guardians, Record of, 1924-1970; Appointment of Trustees under Wills, 1941-1970; 3 reels.
Inheritance Tax Records, 1923-1966; 2 reels.
Inventories and Accounts of Sale, Record of, 1869-1965; 3 reels.
Receivership of Minors' Accounts, Record of, 1918-1922, 1931-1966; 1 reel.
Settlements, Record of, 1846-1965; 12 reels.
Widows' Year's Support, Record of, 1946-1962; 1 reel.

LAND RECORDS

Deeds, Index to, Grantee, 1892-1967; 12 reels.
Deeds, Index to, Grantor, 1892-1967; 12 reels.
Deeds, Index to, Grantor and Grantee, 1792-1891; 1 reel.
Deeds, Record of, 1784-1962; 122 reels.
Plats, 1914-1923, 1933-1964; 3 reels.
Plats, Index to, 1894-1964; 1 reel.
Registration of Titles, 1914-1923; 1 reel.
Resale of Land under Mortgagees and Trustees, Record of, 1921-1966; 3 reels.

MARRIAGE, DIVORCE, AND VITAL STATISTICS

Births, Index to, 1914-1981; 3 reels.
Deaths, Index to, 1913-1981; 3 reels.
Delayed Births, Index to, various years; 1 reel.
Maiden Names of Divorced Women, 1938-1966; 1 reel.
Marriage Bonds, 1792-1868; 7 reels.
Marriage Licenses, 1864-1965; 13 reels.
Marriage Registers, 1867-1982; 3 reels.

MILITARY AND PENSION RECORDS

Eleventh Company, N.C. Reserve Militia, Minutes, 1909-1915; 1 reel.
Pensions, Record of, 1889-1940; 1 reel.

MISCELLANEOUS RECORDS

Alien Registration, 1921, 1940-1941; 1 reel.
Appointment of Receivers, 1915-1917; 1 reel.
Lunacy, Record of, 1899-1946; 1 reel.
Naturalization, Record of, 1918-1921; 1 reel.
Orders and Decrees, 1868-1957; 14 reels.
Special Proceedings, Index to, Defendant, 1868-1970; 2 reels.
Special Proceedings, Index to, Plaintiff, 1868-1970; 2 reels.

OFFICIALS, COUNTY

Board of County Commissioners, Minutes, 1868-1961; 7 reels.

SCHOOL RECORDS

Association of Teachers, Records of, 1901-1915; 1 reel.
Board of Superintendents of Common Schools, Minutes, 1841-1885; 1 reel.
Common School Register, 1857-1903; 1 reel.
County Board of Education, Minutes, 1885-1966; 2 reels.

TAX AND FISCAL RECORDS

Board of Assessors, Record of Assessment List, 1860, 1863-1868; 1 reel.
Tax Lists, 1881-1884; 1 reel.
Tax Scrolls, 1872-1900, 1905, 1915; 7 reels.

WILLS

Wills, Index to, Devisee, 1794-1970; 1 reel.
Wills, Index to, Devisor, 1794-1970; 1 reel.
Wills, Record of, 1798-1966; 6 reels.

CALDWELL COUNTY

Established in 1841 from Burke and Wilkes counties.

ORIGINAL RECORDS

Bonds

Apprentice Bonds and Records, 1841-1906; 1 Fibredex box.
Bastardy Bonds and Records, 1843-1925; 3 Fibredex boxes.
Officials' Bonds and Records, 1841-1917; 3 Fibredex boxes.
Sheriffs' Bonds and Records, 1841-1903; 1 Fibredex box.

Court Records

County Court of Pleas and Quarter Sessions
- Execution Docket, 1841-1848, 1863; 1 volume.
- Minutes, 1841-1868; 3 volumes.
- State Docket, 1848-1868; 1 volume.

Superior Court
- Civil Action Papers, 1838-1934; 23 Fibredex boxes.
- Civil Action Papers Concerning Land, 1840-1930; 13 Fibredex boxes.
- Criminal Action Papers, 1840-1932; 26 Fibredex boxes. [*See also* **CRX RECORDS**]
- Equity Minutes, 1844-1868; Civil and Criminal Issues Dockets, 1883-1887; 1 volume.
- Minutes, 1843-1911; 10 volumes.

Election Records

Elections, Record of, 1898-1932; 4 volumes.

Estates Records

Accounts, Record of, 1868-1914; 2 volumes.
Appointment of Administrators, Executors, Guardians, and Masters, 1868-1911; 1 volume.
Estates, Record of, 1847-1867; 1 volume.
Estates Records, 1841-1934; 47 Fibredex boxes.
Guardians' Records, 1842-1934; 3 Fibredex boxes.
Settlements, Record of, 1868-1913; 1 volume.

Land Records

Deeds of Sale, 1849-1920; 1 Fibredex box.
Ejectments, 1841-1904; 1 Fibredex box.
Miscellaneous Deeds, 1841-1931; 1 Fibredex box.
Miscellaneous Land Records, 1841-1934; 2 Fibredex boxes.

Marriage, Divorce, and Vital Statistics

Disinterment/Reinterment Permits, 1974-1978; 1 manuscript box.
Divorce Records, 1850-1925; 3 Fibredex boxes.
Miscellaneous Marriage Records, 1867-1933; 1 Fibredex box.

Miscellaneous Records

Alien Registration, 1940; 1 volume.
Assignees, Receivers, and Trustees, Records of, 1841-1930; 2 Fibredex boxes.
Board of County Commissioners, Minutes, 1868-1870; Common School Register, 1858; 1 volume.
Grand Jury Records, 1843-1924; 1 Fibredex box.

Licenses to Trades, Registry of, 1901-1916; 1 volume.
Magistrates' Records, 1849-1915; 1 Fibredex box.
Miscellaneous Records, 1837-1934; 5 Fibredex boxes.
Orders and Decrees, 1869-1906; 3 volumes.
Railroad Records, 1876-1911; 3 Fibredex boxes.
Road Records, 1838-1913; 2 Fibredex boxes.
Slave Records, 1842-1866; 1 Fibredex box.

OFFICIALS, COUNTY [*See* **MISCELLANEOUS RECORDS**]

SCHOOL RECORDS [*See* **MISCELLANEOUS RECORDS**]

TAX AND FISCAL RECORDS
Lists of Taxables, 1841-1853, 1868; 2 volumes.

WILLS
Wills, 1830-1925; 3 Fibredex boxes.

CRX RECORDS
Criminal Actions, 1906; 1 folder.

MICROFILM RECORDS

CORPORATIONS AND PARTNERSHIPS
Corporations, Record of, 1885-1945; 1 reel.

COURT RECORDS
County Court of Pleas and Quarter Sessions
Minutes, 1841-1868; 2 reels.
Superior Court
Equity Minutes, 1844-1868; 1 reel.
Judgments, Index to, Defendant, 1940-1963; 5 reels.
Judgments, Index to, Plaintiff, 1940-1963; 5 reels.
Minutes, 1843-1954; 12 reels.

ELECTION RECORDS
Elections, Record of, 1898-1968; 1 reel.

ESTATES RECORDS
Accounts, Record of, 1868-1966; 7 reels.
Administrators, Record of, 1897-1966; 4 reels.
Appointment of Administrators, Executors, and Guardians, 1868-1948; 2 reels.
Appointment of Executors, 1948-1966; 1 reel.
Appointment of Guardians, 1941-1966; 1 reel.
Inheritance Tax Records, 1920-1967; 1 reel.
Inventories of Estates, 1847-1867, 1885-1966; 5 reels.
Minors' Accounts, Record of, 1944-1956; 1 reel.
Settlements, Record of, 1868-1966; 6 reels.

LAND RECORDS
Deeds, Record of, 1841-1956; 78 reels.
Land Entries, 1841-1954; 1 reel.
Plat Books, 1913-1946; 1 reel.
Plats, Index to, 1915-1980; 1 reel.
Real Estate Conveyances, Index to, Grantee, 1841-1971; 10 reels.

Real Estate Conveyances, Index to, Grantor, 1841-1971; 13 reels.
Sales by Trustees, Mortgagees, and Executors, Record of, 1917-1959; 2 reels.
Surveys, Record of, 1905-1937; 1 reel.

Marriage, Divorce, and Vital Statistics

Births, Index to, 1914-1980; 3 reels.
Cohabitation and Marriage Records, 1866-1872; 1 reel.
Deaths, Index to, 1914-1980; 2 reels.
Delayed Births, Index to, various years; 1 reel.
Marriage Licenses, 1841-1961; 15 reels.
Marriage Registers, 1851-1969; 3 reels.

Miscellaneous Records

Lunacy, Record of, 1908-1959; 1 reel.
Orders and Decrees, 1869-1938; 3 reels.
Special Proceedings, 1903-1952; 7 reels.

Officials, County

Board of County Commissioners, Minutes, 1870-1964; 7 reels.

School Records

Board of Education, City of Lenoir, Minutes, 1903-1957; 1 reel.
County Board of Education, Minutes, 1885-1952; 1 reel.

Tax and Fiscal Records

Tax Lists, 1841-1853; 1 reel.

Wills

Wills, Index to, 1841-1966; 1 reel.
Wills, Record of, 1827-1966; 5 reels.

CAMDEN COUNTY

Established in 1777 from Pasquotank County.
Some records were said to have been destroyed in a storage room fire; many records missing.

ORIGINAL RECORDS

BONDS

- Apprentice Bonds, 1871-1886; 1 volume.
- Bastardy Bonds, 1871-1879; 1 volume.

COURT RECORDS

- County Court of Pleas and Quarter Sessions
  - Execution Docket, 1858-1862, 1866-1868; 1 volume.
  - Minutes, 1855-1868; 1 volume.
  - Trial, Appearance, and Petition Dockets, 1857-1862, 1865-1868; 2 volumes.
- Superior Court
  - Civil Action Papers, 1802-1929; 2 Fibredex boxes.
  - Criminal Action Papers, 1808-1928; 1 Fibredex box.
  - Equity Minutes, 1807-1861, 1866-1868; 2 volumes.
  - Equity Trial Dockets, 1807-1861; 2 volumes.
  - Execution Docket, 1854-1860, 1866-1869; 1 volume.
  - Minutes, 1853-1861, 1866-1911; 4 volumes.
  - State Docket, 1854-1861, 1866-1869; 1 volume.
  - Trial and Appearance Dockets, 1842-1861, 1866-1869; 2 volumes.

ELECTION RECORDS [*See also* **CRX RECORDS**]

- Elections, Record of, 1878-1916; 3 volumes.

ESTATES RECORDS

- Accounts, Record of, 1866-1906; 3 volumes.
- Administrators' Bonds, 1853-1872, 1895-1916; 4 volumes.
- Estates, Record of, 1853-1869; 1 volume.
- Estates Records, 1790-1929; 22 Fibredex boxes.
- Fiduciary Account Book, 1850-1860, 1881; 1 volume.
- Guardians' Accounts, 1805-1809, 1858-1869; 2 volumes.
- Guardians' Bonds, 1856-1918; 3 volumes.
- Guardians' Records, 1809-1925; 5 Fibredex boxes.
- Inventories, Record of, 1853-1868; 1 volume.
- Settlements, Record of, 1869-1914; 1 volume.
- Widows' Dowers, 1894-1918; 1 volume.

LAND RECORDS

- Deeds, 1739-1912; 1 Fibredex box.
- Miscellaneous Land Records, 1807-1925; 1 Fibredex box.
- Processioners' Record, 1874-1904; 1 volume.

MISCELLANEOUS RECORDS

- Assignees, Receivers, and Trustees, Records of, 1859-1928; 1 Fibredex box.
- Board of County Highway Commissioners, Minutes, 1917-1931; 1 volume.
- Board of Supervisors of Public Roads, Minutes, 1879-1903; 1 volume.
- Miscellaneous Records, 1786-1928; 3 Fibredex boxes.
- Orders and Decrees, 1869-1904; 3 volumes.

Officials, County [*See* **Miscellaneous Records**]

Roads and Bridges [*See* **Miscellaneous Records**]

Tax and Fiscal Records

Miscellaneous Tax Records, 1848-1890; 1 Fibredex box.

Wills

Wills, 1766-1922; 5 Fibredex boxes. [*See also* **CRX Records**]
Wills, Record of, 1822-1868; 2 volumes.

CRX Records

Voter Registration Book—Town of South Mills, 1903-1915; 1 volume in manuscript box.
Will (James Ferrebee), 1778; 1 folder.

MICROFILM RECORDS

Bonds

Apprentice Bonds, 1871-1886; 1 reel.
Bastardy Bonds, 1871-1879; 1 reel.

Corporations and Partnerships

Corporations, Record of, 1908-1972; 1 reel.

Court Records

County Court of Pleas and Quarter Sessions
 Minutes, 1855-1868; 1 reel.
Superior Court
 Civil Actions, Index to, Defendant, 1966-1983; 1 reel.
 Civil Actions, Index to, Plaintiff, 1966-1983; 1 reel.
 Criminal Actions, Index to, 1966-1983; 1 reel.
 Equity Minutes, 1807-1868; 1 reel.
 Judgment Dockets, 1869-1912; 1 reel.
 Judgments, Index to, 1929-1966; 1 reel.
 Minutes, 1853-1959; 4 reels.

Election Records

Elections, Record of, 1878-1968; 1 reel.

Estates Records

Accounts, Record of, 1866-1966; 4 reels.
Accounts and Sales of Estates, 1853-1869; 1 reel.
Administrators' Bonds, 1853-1916; 2 reels.
Administrators, Executors, and Guardians, Record of, 1915-1966; 1 reel.
Administrators, Record of, 1929-1966; 1 reel.
Guardians' Accounts, 1849-1860; 1 reel.
Guardians' Bonds, 1871-1918; 1 reel.
Guardians, Record of, 1858-1869; 1 reel.
Inheritance Tax Records, 1923-1966; 1 reel.
Inventories of Estates, 1853-1868; 1 reel.
Orphans' Accounts, 1800-1809; 1 reel.
Settlements, Record of, 1862-1967; 2 reels.
Widows' Dowers, Record of, 1894-1914; 1 reel.

LAND RECORDS

Deeds, General Index to, Grantor and Grantee, 1777-1927; 1 reel.
Deeds, Record of, 1777-1949; 36 reels.
Land Entries, 1866-1903; 1 reel.
Processioners' Record, 1875-1904; 1 reel.
Real Estate Conveyances, Index to, Grantee, 1927-1946; 1 reel.
Real Estate Conveyances, Index to, Grantor, 1927-1946; 1 reel.

MARRIAGE, DIVORCE, AND VITAL STATISTICS

Births, Index to, 1913-1982; 1 reel.
Deaths, Index to, 1913-1982; 1 reel.
Delayed Births, Index to, various years; 1 reel.
Maiden Names of Divorced Women, 1945-1965; 1 reel.
Marriage Licenses, 1868-1945; 32 reels.
Marriage Registers, 1840-1967; 3 reels.

MISCELLANEOUS RECORDS

Committee of Finance, Minutes, 1861-1877; 1 reel.
Lunacy, Record of, 1907-1967; 1 reel.
Orders and Decrees, 1869-1966; 5 reels.

OFFICIALS, COUNTY

Board of County Commissioners, Minutes, 1868-2002; 5 reels.

SCHOOL RECORDS

Board of Superintendents of Common Schools, Minutes, 1857-1867; 1 reel.
County Board of Education, Minutes, 1872-1998; 3 reels.

TAX AND FISCAL RECORDS

Tax Scrolls, 1872-1893, 1915, 1925, 1935, 1945; 3 reels.

WILLS

Wills, Index to, 1822-1966; 1 reel.
Wills, Record of, 1815-1966; 3 reels.

CARTERET COUNTY

Established in 1722 from Craven Precinct as a precinct of Bath County.

ORIGINAL RECORDS

BONDS

Bastardy Bonds and Records, 1771-1906; 2 Fibredex boxes.
Officials' Bonds and Records, 1755-1909; 2 Fibredex boxes.

COURT RECORDS

County Court of Pleas and Quarter Sessions
- Appearance Dockets, 1793-1868; 4 volumes, 1 manuscript box.
- Clerk's Fee Book, 1849-1862; 1 pamphlet.
- Execution Dockets, 1785-1839, 1847-1856, 1867-1868; 8 volumes, 1 manuscript box.
- Minutes, 1723-1868; 19 volumes.
- State Dockets, 1775-1850; 1 volume, 1 manuscript box.
- Trial and Appearance Dockets, 1731-1792; 4 volumes, 1 manuscript box.
- Trial Dockets, 1793-1868; 3 volumes, 1 manuscript box.

Superior Court
- Appearance Dockets, 1816-1869; 1 volume, 1 manuscript box.
- Civil Action Papers, 1741-1913; 18 Fibredex boxes.
- Civil Action Papers Concerning County and Municipal Officials, 1869-1894; 1 Fibredex box.
- Civil Action Papers Concerning Land, 1779-1938; 6 Fibredex boxes.
- Civil Issues Dockets, 1869-1922; 3 volumes.
- Criminal Action Papers, 1771-1913; 6 Fibredex boxes.
- Equity Execution Docket, 1818-1859; 1 volume.
- Equity Minutes, 1816-1847, 1859-1867; 2 volumes.
- Equity Trial and Appearance Dockets, 1810-1868; 3 volumes.
- Execution Dockets, 1833-1868; 2 volumes.
- Judgment Docket, 1869-1904; 1 volume.
- Minutes, 1809-1907, 1919; 6 volumes, 1 manuscript box.
- Prosecution Bonds, 1836-1845; 1 volume.
- State Docket, 1866-1881; 1 volume.
- Trial Dockets, 1816-1868; 1 manuscript box.

ELECTION RECORDS

Elections, Record of, 1896-1944; 2 volumes.

ESTATES RECORDS

Accounts, Record of, 1868-1915; 1 volume.
Administrators' Bonds, 1884-1902; 1 volume.
Estates, Record of, 1829-1862; 6 volumes.
Estates Records, 1744-1957; 40 Fibredex boxes.
Guardians' Bonds, 1884-1903; 1 volume.
Guardians' Dockets, 1818-1846; 1 manuscript box.
Guardians' Records, 1789-1962; 16 Fibredex boxes.

LAND RECORDS [*See also* **CRX RECORDS**]

Deeds, 1803-1952; 3 Fibredex boxes.
Deeds, Record of, 1721-1839, 1845-1852; 47 volumes.

Grants and Miscellaneous Papers, 1717-1844; 1 volume.
Miscellaneous Land Records, 1743-1948; 1 Fibredex box.

MARRIAGE, DIVORCE, AND VITAL STATISTICS

Disinterment/Reinterment Permits, 1976-1980; 1 manuscript box.
Divorce Records, 1877-1939; 1 Fibredex box.
Marriage Bonds, 1746-1868; 8 Fibredex boxes.
Marriages, Record of, 1864-1872; 1 volume.

MISCELLANEOUS RECORDS

Assignees, Receivers, and Trustees, Records of, 1795-1918; 2 Fibredex boxes.
Beaufort Peabody Educational Association, Minutes, 1871-1872; 1 volume.
Board of Superintendents of Common Schools, Minutes, 1841-1860; 1 volume.
Declaration of Intent (to Become a Citizen), 1910-1911, 1940; 1 volume.
Miscellaneous Papers, 1717-1844. [*See* **LAND RECORDS**, Grants and Miscellaneous Papers]
Miscellaneous Records, 1741-1919; 3 Fibredex boxes. [*See also* **CRX RECORDS**]
Oyster Bed Records, 1879-1906; 1 volume, 1 Fibredex box.
Professional Certificates of Registration, 1889-1971; 1 manuscript box.
Railroad Records, 1858-1913; 2 Fibredex boxes.
Road Records, 1811-1911; 2 Fibredex boxes.
Slave Records, 1793-1867; 1 Fibredex box.
Vestry Books (St. John's Parish, Beaufort), 1742-1843; 3 volumes.
Wardens of the Poor, Minutes, 1844-1866; 1 volume.

OFFICIALS, COUNTY [*See* **CRX RECORDS**]

ROADS AND BRIDGES [*See* **MISCELLANEOUS RECORDS**]

SCHOOL RECORDS [*See* **MISCELLANEOUS RECORDS**]

TAX AND FISCAL RECORDS

Lists of Taxables, 1802-1860; 10 volumes.
Tax Records, 1745-1899; 1 Fibredex box.

WILLS

Wills, 1744-1921; 10 Fibredex boxes.

CRX RECORDS

Board of County Commissioners, Minutes (rough), 1882; 1 folder.
Deeds and Land Division, 1817-1869; 2 folders.
Miscellaneous Records, 1747, 1799-1874; 1 volume, 4 folders.

MICROFILM RECORDS

CORPORATIONS AND PARTNERSHIPS

Corporations, Index to, 1878-1982; 1 reel.
Corporations, Record of, 1878-1957; 1 reel.
Dissolutions and Agreements, Record of, 1924-1946; 1 reel.
Partnerships, Record of, 1917-1982; 1 reel.

COURT RECORDS

County Court of Pleas and Quarter Sessions
    Minutes, 1723-1868; 11 reels.
Superior Court
    Equity Minutes, 1816-1868; 1 reel.

Judgments, Index to, Defendant, 1869-1968; 2 reels.
Judgments, Index to, Plaintiff, 1869-1968; 2 reels.
Minutes, 1809-1949; 8 reels.
Prosecution Bonds, 1836-1845; 1 reel.

ELECTION RECORDS
Elections, Record of, 1897-1958; 1 reel.

ESTATES RECORDS
Accounts, Record of, 1868-1961; 3 reels.
Administrators' Bonds, 1884-1936; 3 reels.
Administrators, Executors, and Guardians, Record of, 1758-1959; 5 reels.
Administrators, Record of, 1926-1936; 1 reel.
Appointment of Executors, 1868-1902; 1 reel.
Estates, Record of, 1829-1862; 2 reels.
Executors and Guardians, Record of, 1928-1959; 1 reel.
Guardians' Bonds, 1884-1903; 1 reel.
Guardians, Record of, 1929-1961; 1 reel.
Inheritance Tax Records, 1923-1955; 1 reel.
Settlements, Record of, 1880-1955; 2 reels.

LAND RECORDS
Land Entries, 1866-1895, 1905-1958; 1 reel.
Plat Books, 1926-1976; 4 reels.
Plats, Index to, 1904-1982; 1 reel.
Real Estate Conveyances, Index to, Grantee, 1722-1972; 10 reels.
Real Estate Conveyances, Index to, Grantor, 1722-1972; 9 reels.
Real Estate Conveyances, Record of, 1722-1947; 79 reels.
Sales and Resales by Mortgagees and Trustees, Record of, 1922-1966; 3 reels.
Sheriffs' Deeds, 1800; 1 reel.

MARRIAGE, DIVORCE, AND VITAL STATISTICS
Births, Index to, 1913-1961; 2 reels.
Deaths, Index to, 1913-1957; 1 reel.
Maiden Names of Divorced Women, 1938-1968; 1 reel.
Marriage Bonds, 1741-1868; 6 reels.
Marriage Registers, 1850-1981; 3 reels.
Marriages, Index to, Female, 1850-1981; 1 reel.
Marriages, Record of, 1864-1872; 1 reel.

MISCELLANEOUS RECORDS
Declaration of Intent (to Become a Citizen), 1910-1911, 1914; 1 reel.
Lunacy, Record of, 1899-1945; 1 reel.
Orders and Decrees, 1868-1968; 7 reels.
Special Proceedings, 1882-1968; 2 reels.
Special Proceedings, Index to, Defendant, 1869-1968; 1 reel.
Special Proceedings, Index to, Plaintiff, 1869-1968; 1 reel.
Wardens of the Poor, Minutes, 1742-1866; 2 reels.

OFFICIALS, COUNTY
Board of County Commissioners, Index to Minutes, 1868-1939; 2 reels.
Board of County Commissioners, Minutes, 1879-1959; 5 reels.

School Records

Beaufort Peabody Educational Association, Minutes, 1871-1872; 1 reel.
Board of Superintendents of Common Schools, Minutes, 1844-1858; 1 reel.
County Board of Education, Minutes, 1872-1956; 1 reel.

Tax and Fiscal Records

Lists of Taxables, 1802-1841; 1 reel.

Wills

Wills, Index to, Devisee, 1745-1968; 1 reel.
Wills, Index to, Devisor, 1745-1968; 1 reel.
Wills, Record of, 1745-1968; 5 reels.

CASWELL COUNTY

Established in 1777 from Orange County.
Some records were said to have been destroyed during occupation
by militia troops during Reconstruction.

ORIGINAL RECORDS

Bonds

- Apprentice Bonds and Records, 1777-1921; 2 volumes, 2 Fibredex boxes.
- Bastardy Bonds and Records, 1780-1905; 1 volume, 2 Fibredex boxes.
- Officials' Bonds and Records, 1777-1907; 1 volume, 3 Fibredex boxes.
- Tavern Bonds, 1777-1868; 1 Fibredex box.

Court Records

- County Court of Pleas and Quarter Sessions
  - Appearance Docket, 1843-1849; 1 volume.
  - Clerk's Fee Book, 1801-1822; 1 volume.
  - Costs Docket (State Prosecutions), 1822-1845; 1 volume.
  - Execution Dockets, 1778-1868; 9 volumes.
  - Minutes, 1777-1868; 17 volumes.
  - Prosecution Bond Docket, 1788-1805; 1 volume.
  - State Dockets, 1777-1789, 1804-1868; 5 volumes.
  - Trial, Appearance, and Reference Dockets, 1777-1843; 10 volumes.
  - Trial Dockets, 1843-1868; 2 volumes.
- Superior Court
  - Civil Action Papers, 1767-1944; 61 Fibredex boxes.
  - Civil Action Papers Concerning Land, 1778-1927; 5 Fibredex boxes.
  - Criminal Action Papers, 1777-1911; 42 Fibredex boxes.
  - Criminal Issues Docket, 1869-1892; 1 volume.
  - Equity Minutes, 1807-1868; 3 volumes.
  - Equity Receipt Books, 1840-1872; 3 volumes.
  - Equity Trial and Appearance Docket, 1856-1868; 1 volume.
  - Execution Dockets, 1823-1868; 4 volumes.
  - Minutes, 1807-1837, 1853-1924; 13 volumes.
  - State Dockets, 1823-1868; 3 volumes.
  - Trial and Appearance Docket, 1834-1848; 1 volume.
  - Trial Dockets, 1854-1873; 2 volumes.

Election Records

- Election Records, 1803-1920; 1 Fibredex box.
- Elections, Record of, 1872-1912; 2 volumes.

Estates Records

- Accounts, Record of, 1868-1930; 8 volumes.
- Administrators' Bonds, 1876-1918; 4 volumes.
- Appointment of Administrators, Executors, and Guardians, 1868-1907; 2 volumes.
- Estates, Cross Index to, 1859-1887; 1 volume.
- Estates Records, 1772-1941; 106 Fibredex boxes.
- Guardians' Accounts, 1794-1868; 5 volumes.
- Guardians' Bonds, 1875-1936; 4 volumes.
- Guardians' Records, 1777-1930; 23 Fibredex boxes.

Receivers of Estates, Record of, 1887-1934; 2 volumes.
Settlements, Record of, 1868-1926; 3 volumes.

LAND RECORDS

Attachments, Executions, Liens, and Levies (on Land), 1799-1900; 1 Fibredex box.
Deeds, 1780-1884; 5 Fibredex boxes.
Deeds of Gift, 1787-1864; Deeds of Trust, 1803-1884; 1 Fibredex box.
Ejectments, 1799-1878; 1 Fibredex box.
Land Entries, 1778-1795, 1841-1863; 1 volume.
Miscellaneous Land Records, 1778-1918; 1 Fibredex box.

MARRIAGE, DIVORCE, AND VITAL STATISTICS

Divorce Records, 1818-1928; 2 Fibredex boxes.
Marriage Bonds, 1778-1868; 17 Fibredex boxes.

MILITARY AND PENSION RECORDS [*See* **MISCELLANEOUS RECORDS**]

MISCELLANEOUS RECORDS

Assignees, Trustees, and Receivers, Records of, 1815-1934; 1 Fibredex box.
Bridge Records, 1787-1872; 1 Fibredex box.
Common School Register, 1859; 1 volume.
County Accounts, 1771-1867; 5 Fibredex boxes.
County Claims Allowed, 1808-1832; 1 volume.
Highway Commission of Caswell County, Minutes, 1919-1923; 1 manuscript box.
Insolvents Records, 1786-1858; 1 Fibredex box.
Jury Lists and Tickets, 1786-1869; 3 Fibredex boxes.
Miscellaneous Records, 1775-1900; 4 Fibredex boxes.
Orders and Decrees, 1868-1924; 5 volumes.
Pension Records, 1909-1937; 1 volume.
Powers of Attorney, 1785-1876; 1 Fibredex box.
Road Dockets, 1801-1867; 8 volumes.
Road Records, 1785-1922; 1 Fibredex box.
School Records, 1816-1877; 3 Fibredex boxes.
Special Proceedings Docket, 1869-1883; 1 volume.

ROADS AND BRIDGES [*See* **MISCELLANEOUS RECORDS**]

SCHOOL RECORDS [*See* **MISCELLANEOUS RECORDS; CRX RECORDS**]

TAX AND FISCAL RECORDS

Lists of Taxables, 1777-1867; 9 volumes, 3 Fibredex boxes.

WILLS

Extracts from County Court Minutes, 1780-1782; 1 volume.
Wills, 1771-1927; 7 Fibredex boxes.

CRX RECORDS

Public School Register District 9, 1891-1899; 1 volume in manuscript box.
School Account Book, 1848-1853; 1 volume.
School Records, 1842-1853; 2 folders.

MICROFILM RECORDS

BONDS

Apprentice Bonds, 1880-1921; 1 reel.
Bastardy Bonds, 1780-1799, 1830-1905; 2 reels.
Officials' Bonds, 1868-1907; 1 reel.

CORPORATIONS AND PARTNERSHIPS

Certificates of Incorporation, 1899-1963; 1 reel.

COURT RECORDS

County Court of Pleas and Quarter Sessions
- Minutes, 1777-1862, 1866-1868; 5 reels.
- Orders of Allowance, 1808-1832; 1 reel.

Superior Court
- Civil Actions, Index to, 1970-1986; 1 reel.
- Criminal Actions, Index to, 1948-1970; 1 reel.
- Equity Minutes, 1807-1868; 1 reel.
- Judgments, Index to, 1948-1970; 1 reel.
- Judgments, Liens, and Lis Pendens, Index to, 1948-1970; 1 reel.
- Minutes, 1807-1826, 1853-1970; 7 reels.

ELECTION RECORDS

Elections, Record of, 1940-1970; 1 reel.

ESTATES RECORDS

Accounts for Indigent Children, 1905-1936; 1 reel.
Accounts, Record of, 1867-1970; 10 reels.
Administrators' Bonds, 1876-1918; 1 reel.
Administrators and Guardians, Index to, 1864-1887, 1924-1948; 1 reel.
Administrators, Record of, 1868-1889, 1919-1951; 2 reels.
Application for Guardianship, 1937-1962, 1967-1970; 1 reel.
Appointment of Administrators, Executors, and Guardians, 1892-1907; 1 reel.
Clerk's Receiver Accounts, 1920-1940; 1 reel.
Estates, Index to, 1948-1963; 1 reel.
Executors and Guardians, Record of, 1868-1892, 1923-1936, 1949-1970; 3 reels.
Final Accounts, Record of, 1890-1958; 4 reels.
Guardians' Accounts, 1794-1868; 3 reels.
Guardians' Bonds, 1875-1929; 2 reels.
Inheritance Tax Records, 1923-1970; 1 reel.
Trustees under Wills, Record of, 1963; 1 reel.

LAND RECORDS

Deeds, Record of, 1777-1963; 52 reels.
Federal Tax Liens, Index to, 1935-1969; 1 reel.
Land Entries, 1778-1795, 1841-1863; 1 reel.
Plat Books, 1914-1968; 3 reels.
Real Estate Conveyances, Index to, Grantee, 1777-1971; 4 reels.
Real Estate Conveyances, Index to, Grantor, 1777-1971; 6 reels.
Sales and Resales by Mortgagees and Trustees, Record of, 1920-1970; 1 reel.

MARRIAGE, DIVORCE, AND VITAL STATISTICS

Births, Index to, 1913-1956; 1 reel.
Deaths, Index to, 1913-1985; 1 reel.

Delayed Birth Certificates, 1941-1946; Index to Delayed Births, various years; 3 reels.
Maiden Names of Divorced Women, 1936-1961; 1 reel.
Marriage Bonds, 1780-1868; 6 reels.
Marriage Licenses, 1867-1965; 23 reels.
Marriage Registers, 1853-1963; 2 reels.

MISCELLANEOUS RECORDS

Lunacy, Record of, 1899-1963; 1 reel.
Orders and Decrees, 1868-1970; 9 reels.
Special Proceedings, 1884-1970; 2 reels.
Special Proceedings, Index to, 1884-1970; 2 reels.

OFFICIALS, COUNTY

Board of County Commissioners, Minutes, 1868-1961; 4 reels.

ROADS AND BRIDGES

County Highway Commission, Minutes, 1919-1923; 1 reel.
Road Docket, 1801-1867; 1 reel.

SCHOOL RECORDS

County Board of Education, Minutes, 1882-1963; 2 reels.
School Census, 1905-1909, 1919; 1 reel.
School Register, Common School, 1859; 1 reel.
School Registers, 1901-1923; 7 reels.

TAX AND FISCAL RECORDS

Lists of Taxables, 1777-1806, 1823-1824, 1838-1839, 1863-1864; 3 reels.
Tax Scrolls, 1866-1867, 1876-1902, 1907, 1911, 1917; 7 reels.

WILLS

Original Wills, 1785-1864; 1 reel.
Wills, Index to, 1777-1970; 3 reels.
Wills, Record of, 1777-1970; 12 reels.

CATAWBA COUNTY

Established in 1842 from Lincoln County.
Many court records missing; reason unknown.

ORIGINAL RECORDS

BONDS

Bastardy Bonds and Records, 1868-1911; 2 Fibredex boxes.

COURT RECORDS

County Court of Pleas and Quarter Sessions
- Appearance Docket, 1843-1868; List of Commissioners of Affidavits, 1883; 1 volume.
- Execution Docket, 1843-1868; 1 volume.
- Levy Docket, 1843-1868; Minutes, Board of County Commissioners, 1868-1880; 1 volume.
- Minutes, 1843-1868; 2 volumes.
- State Docket, 1843-1868; 1 volume.

Superior Court
- Appearance Docket, 1844-1868; 1 volume.
- Civil Action Papers, 1858-1926; 22 Fibredex boxes.
- Civil Action Papers Concerning Land, 1867-1925; 6 Fibredex boxes.
- Civil Issues Docket, 1869-1891; 1 volume.
- Criminal Action Papers, 1866-1923; 14 Fibredex boxes.
- Equity Execution Docket, 1845-1868; Special Proceedings Judgment Docket, 1875-1886; 1 volume. [*See also* **MISCELLANEOUS RECORDS**, Special Proceedings Judgment Docket, 1885-1900]
- Equity Minutes, 1843-1868; Record of Widows' Year's Support, 1871-1893; 1 volume.
- Equity Trial Docket, 1844-1868; 1 volume.
- Execution Docket, 1844-1868; Levy Docket, 1878-1879; 1 volume.
- Execution Docket, 1878-1885; 1 volume.
- Judgment Dockets, 1880-1941; 21 volumes.
- Minutes, 1843-1915; 11 volumes.
- State Docket, 1845-1868; 1 volume.
- Trial Docket, 1844-1868; Motion Docket, 1873-1883; 1 volume.

ELECTION RECORDS

Elections, Record of, 1878-1924; 3 volumes.
Permanent Registration of Voters, 1902-1908; 1 volume.

ESTATES RECORDS

Accounts and Inventories, Record of, 1868-1898; 5 volumes.
Clerk's Receipt Book (Trust Funds), 1912-1915; 1 volume.
Dowers and Land Divisions, Record of, 1875-1907; 2 volumes.
Estates, Record of, 1843-1868; 2 volumes.
Estates Records, 1851-1982; 101 Fibredex boxes.
Executors and Administrators, Cross Index to, 1843-1927; 1 volume.
Guardians' Records, 1856-1912; 9 Fibredex boxes.
Guardians and Wards, Cross Index to, 1843-1937; 1 volume.

Settlements, Record of, 1868-1908; 3 volumes.
Widows' Year's Support, Record of, 1871-1907; 1 volume. [*See also* **COURT RECORDS**, Superior Court, Equity Minutes, 1843-1868]

LAND RECORDS
Miscellaneous Land Records, 1864-1906; 1 Fibredex box.

MARRIAGE, DIVORCE, AND VITAL STATISTICS
Disinterment/Reinterment Permits, 1968-1984; 1 manuscript box.
Divorce Records, 1869-1927; 4 Fibredex boxes.
Marriage Bonds, 1843-1868; 1 Fibredex box.

MISCELLANEOUS RECORDS
Assignees, Trustees, and Receivers, Records of, 1853-1911; 2 Fibredex boxes.
Board of County Commissioners, Minutes, 1868-1880. [*See* **COURT RECORDS**, Court of Pleas and Quarter Sessions, Levy Docket, 1843-1868]
Commissioners of Affidavits, List of, 1883. [*See* **COURT RECORDS**, Court of Pleas and Quarter Sessions, Levy Docket]
County Board of Education, Minutes, 1881-1884; 1 volume.
Lunacy, Record of, 1899-1919; 1 volume.
Miscellaneous Records, 1851-1922; 3 Fibredex boxes.
Orders and Decrees, 1870-1885; 1 volume.
Road and Bridge Records, 1869-1911; 1 Fibredex box.
Road Docket, 1843-1869; 1 volume.
School Fund Account Book, 1899-1908; 1 volume.
Special Proceedings Dockets, 1880-1915; 2 volumes.
Special Proceedings Judgment Docket, 1885-1900; 1 volume. [*See also* **COURT RECORDS**, Superior Court, Equity Execution Docket, 1845-1868]

OFFICIALS, COUNTY [*See* **COURT RECORDS; MISCELLANEOUS RECORDS**]

ROADS AND BRIDGES [*See* **MISCELLANEOUS RECORDS**]

SCHOOL RECORDS [*See* **MISCELLANEOUS RECORDS**]

TAX AND FISCAL RECORDS
Lists of Taxables, 1857-1868; 1 volume.
Tax Records, 1894-1912; 2 Fibredex boxes.

WILLS
Wills, 1843-1966; 48 Fibredex boxes.
Wills, Cross Index to, 1843-1926; 1 volume.

MICROFILM RECORDS

CORPORATIONS AND PARTNERSHIPS
Corporations, Index to, 1883-1968; 1 reel.
Corporations, Record of, 1883-1949; 3 reels.
Partnerships, Record of, 1913-1968; 1 reel.

COURT RECORDS
County Court of Pleas and Quarter Sessions
Minutes, 1843-1868; 1 reel.
Superior Court
Civil Actions, Index to, Defendant, 1966-1974; 3 reels.
Civil Actions, Index to, Plaintiff, 1966-1980; 2 reels.

Equity Minutes, 1843-1868; Widows' Year's Support, 1871-1893; 1 reel.
Judgments, Index to, Defendant, 1912-1967; 3 reels.
Minutes, 1843-1960; 15 reels.

ELECTION RECORDS

Elections, Record of, 1906-1966; 1 reel.

ESTATES RECORDS

Accounts and Inventories, Record of, 1869-1966; 14 reels.
Administrators, Executors, and Guardians, Index to, 1843-1966; 2 reels.
Administrators, Executors, and Guardians, Record of, 1868-1925; 6 reels.
Administrators, Record of, 1916-1966; 9 reels.
Dowers, Record of, 1871-1948; 1 reel.
Estates Not Exceeding $300, Record of, 1930-1942; 1 reel.
Estates, Record of, 1843-1868; 2 reels.
Executors, Record of, 1925-1966; 4 reels.
Guardians, Record of, 1925-1966; 3 reels.
Guardians of World War I Veterans, Record of, 1930-1938; 1 reel.
Inheritance Tax Records, 1923-1968; 2 reels.
Settlements, Record of, 1868-1966; 10 reels.
Widows' Year's Support, Record of, 1894-1907; 1 reel. [*See also* **COURT RECORDS**, Superior Court, Equity Minutes]

LAND RECORDS

Deeds, Record of, 1843-1955; 103 reels.
Entry Takers' Book, 1904-1918; 1 reel.
Federal Tax Liens, Index to, 1906-1969; 1 reel.
Maps, 1911-1946; 1 reel.
Plats, Index to, 1842-1980; 1 reel.
Real Estate Conveyances, Index to, Grantee, 1837-1954; 7 reels.
Real Estate Conveyances, Index to, Grantor, 1837-1954; 7 reels.
Sale and Resale, Record of, 1925-1967; 3 reels.
Tax Levies on Land, 1843-1868; 1 reel.

MARRIAGE, DIVORCE, AND VITAL STATISTICS

Births, Index to, 1913-1967; 3 reels.
Deaths, Index to, 1909-1979; 1 reel.
Delayed Births, Index to, various years; 1 reel.
Freedmen's Marriage Records, 1866; 1 reel.
Marriage Bond Abstracts, 1842-1868; 1 reel.
Marriage Bonds, 1842-1868; 1 reel.
Marriage Licenses, 1864-1946; 8 reels.
Marriage Registers, 1851-1968; 2 reels.

MILITARY AND PENSION RECORDS [*See* **MISCELLANEOUS RECORDS**]

MISCELLANEOUS RECORDS

Clerk's Minute Dockets, 1927-1966; 3 reels.
Lunacy, Record of, 1899-1959; 2 reels.
Orders and Decrees, 1868-1966; 19 reels.
Orders and Decrees, Index to, Defendant, 1868-1966; 1 reel.
Orders and Decrees, Index to, Plaintiff, 1868-1966; 1 reel.

Special Proceedings Dockets, 1880-1915; 1 reel.
Special Proceedings, Index to, 1966-1980; 1 reel.

OFFICIALS, COUNTY

Board of County Commissioners, Minutes, 1880-1960; 4 reels.

SCHOOL RECORDS

County Board of Education, Minutes, 1881-1968; 2 reels.

TAX AND FISCAL RECORDS

List of Taxables, 1857-1868; 1 reel.
Tax Scrolls, 1869-1896, 1905, 1915, 1925, 1935, 1945, 1955, 1965; 7 reels.

WILLS

Wills, Index to, Devisor, 1843-1966; 1 reel.
Wills, Record of, 1843-1966; 5 reels.

CHATHAM COUNTY

Established in 1771 from Orange County.
Many court records missing; reason unknown.

ORIGINAL RECORDS

BONDS

Apprentice Bonds and Records, 1784-1920; 3 volumes, 2 Fibredex boxes.
Bastardy Bonds and Records, 1869-1931; 2 Fibredex boxes. [*See also* **CRX RECORDS**]
Constables' Bonds, 1771-1928; 3 Fibredex boxes.
Officials' Bonds, 1782-1904; 1 Fibredex box.

COURT RECORDS

County Court of Pleas and Quarter Sessions
- Appearance Dockets, 1839-1867; 3 volumes.
- Execution Dockets, 1807-1868; 7 volumes.
- Minutes, 1774-1864; 16 volumes.
- State and Recognizance Dockets, 1824-1866; 2 volumes.
- Trial, Appearance, and Reference Dockets, 1774-1821; 6 volumes.
- Trial Dockets, 1839-1866; 3 volumes.

General County Court
- Minutes, 1929-1948; 2 volumes.

Inferior Court
- Criminal Issues Docket, 1878-1885; 1 volume.
- Execution Docket, 1878-1885; 1 volume.

Superior Court
- Civil Action Papers, 1772-1937; 15 Fibredex boxes. [*See also* **CRX RECORDS**]
- Civil Action Papers Concerning Land, 1868-1940; 17 Fibredex boxes.
- Civil Action Papers Concerning Mines, 1863-1930; 1 Fibredex box.
- Civil Issues Dockets, 1868-1898; 4 volumes.
- Criminal Action Papers, 1846-1934; 15 Fibredex boxes.
- Criminal Issues Docket, 1894-1898; 1 volume.
- Equity Costs Docket, 1860-1868; 1 volume.
- Equity Minutes, 1821-1842, 1859-1868; 2 volumes.
- Equity Trial Dockets, 1854-1868; 2 volumes.
- Execution Dockets, 1816-1874; 6 volumes.
- Judgment Dockets, 1868-1909; 8 volumes. [*See also* **LAND RECORDS**]
- Minutes, 1807-1949; 17 volumes, 1 manuscript box.
- State Dockets, 1849-1892; 3 volumes.
- Trial and Appearance Dockets, 1821-1868; 3 volumes.

ELECTION RECORDS

Democratic Canvass Book, 1888-1890; Registration Book, 1890, 1892, 1896; 1 manuscript box.
Elections, Record of, 1878-1942; 4 volumes.

ESTATES RECORDS [*See also* **WILLS**]

Accounts, Record of, 1868-1968; 14 volumes.
Administrators' Bonds, 1867-1896; 4 volumes.
Administrators, Record of, 1896-1928; 3 volumes.

Appointment of Executors, Administrators, Guardians, and Masters, 1868-1903; 1 volume.
Estates, Record of, 1799-1868; 16 volumes.
Estates Records, 1771-1948, 1955; 164 Fibredex boxes. [*See also* **CRX RECORDS**]
Executors, Record of, 1915-1949; 1 volume.
Guardians' Accounts, 1800-1868; 3 volumes.
Guardians' Bonds, 1874-1911; 3 volumes.
Guardians, Record of, 1906-1958; 2 volumes.
Guardians' Records, 1775, 1784-1939; 17 Fibredex boxes.
Probate Court Docket, 1868-1902; 1 volume.
Settlements, Record of, 1869-1944; 5 volumes.

LAND RECORDS [*See also* **WILLS**]
Attachments, Executions, Liens, and Levies on Land, 1800-1937; 5 Fibredex boxes.
Deeds, 1775-1952; 5 Fibredex boxes.
Deeds, Index to, 1771-1873; 2 manuscript boxes.
Deeds of Trust, 1821-1867, 1913-1939; 1 Fibredex box.
Ex Parte Proceedings Concerning Land, 1872-1930; 1 Fibredex box.
Judgment Docket, Land Tax Sales, 1929-1961; 4 volumes. [*See also* **COURT RECORDS**, Superior Court]
Judgment Docket, Land Tax Sales, Cross Index to, 1929-1941; 1 volume.
Land Entry Book, 1843-1913; 1 manuscript box.
Land Grants, 1779-1870; 1 oversized manuscript box.
Levies on Land, 1853-1944; 4 Fibredex boxes.
Miscellaneous Land Records, 1778-1938; 2 Fibredex boxes.

MARRIAGE, DIVORCE, AND VITAL STATISTICS
Applications for Marriage Licenses, Record of, 1929-1932; 1 volume.
Divorce Records, 1829-1934; 7 Fibredex boxes.
Maiden Names of Divorced Women, 1945-1988; 1 volume.
Marriage Bonds, 1778-1867; 5 Fibredex boxes.
Marriage Certificates, Record of, 1851-1868; 1 volume.
Marriage Registers, 1868-1940; 6 volumes.

MISCELLANEOUS RECORDS
Accounts of Outside Poor and Lunatics, 1879-1916; 3 volumes.
Assignees, Trustees, and Receivers, Records of, 1872-1935; 5 Fibredex boxes.
Board of County Commissioners, Minutes, 1868-1874; 1 volume.
Board of Magistrates, Minutes, 1877-1894; 1 volume.
Coroners' Inquests, 1796-1971; 3 Fibredex boxes.
County Accounts and Claims, 1868-1910; 2 volumes.
County Commissioners, Records Relating to, 1871-1930; 1 Fibredex box.
County Superintendent of Public Instruction, Record of Expenditures, 1883-1887; 1 volume.
Homestead and Personal Property Exemptions, 1869-1939; 2 Fibredex boxes.
Homestead Returns, 1888-1945; 1 volume.
Lunacy, Record of, 1899-1946; 2 volumes.
Miscellaneous Records, 1772-1956; 4 Fibredex boxes. [*See also* **CRX RECORDS**]
Miscellaneous School Records, 1843-1934; 1 Fibredex box.
Official Reports, Record of, 1875-1908; 1 volume.

Orders and Decrees, 1870-1922; 6 volumes.
Railroad Records, 1874-1933; 4 Fibredex boxes.
Road and Bridge Records, 1781-1921; 1 Fibredex box.
Slaves and Free Persons of Color, Records of, 1782-1870; 1 Fibredex box.

OFFICIALS, COUNTY [*See* **MISCELLANEOUS RECORDS**]

ROADS AND BRIDGES [*See* **MISCELLANEOUS RECORDS**]

SCHOOL RECORDS [*See* **MISCELLANEOUS RECORDS**]

TAX AND FISCAL RECORDS
Poll Tax Register, 1902-1908; 1 volume.

WILLS
Deeds, Bills of Sale, Inventories, and Wills, 1782-1794; 1 volume.
Wills, 1771-1964; 27 Fibredex boxes.
Wills, Cross Index to, 1792-1915; 1 volume.
Wills, Record of, 1794-1905; 8 volumes.

CRX RECORDS
Bastardy Bonds and Records, 1787-1911; 1 Fibredex box.
Civil Action, 1832; 1 folder.
County of Chatham Funding Bonds, 1909; 1 folder.
Estates Records, 1807-1830; 5 folders.
Miscellaneous Records, 1774-1910; 1 Fibredex, 31 folders.

MICROFILM RECORDS

BONDS
Apprentice Bonds, 1875-1920; 1 reel.
Officials' Bonds, 1868-1892; 1 reel.

CORPORATIONS AND PARTNERSHIPS
Corporations, Record of, 1889-1977; 3 reels.
Partnerships, Record of, 1913-1952; 1 reel.

COURT RECORDS
County Court of Pleas and Quarter Sessions
Minutes, 1774-1864; 5 reels.
General County Court
Minutes, 1929-1959; 2 reels.
Superior Court
Civil Actions, Index to, 1968-1977; 1 reel.
Criminal Actions, Index to, 1968-1977; 1 reel.
Equity Minutes, 1821-1842, 1858-1868; 2 reels.
Judgment Dockets, 1900-1909; 1 reel.
Judgments, Cross Index to, 1868-1956; 1 reel.
Judgments, Index to, Defendant, 1956-1968; 1 reel.
Judgments, Index to, Plaintiff, 1956-1968; 1 reel.
Minutes, 1827-1839, 1867-1960; 10 reels.

ELECTION RECORDS
Elections, Record of, 1878-1968; 3 reels.

ESTATES RECORDS

Accounts for Indigent Children, 1922-1926; 1 reel.
Accounts, Record of, 1868-1968; 8 reels.
Administrators' Bonds, 1867-1894; 1 reel.
Administrators, Executors, and Guardians, Index to, 1867-1966; 1 reel.
Administrators, Record of, 1896-1954; 4 reels.
Appointment of Executors, 1868-1903, 1915-1968; 2 reels.
Dowers and Widows' Year's Support, Record of, 1888-1968; 1 reel.
Estates, Record of, 1782-1857, 1862-1868; 5 reels.
Guardians' Bonds, 1874-1907; 1 reel.
Guardians, Record of, 1800-1868, 1906-1958; 2 reels.
Inheritance Tax Records, 1923-1971; 1 reel.
Settlements, Record of, 1868-1968; 5 reels.

LAND RECORDS

Deeds, Record of, 1771-1950; 60 reels.
Federal Farm Loan Mortgages, 1923-1930; 1 reel.
Land Entry Book, 1843-1913; 1 reel.
Land Grants, 1837-1858; 1 reel.
Maps, 1911-1949; 1 reel.
Plats, Index to, 1814-1986; 1 reel.
Real Estate Conveyances, Index to, Grantee, 1771-1974; 7 reels.
Real Estate Conveyances, Index to, Grantor, 1771-1974; 7 reels.
Sales by Trustees and Mortgagees, Record of, 1921-1969; 3 reels.
Tax Liens, Index to [Federal], 1932-1959; 1 reel.

MARRIAGE, DIVORCE, AND VITAL STATISTICS

Births, Index to, 1913-1985; 2 reels.
Deaths, Index to, 1913-1976; 1 reel.
Delayed Births, Index to, various years; 1 reel.
Maiden Names of Divorced Women, 1945-1959; 1 reel.
Marriage Bonds, 1772-1868; 3 reels.
Marriage Licenses, 1877-1960; 8 reels.
Marriage Registers, 1851-1977; 3 reels.
Marriages, Index to, 1903-1971; 2 reels.

MISCELLANEOUS RECORDS

Accounts of Outside Poor and Lunatics, 1879-1932; 1 reel.
Homestead Returns, 1888-1916; 1 reel.
Lunacy, Record of, 1899-1947; 1 reel.
Notaries Public, Index to, 1969-1971; 1 reel.
Orders and Decrees, 1870-1968; 9 reels.
Poor House Book, 1871-1885; 1 reel.
Revolutionary History of Chatham, 1876; 1 reel.
Special Proceedings, 1905-1968; 2 reels.
Special Proceedings, Index to, 1935-1968; 1 reel.

OFFICIALS, COUNTY

Board of County Commissioners, Index to Minutes, 1875-1978; 1 reel.
Board of County Commissioners, Minutes, 1869-1962; 5 reels.
Commissioners' Ledgers, 1878-1909; 1 reel.
Magistrates, Record of, 1877-1894; 1 reel.

ROADS AND BRIDGES

Road Overseers, Record of, 1869; 1 reel.

SCHOOL RECORDS

Board of Superintendents of Common Schools, Minutes, 1841-1863; County Board of Education, Minutes, 1885-1954; 1 reel.

TAX AND FISCAL RECORDS

Tax Lists, 1874-1896, 1905; 5 reels.

Tax Scrolls, 1865, 1875-1945; 12 reels.

WILLS

Wills, Index to, 1792-1971; 2 reels.

Wills, Index to, Devisee, 1970-1977; 1 reel.

Wills, Record of, 1780-1968; 7 reels.

CHEROKEE COUNTY

Established in 1839 from Macon County.
Courthouse fires of 1865 (Federal troops), 1895, and 1926 destroyed many court records.

ORIGINAL RECORDS

Bonds

Apprentice Bonds, 1896, 1906; Bastardy Bonds, 1866-1912; Officials' Bonds, 1866-1948; 1 Fibredex box.

Court Records

County Court of Pleas and Quarter Sessions

- Minutes, 1865-1868; Minutes, Board of County Commissioners, 1870-1882; Merchants' Taxes, 1873-1882; 1 volume.

Superior Court

- Civil Action Papers, 1846-1919; 10 Fibredex boxes.
- Civil Action Papers Concerning Land, 1862-1926; 23 Fibredex boxes.
- Criminal Action Papers, 1863-1913; 12 Fibredex boxes.
- Equity Enrolling Docket, 1866-1868; Minutes, Superior Court, 1868-1869; 1 volume.
- Equity Minutes, 1866-1868. [*See* **Land Records**, Record of Probate, 1869-1880]
- Minutes, 1869-1913; 8 volumes.

Election Records

Elections, Record of, 1878-1934; 6 volumes.

Estates Records

Accounts, Record of, 1868-1928; 1 volume.
Administrators' Bonds, 1914-1936; 1 volume.
Estates Records, 1843-1940; 24 Fibredex boxes.
Guardians' Records, 1869-1936; 2 Fibredex boxes.

Land Records

Deeds, 1889-1950; 2 Fibredex boxes.
Deeds, Cross Index to, [1839-1897]; 2 volumes.
Deeds, Record of, 1839-1856, 1859-1889, 1897-1898; 20 volumes.
Deeds of Trust and Mortgage Deeds, 1893-1954; 1 Fibredex box.
Land Entries, 1883-1931; 3 Fibredex boxes.
Miscellaneous Land Records, 1869-1946; 1 Fibredex box.
Pre-emption Bond Book, 1838-1857; 1 volume.
Probate, Record of, 1869-1880; Equity Minutes, 1866-1868; 1 volume.
Solvent and Insolvent Principals, Record of, 1844-1845; 1 volume.

Marriage, Divorce, and Vital Statistics

Divorce Records, 1869-1914, 1942; 3 Fibredex boxes.
Marriage Licenses Issued, Record of, 1865-1870; Registry of Licenses to Trades, 1869-1870, 1883-1890; 1 volume.
Marriage Registers, 1868-1906; 2 volumes.

Miscellaneous Records

Alien Registration, 1927, 1940, 1957; 1 volume.
Assignees, Receivers, and Trustees, Records of, 1872-1919; 6 Fibredex boxes.

Board of County Commissioners, Minutes, 1870-1882. [*See* **COURT RECORDS**, Court of Pleas and Quarter Sessions, Minutes, 1865-1868]
Ear Marks and Brands, Record of, 1888-1918; 1 volume.
Homestead and Personal Property Exemptions, 1869-1926; 1 Fibredex box.
Licenses to Trades, Registry of, 1869-1870, 1883-1890. [*See* **MARRIAGE, DIVORCE, AND VITAL STATISTICS**, Marriage Licenses Issued, Record of, 1865-1870]
Miscellaneous Records, 1866-1948; 3 Fibredex boxes.
Orders and Decrees, 1869-1914; 2 volumes.
Railroad Records, 1880-1914; 4 Fibredex boxes.
Road Records, 1874-1927; 1 Fibredex box.
Wardens of the Poor Account Book, 1843-1868; 1 volume.

OFFICIALS, COUNTY [*See* **MISCELLANEOUS RECORDS**]

ROADS AND BRIDGES [*See* **MISCELLANEOUS RECORDS**]

TAX AND FISCAL RECORDS

Merchants' Taxes, 1873-1882. [*See* **COURT RECORDS**, Court of Pleas and Quarter Sessions, Minutes, 1865-1868]
Tax Book, 1867-1869; 1 volume.
Tax Records, 1870-1946; 1 Fibredex box.
Tax Scrolls, 1933, 1936, 1937; 3 volumes.

WILLS

Wills, 1857-1941; 5 Fibredex boxes.

MICROFILM RECORDS

CORPORATIONS AND PARTNERSHIPS

Corporations, Record of, 1898-1963; 2 reels.
Partnerships, Record of, 1913-1957; 1 reel.

COURT RECORDS

County Court of Pleas and Quarter Sessions
Minutes, 1865-1868; 1 reel.
Superior Court
Civil Actions, Index to, 1890-1979; 3 reels.
Criminal Actions, Index to, 1966-1979; 1 reel.
Equity Minutes, 1866-1868; 1 reel.
Judgment Dockets, 1925-1933; 2 reels.
Judgments, Index to, 1898-1966; 4 reels.
Minutes, 1868-1945; 12 reels.

ELECTION RECORDS

Elections, Record of, 1878-1966; 2 reels.

ESTATES RECORDS

Accounts, Record of, 1868-1966; 3 reels.
Administrators' Bonds, 1914-1936; 1 reel.
Administrators, Executors, and Guardians, Record of, 1925-1956; 2 reels.
Administrators, Record of, 1948-1966; 1 reel.
Appointment of Executors, 1868-1925; 1 reel.
Executors and Guardians, Record of, 1956-1966; 1 reel.
Guardians, Record of, 1947-1966; 1 reel.

Inheritance Tax Records, 1919-1967; 1 reel.
Settlements, Record of, 1871-1966; 2 reels.

LAND RECORDS

Deeds, Index to, Grantee, 1839-1967; 8 reels.
Deeds, Index to, Grantor, 1839-1967; 8 reels.
Deeds, Record of, 1839-1955; 61 reels.
Land Entries, 1853-1936; 2 reels.
Plat Book, various years; 1 reel.
Plats, Index to, various years; 1 reel.
Pre-emption Bonds, 1838-1857; 2 reels.
Sales and Resales by Mortgagees and Trustees, Record of, 1920-1966; 1 reel.
Solvent and Insolvent Purchasers, Record of, 1844-1845; 1 reel.
Surveys, Record of, 1905-1915; 1 reel.

MARRIAGE, DIVORCE, AND VITAL STATISTICS

Births, Index to, 1913-1945; 1 reel.
Deaths, Index to, 1913-1945; 1 reel.
Marriage Licenses, 1868-1961; 7 reels.
Marriage Registers, 1869-1978; 4 reels.

MISCELLANEOUS RECORDS

Alien Registration, 1927, 1940, 1957; 1 reel.
Ear Marks and Brands, Record of, 1888-1918; 1 reel.
Lunacy, Record of, 1919-1966; 1 reel.
Memorials, Record of, 1927-1965; 1 reel.
Orders and Decrees, 1869-1958; 5 reels.
Special Proceedings, 1921-1951; 1 reel.
Special Proceedings, Index to, 1869-1967; 3 reels.
Wardens of the Poor, Record of, 1843-1868; 1 reel.

OFFICIALS, COUNTY

Board of County Commissioners, Minutes, 1870-1965; 5 reels.

TAX AND FISCAL RECORDS

Tax List, 1867-1869; 1 reel.
Tax Scrolls, 1933, 1936-1937; 1 reel.

WILLS

Wills, Cross Index to, 1869-1966; 1 reel.
Wills, Record of, 1869-1966; 2 reels.

CHOWAN COUNTY

Established by 1670 as a precinct of Albemarle County.
Many court records were said to have been destroyed by acting clerk of court in 1848.

ORIGINAL RECORDS

BONDS

Apprentice Bonds and Records, 1737-1909; 1 volume, 4 Fibredex boxes.
Bastardy Bonds and Records, 1736-1933; 1 volume, 4 Fibredex boxes.
Officials' Bonds and Records, 1737-1921; 5 Fibredex boxes.
Ordinary Bonds and Records, 1739-1867; 2 Fibredex boxes.

COURT RECORDS

County Court of Pleas and Quarter Sessions
- Clerk's Account Book, 1804-1811; 1 volume.
- Clerk's Account and Receipt Book, 1840-1850; 1 volume.
- Costs Dockets, 1806-1813, 1841-1850; 2 volumes.
- Execution Dockets, 1757-1859; 11 volumes, 1 manuscript box.
- Levy Docket, 1849-1850; 1 volume.
- Minutes, 1714-1868; 21 volumes.
- State (Crown) Dockets, 1774-1862; 4 volumes, 1 manuscript box.
- Trial, Appearance, and Reference Dockets, 1757-1868; 18 volumes, 2 manuscript boxes.

Superior Court
- Civil Action Papers, 1730-1922; 103 Fibredex boxes.
- Civil Action Papers Concerning Land, 1761-1911; 12 Fibredex boxes.
- Civil Action Papers Concerning Timber, 1795-1908; 1 Fibredex box.
- Criminal Action Papers, 1720-1933; 38 Fibredex boxes.
- Equity Minutes, 1816-1861, 1866-1868; 2 volumes. [*See also* CRX RECORDS]
- Equity Trial Docket, 1849-1868; 1 volume.
- Execution Dockets, 1814-1868; 2 volumes.
- Minutes, 1809-1910; 11 volumes, 1 manuscript box.
- Rough Minutes and Dockets, 1725-1867; 1 Fibredex box.
- State Docket, 1826-1868; 1 volume.
- Trial, Appearance, and Reference Dockets, 1807-1868; 5 volumes, 1 manuscript box.

ELECTION RECORDS

Election Returns and Lists of Voters, 1772-1914; 2 Fibredex boxes.
Elections, Record of, 1878-1912; 2 volumes.

ESTATES RECORDS

Accounts of Sale, 1779-1796, 1812-1868; 7 volumes.
Administrators' Bonds, 1867-1911; 4 volumes.
Appointment of Administrators, 1777-1784; 1 pamphlet.
Appointment of Administrators, Executors, Guardians, and Masters, 1868-1911; 1 volume.
Dowers and Widows' Year's Support, 1815-1858; 2 volumes.
Estates, Record of, 1811-1868; 2 volumes.
Estates Records, 1728-1951; 118 Fibredex boxes.
Guardians' Accounts, 1812-1868; 3 volumes.

Guardians' Bonds, 1850-1911; 2 volumes.
Guardians' Records, 1741-1913; 7 Fibredex boxes.
Hiring of Slaves Belonging to Estates, Record of, 1808-1817; 1 volume.
Inheritance Tax, Record of, 1919; 1 volume.
Inventories of Estates, 1811-1866; 1 volume.
Orphans' Court Docket, 1766-1775; 1 volume.

LAND RECORDS

Deeds, 1714-1900; 2 Fibredex boxes.
Deeds Proved, Record of, 1811-1852; 1 volume.
Deeds, Record of, 1715-1758; 8 volumes.
Ejectments, 1767-1879; 1 Fibredex box.
Entry Book, 1794-1801; 1 volume.
Miscellaneous Deeds, 1678-1893; 1 Fibredex box.
Miscellaneous Land Records, 1708-1923; 2 Fibredex boxes.

MARRIAGE, DIVORCE, AND VITAL STATISTICS

Divorce Records, 1823-1909; 2 Fibredex boxes.
Marriage Bonds, 1747-1868; 8 Fibredex boxes.
Marriage Certificates, Record of, 1851-1867; 1 volume.
Miscellaneous Marriage Records, 1754-1909; 1 Fibredex box.

MISCELLANEOUS RECORDS

Accounts, Letters, and Receipts of Edmund Hoskins, 1801-1835; 4 Fibredex boxes.
Accounts, Letters, and Receipts of Elisha Norfleet, Clerk of Court of Pleas and Quarter Sessions, 1796-1811; 1 Fibredex box.
Assignees, Receivers, and Trustees, Records of, 1763-1918; 2 Fibredex boxes.
Common School Records, 1839-1897; 1 Fibredex box.
County Accounts, 1742-1929; 2 Fibredex boxes.
County Road Commissioners, Minutes, 1921-1929; 1 volume.
Ferriage Docket, 1781-1783; 1 volume.
Insolvent Debtors, 1769-1869; 4 Fibredex boxes.
Jury Lists, 1722-1877; 1 Fibredex box.
Jury Tickets, Record of, 1873-1906; 1 volume.
Justices of the Peace Records, 1753-1920; 1 Fibredex box.
Loyalty Oath Stubs, 1865; 1 volume.
Miscellaneous Accounts, 1752-1879; 1 Fibredex box.
Miscellaneous Records, 1685-1916; 20 volumes, 5 Fibredex boxes. [*See also* **CRX RECORDS**]
Personal Accounts, 1700-1895; 2 Fibredex boxes.
Promissory Notes and Receipts, 1721-1909; 1 Fibredex box.
Road Records, 1717-1912; 6 Fibredex boxes.
Shipping Records, 1731-1894; 5 Fibredex boxes.
Slave Records, 1730-1869; 7 Fibredex boxes.
Special Proceedings, 1870-1895; 2 volumes.
Strays, Record (Entry) of, 1906-1919; 1 volume.

OFFICIALS, COUNTY [*See* **MISCELLANEOUS RECORDS**]

ROADS AND BRIDGES [*See* **MISCELLANEOUS RECORDS**]

SCHOOL RECORDS [*See* **MISCELLANEOUS RECORDS**]

TAX AND FISCAL RECORDS

Tax Lists, 1801-1826, 1869; 2 volumes.
Taxables, Lists of, 1717-1909, 9 Fibredex boxes.

WILLS

Wills, 1694-1938; 24 Fibredex boxes.

CRX RECORDS

Equity Court Minutes, Edenton District Superior Court, 1800-1804, Chowan County Superior Court, 1844, 1850; 1 volume.
Miscellaneous Records, 1747-1830; 13 folders.

MICROFILM RECORDS

BONDS

Apprentice Bonds, 1871-1909; 1 reel.
Bastardy Bonds, 1755-1878; 2 reels.
Officials' Bonds, 1690-1959; 3 reels.
Tavern Bonds, 1785-1837; 1 reel.

CORPORATIONS AND PARTNERSHIPS

Corporations, Record of, 1888-1950; 1 reel.
Partnerships, Record of, 1922-1976; 1 reel.

COURT RECORDS

County Court of Pleas and Quarter Sessions
- Court Letterbook, 1816-1858; 1 reel.
- Minutes, 1714-1719, 1730-1868; 11 reels.
- Orders of the Court, 1780-1830; 1 reel.
- Trial Dockets, 1788-1804; 1 reel.

Superior Court
- Civil Actions, Index to, 1966-1984; 3 reels.
- Criminal Actions, Index to, 1966-1984; 1 reel.
- Equity Minutes, 1807-1810, 1816-1868; 2 reels.
- Judgments, Index to, 1872-1985; 3 reels.
- Judgments, Liens, and Lis Pendens, Index to, 1966-1985; 1 reel.
- Minutes, 1810-1956; 6 reels.

ELECTION RECORDS

Elections, Record of, 1880-1914, 1924-1958; 1 reel.

ESTATES RECORDS

Accounts, Record of, 1785-1794, 1868-1958; 5 reels.
Accounts of Sale of Estates, 1811-1868; 2 reels. [*See also* Auction Sales, Record of; Vendue books]
Administrators' Bonds, 1748-1807, 1870-1911; 2 reels.
Administrators, Executors and Guardians, Index to, 1811-1966; 1 reel.
Administrators, Executors and Guardians, Record of, 1911-1943; 1 reel.
Administrators and Executors, Record of, 1811-1868; 1 reel.
Administrators, Record of, 1919-1966; 3 reels.
Appointment of Executors, 1868-1911; 1 reel.
Auction Sales, Record of, 1785-1794; 1 reel. [*See also* Accounts of Sale of Estates; Vendue Books]
Estates, Division of, ca. 1742-1831; 2 reels.

Estates, Index to, 1811-1966; 1 reel.
Estates, Record of, 1707-1790; 2 reels.
Executors and Guardians, Record of, 1936-1966; 2 reels.
Guardians' Bonds, 1787, 1811-1911; 3 reels.
Guardians, Record of, 1877-1883; 1 reel.
Inheritance Tax Records, 1914-1967; 2 reels.
Inventories of Estates, 1811-1866; 1 reel.
Orphans' Court Docket, 1767-1775; 1 reel.
Settlements, Record of, 1859-1969; 3 reels.
Vendue Books, 1779-1796; 2 reels. [*See also* Accounts of Sale of Estates; Auction Sales, Record of]
Widows' Dowers, 1786-1843; 1 reel. [*See also* **MISCELLANEOUS RECORDS**, Special Proceedings]
Widows' Year's Support, Record of, 1869-1966; 2 reels.

LAND RECORDS

Deeds, Index to, Grantee, 1695-1975; 3 reels.
Deeds, Index to, Grantor, 1695-1975; 3 reels.
Deeds Proved, Record of, 1811-1852; 1 reel.
Deeds, Record of, 1700-1946; 36 reels.
Land Entries, 1787-1941; 1 reel.
Processioners' Record, 1756, 1795-1808; 1 reel.
Sales and Resales of Land under Mortgagees and Trustees, 1926-1966; 2 reels.

MARRIAGE, DIVORCE, AND VITAL STATISTICS

Births, Index to, 1913-1993; 1 reel.
Deaths, Index to, 1913-1993; 1 reel.
Delayed Births, Index to, various years; 1 reel.
Divorce, Record of, 1868-1960; 1 reel.
Marriage Bonds, 1741-1868; 2 reels.
Marriage Registers, 1851-1947; 1 reel.

MISCELLANEOUS RECORDS

Clerk's Minute Docket, 1921-1966; 1 reel.
Ferriage Docket, 1781-1783; 1 reel.
Licenses to Trades, Registry of, 1873-1902; 1 reel.
Lunacy, Record of, 1899-1966; 1 reel.
Miscellaneous Records, 1685-1805; 10 reels.
Orders and Decrees, 1868-1968; 2 reels.
Petitions, Record of, 1770-1887; 3 reels.
Special Proceedings, 1868-1895, 1911-1967; Widows' Dowers and Year's Provisions, 1859-1868; 2 reels.

OFFICIALS, COUNTY

Board of County Commissioners, Minutes, 1868-1953; 3 reels.
Commissioners and Magistrates, Minutes, 1876-1896; 1 reel.

ROADS AND BRIDGES

County Road Commissioners, Minutes, 1921-1929; 1 reel.

SCHOOL RECORDS

Board of Superintendents of Common Schools, Minutes, 1841-1861; 1 reel.
County Board of Education, Minutes, 1885-1982; 2 reels.

TAX AND FISCAL RECORDS

Constables' Levies, 1849-1950; 1 reel.
Lists of Taxables, 1801-1810, 1814-1826; 1 reel.
Tax Ledger, 1865-1867; 1 reel.
Tax Scrolls, 1888-1892; 1 reel.

WILLS

Wills, Index to, Devisee, 1760-1966; 1 reel.
Wills, Index to, Devisor, 1760-1966; 1 reel.
Wills, List of, 1777-1784; 1 reel.
Wills, Record of, 1694-1966; 7 reels.

CLAY COUNTY

Established in 1861 from Cherokee County.
Fire (not courthouse) destroyed all records of the county in 1870.

ORIGINAL RECORDS

Bonds

Apprentice Bonds, 1871-1910; 1 volume.
Bastardy Bonds, 1879; 1 volume.
Officials' Bonds and Records, 1879-1939; 1 Fibredex box.

Court Records

Superior Court
- Civil Action Papers, 1868-1911; 2 Fibredex boxes.
- Civil Action Papers Concerning Land, 1870-1942; 4 Fibredex boxes.
- Criminal Action Papers, 1870-1909; 6 Fibredex boxes.
- Minutes, 1870-1902; 2 volumes.

Election Records

Elections, Record of, 1878-1932; 4 volumes.

Estates Records

Administrators' Bonds, 1870-1915; 2 volumes.
Dowers, Record of, 1871-1901; 1 volume.
Estates Records, 1862-1943; 16 Fibredex boxes.
Guardians' Bonds, 1870-1921; 2 volumes.
Guardians' Records, 1869-1921; 2 Fibredex boxes.

Land Records

Deeds, 1845-1937; 1 Fibredex box.
Deeds, Cross Index to, 1870-1906; 1 volume.
Entry Books, 1871-1929; 4 volumes.
Land Entries, 1877-1928; 1 Fibredex box.
Probate of Deeds, 1870-1908; 2 volumes.
Processioners of Land, Record of, 1881-1891; 1 volume.

Military and Pension Records [*See* Miscellaneous Records]

Miscellaneous Records

Board of Pensions, Minutes, 1908-1939; 1 volume.
Licenses to Trades, Registry of, 1876-1904; 1 volume.
Miscellaneous Records, 1845-1945; 1 Fibredex box.
Road Records, 1871-1903; 1 Fibredex box.

Roads and Bridges [*See* Miscellaneous Records]

Wills

Wills, 1870-1928; 1 Fibredex box.

MICROFILM RECORDS

Bonds

Apprentice Bonds, 1871-1910; 1 reel.

Corporations and Partnerships

Corporations, Record of, 1919-1970; 1 reel.
Partnerships, Record of, 1919-1960; 1 reel.

Court Records

Superior Court

- Judgment Docket, 1870-1889; 1 reel.
- Judgments, Cross Index to, 1870-1966; 1 reel.
- Minutes, 1870-1966; 4 reels.

Election Records

Elections, Record of, 1878-1966; 1 reel.

Estates Records

Accounts, Record of, 1870-1966; 2 reels.
Administrators' Bonds, 1870-1910; 1 reel.
Administrators' and Executors' Bonds, 1877-1915; 1 reel.
Administrators, Executors, and Guardians, Record of, 1915-1966; 1 reel.
Administrators, Record of, 1939-1966; 1 reel.
Dowers, Record of, 1871-1931; 1 reel.
Guardians' Bonds, 1870-1921; 1 reel.
Guardians, Record of, 1952-1966; 1 reel.
Inheritance Tax Records, 1920-1966; 1 reel.
Settlements, Record of, 1873-1946; 1 reel.

Land Records

Deeds, Cross Index to, 1870-1944; 1 reel.
Deeds, Record of, 1870-1958; 23 reels.
Federal Farm Loan Mortgages, 1922-1929; 1 reel.
Land Entry Books, 1871-1929; 1 reel.
Processioners of Land, Record of, 1881-1891; 1 reel.
Real Estate Conveyances, Index to, Grantee, 1945-1977; 1 reel.
Real Estate Conveyances, Index to, Grantor, 1945-1977; 1 reel.
Registration of Land Titles, 1945-1968; 1 reel.
Sales and Resales by Mortgagees and Trustees, Record of, 1933-1966; 1 reel.
Taxes for Mortgages, Record of, 1927-1932; 1 reel.

Marriage, Divorce, and Vital Statistics

Births, Index to, 1913-1970; 1 reel.
Deaths, Index to, 1913-1970; 1 reel.
Marriage Licenses, 1889-1964; 2 reels.
Marriage Registers, 1870-1970; 1 reel.

Military and Pension Records

Board of Pensions, Minutes, 1908-1939; 1 reel.

Miscellaneous Records

Clerk's Minute Docket, 1909-1966; 1 reel.
Licenses to Trades, Registry of, 1876-1904; 1 reel.
Orders and Decrees, 1870-1966; 3 reels.
Special Proceedings and Orders and Decrees, Cross Index to, 1870-1966; 1 reel.

Officials, County

Board of County Commissioners, Minutes, 1874-1972; 3 reels.

School Records

County Board of Education, Minutes, 1921-1979; 1 reel.

Wills

Wills, Cross Index to, 1870-1966; 1 reel.
Wills, Record of, 1870-1966; 1 reel.

CLEVELAND COUNTY

Established in 1841 from Lincoln and Rutherford counties.

ORIGINAL RECORDS

Bonds

- Apprentice Bonds and Records, 1841-1888; 1 volume, 1 Fibredex box.
- Bastardy Bonds and Records, 1841-1919; 3 Fibredex boxes.
- Officials' Bonds and Records, 1841-1909; 1 Fibredex box.

Court Records

- County Court of Pleas and Quarter Sessions
  - Appearance Docket, 1844-1868; 1 volume.
  - Execution Dockets, 1841-1868; 3 volumes.
  - Levy Docket, 1841-1868, 1876; 1 volume.
  - Minutes, 1841-1867; 4 volumes.
  - State Docket, 1841-1859; 1 volume.
  - Trial Dockets, 1841-1868; 2 volumes.
- Superior Court
  - Civil Action Papers, 1838-1921; 30 Fibredex boxes.
  - Civil Action Papers Concerning Land, 1842-1911; 11 Fibredex boxes.
  - Criminal Action Papers, 1841-1879; 19 Fibredex boxes.
  - Equity Enrolling Docket, 1856-1867; 1 volume.
  - Equity Execution Docket, 1843-1868; 1 volume.
  - Equity Trial Docket, 1842-1857; 1 volume.
  - Execution Docket, 1854-1867; 1 volume.
  - Minutes, 1841-1910; 12 volumes.
  - Trial and Appearance Docket, 1841-1854; 1 volume.

Election Records

- Election Records, 1841-1922; 2 Fibredex boxes.
- Elections, Record of, 1878-1908; 1 volume.

Estates Records

- Accounts, Record of, 1868-1909; 4 volumes.
- Estates, Record of, 1841-1868; 4 volumes.
- Estates Records, 1795-1915; 56 Fibredex boxes.
- Guardians' Accounts, 1841-1867; 2 volumes.
- Guardians' Records, 1845-1910; 4 Fibredex boxes.
- Settlements, Record of, 1869-1919; 4 volumes.

Land Records

- Attachments, Executions, Levies, and Liens on Land, 1841-1899; 2 Fibredex boxes.
- Deeds and Grants, 1775-1898; 1 Fibredex box.
- Ejectments, 1841-1895; 3 Fibredex boxes.
- Miscellaneous Land Records, 1790-1905; 1 Fibredex box.
- Processioners' Returns, 1841-1860, 1867; 1 volume.

Marriage, Divorce, and Vital Statistics

- Divorce Records, 1842-1907; 4 Fibredex boxes.
- Marriage Bonds, 1865-1866; 1 Fibredex box.
- Marriage Register, 1905-1917; 1 volume.

MISCELLANEOUS RECORDS

Assignees, Receivers, and Trustees, Records of, 1860-1909; 1 Fibredex box.
County Accounts, Claims, and Court Orders, 1841-1889; 2 Fibredex boxes.
Insolvent Debtors and Homestead and Personal Property Exemptions, 1841-1891; 1 Fibredex box.
Lunacy Records, 1845-1907; 1 Fibredex box.
Mill Records, 1850-1896; 1 Fibredex box.
Miscellaneous Records, 1833, 1841-1938; 3 Fibredex boxes.
Orders and Decrees, 1869-1904; 5 volumes.
Overseers of Roads and Hands, 1829-1867; 3 Fibredex boxes.
Railroad Records, 1857-1908; 4 Fibredex boxes.
Road Petitions, 1841-1899; 2 Fibredex boxes.
School Records, 1841-1905; 1 Fibredex box.
Slaves and Free Persons of Color, Records of, 1841-1869; 2 Fibredex boxes.
Wardens of the Poor, Minutes, 1847-1868; 1 volume.

ROADS AND BRIDGES [*See* **MISCELLANEOUS RECORDS**]

SCHOOL RECORDS [*See* **MISCELLANEOUS RECORDS; CRX RECORDS**]

TAX AND FISCAL RECORDS [*See also* **CRX RECORDS**]

Tax List, 1918; 1 volume.
Tax Records, 1823-1896; 1 Fibredex box.

WILLS

Wills, 1841-1919; 12 Fibredex boxes.

CRX RECORDS

Common School Reports, 1858-1867; 1 binder.
Tax Scrolls, 1840-1857; 3 volumes.

MICROFILM RECORDS

BONDS

Apprentice Bonds, 1869-1888; 1 reel.

CORPORATIONS AND PARTNERSHIPS

Corporations, Index to, 1883-1977; 1 reel.
Corporations, Record of, 1888-1960; 2 reels.
Partnerships, Record of, 1913-1961; 1 reel.

COURT RECORDS

County Court of Pleas and Quarter Sessions
- Minutes, 1841-1867; 3 reels.

Superior Court
- Civil Actions, Index to, 1939-1978; 3 reels.
- Criminal Actions, Index to, 1968-1978; 1 reel.
- Judgments and Liens, Index to, Defendant, 1921-1968; 4 reels.
- Judgments and Liens, Index to, Plaintiff, 1921-1968; 3 reels.
- Minutes, 1841-1950; 11 reels.
- Minutes, Criminal, 1866-1906; 2 reels.

ELECTION RECORDS

Elections, Record of, 1878-1908, 1924-1936; 2 reels.

ESTATES RECORDS

Accounts, Record of, 1868-1959; 7 reels.
Administrators, Record of, 1896-1956; 5 reels.
Appointment of Executors, 1868-1968; 3 reels.
Estates, Record of, 1841-1868; 2 reels.
Executors and Administrators, Cross Index to, 1869-1964; 1 reel.
Inheritance Tax Records, 1923-1960; 1 reel.
Guardians, Cross Index to, 1870-1960; 1 reel.
Guardians, Record of, 1897-1959; 2 reels.
Settlements, Record of, 1869-1965; 8 reels.

LAND RECORDS

Deeds, Index to, Grantee, 1841-1959; 5 reels.
Deeds, Index to, Grantor, 1841-1959; 5 reels.
Deeds, Record of, 1841-1957; 77 reels.
Entry Book, 1888-1925; 1 reel.
Federal Tax Lien Index, 1935-1941, 1951-1964; 1 reel.
Land Sales, Record of, 1924-1960; 2 reels.
Plats, 1912-1957; 1 reel.
Plats, Index to, various years; 1 reel.
Processioners' Returns, 1841-1859; 1 reel.

MARRIAGE, DIVORCE, AND VITAL STATISTICS

Births and Deaths, Index to, 1913-1962; 3 reels.
Delayed Births, Index to, 1908-1935, various years; 3 reels.
Maiden Names of Divorced Women, 1945-1970; 1 reel.
Marriage Licenses, 1882-1906; 5 reels.
Marriage Registers, 1870-1945; 1 reel.
Marriages, Record of, 1851-1866; 1 reel.

MISCELLANEOUS RECORDS

Lunacy, Record of, 1899-1963; 2 reels.
Orders and Decrees, 1868-1968; 17 reels.
Special Proceedings, 1875-1968; 2 reels.
Special Proceedings, Cross Index to, 1874-1910, 1968-1978; 2 reels.
Wardens of the Poor, Minutes, 1847-1868; 1 reel.

OFFICIALS, COUNTY

Board of County Commissioners, Minutes, 1868-1955; 5 reels.

SCHOOL RECORDS

County Board of Education, Minutes, 1913-1977; 1 reel.

TAX AND FISCAL RECORDS

Tax List, 1918; 1 reel.
Taxes, Record of, 1840-1857; 1 reel.

WILLS

Wills, Cross Index to, 1841-1960; 1 reel.
Wills, Record of, 1841-1965; 5 reels.

COLUMBUS COUNTY

Established in 1808 from Bladen and Brunswick counties.

ORIGINAL RECORDS

BONDS

Apprentice Bonds, 1874-1891; 1 volume.
Officials' Bonds, 1868-1881, 1891-1914; 2 volumes.

CENSUS RECORDS (County Copy)

Census (partial), 1810; 1 volume of photostats.

COURT RECORDS

County Court of Pleas and Quarter Sessions
- Appeal Docket, 1856-1868; 1 volume.
- Appearance Docket, 1856-1868; 1 volume.
- Execution Dockets, 1842-1868; 2 volumes.
- Minutes, 1819-1868; 6 volumes.
- State Docket, 1856-1868; 1 volume.
- Trial Docket, 1856-1868; 1 volume.

Superior Court
- Appearance Docket, 1858-1869; 1 volume.
- Civil Issues Docket, 1921-1933; 1 volume.
- Clerk's Minute Dockets, 1921-1968; 9 volumes.
- Criminal Issues Docket, 1896-1905; 1 volume.
- Equity Decrees, 1858-1860; 1 volume.
- Equity Execution Docket, 1858-1868; 1 volume.
- Equity Minutes, 1843-1868; 1 volume.
- Equity Trial Docket, 1859-1861, 1866-1868; 1 volume.
- Judgment Dockets, 1905-1944; 15 volumes. [*See also* **LAND RECORDS**, Tax Suit Judgment Dockets]
- Minutes, 1817-1968; 41 volumes.
- State Docket, 1847-1868; 1 volume.

ELECTION RECORDS

Elections, Record of, 1878-1900, 1906-1936; 4 volumes.

ESTATES RECORDS

Accounts, Record of, 1869-1968; 14 volumes.
Administrators' Bonds, 1873-1912; 4 volumes.
Administrators and Executors, Record of, 1912-1936; 1 volume.
Administrators, Record of, 1920-1968; 8 volumes.
Amounts Paid for Indigent Children, Record of, 1912-1935; 1 volume.
Appointment of Administrators, Executors, and Guardians, 1868-1915; 1 volume.
Division of Estates, 1887-1935; 2 volumes.
Estates Records, 1812-1969; 31 Fibredex boxes.
Executors, Record of, 1937-1968; 3 volumes.
Guardians' Accounts, 1857-1868; 1 volume.
Guardians, Record of, 1902-1968; 5 volumes.
Guardians' Records, 1844-1968; 4 Fibredex boxes.
Guardians of World War Veterans, Record of, 1931-1946; 1 volume.
Settlements, Record of, 1869-1899; 1 volume.

LAND RECORDS

Entry Books, 1809-1900; 4 volumes.
Sale and Resale of Land, Record of, 1928-1940; 2 volumes.
Tax Suit Judgment Dockets, 1930-1958; 2 volumes. [*See also* **COURT RECORDS**, Superior Court, Judgment Dockets]

MARRIAGE, DIVORCE, AND VITAL STATISTICS

Disinterment/Reinterment Permits, 1967-1987; 1 manuscript box.
Maiden Names of Divorced Women, 1939-1969; 1 volume.

MILITARY AND PENSION RECORDS [*See* **ESTATES RECORDS**]

MISCELLANEOUS RECORDS

Alien Registration, 1927, 1940, 1946, 1958; 1 volume.
Licenses to Trades, Registry of, 1876-1893; 1 volume.
Lunacy, Record of, 1923-1968; 3 volumes.
Magistrates, Record of, 1913-1968; 1 volume.
Miscellaneous Records, 1816, 1884; 1 manuscript box.
Notaries Public, Record of, 1914-1945; 1 volume.
Officials' Oaths, Record of, 1938-1973; 1 volume.
Orders and Decrees, 1875-1943; 13 volumes.
Settlement of County Accounts, Committee of Finance, 1824-1857; 1 volume.
Special Proceedings Dockets, 1899-1936; 2 volumes.

OFFICIALS, COUNTY [*See* **MISCELLANEOUS RECORDS**]

TAX AND FISCAL RECORDS

Poll Tax Record, 1910-1916; 1 volume.

WILLS

Wills, 1808-1917; 3 Fibredex boxes.

MICROFILM RECORDS

CENSUS RECORDS (County Copy)

Census, 1860; 1 reel.

CORPORATIONS AND PARTNERSHIPS

Corporations, Assumed Names, and Partnerships, Index to, 1913-1974; 1 reel.
Incorporations, Record of, 1887-1974; 3 reels.

COURT RECORDS

County Court of Pleas and Quarter Sessions
Minutes, 1819-1868; 3 reels.
Superior Court
Equity Minutes, 1817-1868; 1 reel.
Judgments, Index to, Defendant, 1940-1968; 1 reel.
Judgments, Index to, Plaintiff, 1940-1968; 1 reel.
Minutes, 1851-1960; 17 reels.

ESTATES RECORDS

Accounts of Executors and Administrators, Record of, 1895-1909; 1 reel.
Accounts, Record of, 1869-1967; 7 reels.
Administrators, Executors, and Guardians, Index to, 1869-1967; 1 reel.
Administrators and Executors, Record of, 1912-1957; 2 reels.
Administrators, Record of, 1920-1967; 4 reels.

Amounts Paid to Indigent Children, Record of, 1912-1967; 1 reel.
Appointment of Executors, 1868-1915; 1 reel.
Division of Estates, 1887-1967; 3 reels.
Guardians, Record of, 1902-1967; 2 reels.
Inheritance Tax Records, 1923-1967; 1 reel.
Settlements, Record of, 1869-1967; 3 reels.

LAND RECORDS

Deeds, Record of, 1805-1960; 113 reels.
Land Entries, 1809-1953; 1 reel.
Plats, 1919-1967; 1 reel.
Real Estate Conveyances, Index to, Grantee, 1808-1966; 8 reels.
Real Estate Conveyances, Index to, Grantor, 1808-1966; 9 reels.
Resale of Land by Trustees and Mortgagees, Record of, 1922-1954; 3 reels.

MARRIAGE, DIVORCE, AND VITAL STATISTICS

Births, Index to, 1913-1974; 3 reels.
Cohabitation Records, 1866-1868; 1 reel.
Delayed Births, Index to, various years; 1 reel.
Maiden Names of Divorced Women, 1939-1969; 1 reel.
Marriage Registers, 1868-1974; 2 reels.
Marriages, Record of, 1851-1868; 1 reel.

MISCELLANEOUS RECORDS

Orders and Decrees, 1869-1953; 9 reels.
Special Proceedings, Cross Index to, 1885-1967; 2 reels.
Special Proceedings Dockets, 1885-1945, 1954-1967; 2 reels.

OFFICIALS, COUNTY

Board of County Commissioners, Minutes, 1868-1954; 7 reels.

SCHOOL RECORDS

County Board of Education, Minutes, 1885-1929; 1 reel.

TAX AND FISCAL RECORDS

Tax Lists and Tax Scrolls, 1869, 1925; 1 reel.

WILLS

Wills, Cross Index to, 1808-1967; 1 reel.
Wills, Record of, 1808-1967; 4 reels.

CRAVEN COUNTY

Established in 1705 as Archdale Precinct of Bath County.
Name changed to Craven in 1712.

ORIGINAL RECORDS

BONDS

Apprentice Bonds and Records, 1748-1910; 2 volumes, 7 Fibredex boxes.
Bastardy Bonds and Records, 1803-1880; 1 volume, 3 Fibredex boxes.
Constables' Bonds, 1850-1859; 1 volume.
Officials' Bonds, 1753-1867; 1 Fibredex box.

COURT RECORDS [*See also* **MISCELLANEOUS RECORDS**]

Circuit Criminal Court/Eastern District Criminal Court
- Criminal Issues Docket, 1895-1901; 1 volume.
- Minutes, 1895-1901; 1 volume.

County Court
- Minutes, 1921-1967; 15 volumes.

County Court of Pleas and Quarter Sessions
- Appearance Dockets, 1791-1868; 9 volumes.
- Clerk's Account Book, 1816-1828; 1 volume.
- Execution Dockets, 1754-1868; 29 volumes (includes Superior Court, Transfer Docket, 1870-1875).
- Levy Docket, 1842-1857; 1 volume.
- Minutes, 1712-1715, 1730-1868; 43 volumes.
- Reference (Trial) and Appearance Dockets, 1778-1791; 2 volumes.
- State Dockets, 1786-1859; 4 volumes.
- Trial and Petition Dockets, 1807-1868; 14 volumes.
- Trial and Reference Dockets, 1789-1807; 3 volumes.
- Writs Docket, 1850-1854; 1 volume.

Superior Court
- Appearance Docket, 1843-1867; 1 volume.
- Clerk and Master in Equity Sale and Hiring Book, 1858-1875; 1 volume.
- Civil Action Papers, 1756-1908; 71 Fibredex boxes.
- Civil Action Papers Concerning Land, 1809-1920; 7 Fibredex boxes.
- Civil Issues Dockets, 1868-1914; 10 volumes.
- Clerk's Receipt Book, 1872-1886; 1 volume. [*See also* Equity Execution Docket]
- Criminal Action Papers, 1778-1906; 20 Fibredex boxes.
- Criminal Docket, 1868-1914; 5 volumes.
- Criminal Judgments, General Index to, 1953-1968; 3 volumes.
- Equity Execution Docket, 1858-1868; Clerk's Receipt Book (Land Sales), 1869-1872; 1 volume. [*See also* Clerk's Receipt Book, 1872-1886]
- Equity Minutes, 1850-1868; 3 volumes.
- Equity Trial and Appearance Dockets, 1850-1868; 2 volumes.
- Execution Dockets, 1806-1830, 1840-1869; 5 volumes.
- Judgment Dockets, 1868-1904; 7 volumes.
- Judgment Dockets, Tax Foreclosure Suits, 1927-1956; 12 volumes.
- Minutes, 1807-1820, 1829-1968; 57 volumes.
- Miscellaneous Court Records, 1857-1858, 1927; 1 manuscript box.

Petition Docket, 1868. [*See* Equity Trial and Appearance Docket]
State Dockets, 1815-1861, 1866-1867, 1869; 4 volumes.
Transfer Docket, 1870-1875. [*See* Court of Pleas and Quarter Sessions, Execution Docket, 1868]
Trial, Appearance, Argument and Reference Docket, 1807-1813; 1 volume.
Trial and Argument Docket, 1814-1832; 1 volume.
Trial Dockets, 1845-1868, 1891-1969; 6 volumes.

ELECTION RECORDS

Election Returns, 1835-1895; 4 Fibredex boxes.
Election Returns for Sheriffs, 1830-1860; 2 Fibredex boxes.
Elections, Record of, 1874-1968; 7 volumes, 1 manuscript box.
Permanent Registration of Voters, 1902-1908; 1 volume.
Poll Tax Register, 1902-1910; 1 volume.

ESTATES RECORDS [*See also* **LAND RECORDS**; **WILLS**]

Accounts, Record of, 1829-1902; 11 volumes.
Administrators' Bonds, 1868-1917; 5 volumes.
Administrators, Executors, and Guardians, Record of, 1879-1900; 1 volume.
Estates Records, 1745-1945; 167 Fibredex boxes.
Fiduciary Account Book (Estate of Major Willis), 1844-1845; 1 volume.
Guardians' Bonds, 1869-1927; 6 volumes.
Guardians, Record of, 1808-1869; 2 volumes.
Guardians' Records, 1766-1945; 16 Fibredex boxes.
Guardians of World War Veterans, 1930-1954; 1 volume.
Inheritance Tax Collections, Record of, 1920-1923; 1 volume.
Inventories and Accounts of Sale, 1781-1789, 1807, 1830-1867; 11 volumes.
Inventories, Accounts of Sale, and Deeds, 1763-1767; 1 volume.
Probate (Estates), Record of, 1877-1885; 1 volume. [*See also* **LAND RECORDS**, Acknowledgment of Deeds and Powers of Attorney]

LAND RECORDS [*See also* **ESTATES RECORDS**; **WILLS**]

Acknowledgment of Deeds and Powers of Attorney (Record of Probate), 1786-1799; 1 volume. [*See also* **ESTATES RECORDS**, Probate, Record of]
Deeds, Index to, 1744-1846; 3 volumes.
Deeds, Inventories, Wills, and Miscellaneous Records, 1729-1855; 21 volumes.
Deeds, Patents, Grants, Deeds of Trust, and Mortgage Deeds, 1720, 1724-1904; 2 Fibredex boxes.
Division and Sale of Land, 1803-1810. [*See* Land Entries]
Ejectments, 1787-1872, 1896; 3 Fibredex boxes.
Grants and Surveys, 1716-1802 (includes Land Entry Book, 1809-1813); 2 volumes.
Land Divisions and Plats, ca. 1790-1868; 1 volume.
Land Entries, 1789-1861, 1893; Division and Sale of Land, 1803-1910; 1 Fibredex box.
Land Entries, 1834-1903; 1 volume.
Land Sales, Record of, 1911-1970; 9 volumes.
Land Sold for Taxes, 1911-1914, 1925-1937; 23 Fibredex boxes.
Land Title Guaranty Proceedings, 1913-1966; 1 volume.
Plats of Survey, 1819, 1823, 1826; 1 Fibredex box.
Plats, Surveys, and Miscellaneous Land Records, 1754-1901; 1 Fibredex box.

Tax Judgments, Index to, Creditor, 1867-1949; 4 volumes.
Tax Judgments, Index to, Debtor, 1895-1948; 3 volumes.
Tax Levies by Sheriff, 1872-1908; 2 volumes.

Marriage, Divorce, and Vital Statistics

Divorce Records, 1828-1897, 1955; 4 Fibredex boxes.
Maiden Names of Divorced Women, 1937-1968; 1 volume.
Marriage Bonds, 1773-1868; 17 Fibredex boxes, 2 volumes.

Military and Pension Records [*See* **Estates Records; Miscellaneous Records**]

Miscellaneous Records

Alien Registration, 1927-1940; 1 volume.
Appointment of Constables and Overseers, 1784-1857; 2 volumes.
Appointment of Receivers [*See* Book of Orders Appointing Receivers of Judgment Debtors]
Blind Pensioners, 1902-1927; 1 volume.
Board of Superintendents of Common Schools, Minutes, 1841-1859; 1 volume.
Book of Orders Appointing Receivers of Judgment Debtors, 1880-1891; 1 volume.
Buildings, Claims, County Lines, and Trustee Settlements, 1780-1918; 1 Fibredex box.
Certificates of Claims, 1829-1846; 2 volumes.
Civil Action Papers Concerning Slaves and Free Persons of Color, 1788, 1806-1860, 1885; 1 Fibredex box.
Clerk's Minute Dockets (Special Proceedings), 1869-1903; 6 volumes.
Commissioners of Affidavits, List of, 1851-1884; 1 volume.
Coroners' Inquests, 1782-1905; 2 Fibredex boxes.
County Trustees' Settlements, 1817-1868; 3 volumes.
Criminal Action Papers Concerning Slaves and Free Persons of Color, 1781-1868; 2 Fibredex boxes.
Inquisition of Lunacy, 1899-1968; 4 volumes.
Insolvent Debtors, 1757-1866; 4 Fibredex boxes.
Jury Lists, 1894-1913; 1 manuscript box.
Letters to Clerk, 1814-1871; 1 Fibredex box.
Magistrates, Record of, 1868-1924; 1 Fibredex box, 1 manuscript box.
Miscellaneous Records, 1757-1929; 5 Fibredex boxes.
Miscellaneous School Records, 1823-1874; 1 Fibredex box.
Naturalization Record, 1904-1905; 1 volume.
Oath Book, 1811-1872, 1885-1896; 1 volume, 1 manuscript box.
Orders and Decrees, 1869-1925; 7 volumes.
Permits for Purchase of Concealed Weapons, Record of, 1919-1959; 1 volume.
Personal Accounts, 1750-1894; 1 Fibredex box.
Physicians' Certificates of Registration, 1951-1966; 1 volume.
Railroad Records, 1855-1908; 2 Fibredex boxes.
Road Records, 1767-1868; 3 Fibredex boxes.
School Committees, 1841-1861; 2 Fibredex boxes.
Schoolchildren and Teacher Applications, Lists of, 1841-1861; 1 Fibredex box.
Sheriffs' Receipt Book, 1836-1845; 1 volume.
Sheriff's Settlements, 1811-1854, and State of County Finance, 1834-1856; 1 Fibredex box.
Ships and Merchants, Records of, 1770-1858; 3 Fibredex boxes.
Slaves and Free Negroes, 1775-1861; 1 Fibredex box.
Special Proceedings, Cross Index to, 1869-1868; 4 volumes.

Special Proceedings Docket, 1869-1891. [*See* **COURT RECORDS**, Superior Court, Equity Trial and Appearance Docket, 1859-1868]
State Pension Book, 1903-1938; 1 volume.
Treasurer of Public Buildings Accounts, 1817-1857; 1 Fibredex box.
Treasurer's Account Book, 1881-1887; 1 volume.
Wardens of the Poor, Minutes, 1837-1871; 1 volume.
Wardens of the Poor, Records of, 1803-1861; 1 Fibredex box.

OFFICIALS, COUNTY [*See* **MISCELLANEOUS RECORDS**]

ROADS AND BRIDGES [*See* **MISCELLANEOUS RECORDS**]

SCHOOL RECORDS [*See* **MISCELLANEOUS RECORDS**]

TAX AND FISCAL RECORDS
Tax Book, 1829-1856; 1 volume.
Tax Records, 1764-1904; 1 Fibredex box.

WILLS
Wills, 1748-1941; 20 Fibredex boxes. [*See also* **ESTATES RECORDS; LAND RECORDS; CRX RECORDS**]
Wills, Cross Index to, 1750-1914; 1 volume.
Wills (includes inventories and deeds), 1737-1868; 12 volumes.

CRX RECORDS
Crop Lien, 1872; 1 folder.
Will (George Kornegy), 1773; 1 folder

MICROFILM RECORDS

BONDS
Apprentice Bonds, 1748-1839, 1868-1910; 3 reels.
Bastardy Bonds, 1784-1880; 3 reel.

COURT RECORDS
County Court of Pleas and Quarter Sessions
Minutes, 1712-1868; 15 reels.
Superior Court
Equity Minutes, 1850-1860; 1 reel.
Judgments, Index to, Creditor, 1862-1968; 4 reels.
Judgments, Index to, Criminal, 1953-1968; 2 reels.
Judgments, Index to, Debtor, 1862-1968; 3 reels.
Minutes, 1801-1820, 1829-1933; 15 reels.

ESTATES RECORDS [*See also* **WILLS**]
Accounts, Record of, 1868-1951; 7 reels.
Administrators' Bonds, 1868-1947; 2 reels.
Administrators, Record of, 1919-1946; 2 reels.
Estates, Record of, 1829-1960; 6 reels.
Executors and Administrators, Cross Index to, 1869-1910; 1 reel.
Fiduciaries, Cross Index to, 1909-1968; 1 reel.
Guardians, Administrators, and Executors, Citations to, 1869-1885; 1 reel.
Guardians' Bonds, 1868-1927; 2 reels.
Guardians, Cross Index to, 1868-1910; 1 reel.
Guardians, Record of, 1919-1960; 2 reels.

Inventories and Accounts of Sale, 1763-1767, 1781-1789, 1807, 1830-1867; 7 reels.
Inventory of the Estate of Major Willis, 1844; 1 reel.
Land Divisions and Plats, ca. 1790-1868; 1 reel.
Miscellaneous Estates Records, 1740-1870; 6 reels.
Settlements, Record of, 1869-1955; 5 reels.

LAND RECORDS [*See also* **WILLS**]
Deeds and Mortgages, Index to, Grantee, 1739-1980; 12 reels.
Deeds and Mortgages, Index to, Grantor, 1739-1980; 13 reels.
Deeds, Record of, 1739-1940; 165 reels.
Land Divisions and Plats, 1803-1868. [*See* **ESTATES RECORDS**]
Land Entries, 1778-1959; 1 reel.
Land Grants, 1783-1809; 1 reel.
Land Grants, Index to, no date; 1 reel.
Land Sales by Mortgagees and Trustees, Record of, 1921-1946; 3 reels.
Patents, Record of, 1770-1859; 2 reels.

MARRIAGE, DIVORCE, AND VITAL STATISTICS
Cohabitation, Record of. [*See* Marriage Registers, 1851-1960]
Marriage Bond Abstracts, 1740-1868; 1 reel.
Marriage Licenses, 1892-1960; 13 reels.
Marriage Registers, 1851-1960; Record of Cohabitation, 1865-1867; 3 reels.
Marriage Registers, Women, 1851-1946; 3 reels.
Vital Statistics, Index to, Births, 1914-1996; 2 reels.
Vital Statistics, Index to, Deaths, 1914-1996; 1 reel.

MISCELLANEOUS RECORDS
Orders and Decrees, 1868-1925; 2 reels.
Special Proceedings, 1869-1949; 9 reels.
Special Proceedings, Cross Index to, 1869-1960; 1 reel.
Wardens of the Poor, Minutes, 1837-1871; 1 reel.

OFFICIALS, COUNTY
Board of County Commissioners, Minutes, 1868-1902; 3 reels.

SCHOOL RECORDS
Board of Superintendents of Common Schools, Minutes, 1839-1860; 1 reel.
School Records, 1841-1874; 3 reels.

TAX AND FISCAL RECORDS
Lists of Taxables, 1829-1856; 1 reel.
Tax Lists, 1881-1893, 1896, 1900, 1916-1917, 1925, 1935; 7 reels.

WILLS
Original Wills, 1746-1890; 3 reels.
Wills, Cross Index to, 1784-1970; 2 reels.
Wills, Deeds, and Inventories, 1749-1766; 2 reels.
Wills and Estates Papers, 1736-1857; 4 reels.
Wills, Record of, 1708-1716, 1784-1968; 14 reels.

CUMBERLAND COUNTY

Established in 1754 from Bladen County.

ORIGINAL RECORDS

BONDS

Apprentice Bonds and Records, 1812-1909; 1 volume, 2 Fibredex boxes.
Bastardy Bonds and Records, 1760-1910; 1 volume, 1 Fibredex box.
Constables' Bonds, 1779-1883, 1920; 1 Fibredex box.
Officials' Bonds, 1777-1954; 2 Fibredex boxes.

CENSUS RECORDS (County Copy)

Census, 1840; 1 volume.

COURT RECORDS [*See also* **CRX RECORDS**]

Circuit Criminal Court/Eastern District Criminal Court
- Minutes, 1897-1901; 1 volume.

County Court of Pleas and Quarter Sessions
- Appeal Dockets, 1791-1834, 1857-1868; 5 volumes.
- Appearance Dockets, 1789-1868; 7 volumes.
- Execution Dockets, 1785-1868; 14 volumes.
- Judgment Docket, 1823-1825; 1 volume.
- Levy Dockets, 1821-1835; 2 volumes.
- Minutes, 1755-1868; 44 volumes.
- Recognizance Docket, 1789-1806; 1 volume.
- State Dockets, 1784-1860; 4 volumes.
- Trial, Appearance, and Reference Dockets, 1774-1787; 2 volumes.
- Trial Dockets, 1788-1868; 11 volumes.

Recorder's Court
- Minutes, 1937-1966; 18 volumes.

Superior Court
- Appearance Docket, 1853-1869; 1 volume.
- Argument Docket, 1807-1816; 1 volume.
- Civil Action Papers, 1759-1914; 4 Fibredex boxes.
- Civil Action Papers Concerning Land, 1857-1945; 2 Fibredex boxes.
- Civil Judgments, Index to, Plaintiff, 1889-1921; 2 volumes.
- Criminal Action Papers, 1772-1927; 3 Fibredex boxes.
- Criminal Actions, Index to, 1927-1966; 2 volumes.
- Criminal Issues Dockets, 1869-1900, 1927-1966; 17 volumes.
- Equity Costs Docket, 1827-1855; 1 volume.
- Equity Enrolling Docket, 1845-1867; 1 volume.
- Equity Execution Docket, 1862-1868; 1 volume.
- Equity Minutes, 1830-1868; 3 volumes.
- Equity Trial Dockets, 1840-1868; 2 volumes.
- Execution Dockets, 1818-1868; 6 volumes.
- Judgment Dockets, 1869-1878, 1893-1961; 26 volumes. [*See also* **LAND RECORDS**, Tax Foreclosure Docket]
- Lien Docket, 1951-1966; 3 volumes.
- Minutes, 1806-1818, 1831-1966; 55 volumes.
- Minutes, Criminal, 1961-1966; 4 volumes.
- Minutes, Divorce, 1960-1966; 3 volumes.

Notice and Claim of Lien, Index to, 1939-1957; 1 volume.
State Dockets, 1816-1847; 3 volumes.
Trial Docket, 1830-1846; 1 volume.

ELECTION RECORDS

Election Records, 1793-1925; 4 Fibredex boxes.
Elections, Record of, 1900-1921; 3 volumes.

ESTATES RECORDS

Accounts and Inventories, Record of, 1868-1966; 33 volumes.
Administrators' Bonds, 1869-1906; 4 volumes.
Administrators, Record of, 1906-1956; 14 volumes.
Appointment of Administrators, Executors, Guardians, and Masters, 1868-1906; 1 volume.
Appointment of Administrators, Guardians, Executors, and Trustees, 1956-1966; 12 volumes.
Assignments, Record of, 1894-1912; 1 volume.
Clerk's Account Book, 1898-1908, 1916-1926; 2 volumes.
Division of Estates, 1818-1860; 1 volume.
Estates, Non Qualified, Record of, 1956-1968; 1 volume.
Estates Not Exceeding $300, Record of, 1930-1956; 1 volume.
Estates, Record of, 1825-1868; 6 volumes.
Estates Records, 1758-1930; 79 Fibredex boxes.
Guardians' Accounts, 1830-1868; 3 volumes.
Guardians' Bonds, 1869-1906; 3 volumes.
Guardians, Record of, 1906-1956; 5 volumes.
Guardians' Records, 1795-1916; 10 Fibredex boxes.
Inheritance Tax Record, 1921-1967; 4 volumes.
Settlements, Record of, 1869-1950; 7 volumes.

LAND RECORDS [*See also* **CRX RECORDS**]

Chattel Mortgages, 1899-1901; 1 volume.
Deeds, 1787-1956; 20 Fibredex boxes.
Deeds, Index to, 1752-1856; 2 volumes.
Deeds of Trust, 1837, 1852, 1903-1956; 1 Fibredex box.
Miscellaneous Land Records, 1784-1955; 1 Fibredex box.
Mortgage Deeds, 1894-1947; 1 Fibredex box.
Tax Foreclosure Docket, (Tax Suit Judgment Docket) 1941-1944; 1 volume. [*See also* **COURT RECORDS**, Superior Court, Judgment Dockets]

MARRIAGE, DIVORCE, AND VITAL STATISTICS

Disinterment/Reinterment Permits, 1953-1981; 1 Fibredex box.
Divorce Minutes, 1960-1966. [*See* **COURT RECORDS**, Superior Court]
Marriage Bonds, 1800-1868; 15 Fibredex boxes.
Marriage Licenses, 1868-1906, 1908; 17 Fibredex boxes.
Marriage Registers, 1851-1941; 8 volumes.

MILITARY AND PENSION RECORDS [*See* **MISCELLANEOUS RECORDS; CRX RECORDS**]

MISCELLANEOUS RECORDS

Account Book, Cumberland Agricultural Society, 1823-1825; 1 volume.
Alien Registration, 1927-1942; 1 volume.
Applications for Naturalization, 1894-1904; 1 volume.

Assignees, Receivers, and Trustees, Records of, 1839-1926; 3 Fibredex boxes.
Claims Allowed, Record of, 1797-1836; 1 volume.
Coroners' Inquests, 1791-1909; 1 Fibredex box.
County Trustee Accounts, 1845-1855; 1 volume.
Miscellaneous Records, 1758-1965; 7 Fibredex boxes. [*See also* **CRX RECORDS**]
Oaths, 1936-1966; 1 volume.
Orders and Decrees, 1869-1966; 46 volumes.
Pensions, Record of, 1915-1926; 1 volume.
Road Dockets, 1825-1855; 2 volumes.

ROADS AND BRIDGES [*See* **MISCELLANEOUS RECORDS**]

TAX AND FISCAL RECORDS [*See also* **CRX RECORDS**]
Lists of Taxables, 1777-1884; 7 volumes.
Poll Tax Register, 1902-1904; 1 volume.

WILLS
Wills, 1757-1967; 58 Fibredex boxes.
Wills, Cross Index to, 1796-1933; 1 volume.

CRX RECORDS
Clerk's Fee Docket, Superior Court, 1879-1904; 1 volume.
Criminal Action Papers, 1822, 1840-1879; 2 Fibredex boxes.
Deeds, 1869-1896; 1 folder.
Equity Trial Dockets, Fayetteville District Superior Court, 1801-1806; Cumberland County Superior Court, 1807-1840; 2 volumes.
Execution Docket, Court of Pleas and Quarter Sessions, 1808-1818; 1 volume.
List of Taxables, 1816-1823; 1 volume.
Miscellaneous Records, 1826-1915; 1 Fibredex box, 10 folders.
Pensions, Record of, 1898-1914; 1 volume.
Plat, no date; 1 folder.
Receivers, Records of, 1910-1916; 1 Fibredex box.
Tax Lists, 1804; 1 folder.
Trial Docket, Superior Court, 1810-1818; 1 volume.
Warrants Returned Docket, Court of Pleas and Quarter Sessions, 1808-1821; 1 volume.

MICROFILM RECORDS

BONDS
Apprentice Bonds, 1873-1894; 1 reel.
Bastardy Bonds, 1867-1883; 1 reel.

CENSUS RECORDS (County Copy)
Census, 1840, 1850; 1 reel.

CORPORATIONS AND PARTNERSHIPS
Incorporations, Record of, 1898-1923; 1 reel.

COURT RECORDS
County Court of Pleas and Quarter Sessions
Minutes, 1755-1868; 9 reels.
Superior Court
Criminal Actions, Index to, 1927-1962; 1 reel.
Equity Minutes, 1830-1868; 1 reel.

Judgments, Index to, Defendant, 1920-1966; 3 reels.
Judgments, Index to, Plaintiff, 1889-1966; 4 reels.
Minutes, 1806-1966; 24 reels.

ELECTION RECORDS

Elections, Record of, 1906-1960; 1 reel.

ESTATES RECORDS

Accounts and Inventories, Record of, 1868-1962; 10 reels.
Administrators' Bonds, 1869-1906; 1 reel.
Administrators, Record of, 1906-1956; 7 reels.
Appointment of Administrators, Executors, and Guardians, 1868-1906; 1 reel.
Appointment of Administrators, Executors, Guardians, and Trustees, 1956-1962; 3 reels.
Appointment of Administrators, Executors, Guardians, and Trustees, Index to, 1849-1962; 1 reel.
Assignment, Record of, 1894-1912; 1 reel.
Clerk's Receipt Book (Estates), 1898-1908; 1 reel.
Division of Estates, Record of, 1808-1860; 1 reel.
Estates, Index to, 1949-1962; 1 reel.
Estates not Exceeding $300, Record of, 1930-1956; 1 reel.
Estates, Record of, 1825-1868; 3 reels.
Guardians' Accounts, 1820-1862; 2 reels.
Guardians' Bonds, 1869-1906; 1 reel.
Guardians, Record of, 1906-1956; 2 reels.
Inheritance Tax Records, 1921-1962; 1 reel.
Settlements, Record of, 1869-1962; 5 reels.

LAND RECORDS

Deeds, Index to, Grantee, 1754-1942; 7 reels.
Deeds, Index to, Grantor, 1754-1942; 7 reels.
Deeds, Record of, 1754-1947; 176 reels.
Grants, Index to Record of, 1774-1927; 1 reel.
Grants, Record of, 1897-1926; 1 reel.
Land Sales by Trustees and Mortgagees, 1921-1962; 5 reels.
Land Sales by Trustees and Mortgagees, Index to, 1956-1962; 1 reel.
Plat Books, 1911-1950, 1957-1962; 2 reels.
Plats, Index to, 1905-1973; 1 reel.
Surveys and Plats, Record of, 1904-1910; 1 reel.

MARRIAGE, DIVORCE, AND VITAL STATISTICS

Births, Index to, 1913-1962; 4 reels.
Deaths, Index to, 1913-1962; 3 reels.
Divorces, Minute Book, 1960-1966; 2 reels.
Marriage Bond Abstracts, 1808-1868; 1 reel.
Marriage Bonds, 1803-1868; 5 reels.
Marriage Licenses, 1868-1961; 19 reels.
Marriage Registers, 1851-1962; 9 reels.

MISCELLANEOUS RECORDS

Orders and Decrees, 1869-1959; 10 reels.
Special Proceedings and Orders and Decrees, Index to, Defendant, 1869-1962; 2 reels.
Special Proceedings and Orders and Decrees, Index to, Plaintiff, 1869-1962; 2 reels.

OFFICIALS, COUNTY

Board of County Commissioners, Index to Minutes, 1871-1940; 1 reel.
Board of County Commissioners, Minutes, 1868-1924; 2 reels.

SCHOOL RECORDS

County Board of Education, Minutes, 1885-1962; 1 reel.

TAX AND FISCAL RECORDS

Lists of Taxables, 1771-1783, 1816-1823, 1837-1849, 1857-1884; 5 reels.
Tax Levies on Land, 1833-1835; 1 reel.

WILLS

Wills, Index to, 1796-1962; 1 reel.
Wills, Record of, 1761-1966; 9 reels.

CURRITUCK COUNTY

Established by 1670 as a precinct of Albemarle County.
Many records of the county are missing; reason unknown.

ORIGINAL RECORDS

BONDS

Apprentice Bonds, 1868-1884, 1888; 2 volumes.
Bastardy Bonds, 1830-1879; 2 volumes.

COURT RECORDS

County Court of Pleas and Quarter Sessions
Execution Dockets, 1821-1868; 5 volumes.
Minutes, 1799-1832, 1838-1868; 12 volumes.
State Dockets, 1807-1868; 2 volumes.
Trial, Appearance, and Reference Dockets, 1806-1861; 5 volumes.
Recorder's Court
Minutes, 1949-1966; 6 volumes.
Superior Court
Civil Action Papers, 1781, 1840-1923; 1 Fibredex box.
Civil Action Papers Concerning Land, 1858-1915; 1 Fibredex box.
Civil Issues Dockets, 1869-1913; 2 volumes.
Criminal Action Papers, 1858-1902; 1 Fibredex box.
Criminal Issues Docket, 1889-1913; 1 volume.
Equity Execution and Costs Docket, and Receipts in Equity, 1841-1857; 1 volume.
Equity Minutes, 1808-1868; 2 volumes.
Execution Dockets, 1847-1862, 1866-1917; 2 volumes.
Judgment Dockets, 1867-1966; 4 volumes. [*See also* **LAND RECORDS**]
Lien Docket, 1879-1912; 1 volume.
Minutes, 1851-1862, 1866-1966; 10 volumes.
Special Proceedings Record, (Torrens Act) Swan Island Club, Inc., 1927-1930; 1 volume.
State Docket, 1856-1861, 1866-1869; 1 volume.
Trial and Appearance Docket, 1856-1861, 1866-1868; 1 volume.

ELECTION RECORDS

Elections, Record of, 1878-1972; 6 volumes.

ESTATES RECORDS

Accounts, Record of, 1869-1967; 5 volumes.
Accounts of Sale, 1830-1918; 5 volumes.
Administrators' Bonds, 1827-1927; 7 volumes.
Administrators, Record of, 1930-1966; 3 volumes.
Appointment of Administrators, Executors, Guardians, and Masters, 1868-1953; 2 volumes.
Dowers and Widows' Year's Support, Record of, 1869-1918; 1 volume.
Estates Records, 1812-1926; 14 Fibredex boxes.
Executors and Guardians, Record of, 1953-1966; 1 volume.
Guardians' Accounts, 1830-1870; 5 volumes.

Guardians' Bonds, 1827-1927; 7 volumes.
Guardians' Records, 1841-1928; 4 Fibredex boxes.
Inheritance Tax Record, 1923-1967; 2 volumes.
Inventories of Estates, 1830-1967; 4 volumes.
Miscellaneous Estates Records, 1772-1827; 1 volume.
Settlements, Record of, 1830-1966; 6 volumes.

LAND RECORDS

Judgment Docket, Tax Suits, 1935-1949; 1 volume. [*See also* **COURT RECORDS**, Superior Court]
Land Divisions, 1877-1911; 1 Fibredex box.
Miscellaneous Land Records, 1808-1899; 1 Fibredex box.
Sale and Resale, Record of, 1961-1968; 1 volume.

MARRIAGE, DIVORCE, AND VITAL STATISTICS

Maiden Names of Divorced Women, 1937-1968; 1 volume.
Marriage Bonds, 1858-1867; 1 Fibredex box.

MILITARY AND PENSION RECORDS [*See* **MISCELLANEOUS RECORDS**]

MISCELLANEOUS RECORDS

Alien Registration, 1940; 1 volume.
County Accounts, 1840-1874; 1 volume.
Drainage Record, 1909; 1 volume.
Lunacy, Record of, 1907-1969; 2 volumes.
Miscellaneous Records, 1787-1914; 1 Fibredex box.
Official Reports, Record of, 1881-1932; 1 volume.
Orders and Decrees, 1868-1966; 7 volumes.
Pensions, Record of, 1908-1925; 1 volume.
Special Proceedings, 1879-1918; 1 volume. [*See also* **COURT RECORDS**, Superior Court]
Wardens of the Poor, Account Book, 1803-1868; 1 volume.

TAX AND FISCAL RECORDS

Oyster Tax Receipts, 1895-1899; 1 volume.

WILLS

Wills, 1841-1924; 4 Fibredex boxes.
Wills, Record of, 1761-1951; 8 volumes.

MICROFILM RECORDS

BONDS

Apprentice Bonds, 1844, 1868-1883; 1 reel.
Bastardy Bonds, 1830-1833, 1872-1879; 1 reel.

CORPORATIONS AND PARTNERSHIPS

Incorporations and Partnerships, Record of, 1868-1966; 1 reel.

COURT RECORDS

County Court of Pleas and Quarter Sessions
Minutes, 1799-1832, 1838-1868; 4 reels.
Superior Court
Equity Minutes, 1808-1847, 1850-1868; 1 reel.
Judgments, Index to, 1867-1966; 3 reels.
Minutes, 1851-1966; 6 reels.

ELECTION RECORDS

Board of Elections, Minutes, 1896-1916; 1 reel.
Elections, Record of, 1880-1968; 1 reel.

ESTATES RECORDS

Accounts, Record of, 1861-1934; 2 reels.
Accounts of Sale, 1830-1918; 3 reels.
Administrators' Bonds, 1827-1847, 1856-1927; 2 reels.
Administrators and Executors, Cross Index to, 1907-1938; 1 reel.
Administrators, Record of, 1795-1820, 1830-1841, 1930-1945; 2 reels.
Appointment of Administrators, Executors, and Guardians, 1907-1953; 1 reel.
Appointment of Executors, 1868-1919; 1 reel.
Executors and Guardians, Record of, 1953-1966; 1 reel.
Guardians' Accounts, 1830-1870; 2 reels.
Guardians' Bonds, 1827-1834, 1840-1927; 3 reels.
Inheritance Tax Records, 1923-1967; 1 reel.
Inventories, Record of, 1830-1967; 2 reels.
Settlements, Record of, 1841-1966; 3 reels.

LAND RECORDS

Deeds, Index to, 1761-1929; 2 reels.
Deeds, Record of, 1739-1965; 61 reels.
Land Entries, 1872-1955; 2 reels.
Real Estate Conveyances, Index to, Grantee, 1928-1977; 2 reels.
Real Estate Conveyances, Index to, Grantor, 1928-1977; 2 reels.

MARRIAGE, DIVORCE, AND VITAL STATISTICS

Cohabitation Certificates, 1866; 1 reel.
Marriage Registers, 1868-1983; 4 reels.
Marriage Registers, Cross Index to, 1852-1972; 1 reel.
Vital Statistics, Index to, 1914-1983; 1 reel.

MISCELLANEOUS RECORDS

Accounts of the Clerk, Treasurer, and Sheriff, 1840-1974; 1 reel.
Clerk's Minute Docket, 1868-1899; 1 reel.
Orders and Decrees, 1868-1966; 3 reels.
Special Proceedings, 1879-1918; 1 reel.
Wardens of the Poor, Record of, 1803-1862; 1 reel.

OFFICIALS, COUNTY

Board of County Commissioners, Minutes, 1868-1951; 2 reels.

SCHOOL RECORDS

County Board of Education, Minutes, 1885-1895, 1915-1960; 1 reel.

TAX AND FISCAL RECORDS

Tax Scrolls, 1915-1970; 7 reels.

WILLS

Wills, Index to, 1761-1966; 2 reels.
Wills, Record of, 1761-1960; 3 reels.

DARE COUNTY

Established in 1870 from Currituck, Hyde, and Tyrrell counties.

ORIGINAL RECORDS

BONDS

Bastardy Bonds and Records, 1869-1957; 1 volume, 1 Fibredex box.
Officials' Bonds and Records, 1871-1917; 1 Fibredex box.

COURT RECORDS

Justices of the Peace

Justices' Criminal and Civil Dockets, 1895-1902, 1913-1915; 2 volumes in manuscript box.

Superior Court

Civil Action Papers, 1869-1966; 14 Fibredex boxes.
Civil Action Papers Concerning Land, 1874-1968; 16 Fibredex boxes.
Criminal Action Papers, 1870-1965; 13 Fibredex boxes.
Minutes, 1870-1924; 3 volumes.

ELECTION RECORDS

Election Records, 1878-1955; 3 Fibredex boxes.
Elections, Record of, 1878-1958; 5 volumes.

ESTATES RECORDS

Accounts, Record of, 1870-1927; 2 volumes.
Administrators' Bonds, 1904-1936; 1 volume.
Dowers, Widows' Year's Support, and Land Partitions, Record of, 1869-1915; 1 volume.
Estates Records, 1832-1964; 8 Fibredex boxes.
Guardians' Records, 1866-1959; 1 Fibredex box.
Settlements, Record of, 1867-1926; 1 volume.

LAND RECORDS

Attachments, Executions, Levies, and Liens on Land, 1874-1965; 1 Fibredex box.
Miscellaneous Land Records, 1804-1962; 1 Fibredex box.
Sheriff's Sale Book, 1890-1911; 1 volume.
Tax Levies on Land, 1872-1949; 1 Fibredex box.

MARRIAGE, DIVORCE, AND VITAL STATISTICS

Divorce Records, 1882-1969; 9 Fibredex boxes.
Marriage Registers, 1870-1903; 2 volumes.

MISCELLANEOUS RECORDS

Assignees, Receivers, and Trustees, Records of, 1875-1961; 2 Fibredex boxes.
Fishing and Shipping Records, 1868-1915; 1 Fibredex box.
Grand Jury Reports, 1870-1966; 1 Fibredex box.
Marks and Brands, 1870-1935; 1 volume.
Miscellaneous Records, 1821-1966; 4 Fibredex boxes.
Official Reports, 1906-1958; 1 volume.

TAX AND FISCAL RECORDS

Miscellaneous Tax Records, 1873-1942; 2 Fibredex boxes.

WILLS

Wills, 1872-1959; 2 Fibredex boxes.

MICROFILM RECORDS

CORPORATIONS AND PARTNERSHIPS

Incorporations, Record of, 1906-1967; 3 reels.

COURT RECORDS

Superior Court

Minutes, 1870-1956; 3 reels.
Minutes, Index to, Defendant, 1870-1967; 1 reel.
Minutes, Index to, Plaintiff, 1870-1967; 1 reel.

ELECTION RECORDS

Elections, Record of, 1878-1948; 1 reel.

ESTATES RECORDS

Accounts, Record of, 1870-1967; 4 reels.
Administrators' Bonds, 1936-1967; 1 reel.
Administrators, Executors, and Guardians, Cross Index to, 1870-1966; 2 reels.
Appointment of Administrators, Executors, and Guardians, 1906-1967; 3 reels.
Guardians' Bonds, 1904-1932, 1937-1967; 1 reel.
Guardians, Cross Index to, 1870-1940; 1 reel.
Inheritance Tax Records, 1923-1967; 1 reel.

LAND RECORDS

Deeds, Record of, 1871-1958; 54 reels.
Entry Takers' Books, 1870-1959; 2 reels.
Real Estate Conveyances, Index to, Grantee, 1870-1966; 3 reels.
Real Estate Conveyances, Index to, Grantor, 1870-1965; 3 reels.
Registration of Land Titles, 1924-1964; 1 reel.
Surveys, Record of, 1905-1923; 1 reel.

MARRIAGE, DIVORCE, AND VITAL STATISTICS

Maiden Names of Divorced Women, 1943-1967; 1 reel.
Marriage Registers, 1870-1964; 2 reels.

MISCELLANEOUS RECORDS

Orders and Decrees, 1871-1966; 2 reels.
Special Proceedings, 1906-1960; 2 reels.

OFFICIALS, COUNTY

Board of County Commissioners, Minutes, 1870-1954; 4 reels.

SCHOOL RECORDS

County Board of Education, Minutes, 1896-1963; 1 reel.

TAX AND FISCAL RECORDS

Tax Lists, 1915, 1920, 1925, 1930, 1935, 1945; 4 reels.
Tax Scrolls, 1872-1879, 1881-1905, 1915, 1920, 1925, 1930, 1935, 1940; 3 reels.

WILLS

Beneficiaries and Devisees, Index to, 1966-1968; 1 reel.
Wills, Index to, 1870-1968; 2 reels.
Wills, Record of, 1870-1966; 3 reels.

DAVIDSON COUNTY

Established in 1822 from Rowan County.
Courthouse fire in 1866 may have destroyed some records.

ORIGINAL RECORDS

BONDS

Apprentice Bonds and Records, 1824-1919; 2 volumes, 1 Fibredex box.
Bastardy Bonds and Records, 1823-1935; 9 Fibredex boxes.
Officials' Bonds and Records, 1827-1930; 3 Fibredex boxes.

CENSUS RECORDS (County Copy)

Census, 1880; 1 pamphlet.

COURT RECORDS

County Court of Pleas and Quarter Sessions
- Appearance Dockets, 1823-1868; 2 volumes.
- Execution Dockets, 1823-1868; 8 volumes.
- Minutes, 1823-1868; 7 volumes.
- Recognizance Dockets, 1827-1861; 2 volumes.
- State Dockets, 1823-1868; 3 volumes.
- Trial Dockets, 1823-1868; 4 volumes.

Superior Court
- Appearance Docket, 1824-1868; 1 volume.
- Civil Action Papers, 1821-1946; 65 Fibredex boxes. [*See also* **CRX RECORDS**]
- Civil Action Papers Concerning Land, 1820-1946; 42 Fibredex boxes.
- Criminal Action Papers, 1822-1940; 33 Fibredex boxes.
- Criminal Dockets, 1943-1955, 1968-1970; 2 volumes.
- Criminal Judgments, Index to, [A-L], 1933-1961; 2 volumes.
- Equity Execution Docket, 1824-1868; 1 volume.
- Equity Minutes, 1824-1856; 2 volumes.
- Equity Trial and Appearance Dockets, 1824-1868; 2 volumes.
- Execution Dockets, 1824-1861; 2 volumes.
- Minutes, 1824-1970; 44 volumes.
- Probation Judgment Docket, 1954-1958, 1963-1970; 1 volume.
- Recognizance Dockets, 1824-1867; 2 volumes.
- State Dockets, 1824-1868; 2 volumes.
- Trial Dockets, 1824-1868; 2 volumes.

Thomasville Recorder's Court
- Judgment Dockets, 1941-1970; 3 volumes.
- Minutes, 1941-1969; 2 volumes.

ELECTION RECORDS

Division of Lexington, Thomasville, and Conrad Hill Townships into Voting Precincts, 1896; 1 volume.
Election Returns, 1823-1888; 3 Fibredex boxes.
Elections, Record of, 1878-1926, 1946-1972; 4 volumes.
Miscellaneous Election Records, 1833-1928; 2 Fibredex boxes.

ESTATES RECORDS

Accounts, Record of, 1868-1970; 43 volumes.
Administrators' Bonds, 1868-1916; 7 volumes.

Appointment of Administrators, Executors, Guardians, and Masters, 1868-1910; 1 volume.
Dowers, Record of, 1915-1952; 1 volume.
Estates, Record of, 1830-1868; 9 volumes.
Estates Records, 1817-1948; 249 Fibredex boxes. [*See also* **CRX RECORDS**]
Executors of Persons Who Died Prior to 1916, Record of, 1915-1916; 1 pamphlet.
Guardians' Accounts, 1830-1868; 3 volumes.
Guardians' Bonds, 1870-1909; 5 volumes.
Guardians, Cross Index to, 1900-1970; 1 volume.
Guardians, Record of, 1912-1970; 6 volumes.
Guardians' Records, 1823-1941; 34 Fibredex boxes.
Inheritance Tax Record, 1923-1970; 6 volumes.
Notice to Guardians to Renew Bonds, Record of, 1877-1895; 1 volume.
Qualification of Trustees under Wills, 1962-1970; 1 volume.
Settlements, Record of, 1869-1970; 30 volumes.
Widows' Year's Support, Record of, 1900-1970; 4 volumes.

LAND RECORDS
Deeds, 1808-1922; 2 Fibredex boxes.
Deeds, Cross Index to, 1826-1902; 5 volumes.
Ejectments, 1822-1935; 4 Fibredex boxes.
Land Entries, 1874-1916; 2 volumes.
Levies on Land, 1831-1938; 6 Fibredex boxes.
Processions, Surveys, and Divisions of Land, 1827-1941; 2 Fibredex boxes.
Miscellaneous Land Records, 1817-1937; 1 Fibredex box.
Mortgage Sales, Record of, 1939-1973; 5 volumes.

MARRIAGE, DIVORCE, AND VITAL STATISTICS [*See also* **ESTATES RECORDS; CRX RECORDS**]
Divorce Records, 1831-1944; 30 Fibredex boxes.
Maiden Names of Divorced Women, 1937-1970; 1 volume.
Marriage Bonds, 1823-1868; 8 Fibredex boxes.
Marriage Certificates, Record of, 1852-1868; 1 volume.
Marriage Licenses, 1869-1893; 1 manuscript box.
Marriage Registers, 1867-1921; 8 volumes.

MILITARY AND PENSION RECORDS [*See* **CRX RECORDS**]

MISCELLANEOUS RECORDS
Alien Registration, 1927, 1940; 1 volume.
Assignees, Receivers, and Trustees, Records of, 1846-1943; 13 Fibredex boxes.
Bridges and Ferries, 1824-1929; 1 Fibredex box.
Certificates of Registration, 1887-1970; 1 manuscript box.
Certificates of Registration for Optometrists, 1909-1916; 1 volume.
County Accounts (County Treasurer), 1876-1882; 1 volume.
County Accounts (County Trustee), 1868; 1 volume.
County Claims, 1823-1867; 2 volumes.
County Treasurer's Reports, 1879-1914; 1 volume.
Homestead and Personal Property Exemptions, 1869-1944; 2 volumes.
Insolvent Debtors, 1831-1933; 3 Fibredex boxes.
Judicial Hospitalization, Index to, 1899-1970; 1 volume.
Jurors, List of, 1875-1906; 1 volume.
Licenses to Trades, Registry of, 1871-1878; 1 volume.

Lunacy, Record of, 1899-1970; 8 volumes.
Mining Records, 1835-1931; 8 Fibredex boxes.
Miscellaneous Records, 1824-1946; 11 Fibredex boxes. [*See also* **CRX RECORDS**]
Orders and Decrees, 1869-1970; 54 volumes.
Railroad Records, 1847-1941; 10 Fibredex boxes.
Road Orders, 1833-1865; 1 volume.
Road Records, 1823-1939; 5 Fibredex boxes.
School Records, 1855-1934; 2 Fibredex boxes.
Slaves and Free Persons of Color, Records of, 1826-1896; 1 Fibredex box.
Special Proceedings, 1871-1938; 4 volumes.
Special Proceedings, Cross Index to, 1886-1936; 1 volume.

ROADS AND BRIDGES [*See* **MISCELLANEOUS RECORDS**]

SCHOOL RECORDS [*See* **MISCELLANEOUS RECORDS**]

TAX AND FISCAL RECORDS
Tax Lists, 1827-1863; 5 volumes, 1 manuscript box.

WILLS
Wills, 1810-1970; 95 Fibredex boxes.
Wills, Cross Index to, 1919-1947; 1 volume.

CRX RECORDS
Civil Action Papers, 1842, 1852, 1857; 1 folder.
Estates Records and Marriage Records, 1826-1867; 4 folders.
Miscellaneous Records, 1814-1889; 1 Fibredex box.
Petitions to be Exempted from Military Service, 1862-1865; 2 folders.

MICROFILM RECORDS

BONDS
Apprentice Bonds, 1870-1919; 1 reel.

CORPORATIONS AND PARTNERSHIPS
Incorporations, Index to, 1884-1966; 1 reel.
Incorporations, Record of, 1884-1957; 5 reels.
Partnerships, Record of, 1913-1958; 1 reel.

COURT RECORDS
County Court of Pleas and Quarter Sessions
Minutes, 1823-1868; 4 reels.
Superior Court
Criminal Actions, Index to, 1933-1969; 3 reels.
Judgment Docket, Criminal, 1961-1970; 1 reel.
Judgments, Index to, Defendant, 1900-1953; 1 reel.
Judgments, Index to, Plaintiff, 1900-1953; 1 reel.
Judgments, Liens, and Lis Pendens, Index to, 1954-1970; 4 reels.
Minutes, 1824-1970; 33 reels.

ESTATES RECORDS
Accounts, Record of, 1868-1961; 12 reels.
Administrators' Bonds, 1868-1916; 1 reel.
Administrators and Executors, Cross Index to, 1868-1966; 1 reel.
Administrators, Record of, 1910-1955; 7 reels.

Appointment of Administrators, Executors, and Guardians, 1868-1912; 2 reels.
Dowry, Record of, 1915-1952; 1 reel.
Estates, Record of, 1830-1866; 3 reels.
Executors, Record of, 1918-1966; 2 reels.
Guardians' Bonds, 1870-1909; 1 reel.
Guardians, Cross Index to, 1900-1970; 1 reel.
Guardians, Record of, 1918-1967; 3 reels.
Inheritance Tax Records, 1923-1956; 1 reel.
Inventories and Accounts of Sale, 1830-1897; 5 reels.
Settlements, Record of, 1866-1960; 14 reels.
Widows' Year's Support, Record of, 1900-1967; 2 reels.

LAND RECORDS

Deeds, Record of, 1822-1953; 124 reels.
Division of Land, 1835-1966; 3 reels.
Real Estate Conveyances, Index to, Grantee, 1823-1953; 18 reels.
Real Estate Conveyances, Index to, Grantor, 1823-1953; 16 reels.
Registration of Land Titles, 1914-1943; 1 reel.

MARRIAGE, DIVORCE, AND VITAL STATISTICS

Delayed Births, Index to, various years; 1 reel.
Maiden Names of Divorced Women, 1937-1966; 1 reel.
Marriage Registers, 1822-1954; 3 reels.
Vital Statistics, Index to, 1914-1980; 4 reels.

MISCELLANEOUS RECORDS

Homestead Returns, 1878-1944; 1 reel.
Orders and Decrees, 1869-1959; 16 reels.
Special Proceedings, 1871-1928; 2 reels.
Special Proceedings, Cross Index to, 1886-1936; 1 reel.

OFFICIALS, COUNTY

Board of County Commissioners, Minutes, 1868-1951; 6 reels.

SCHOOL RECORDS

Board of Superintendents of Common Schools, Minutes, 1843-1864; County Board of Education, Minutes, 1885-1906, 1931-1963; 1 reel.

TAX AND FISCAL RECORDS

Tax Lists, 1827-1863; 2 reels.

WILLS

Wills, Cross Index to, 1823-1955; 1 reel.
Wills, Index to, Devisee, 1956-1966; 1 reel.
Wills, Index to, Devisor, 1956-1966; 1 reel.
Wills, Record of, 1823-1967; 12 reels.

DAVIE COUNTY

Established in 1836 from Rowan County.

ORIGINAL RECORDS

BONDS

Apprentice Bonds and Records, 1829-1925; 1 volume, 2 Fibredex boxes.
Bastardy Bonds and Records, 1837-1897; 2 Fibredex boxes.
Officials' Bonds and Records, 1830-1908; 3 Fibredex boxes.

COURT RECORDS

County Court of Pleas and Quarter Sessions
- Appearance Dockets, 1837-1868; 2 volumes.
- Execution Dockets, 1837-1859; 2 volumes.
- Levy Docket, 1843-1868; 1 volume.
- State Docket, 1847-1868; 1 volume.
- Trial Dockets, 1837-1853; 2 volumes.

Inferior Court
- Minutes, 1877-1883; 1 volume.

Superior Court
- Civil Action Papers, 1829-1913; 23 Fibredex boxes.
- Civil Action Papers Concerning Land, 1869-1913; 9 Fibredex boxes.
- Criminal Action Papers, 1837-1905; 12 Fibredex boxes.
- Equity Enrolling Docket, 1837-1839, 1858; 1 volume.
- Equity Minutes, 1837-1868; 1 volume.
- Equity Trial and Appearance Docket, 1837-1867; 1 volume.
- Minutes, 1837-1905; 8 volumes, 1 manuscript box.

ELECTION RECORDS

Election Records, 1838-1898; 4 Fibredex boxes.
Elections, Record of, 1878-1928; 5 volumes.

ESTATES RECORDS

Accounts, Record of, 1868-1895; 2 volumes.
Appointment of Administrators, Executors, Guardians, and Masters, 1868-1917; 1 volume.
Estates, Record of, 1855-1868; 1 volume.
Estates Records, 1809-1936; 77 Fibredex boxes.
Guardians' Accounts, 1846-1868; 1 volume.
Guardians' Records, 1834-1918; 9 Fibredex boxes.
Settlements, Record of, 1840-1904, 1923; 3 volumes.

LAND RECORDS

Miscellaneous Land Records, 1792-1914; 2 Fibredex boxes.
Probate, Record of, 1891-1894; 1 volume.
Processioners' Records, 1840-1885; 1 volume.

MARRIAGE, DIVORCE, AND VITAL STATISTICS

Divorce Records, 1849-1908; 3 Fibredex boxes.

MILITARY AND PENSION RECORDS [*See* **CRX RECORDS**]

MISCELLANEOUS RECORDS

Assignees, Receivers, and Trustees, Records of, 1872-1897; 1 Fibredex box.
Board of Superintendents of Common Schools, Minutes, 1841-1864; 1 volume.
Bridge, Ferry, and Road Records, 1837-1909; 3 Fibredex boxes.
Homestead and Personal Property Exemptions, 1869-1899; 3 Fibredex boxes.
Insolvent Debtors, 1837-1890; 1 Fibredex box.
Miscellaneous Records, 1813-1927; 8 Fibredex boxes.
Orders and Decrees, 1868-1883; 1 volume.
Railroad Records, 1878-1910; 1 Fibredex box.
School Records, 1839-1908; 3 Fibredex boxes.
Special Proceedings, 1883-1906; 2 volumes.

ROADS AND BRIDGES [*See* **MISCELLANEOUS RECORDS**]

SCHOOL RECORDS [*See* **MISCELLANEOUS RECORDS**]

TAX AND FISCAL RECORDS

Tax Records, 1838-1905; 3 Fibredex boxes.

WILLS

Wills, 1808-1902; 2 Fibredex boxes.

CRX RECORDS

Petitions to be Exempted from Military Service, 1862-1865; 2 folders.

MICROFILM RECORDS

BONDS

Apprentice Bonds, 1889-1925; 1 reel.

CORPORATIONS AND PARTNERSHIPS

Incorporations, Record of, 1891-1962; 1 reel.
Partnerships, Record of, 1913-1967; 1 reel.

COURT RECORDS

County Court of Pleas and Quarter Sessions
- Minutes, 1837-1868; 2 reels.

Superior Court
- Equity Minutes, 1837-1868; 1 reel.
- Minutes, 1837-1948; 5 reels.

ELECTION RECORDS

Elections, Record of, 1880-1967; 1 reel.

ESTATES RECORDS

Accounts of Indigent Orphans, 1917-1967; 1 reel.
Accounts of Sale, 1846-1854; 1 reel.
Accounts, Record of, 1868-1967; 5 reels.
Administrators and Estates, Index to, 1837-1967; 1 reel.
Administrators and Executors, Cross Index to, 1869-1937; 1 reel.
Administrators, Executors, and Guardians, Record of, 1912-1931; 1 reel.
Administrators, General Index to, 1837-1967; 1 reel.
Administrators, Record of, 1920-1967; 2 reels.
Estates, Record of, 1855-1868; 1 reel.
Executors, Record of, 1868-1916, 1925-1964; 1 reel.

Guardians, Record of, 1925-1967; 1 reel.
Guardians' Settlements, 1846-1868; 1 reel.
Guardians and Wards, Index to, 1868-1935; 1 reel.
Inheritance Tax Records, 1923-1957; 1 reel.
Settlements, Record of, 1846-1967; 5 reels.
Widows' Year's Support, Record of, 1955-1966; 1 reel.

LAND RECORDS

Deeds, Record of, 1837-1953; 27 reels.
Land Entries, 1837-1910; 1 reel.
Real Estate Conveyances, Index to, Grantee, 1837-1967; 4 reels.
Real Estate Conveyances, Index to, Grantor, 1837-1967; 4 reels.
Resale, Record of, 1920-1967; 1 reel.

MARRIAGE, DIVORCE, AND VITAL STATISTICS

Births, Index to, 1912-1966; 2 reels.
Cohabitation Record, 1866-1867; 1 reel.
Deaths, Index to, 1913-1966; 1 reel.
Delayed Births, Index to, various years; 1 reel.
Maiden Names of Divorced Women, 1940-1966; 1 reel.
Marriage Bonds, 1836-1868; 2 reels.
Marriage Registers, 1851-1959; 3 reels.

MISCELLANEOUS RECORDS

Lunacy Docket, 1908-1970; 1 reel.
Special Proceedings, 1883-1946; 4 reels.
Special Proceedings, Index to, Defendant, 1883-1967; 1 reel.
Special Proceedings, Index to, Plaintiff, 1883-1967; 1 reel.
Wardens of the Poor, Minutes, 1839-1854; 1 reel.

OFFICIALS, COUNTY

Board of County Commissioners, Minutes, 1868-1967; 2 reels.

SCHOOL RECORDS

Board of Superintendents of Common Schools, Minutes, 1841-1864; 1 reel.
County Board of Education, Minutes, 1885-1967; 1 reel.

TAX AND FISCAL RECORDS

Tax Lists, 1843-1860, 1866-1872; 4 reels.
Tax Scrolls, 1869-1896, 1905, 1915; 8 reels.

WILLS

Wills, Index to, 1837-1967; 2 reels.
Wills, Record of, 1837-1967; 2 reels.

DOBBS COUNTY

Established in 1758 (effective 1759) from Johnston County.
Divided into Glasgow and Lenoir counties in 1791.
Land records destroyed by fire at Lenoir County Courthouse in 1880.

ORIGINAL RECORDS

COURT RECORDS [*See* **CRX RECORDS**]

LAND RECORDS

Deeds, Index to, no date; 4 volumes.

MISCELLANEOUS RECORDS

Miscellaneous Records, 1762-1791; 1 Fibredex box.

CRX RECORDS

Civil Action Papers, 1767; 1 folder.

MICROFILM RECORDS

LAND RECORDS (includes records of Johnston County, 1746-1759, and Lenoir County, 1792-1880)

Deeds, Index to, Grantee, 1746-1880; 1 reel.
Deeds, Index to, Grantor, 1746-1880; 1 reel.

DUPLIN COUNTY

Established in 1750 from New Hanover County.
Many court records are missing; reason unknown.

ORIGINAL RECORDS

BONDS

Apprentice Bonds, 1871-1916; 1 volume.
Apprentice Bonds and Records, 1801-1908; Bastardy Bonds and Records, 1868-1921; 1 Fibredex box.
Officials' Bonds and Records, 1779-1936; 2 Fibredex boxes.

COURT RECORDS

County Court
- Minutes, 1928-1968; 16 volumes.

County Court of Pleas and Quarter Sessions
- Appearance Dockets, 1847-1868; 2 volumes.
- Execution Dockets, 1847-1868; 5 volumes.
- Minutes, 1784-1868; 20 volumes.
- Prosecution Bonds, 1866-1868; 1 volume.
- State Docket, 1847-1868; 1 volume.
- Trial Dockets, 1847-1868; 3 volumes.

Inferior Court
- Minutes, 1881-1885; 1 volume.

Superior Court
- Civil Action Papers, 1799-1935; 7 Fibredex boxes.
- Civil Action Papers Concerning Land, 1868-1946; 25 Fibredex boxes.
- Criminal Action Papers, 1871-1927; 6 Fibredex boxes.
- Criminal Issues Docket, 1869-1887; 1 volume.
- Execution Docket, 1864-1870; 1 volume.
- Equity Minutes, 1824-1868; 2 volumes.
- Equity Trial Docket, 1824-1868; 1 volume.
- Judgment Dockets, 1935-1947; 4 volumes. [*See also* **LAND RECORDS**]
- Minutes, 1815-1968; 33 volumes.
- Trial Docket, 1851-1867; 1 volume.

ELECTION RECORDS

Elections, Record of, 1878-1932; 4 volumes.

ESTATES RECORDS

Administrators' Bonds, 1846-1871, 1885-1923; 7 volumes.
Committees to Divide Real Estate, General Index to Reports of, 1800-1967; 1 volume.
Committees to Divide Real Estate, Record of, 1854-1861; 1 volume.
Estates, Record of, 1830-1876; 6 volumes.
Estates Records, 1752-1930; 100 Fibredex boxes.
Guardians' Accounts, 1854-1882; 2 volumes.
Guardians' Bonds, 1846-1856, 1871-1919; 3 volumes.
Guardians' Records, 1787-1943; 12 Fibredex boxes.
Inheritance Tax Collections, Record of, 1919-1948; 2 volumes.
Probate (Estates), Record of, 1868-1878; 1 volume.

LAND RECORDS

Attachments, Executions, Levies, and Liens on Land, 1804-1950; 3 Fibredex boxes.
Judgment Dockets, Tax Foreclosure Sales, 1938-1948; 3 volumes. [*See also* **COURT RECORDS**, Superior Court]
Land Divisions, Partitions, and Sales, 1796-1936; 2 Fibredex boxes.
Land Sales for Taxes, 1933; 1 volume.
Maps of Land Divisions, 1919-1962; 2 volumes.
Meridian Record, 1902-1932; 1 volume.
Miscellaneous Land Records, 1776-1935; 2 Fibredex boxes.
Mortgage Sales, Record of, 1923-1948; 5 volumes.
Processioners' Record, 1859-1877; 1 volume.

MARRIAGE, DIVORCE, AND VITAL STATISTICS

Divorce Records, 1869-1952; 4 Fibredex boxes.
Maiden Names of Divorced Women, 1944-1969; 1 volume.
Marriage Bonds, 1755-1869; 5 Fibredex boxes.
Marriage Registers, 1867-1928; 4 volumes.

MISCELLANEOUS RECORDS [*See also* **CRX RECORDS**]

Alien Registration, 1940; 1 volume.
Assignees, Receivers, and Trustees, Records of, 1822-1930; 2 Fibredex boxes.
Board of County Commissioners, Minutes, 1878-1906; 4 volumes.
Homestead and Personal Property Exemptions, 1869-1942; 2 Fibredex boxes.
Miscellaneous Records, 1754-1947; 4 Fibredex boxes.
Officials' Reports, Record of, 1868-1893; 1 volume.
Orders and Decrees, 1872-1950; 19 volumes.
Railroad Records, 1877-1922; 6 Fibredex boxes.
St. Gabriel's Parish Wardens' Records, 1799-1817; 1 volume.
School Records, 1861-1921; 1 Fibredex box.
Special Proceedings Docket, 1891-1906; 1 volume.
Timber Records, 1903-1918; 2 Fibredex boxes.

OFFICIALS, COUNTY [*See* **MISCELLANEOUS RECORDS**]

ROADS AND BRIDGES [*See* **MISCELLANEOUS RECORDS**]

SCHOOL RECORDS [*See* **MISCELLANEOUS RECORDS**]

TAX AND FISCAL RECORDS

Lists of Taxables, 1783-1838; 2 volumes, 1 manuscript box.
Tax Returns, 1895-1925; 2 volumes.

WILLS [*See also* **SAMPSON COUNTY, WILLS**]

Wills, 1759-1913; 12 Fibredex boxes.
Wills, Cross Index to, 1931-1970; 1 volume.
Wills, Record of, ca. 1760-1910; 5 volumes.

CRX RECORDS

Miscellaneous Records, 1762-1918; 1 Fibredex box.

MICROFILM RECORDS

BONDS

Apprentice Bonds, 1871-1916; 1 reel.

COURT RECORDS

County Court of Pleas and Quarter Sessions

Minutes, 1784-1868; 5 reels.

Superior Court

Equity Minutes, 1824-1868; 1 reel.
Judgments, Criminal, Index to, 1928-1968; 2 reels.
Judgments, Index to, Defendant, 1927-1968; 2 reels.
Judgments, Index to, Plaintiff, 1927-1968; 2 reels.
Minutes, 1815-1930; 8 reels.

ELECTION RECORDS

Elections, Record of, 1880-1952; 1 reel.

ESTATES RECORDS

Accounts, Record of, 1869-1962; 6 reels.
Administrators' Bonds, 1846-1923; 1 reel.
Administrators, Record of, 1918-1962; 4 reels.
Committees to Divide Real Estate, General Index to Record of, 1800-1968; 1 reel.
Committees to Divide Real Estate, Record of, 1800-1960; 3 reels.
Estates, Record of, 1830-1874; 2 reels.
Guardians' Accounts, 1854-1882; 1 reel.
Guardians' Bonds, 1846-1918; 1 reel.
Guardians, Record of, 1918-1962; 1 reel.
Inheritance Tax Records, 1919-1962; 1 reel.
Inventories and Accounts of Estates, 1754-1800; 3 reels.
Settlements, Record of, 1869-1961; 3 reels.

LAND RECORDS [*See also* **SAMPSON COUNTY, LAND RECORDS**]

Deeds, Record of, 1784-1935; 91 reels.
Divisions of Land, 1800-1860; 1 reel.
Land Entries, 1896-1941; 1 reel.
Mortgage Resales, Record of, 1922-1933; 1 reel.
Plat Books, 1784-1962; 1 reel.
Plat Books, Index to, 1784-1962; 1 reel.
Processioners' Records, 1859-1877; 1 reel.
Real Estate Conveyances, Index to, Grantee, 1784-1940; 3 reels.
Real Estate Conveyances, Index to, Grantor, 1784-1940; 3 reels.
Registration of Land Titles, 1929-1967; 1 reel.

MARRIAGE, DIVORCE, AND VITAL STATISTICS

Births, Index to, 1913-1981; 3 reels.
Cohabitation, Record of, 1866; 1 reel.
Deaths, Index to, 1913-1981; 2 reels.
Delayed Births, Index to, 1913-1981; 1 reel.
Maiden Names of Divorced Women, 1944-1969; 1 reel.
Marriage Bond Abstracts, 1755-1868; 1 reel.
Marriage Bonds, 1755-1868; 1 reel.
Marriage Licenses, 1893-1961; 9 reels.
Marriage Registers, 1867-1981; 6 reels.
Marriages, Record of, 1866-1868; 1 reel.

Miscellaneous Records

Home Demonstration Club, Calypso, Record of, 1952-1962; 1 reel.
Miscellaneous Historical Essays: County and People, no date; 1 reel.
Orders and Decrees, 1872-1938; 6 reels.
Special Proceedings, 1872-1962; Cross Index to Special Proceedings, 1872-1926; 3 reels.

Officials, County

Board of County Commissioners, Minutes, 1878-1932; 4 reels.
County Board of Social Services, Minutes, 1946-1962; 1 reel.

School Records

County Board of Education, Minutes, 1872-1935; 1 reel.

Tax and Fiscal Records

Tax Lists, 1786-1838, 1895-1925; 2 reels.

Wills

Wills, Cross Index to, 1760-1970; 2 reels.
Wills, Record of, 1760-1968; 7 reels.

DURHAM COUNTY

Established in 1881 from Orange and Wake counties.

ORIGINAL RECORDS

BONDS

Apprentice Bonds, 1882-1913; 1 volume.

COURT RECORDS

Superior Court

Civil Action Papers, 1879-1926; 2 Fibredex boxes.
Criminal Action Papers, 1882-1936; 4 Fibredex boxes.
Minutes, 1887-1924; 17 volumes.

ELECTION RECORDS

Election Returns and Vote Abstracts, 1896-1936; 3 Fibredex boxes.
Elections, Record of, 1881-1904; 1 volume.

ESTATES RECORDS

Accounts, Record of, 1881-1946; 10 volumes.
Administrators' Bonds, 1891-1896; 1 volume.
Administrators and Executors, Index to, 1881-1890; 1 volume.
Amounts Paid for Indigent Children, Record of, 1915-1916; 1 pamphlet.
Appointment of Administrators, Executors, and Guardians, 1881-1892; 1 volume.
Estates Records, 1875-1926; 1 Fibredex box.
Guardians' Accounts, 1881-1909, 1921-1950; 7 volumes.
Guardians' Bonds, 1881-1898; 2 volumes.
Guardians, Record of, 1898-1912; 1 volume.
Settlements, Record of, 1882-1939; 9 volumes.
Widows' Dowers and Year's Support, Record of, 1881-1944; 1 volume.

LAND RECORDS

Record of Partition, 1882-1898; 1 volume.

MISCELLANEOUS RECORDS

Alien, Naturalization, and Citizenship Records, 1882-1904; 2 Fibredex boxes.
Alien Registration, 1927-1928, 1940-1941; 1 volume.
Board of Justices, Minutes, 1881-1894; 1 volume.
Justices of the Peace Oaths, 1889-1900; 1 volume.
Licenses to Trades, Registry of, 1881-1913; 1 volume.
Miscellaneous Records, 1825-1934; 1 Fibredex box.
Officials' Reports, Record of, 1885-1917; 1 volume.
Orders and Decrees, 1881-1892; 1 volume.
Petitions for Naturalization, 1909-1922, 1943-1944; 2 volumes.
Special Licenses Issued, Record of, 1908-1918; 4 volumes.

OFFICIALS, COUNTY [*See* **MISCELLANEOUS RECORDS**]

SCHOOL RECORDS [*See* **CRX RECORDS**]

WILLS

Wills, Cross Index to, 1881-1915; 1 volume.

CRX RECORDS
Agreement, 1917; 1 folder.
Public School Register (colored), District 15, 1892-1896; 1 volume.

MICROFILM RECORDS

BONDS
Apprentice Bonds, 1882-1913; 1 reel.

CORPORATIONS AND PARTNERSHIPS
Incorporations, Index to, 1890-1968; 1 reel.
Incorporations, Record of, 1905-1945; 2 reels.

COURT RECORDS
Superior Court
Judgments, Index to, Defendant, 1929-1966; 3 reels.
Judgments, Index to, Plaintiff, 1929-1966; 2 reels.
Minutes, 1884-1959; 26 reels.

ELECTION RECORDS
Elections, Record of, 1881-1904; 1 reel.

ESTATES RECORDS
Accounts, Record of, 1881-1965; 16 reels.
Administrators' Bonds, 1891-1896; 1 reel.
Administrators and Executors, Index to, 1881-1890; 1 reel.
Administrators, Record of, 1896-1966; 14 reels.
Appointment of Administrators, Executors, and Guardians, 1881-1892; 1 reel.
Estates, General Index to, 1881-1968; 2 reels.
Guardians' Accounts, 1881-1966; 10 reels.
Guardians' Bonds, 1881-1898; 1 reel.
Guardians, Record of, 1898-1964; 6 reels.
Inheritance Tax Records, 1922-1966; 3 reels.
Next Friend of Minors and Incompetents, Record of, 1935-1967; 1 reel.
Settlements, Record of, 1882-1966; 14 reels.
Trust Funds of Estates and Special Proceedings, Record of, 1920-1966; 4 reels.
Trustees under Wills, Record of, 1941-1966; 1 reel.
Widows' Dowers and Year's Support, Record of, 1881-1969; 2 reels.

LAND RECORDS
Deeds, Index to, Grantee, 1881-1961; 6 reels.
Deeds, Index to, Grantor, 1881-1961; 6 reels.
Deeds, Record of, 1881, 1883-1961; 168 reels.
Sales of Trustees and Mortgagees, Record of, 1923-1967; 10 reels.

MARRIAGE, DIVORCE, AND VITAL STATISTICS
Maiden Names of Divorced Women, 1937-1969; 1 reel.
Marriage Licenses, Colored, 1898-1968; 14 reels.
Marriage Licenses, White, 1898-1968; 22 reels.
Marriage Registers, 1881-1969; 3 reels.

MISCELLANEOUS RECORDS
Homesteads, Record of, 1882-1939; 1 reel.
Special Proceedings, 1892-1961; 18 reels.

Special Proceedings, Cross Index to, 1883-1966; 1 reel.
Special Proceedings Dockets, 1881-1952; 3 reels.

OFFICIALS, COUNTY

Board of County Commissioners, Minutes, 1881-1950; 7 reels.

SCHOOL RECORDS

County Board of Education, Minutes, 1881-1967; 4 reels.

TAX AND FISCAL RECORDS

Tax Scrolls, 1882-1902, 1905, 1910, 1915, 1925, 1935, 1945; 14 reels.

WILLS

Beneficiaries, Index to, 1966-1968; 1 reel.
Wills, Index to, 1881-1968; 1 reel.
Wills, Record of, 1881-1966; 8 reels.

EDGECOMBE COUNTY

Established in 1741 from Bertie County.
Land records prior to 1759 are among those of Halifax County.

ORIGINAL RECORDS

BONDS

Apprentice Bonds, 1875-1924; 2 volumes.
Bastardy Bonds and Records, 1771-1909; 3 volumes, 1 Fibredex box.

COURT RECORDS

Circuit Criminal Court/Eastern District Criminal Court
 Minutes, 1895-1901; 1 volume.
County Court of Pleas and Quarter Sessions
 Canal Docket, 1867-1868; 1 volume.
 Clerk's Docket, 1745-1746; 1 manuscript box.
 Clerk's Fee Books, 1753-1765; 2 volumes.
 Execution Dockets, 1769-1856; 4 volumes, 1 manuscript box.
 Minutes, 1744-1746, 1757-1868; 27 volumes.
 Reference (Trial) and Appearance Dockets, 1758-1790; 1 volume, 2 manuscript boxes.
 State (and Crown) Dockets, 1755-1762, 1778-1868; 3 volumes, 1 manuscript box.
 Trial and Appearance Dockets, 1794-1868; 15 volumes, 1 pamphlet.
Inferior Court
 Minutes, 1877-1895; 2 volumes.
Superior Court
 Civil Action Papers, 1756-1910; 116 Fibredex boxes.
 Civil Action Papers Concerning Land, 1791-1918; 13 Fibredex boxes.
 Criminal Action Papers, 1756-1910; 14 Fibredex boxes.
 Criminal Issues Docket, 1906-1927; 1 volume.
 Equity Enrolling Docket, 1807-1814; 1 manuscript box.
 Equity Minutes, 1807-1868; 3 volumes.
 Equity Trial Dockets, 1826-1868; 2 volumes, 1 manuscript box.
 Execution Dockets, 1807-1817, 1867-1868; 1 volume, 1 manuscript box.
 Minutes, 1807-1834, 1862-1910; 14 volumes.
 Receipts in Equity, 1866-1874; 1 volume.
 State Dockets, 1807-1841, 1866-1868; 2 volumes, 1 manuscript box.
 Trial and Appearance Dockets, 1807-1817, 1866-1868; 2 volumes.

ELECTION RECORDS

Elections, Record of, 1878-1942; 5 volumes.

ESTATES RECORDS

Administrators' Bonds, 1866-1907; 6 volumes.
Appointment of Administrators, Executors, Guardians, and Masters, 1868-1915; 2 volumes.
Estates, Record of, 1730-1896; 30 volumes.
Estates Records, 1748-1917; 139 Fibredex boxes. [*See also* **CRX RECORDS**]
Guardians' Accounts, 1764-1778, 1820-1914; 11 volumes.
Guardians' Bonds, 1867-1916; 6 volumes.

Guardians' Records, 1787-1917; 20 Fibredex boxes.
Settlements, Record of, 1869-1916; 4 volumes.

LAND RECORDS [*See also* **CRX RECORDS; HALIFAX COUNTY, LAND RECORDS**]
Deeds, Record of, 1732-1741; 4 volumes.
Land Entries, 1795-1853; 1 volume.
Miscellaneous Land Records, 1742-1913; 1 Fibredex box.

MARRIAGE, DIVORCE, AND VITAL STATISTICS
Cohabitation Certificates, 1866; 2 Fibredex boxes.
Divorce Records, 1835-1901; 3 Fibredex boxes.
Marriage Bonds, 1760-1868; 9 Fibredex boxes.

MILITARY AND PENSION RECORDS [*See* **MISCELLANEOUS RECORDS**]

MISCELLANEOUS RECORDS
Alien Registration, 1940; 1 volume.
Assignees, Receivers, and Trustees, Records of, 1891-1922; 2 Fibredex boxes.
Board of Superintendents of Common Schools, Minutes, 1846-1860; 1 volume.
Bridge and Mill Records, 1760-1891; 1 Fibredex box.
Canal and Drainage Records, 1821-1912; 1 Fibredex box.
Committee of Finance, Minutes, 1852-1866; 1 volume.
County Board of Education, Minutes, 1883-1886; 1 volume.
County Claims, 1839-1855; 1 volume.
Declaration of Intent (to Become a Citizen), Record of, 1907-1920; 1 volume.
Insolvents, 1788-1857; 1 Fibredex box.
Miscellaneous Records, 1769-1929; 4 Fibredex boxes.
Orders and Decrees, 1868-1922; 1 volume.
Pension Records, 1878-1927; 2 volumes.
Petitions for Naturalization, 1903-1920; 1 volume.
Promissory Notes, 1753-1876; 1 Fibredex box.
Railroad Records, 1837-1905; 3 Fibredex boxes.
Road Records, 1761-1897; 2 Fibredex boxes.
Slave Records, 1780-1857, 1871; 1 Fibredex box.
Stock Marks, 1732-1809, 1835; 1 volume.
Wardens of the Poor, Minutes, 1859-1869; 1 volume.

SCHOOL RECORDS [*See* **MISCELLANEOUS RECORDS**]

TAX AND FISCAL RECORDS
Federal Direct Taxes Collected, Record of, 1866; 1 volume.
Poll Tax Records, 1908, no date; 2 volumes.

WILLS
Wills, 1750-1945; 34 Fibredex boxes.

CRX RECORDS
Estates Records, 1842, 1883; 2 folders.
Land Grant, 1745; 1 folder.

MICROFILM RECORDS

COURT RECORDS
County Court of Pleas and Quarter Sessions
Minutes, 1744-1746, 1757-1868; 10 reels.

Superior Court

Criminal Actions, Index to, 1946-1968; 2 reels.
Judgments, Liens, and Lis Pendens, Index to, 1920-1968; 6 reels.
Minutes, 1862-1924; 8 reels.

ELECTION RECORDS

Elections, Record of, 1878-1960; 1 reel.

ESTATES RECORDS

Administrators, Record of, 1897-1968; 10 reels.
Appointment of Administrators, Executors, and Guardians, 1868-1949; 4 reels.
Estates Not Exceeding $300, 1929-1953; 1 reel.
Estates Not Exceeding $500, 1948-1961; 1 reel.
Estates, Record of, 1733-1867; 11 reels.
Estates, Wills, Guardians, and Trustees, Index to, 1930-1968; 1 reel.
Executors, Record of, 1936-1961; 1 reel.
Guardians' Bonds, 1908-1915; 1 reel.
Guardians, Cross Index to, 1887-1937; 1 reel.
Inheritance Tax Records, 1920-1961; 1 reel.
Inventories and Accounts of Sale, 1867-1896; 1 reel.
Inventories and Accounts of Trustees, 1894-1951; 4 reels.
Inventories, Record of, 1830-1836; 1 reel.
Payments to Indigent Children, Record of, 1900-1961; 1 reel.
Settlements, Record of, 1869-1968; 8 reels.
Widows' Year's Allowance, Record of, 1928-1961; 1 reel.

LAND RECORDS

Deeds and Mortgages, General Index to, 1759-1920; 4 reels.
Maps, 1891-1973; 4 reels.
Maps, Index to, 1759-1974; 1 reel.
Real Estate Conveyances, Record of, 1759-1937; 113 reels.

MARRIAGE, DIVORCE, AND VITAL STATISTICS

Births, Index to, 1914-1961; 2 reels.
Cohabitation, Record of, 1866; 1 reel.
Deaths, Index to, 1914-1972; 2 reels.
Delayed Births, Index to, 1909-1981; 1 reel.
Maiden Names of Divorced Women, 1948-1960; 1 reel.
Marriage Bonds, 1760-1868; 3 reels.
Marriage Licenses, 1866-1961; 17 reels.
Marriage Registers, 1851-1937, 1950-1961; 4 reels.

MILITARY AND PENSION RECORDS

Pensions, Record of, 1878-1893, 1903-1927; 1 reel.

MISCELLANEOUS RECORDS

Alien Registration Record, 1940; 1 reel.
Declaration of Intent (to Become a Citizen), Record of, 1907-1920; 1 reel.
Inquisitions of Lunacy, 1899-1952; 2 reels.
Orders and Decrees, 1868-1928; 1 reel.
Petitions for Naturalization, 1903-1920; 1 reel.
Special Proceedings, 1874-1931; 8 reels.
Special Proceedings, Cross Index to, 1887-1961; 1 reel.

OFFICIALS, COUNTY

Board of County Commissioners, Minutes, 1868-1971; 11 reels.

SCHOOL RECORDS

Board of Superintendents of Common Schools, Minutes, 1846-1860; 1 reel.
County Board of Education, Minutes, 1883-1907, 1962-1973; 3 reels.

WILLS

Wills, Index to, 1760-1936; 1 reel.
Wills, Record of, 1749-1968; 10 reels.

FORSYTH COUNTY

Established in 1849 from Stokes County.

ORIGINAL RECORDS

BONDS

Apprentice Bonds, 1875-1891; 1 volume.
Apprentice Bonds, 1850-1916; Bastardy Bonds, 1849-1927; Officials' Bonds, 1877; 1 Fibredex box.

COURT RECORDS

County Court of Pleas and Quarter Sessions
  Minutes, 1849-1868; 3 volumes.
Forsyth County Court
  Clerk's Minute Dockets, 1931-1933, 1938-1940; 2 volumes.
Inferior Court
  Judgment Docket, 1878-1885; 1 volume.
  Minutes, 1878-1885; 1 volume.
Superior Court
  Civil Action Papers, 1851-1930; 16 Fibredex boxes.
  Civil Action Papers Concerning Land, 1849-1930; 5 Fibredex boxes.
  Clerk's Minute Dockets, 1926-1947; 4 volumes.
  Equity Minutes, 1849-1868; 1 volume.
  Judgment Dockets, 1869-1877; 2 volumes. [*See also* **LAND RECORDS**, Tax Suit Judgment Dockets]
  Minutes, 1848-1941; 61 volumes.
  State Docket, 1849-1872; 1 volume.
Western District Criminal Court
  Minutes, 1899-1901; 1 volume.

ELECTION RECORDS

Elections, Record of, 1898-1900, 1908-1924; 3 volumes.
Permanent Registration of Voters, 1902-1908; 1 volume.

ESTATES RECORDS

Accounts, Record of, 1868-1926; 16 volumes.
Administrators and Executors, Cross Index to, 1868-1929; 1 volume.
Administrators, Executors, and Guardians, Index to, 1849-1940; 4 volumes.
Estates Records, 1845-1956; 419 Fibredex boxes.
Guardians, Cross Index to, 1868-1929; 1 volume.
Inventories of Estates, 1849-1868; 4 volumes.

LAND RECORDS

Deeds, Cross Index to, 1849-1907; 5 volumes.
Land Records, 1876-1947; 15 Fibredex boxes.
Processioners' Record, 1884-1886; 1 volume.
Street Assessment Judgment Docket, 1936-1939; 1 volume.
Tax Suit Judgment Dockets, 1936-1945; 3 volumes. [*See also* **COURT RECORDS**, Superior Court, Judgment Dockets]

MARRIAGE, DIVORCE, AND VITAL STATISTICS

Divorce Records, 1871-1929; 2 Fibredex boxes.
Marriage Bonds, 1850-1859; 1 Fibredex box.

MILITARY AND PENSION RECORDS [*See* **MISCELLANEOUS RECORDS; CRX RECORDS**]

MISCELLANEOUS RECORDS

Alien Registration, 1927-1940; 1 volume.
Assignees, Receivers, and Trustees, Records of, 1858-1930; 6 Fibredex boxes.
Board of Road Supervisors, Minutes, 1907-1912; 1 volume.
Board of Superintendents of Common Schools, Minutes, 1851-1854; 1 volume.
County Claims, 1849-1878; 1 volume.
Declaration of Intent (to Become a Citizen), Record of, 1908-1919; 1 volume.
Homestead and Personal Property Exemptions, 1877-1943; 4 Fibredex boxes.
Justices of the Peace, Record of, 1883-1924; 1 volume.
Lunacy Records, 1852-1949; 4 Fibredex boxes.
Miscellaneous Records, 1849-1954; 6 Fibredex boxes.
Notaries Public, Record of, 1924-1936; 1 volume. [*See also* **COURT RECORDS**, Superior Court, Minutes, 1911-1912]
Petitions to Change Name, 1891-1949; 2 Fibredex boxes.
Petitions for Naturalization, 1891-1921; 1 volume.
Railroad Records, 1870-1930; 2 Fibredex boxes.
Road Docket, 1850-1879; 1 volume.
Roster of Norfleet Camp, No. 436, Confederate Veterans, 1902-1926; 1 volume.
Salem Militia Record Book, 1831-1861; 1 volume.
Special Proceedings, 1903-1942; 1 Fibredex box.
Stokes County Records (includes civil actions, estates), 1808-1848; 1 Fibredex box.

OFFICIALS, COUNTY [*See* **MISCELLANEOUS RECORDS**]

ROADS AND BRIDGES [*See* **MISCELLANEOUS RECORDS**]

SCHOOL RECORDS [*See* **MISCELLANEOUS RECORDS**]

WILLS

Wills, 1840-1900; 7 Fibredex boxes.
Wills, Cross Index to, 1857-1929; 2 volumes.

CRX RECORDS

Petitions to be Exempted from Military Service, 1862-1865; 2 folders.

MICROFILM RECORDS

BONDS

Apprentice Bonds, 1875-1920; 2 reels.
Bastardy Bonds, 1849-1879, 1915-1927; 2 reels.

CORPORATIONS AND PARTNERSHIPS

Corporations, Index to, 1884-1969; 1 reel.
Corporations, Record of, 1884-1957; 7 reels.

COURT RECORDS

County Court of Pleas and Quarter Sessions
Minutes, 1849-1868; 2 reels.
Forsyth County Court
Minutes, 1915-1931; 5 reels.
Superior Court
Civil Actions, Index to, Defendant, 1849-1968; 4 reels.
Civil Actions, Index to, Plaintiff, 1849-1968; 3 reels.

Equity Minutes, 1849-1868; 1 reel.
Judgments, Index to, 1878-1942; 1 reel.
Judgments, Index to, Defendant, 1869-1968; 11 reels.
Judgments, Index to, Plaintiff, 1869-1968; 9 reels.
Minutes, 1849-1932; 26 reels.

Election Records

Elections, Record of, 1878-1952; 1 reel.

Estates Records

Accounts, Record of, 1868-1932; 12 reels.
Accounts in Trust, Index to, 1924-1969; 1 reel.
Administrators' Bonds, 1882-1893; 1 reel.
Administrators, Executors, and Guardians, Reports of, 1902-1914, 1932-1935; 7 reels.
Administrators, Executors, Guardians, and Trustees, Index to, 1849-1968; 5 reels.
Administrators, Record of, 1893-1952; 7 reels.
Appointment of Administrators, Executors, and Guardians, 1899-1936; 4 reels.
Appointment of Executors, 1868-1928; 2 reels.
Appointment of Guardians, and Guardians' Oath Book, 1903-1910; 1 reel.
Bonds of Administrators, Surviving Partners, and Collectors, 1936-1950; 9 reels.
Final Settlements, Record of, 1868-1934; 8 reels.
Guardians' Bonds, 1875-1903, 1910-1946; 9 reels.
Guardians, Record of, 1946-1953; 2 reels.
Inheritance Tax Records, 1923-1949; 2 reels.
Inventories and Accounts of Fiduciaries, 1935-1949; 20 reels.
Inventories of Estates, 1849-1868; 2 reels.
Receivers for Estates, Record of, 1912-1930; 1 reel.
Trustees under Wills, Record of, 1933-1949; 1 reel.
Widows' Year's Allowances, Record of, 1934-1939; 1 reel.

Land Records

Deeds, Record of, 1849-1957; 316 reels.
Federal Tax Lien Index, 1932-1966; 1 reel.
Foreclosure Sales, Record of, 1932-1935; 1 reel.
Land Title Guaranty Proceeding Docket, 1914-1927; 1 reel.
Processioners, Record of, 1884-1886; 1 reel.
Real Estate Conveyances, Index to, Grantee, 1849-1956; 18 reels.
Real Estate Conveyances, Index to, Grantor, 1849-1956; 18 reels.
Sales by Mortgagees, Trustees, and Executors, Record of, 1917-1949; 6 reels.
Sales by Trustee and Commissioner, Index to, 1917-1968; 1 reel.
Sales by Trustee, Commissioner, and Owner, Index to, 1917-1968; 1 reel.

Marriage, Divorce, and Vital Statistics

Cohabitation Certificates, 1866; 1 reel.
Maiden Names of Divorced Women, 1937-1969; 1 reel.
Marriage Bonds and Licenses, 1849-1869; 3 reels.
Marriage License Index, 1849-1969; 7 reels.
Marriage Licenses, 1870-1967; 78 reels.

Military and Pension Records

Militia Records, 1831-1861; 1 reel.

MISCELLANEOUS RECORDS

Appointment of Receivers, 1910-1940; 1 reel.
Assignments, Record of, 1894-1948; 2 reels.
Clerk's Minute Dockets, 1931-1940; 1 reel.
Inventories and Accounts of Receivers, 1930-1949; 1 reel.
Lunacy, Record of, 1899-1960; 4 reels.
Miscellaneous Index, 1849-1968; 2 reels.
Orders and Decrees, 1869-1952; 24 reels.
Persons Adjudged Mentally Disordered, Index to, 1899-1968; 1 reel.
Receiverships and Assignments, Index to, 1956-1960; 1 reel.
Special Proceedings, 1879-1935; 4 reels.
Special Proceedings, Cross Index to, 1849-1953; 1 reel.
Special Proceedings, Index to, Defendant, 1849-1953; 1 reel.
Special Proceedings, Index to, Plaintiff, 1849-1953; 1 reel.

SCHOOL RECORDS

Board of Graded Schools, Town of Winston, Minutes, 1883-1890; 1 reel.

TAX AND FISCAL RECORDS

Tax Scrolls, 1945-1955; 10 reels.

WILLS

Wills, Index to, Devisee, 1849-1969; 2 reels.
Wills, Index to, Devisor, 1849-1969; 1 reel.
Wills, Record of, 1842-1953; 15 reels.

FRANKLIN COUNTY

Established in 1779 from Bute County.

ORIGINAL RECORDS

BONDS

Bastardy Bonds and Records, 1784-1906; 2 Fibredex boxes.
Officials' Bonds, 1820-1898; 3 volumes, 2 Fibredex boxes.

COURT RECORDS

County Court of Pleas and Quarter Sessions
- Execution Dockets, 1785-1828, 1846-1858; 5 volumes.
- Minutes, 1785-1868; 23 volumes.
- State Dockets, 1786-1794, 1803-1868; 5 volumes.
- Trial and Appearance Dockets, 1798-1868; 15 volumes.

Superior Court
- Civil Action Papers, 1774-1932; 34 Fibredex boxes.
- Civil Action Papers Concerning Land, 1792-1934; 4 Fibredex boxes.
- Criminal Action Papers, 1779, 1784-1914; 9 Fibredex boxes.
- Equity Minutes, 1818-1863; 3 volumes.
- Equity Receipts, 1839-1856; 1 volume.
- Equity Trial Dockets, 1827-1868; 3 volumes.
- Execution Docket, 1850-1869, 1903-1915; 1 volume.
- Minutes, 1807-1836, 1846-1883; 6 volumes.
- State Dockets, 1818-1868; 2 volumes.
- Trial and Appearance Dockets, 1807-1868; 5 volumes.

ELECTION RECORDS

Election Records, 1810-1926; 4 Fibredex boxes.
Elections, Record of, 1897-1932; 3 volumes.

ESTATES RECORDS

Accounts, Record of, 1868-1901; 4 volumes.
Administrators' Bonds, 1866-1869, 1900-1913; 3 volumes.
Administrators, Executors, and Guardians, Record of, 1890-1893; 1 volume.
Appointment of Administrators, Executors, Guardians, and Masters, 1868-1902; 2 volumes.
Estates Records, 1781-1934; 88 Fibredex boxes.
Guardians' Bonds, 1866-1869, 1913-1914; 2 volumes.
Guardians' Records, 1793-1916; 4 Fibredex boxes.
Settlements, Record of, 1869-1901; 1 volume.

LAND RECORDS

Deeds, 1784-1925; 2 Fibredex boxes.
Deeds, Record of, 1797-1800; 2 volumes.
Deeds of Trust, 1820-1927; 1 Fibredex box.
Ejectments, 1804-1899; 1 Fibredex box.
Miscellaneous Land Records, 1793-1931; 1 Fibredex box.
Mortgage Deeds, 1870-1924; 1 Fibredex box.

MARRIAGE, DIVORCE, AND VITAL STATISTICS

Cohabitation Certificates, 1866; 1 volume.
Divorce Records, 1820-1928; 3 Fibredex boxes.
Marriage Bonds, 1789-1868; 10 Fibredex boxes.
Marriage Licenses and Certificates, Record of, 1851-1867; 1 volume.
Marriage Registers, 1872-1919; 3 volumes.

MILITARY AND PENSION RECORDS [*See* **MISCELLANEOUS RECORDS**]

MISCELLANEOUS RECORDS

Assignees, Receivers, and Trustees, Records of, 1844-1931; 1 Fibredex box.
Audit of County Claims, 1868-1879; 1 volume.
Board of Superintendents of Common Schools, Minutes, 1841-1864; 1 volume.
Committee of Finance, Minutes and Accounts, 1853-1868; 1 volume.
County Board of Education, Minutes, 1872-1882; 1 volume.
Court Martial Minutes, 1820-1852; 1 volume.
Incorporations, Record of, 1905-1924; 1 volume.
Insolvents, Homestead and Personal Property Exemptions, 1820-1900; 1 Fibredex box.
Louisburg Dispensary Records, 1897-1908; 3 Fibredex boxes.
Miscellaneous Records, 1784-1933; 4 Fibredex boxes.
Personal and Merchants' Accounts, 1788-1900; 1 Fibredex box.
Special Proceedings Dockets, 1868-1909; 2 volumes.

SCHOOL RECORDS [*See* **MISCELLANEOUS RECORDS**]

TAX AND FISCAL RECORDS

Assessment of Land and Slaves for Taxation, 1859-1868; 1 volume.
Poll Tax Register, 1902-1904; 1 volume.
Tax Lists, 1804-1836, 1855-1871; 5 volumes.
Tax Records, 1785-1898; 1 Fibredex box.

WILLS

Wills, 1787-1929; 8 Fibredex boxes.
Wills, Cross Index to, 1789-1945; 1 volume.

MICROFILM RECORDS

COURT RECORDS

County Court of Pleas and Quarter Sessions
  Minutes, 1785-1868; 7 reels.
Superior Court
  Minutes, 1884-1945; 5 reels.

ELECTION RECORDS

Elections, Record of, 1924-1932; 1 reel.

ESTATES RECORDS

Accounts, Record of, 1901-1964; 3 reels.
Administrators, Executors, and Guardians, Index to, 1872-1964; 1 reel.
Appointment of Administrators, 1920-1964; 4 reels.
Appointment of Administrators, Executors, and Guardians, 1902-1922; 1 reel.
Appointment of Executors, 1913-1964; 1 reel.
Appointment of Guardians, 1914-1964; 1 reel.
Dowers and Widows' Year's Support, Record of, 1925-1964; 1 reel.

Inheritance Tax Records, 1920-1964; 1 reel.
Settlements, Record of, 1898-1964; 3 reels.

Land Records

Deeds, Record of, 1779-1952; 101 reels.
Land Entries, 1778-1898; 2 reels.
Land Sold for Taxes, 1926-1933; 1 reel.
Real Estate Conveyances, Index to, Grantee, 1776-1949; 11 reels.
Real Estate Conveyances, Index to, Grantor, 1776-1949; 10 reels.
Sales by Trustees and Mortgagees, Record of, 1922-1964; 2 reels.
Taxes for Mortgagees, Record of, 1931-1932; 1 reel.

Marriage, Divorce, and Vital Statistics

Cohabitation Certificates, 1866; 1 reel.
Delayed Births, Index to, various years; 1 reel.
Marriage Bonds, 1779-1868; 5 reels.
Marriage Licenses, 1869-1961; 25 reels.
Marriage Registers, 1851-1995; 3 reels.
Vital Statistics, Index to Births, 1913-1960; 1 reel.
Vital Statistics, Index to Deaths, 1913-1977; 1 reel.

Military and Pension Records

Militia Court Martial Minutes, 1820-1852; 1 reel.

Miscellaneous Records

Inquisition of Lunacy, 1900-1964; 1 reel.
Orders and Decrees and Index, 1868-1968; 12 reels.
Owelty Docket, Special Proceedings, 1900-1963; 1 reel.
Special Proceedings, 1910-1964; 1 reel.

Officials, County

Board of County Commissioners, Minutes, 1868-1940; 4 reels.

School Records

Board of Superintendents of Common Schools, Minutes, 1841-1864; 1 reel.
County Board of Education, Minutes, 1885-1941; 1 reel.

Tax and Fiscal Records

Assessment of Real Property for Taxation, 1859-1868; 1 reel.
Lists of Taxables, 1804-1871; 3 reels.
Tax List, 1874; 1 reel.
Tax Maps, various years; 1 reel.
Tax Scrolls, 1915, 1925; 1 reel.

Wills

Original Wills, 1787-1838; 1 reel.
Wills, Index to, Devisee, 1785-1978; 1 reel.
Wills, Index to, Devisor, 1785-1978; 1 reel.
Wills, Record of, 1785-1964; 12 reels.

GASTON COUNTY

Established in 1846 from Lincoln County.
Courthouse fire of 1874 destroyed many court records.

ORIGINAL RECORDS

Bonds

- Bastardy Bonds and Records, 1849-1905; 1 volume, 2 Fibredex boxes.
- Officials' Bonds, Record of, 1868-1889; 1 volume.

Court Records

- County Court of Pleas and Quarter Sessions
  - Appearance Docket, 1847-1868; 1 volume.
  - Minutes, 1847-1860; 1 volume.
  - State Docket, 1847-1868; 1 volume.
- Superior Court
  - Civil Action Papers, 1850-1912; 16 Fibredex boxes.
  - Civil Action Papers Concerning Land, 1868-1912; 6 Fibredex boxes.
  - Civil Issues Dockets, 1870-1968; 14 volumes.
  - Civil Issues Dockets, Index to, 1913-1963; 3 volumes.
  - Criminal Action Papers, 1860-1910; 32 Fibredex boxes.
  - Equity Minutes, 1847-1868; 1 volume.
  - Execution Dockets, 1848-1876; 2 volumes.
  - Minutes, 1847-1885, 1897-1965; 39 volumes.
  - Minutes—Divorces, 1952-1965; 2 volumes.
  - Miscellaneous Court Records, 1870-1902; 1 Fibredex box.

Election Records

- Election Records, 1856-1888; 1 Fibredex box.
- Elections, Record of, 1880-1960; 4 volumes.
- Permanent Roll of Registered Voters, 1902-1908; 1 volume.

Estates Records

- Accounts, Record of, 1869-1942; 14 volumes.
- Administrators, Executors, and Guardians, Record of, 1901-1924; 3 volumes.
- Administrators, Index to, 1906-1936; 1 volume.
- Administrators, Record of, 1913-1941; 7 volumes.
- Appointment of Administrators, Executors, Guardians, and Masters, 1869-1901; 1 volume.
- Estates Records, 1839-1928; 60 Fibredex boxes. [*See also* **CRX Records**]
- Executors and Guardians, Record of, 1913-1936; 1 volume.
- Executors, Index to, 1910-1936; 1 volume.
- Executors, Record of, 1936-1953; 1 volume.
- Guardians, Index to, 1902-1936; 1 volume.
- Guardians, Record of, 1924-1968; 6 volumes.
- Guardians' Records, 1849-1933; 4 Fibredex boxes.
- Settlements, Record of, 1869-1941; 8 volumes.

Land Records

- Deeds, Cross Index to, 1847-1898; 5 volumes.
- Deeds of Sale and Miscellaneous Deeds, 1860-1944; 1 Fibredex box.

Probate, Record of, 1883-1885; 1 volume.
Sale and Resale of Land, Record of, 1919-1951; 7 volumes.

MARRIAGE, DIVORCE, AND VITAL STATISTICS [*See also* **COURT RECORDS**, Superior Court, Minutes]
Divorce Records, 1859-1910; 3 Fibredex boxes.
Maiden Names of Divorced Women, Record of, 1939-1969; 1 volume.
Marriage Certificates, Record of, 1865-1871; 1 manuscript box.
Marriage Registers, 1871-1905; 2 volumes.

MISCELLANEOUS RECORDS
Assignees, Receivers, and Trustees, Records of, 1869-1911; 2 Fibredex boxes.
Commissioners of Affidavits, Record of, 1875-1883; 1 volume.
Lunacy, Record of, 1899-1941; 3 volumes.
Miscellaneous Records, 1847-1910; 4 Fibredex boxes.
Orders and Decrees, 1869-1941; 14 volumes.
Railroad Records, 1872-1912; 3 Fibredex boxes.
Road and Bridge Records, 1859-1909; 1 Fibredex box.
School Records, 1855-1884; 2 Fibredex boxes.
Special Proceedings, 1848-1911; 33 Fibredex boxes.
Special Proceedings Dockets, 1883-1943; 3 volumes.

ROADS AND BRIDGES [*See* **MISCELLANEOUS RECORDS**]

SCHOOL RECORDS [*See* **MISCELLANEOUS RECORDS**]

TAX AND FISCAL RECORDS
Tax Lists, 1847-1868; 3 volumes.
Tax Records, 1851-1902; 1 Fibredex box.

WILLS
Wills, 1849-1924; 9 Fibredex boxes.

CRX RECORDS
Estates Records, 1914; 1 folder.

MICROFILM RECORDS

BONDS
Apprentice Bonds, 1869-1919; 1 reel.
Bastardy Bonds, 1869-1882; 1 reel.

CORPORATIONS AND PARTNERSHIPS
Incorporations, Record of, 1883-1945; 3 reels.

COURT RECORDS
County Court of Pleas and Quarter Sessions
Minutes, 1847-1860; 1 reel.
Superior Court
Civil Actions, Index to, Plaintiff, 1963-1968; 2 reels.
Equity Minutes, 1847-1868; 1 reel.
Judgments, Index to, 1873-1966; 1 reel.
Judgments, Index to, Defendant, 1920-1962; 4 reels.
Judgments, Index to, Plaintiff, 1920-1968; 5 reels.
Minutes, 1847-1968; 30 reels.

ELECTION RECORDS

Elections, Record of, 1890-1932; 1 reel.

ESTATES RECORDS

Accounts, Record of, 1869-1963; 11 reels.
Administrators' Bonds, 1868-1904; 1 reel.
Administrators, Executors, Guardians, and Trustees, Index to, 1963; 1 reel.
Administrators, Executors, Trustees, and Guardians, 1963; 2 reels.
Administrators, Record of, 1913-1963; Index to Administrators, 1925-1936; 8 reels.
Appointment of Administrators, Executors, and Guardians, 1901-1918; 1 reel.
Appointment of Executors and Guardians, 1913-1953; 1 reel.
Estates, Index to, 1963; 1 reel.
Estates, Record of, 1847-1869; 1 reel.
Executors, Index to, 1921-1936; 1 reel.
Executors, Record of, 1913-1961; 2 reels.
Guardians' Bonds, 1868-1908; 1 reel.
Guardians, Record of, 1925-1963; Index to Guardians, 1917-1933; 2 reels.
Inheritance Tax Records, 1923-1959; 1 reel.
Settlements, Record of, 1869-1963; 7 reels.

LAND RECORDS

Deeds and Mortgages, Index to, Grantee, 1846-1961; 16 reels.
Deeds and Mortgages, Index to, Grantor, 1846-1961; 13 reels.
Deeds, Record of, 1847-1953; 121 reels.
Plat Books, 1913-1964; 4 reels.
Processions, Record of, 1847-1886; 1 reel.
Resale of Land, Record of, 1919-1963; 5 reels.
State Grants, Record of, 1845-1891; 1 reel.

MARRIAGE, DIVORCE, AND VITAL STATISTICS

Births, Index to, 1913-1977; 5 reels.
Deaths, Index to, 1913-1962; 2 reels.
Delayed Births, Index to, various years; 1 reel.
Maiden Names of Divorced Women, 1939-1963; 1 reel.
Marriage Licenses, 1848-1963; 16 reels.
Marriage Registers, 1848-1991; 4 reels.

MISCELLANEOUS RECORDS

Orders and Decrees, 1869-1962; 12 reels.
Special Proceedings Dockets, 1883-1968; 4 reels.
Special Proceedings, Index to, 1963-1968; 2 reels.

OFFICIALS, COUNTY

Board of County Commissioners, Minutes, 1868-1955; 6 reels.

SCHOOL RECORDS

County Board of Education, Minutes, 1885-1964; 1 reel.

WILLS

Wills, Cross Index to, 1847-1963; 1 reel.
Wills, Record of, 1847-1963; 5 reels.

GATES COUNTY

Established in 1779 from Chowan, Hertford, and Perquimans counties.

ORIGINAL RECORDS

BONDS [*See also* **CRX RECORDS**]

Apprentice Bonds and Records, 1779-1911; 2 volumes, 2 Fibredex boxes.
Bastardy Bonds and Records, 1779-1910; 3 Fibredex boxes.
Constables' Bonds, 1834-1838, 1846-1861; 2 volumes.
Officials' Bonds and Records, 1779-1897; 7 Fibredex boxes.

COURT RECORDS

County Court of Pleas and Quarter Sessions
- Clerk's Fee Books, 1791-1807; 2 volumes.
- Execution Dockets, 1786-1860; 4 volumes, 2 manuscript boxes.
- Minutes, 1779-1868; 15 volumes.
- State Dockets, 1779-1854; 5 volumes. [*See also* Trial and Appearance Docket, 1857-1867]
- Trial and Appearance Dockets, 1779-1867; 9 volumes, 1 manuscript box.

County Criminal Court
- Minutes, 1931-1966; 4 volumes.

Recorder's Court
- Judgment Dockets, 1939-1966; 11 volumes.
- Judgments, Cross Index to, 1942-1966; 2 volumes.

Superior Court
- Civil Action Papers, 1768-1911; 36 Fibredex boxes.
- Civil Action Papers Concerning Land, 1780-1912; 6 Fibredex boxes.
- Civil Action Papers Concerning Timber, 1849-1911; 2 Fibredex boxes.
- Civil Issues Dockets, 1887-1968; 2 volumes. [*See also* Trial and Appearance Docket, 1859-1868]
- Criminal Action Papers, 1775-1912; 23 Fibredex boxes.
- Criminal Issues Docket, 1869-1919; 1 volume.
- Equity Execution Docket and Receipts in Equity, 1847-1878; 1 volume.
- Equity Minutes, 1808-1830, 1855-1868; 2 volumes.
- Equity Trial Docket, 1831-1867; 1 volume.
- Execution Dockets, 1814-1869; 4 volumes. [*See also* Trial and Appearance Docket, 1807-1813]
- Judgment Dockets, 1868-1966; 11 volumes. [*See also* **LAND RECORDS**]
- Judgments, Index to, 1868-1966; 4 volumes.
- Minutes, 1807-1966; 11 volumes.
- Parties to Actions, Cross Index to, 1961-1964; 1 volume.
- State Dockets, 1807-1860; 2 volumes.
- Summons Docket, 1934-1966; 1 volume.
- Trial and Appearance Dockets, 1807-1868; 4 volumes.

ELECTION RECORDS

Election Records, 1783-1882; 1 Fibredex box.
Elections, Record of, 1878-1974; 7 volumes.
Permanent Voter Registration, 1902-1908; 1 volume.

ESTATES RECORDS

Accounts, Record of, 1869-1966; 9 volumes.
Administrators' Bonds, 1812-1847, 1892-1914, 1934-1966; 7 volumes.
Administrators and Executors, Cross Index to, 1919-1934; 1 volume.
Administrators and Executors, Index to, no date; 4 volumes.
Estates, Record of, 1807-1868; 8 volumes.
Estates Records, 1765-1920; 134 Fibredex boxes.
Guardians' Accounts, 1808-1863; 6 volumes.
Guardians' Bonds, 1810-1904; 13 volumes.
Guardians, Cross Index to, 1910-1934; 1 volume.
Guardians, Index to, no date; 1 volume.
Guardians' Records, 1785-1915; 21 Fibredex boxes.
Inheritance Tax Record, 1960-1968; 1 volume.
Settlements, Record of, 1807-1966; 9 volumes.

LAND RECORDS

Deeds of Sale, 1788-1903; 2 Fibredex boxes.
Ejectments, 1795-1911; 2 Fibredex boxes.
Judgment Docket, Land Tax Sales, 1931-1954; 1 volume. [*See also* **COURT RECORDS**, Superior Court]
Land Divisions, 1810-1911; 1 Fibredex box.
Land Entries, 1811-1817, 1831-1833; 1 volume.
Land Registration, 1958-1959; 1 volume.
Land Sold by Mortgagees and Trustees, Record of, 1927-1970; 2 volumes.
Miscellaneous Deeds, 1776-1908; 1 Fibredex box.
Probate, Record of, 1868-1882; 3 volumes.

MARRIAGE, DIVORCE, AND VITAL STATISTICS

Divorce Records, 1817-1911; 1 Fibredex box.
Maiden Names of Divorced Women, Record of, 1945-1963; 1 volume.
Marriage Bonds, 1779-1868; 11 Fibredex boxes.
Marriage Certificates, Record of, 1851-1867; 1 volume.
Miscellaneous Marriage Records, 1784, 1821-1908; 1 Fibredex box.

MISCELLANEOUS RECORDS

Assignees, Receivers, and Trustees, Records of, 1796-1915; 4 Fibredex boxes.
Board of Superintendents of Common Schools, Minutes, 1841-1861; 1 volume.
Bridge Records, 1786-1910; 1 Fibredex box.
Claims Allowed by County Court, Record of, 1845-1868; 1 volume.
Clerk's Minute Docket, 1955-1966; 1 volume.
Drainage Record, 1930-1989; 2 volumes.
Inquisition of Lunacy, Record of, 1900-1966; 2 volumes.
Miscellaneous Records, 1780-1912; 5 Fibredex boxes.
Notaries and Justices, Record of, 1929-1965; 1 volume.
Officials' Oaths, Record of, 1938-2006; 1 volume.
Orders and Decrees, 1868-1966; 6 volumes.
Railroad Records, 1849-1912; 2 Fibredex boxes.
Road Records, 1779-1912; 2 Fibredex boxes.
Slave Records, 1783-1867; 3 Fibredex boxes.
Slaves to Work in Great Dismal Swamp, Register of, 1847-1861; 1 volume.
Special Proceedings, 1868-1966; 4 volumes.
Special Proceedings, Cross Index to, 1869-1963; 1 volume.

ROADS AND BRIDGES [*See* **MISCELLANEOUS RECORDS**]

SCHOOL RECORDS [*See* **MISCELLANEOUS RECORDS**]

TAX AND FISCAL RECORDS
Lists of Taxables, 1784-1868; 6 volumes.
Tax Lists, 1924, 1926, 1935; 3 volumes.

WILLS
Wills, 1762-1904; 12 Fibredex boxes.

CRX RECORDS
Bonds, 1773-1774, 1800; 2 folders.

MICROFILM RECORDS

BONDS
Apprentice Bonds, 1878-1917; 1 reel.

CORPORATIONS AND PARTNERSHIPS
Incorporations, Record of, 1866-1964; 1 reel.

COURT RECORDS
County Court of Pleas and Quarter Sessions
Minutes, 1779-1868; 4 reels.
Superior Court
Equity Minutes, 1808-1830, 1855-1868; Equity Minutes and Trial Docket, 1831-1867; 2 reels.
Minutes, 1807-1964; 5 reels.

ELECTION RECORDS
Elections, Record of, 1880-1964; 1 reel.

ESTATES RECORDS
Accounts, Record of, 1869-1964; 5 reels.
Administrators' Bonds, 1822-1847, 1870-1914; 2 reels.
Administrators and Executors, Cross Index to, 1868-1934; 1 reel.
Appointment of Administrators, Executors, and Guardians, 1868-1964; 2 reels.
Estates, Record of, 1806-1851; 3 reels.
Guardians' Accounts, 1808-1868; 2 reels.
Guardians' Accounts and Minutes of Probate Court, 1857-1888; 1 reel.
Guardians' Bonds, 1810-1904; 3 reels.
Guardians, Cross Index to, 1868-1944; 1 reel.
Guardians' Returns, 1828-1837; 1 reel.
Inheritance Tax Records, 1923-1964; 1 reel.
Inventories of Estates, 1819-1842; 1 reel.
Settlements, Record of, 1804-1841, 1867-1964; 4 reels.

LAND RECORDS
Deeds, Cross Index to, 1776-1910; 1 reel.
Deeds, Index to, Grantee, 1910-1964; 1 reel.
Deeds, Index to, Grantor, 1910-1964; 1 reel.
Deeds, Record of, 1776-1964; 51 reels.
Federal Tax Lien Index, 1950-1964; 1 reel.
Plats, 1928-1964; 1 reel.

Registration of Land Titles, 1923-1964; 1 reel.
Surveyors' Book, 1894-1922; 1 reel.

Marriage, Divorce, and Vital Statistics

Marriage Bonds, 1778-1868; 4 reels.
Marriage Licenses, 1886-1963; 5 reels.
Marriage Registers, 1867-1964; 2 reels.
Vital Statistics, Index to, 1913-1964; 1 reel.

Miscellaneous Records

Orders and Decrees, 1868-1964; 3 reels.
Registration of Slaves to Work in Great Dismal Swamp, 1847-1861; 1 reel.
Special Proceedings, 1910-1966; 1 reel.
Special Proceedings, Cross Index to, 1869-1964; 1 reel.

Officials, County

Board of County Commissioners, Minutes, 1887-1922; 1 reel.

School Records

County Board of Education, Minutes, 1885-1927; 1 reel.

Tax and Fiscal Records

Tax Lists, 1784-1868, 1874, 1890, 1897, 1900, 1924-1926, 1935; 6 reels.

Wills

Wills, Cross Index to, 1779-1964; 1 reel.
Wills, Record of, 1779-1964; 4 reels.

GRAHAM COUNTY

Established in 1872 from Cherokee County.

ORIGINAL RECORDS

BONDS

Bastardy Bonds, 1873-1893; 1 folder.
Officials' Bonds, 1871-1914; 1 Fibredex box.

COURT RECORDS [*See also* **CRX RECORDS**]

Superior Court

Civil Action Papers, 1864-1931; 2 Fibredex boxes.
Civil Action Papers Concerning Land, 1872-1928; 3 Fibredex boxes.
Civil Action Papers, Series II, 1874-1951; 29 Fibredex boxes.
Criminal Action Papers, 1874-1920; 1 Fibredex box.
Minutes, 1873-1908; 4 volumes.

ELECTION RECORDS

Elections, Record of, 1878-1938; 3 volumes.

ESTATES RECORDS

Administrators' Bonds, 1879-1887; 1 volume.
Estates Records, 1847-1930; 3 Fibredex boxes.
Guardians' Bonds, 1877-1898; 1 volume.

LAND RECORDS

Deeds, 1789-1921; 1 Fibredex box.
Deeds, Cross Index to, 1873-1933; 4 volumes.
Deeds, Record of, 1867-1924; 11 volumes.
Land Entry Books, 1872-1919; 2 volumes.

MARRIAGE, DIVORCE, AND VITAL STATISTICS

Marriage Register, 1873-1926; 1 volume.

MISCELLANEOUS RECORDS

Miscellaneous Records (including wills), 1836-1940; 3 Fibredex boxes.

TAX AND FISCAL RECORDS

Miscellaneous Tax Records, 1874-1921; 1 Fibredex box.

WILLS [*See* **MISCELLANEOUS RECORDS**]

CRX RECORDS

Civil Action Papers, 1879; 1 folder.

MICROFILM RECORDS

CORPORATIONS AND PARTNERSHIPS

Corporations, Record of, 1907-1970; 1 reel.
Partnerships, Record of, 1927-1928; 1 reel.

COURT RECORDS

Superior Court

Civil Files, Index to, 1873-1966; 1 reel.
Judgments, Index to, 1873-1966; 1 reel.

Judgments, Index to, Criminal, 1873-1966; 2 reels.
Minutes, 1873-1960; 5 reels.

ELECTION RECORDS

Elections, Record of, 1878-1966; 1 reel.

ESTATES RECORDS

Accounts, Record of, 1873-1966; 2 reels.
Administrators' Bonds, 1879-1966; 1 reel.
Guardians' Bonds, 1877-1898, 1910-1966; 1 reel.
Inheritance Tax Records, 1928-1966; 1 reel.
Settlements, Record of, 1886-1903, 1928-1961; 1 reel.

LAND RECORDS

Deeds, Index to, Grantee, 1873-1967; 3 reels.
Deeds, Index to, Grantor, 1873-1967; 3 reels.
Deeds, Record of, 1873-1966; 31 reels.
Land Entry Books, 1872-1961; 1 reel.
Land Sales for Taxes, 1929-1966; 3 reels.
Sales and Foreclosures, Record of, 1934-1944; 1 reel.
Sales by Mortgagees, Record of, 1934-1966; 1 reel.

MARRIAGE, DIVORCE, AND VITAL STATISTICS

Births, Index to, 1913-1979; 1 reel.
Deaths, Index to, 1913-1979; 1 reel.
Marriage Registers, 1873-1979; 2 reels..

MISCELLANEOUS RECORDS

Orders and Decrees, 1878-1951; 1 reel.
Special Proceedings, 1915-1953; 1 reel.

OFFICIALS, COUNTY

Board of County Commissioners, Minutes, 1873-1961; 4 reels.

WILLS

Wills, Record of, 1873-1966; 1 reel.

GRANVILLE COUNTY

Established in 1746 from Edgecombe County.

ORIGINAL RECORDS

BONDS

Apprentice Bonds and Records, 1749-1913; 1 volume, 6 Fibredex boxes.
Bastardy Bonds and Records, 1746-1910; 1 volume, 5 Fibredex boxes. [*See also* **MISCELLANEOUS RECORDS**, Record of Jurors, 1849-1863]
Constables' Bonds, 1781-1886; 3 Fibredex boxes.
Officials' Bonds, 1754-1898; 3 Fibredex boxes.
Ordinary Bonds, 1748-1838; 1 Fibredex box.
Sheriffs' Bonds, 1748-1887; 1 Fibredex box.

COURT RECORDS

County Court of Pleas and Quarter Sessions
- Appeal Docket, 1792-1807; 1 manuscript box.
- Clerk's Fee Books, 1764-1769, 1830-1857; 3 volumes.
- Clerk's Receipt Book, 1795-1796; 1 volume.
- Costs Docket, State Cases, 1859-1868; 1 volume.
- Execution Dockets, 1765-1867; 14 volumes.
- Levy Docket, 1795-1801, 1837-1838; 1 volume.
- Minutes, 1754-1868; 24 volumes.
- Minutes (Rough), 1867-1868; Minutes (Rough), Superior Court, 1868-1869; Record of Probate, 1868-1869; 1 volume.
- State Dockets, 1774-1868; 10 volumes.
- Trial and Appearance Dockets, 1853-1868; 3 volumes.
- Trial, Appearance, and Reference Dockets, 1753-1853; 26 volumes.
- Witness Ticket Books, 1814-1848; 2 volumes.

Inferior Court
- Costs Docket, 1878-1885; 1 volume.
- Criminal Issues Docket, 1878-1885; 1 volume.
- Minutes, 1877-1885; 1 volume.

Superior Court [*See also* **MISCELLANEOUS RECORDS**]
- Account Book, Clerk and Master in Equity, 1854-1874; 1 volume.
- Civil Action Papers, 1742-1916; 153 Fibredex boxes.
- Civil Action Papers Concerning Land, 1778-1913; 7 Fibredex boxes.
- Civil Issues Dockets, 1869-1882, 1887-1918; 5 volumes.
- Clerk's Fee Book, 1917-1923; 1 volume.
- Clerk's Receipt Book, 1832-1857, 1866-1867; Half Fee Docket, 1879-1886; 1 volume.
- Criminal Action Papers, 1746-1921; 63 Fibredex boxes.
- Criminal Issues Dockets, 1869-1907; 5 volumes.
- Equity Minutes, 1807-1867; 4 volumes.
- Equity Trial and Appearance Dockets, 1807-1868; 5 volumes.
- Execution Dockets, 1807-1813, 1854-1866; 2 volumes.
- Minutes, 1807-1900; 18 volumes.
- Receipt Books, Clerk and Master in Equity, 1844-1868; 3 volumes.
- State Dockets, 1812-1868; 4 volumes.

Transfer Docket, 1869-1879; 1 volume.
Trial, Appearance, and Reference Dockets, 1807-1847; 3 volumes.

ELECTION RECORDS

Election Records, 1790-1878; 3 Fibredex boxes.
Miscellaneous Election Records, 1817-1917; 1 Fibredex box.
Permanent Registration of Voters, 1902-1908; 1 volume.

ESTATES RECORDS [*See also* **CRX RECORDS**]

Accounts, Record of, 1869-1922; 9 volumes.
Administrators' Bonds, 1868-1891; 3 volumes.
Appointment of Administrators, Executors, and Guardians, Record of, 1898-1901; 1 volume.
Appointment of Guardians, Record of, 1791-1850, 1860-1868; 2 volumes.
Clerk's Receipt Books (Estates), 1899-1928; 3 volumes.
Clerk's Receiver Accounts, 1891-1928; 2 volumes.
Estates Records, 1746-1919, 1922; 200 Fibredex boxes.
Executors, Record of, 1868-1874, 1899-1921; 2 volumes.
Guardians' Accounts, 1810-1868; 8 volumes.
Guardians' Bonds, 1888-1897; 1 volume.
Guardians, Record of, 1899-1919; 1 volume.
Guardians' Records, 1758-1913, 1927; 25 Fibredex boxes.
Settlements, Record of, 1869-1875, 1881-1925; 5 volumes.

LAND RECORDS

Attachments, Executions, Levies, and Liens on Land, 1785-1918; 9 Fibredex boxes.
Bills of Sale, Mortgage Deeds, and Deeds of Trust, 1757-1912; 1 Fibredex box.
Deeds, 1742-1874; 4 Fibredex boxes.
Ejectments, 1788-1886; 5 Fibredex boxes.
Land Entries, 1778-1877; 3 volumes.
Miscellaneous Land Records, 1748-1914; 2 Fibredex boxes.
Probate Fee Books, 1886-1890, 1905-1910; 2 volumes.

MARRIAGE, DIVORCE, AND VITAL STATISTICS

Cohabitation, Record of, 1866-1867; 3 volumes.
Divorce Records, 1819-1895, 1914; 2 Fibredex boxes.
Marriage Bonds, 1758-1868; 17 Fibredex boxes.

MILITARY AND PENSION RECORDS [*See* **MISCELLANEOUS RECORDS**]

MISCELLANEOUS RECORDS

Alien Registration, 1940; 1 volume.
Attachments and Levies on Slaves, 1794-1863; 2 Fibredex boxes.
Bankruptcy Proceedings, 1804-1884; 1 Fibredex box.
Board of Justices of the Peace, Minutes, 1899-1904; 1 volume.
Bridge Records, 1748-1868; 1 Fibredex box.
Civil Action Papers Concerning Slaves and Free Persons of Color, 1754-1875; 4 Fibredex boxes.
Common School Register, 1860-1861; 1 volume.
Coroners' Inquests, 1755-1905, 1920; 2 Fibredex boxes.
Correspondence, 1759-1914; 1 Fibredex box.
County Accounts, Court Orders, and Memoranda, 1746-1908; 5 Fibredex boxes.
County Claims Allowed, 1829-1866; 2 volumes.

Criminal Action Papers Concerning Slaves and Free Persons of Color, 1764-1876; 6 Fibredex boxes.
Declaration of Intent (to Become a Citizen), 1909-1929; 1 volume.
Grand Jury Presentments and Reports, 1749-1901; 1 Fibredex box.
Homestead and Personal Property Exemptions, 1844-1908; 1 Fibredex box.
Insolvent Debtors, 1746-1871; 12 Fibredex boxes.
Jurors, Record of, 1849-1868; 2 volumes.
Jury Lists, 1746-1881; 1 Fibredex box.
Jury and Witness Tickets, 1757-1865; 2 Fibredex boxes.
Justices of the Peace, Record of, 1869-1904; 2 volumes.
Justices of the Peace Records, 1749-1886; 1 Fibredex box.
Lists of Schoolchildren, 1825-1878; 3 Fibredex boxes.
Lunacy, Record of, 1899-1930; 1 volume.
Lunacy Records, 1798-1913; 1 Fibredex box.
Mill Records, 1747-1865; 2 Fibredex boxes.
Miscellaneous Records, 1722, 1747-1920; 5 Fibredex boxes.
Miscellaneous Records of Slaves and Free Persons of Color, 1755-1871; 1 Fibredex box.
Miscellaneous School Records, 1804-1895; 2 Fibredex boxes.
Naturalization Certificates, 1915-1927; 1 volume.
Oaths of Allegiance, 1865; 1 volume.
Pensions, Record of, 1907-1931; 1 volume.
Personal and Merchants' Accounts, 1742-1906; 2 Fibredex boxes.
Petitions for Naturalization, 1913-1927; 1 volume.
Powers of Attorney, 1749-1877; 2 Fibredex boxes.
Public School Register, Oxford Graded School, 1893-1904; 1 volume.
Railroad Records, 1837-1891; 1 Fibredex box.
Road Records, 1747-1905; 7 Fibredex boxes.
Wardens of the Poor, 1787-1868; 1 Fibredex box.
Wardens of the Poor, County Home, and Outside Paupers List, 1851-1921; 3 volumes.

OFFICIALS, COUNTY [*See* **MISCELLANEOUS RECORDS**]

ROADS AND BRIDGES [*See* **MISCELLANEOUS RECORDS**]

SCHOOL RECORDS [*See* **MISCELLANEOUS RECORDS**]

TAX AND FISCAL RECORDS

Federal Direct Tax Collected, Record of, 1866; 1 volume.
Lists of Taxables, 1796-1864; 19 volumes.
Miscellaneous Tax Records, 1754-1886; 3 Fibredex boxes.
Poll Tax, Record of, 1902; 1 volume.
Taxables, 1747-1887; 9 Fibredex boxes.

WILLS

Wills, 1749-1968; 42 Fibredex boxes.

CRX RECORDS

Estate Settlement, 1828; 3 folders.
List of Tithables, 1758; 2 folders.

MICROFILM RECORDS

BONDS
- Apprentice Bonds, 1802-1913; 1 reel.
- Bastardy Bonds, 1869-1879; 1 reel.

CENSUS RECORDS
- State Census, Granville County, 1786; 1 reel.

CORPORATIONS AND PARTNERSHIPS
- Corporations, Record of, 1895-1961; 1 reel.
- Partnership Record Index, 1916-1971; 1 reel.

COURT RECORDS
- County Court of Pleas and Quarter Sessions
  - Minutes, 1746-1868; 12 reels.
- Superior Court
  - Civil Actions, Index to, 1968-1990; 1 reel.
  - Criminal Actions, Index to, 1968-1990; 1 reel.
  - Equity Minutes, 1807-1867; 2 reels.
  - Equity Minutes, Index to, 1852-1867; 1 reel.
  - Judgment Docket, 1868-1877; 1 reel.
  - Judgments, Index to, 1868-1968; 2 reels.
  - Minutes, 1807-1947; 12 reels.

ESTATES RECORDS
- Accounts, Record of, 1868-1968; 11 reels.
- Administrators' Bonds, 1868-1891; 1 reel.
- Administrators, Executors, and Guardians, Index to, 1896-1961; 1 reel.
- Appointment of Administrators, 1896-1968; 6 reels.
- Appointment of Administrators, Executors, Collectors, and Masters, 1888-1901; 1 reel.
- Appointment of Executors, 1868-1869, 1896-1933; 2 reels.
- Estates, Record of, 1810-1868; 2 reels.
- Guardians' Accounts, 1849-1864; 1 reel.
- Guardians' Bonds, 1790-1917; 1 reel.
- Guardians, Record of, 1899-1940; 2 reels.
- Inheritance Tax Records, 1923-1963; 2 reels.
- Settlements, Record of, 1868-1961; 9 reels.

LAND RECORDS
- Deeds, Index to, Grantee, 1746-1947; 3 reels.
- Deeds, Index to, Grantor, 1746-1947; 3 reels.
- Deeds, Record of, 1746-1946; 76 reels.
- Federal Tax Liens, Index to, 1925-1969; 1 reel.
- Land Entries, 1778-1904; 2 reels.
- Sale and Resale of Land by Mortgagees and Trustees, Record of, 1920-1948; 2 reels.

MARRIAGE, DIVORCE, AND VITAL STATISTICS
- Delayed Births, Index to, various years; 1 reel.
- Marriage Bonds, 1753-1868; 5 reels.
- Marriage Bonds, Index to, 1753-1868; 1 reel.
- Marriage Certificates, 1851-1868; 1 reel.
- Marriage Registers, 1867-1961; 2 reels.
- Marriages of Freed People, 1866-1867; 1 reel.

Vital Statistics, Index to, Births, 1914-1961; 1 reel.
Vital Statistics, Index to, Deaths, 1913-1977; 2 reels.

MISCELLANEOUS RECORDS

Special Proceedings, 1868-1925; 6 reels.
Special Proceedings, Cross Index to, 1868-1961; 1 reel.
Special Proceedings and Orders and Decrees, 1960-1961; 1 reel.

OFFICIALS, COUNTY

Board of County Commissioners, Minutes, 1868-1925; 6 reels.

SCHOOL RECORDS

Board of Superintendents of Common Schools, Minutes, 1842-1865; 1 reel.
County Board of Education, Minutes, 1885-1975; 2 reels.
Oxford Graded School Board of Trustees, Minutes, 1903-1959; 1 reel.

TAX AND FISCAL RECORDS

Tax Lists, 1755-1902, 1915, 1925, 1935, 1945, 1955; 16 reels.

WILLS

Unrecorded Wills, 1749-1771; 1 reel.
Wills, Cross Index to, 1762-1971; 2 reels.
Wills (Original), 1749-1968; 11 reels.
Wills, Record of, 1772-1968; 19 reels.

GREENE COUNTY

Established in 1791 as Glasgow County from Dobbs County.
Name changed to Greene in 1799.
Courthouse fire of 1876 destroyed many court records and all land records.

ORIGINAL RECORDS

BONDS

Apprentice Bonds, 1869-1888, 1911-1912; 2 volumes.
Magistrates' Bonds, 1910-1938; 1 volume.
Officials' Bonds and Records, 1874-1933; 2 Fibredex boxes.

COURT RECORDS

County Court
- Criminal Issues Docket, 1916-1926; 1 volume.

County Court of Pleas and Quarter Sessions
- Execution Docket, 1861-1862, 1866-1868; 1 volume.
- Trial Docket, 1867-1868; 1 volume.

Inferior Court
- Criminal Issues Docket, 1877-1883; 1 volume.
- Minutes, 1877-1884; 1 volume.

Superior Court
- Civil Action Papers, 1868-1959; 16 Fibredex boxes.
- Civil Action Papers Concerning Land, 1871-1967; 22 Fibredex boxes.
- Clerk's Receipt Book, 1868-1871; 1 volume.
- Criminal Issues Docket, 1909-1926; 1 volume.
- Judgment Dockets, 1868-1931, 1936; 11 volumes.
- Minutes, 1869-1968; 13 volumes.

ELECTION RECORDS

Elections, Record of, 1878-1968; 6 volumes.
Permanent Registration of Voters, 1902-1908; 1 volume.

ESTATES RECORDS

Accounts, Record of, 1869-1905; 2 volumes.
Amounts Paid for Indigent Children, Record of, 1912-1913; 1 volume.
Appointment of Administrators, Executors, Guardians, and Masters, 1869-1871, 1891-1918; 1 volume.
Appointment of Receivers and Receivers' Accounts, 1906-1934; 3 volumes.
Estates, Record of, 1839-1845; 1 volume.
Estates Records, 1809-1967; 68 Fibredex boxes.
Guardians' Bonds, 1857-1918; 4 volumes.
Guardians' Records, 1860-1947; 9 Fibredex boxes.
Inheritance Tax Records, 1916-1968; 3 volumes.
Qualification of Trustees under Wills, 1962-1968; 1 volume.
Renounced Estates, Cross Index to, 1965-1968; 1 volume.
Settlements, Record of, 1869-1908; 1 volume.

LAND RECORDS [*See also* CRX RECORDS]

Attachments, Executions, Levies, and Liens on Land, 1876-1969; 3 Fibredex boxes.
Deeds, 1857-1926; 2 Fibredex boxes.
Land Entries, 1906-1913; 1 volume.

Miscellaneous Land Records, 1880-1958; 1 Fibredex box.
Mortgage Deeds, 1875-1927; 1 Fibredex box.
Sales and Resales, Record of, 1921-1968; 2 volumes.
Tax Liens on Land, 1892-1943; 2 Fibredex boxes.

MARRIAGE, DIVORCE, AND VITAL STATISTICS
Divorce Records, 1875-1959; 23 Fibredex boxes.
Marriage Registers, 1875-1958; 6 volumes.

MISCELLANEOUS RECORDS
Alien Registration, 1927, 1940; 1 volume.
Assignees, Receivers, and Trustees, Records of, 1872-1947; 6 Fibredex boxes.
Bankruptcy Proceedings, 1879-1943; 1 Fibredex box.
Homestead and Personal Property Exemptions, 1881-1966; 1 Fibredex box.
Licenses to Trades, Registry of, 1875-1899; 1 volume.
Lunacy, Record of, 1906-1968; 2 volumes.
Miscellaneous Records, 1802-1956; 5 Fibredex boxes.
Railroad Records, 1874-1942; 3 Fibredex boxes.
Road Records, 1874-1940; 1 Fibredex box.
Special Proceedings Docket, 1871-1918; 1 volume.

ROADS AND BRIDGES [*See* **MISCELLANEOUS RECORDS**]

TAX AND FISCAL RECORDS
Tax Records, 1875-1894; 1 Fibredex box.

WILLS
Wills, 1842-1972; 17 Fibredex boxes. [*See also* **CRX RECORDS**]
Wills, Cross Index to, 1869-1935; 1 volume.

CRX RECORDS
Deed of Trust, 1848; 1 folder.
Wills, 1800-1835; 3 folders.

MICROFILM RECORDS

BONDS
Apprentice Bonds, 1869-1888; 1 reel.
Officials' Bonds, Record of, 1860-1937; 1 reel.

CORPORATIONS AND PARTNERSHIPS
Incorporations, Record of, 1915-1966; 1 reel.
Partnerships, Record of, 1917-1936; 1 reel.

COURT RECORDS
Superior Court
Minutes, 1869-1963; 6 reels.
Minutes, Index to, Defendant, 1875-1966; 2 reels.
Minutes, Index to, Plaintiff, 1875-1966; 1 reel.

ELECTION RECORDS
Elections, Record of, 1878-1966; 1 reel.

ESTATES RECORDS
Accounts and Inventories, Record of, 1924-1956; 4 reels.
Accounts, Record of, 1868-1923; 3 reels.

Administrators and Executors, Cross Index to, 1869-1920; 1 reel.
Administrators, Executors, and Guardians, Record of, 1918-1926; 1 reel.
Administrators, Record of, 1921-1964; 2 reels.
Amounts Paid for Indigent Children, Record of, 1912-1913; 1 reel.
Appointment and Accounts of Receivers of Estates, 1905-1934; 1 reel.
Appointment of Executors, 1869-1918; 1 reel.
Estates, Record of, 1839-1845; 1 reel.
Executors, Record of, 1942-1967; 1 reel.
Guardians' Bonds, 1869-1918; 1 reel.
Guardians, Cross Index to, 1872-1917; 1 reel.
Guardians, Record of, 1926-1966; 1 reel.
Inheritance Tax Records, 1923-1967; 1 reel.
Qualifications, Inventories, Accounts, and Wards, 1869-1966; 1 reel.
Settlements, Record of, 1869-1952; 3 reels.

LAND RECORDS

Deeds, Record of, 1861-1960; 23 reels.
Deeds of Trust, 1875-1965; 40 reels.
Real Estate Conveyances, Index to, Grantee, 1875-1966; 3 reels.
Real Estate Conveyances, Index to, Grantor, 1875-1966; 3 reels.
Sale and Resale, Record of, 1921-1966; 1 reel.

MARRIAGE, DIVORCE, AND VITAL STATISTICS

Births, Index to, 1913-1981; 2 reels.
Deaths, Index to, 1913-1966; 1 reel.
Delayed Births, Index to, 1880-1966; 1 reel.
Marriage Licenses, 1870-1999; 7 reels.
Marriages, Index to, 1876-1982; 2 reels.

MISCELLANEOUS RECORDS

Orders and Decrees, 1869-1948; 8 reels.
Special Proceedings, 1871-1894; 1 reel.
Special Proceedings, Cross Index to, 1868-1967; 1 reel.
Special Proceedings, Index to, Defendant, 1875-1967; 1 reel.
Special Proceedings, Index to, Plaintiff, 1875-1967; 1 reel.

OFFICIALS, COUNTY

Board of County Commissioners, Minutes, 1875-1931; 5 reels.

SCHOOL RECORDS

County Board of Education, Minutes, 1911-1967; 1 reel.

TAX AND FISCAL RECORDS

Tax Lists, 1881-1908, 1917-1924, 1935-1955; 2 reels.

WILLS

Wills, Index to, 1868-1966; 1 reel.
Wills, Record of, 1868-1966; 3 reels.

GUILFORD COUNTY

Established in 1771 from Orange and Rowan counties.
Courthouse fire of 1872 resulted in slight loss of records.

ORIGINAL RECORDS

BONDS

Apprentice Bonds and Records, 1817-1922; 3 volumes, 4 Fibredex boxes.
Bastardy Bonds and Records, 1779, 1816-1877, 1923; 3 Fibredex boxes.
Officials' Bonds, 1774-1892; 4 Fibredex boxes.

CORPORATIONS AND PARTNERSHIPS [*See* **MISCELLANEOUS RECORDS**]

COURT RECORDS

County Court of Pleas and Quarter Sessions
- Execution Dockets, 1813-1868; 12 volumes.
- Minutes, 1781-1868; 18 volumes, 2 manuscript boxes.
- State Dockets, 1811-1868; 7 volumes.
- Trial and Appearance Dockets, 1817-1868; 9 volumes.
- Trial Dockets, 1779-1817; 4 volumes.

Superior Court
- Civil Action Papers, 1774-1930; 9 Fibredex boxes.
- Civil Action Papers Concerning Land, 1817-1935; 8 Fibredex boxes.
- Civil Action Papers Concerning Mines, 1845-1892; 1 Fibredex box.
- Clerk's Fee Dockets, 1853-1860; 2 volumes.
- Clerk's Receipt Docket, 1886-1890; 1 volume.
- Equity Execution Docket, 1858-1868; 1 volume.
- Equity Minutes, 1826-1867; 2 volumes.
- Equity Trial and Appearance Docket, 1822-1824; 1 volume.
- Equity Trial Dockets, 1833-1868; 2 volumes.
- Execution Dockets, 1858-1887; 2 volumes.
- Minutes, 1850-1924; 21 volumes.
- State Docket, 1855-1868; 1 volume.
- Supplementary Proceedings, 1894-1899; 1 volume.
- Trial and Appearance Dockets, 1852-1869; 3 volumes.

ELECTION RECORDS

Election Returns, 1841-1918; 5 Fibredex boxes.
Elections, Record of, 1880-1922; 3 volumes.

ESTATES RECORDS

Accounts, Record of, 1869-1903; 7 volumes.
Administrators' Bonds, 1871-1899; 6 volumes.
Appointment of Administrators, Executors, and Guardians, 1890-1897; 1 volume.
Appointment of Administrators, Executors, Guardians, and Masters, 1868-1890; 1 volume.
Clerk's Receipt Book (Estates), 1890-1930; 1 volume.
Dowers, Record of, 1887-1897; 1 volume.
Estates, Record of, 1816-1868; 17 volumes.
Estates Records, 1778-1942; 275 Fibredex boxes. [*See also* **CRX RECORDS**]

Guardian Summons Docket, 1828-1850; 1 volume. [*See also* **COURT RECORDS**, Court of Pleas and Quarter Sessions, Trial Docket, 1817-1822]
Guardians' Accounts, 1821-1868, 1879-1897; 8 volumes.
Guardians' Bonds, 1871-1899; 4 volumes.
Guardians' Records, 1775-1933; 31 Fibredex boxes.
Probate Fee Docket, 1868-1869, 1880-1890; 1 volume.
Settlements, Record of, 1816-1862, 1869-1898; 9 volumes.
Widows' Year's Support, Record of, 1886-1921; 1 volume.

LAND RECORDS

Deeds, 1785-1930; 16 Fibredex boxes. [*See also* **CRX RECORDS**]
Deeds Proved, Record of, 1853-1872; 1 volume.
Deeds of Trust and Mortgage Deeds, 1816-1926; 6 Fibredex boxes.
Ejectments, 1808-1908; 5 Fibredex boxes.
Land Condemnations, 1909-1937; 3 Fibredex boxes.
Land Divisions, Partitions, and Surveys, 1825-1939; 9 Fibredex boxes.
Land Foreclosures and Mortgage Sales, 1873-1931; 15 Fibredex boxes.
Miscellaneous Land Records, 1784-1959; 2 Fibredex boxes.

MARRIAGE, DIVORCE, AND VITAL STATISTICS [*See also* **CRX RECORDS**]

Divorce Records, 1820-1929; 7 Fibredex boxes.
Maiden Names of Divorced Women, 1937-1969; 1 volume.
Marriage Bonds, 1770-1868; 21 Fibredex boxes.
Marriage Certificates, Record of, 1853-1867; Record of Cohabitation, 1866-1867; 1 volume.
Marriage Registers (Colored), 1867-1937; 3 volumes.
Marriage Registers (White), 1867-1937; 7 volumes.

MILITARY AND PENSION RECORDS [*See* **MISCELLANEOUS RECORDS; CRX RECORDS**]

MISCELLANEOUS RECORDS

Alien Registration, 1927, 1935, 1940-1941; 2 volumes.
Assignees, Trustees, and Receivers, Records of, 1867-1935; 2 Fibredex boxes.
Confederate Pension Records, 1890-1972; 4 Fibredex boxes.
County Board of Education, Minutes, 1872-1899; 1 volume.
Court Martial Minutes, 1806-1852; 1 volume.
Homestead and Personal Property Exemptions, 1869-1931; 1 Fibredex box.
Incorporations, Record of, 1885-1896; 1 volume.
Insolvent Debtors, 1846-1868; 3 Fibredex boxes.
Lunacy Records, 1826-1930; 2 Fibredex boxes.
Miscellaneous Records, 1771-1934; 5 Fibredex boxes.
Orders and Decrees, 1869-1901; 3 volumes.
Powers of Attorney, 1805-1929; 1 Fibredex box.
Road and Bridge Records, 1799-1890; 3 Fibredex boxes.
Road Dockets, 1824-1827, 1832-1869; 4 volumes.
School Records, 1853-1929; 2 Fibredex boxes.
Slaves and Free Persons of Color, Records of, 1781-1864; 1 Fibredex box.
Special Proceedings Dockets, 1871-1900; 2 volumes.
Wardens of the Poor, Minutes, 1838-1868; 1 volume.

ROADS AND BRIDGES [*See* **MISCELLANEOUS RECORDS**]

SCHOOL RECORDS [*See* **MISCELLANEOUS RECORDS**]

WILLS

Wills, 1771-1968; 228 Fibredex boxes. [*See also* **CRX RECORDS**]
Wills, Cross Index to, 1771-1934; 3 volumes.

CRX RECORDS

Deeds, 1835, 1873; 2 folders.
Estates Records, 1873-1874; 2 folders.
Marriage License, 1846; 1 folder.
Petitions to be Exempted from Military Service, 1862-1865; 2 folders.
Will, 1891; 1 folder.

MICROFILM RECORDS

BONDS

Apprentice Bonds, 1871-1922; 1 reel.

CORPORATIONS AND PARTNERSHIPS

Incorporations, Index to, 1885-1970; 1 reel.
Incorporations, Record of, 1886-1962; 37 reels.

COURT RECORDS

County Court of Pleas and Quarter Sessions
  Minutes, 1781-1868; 8 reels.
Superior Court
  Civil Actions, Index to, Defendant, 1900-1962; 3 reels.
  Civil Actions, Index to, Plaintiff, 1900-1968; 4 reels.
  Criminal Actions, Index to, 1900-1967; 3 reels.
  Equity Minutes, 1826-1867; 1 reel.
  Judgment Docket, 1930-1933; 1 reel.
  Judgments, Index to, Defendant, 1925-1968; 6 reels.
  Judgments, Index to, Plaintiff, 1925-1968; 6 reels.
  Minutes, 1850-1932; 15 reels.
  Minutes, Civil, 1932-1952, 1959-1964; 7 reels.
  Minutes, Criminal, 1932-1969; 8 reels.

ELECTION RECORDS

Board of Elections, Minutes, 1948-1969; 1 reel.
Elections, Record of, 1880-1968; 1 reel.

ESTATES RECORDS

Accounts and Final Settlements (Wachovia and Security National Banks),
  Record of, 1940-1962; 26 reels.
Accounts, Record of, 1879-1962; 27 reels.
Accounts and Settlements, Record of, 1857-1863, 1889-1893, 1939-1942; 2 reels.
Administrators' Bonds, 1871-1899; 1 reel.
Administrators' Bonds, Index to, 1871-1899; 1 reel.
Administrators, Executors, and Guardians, Record of, 1868-1908; 3 reels.
Administrators' and Guardians' Bonds, Record of, 1935-1969; 5 reels.
Annual Accounts of Administrators, Executors, and Trustees, 1887-1903; 1 reel.
Appointment of Administrators, 1899-1968; 23 reels.
Appointment of Administrators, Executors, and Guardians, 1966-1968; 1 reel.

Appointment of Executors, 1957-1968; 2 reels.
Appointment of Guardians, 1899-1968; 7 reels.
Dowers, Record of, 1887-1891; 1 reel.
Estates, Index to, 1818-1970; 5 reels.
Estates, Record of, 1820-1879, 1886-1932; 13 reels.
Executors, Record of, 1844-1848, 1868-1887, 1915-1968; 6 reels.
Guardians' Bonds, 1871-1899; 1 reel.
Guardians' Docket, 1821-1868; 1 reel.
Guardians, Record of, 1821-1849, 1864-1866, 1914-1926; 4 reels.
Inheritance Tax Records, 1912-1968; 7 reels.
Inheritance Tax Records, General Index to, 1912-1970; 1 reel.
Qualifications of Trustees Under Wills, 1934-1968; 1 reel.
Renunciations and Disclaimers, Index to, 1961-1968; 1 reel.
Settlements, Record of, 1820-1825, 1836-1862, 1869-1888, 1898-1962; 17 reels.
Widows' Year's Support, Record of, 1886-1962; 2 reels.

LAND RECORDS

Deeds, Record of, 1771-1957; 386 reels.
Land Divisions, 1873-1893, 1921-1930; 1 reel.
Land Entries, 1779-1795; 1 reel.
Maps, Hamilton Lakes, 1926; 1 reel.
Plat Books, 1895-1954; 5 reels.
Plats, Index to, 1853-1984; 1 reel.
Real Estate Conveyances, Index to, Grantee, 1771-1951; 12 reels.
Real Estate Conveyances, Index to, Grantor, 1771-1951; 13 reels.

MARRIAGE, DIVORCE, AND VITAL STATISTICS

Births, Index to, 1913-1981; 10 reels.
Deaths, Index to, 1913-1980; 5 reels.
Delayed Births, Index to, various years; 1 reel.
Maiden Names of Divorced Women, 1937-1969; 1 reel.
Marriage Bond Abstracts, 1770-1868; 1 reel.
Marriage Bonds, 1770-1868; 6 reels.
Marriage Licenses (Black), 1871-1961; 15 reels.
Marriage Licenses (White), 1871-1961; 56 reels.
Marriage Registers (Black), 1867-1970; 2 reels.
Marriage Registers (White), 1867-1970; 4 reels.
Marriage Registers (White and Black), 1971-1981; 3 reels.
Marriages, Record of, 1853-1867; 1 reel.
Non-Jury Divorce Judgments, 1966-1967; 1 reel.

MILITARY AND PENSION RECORDS

Court Martial Proceedings, Record of, 1806-1852; 1 reel.

MISCELLANEOUS RECORDS

Accounts of Receivers, 1911-1931; 1 reel.
Appointment of Receivers of Judgment Debtors, 1894-1899; 1 reel.
Commissioners' Bonds in Special Proceedings, 1940-1954; 1 reel.
Final Reports of Receivers, 1933-1949; 1 reel.
Inquisition of Inebriety, 1938-1958; 1 reel.
Inventories, Reports, and Accounts of Receivership, 1950-1962; 1 reel.

Liquidations (N.C. Bank and Trust Company and United Bank and Trust Company), Index to, 1930-1946; 1 reel.
Lunacy and Inebriety, Index to, 1908-1968; 1 reel.
Lunacy, Record of, 1899-1946; 3 reels.
Orders and Decrees, 1869-1962; 38 reels.
Special Proceedings Dockets, 1884-1968; 6 reels.
Special Proceedings and Orders and Decrees, Index to, 1869-1968; 5 reels.
Wardens of the Poor, Minutes, 1838-1868; 1 reel.

OFFICIALS, COUNTY

Board of County Commissioners, Index to Minutes, 1899-1966; 1 reel.
Board of County Commissioners, Minutes, 1868-1970; 15 reels.
Oaths, Index to, 1968-1981; 1 reel.
Officials' Oaths, 1936-1962; 1 reel.

ROADS AND BRIDGES

Road Dockets, 1824-1869; 2 reels.
Road Overseers, 1832-1937; 1 reel.

SCHOOL RECORDS

County Board of Education, Minutes, 1872-1965; 3 reels.

WILLS

Wills, Index to, 1771-1969; 4 reels.
Wills, Record of, 1779-1963; 24 reels.

HALIFAX COUNTY

Established in 1758 (effective 1759) from Edgecombe County.
Many court records are missing; reason unknown.
Land records of Edgecombe County and Bertie Precinct are included in the Record of Deeds series.

ORIGINAL RECORDS

BONDS

Bastardy Bonds and Records, 1858-1899; 1 Fibredex box.
Officials' Bonds and Records, 1820-1913; 1 Fibredex box.

CORPORATIONS AND PARTNERSHIPS [*See* **MISCELLANEOUS RECORDS**]

COURT RECORDS

Circuit Criminal Court
- Minutes, 1899-1901; 1 volume.

County Court of Pleas and Quarter Sessions
- Crown Docket, 1759-1770; 1 volume.
- Execution Dockets, 1836-1840, 1848-1868; 4 volumes.
- Minutes, 1784-1787, 1796-1802, 1822-1868; 9 volumes.
- Trial and Appearance Dockets, 1766-1770, 1837-1868; 6 volumes.

Superior Court
- Civil Action Papers, 1765-1829, 1860-1922; 41 Fibredex boxes.
- Civil Action Papers Concerning Land, 1868-1922; 25 Fibredex boxes.
- Criminal Action Papers, 1844-1898; 1 Fibredex box.
- Equity Minutes, 1822-1851; 1 volume.
- Execution Docket, 1846-1869; Land Entries, 1844-1859; 1 volume.
- Minutes, 1868-1902; 17 volumes.
- State Docket, 1848-1868; 1 volume.
- Trial and Appearance Docket, 1846-1866; 1 volume.

ELECTION RECORDS

Elections, Record of, 1878-1922; 2 volumes.

ESTATES RECORDS

Accounts, Record of, 1868-1898; 7 volumes.
Estates, Record of, 1773-1779, 1828-1862; 6 volumes.
Estates Records, 1762-1924; 108 Fibredex boxes. [*See also* **CRX RECORDS**]
Guardians' Records, 1808-1922; 12 Fibredex boxes.
Settlements, Record of, 1870-1900; 3 volumes.

LAND RECORDS

Attachments, Executions, Levies, and Liens on Land, 1867-1917; 1 Fibredex box.
Deeds and Bills of Sale, 1729-1855; 4 manuscript boxes.
Deeds, Cross Index to, 1732-1893; 9 volumes.
Deeds, Record of, 1758-1856; 10 volumes, 1 manuscript box.
Land Entries, 1844-1859. [*See* **COURT RECORDS**, Superior Court, Execution Docket]
Miscellaneous Land Records, 1761-1917; 1 Fibredex box.
Petitions to Divide and Sell Land, 1872-1922; 4 Fibredex boxes.
Probate, Record of, 1869-1873; 1 volume.

MARRIAGE, DIVORCE, AND VITAL STATISTICS
- Divorce Records, 1870-1922; 16 Fibredex boxes.
- Marriage Bonds, 1770-1868; 10 Fibredex boxes.
- Marriage Register, 1872-1895; 1 volume.

MISCELLANEOUS RECORDS
- Assignees, Receivers, and Trustees, Records of, 1868-1920; 6 Fibredex boxes.
- County Accounts, 1826-1851; 1 volume.
- Homestead and Personal Property Exemptions, 1869-1911; 1 Fibredex box.
- Incorporation Records, 1889-1894; 1 Fibredex box.
- Miscellaneous Records, 1761-1927; 6 Fibredex boxes.
- Naturalization Record, 1916-1925; 1 volume.
- Railroad Records, 1868-1921; 7 Fibredex boxes.
- Roanoke Navigation and Water Power Company Records, 1818-1913; 2 Fibredex boxes.

ROADS AND BRIDGES [*See* **MISCELLANEOUS RECORDS**]

SCHOOL RECORDS [*See* **CRX RECORDS**]

TAX AND FISCAL RECORDS
- Lists of Taxables, 1784-1863; 2 volumes, 1 manuscript box.

WILLS
- Wills, 1772-1916; 12 Fibredex boxes.
- Wills, Cross Index to, 1759-1963; 3 volumes.
- Wills, Record of, 1759-1779; 2 volumes.

CRX RECORDS
- Estates Record, 1838; 1 folder.
- School Records, 1839-1865; 3 Fibredex boxes.

MICROFILM RECORDS

CORPORATIONS AND PARTNERSHIPS
- Corporations, Record of, 1887-1947; 1 reel.

COURT RECORDS
- Circuit Criminal Court
  - Minutes, 1899-1901; 1 reel.
- County Court of Pleas and Quarter Sessions
  - Minutes, 1784-1787, 1796-1802, 1822-1824, 1832-1868; 4 reels.
- Superior Court
  - Equity Minutes, 1822-1851; 1 reel.
  - Minutes, 1868-1940; 17 reels.
  - Trial and Appearance Docket, 1846-1866; 1 reel.

ELECTION RECORDS
- Elections, Record of, 1878-1968; 3 reels.

ESTATES RECORDS
- Accounts, Record of, 1868-1954; 9 reels.
- Administrators, Executors, and Guardians, Index to, 1934-1968; 1 reel.
- Administrators, Record of, 1903-1946; 3 reels.
- Appointment of Administrators, Executors, and Guardians, 1868-1909; 1 reel.
- Estates, Record of, 1828-1862; 3 reels.

Executors, Record of, 1903-1963; 1 reel.
Guardians, Record of, 1904-1950; 1 reel.
Inheritance Tax Records, 1920-1963; 1 reel.
Inventories, Record of, 1773-1779, 1931-1950; 2 reels.
Qualification of Trustees under Wills, 1962; 1 reel.
Settlements, Record of, 1867-1950; 5 reels.

LAND RECORDS

Deeds and Mortgages, Index to, Grantee, 1732-1934; 7 reels.
Deeds and Mortgages, Index to, Grantor, 1732-1934; 7 reels.
Deeds, Record of, 1732-1934; 123 reels.
Resale of Land by Trustees, Record of, 1913-1940; 2 reels.

MARRIAGE, DIVORCE, AND VITAL STATISTICS

Births, Index to, 1913-1981; 4 reels.
Deaths, Index to, 1913-1981; 3 reels.
Delayed Births, Index to, various years; 1 reel.
Maiden Names of Divorced Women, 1938-1963; 1 reel.
Marriage Bonds, 1758-1868; 2 reels.
Marriage Registers, 1867-1974; 6 reels.
Marriage Registers, Index to, 1867-1962; 2 reels.
Marriages, Record of, 1851-1903; 1 reel.

MISCELLANEOUS RECORDS

Miscellaneous Records, Index to, 1968-1981; 1 reel.
Orders and Decrees, 1932-1938; 1 reel.
Special Proceedings, 1868-1947; 7 reels.
Special Proceedings, Cross Index to, 1868-1963, 1968-1981; 2 reels.

OFFICIALS, COUNTY

Board of County Commissioners, Minutes, 1873-1921; 4 reels.

SCHOOL RECORDS

County Board of Education, Minutes, 1909-1951; 1 reel.

TAX AND FISCAL RECORDS

Lists of Taxables, 1784-1834; 1 reel.
Tax Scrolls, 1915, 1925, 1935; 2 reels.

WILLS

Wills, Index to, 1759-1968; 4 reels.
Wills, Record of, 1758-1968; 7 reels.

HARNETT COUNTY

Established in 1855 from Cumberland County.
Courthouse fires of 1892 and 1894 destroyed court records and many of the land records.

ORIGINAL RECORDS

BONDS

Officials' Bonds, 1893-1918; 1 volume.

COURT RECORDS

Superior Court

Civil Action Papers, 1880-1907; 21 Fibredex boxes. [*See also* **CRX RECORDS**]

ELECTION RECORDS

Elections, Record of, 1896-1932; 4 volumes.

ESTATES RECORDS

Amounts Paid for Indigent Children, 1929-1948; 1 volume.
Appointment of Administrators, Executors, and Guardians, 1892-1908; 1 volume.
Guardians, Record of, 1910-1927; 1 volume.

TAX AND FISCAL RECORDS [*See also* **MISCELLANEOUS RECORDS**]

Tax List, 1915; 1 volume.

MISCELLANEOUS RECORDS

Coroners' Inquests, 1906-1968; 7 Fibredex boxes.
Miscellaneous Records, 1855; 1 manuscript box.
Official Reports, Record of, 1875-1906; 1 volume.
Released Polls, Record of, 1887-1927; 1 volume.
Settlement of County Accounts, Record of, 1891-1900; 1 volume.

CRX RECORDS

Civil Action Papers, 1909-1947; 1 folder.

MICROFILM RECORDS

CORPORATIONS AND PARTNERSHIPS

Corporations, Record of, 1901-1939; 1 reel.

COURT RECORDS

Superior Court

Civil Actions, Index to, 1855-1967; 1 reel.
Criminal Judgments, Index to, 1943-1968; 1 reel.
Judgments, Index to, Defendant, 1890-1968; 2 reels.
Judgments, Index to, Plaintiff, 1890-1968; 2 reels.
Minutes, 1892-1956; 8 reels.

ELECTION RECORDS

Elections, Record of, 1936-1966; 1 reel.

ESTATES RECORDS

Accounts, Record of, 1884-1956; 5 reels.
Administrators, Executors, and Guardians, Cross Index to, 1919-1954; 1 reel.
Administrators, Record of, 1910-1959; 4 reels.
Amounts Paid Indigent Children, 1929-1948; 1 reel.

Dowers, Record of, 1893-1938; 1 reel.
Estates, Index to, 1950-1967; 1 reel.
Estates Not Exceeding $300, 1930-1966; Estates Not Exceeding $1,000, 1966-1967; 1 reel.
Guardians, Record of, 1927-1967; 1 reel.
Inheritance Tax Records, 1947-1967; 1 reel.
Inventories, Record of, 1908-1962; 2 reels.
Settlements, Record of, 1889-1957; 4 reels.
Trust Funds for Minors and Incompetents, 1943-1966; 2 reels.
Widows' Year's Support, Record of, 1938-1967; 1 reel.

LAND RECORDS

Deeds, Record of, 1877-1952; 109 reels.
Division and Partition of Land, Record of, 1898-1921; 1 reel.
Real Estate Conveyances, Index to, Grantee, 1855-1955; 6 reels.
Real Estate Conveyances, Index to, Grantor, 1855-1955; 5 reels.
Resale of Land by Trustees and Mortgagees, Record of, 1919-1957; 6 reels.

MARRIAGE, DIVORCE, AND VITAL STATISTICS

Births, Index to, 1914-1974; 4 reels.
Deaths, Index to, 1924-1966; 1 reel.
Delayed Births, Index to, 1914-1973; 2 reels.
Maiden Names of Divorced Women, 1936-1967; 1 reel.
Marriage Registers, 1892-1967; 1 reel.

MISCELLANEOUS RECORDS

Orders and Decrees, 1892-1956; 11 reels.
Reports of Receivers, 1922-1942; 1 reel.
Special Proceedings, Cross Index to, 1892-1967; 1 reel.
Special Proceedings Dockets, 1894-1952; 2 reels.

OFFICIALS, COUNTY

Board of County Commissioners, Minutes, 1876-1943; 4 reels.

SCHOOL RECORDS

County Board of Education, Minutes, 1885-1931; 1 reel.
Old Teachers' Register, 1857-1860; 1 reel.

WILLS

Wills, Index to, 1883-1967; 1 reel.
Wills, Record of, 1885-1967; 6 reels.

HAYWOOD COUNTY

Established in 1808 from Buncombe County.

ORIGINAL RECORDS

BONDS

Apprentice Bonds and Records, 1812-1861, 1870, 1905, 1908; 1 Fibredex box.
Bastardy Bonds and Records, 1814-1936; 4 Fibredex boxes.
Officials' Bonds and Records, 1812-1942; 2 Fibredex boxes.

COURT RECORDS

Circuit Criminal Court/Western District Criminal Court
- Judgment Docket, 1895-1902; 1 volume.
- Minutes, 1895-1900; 1 volume.

County Court of Pleas and Quarter Sessions
- Execution Dockets, 1816-1868; 3 volumes, 1 manuscript box.
- Minutes, 1809-1815, 1820-1868; 9 volumes.
- Miscellaneous Dockets, 1843-1868; 1 manuscript box.
- State Dockets, 1811-1868; 2 volumes, 1 manuscript box.
- Trial and Appearance Dockets, 1809-1834; 1 manuscript box.
- Trial Dockets, 1835-1866; 3 volumes.

Recorder's Court
- Judgment Dockets, 1924-1927, 1957-1966; 12 volumes.
- Minutes, 1924-1927, 1957-1966; 5 volumes.

Superior Court
- Appearance and Motion Docket, 1847-1882; 1 volume.
- Civil Action Papers, 1802, 1810-1939; 87 Fibredex boxes. [*See also* **CRX RECORDS**]
- Civil Action Papers Concerning Land, 1815-1948; 29 Fibredex boxes.
- Civil Issues Docket, Cross Index to, 1869-1879; 1 volume.
- Civil Issues Dockets, 1869-1898; 3 volumes.
- Criminal Action Papers, 1814-1944; 35 Fibredex boxes.
- Criminal Issues Docket, 1870-1889; 1 volume. [*See also* Civil Issues Dockets]
- Equity Minutes, 1846-1868; 1 volume.
- Equity Trial Docket, 1843-1868; 1 volume.
- Execution Dockets, 1838-1877; 3 volumes.
- Judgment Dockets, 1868-1944; 41 volumes.
- Judgments, Cross Index to, 1868-1923; 7 volumes.
- Minutes, 1815-1966; 36 volumes, 2 manuscript boxes.
- Miscellaneous Dockets, 1810-1845; 1 manuscript box.
- State Dockets, 1840-1869; 2 volumes.
- Summons Docket, 1884-1887. [*See* Civil Issues Dockets]
- Trial Docket, 1840-1867; 1 volume.

ELECTION RECORDS

Certificates of Permanent Registration and Oaths, 1902-1908; 3 Fibredex boxes.
Elections, Record of, 1878-1902, 1924-1930, 1940; 3 volumes.
Miscellaneous Election Records, 1832-1936; 2 Fibredex boxes.
Permanent Registration of Voters, 1902-1916; 1 volume.

ESTATES RECORDS

Accounts, Record of, 1866-1909, 1916-1966; 15 volumes.
Appointment of Administrators, Executors, Guardians, and Masters, 1868-1909; 1 volume.
Estates Records, 1809-1942; 82 Fibredex boxes.
Guardians' Records, 1815-1941; 9 Fibredex boxes.
Inheritance Tax, Record of, 1921-1956; 3 volumes.
Settlements, Record of, 1869-1921; 2 volumes.

LAND RECORDS

Agreements, Contracts, and Leases, 1832-1948; 1 Fibredex box.
Attachments, Executions, Levies, and Liens on Land, 1809-1938; 4 Fibredex boxes.
Deeds, 1801-1948; 9 Fibredex boxes.
Deeds, Cross Index to, 1809-1877; 1 volume.
Deeds, Record of, 1809-1865; 13 volumes.
Deeds of Trust, Mortgage Deeds, and Land Grants, 1786-1948; 1 Fibredex box.
Ejectments, 1812-1935; 3 Fibredex boxes.
Land Entries, 1809-1904; 3 volumes.
Miscellaneous Land Records, 1809-1946; 2 Fibredex boxes.
Probate of Deeds, 1885-1887; 1 volume.
Sales and Resales by Trustees and Mortgages, Record of, 1924-1966; 5 volumes.
Tax Levies on Land, 1927-1936; 9 Fibredex boxes.

MARRIAGE, DIVORCE, AND VITAL STATISTICS

Divorce Records, 1829-1944; 19 Fibredex boxes.
Maiden Names of Divorced Women, 1939-1966; 1 volume.
Marriage Bonds, 1808-1868; 5 Fibredex boxes.
Marriage Licenses, 1857-1925; 19 Fibredex boxes.
Marriage Registers, 1868-1938; 4 volumes.

MISCELLANEOUS RECORDS

Alien Registration, 1940-1943; 1 volume.
Assignees, Receivers, and Trustees, Records of, 1852-1942; 9 Fibredex boxes.
Clerk's Minute Dockets, 1921-1966; 6 volumes.
Coroners' Inquests, 1822-1967; 2 Fibredex boxes.
County Accounts, Claims, and Correspondence, 1809-1938; 1 Fibredex box, 1 manuscript box.
Grand Jury Presentments and Reports, 1823-1966; 2 Fibredex boxes.
Indian Records, 1821-1925; 1 Fibredex box.
Inquisition of Lunacy, Record of, 1899-1966; 6 volumes.
Insolvent Debtors, 1814-1896; 7 Fibredex boxes.
Miscellaneous Records, 1815-1966; 5 Fibredex boxes.
Orders and Decrees, 1870-1921; 1 volume.
Petitions for Naturalization, 1906-1918; 4 volumes.
Railroad Records, 1869-1933; 5 Fibredex boxes.
Roads, Cartways, and Bridges, 1838-1932; 1 Fibredex box.
Road Records, 1811-1927; 1 Fibredex box.
School Records, 1830-1950; 1 Fibredex box.
Slaves and Free Persons of Color, Records of, 1823-1868; 1 Fibredex box.
Special Proceedings Dockets, 1913-1946; 15 volumes.
Special Proceedings, Index to, 1875-1917; 1 volume.

ROADS AND BRIDGES [*See* **MISCELLANEOUS RECORDS**]

SCHOOL RECORDS [*See* **MISCELLANEOUS RECORDS**]

TAX AND FISCAL RECORDS

Miscellaneous Tax Records, 1820-1933; 2 Fibredex boxes.
Tax List, 1866-1868; 1 volume.

WILLS

Wills, 1803-1966; 52 Fibredex boxes.

CRX RECORDS

Civil Action Papers, 1842; 1 folder.

MICROFILM RECORDS

CORPORATIONS AND PARTNERSHIPS

Corporations, Record of, 1885-1941; 1 reel.

COURT RECORDS

Circuit Criminal Court/ Western District Criminal Court
Minutes, 1895-1900; 1 reel.
County Court of Pleas and Quarter Sessions
Minutes, 1809-1815, 1820-1868; 3 reels.
Superior Court
Civil Actions, Index to, Defendant, 1920-1966; 2 reels.
Civil Actions, Index to, Plaintiff, 1920-1966; 1 reel.
Criminal Actions, Index to, 1921-1966; 2 reels.
Minutes, 1815-1955; 15 reels.

ESTATES RECORDS

Accounts of Indigent Orphans, 1921-1941; 1 reel.
Accounts, Record of, 1874-1966; 8 reels.
Administrators and Executors, Cross Index to, 1870-1966; 1 reel.
Appointment and Bonds of Administrators, 1902-1966; 6 reels.
Appointment and Bonds of Guardians, 1909-1966; 3 reels.
Appointment of Executors, 1927-1966; 2 reels.
Estates, Index to, 1808-1939; 1 reel.
Guardians' Bonds, 1909-1926; 1 reel.
Guardians, Cross Index to, 1870-1966; 1 reel.
Inheritance Tax Records, 1921-1966; 2 reels.
Qualification of Trustees under Wills, 1963-1966; 1 reel.
Settlements, Record of, 1869-1966; 6 reels.

LAND RECORDS

Deeds, Record of, 1809-1958; 99 reels.
Federal Tax Lien Index, 1925-1969; 1 reel.
Land Entries, Record of, 1809-1887; 1 reel.
Land Sold for Taxes, Record of, 1925-1927; 1 reel.
Real Estate Conveyances, Index to, Grantee, 1808-1966; Index to Deeds of Trust, 1959-1966; 10 reels.
Real Estate Conveyances, Index to, Grantor, 1808-1966; 10 reels.
Resales, Record of, 1924-1966; 3 reels.

MARRIAGE, DIVORCE, AND VITAL STATISTICS

Births, Index to, 1913-1978; 4 reels.
Deaths, Index to, 1913-1972; 2 reels.
Delayed Births, Index to, various years; 1 reel.
Maiden Names of Divorced Women, 1939-1966; 1 reel.
Marriage Bonds, 1806-1868; 3 reels.
Marriage Licenses, 1857-1965; 27 reels.
Marriage Registers, 1868-1921, 1939-1965; 3 reels.
Marriages, Index to, 1850-1939; 2 reels.

MISCELLANEOUS RECORDS

Clerk's Minute Dockets, 1921-1966; 3 reels.
Orders and Decrees, 1870-1921; 1 reel.
Special Proceedings, 1875-1951; 12 reels.
Special Proceedings, Cross Index to, 1874-1966; 2 reels.

OFFICIALS, COUNTY

Board of County Commissioners, Minutes, 1868-1966; 4 reels.

SCHOOL RECORDS

County Board of Education, Minutes, 1885-1921; 1 reel.

TAX AND FISCAL RECORDS

Tax List, 1866-1868; 1 reel.

WILLS

Wills and Inventories, Record of, 1808-1878; 1 reel.
Wills, Index to, 1829-1966; 1 reel.
Wills, Record of, 1869-1966; 4 reels.

HENDERSON COUNTY

Established in 1838 from Buncombe County.

ORIGINAL RECORDS

BONDS

- Apprentice Bonds, 1875-1885; 1 volume.
- Bastardy Bonds and Records, 1840-1936, 1953; 1 volume, 2 Fibredex boxes.
- Officials' Bonds and Records, 1839-1931; 8 Fibredex boxes.

CORPORATIONS AND PARTNERSHIPS [*See* **MISCELLANEOUS RECORDS**]

COURT RECORDS

- Circuit Criminal Court/Western District Criminal Court
  - Judgment Docket, 1895-1901; 1 volume.
  - Minutes, 1895-1901; 1 volume.
- County Court of Pleas and Quarter Sessions
  - Execution Dockets, 1839-1859, 1866-1868; 3 volumes.
  - Minutes, 1839-1868; 5 volumes.
  - State Docket, 1840-1868; 1 volume.
- General County Court
  - Minutes, 1926-1931; 1 volume.
- Superior Court
  - Civil Action Papers, 1808-1959; 59 Fibredex boxes.
  - Civil Action Papers Concerning Land, 1835-1933; 17 Fibredex boxes.
  - Criminal Action Papers, 1839-1955; 38 Fibredex boxes.
  - Equity Enrolling Docket, 1844-1868; 1 volume.
  - Equity Minutes, 1841-1868; 1 volume.
  - Execution Docket, 1842-1846; 1 volume.
  - Judgment Dockets, 1869-1928; 18 volumes.
  - Judgments, Cross Index to, 1857-1899; 2 volumes.
  - Minutes, 1841-1968; 33 volumes.
  - Miscellaneous Court Records, 1861-1966; 1 Fibredex box.
  - State Docket, 1841-1856; 1 volume.
  - Trial Dockets, 1851-1868; 2 volumes.

ELECTION RECORDS

- Election Records, 1844-1927; 1 Fibredex box.
- Elections, Record of, 1878-1970; 5 volumes.

ESTATES RECORDS

- Accounts of Indigent Orphans, Record of, 1910-1937; 1 volume.
- Accounts, Record of, 1870-1968; 17 volumes.
- Administrators' Bonds, 1871-1922; 2 volumes.
- Estates Records, 1838-1968; 119 Fibredex boxes.
- Guardians' Accounts, 1846-1869; 1 volume.
- Guardians' Bonds, 1872-1967; 3 volumes.
- Guardians' Records, 1838-1968; 23 Fibredex boxes.
- Probate (Estates), Record of, 1868-1896; 1 volume.
- Settlements, Record of, 1869-1968; 13 volumes.

LAND RECORDS

Deeds, Record of, 1839-1841; 1 volume.
Deeds of Sale, 1795-1959; 10 Fibredex boxes.
Deeds of Trust, 1848-1955; 1 Fibredex box.
Ejectments, 1838-1957; 5 Fibredex boxes.
Levies on Land, 1840-1926; 5 Fibredex boxes.
Miscellaneous Deeds, 1799-1949; 1 Fibredex box.
Miscellaneous Land Records, 1847-1959; 9 Fibredex boxes.
Probate of Deeds, Record of, 1839-1876; 2 volumes.
Quitclaim Deeds, 1835-1959; 1 Fibredex box.
Sales and Resales by Mortgagees and Trustees, Record of, 1916-1970; 8 volumes.

MARRIAGE, DIVORCE, AND VITAL STATISTICS

Divorce Records, 1842-1931; 3 Fibredex boxes.
Marriage Records, 1838-1967; 1 Fibredex box.

MILITARY AND PENSION RECORDS [*See* **MISCELLANEOUS RECORDS**]

MISCELLANEOUS RECORDS

Alien Registration, 1927-1948; 1 volume.
Appointment of Receivers, Record of, 1913-1968; 2 volumes.
Assignees, Receivers, and Trustees, Records of, 1857-1944; 1 Fibredex box.
Business, Corporation, and Partnership Records, 1844-1959; 2 Fibredex boxes.
Clerk of Court Correspondence, 1873-1962; 10 Fibredex boxes.
Clerk's Minute Dockets (Special Proceedings), 1885-1968; 9 volumes.
Confederate Pensions, Record of, 1885-1905; 1 volume.
Coroners' Inquests, 1872-1934; 1 Fibredex box.
Coroners' Inquests, Record of, 1853-1926; 1 volume.
County Accounts, 1909-1968; 1 volume.
Declaration of Intent (to Become a Citizen), 1913-1925; 1 volume.
Grand Jury Records, 1840-1954; 1 Fibredex box.
Homestead Records, 1867-1927; 1 Fibredex box.
Insolvent Debtors, 1838-1929; 1 Fibredex box.
Justices of the Peace Records, 1853-1955; 2 Fibredex boxes.
Lunacy, Record of, 1899-1927; 1 volume.
Lunacy Records, 1849-1929; 1 Fibredex box.
Medical Examinations, Record of, 1911-1927; 1 volume.
Miscellaneous Correspondence, 1846-1930; 2 Fibredex boxes.
Miscellaneous Records, 1840-1956; 4 Fibredex boxes.
Orders and Decrees, 1869-1885, 1931-1957; 3 volumes.
Partnership, Record of, 1913-1963; 1 volume.
Pension Records, 1885-1939; 3 Fibredex boxes.
Petitions for Naturalization, 1910-1927; 1 volume.
Railroad Records, 1896-1909; 3 Fibredex boxes.
Road Records, 1842-1927; 3 Fibredex boxes.
Special Proceedings Dockets, 1880-1968; 3 volumes.

ROADS AND BRIDGES [*See* **MISCELLANEOUS RECORDS**]

TAX AND FISCAL RECORDS

Tax Records, 1841-1955; 1 Fibredex box.

WILLS

Wills, 1797, 1817, 1835-1969; 62 Fibredex boxes.
Wills, Cross Index to, 1841-1949; 1 volume.

MICROFILM RECORDS

CORPORATIONS AND PARTNERSHIPS

Corporations, Record of, 1874-1957; 2 reels.
Partnership Records, 1913-1963; 1 reel.

COURT RECORDS

County Court of Pleas and Quarter Sessions
 Minutes, 1839-1868; 3 reels.
Superior Court
 Judgment Dockets, 1924-1928, 1934-1938; 2 reels.
 Judgments, Index to, Defendant, 1933-1968; 1 reel.
 Judgments, Index to, Plaintiff, 1933-1968; 1 reel.
 Minutes, 1841-1956; 14 reels.
 Tax Judgments, Index to, 1926-1964; 1 reel.

ELECTION RECORDS

Elections, Record of, 1928-1966; 1 reel.

ESTATES RECORDS

Accounts of Indigent Orphans, 1910-1937; 1 reel.
Accounts, Record of, 1871-1967; 9 reels.
Administrators' and Executors' Bonds, 1917-1929; 1 reel.
Administrators, Executors, and Guardians, Record of, 1903-1928; 1 reel.
Administrators, Record of, 1919-1968; 4 reels.
Appointment of Administrators, Record of, 1895-1930; 1 reel.
Executors, Record of, 1927-1968; 2 reels.
Guardians' Bonds, 1928-1967; 1 reel.
Guardians, Record of, 1925-1967; 2 reels.
Inheritance Tax Records, 1915-1956; 1 reel.
Probate, Record of (Estates).
Settlements, Record of, 1869-1968; 7 reels.
Widows' Year's Support [*See* Appointment of Administrators, Record of]

LAND RECORDS

Deeds, Record of, 1838-1959; 187 reels. [*See* Appointment of Administrators, Record of]
Real Estate Conveyances, Index to, Grantee, 1838-1962; 6 reels.
Real Estate Conveyances, Index to, Grantor, 1838-1968; 7 reels.
Sales and Resales, Record of, 1916-1967; 4 reels.
Surveys and Land Entries, Record of, 1921-1950; 1 reel.

MARRIAGE, DIVORCE, AND VITAL STATISTICS

Births, Index to, 1914-1967; 1 reel.
Deaths, Index to, 1914-1967; 1 reel.
Delayed Births, Index to, various years; 1 reel.
Marriage Licenses, 1906-1967; 9 reels.
Marriage Licenses, Record of, 1921-1939; 2 reels.
Marriage Registers, 1851-1967; 5 reels.

MISCELLANEOUS RECORDS

Appointment of Receivers, Record of, 1916-1967; 1 reel.
Clerk's Minute Docket, 1921-1968; 3 reels.
Orders and Decrees, 1869-1957; 2 reels.
Special Proceedings, 1905-1957; 5 reels.
Special Proceedings, Cross Index to, 1869-1967; 1 reel.

OFFICIALS, COUNTY

Board of County Commissioners, Minutes, 1868-1941; 5 reels.

SCHOOL RECORDS

County Board of Education, Minutes, 1885-1967; 1 reel.

WILLS

Wills, Index to, 1843-1967; 1 reel.
Wills, Record of, 1841-1967; 10 reels.

HERTFORD COUNTY

Established in 1759 (effective 1760) from Chowan County.
Courthouse fires of 1830 and 1862 destroyed a majority of the county's records.

ORIGINAL RECORDS

BONDS [*See also* **CRX RECORDS**]
- Apprentice Bonds, 1861-1868; 1 Fibredex box.
- Bastardy Bonds, 1865-1898; 1 Fibredex box.

COURT RECORDS
- County Court of Pleas and Quarter Sessions
  - Execution Dockets, 1846-1868; 2 volumes.
  - Minutes, 1830-1868; 5 volumes.
  - State Docket, 1845-1868; 1 volume.
  - Trial and Appearance Dockets, 1830-1868; 3 volumes.
- Inferior Court/Criminal Court of Hertford County
  - Criminal Issues Docket, Inferior Court, 1879-1891; Criminal Issues Docket, Criminal Court, 1891-1897; 1 volume.
  - Minutes, Board of Justices of the Peace, 1878-1885; 1 volume.
  - Minutes, Inferior Court, 1877-1891; Minutes, Criminal Court, 1891-1897;
- Superior Court
  - Civil and Criminal Action Papers, 1802-1824, 1855-1914; 11 Fibredex boxes.
  - Minutes, 1868-1915; 5 volumes.
  - Supreme Court Opinions, 1859-1898; 1 manuscript box.
  - Trial Docket, 1830-1836; Trial and Appearance Docket, 1842-1868; 1 volume.

ELECTION RECORDS
- Elections, Record of, 1880-1908, 1924-1932; 4 volumes.

ESTATES RECORDS
- Accounts, Record of, 1868-1896; 4 volumes.
- Administrators' Bonds, 1869-1915; 5 volumes.
- Estates, Record of, 1830-1866; 4 volumes.
- Estates Records, 1858-1914; 48 Fibredex boxes.
- Guardians' Accounts, 1823-1866; 3 volumes.
- Guardians' Bonds, 1869-1915; 2 volumes.
- Guardians' Records, 1858-1914; 1 Fibredex box.
- Settlements, Record of, 1868-1910; 1 volume.

LAND RECORDS
- Deeds, 1775-1940; 9 Fibredex boxes. [*See also* **CRX RECORDS**]
- Deeds of Trust and Mortgage Deeds, 1871-1940; 2 Fibredex boxes.
- Real Estate Conveyances, Cross Index to, 1862-1920; 9 volumes.

MARRIAGE, DIVORCE, AND VITAL STATISTICS
- Divorce Records, 1871-1914; 2 Fibredex boxes.

MISCELLANEOUS RECORDS
- Miscellaneous Records, 1787-1939; 3 Fibredex boxes.

TAX AND FISCAL RECORDS
- Tax Lists, 1782, 1859-1860; 1 volume, 1 manuscript box.

WILLS

Wills, 1763, 1861-1903; 4 Fibredex boxes. [*See also* **CRX RECORDS**]

CRX RECORDS

Bond, 1778; 1 folder.
Deeds, 1845-1873; 1 folder.
Will, 1825; 1 folder.

MICROFILM RECORDS

CORPORATIONS AND PARTNERSHIPS

Corporations, Record of, 1878-1962; 1 reel.
Partnership Records, 1918-1952; 1 reel.

COURT RECORDS

County Court of Pleas and Quarter Sessions
 Minutes, 1830-1868; 1 reel.
Superior Court
 Minutes, 1868-1950; 6 reels.
 Trial Docket, 1830-1836; Trial and Appearance Docket, 1842-1868; 1 reel.

ELECTION RECORDS

Elections, Record of, 1880-1962; 1 reel.

ESTATES RECORDS

Accounts, Record of, 1830-1840, 1891-1959; 4 reels.
Accounts and Inventories, Record of, 1895-1963; 2 reels.
Administrators' Bonds, 1869-1915; 1 reel.
Administrators, Record of, 1918-1963; 2 reels.
Appointment of Administrators, Executors, and Guardians, 1868-1933; 1 reel.
Executors, Record of, 1933-1963; Record of Guardians, 1931-1962; 1 reel.
Guardians' Accounts, 1823-1845; 1 reel.
Guardians' Bonds, 1869-1914; 1 reel.
Inheritance Tax Collections, Record of, 1920-1963; 1 reel.
Settlements, Record of, 1868-1963; 3 reels.

LAND RECORDS

Deeds, Record of, 1862-1946; 54 reels.
Real Estate Transfers, Index to, Grantee, 1862-1960; 2 reels.
Real Estate Transfers, Index to, Grantor, 1862-1960; 2 reels.
Resale of Land by Trustees and Mortgagees, Record of, 1920-1963; 2 reels.
Taxes for Mortgagees, Record of, 1931-1934; 1 reel.

MARRIAGE, DIVORCE, AND VITAL STATISTICS

Maiden Names of Divorced Women, 1939-1962; 1 reel.
Marriage Licenses, 1904-1961; 5 reels.
Marriage Registers, 1868-1971; 1 reel.
Vital Statistics, Index to, 1913-1954; 1 reel.

MILITARY AND PENSION RECORDS

Confederate Soldiers, Register of, 1861-1865; 1 reel.

MISCELLANEOUS RECORDS

Civil Actions and Special Proceedings, Index to, 1881-1968; 1 reel.
Orders and Decrees, 1868-1950; 4 reels.
Special Proceedings, 1881-1968; 3 reels.

OFFICIALS, COUNTY

Board of County Commissioners, Minutes, 1868-1939; 2 reels.

TAX AND FISCAL RECORDS [*See* **ESTATES RECORDS; LAND RECORDS**]

WILLS

Wills, Cross Index to, 1830-1963; 1 reel.
Wills, Record of, 1829-1963; 3 reels.

HOKE COUNTY

Established in 1911 from Cumberland and Robeson counties.

ORIGINAL RECORDS

Court Records

Superior Court

Minutes, 1911-1949; 4 volumes.

Election Records

Elections, Record of, 1920-1966; 2 volumes.

Estates Records

Amounts Paid for Indigent Children, Record of, 1912-1955; 1 volume.

Land Records

Land Entries, 1913-1929; 1 volume, 1 manuscript box.

Marriage, Divorce, and Vital Statistics

Maiden Names of Divorced Women, 1944-1965; 1 volume.

Miscellaneous Records

Alien Registration, 1927; 1 volume.
Clerk's Minute Dockets (Special Proceedings), 1921-1956; 3 volumes.
Dentists' Certificates of Registration, 1912-1943; 1 volume.
Nurses' Certificates of Registration, 1918-1942; 1 volume.
Optometrists' and Chiropractors' Certificates of Registration, 1911-1949; 1 volume.
Physicians' and Surgeons' Certificates of Registration, 1911-1964; 1 volume.

MICROFILM RECORDS

Corporations and Partnerships

Corporations, Record of, 1911-1970; 1 reel.
Partnerships, Record of, 1943-1970; 1 reel.

Court Records

Superior Court

Judgment Docket, Land Tax Sales, 1930-1942; 1 reel.
Minutes, 1911-1966; 4 reels.

Election Records

Board of Elections, Minutes, 1956-1970; 1 reel.
Elections, Record of, 1916-1966; 1 reel.

Estates Records

Accounts, Record of, 1911-1966; 3 reels.
Administrators and Executors, Cross Index to, 1911-1966; 1 reel.
Administrators, Executors, and Guardians, Record of, 1911-1953; 1 reel.
Administrators, Record of, 1921-1966; 2 reels.
Amounts Paid for Indigent Children, Record of, 1912-1955; 1 reel.
Executors, Record of, 1953-1966; 1 reel.
Guardians, Cross Index to, 1911-1966; 1 reel.
Guardians, Record of, 1928-1966; 1 reel.
Inheritance Tax Records, 1919-1970; 1 reel.

Settlements, Record of, 1911-1965; 3 reels.
Trustee Ledger for Minors, 1943-1966; 1 reel.

LAND RECORDS

Deeds, Record of, 1911-1959; 21 reels.
Easements and Rights-of-Way, 1929-1966; 2 reels.
Federal Tax Lien Index, 1924-1969; 1 reel.
Real Estate Conveyances, General Index to, Grantee, 1911-1970; 2 reels.
Real Estate Conveyances, General Index to, Grantor, 1911-1970; 2 reels.
Report of Land Sales under Foreclosures, 1923-1966; 1 reel.

MARRIAGE, DIVORCE, AND VITAL STATISTICS

Maiden Names of Divorced Women, 1944-1965; 1 reel.
Marriage Registers, 1911-1970; 1 reel.
Vital Statistics, Index to, 1913-1968; 1 reel.

MISCELLANEOUS RECORDS

Clerk's Minute Dockets, 1921-1966; 2 reels.
Lunacy Docket, 1911-1966; 1 reel.
Orders and Decrees, 1911-1967; 3 reels.
Special Proceedings, 1911-1970; 2 reels.
Special Proceedings, Cross Index to, 1911-1966; 1 reel.

OFFICIALS, COUNTY

Board of County Commissioners, Minutes, 1911-1970; 2 reels.

SCHOOL RECORDS

County Board of Education, Minutes, 1911-1970; 1 reel.

TAX AND FISCAL RECORDS

Tax Scrolls, 1915, 1925, 1965; 1 reel.

WILLS

Wills, Record of, 1911-1966; 1 reel.

HYDE COUNTY

Established in 1705 as Wickham Precinct of Bath County.
Name changed to Hyde in 1712.

ORIGINAL RECORDS

BONDS

Apprentice Bonds and Records, 1771-1911; 1 volume, 2 Fibredex boxes.
Bastardy Bonds and Records, 1740-1907; 1 volume, 2 Fibredex boxes.
Officials' Bonds, 1755-1910; 1 volume, 3 Fibredex boxes.

COURT RECORDS

County Court of Pleas and Quarter Sessions
- Appearance Dockets, 1820-1868; 4 volumes.
- Appearance, Reference (Trial), Crown (State), and Execution Dockets, 1744-1797; 4 volumes, 1 manuscript box.
- Appearance and Trial Dockets, 1790-1820; 3 volumes, 1 manuscript box.
- Execution Dockets, 1765-1861; 6 volumes.
- Minutes, 1736-1737, 1744-1868; 19 volumes, 1 manuscript box.
- State Docket, 1825-1828; 1 volume. [*See also* Appearance and Trial Dockets]
- Trial Dockets, 1818-1868; 9 volumes, 1 manuscript box.

Recorder's Court
- Minutes, 1913-1968; 4 volumes.

Superior Court
- Appearance Docket, 1822-1860; 1 volume.
- Civil Action Papers, 1736-1914; 7 Fibredex boxes. [*See also* **CRX RECORDS**]
- Civil Action Papers Concerning Land, 1791-1914; 6 Fibredex boxes.
- Criminal Action Papers, 1741-1909; 4 Fibredex boxes.
- Criminal Issues Docket, 1869-1903; 1 volume.
- Equity Enrolling Docket, 1808-1852; 1 volume.
- Equity Execution Docket, 1808-1868; 1 volume.
- Equity Minutes, 1808-1868; 1 volume.
- Equity Trial Dockets, 1816-1868; 2 volumes.
- Execution Dockets, 1808-1875; 4 volumes.
- Executions, 1737-1898, 1909; 11 Fibredex boxes.
- Judgment Dockets, 1867-1968; 15 volumes. [*See also* **LAND RECORDS**, Tax Suit Judgment Dockets]
- Judgments, Index to, 1867-1968; 4 volumes.
- Minutes, 1807-1968; 14 volumes.
- State Dockets, 1813-1859; 3 volumes.
- Trial and Appearance Docket, 1807-1822; 1 volume.
- Trial Dockets, 1822-1869; 3 volumes.

ELECTION RECORDS

Election Records, 1755, 1800-1844, 1920; 1 Fibredex box.
Elections, Record of, 1878-1970; 6 volumes.

ESTATES RECORDS

Accounts, Record of, 1869-1939; 7 volumes.
Accounts of Trust Funds and Funds of Indigent Children, 1918-1926; 1 volume.
Administrators' Bonds, 1868-1919, 1926-1950; 4 volumes.

Estates, Record of, 1837-1868; 3 volumes.
Estates Records, 1735-1933, 1944; 82 Fibredex boxes.
Funds for Indigent Orphans and Non-Residents, Record of, 1935-1966; 1 volume.
Guardians' Bonds, 1884-1919; 1 volume.
Guardians, Cross Index to, 1869-1959; 1 volume.
Guardians, Executors, and Administrators, Index to, 1907-1947; 1 volume.
Guardians, Record of, 1962-1968; 1 volume.
Guardians' Records, 1744-1925, 1946, 1951; 4 Fibredex boxes.
Inheritance Tax Record, 1925-1969; 1 volume.
Settlements, Record of, 1869-1905, 1926-1942; 2 volumes.
Widows' Year's Support, Record of, 1961-1968; 1 volume. [*See also* **COURT RECORDS**, Superior Court, Judgment Dockets]

LAND RECORDS

Deeds, Cross Index to, 1736-1840; 1 volume.
Deeds and Miscellaneous Deeds, 1759-1927; 1 Fibredex box.
Deeds, Record of, 1736-1840; 9 volumes.
Ejectments, 1786-1887; 2 Fibredex boxes.
Federal Tax Lien Index, 1935-1970; 1 volume.
Foreclosures, 1842-1934; 1 Fibredex box.
Judgments [Tax Foreclosures], Index to, 1929-1953; 1 volume.
Land Entries, 1778-1795; 1 volume.
Land Grants, 1779-1857; 2 volumes.
Land Sales for Taxes, 1837, 1851, 1870-1920; 1 Fibredex box.
Miscellaneous Land Records, 1758-1916, 1933, 1952; 2 Fibredex boxes.
Petitions for Partition and Sale of Land, 1757, 1801-1916; 1 Fibredex box.
Sale and Resale of Land, Record of, 1918-1967; 2 volumes.
Tax Suit Judgment Dockets, 1929-1968; 5 volumes. [*See also* **COURT RECORDS**, Superior Court, Judgment Dockets]

MARRIAGE, DIVORCE, AND VITAL STATISTICS

Cohabitation Records, 1866; 1 volume.
Divorce Records, 1829-1914; 2 Fibredex boxes.
Marriage Bonds, 1742-1868; 1 Fibredex box.
Marriage Register, 1868-1873; 1 volume.

MISCELLANEOUS RECORDS

Alien Registration, 1940; 1 volume.
Assignees, Receivers, and Trustees, Records of, 1841-1926; 1 Fibredex box.
Board of County Commissioners, Minutes (Rough), 1878-1885; 1 volume.
Board of Superintendents of Common Schools, Minutes, 1841-1861; 1 volume.
Bridge Records, 1748-1928; 1 Fibredex box.
Canal and Drainage Records, 1792-1935; 2 Fibredex boxes.
Clerk's Minute Dockets, 1935-1968; 2 volumes.
County Accounts, 1746-1926; 1 Fibredex box.
County Accounts and Claims, 1853-1873; 1 volume.
County Board of Education, Minutes, 1880-1885; 1 volume.
County Claims, 1752-1928, 1933; 2 Fibredex boxes.
Franklin Society, Minutes, 1861; 1 volume.
Insolvent Debtors and Homestead and Personal Property Exemptions, 1795-1916; 1 Fibredex box.
Jury Lists and Records, 1742-1918; 1 Fibredex box.

Justices of the Peace, Records of, 1760-1917; 1 Fibredex box.
Lake Landing Township Minutes, 1869-1877; 1 volume.
Licenses to Catch Oysters, 1895-1902; 2 volumes.
Licenses to Trades, Registry of, 1881-1903; 1 volume.
Lunacy, Record of, 1899-1968; 2 volumes.
Magistrates and Notaries Public, Record of, 1953-1969; 1 volume.
Miscellaneous Records, 1735-1952; 5 Fibredex boxes.
Orders and Decrees, 1868-1941; 2 volumes.
Paupers, Records of, 1763, 1769, 1849-1935; 2 Fibredex boxes.
Railroad Records, 1901-1923; 1 Fibredex box.
Road Docket, 1855-1879, 1923; 1 volume.
Road Records, 1742-1928, 1935; 4 Fibredex boxes.
Special Proceedings Summons Docket, 1883-1938; 1 volume.
Wardens of the Poor, Minutes, 1837-1868; 1 volume.

OFFICIALS, COUNTY [*See* **MISCELLANEOUS RECORDS**]

ROADS AND BRIDGES [*See* **MISCELLANEOUS RECORDS**]

SCHOOL RECORDS [*See* **MISCELLANEOUS RECORDS**]

TAX AND FISCAL RECORDS
Lists of Taxables, 1837-1868, 1910; 5 volumes, 1 manuscript box.
Merchants' Returns of Purchases, 1883-1903; 1 Fibredex box.
Receipts from Oyster License Tax, 1895-1904; 1 volume.
Tax Records, 1740-1936; 1 Fibredex box.

WILLS
Wills, 1760-1968; 19 Fibredex boxes.
Wills and Estates, Record of, 1755-1818; 9 volumes.

CRX RECORDS
Civil Action Paper, 1814; 1 folder.

MICROFILM RECORDS

BONDS
Apprentice Bonds, 1868-1912; 1 reel.

COURT RECORDS
County Court of Pleas and Quarter Sessions
- Appearance, Crown, Reference, and Execution Dockets, 1744-1761; 1 reel.
- Minutes, 1736-1815, 1820-1844; 4 reels.

Superior Court
- Equity Enrolling Docket, 1808-1852; 1 reel.
- Equity Minutes, 1808-1868; 1 reel.
- Judgments, Index to, 1913-1935; 1 reel.
- Judgments, Index to, Defendant, 1936-1968; 1 reel.
- Judgments, Index to, Plaintiff, 1936-1968; 1 reel.

Minutes, 1869-1921; 3 reels.

ELECTION RECORDS
Elections, Record of, 1880-1956; 1 reel.

Estates Records [*See also* **Wills**]

Accounts, Record of, 1869-1921; 4 reels.
Administrators' Bonds, 1869-1919; 1 reel.
Administrators and Executors, Cross Index to, 1870-1960; 1 reel.
Appointment of Administrators, Executors, and Guardians, 1868-1919; 1 reel.
Estates, Record of, 1845-1868; 2 reels.
Guardians' Bonds, 1884-1919; 1 reel.
Guardians, Cross Index to, 1870-1960; 1 reel.
Guardians' Settlements, 1837-1845; 1 reel.
Orphans' Book, 1756-1762; 1 reel.
Settlements, Record of, 1856-1905; 1 reel.

Land Records

Deeds, Record of, 1736-1946; 45 reels.
Entry Takers' Book, 1891-1892; 1 reel.
Grant Book, 1782-1787; 1 reel.
Mortgages and Deeds of Trust, Record of, 1882-1915; 6 reels.
Real Estate Conveyances, Index to, Grantee, 1736-1937; 4 reels.
Real Estate Conveyances, Index to, Grantor, 1736-1937; 4 reels.

Marriage, Divorce, and Vital Statistics

Marriage Bonds, 1741-1868; 2 reels.
Marriage Registers, 1855-1975; 1 reel.
Vital Statistics, Index to, 1877-1958; 1 reel.

Miscellaneous Records

Orders and Decrees, 1869-1941; 1 reel.
Special Proceedings, 1885-1968; 8 reels.
Special Proceedings, Cross Index to, 1859-1960; 1 reel.
Wardens of the Poor, Minutes, 1837-1868; 1 reel.

Roads and Bridges

Road Overseers' Book, 1858-1879; 1 reel.

Tax and Fiscal Records

Lists of Taxables, 1837-1868; 2 reels.

Wills

Wills, Cross Index to, 1764-1970; 1 reel.
Wills, Inventories, and Sales of Estates, Record of, 1756-1762, 1765-1818; 4 reels.
Wills, Record of, 1764-1968; 7 reels.

IREDELL COUNTY

Established in 1788 from Rowan County.
Courthouse fire of 1854 destroyed many court records.

ORIGINAL RECORDS

BONDS

Bastardy Bonds and Records, 1855-1937; 1 volume, 3 Fibredex boxes.
Constables' Bonds, 1847-1866; 1 volume.
Officials' Bonds, 1868-1903; 1 volume.

COURT RECORDS

County Court of Pleas and Quarter Sessions
- Appearance Dockets, 1810-1868; 4 volumes.
- Execution Dockets, 1791-1801, 1835-1844; 4 volumes.
- Indictment and Recognizance Docket, 1802-1821; 1 volume.
- Levy Dockets, 1845-1858; 2 volumes.
- Minutes, 1789-1868; 7 volumes.
- State Docket, 1857-1868; 1 volume.
- Trial Dockets, 1810-1841, 1855-1868; 5 volumes.

Superior Court
- Appearance and Reference Docket, 1808-1825; 1 volume.
- Civil Action Papers, 1808-1941; 30 Fibredex boxes.
- Civil Action Papers Concerning Land, 1845-1934; 11 Fibredex boxes.
- Criminal Action Papers, 1814-1937; 36 Fibredex boxes.
- Equity Enrolling Dockets, 1837-1841, 1862-1868; 2 volumes.
- Equity Minutes, 1828-1868; 2 volumes.
- Equity Trial Dockets, 1807-1827, 1854-1868; 2 volumes.
- Execution Dockets, 1808-1833, 1841-1861; 4 volumes.
- Judgment Dockets (Criminal), 1882-1899; 2 volumes.
- Minutes, 1807-1845, 1869-1909; 15 volumes.
- State and Recognizance Docket, 1808-1826; 1 volume.
- Trial Dockets, 1808-1857; 3 volumes.

ELECTION RECORDS

Election Records, 1886-1926; 1 Fibredex box.
Elections, Record of, 1878-1928; 3 volumes.

ESTATES RECORDS

Accounts, Record of, 1868-1889; 3 volumes.
Administrators' Bonds, 1846-1931; 8 volumes.
Appointment of Administrators, Executors, and Guardians, 1868-1876, 1888-1905; 3 volumes.
Estates, Record of, 1843-1868; 3 volumes.
Estates Records, 1790-1970; 264 Fibredex boxes. [*See also* **CRX RECORDS**]
Fiduciary Account Book, 1833-1867; 1 volume.
Guardians' Accounts, 1894-1907; 1 volume.
Guardians' Bonds, 1846-1939; 5 volumes.
Guardians' Records, 1803-1964; 21 Fibredex boxes.
Petitions and Orders, 1901-1905, 1921; 1 volume.

Settlements, Record of, 1868-1895; 2 volumes.
Widows' Year's Support, Record of, 1871-1895; 1 volume.

LAND RECORDS [*See also* **CRX RECORDS**]
Attachments, Executions, Liens, and Levies on Land, 1843-1926; 4 Fibredex boxes.
Boundary Line Disputes, 1901-1936; 1 Fibredex box.
Condemnation of Land, 1903-1919; 1 Fibredex box.
Deeds, 1811-1945; 6 Fibredex boxes.
Ejectments, 1853-1906, 1918; 1 Fibredex box.
Foreclosures, 1901-1939; 2 Fibredex boxes.
Land Entries, 1855-1905; 2 volumes.
Miscellaneous Land Records, 1846-1953; 2 Fibredex boxes.
Mortgage Deeds and Deeds of Trust, 1857-1952; 1 Fibredex box.
Petitions for Partition of Land, 1862-1941; 2 Fibredex boxes.
Petitions for Sale of Land, 1863-1941; 7 Fibredex boxes.
Probate of Deeds, 1868-1886; 3 volumes.

MARRIAGE, DIVORCE AND VITAL STATISTICS
Cohabitation, Record of. [*See* Marriage Certificates, Record of]
Divorce Records, 1855-1934, 1952; 6 Fibredex boxes.
Maiden Names of Divorced Women, 1938-1970; 1 Fibredex box.
Marriage Bonds, 1788-1868; 1 Fibredex box.
Marriage Certificates, Record of, 1851-1867, 1899; Record of Cohabitation, 1866; 1 volume.
Marriage Registers, 1867-1939; 5 volumes.

MILITARY AND PENSION RECORDS [*See* **MISCELLANEOUS RECORDS**]

ROADS AND BRIDGES [*See* **MISCELLANEOUS RECORDS**]

MISCELLANEOUS RECORDS
Architects' Certificates of Registration, 1949-1981; 1 volume.
Assignees, Receivers, and Trustees, Records of, 1843-1941; 8 Fibredex boxes.
Chiropractors' Certificates of Registration, 1921-1975; 1 manuscript box.
Coroners' Inquests, 1854-1968; 9 Fibredex boxes.
County Accounts and Buildings, 1815-1918; 1 Fibredex box.
County Home Account Books, 1903-1908, 1914-1916; 1 manuscript box.
Court Martial Minutes, 1808-1862; 1 volume.
Dentists' Certificates of Registration, 1923-1938; 1 volume.
Homestead and Personal Property Exemptions, 1869-1899, 1933; 1 Fibredex box.
Lunacy Records, 1871-1939; 2 Fibredex boxes.
Miscellaneous Records, 1808-1949; 6 Fibredex boxes.
Nurses' Certificates of Registration, 1905-1974; 1 manuscript box.
Orders and Decrees, 1869-1888, 1901; 3 volumes.
Pensions, Record of, 1929-1968; 1 volume.
Personal Accounts, 1819, 1854-1892; 1 Fibredex box.
Physicians' and Surgeons' Certificates of Registration, 1889-1978; 1 manuscript box.
Physicians, Surgeons, and Dentists, Registry of, 1888-1902; 1 volume.
Railroad Records, 1860-1928; 8 Fibredex boxes.
Road Records, 1855-1869, 1902-1917; 1 Fibredex box.
Slave Records, 1823-1872; 1 Fibredex box.
Timber Records, 1902-1936; 1 Fibredex box.

TAX AND FISCAL RECORDS

List of Taxables, 1837-1842; 1 volume.
Miscellaneous Tax Records, 1790-1918; 1 Fibredex box.

WILLS

Wills, 1787-1917; 13 Fibredex boxes.
Wills, Cross Index to, [1790-1868, 1894-1907]; 1 volume.

CRX RECORDS

County Home Account Books and Registers of Inmates, 1904-1932; 3 volumes.
Deeds, Mortgage Deeds, and Power of Attorney, 1825-1888; 3 folders.
Estates Records, 1876; 1 folder.

MICROFILM RECORDS

BONDS

Bastardy Bonds, 1870-1879; 1 reel.
Officials' Bonds, 1868-1903; 1 reel.

CORPORATIONS AND PARTNERSHIPS

Corporations, Record of, 1888-1956; 4 reels.
Partnership Records, 1913-1965; 1 reel.

COURT RECORDS

County Court of Pleas and Quarter Sessions
- Minutes, 1789-1868; 2 reels.

Superior Court
- Civil Actions, Index to, Defendant, 1951-1970; 1 reel.
- Civil Actions, Index to, Plaintiff, 1951-1970; 1 reel.
- Equity Minutes, 1828-1868; 1 reel.
- Judgments, Index to, 1866-1970; 1 reel.
- Judgments, Index to, Defendant, 1925-1965; 4 reels.
- Judgments, Index to, Plaintiff, 1925-1965; 5 reels.
- Minutes, 1807-1954; 14 reels.

ELECTION RECORDS

Elections, Record of, 1908-1964; 1 reel.

ESTATES RECORDS

Accounts of Indigent Orphans, 1913; 1 reel.
Accounts, Record of, 1869-1965; 17 reels.
Administrators' Bonds, 1846-1965; 5 reels.
Appointment of Administrators and Executors, 1931-1965; 4 reels.
Appointment of Administrators, Executors, and Guardians, 1888-1931; Appointment of Guardians, 1928-1964; 4 reels.
Appointment of Executors, 1964-1968; Appointment of Executors and Guardians, 1962-1968; 1 reel.
Dowers and Widows' Year's Support, 1867-1959; 2 reels.
Estates, Record of, 1843-1867; 2 reels.
Final Accounts, Index to, 1788-1970; 3 reels.
Guardians' Accounts, 1894-1965; 5 reels.
Guardians' Bonds, 1846-1939; 2 reels.
Inheritance Tax Records, 1920-1965; 2 reels.
Settlements, Record of, 1868-1894; 1 reel.

LAND RECORDS

Deeds, Index to, Grantee, 1788-1965; 14 reels.
Deeds, Index to, Grantor, 1788-1965; 15 reels.
Deeds, Record of, 1788-1960; 181 reels.
Land Entries, 1789-1794, 1855-1905; 1 reel.
Sales and Resales, Record of, 1921-1965; 3 reels.

MARRIAGE, DIVORCE, AND VITAL STATISTICS

Births, Index to, 1913-1981; 5 reels.
Cohabitation, Record of, 1866; 1 reel.
Deaths, Index to, 1913-1965; 3 reels.
Delayed Births, Index to, various years; 1 reel.
Marriage Bonds, 1790-1866; 1 reel.
Marriage Licenses, 1893-1964; 14 reels.
Marriage Registers, Female, 1851-1965; 2 reels.
Marriage Registers, Male, 1851-1972; 3 reels.

MISCELLANEOUS RECORDS

Orders and Decrees, 1869-1893; 1 reel.
Special Proceedings, 1887-1949; 16 reels.
Special Proceedings, Index to, 1970-1981; 1 reel.
Special Proceedings, Index to, Defendant, 1868-1965; 1 reel.
Special Proceedings, Index to, Plaintiff, 1868-1965; 2 reels.

OFFICIALS, COUNTY

Board of County Commissioners, Minutes, 1868-1982; 7 reels.

SCHOOL RECORDS

County Board of Education, Minutes, 1885-1899, 1907-1950; 1 reel.

TAX AND FISCAL RECORDS

Land Valuations for Direct Tax, 1800; 1 reel.

WILLS

Wills, Index to, Devisee, 1788-1970; 2 reels.
Wills, Index to, Devisor, 1788-1970; 1 reel.
Wills, Record of, 1790-1965; 9 reels.

JACKSON COUNTY

Established in 1851 from Haywood and Macon counties.
Many records missing; reason unknown.

ORIGINAL RECORDS

COURT RECORDS

County Court of Pleas and Quarter Sessions
- Execution Docket, 1860-1868; 1 volume.
- Minutes, 1853-1868; 2 volumes.
- State Docket, 1853-1866; 1 volume.
- Trial Docket, 1853-1868; 1 volume.

Superior Court
- Civil Issues Docket, 1869-1900; 1 volume.
- Equity Minutes, 1853-1864; 1 volume.
- Execution Docket, 1869-1885. [*See* Court of Pleas and Quarter Sessions, Execution Docket]
- Judgment Dockets, 1869-1887; 2 volumes. [*See also* **LAND RECORDS**, Tax Suit Judgment Dockets]
- Judgments, Index to, 1868-1879; 1 volume.
- Minutes, 1869-1910; 9 volumes.

ELECTION RECORDS

Elections, Record of, 1878-1938; 4 volumes.
Permanent Registration of Voters, 1902-1908; 1 volume.

ESTATES RECORDS

Administrators, Record of, 1870-1914, 1924; 1 volume.
Appointment of Administrators, Executors, Guardians, and Masters, 1868-1913; 1 volume.
Estates, Record of, 1853-1879, 1885; 1 volume.
Guardians, Record of, 1871-1915; 1 volume.

LAND RECORDS

Deeds, Cross Index to, [1853-1891]; 2 volumes.
Deeds, Record of, 1853-1875; 4 volumes.
Probate of Deeds, 1872-1894; 2 volumes.
Tax Suit Judgment Dockets, 1939-1961; 7 volumes. [*See also* **COURT RECORDS**, Superior Court, Judgment Dockets]

MARRIAGE, DIVORCE, AND VITAL STATISTICS

Maiden Names of Divorced Women, Record of, 1940-1971; 1 volume.

MISCELLANEOUS RECORDS

County Board of Education, Minutes and Records of, 1881-1922; 4 volumes.
Licenses to Trades, Registry of, 1873-1904; 1 volume.
Lunacy, Record of, 1899-1967; 3 volumes.
Orders and Decrees, 1869-1908; 1 volume.
Special Proceedings Dockets, 1886-1941; 6 volumes.
Treasurer's Book of Fines Received, 1884-1907; 1 volume.

SCHOOL RECORDS [*See* **MISCELLANEOUS RECORDS**]

WILLS
Wills, 1860-1966; 10 Fibredex boxes.

MICROFILM RECORDS

CORPORATIONS AND PARTNERSHIPS
Incorporations, Record of, 1891-1970; 1 reel.
Partnership Records, 1913-1960; 1 reel.

COURT RECORDS
County Court of Pleas and Quarter Sessions
    Minutes, 1853-1868; 1 reel.
Superior Court
    Criminal Actions, Index to, 1963-1966; 1 reel.
    Equity Minutes, 1853-1864; 1 reel.
    Judgments, Index to, 1868-1966; 2 reels.
    Minutes, 1869-1957; 9 reels.

ELECTION RECORDS
Elections, Record of, 1878-1968; 1 reel.

ESTATES RECORDS
Administrators, Executors, and Guardians, Record of, 1870-1966; 3 reels.
Administrators and Executors, Index to, 1911-1966; 1 reel.
Appointment of Executors, 1868-1914; 1 reel.
Guardians, Cross Index to, 1911-1966; 1 reel.
Guardians, Record of, 1871-1915, 1930-1966; 2 reels.
Inheritance Tax Records, 1923-1970; 1 reel.
Inventories, Record of, 1863-1875; 1 reel.
Qualification of Trustees Under Wills, 1964; 1 reel.
Settlements, Record of, 1868-1966; 3 reels.
Trust Fund Records, 1928-1966; 1 reel.

LAND RECORDS
Deeds, Record of, 1853-1960; 68 reels.
Land Entries, Index to, 1853-1968; 1 reel.
Land Entry Books, 1853-1968; 1 reel.
Real Estate Conveyances, Index to, Grantee, 1853-1970; 14 reels.
Real Estate Conveyances, Index to, Grantor, 1853-1970; 14 reels.

MARRIAGE, DIVORCE, AND VITAL STATISTICS
Births, Index to, 1913-1992; 2 reels.
Deaths, Index to, 1913-1992; 1 reel.
Delayed Births, Index to, 1877-1991; 1 reel.
Maiden Names of Divorced Women, 1940-1968; 1 reel.
Marriage Registers, 1853-1974; 1 reel.

MISCELLANEOUS RECORDS
Orders and Decrees, 1869-1908; 1 reel.
Receipts and Disbursements by Clerk for Special Proceedings, 1919-1931; 1 reel.
Special Proceedings, 1885-1970; Index to Special Proceedings, 1885-1966; 5 reels.

WILLS
Wills, Index to, 1853-1966; 1 reel.
Wills, Record of, 1868-1966; 2 reels.

JOHNSTON COUNTY

Established in 1746 from Craven County.
No record of fires, but many records missing.

ORIGINAL RECORDS

BONDS

Apprentice Bonds, 1850-1911; 4 volumes.
Bastardy Bonds, 1850-1895; 2 volumes.
Officials' Bonds and Records. [*See* **CRX RECORDS**]

COURT RECORDS

County Court of Pleas and Quarter Sessions
- Appearance Dockets, 1820-1868; 3 volumes.
- Execution Dockets, 1790-1868; 6 volumes.
- Minutes, 1759-1868; 16 volumes.
- State Dockets, 1793-1868; 6 volumes.
- Trial and Appearance Dockets, 1786-1820; 6 volumes.
- Trial Dockets, 1820-1868; 6 volumes.
- Witness Ticket Book, 1818-1840; 1 volume.

Recorder's Court
- Minutes, 1911-1968; 25 volumes.
- Orders, Decrees, and Judgments, 1932-1953; 1 volume.
- Summons Docket, 1911-1921; 1 volume.
- Summons Dockets, Taxes, 1930-1940; 5 volumes.

Recorder's Court, Smithfield
- Minutes, 1955-1968; 5 volumes.

Recorder's Court, Town of Benson
- Minutes, 1953-1968; 5 volumes.

Recorder's Court, Town of Kenly
- Minutes, 1955-1968; 2 volumes.

Recorder's Court, Town of Selma
- Minutes, 1955-1968; 4 volumes.

Superior Court [*See also* **CRX RECORDS**]
- Appearance Docket, 1852-1869; 1 volume.
- Civil Action Papers, 1771-1927; 13 Fibredex boxes.
- Civil Action Papers Concerning Land, 1853-1930; 9 Fibredex boxes.
- Civil Issues Dockets, 1921-1936; 3 volumes.
- Civil Issues Dockets, Index to, 1921-1930; 1 volume.
- Criminal Action Papers, 1769-1936; 7 Fibredex boxes.
- Equity Minutes, 1807-1868; 2 volumes.
- Equity Trial and Appearance Docket, 1848-1868; 1 volume.
- Judgment Dockets, 1868-1948; 20 volumes. [*See also* **LAND RECORDS**]
- Judgment Dockets, Tax Non-Suits, 1935-1968; 5 volumes.
- Judgments, Index to, 1867-1932; 6 volumes.
- Minutes, 1807-1913; 11 volumes.
- State Docket, 1861-1868; 1 volume.
- Statement and Account of Fines and Forfeitures Received, 1870-1881; 1 volume.
- Summons Dockets, 1868-1968; 13 volumes.
- Trial Docket, 1852-1868; 1 volume.
- Witness Books, 1924-1968; 6 volumes.

ELECTION RECORDS

Elections, Record of, 1878-1921; 3 volumes.
Permanent Registration of Voters, 1902-1908; 1 volume.

ESTATES RECORDS

Accounts of Commissioners, 1907-1968; 3 volumes.
Accounts Ledger, 1926-1936; 1 volume.
Accounts, Record of, 1868-1968; 33 volumes.
Administrators' Bonds, 1849-1914; 8 volumes.
Appointment of Administrators, Executors, and Guardians, 1868-1923; 2 volumes.
Estates, Record of, 1781-1868; 27 volumes.
Estates Records, 1771-1962; 91 Fibredex boxes. [*See also* **CRX RECORDS**]
Guardians' Accounts, 1903-1914; 1 volume.
Guardians' Bonds, 1847-1868; 2 volumes.
Guardians, Record of, 1898-1912; 1 volume.
Guardians' Records, 1793-1939; 18 Fibredex boxes.
Guardians' Scire Facias Docket, 1817-1851; 1 volume.
Money Paid into Court by Administrators for Minors and Others, Record of, 1899-1926; 1 volume.
Settlements, Record of, 1868-1925; 5 volumes.
Widows' Year's Support, Record of, 1902-1968; 5 volumes.

LAND RECORDS [*See also* **CRX RECORDS**; **DOBBS COUNTY, LAND RECORDS**]

Deeds, 1748-1939; 7 Fibredex boxes.
Deeds, Record of, 1759-1765, 1779-1782; 2 volumes.
Deeds of Trust and Mortgage Deeds, 1830-1930; 2 Fibredex boxes.
Judgment Docket, Foreclosures, 1937-1941; 1 volume. [*See also* **COURT RECORDS**, Superior Court]
Land Divisions, Record of, 1789-1883; 3 volumes.
Land Entry Books, 1778-1903; 3 volumes.
Land Title Guaranty Proceedings, 1914; 1 volume.
Lis Pendens, Record of, 1913-1959; 1 volume.
Miscellaneous Land Records, 1772-1954; 2 Fibredex boxes.
Probate, Record of, 1869-1880; 1 volume, 1 pamphlet.
Sale and Resale, Record of, 1922-1969; 10 volumes.
Tax Suits, Index to, 1928-1968; 2 volumes.

MARRIAGE, DIVORCE, AND VITAL STATISTICS

Cohabitation, Record of, 1866; 1 volume.
Divorce Records, 1853-1926; 5 Fibredex boxes.
Marriage Bonds, 1746-1868; 12 Fibredex boxes.

MILITARY AND PENSION RECORDS [*See* **MISCELLANEOUS RECORDS**]

MISCELLANEOUS RECORDS [*See also* **CRX RECORDS**]

Assignees, Receivers, and Trustees, Records of, 1884-1952; 5 Fibredex boxes.
Assignments, Record of, 1894-1951; 2 volumes.
Clerk's Minute Dockets (Special Proceedings), 1869-1883, 1895-1912; 2 volumes.
Confederate Soldiers from Johnston County, Record of, 1861-1864; 1 volume.
Court Martial Minutes, 1761-1779; 1 volume.
Drainage Record, 1959-1968; 1 volume.
Ex-Confederate Soldiers and Widows, List of, 1900-1904; 1 volume.
Inquisition of Inebriety, Record of, 1939-1968; 2 volumes.

Lunacy, Record of, 1899-1968; 5 volumes.
Magistrates' Record, 1906-1923; 1 volume.
Miscellaneous Certificates of Registration, 1924-1969; 4 volumes in manuscript box.
Miscellaneous Records, 1764-1930; 3 Fibredex boxes.
Opticians' Certificates of Registration, 1952; 1 volume.
Optometrists' Certificates of Registration, 1909-1954; 1 volume.
Orders and Decrees, 1868-1944; 17 volumes.
Pensions, Record of, 1903-1938; 1 volume.
Physicians' Certificates of Registration, 1883-1957; 1 volume.
Railroad Records, 1853-1921; 4 Fibredex boxes.
Receivers' Accounts, 1905-1953; 1 volume.
Sheriffs' and Clerks' Settlement Book, 1825-1837; 1 volume.
Soldiers in World War I, Record of, 1917-1918; 1 volume.

OFFICIALS, COUNTY [*See* **MISCELLANEOUS RECORDS; CRX RECORDS**]

ROADS AND BRIDGES [*See* **MISCELLANEOUS RECORDS**]

SCHOOL RECORDS [*See* **CRX RECORDS**]

TAX AND FISCAL RECORDS

Lists of Taxables, 1809-1819, 1859-1868; 4 volumes.
Taxables, 1786-1863; 4 Fibredex boxes.

WILLS

Wills, 1760-1922; 11 Fibredex boxes.
Wills, Cross Index to, 1760-1904; 1 volume.
Will, Record of, 1787-1860; 2 volumes.

CRX RECORDS

Board of County Commissioners, Minutes (Rough), 1906-1912; 1 volume.
Civil Action Paper, 1767; 1 folder.
Clerk's Fee Book, Superior Court, 1890-1896; 1 volume.
Clerk's Receipt Book, Superior Court, 1872-1874; 1 volume.
County Accounts and Claims, 1799-1805; 1 volume.
Deeds of Sale, 1867, 1869; 1 folder.
Estates Records, 1959, n.d.; 21 folders.
Land Divisions, 1810-1864; 1 volume.
Miscellaneous Land Records, 1885, 1919; 2 folders.
Miscellaneous Records, 1902-1933; 6 folders.
Officials' Bonds and Records, 1931-1932; 1 folder.
School Records, 1846-1864; 10 folders.

MICROFILM RECORDS

BONDS

Apprentice Bonds, 1850-1911; 1 reel.

CORPORATIONS AND PARTNERSHIPS

Incorporations, Record of, 1890-1962; 2 reels.
Partnership Records, 1913-1972; 1 reel.

COURT RECORDS

County Court of Pleas and Quarter Sessions
Minutes, 1759-1868; 5 reels.

Superior Court
Equity Minutes, 1807-1866; 1 reel.
Minutes, 1807-1968; 17 reels.

ELECTION RECORDS
Elections, Record of, 1878-1926; 1 reel.

ESTATES RECORDS
Accounts, Record of, 1868-1946; 10 reels.
Administrators' Bonds, 1849-1940; 6 reels.
Appointment of Administrators, Executors, and Guardians, 1868-1923; 1 reel.
Dowers, Record of, 1902-1949; 1 reel.
Estates, Record of, 1781-1868; 11 reels.
Guardians' Bonds, 1898-1962; 3 reels.
Guardians' Records, 1866-1868; Guardians' Accounts, 1903-1924; 1 reel.
Monies Paid into Court by Administrators, Record of, 1900-1942; 1 reel.
Settlements, Record of, 1868-1923; 2 reels.
Widows' Year's Support, Record of, 1902-1939; 1 reel.

LAND RECORDS
Accounts of Land Sales by Commissioners, 1907-1968; 1 reel.
Certificate Record of Land Sold for Taxes, 1933; 1 reel.
Deeds and Grants, Record of, 1749-1842; 13 reels.
Deeds, Record of, 1842-1926, 1944-1946; 141 reels.
Federal Tax Lien Index, 1925-1969; 1 reel.
Foreclosures, Record of, 1927-1982; 3 reels.
Heirs' Land Divisions, Index to, 1789-1925; 1 reel.
Land Division Books, 1789-1968; 7 reels.
Land Entries, 1778-1926; 1 reel.
Land Grants, 1779-1782; 1 reel.
Plat Books, 1914-1962; 1 reel.
Plats, Index to, 1914-1979; 1 reel.
Real Estate Conveyances, General Index to, Grantee, 1749-1979; 7 reels.
Real Estate Conveyances, General Index to, Grantor, 1749-1979; 9 reels.
Resale of Land by Mortgagees and Trustees, Record of, 1919-1962; 5 reels.

MARRIAGE, DIVORCE, AND VITAL STATISTICS
Births, Index to, 1913-1972; 3 reels.
Deaths, Index to, 1913-1988; 1 reel.
Delayed Births, Index to, 1941-1988; 1 reel.
Maiden Names of Divorced Women, 1940-1968; 1 reel.
Marriage Bond Abstracts, 1768-1868; 1 reel.
Marriage Bonds, 1768-1868; 4 reels.
Marriage Licenses, 1894-1961; 16 reels.
Marriage Registers, 1760-1988; 5 reels.

MILITARY AND PENSION RECORDS
Civil War Veterans, Record of, 1861-1865; 1 reel.
Courts-Martial Proceedings, Record of, 1761-1779; 1 reel.

MISCELLANEOUS RECORDS
Assignments, Record of, 1894-1951; 1 reel.
Bonds of Trustees in Assignments, 1913-1916; 1 reel.

Clerk's Minute Docket, 1921-1954; 1 reel.
Inquisition of Inebriety, 1939-1969; 1 reel.
Lunacy, Record of, 1899-1963; 3 reels.
Orders and Decrees, 1868-1944; 7 reels.
Receivers' Accounts, 1905-1953; 1 reel.
Special Proceedings, 1869-1962; 3 reels.
Special Proceedings, Index to, 1869-1988; 4 reels.

OFFICIALS, COUNTY

Board of County Commissioners, Minutes, 1868-1979; 7 reels.

SCHOOL RECORDS

County Board of Education, Minutes, 1885-1987; 5 reels.

TAX AND FISCAL RECORDS

List of Taxables, 1809-1819, 1863; 1 reel.
Tax Lists, 1859-1905, 1915; 11 reels.

WILLS

Wills, Index to, Devisee, 1760-1968; 1 reel.
Wills, Index to, Devisor, 1760-1968; 1 reel.
Wills, Record of, 1760-1968; 13 reels.

JONES COUNTY

Established in 1779 from Craven County.
In 1862, courthouse burned during Civil War battle; many court records destroyed.

ORIGINAL RECORDS

BONDS

Apprentice Bonds, 1847-1902; 1 volume, 1 Fibredex box.
Bastardy Bonds, 1812-1914; 1 volume, 1 Fibredex box.

COURT RECORDS

County Court of Pleas and Quarter Sessions
- Appearance Dockets, 1807-1868; 3 volumes.
- Clerk's Fee Book, 1858-1875; 1 volume.
- Execution Dockets, 1847-1868; 4 volumes.
- Minutes, 1807-1868; 7 volumes.
- State Dockets, 1821-1868; 3 volumes.
- Trial Dockets, 1807-1868; 3 volumes.

Superior Court
- Appearance Docket, 1861-1868; 1 volume.
- Civil Action Papers, 1853-1905, 1915, 1931; 7 Fibredex boxes.
- Civil Action Papers Concerning Land, 1858-1944; 5 Fibredex boxes.
- Criminal Action Papers, 1800, 1853-1905, 1938; 4 Fibredex boxes.
- Equity Execution Docket, 1852-1868; 1 volume.
- Equity Minutes, 1826-1868; 2 volumes.
- Equity Trial and Appearance Dockets, 1820-1868; 3 volumes.
- Execution Dockets, 1842-1868; 2 volumes. [*See also* Court of Pleas and Quarter Sessions, Execution Dockets, 1861-1868]
- Minutes, 1807-1932; 11 volumes.
- State Docket, 1847-1868; 1 volume.
- Trial Docket, 1842-1865; 1 volume.

ELECTION RECORDS

Elections, Record of, 1878-1922; 4 volumes.

ESTATES RECORDS

Accounts, Record of, 1868-1925; 2 volumes.
Administrators' Bonds, 1869-1938; 3 volumes.
Estates, Record of, 1780-1854; 6 volumes.
Estates Records, 1783-1939, 1949; 38 Fibredex boxes.
Guardians' Accounts, 1908-1933; 1 volume.
Guardians' Bonds, 1869-1913; 1 volume.
Guardians' Records, 1779-1935; 14 Fibredex boxes.
Settlements and Divisions of Estates, Record of, 1830-1902; 5 volumes.

LAND RECORDS

Deeds, Index to, 1779-1810; 2 volumes.
Deeds, Record of, 1779-1828; 12 volumes.
Ejectments, 1853-1905, 1915; 1 Fibredex box.
Land Entries, 1841-1898; 1 volume.
Land Grants, 1788-1795; 1 volume.
Miscellaneous Land Records, 1796-1940; 4 Fibredex boxes.

MARRIAGE, DIVORCE, AND VITAL STATISTICS
Divorce Records, 1871-1905; 2 Fibredex boxes.
Marriage Certificates, Record of, 1851-1874; 1 volume.
Marriage Registers, 1874-1941; 3 volumes.

MILITARY AND PENSION RECORDS [*See* **CRX RECORDS**]

MISCELLANEOUS RECORDS
Assignees, Receivers, and Trustees, Records of, 1895-1934; 2 Fibredex boxes.
Licenses to Trades, Registry of, 1874-1903; 1 volume.
Lunacy Records, 1884-1934; 1 Fibredex box.
Miscellaneous Records, 1785-1935; 1 Fibredex box.
Special Proceedings Docket, 1869-1912; 1 volume.

TAX AND FISCAL RECORDS
Federal Direct Taxes Collected, Record of, 1866; 1 volume.

WILLS
Wills, 1779-1935; 10 Fibredex boxes.

CRX RECORDS
Letter Inquiring about Confederate Soldiers, 1924; 1 folder.

MICROFILM RECORDS

BONDS
Bastardy Bonds, 1869-1892; 1 reel.

CORPORATIONS AND PARTNERSHIPS
Corporations, Record of, 1891-1980; 2 reels.
Partnerships, Record of, 1923-1949; 1 reel.

COURT RECORDS
County Court of Pleas and Quarter Sessions
Minutes, 1807-1868; 1 reel.
Superior Court
Judgments, Index to, Defendant, 1868-1968; 1 reel.
Judgments, Index to, Plaintiff, 1868-1968; 1 reel.
Minutes, 1820-1964; 5 reels.

ELECTION RECORDS
Elections, Record of, 1878-1916, 1924-1964; 1 reel.

ESTATES RECORDS
Accounts of Indigent Orphans, 1908-1933; 1 reel.
Accounts, Record of, 1854-1968; 4 reels.
Administrators' Bonds, 1869-1938; 2 reels.
Administrators', Executors', and Guardians' Bonds, 1915-1937; 1 reel.
Administrators, Executors, and Guardians, Cross Index to, 1920-1964; 1 reel.
Administrators, Executors, and Guardians, Record of, 1921-1969; 2 reels.
Appointment of Executors, 1868-1923; 1 reel.
Appointment of Receivers of Estates, 1905-1957; 1 reel.
Division and Settlement of Estates, 1830-1957; 3 reels.
Estates, Record of, 1792-1868; 4 reels.
Guardians' Bonds, 1869-1913; 1 reel.

Guardians, Record of, 1921-1964; 1 reel.
Inheritance Tax Records, 1924-1964; 1 reel.

LAND RECORDS

Deeds, Record of, 1779-1964; 73 reels.
Grants, Record of, 1780-1783; 1 reel.
Land Entry Books, 1779-1795, 1841-1959; 1 reel.
Real Estate Conveyances, General Index to, Grantee, 1779-1977; 3 reels.
Real Estate Conveyances, General Index to, Grantor, 1779-1964; 2 reels.
Sales and Resales, Record of, 1924-1963; 1 reel.

MARRIAGE, DIVORCE, AND VITAL STATISTICS

Delayed Births, Index to, various years; 1 reel.
Maiden Names of Divorced Women, 1946-1963; 1 reel.
Marriage Licenses, 1867-1961; 4 reels.
Marriage Registers, 1851-1964; 1 reel.
Vital Statistics, Index to, 1914-1961; 1 reel.

MILITARY AND PENSION RECORDS

Pensions, Record of, 1912-1926; 1 reel.

MISCELLANEOUS RECORDS

Orders and Decrees, 1869-1960; 1 reel.
Special Proceedings, 1869-1964; 3 reels.

OFFICIALS, COUNTY

Board of County Commissioners, Minutes, 1868-1964; 3 reels.

SCHOOL RECORDS

County Board of Education, Minutes, 1873-1879, 1885-1964; 1 reel.

TAX AND FISCAL RECORDS

List of Taxables, 1866; 1 reel.
Tax List, 1779; 1 reel.

WILLS

Original Wills, 1760-1842; 1 reel.
Wills, Index to, 1779-1964; 1 reel.
Wills, Record of, 1779-1964; 2 reels.

LEE COUNTY

Established in 1907 from Chatham and Moore counties.

ORIGINAL RECORDS

BONDS

Apprentice Bonds, 1911-1923; 1 volume.

COURT RECORDS

Superior Court

Minutes, 1908-1913; 1 volume.

ELECTION RECORDS

Elections, Record of, 1908-1924; 1 volume.

MILITARY AND PENSION RECORDS [*See* **MISCELLANEOUS RECORDS**]

MISCELLANEOUS RECORDS

Alien Registration, 1928, 1940; 1 volume.
Miscellaneous Records, 1928-1946; 1 manuscript box.
Pensions, Record of, 1908, 1926-1940; 2 volumes.

WILLS

Wills, Cross Index to, 1908-1923; 1 volume.

MICROFILM RECORDS

BONDS

Apprentice Bonds, 1911-1923; 1 reel.

CORPORATIONS AND PARTNERSHIPS

Corporations, Assumed Names, and Partnerships, Index to, 1907-1970; 1 reel.
Corporations, Record of, 1907-1966; 2 reels.

COURT RECORDS

Superior Court

Minutes, 1908-1959; 6 reels.

ELECTION RECORDS

Elections, Record of, 1908-1946; 1 reel.

ESTATE RECORDS

Accounts of Indigent Orphans, 1909-1930; 1 reel.
Accounts, Record of, 1907-1934; 1 reel.
Administrators and Executors, Cross Index to, 1908-1919; 1 reel.
Administrators, Executors, and Guardians, Record of, 1908-1922; 1 reel.
Administrators and Executors, Index to, 1908-1924; 1 reel.
Administrators, Record of, 1914-1968; 8 reels.
Dowers, Record of, 1908-1951; 1 reel.
Executors and Guardians, Record of, 1927-1936; 1 reel.
Executors, Record of, 1952-1968; 1 reel.
Guardians, Record of, 1935-1968; 2 reels.
Guardians and Wards, Index to, 1912-1923; 2 reels.
Guardians of World War Veterans, 1931-1948; 1 reel.

Inheritance Tax Records, 1921-1968; 2 reels.
Settlements, Record of, 1912-1926; 1 reel.

LAND RECORDS

Deeds, Record of, 1908-1962; 36 reels.
Federal Tax Lien Index, 1925-1970; 1 reel.
Real Estate Conveyances, Index to, Grantee, 1908-1970; 9 reels.
Real Estate Conveyances, Index to, Grantor, 1908-1970; 10 reels.
Real Estate Conveyances, Index to, Trustee, 1953-1970; 2 reels.
Resale of Land by Trustees and Mortgagees, Record of, 1920-1962; 3 reels.
Surveys, Record of, 1908-1928; 1 reel.
Taxes for Mortgagees, Record of, 1931-1934; 1 reel.

MARRIAGE, DIVORCE, AND VITAL STATISTICS

Births, Index to, 1913-1987; 3 reels.
Deaths and Delayed Births, Index to, 1913-1968; 1 reel.
Deaths, Index to, 1969-1987; 1 reel.
Delayed Births, Index to, various years; 1 reel.
Maiden Names of Divorced Women, 1942-1968; 1 reel.
Marriage Licenses, 1908-1970; 8 reels.
Marriages, Index to, 1908-1987; 2 reels.

MILITARY AND PENSION RECORDS [*See also* **ESTATES RECORDS**]

Pensions, Record of, 1908-1940; 1 reel.

MISCELLANEOUS RECORDS

Appointment of Receivers, 1908-1919; 1 reel.
Clerk's Minute Dockets, 1921-1968; 7 reels.
Clerk's Minute Dockets and Wills, Index to, 1908-1968; 3 reels.
Homestead Proceedings, 1927-1949; 1 reel.
Lunacy Dockets, 1908-1969; 3 reels.
Official Reports, Record of, 1908-1920; 1 reel.
Orders and Decrees, 1908-1968; 7 reels.

OFFICIALS, COUNTY

Board of County Commissioners, Minutes, 1908-1970; 3 reels.

SCHOOL RECORDS

County Board of Education, Minutes, 1908-1970; 2 reels.

TAX AND FISCAL RECORDS

Board of Equalization and Review, Minutes, 1963-1970; 1 reel.
Tax Scrolls, 1965; 2 reels.

WILLS

Wills, Index to, 1908-1924; 1 reel. [*See also* **MISCELLANEOUS RECORDS**, Clerk's Minute Dockets and Wills, Index to, 1908-1968]
Wills, Record of, 1908-1968; 3 reels.

LENOIR COUNTY

Established in 1791 from Dobbs County.
Most court records destroyed in fires of 1878 and 1880.

ORIGINAL RECORDS

BONDS

Apprentice Bonds and Records, 1879-1917; 2 volumes, 1 Fibredex box.
Officials' Bonds and Records, 1802-1937; 1 volume, 3 Fibredex boxes.

COURT RECORDS

Inferior Court
Minutes, 1878-1885; 1 volume.
Superior Court
Civil Action Papers, 1866-1939; 14 Fibredex boxes.
Civil Action Papers Concerning Land, 1878-1939; 4 Fibredex boxes.
Criminal Action Papers, 1901-1928; 1 Fibredex box.
Judgment Dockets, 1891-1946; 26 volumes.
Judgment Dockets, Divorces, 1924-1969; 8 volumes.
Minutes, 1880-1968; 51 volumes.

ELECTION RECORDS

Election Records, 1880-1908; 2 Fibredex boxes.
Elections, Record of, 1880-1932, 1960-2000; 4 volumes.

ESTATES RECORDS

Accounts, Record of, 1880-1944; 15 volumes.
Administrators' Bonds, 1879-1891, 1900-1935; 6 volumes.
Estates Records, 1830-1956; 94 Fibredex boxes. [*See also* **CRX RECORDS**]
Guardians' Bonds, 1879-1933; 4 volumes.
Guardians' Records, 1868, 1874-1952; 26 Fibredex boxes.
Inheritance Tax Records, 1923-1974; 3 volumes.
Settlements, Record of, 1880-1904; 2 volumes.
Widows' Year's Support, Record of, 1927-1958; 2 volumes.

LAND RECORDS [*See also* CRX RECORDS; DOBBS COUNTY, LAND RECORDS]

Attachments, Executions, Levies, and Liens on Land, 1873-1919; 1 Fibredex box.
Boundary Line Disputes, 1885-1938; 1 Fibredex box.
Deeds, Cross Index to, 1879-1893; 1 volume.
Deeds of Sale, 1792-1941; 4 Fibredex boxes.
Foreclosures, 1890-1955; 3 Fibredex boxes.
Land Entries, 1879-1915; 1 volume.
Miscellaneous Deeds, 1816-1939; 1 Fibredex box.
Miscellaneous Land Records, 1879-1943; 1 Fibredex box.
Petitions for Partition of Land, 1877-1939; 2 Fibredex boxes.
Petitions for Sale of Land, 1884-1939; 3 Fibredex boxes.
Sale and Resale of Land, Record of, 1921-1969; 6 volumes.

MARRIAGE, DIVORCE, AND VITAL STATISTICS

Divorce Records, 1880-1914, 1922-1969; 94 Fibredex boxes. [*See also* **COURT RECORDS**, Superior Court, Judgment Dockets]
Marriage Bonds, 1791-1868; 1 Fibredex box.
Marriage Registers, 1873-1937; 2 volumes.

Marriages Performed by K. F. Foscue, Justice of the Peace, Record of, 1924-1935; 1 volume.
Vital Statistics, Index to, 1914-1928; 1 volume.

MISCELLANEOUS RECORDS

Alien Registration, 1927, 1940; 1 volume.
Appointment of Road Overseers, Record of, 1826-1862; 1 volume.
Assignees, Receivers, and Trustees, Records of, 1878-1942; 5 Fibredex boxes.
Assumed Business Names, Corporations, and Partnership Records, 1878-1938; 1 Fibredex box.
Canal Records, 1883-1927; 1 Fibredex box.
Clerk's Minute Dockets, 1921-1941; 8 volumes.
Inebriates, Record of, 1939-1963; 1 volume.
Lunacy, Record of, 1904-1968; 5 volumes.
Lunacy Records, 1881-1934; 5 Fibredex boxes.
Miscellaneous Records, 1868-1949; 2 Fibredex boxes. [*See also* **CRX RECORDS**]
Official Reports, Record of, 1888-1914; 1 volume.
Proceedings of the Committee of Finance, Record of, 1855-1868; 1 volume.
Railroad Records, 1889-1937; 2 Fibredex boxes.
Receivers, Record of, 1930-1968; 5 volumes.
Record Book, 1738-1866; 1 volume.
Road, Bridge, and Ferry Records, 1878-1921; 2 Fibredex boxes.
School Records, 1879-1935; 1 Fibredex box.
Timber Records, 1903-1929; 1 Fibredex box.

ROADS AND BRIDGES [*See* **MISCELLANEOUS RECORDS**]

SCHOOL RECORDS [*See* **MISCELLANEOUS RECORDS**]

TAX AND FISCAL RECORDS

Tax Records, 1880-1937; 2 Fibredex boxes.

WILLS

Wills, 1824-1916; 1 Fibredex box. [*See also* **CRX RECORDS**]
Wills, Cross Index to, 1868-1936; 1 volume.

CRX RECORDS

Deeds, 1823, 1855; 2 folders.
Estates Records, 1808, 1871; 2 folders.
Miscellaneous Record, 1902; 1 folder.
Wills, 1864, no date; 2 folders.

MICROFILM RECORDS

CORPORATIONS AND PARTNERSHIPS

Corporations, Record of, 1900-1935; 1 reel.
Partnership Records, 1916-1946; 1 reel.

COURT RECORDS

Superior Court
Minutes, 1880-1953; 17 reels.
Judgments, Index to, Defendant, 1800-1968; 5 reels.
Judgments, Index to, Plaintiff, 1880-1968; 5 reels.

ELECTION RECORDS

Elections, Record of, 1924-1966; 1 reel.

ESTATES RECORDS

Accounts, Record of, 1880-1966; 13 reels.
Administrators' Bonds, 1905-1955; 4 reels.
Amounts Paid for Indigent Children, Record of, 1913-1942; 1 reel.
Appointment of Administrators, Executors, and Guardians, 1894-1955; 1 reel.
Divisions, Dowers, and Year's Provisions, 1868-1956; 2 reels.
Estates: Titles, Index to, 1870-1966; 3 reels.
Estates: Wards, Index to, 1870-1966; 4 reels.
Guardians' Bonds, 1905-1955; 2 reels.
Inheritance Tax Records, 1923-1966; 1 reel.
Settlements, Record of, 1880-1966; 8 reels.
Widows' Year's Allowance, Record of, 1927-1958; 1 reel.

LAND RECORDS

Deeds, Record of, 1880-1955; 89 reels.
Plat Books, 1913-1966; 3 reels.
Plat Books, Index to, 1870-1966; 1 reel.
Real Estate Conveyances, Index to, Grantee, 1746-1966; 9 reels.
Real Estate Conveyances, Index to, Grantor, 1746-1964; 9 reels.
Resale of Land, Record of, 1921-1966; 4 reels.

MARRIAGE, DIVORCE, AND VITAL STATISTICS

Births, Index to, 1914-1981; 9 reels.
Deaths, Index to, 1914-1981; 6 reels.
Delayed Births, Index to, various years; 1 reel.
Marriage Bonds, 1791-1868; 1 reel.
Marriage Registers, 1873-1966; 3 reels.

MISCELLANEOUS RECORDS

Burials, Record of, 1915-1966; Cemetery Lot Map, no date; 1 reel.
Cemetery Lots, Kinston, Record of, 1848-1915; 1 reel.
Homestead Returns, 1937-1964; 1 reel.
Orders and Decrees, 1880-1942; 13 reels.
Record Book, 1738-1866; 1 reel.
Special Proceedings, 1874-1941; 1 reel.
Special Proceedings and Orders and Decrees, Index to, Defendant, 1874-1966; 4 reels.
Special Proceedings and Orders and Decrees, Index to, Plaintiff, 1874-1968; 3 reels.

OFFICIALS, COUNTY

Board of County Commissioners, Minutes, 1873-1966; 4 reels.

SCHOOL RECORDS

County Board of Education, Minutes, 1884-1957; 1 reel.

WILLS

Wills, Index to, Devisee, 1869-1966; 1 reel.
Wills, Index to, Devisor, 1869-1966; 1 reel.
Wills, Record of, 1869-1966; 6 reels.

LINCOLN COUNTY

Established in 1779 from Tryon County.
No known losses but many records are missing.

ORIGINAL RECORDS

Bonds

Apprentice Bonds, 1783-1917; 2 volumes, 3 Fibredex boxes.
Bastardy Bonds, 1784-1893; 3 Fibredex boxes.
Officials' Bonds, 1769-1883; 5 Fibredex boxes.

Court Records

County Court of Pleas and Quarter Sessions
- Appearance Docket, 1843-1868; 1 volume.
- Execution Dockets, 1806-1868; 4 volumes.
- Levy Docket, 1838-1846; 1 volume.
- Minutes, 1781-1868; 15 volumes.
- Recognizance Docket, 1817-1825; 1 volume.
- State Dockets, 1792-1806, 1835-1868; 3 volumes.
- Trial and Appearance Dockets, 1783-1843; 5 volumes, 2 manuscript boxes.
- Trial Docket, 1843-1868; 1 volume.

Superior Court
- Appearance Docket, 1843-1870; 1 volume.
- Civil Action Papers, 1771-1917; 36 Fibredex boxes.
- Civil Action Papers Concerning Gold, Iron, and Railroads, 1831-1899; 1 Fibredex box.
- Civil Action Papers Concerning Land, 1790-1918; 8 Fibredex boxes.
- Civil Action Papers Concerning Land and Gold Mining, Andrew Falls, Plaintiff, 1832; 1 Fibredex box.
- Criminal Action Papers, 1782-1894; 9 Fibredex boxes.
- Equity Enrolling Dockets, 1812-1867; 3 volumes.
- Equity Execution Docket, 1857-1868; 1 volume.
- Equity Minutes, 1830-1868; 2 volumes. [*See also* Minutes, 1816-1841]
- Equity Trial and Appearance Dockets, 1810-1868; 3 volumes.
- Execution Dockets, 1813-1871; 5 volumes.
- Lien Docket, 1893-1931; 1 volume. [*See also* Equity Minutes, 1860-1868]
- Minutes, 1816-1911; 12 volumes, 1 manuscript box.
- Recognizance Docket, 1817-1841; 1 volume.
- State Dockets, 1823-1869; 3 volumes.
- Trial and Appearance Dockets, 1807-1842; 2 volumes.
- Trial Dockets, 1843-1870; 3 volumes.

Election Records

Election Records, 1798-1922; 6 Fibredex boxes.
Elections, Record of, 1878-1934; 5 volumes.
Permanent Roll of Registered Voters, 1902-1908; 1 volume.

Estates Records

Accounts, Record of, 1868-1907; 6 volumes.
Administrators' Bonds, 1868-1913; 3 volumes.
Amounts Paid for Indigent Children, Record of, 1924-1930; 1 volume.

Estates, Record of, 1812-1819, 1831-1868; 3 volumes.
Estates Records, 1803-1937; 137 Fibredex boxes.
Guardians' Bonds, 1868-1924; 3 volumes.
Guardians' Records, 1777-1925; 15 Fibredex boxes.

LAND RECORDS

Deeds, 1777-1925; 2 Fibredex boxes. [*See also* **CRX RECORDS**]
Deeds, Record of, 1770-1810; 8 volumes.
Ejectments, 1800-1895; 2 Fibredex boxes.
Land Entries, 1788-1825; 2 volumes.
Land Grants, 1763-1813; 4 volumes.

MARRIAGE, DIVORCE, AND VITAL STATISTICS

Cohabitation, Record of, 1866; 1 volume.
Divorce Records, 1811-1921; 2 Fibredex boxes.
Marriage Bonds, 1779-1868; 20 Fibredex boxes. [*See also* **CRX RECORDS**]
Marriage Certificates, Record of, 1851-1870; 1 volume.

MILITARY AND PENSION RECORDS [*See* **MISCELLANEOUS RECORDS**]

MISCELLANEOUS RECORDS

Board of County Commissioners, Minutes, 1868-1870; 1 volume.
Board of Road Commissioners, Minutes, 1913-1915; 1 volume.
Board of Superintendents of Common Schools, Minutes, 1845-1865; 1 volume.
Civil War Records, 1864-1923; 1 Fibredex box.
County Accounts and Claims, 1773-1891; 1 Fibredex box.
Drainage Record, 1912-1925; 1 volume.
Insolvent Debtors and Homestead and Personal Property Exemptions, 1788-1895; 1 Fibredex box.
Jurors, Lists of, 1785-1919; 1 Fibredex box.
Miscellaneous Records, 1764-1923; 8 Fibredex boxes. [*See also* **CRX RECORDS**]
Pension Records, 1885-1894, 1901-1907; 1 Fibredex box.
Public School Register, 1893-1897; 1 volume.
Record Book, Company A, 34th Regiment N.C. Troops, 1861-1865; 1 volume.
Road Records, 1781-1869; 4 Fibredex boxes.
Schoolchildren, Lists of, 1845-1862, 1883, 1895; 10 manuscript boxes.
Treasurer's Account of County Funds, 1892-1902; 1 volume.
Wardens of the Poor, Minutes, 1820-1868; 1 volume.

OFFICIALS, COUNTY [*See* **MISCELLANEOUS RECORDS**]

ROADS AND BRIDGES [*See* **MISCELLANEOUS RECORDS**]

SCHOOL RECORDS [*See* **MISCELLANEOUS RECORDS**]

TAX AND FISCAL RECORDS

Tax Lists, 1784-1886, 1916-1917, 1920, 1922-1923, 1926, 1929; 11 volumes, 4 Fibredex boxes.

WILLS

Wills, 1769-1926; 28 Fibredex boxes. [*See also* **CRX RECORDS**]
Wills, Cross Index to, 1765-1940; 1 volume.

CRX RECORDS

Deed, 1830; 1 folder.
Miscellaneous Records, 1778-1851; 3 Fibredex boxes.
Will, 1798; 1 folder.
Wills, Marriage Bonds, and Miscellaneous Items, 1786-1867; 1 volume.

MICROFILM RECORDS

BONDS

Apprentice Bonds, 1869-1917; 1 reel.
Officials' Bonds, 1883-1921; 2 reels.

CORPORATIONS AND PARTNERSHIPS

Incorporations, Record of, 1887-1941; 1 reel.

COURT RECORDS

County Court of Pleas and Quarter Sessions
- Minutes, 1782-1868; 5 reels.
- Trial and Appearance Docket, 1799-1807; 1 reel.

Superior Court
- Equity Enrolling Dockets, 1830-1868; 2 reels.
- Equity Minutes, 1816-1867; 2 reels.
- Judgments, Index to, 1868-1931; 1 reel.
- Judgments, Index to, Defendant, 1924-1968; 2 reels.
- Judgments, Index to, Plaintiff, 1924-1968; 2 reels.
- Minutes, 1842-1960; 8 reels.

ELECTION RECORDS

Elections, Record of, 1878-1962; 1 reel.

ESTATES RECORDS

Accounts, Record of, 1868-1964; 9 reels.
Accounts and Settlements, Index to, 1868-1964; 1 reel.
Administrators' Bonds, 1868-1913; 1 reel.
Administrators and Executors, Record of, 1909-1937; 1 reel.
Administrators, Record of, 1936-1964; 2 reels.
Estates, Record of, 1812-1819; 1 reel.
Executors, Record of, 1869-1908, 1924-1964; 1 reel.
Guardians' Bonds, 1868-1925; 1 reel.
Guardians, Record of, 1924-1964; 1 reel.
Inheritance Tax Records, 1921-1964; 1 reel.
Inventories and Accounts of Estates, 1831-1868; 1 reel.
Receivers of Estates, Record of, 1907-1930; 1 reel.
Settlements, Record of, 1869-1964; 5 reels.

LAND RECORDS

Deeds, Record of, 1769-1961; 119 reels.
Grants, Index to, 1763-1923; 1 reel.
Land Entries, 1788-1853; 3 reels.
Land Grants, 1763-1923; 4 reels.
Levies on Land, 1838-1846; 1 reel.
Procession of Land, 1794-1834; 2 reels.
Real Estate Conveyances, Index to, Grantee, 1769-1964; 4 reels.

Real Estate Conveyances, Index to, Grantor, 1769-1964; 4 reels.
Sales and Resales of Land, Record of, 1921-1964; 2 reels.

MARRIAGE, DIVORCE, AND VITAL STATISTICS

Births, Index to, 1913-1964; 1 reel.
Cohabitation, Record of, 1866; 1 reel.
Deaths, Index to, 1913-1964; 1 reel.
Maiden Names of Divorced Women, 1942-1964; 1 reel.
Marriage Bonds, 1779-1868; 8 reels.
Marriage Licenses, 1868-1961; 8 reels.
Marriage Register, 1869-1976; 1 reel.
Marriages, Record of, 1851-1869; 1 reel.

MILITARY AND PENSION RECORDS

Record Book, Company A, 34th Regiment N.C. Troops, 1861-1865; 1 reel.

MISCELLANEOUS RECORDS

Orders and Decrees, 1868-1954; 16 reels.
Orders and Decrees, Special Proceedings, and Lunacy, Index to, 1868-1964; 1 reel.
Special Proceedings, Index to, 1968-1977; 1 reel.
Wardens of the Poor, 1820-1868; 1 reel.

OFFICIALS, COUNTY

Board of County Commissioners, Minutes, 1870-1964; 6 reels.

SCHOOL RECORDS

County Board of Education, Minutes, 1885-1964; 1 reel.

TAX RECORDS

Tax Lists, 1837-1858; 1 reel.

WILLS

Wills, Index to, 1772-1968; 2 reels.
Wills, Record of, 1824-1964; 4 reels.

MACON COUNTY

Established in 1828 from Haywood County.
No known losses but many records are missing.

ORIGINAL RECORDS

BONDS [*See also* **CRX RECORDS**]
Bastardy Bonds and Records, 1838-1897; 1 volume, 1 Fibredex box.

COURT RECORDS [*See also* **CRX RECORDS**]
County Court of Pleas and Quarter Sessions
Execution Dockets, 1838-1868; 2 volumes.
Minutes, 1829-1868; 4 volumes.
State Docket, 1829-1844; 1 volume.
Trial Docket, 1845-1868; 1 volume.
Justice's Court
Judgment Dockets, 1925-1966; 4 volumes.
Superior Court
Appearance Docket, 1840-1868; 1 volume.
Civil Action Papers, 1822-1924; 31 Fibredex boxes.
Civil Action Papers Concerning Land, 1825-1926; 8 Fibredex boxes.
Civil Issues Docket, 1869-1903; 1 volume.
Criminal Action Papers, 1743-1971; 24 Fibredex boxes.
Criminal Issues Dockets, 1869-1884; 2 volumes.
Equity Appearance Docket, 1835-1854; 1 volume.
Equity Execution Docket, 1837-1868; 1 volume.
Equity Minutes, 1833-1868; 2 volumes.
Execution Dockets, 1846-1870; 2 volumes.
Judgment Dockets, 1868-1966; 25 volumes. [*See also* **LAND RECORDS**]
Judgments in Civil Actions, Index to, 1867-1877; 1 volume.
Judgments, Cross Index to, 1868-1937; 5 volumes.
Minutes, 1843-1966; 19 volumes.
Minutes, Index to, undated, 1950-1966; 4 volumes.
State Dockets, 1840-1869; 2 volumes.
Summons Dockets, 1869-1966; 4 volumes.
Trial Dockets, 1840-1868; 2 volumes.

ELECTION RECORDS [*See also* **MISCELLANEOUS RECORDS; CRX RECORDS**]
Election Records, 1829-1874; 1 Fibredex box.
Elections, Record of, 1878-1914; 4 volumes.
Permanent Voter Registration, 1902-1908; 1 volume.

ESTATES RECORDS [*See also* **CRX RECORDS**]
Accounts, Record of, 1868-1966; 8 volumes.
Administrators' Bonds, 1870-1920; 3 volumes.
Amounts Paid for Indigent Children, Record of, 1903-1945; 1 volume.
Estates, Record of, 1866-1868; 1 volume.
Estates Records, 1831-1920; 27 Fibredex boxes.
Guardians' Bonds, 1870-1919; 2 volumes.
Guardians' Records, 1845-1937; 3 Fibredex boxes.

Inheritance Tax Records, 1924-1969; 2 volumes.
Settlements, Record of, 1870-1913; 1 volume.

LAND RECORDS [*See also* **CRX RECORDS**]
Cherokee Lands Surveyed, 1837; 1 volume.
Deeds, 1828-1920; 2 Fibredex boxes.
Entry Takers' Books, 1836-1937; 10 volumes.
Ejectments, 1833-1890; 1 Fibredex box.
Judgment Docket, Tax Suits, 1931-1945; 2 volumes. [*See also* **COURT RECORDS**, Superior Court]
Land Grants, 1836-1919; 1 Fibredex box.
Miscellaneous Deeds, 1843-1930; 1 Fibredex box.
Miscellaneous Land Records, 1837-1924; 1 Fibredex box.
Probate, Record of, 1827-1875; 2 volumes.
Sales and Resales, Record of, 1925-1966; 3 volumes.

MARRIAGE, DIVORCE, AND VITAL STATISTICS
Divorce Records, 1835-1913; 3 Fibredex boxes.
Marriage Bonds, 1828-1868; 4 Fibredex boxes.
Marriage Licenses, 1869-1891, 1908; 1 Fibredex box.
Marriage Registers, 1831-1943; 4 volumes.

MILITARY AND PENSION RECORDS [*See* **MISCELLANEOUS RECORDS**]

MISCELLANEOUS RECORDS [*See also* **CRX RECORDS**]
Alien Registration, 1940; 1 volume.
Board of Elections, Minutes, 1900-1928; 1 volume.
Cherokee Bond Account Books, 1820-1851; 3 volumes.
Clerk's Minute Docket (Special Proceedings), 1875-1884; 1 volume.
Inquisition of Lunacy, Record of, 1899-1965; 3 volumes.
Insolvent Debtors, 1831-1860; 1 Fibredex box.
Miscellaneous Records, 1829-1964; 3 Fibredex boxes.
Orders and Decrees, 1869-1904; 2 volumes.
Pension Roll, 1903-1910; 1 volume.
Public School Statistical Records, 1885-1896; 1 volume.
Railroad Records, 1855-1914; 1 Fibredex box.
Road Record (Overseers), 1838-1861; 1 volume.
Road Records, 1829-1905; 2 Fibredex boxes.
School Records, 1835-1928; 1 Fibredex box.

OFFICIALS, COUNTY [*See* **CRX RECORDS**]

ROADS AND BRIDGES [*See* **MISCELLANEOUS RECORDS**]

SCHOOL RECORDS [*See* **MISCELLANEOUS RECORDS**]

TAX AND FISCAL RECORDS [*See also* **CRX RECORDS**]
Tax Lists, 1857-1868; 1 volume.

WILLS
Wills, 1830-1905, 1933; 3 Fibredex boxes.

CRX RECORDS
Apprentice Bonds, 1829-1881; 1 Fibredex box.
Bastardy Bonds, 1829-1906; 1 Fibredex box.

Civil Action Papers, 1828-1880; 5 Fibredex boxes.
County Accounts and Claims, 1830-1925; 3 Fibredex boxes.
Criminal Action Papers, 1829-1906; 3 Fibredex boxes.
Election Records, 1837-1922; 4 Fibredex boxes.
Estates Records, 1825-1880, 1924, 1933; 3 Fibredex boxes.
Executions, 1830-1874; 9 Fibredex boxes.
Guardians' Records, 1832-1877; 1 Fibredex box.
Jury Records, 1829-1916; 2 Fibredex boxes.
Justices of the Peace, Records of, 1841-1905; 1 Fibredex box.
Land Records, 1832-1839; 1 Fibredex box.
Merchants' Purchase Returns, 1874-1877, 1887-1895; 1 Fibredex box.
Miscellaneous Records, 1829-1943; 2 Fibredex boxes.
Officials' Bonds, 1829-1869, 1900, 1905, 1925; 1 Fibredex box.
Road and Bridge Records, 1823-1925; 4 Fibredex boxes.
School Records, 1840-1924; 1 Fibredex box.
Tax Records, 1840-1936; 1 Fibredex box.

MICROFILM RECORDS

CORPORATIONS AND PARTNERSHIPS

Incorporations, Record of, 1887-1971; 1 reel.
Partnership Records, 1915-1973; 1 reel.

COURT RECORDS

County Court of Pleas and Quarter Sessions
  Minutes, 1829-1868; 1 reel.
Superior Court
  Judgments, Index to, Defendant, 1938-1966; 1 reel.
  Judgments, Index to, Plaintiff, 1938-1966; 1 reel.
  Minutes, 1869-1963; 8 reels.
  Minutes, Cross Index to, 1869-1963; 2 reels.

ESTATES RECORDS

Accounts, Record of, 1868-1966; 4 reels.
Amounts Paid for Indigent Children, Record of, 1903-1945; 1 reel.
Administrators, Executors, and Guardians, Record of, 1913-1930; 1 reel.
Administrators, Record of, 1931-1966; 2 reels.
Appointment of Administrators, Executors, and Guardians, 1868-1913; 1 reel.
Estates, Index to, 1868-1966; 1 reel.
Executors, Record of, 1930-1966; 1 reel.
Guardians, Record of, 1927-1966; 1 reel.
Inheritance Tax Records, 1920-1966; 1 reel.
Settlements, Record of, 1870-1966; 3 reels.

LAND RECORDS

Deeds, Record of, 1828-1960; 71 reels.
Real Estate Conveyances, Index to, Grantee, 1829-1966; 11 reels.
Real Estate Conveyances, Index to, Grantor, 1829-1966; 11 reels.
Sale of Land, Record of, 1925-1966; 2 reels.
State Grant Index, 1826-1926; 1 reel.
Surveys, Record of, 1905-1927; 1 reel.

Marriage, Divorce, and Vital Statistics

Births, Index to, 1913-1966; 1 reel.
Deaths, Index to, 1913-1966; 1 reel.
Delayed Births, Index to, various years; 1 reel.
Maiden Names of Divorced Women, 1940-1965; 1 reel.
Marriage Bonds, 1828-1868; 5 reels.
Marriage Registers, 1829-1966; 2 reels.

Miscellaneous Records

Orders and Decrees, 1869-1955; 10 reels.
Special Proceedings, Cross Index to, 1869-1939; 1 reel.
Special Proceedings Dockets, 1875-1928; 1 reel.
Special Proceedings, Index to, 1940-1966; 1 reel.

Officials, County

Board of County Commissioners, Minutes, 1868-1922; 4 reels.

School Records

County Board of Education, Minutes, 1885-1966; 1 reel.

Wills

Wills, Cross Index to, 1830-1966; 1 reel.
Wills, Record of, 1830-1966; 3 reels.

MADISON COUNTY

Established in 1851 from Buncombe and Yancey counties.

ORIGINAL RECORDS

BONDS

Apprentice Bonds, 1874-1914; 1 volume.
Apprentice Bonds and Records, 1851-1907; Bastardy Bonds and Records, 1851-1910; 1 Fibredex box.
Bastardy Bonds, 1874-1910; 1 volume.
Officials' Bonds, 1851-1894; 1 Fibredex box.

COURT RECORDS

Circuit Criminal Court/Western District Criminal Court
- Minutes, 1895-1899; 1 volume. [*See also* Superior Court, Minutes, 1900-1902]

County Court of Pleas and Quarter Sessions
- Appearance Docket, 1852-1867; 1 volume.
- Execution Docket, 1863-1868; 1 volume.
- Minutes, 1865-1868; 1 volume.

Inferior Court
- Minutes, 1883-1888, 1894-1895; 1 volume.

Superior Court
- Civil Action Papers, 1837-1925; 13 Fibredex boxes.
- Civil Action Papers Concerning Land, 1856-1940; 8 Fibredex boxes.
- Criminal Action Papers, 1849-1936; 12 Fibredex boxes.
- Minutes, 1851-1913; 11 volumes.

ELECTION RECORDS

Elections, Record of, 1878-1914, 1928-1936; 4 volumes.
Voter Registration Books, 1932-1964; 22 volumes.

ESTATES RECORDS

Accounts, Record of, 1873-1909; 1 volume.
Administrators' Bonds, 1874-1904; 2 volumes.
Appointment of Administrators, Executors, Guardians, and Masters, 1868-1913; 1 volume.
Estates, Record of, 1852-1862; 1 volume.
Estates Records, 1833, 1851-1943; 37 Fibredex boxes.
Guardians' Bonds, 1874-1896; 2 volumes.
Guardians' Records, 1855-1928; 5 Fibredex boxes.

LAND RECORDS

Attachments, Executions, Liens, and Levies on Land, 1851-1932; 1 Fibredex box.
Deeds, Record of, 1851-1858, 1862-1891; 2 volumes.
Ejectments, 1851-1907; 1 Fibredex box.
Miscellaneous Land Records, 1817-1932; 1 Fibredex box.
Probate of Deeds, 1894-1902; 1 volume.

MARRIAGE, DIVORCE, AND VITAL STATISTICS

Divorce Records, 1854-1926; 6 Fibredex boxes.
Marriage Bonds, 1851-1868; 3 Fibredex boxes.

Marriage Licenses, 1868-1945, 1956; 33 Fibredex boxes. [*See also* **CRX RECORDS**]
Marriage Register, 1862-1895; 1 volume.

MISCELLANEOUS RECORDS
Assignees, Receivers, and Trustees, Records of, 1851-1913; 1 Fibredex box.
County Highway Commission, Minutes, 1915-1919; 2 volumes.
Insolvents and Homestead and Personal Property Exemptions, 1852-1916; 1 Fibredex box.
Miscellaneous Records, 1851-1932; 4 Fibredex boxes.
Road Reports and Records, 1854-1937; Railroad Records, 1855-1907; 1 Fibredex box.

ROADS AND BRIDGES [*See* **MISCELLANEOUS RECORDS**]

SCHOOL RECORDS [*See* **CRX RECORDS**]

WILLS
Wills, 1851-1915; 2 Fibredex boxes.

CRX RECORDS
Marriage Licenses, 1873, 1884, 1929; 2 folders.
School Fund Ledger, 1882-1891; 1 volume.

MICROFILM RECORDS

BONDS
Apprentice Bonds, 1874-1914; 1 reel.
Officials' Bonds, Record of, 1894-1969; 1 reel.

CORPORATIONS AND PARTNERSHIPS
Corporations, Record of, 1890-1969; 1 reel.

COURT RECORDS
County Court of Pleas and Quarter Sessions
Minutes, 1851-1868; 2 reels.
Superior Court
Equity Minutes, 1851-1868; 1 reel.
Judgments, Index to, 1928-1968; 1 reel.
Minutes, 1851-1900; 4 reels.
Minutes, Civil, 1900-1958; 4 reels.
Minutes, Criminal, 1899-1955; 5 reels.

ELECTION RECORDS
Elections, Record of, 1878-1968; 1 reel.

ESTATES RECORDS
Accounts of Indigent Orphans, 1911-1915; 1 reel.
Accounts, Record of, 1873-1968; 4 reels.
Administrators' Bonds, 1874-1904; 1 reel.
Administrators and Executors, Index to, 1851-1968; 1 reel.
Administrators, Record of, 1904-1968; 3 reels.
Appointment of Administrators, Executors, and Guardians, 1868-1913; 1 reel.
Appointment and Record of Executors, 1914-1968; 1 reel.
Estates, Index to, 1968-1969; 1 reel.
Guardians' Bonds, 1874-1892, 1917-1968; 1 reel.

Guardians, Cross Index to, 1851-1968; 1 reel.
Guardians, Record of, 1904-1968; 2 reels.
Inheritance Tax Records, 1924-1968; 1 reel.
Inventory Docket, 1852-1862; 1 reel.
Settlements, Record of, 1868-1968; 3 reels.

LAND RECORDS

Deeds, Record of, 1851-1967; 55 reels.
Real Estate Conveyances, Index to, Grantee, 1851-1969; 4 reels.
Real Estate Conveyances, Index to, Grantor, 1851-1969; 4 reels.
Resale of Land by Trustees and Mortgagees, Record of, 1923-1969; 1 reel.

MARRIAGE, DIVORCE, AND VITAL STATISTICS

Births, Index to, 1913-1993; 2 reels.
Deaths, Index to, 1913-1993; 1 reel.
Delayed Births, Index to, various years; 1 reel.
Maiden Names of Divorced Women, 1939-1967; 1 reel.
Marriage Bonds, 1851-1868; 3 reels.
Marriage Registers, 1851-1989; 3 reels.

MISCELLANEOUS RECORDS

Lunacy, Record of, 1899-1969; 1 reel.
Orders and Decrees, 1868-1928; 1 reel.
Special Proceedings, 1883-1968; 8 reels.
Special Proceedings, Index to, 1899-1969; 1 reel.

OFFICIALS, COUNTY

Board of County Commissioners, Minutes, 1868-1943; 5 reels.

WILLS

Wills, Cross Index to, 1851-1969; 1 reel.
Wills, Record of, 1851-1968; 2 reels.

MARTIN COUNTY

Established in 1774 from Halifax and Tyrrell counties.
Courthouse fire of 1884 destroyed many court records.

ORIGINAL RECORDS

COURT RECORDS

County Court of Pleas and Quarter Sessions
- Execution Docket, 1844-1859; 1 volume.
- Minutes, 1847; 1 volume.
- Trial and Appearance Docket, 1852-1860; 1 volume.

Inferior Court
- Criminal Issues Docket, 1878-1884; 1 volume.
- Minutes, 1877-1885; 1 volume.

Superior Court
- Civil Action Papers, 1885-1903; 2 Fibredex boxes.
- Civil Action Papers Concerning Land, 1882-1903; 4 Fibredex boxes.
- Criminal Action Papers, 1884-1903; 1 Fibredex box.
- Equity Minutes, 1809-1829; 1 volume.
- Equity Trial Docket, 1834-1861; 1 volume.
- Minutes, 1838-1912; 8 volumes.

ELECTION RECORDS

Elections, Record of, 1874-1922; 4 volumes.

ESTATES RECORDS

Accounts, Record of, 1869-1904; 3 volumes.
Administrators' Bonds, 1867-1870, 1885-1913; 4 volumes.
Appointment of Administrators, Executors, Guardians, and Masters, 1869-1886; 1 volume.
Estates Records, 1820-1906; 6 Fibredex boxes.
Guardians' Bonds, 1866-1870, 1885-1913; 3 volumes.
Guardians' Records, 1887-1904; 4 Fibredex boxes.
Settlements, Record of, 1869-1916; 2 volumes.
Widows' Year's Support, Record of, 1885-1901; 1 volume.

LAND RECORDS

Deeds, Record of, 1774-1787; 1 volume.
Land Entries, Record of, 1866-1900; 1 volume.
Land Records, 1779-1917; 1 Fibredex box.

MARRIAGE, DIVORCE, AND VITAL STATISTICS

Divorce Records, 1882-1903; 2 Fibredex boxes.

MISCELLANEOUS RECORDS

Alien Registration, 1940; 1 volume.
Miscellaneous Records, 1774-1906; 1 Fibredex box.

WILLS

Wills, 1885-1925; 10 Fibredex boxes.

MICROFILM RECORDS

CORPORATIONS AND PARTNERSHIPS

Incorporations, Record of, 1890-1963; 1 reel.
Partnerships, Record of, 1913-1968; 2 reels.

COURT RECORDS

Superior Court
Minutes, 1838-1939; 6 reels.

ELECTION RECORDS

Elections, Record of, 1878-1962; 2 reels.

ESTATES RECORDS

Accounts of Indigent Orphans, 1907-1934; 1 reel.
Accounts, Record of, 1869-1965; 5 reels.
Accounts of Sale and Inventories, 1905-1963; 1 reel.
Administrators, Record of, 1914-1963; 4 reels.
Appointment of Administrators and Executors, 1887-1928; 1 reel.
Final Accounts, 1869-1963; 5 reels.
Guardians, Record of, 1914-1968; 2 reels.
Guardians of World War Veterans, 1930-1956; 1 reel.
Inheritance Tax Records, 1923-1962; 1 reel.
Widows' Dowers, Record of, 1904-1924; 1 reel.
Widows' Year's Support, Record of, 1885-1947; 1 reel.

LAND RECORDS

Deeds, Record of, 1774-1941; 61 reels.
Federal Tax Lien Index, 1934-1963; 1 reel.
Land Divisions, Record of, 1885-1966; 1 reel.
Land Entries, Record of, 1901-1933; 1 reel.
Plat Books, 1890-1975; 4 reels.
Plats, Index to, 1890-1985; 1 reel.
Real Estate Conveyances, Index to, Grantee, 1772-1975; 3 reels.
Real Estate Conveyances, Index to, Grantor, 1772-1975; 4 reels.
Registration of Land Titles (Torrens Act), 1933-1962; 1 reel.
Resale by Trustees and Mortgagees, Record of, 1924-1963; 2 reels.
Surveys, Record of, 1908-1923; 1 reel.

MARRIAGE, DIVORCE, AND VITAL STATISTICS

Delayed Births, Index to, 1937-1985; 2 reels.
Maiden Names of Divorced Women, 1937-1968; 1 reel.
Marriage Licenses, 1882-1963; 10 reels.
Marriage Registers, 1872-1963; 2 reels.
Vital Statistics, Index to, Births, 1958-1985; 1 reel.
Vital Statistics, Index to, Births and Deaths, 1913-1957; 1 reel.
Vital Statistics, Index to, Deaths, 1937-1973; 1 reel.

MILITARY AND PENSION RECORDS [*See* ESTATES RECORDS]

MISCELLANEOUS RECORDS

Homesteads, Record of, 1886-1958; 1 reel.
Orders and Decrees, 1868-1945, 1961-1966; 8 reels.
Special Proceedings Dockets, 1868-1963; 2 reels.

Officials, County

Board of County Commissioners, Minutes, 1876-1922; 2 reels.
County Board of Social Services, Minutes, 1937-1963; 1 reel.

School Records

County Board of Education, Minutes, 1884-1963; 1 reel.

Tax and Fiscal Records

Tax Scrolls, 1885-1894, 1900-1904, 1914-1915; 4 reels.

Wills

Wills, Cross Index to, 1774-1970; 2 reels.
Wills, Record of, 1774-1963; 4 reels.

MCDOWELL COUNTY

Established in 1842 from Burke and Rutherford counties.

ORIGINAL RECORDS

BONDS

Apprentice Bonds and Records, 1798, 1842-1917; 1 Fibredex box.
Bastardy Bonds and Records, 1842-1932; 2 Fibredex boxes.
Officials' Bonds and Records, 1843-1922; 3 Fibredex boxes.

COURT RECORDS

Circuit Criminal Court/Western District Criminal Court
- Minutes, 1897-1901; 1 volume.

County Court of Pleas and Quarter Sessions
- Execution Dockets, 1843-1868; 3 volumes.
- Minutes, 1843-1867; 2 volumes.
- State Docket, 1857-1868; 1 volume.
- Trial and Appearance Dockets, 1844-1860; 2 volumes.

Superior Court
- Civil Action Papers, 1822-1933; 29 Fibredex boxes.
- Civil Action Papers Concerning Land, 1846-1935; 25 Fibredex boxes.
- Criminal Action Papers, 1843-1936; 38 Fibredex boxes.
- Equity Execution Docket, 1853-1868; 1 volume.
- Equity Minutes, 1852-1866; 1 volume.
- Equity Minutes (Rough), 1851-1855; 1 volume.
- Equity Trial Docket, 1852-1868; 1 volume.
- Execution Dockets, 1846-1862; 2 volumes.
- Minutes, 1845-1925; 18 volumes.
- State Docket, 1845-1867; 1 volume.
- Trial, Appearance, and Reference Dockets, 1845-1869; 4 volumes.

ELECTION RECORDS

Elections, Record of, 1896-1901, 1920-1968; 5 volumes.

ESTATES RECORDS

Accounts, Record of, 1869-1900; 1 volume.
Appointment of Administrators, Executors, and Guardians, 1868-1910; 1 volume.
Estates, Record of, 1859-1879; 1 volume.
Estates Records, 1830, 1832, 1842-1939; 88 Fibredex boxes.
Guardians' Accounts, 1910-1934; 2 volumes.
Guardians' Records, 1843-1937; 14 Fibredex boxes.
Settlements, Record of, 1872-1925; 1 volume.

LAND RECORDS

Attachments, Executions, Levies, and Liens on Land, 1843-1935; 4 Fibredex boxes.
Deeds, 1813-1916; 1 Fibredex box.
Deeds, Cross Index to, 1843-1917; 5 volumes.
Ejectments, 1844-1909; 5 Fibredex boxes.
Land Entry Books, 1843-1915; 7 volumes.
Mineral Lease Book, 1891-1892; 1 volume.
Mineral Lease Book, Index to, 1891-1892; 1 volume.

Miscellaneous Land Records, 1797-1939; 3 Fibredex boxes.
Surveys, Record of, 1905-1914; 1 volume.

MARRIAGE, DIVORCE, AND VITAL STATISTICS
Divorce Records, 1849-1941; 9 Fibredex boxes.
Marriage Bonds, 1842-1868; 2 Fibredex boxes.

MILITARY AND PENSION RECORDS [*See* **MISCELLANEOUS RECORDS**]

MISCELLANEOUS RECORDS
Alien Registration, 1927, 1940, 1942; 1 volume.
Assignees, Receivers, and Trustees, Records of, 1844-1942; 8 Fibredex boxes.
Clerk's Minute Dockets (Special Proceedings), 1921-1968; 4 volumes.
County Accounts and Correspondence, 1843-1941; 1 Fibredex box.
County Board of Education, Minutes, 1873-1885; 1 volume.
Homestead and Personal Property Exemptions, 1858-1926; 1 Fibredex box.
Lunacy Records, 1848-1951; 1 Fibredex box.
Miscellaneous Railroad Records, 1860-1917; 1 Fibredex box.
Miscellaneous Records, 1843-1938; 5 Fibredex boxes.
Pension Records, 1852-1939; 2 Fibredex boxes.
Railroad Bonds, 1867, 1887, 1907; 4 Fibredex boxes.
Railroad Records, 1860-1925; 16 Fibredex boxes.
Road Records, 1843-1921; 2 Fibredex boxes.
Slaves and Free Persons of Color, Records of, 1843-1873; 1 Fibredex box.
Special Proceedings, 1870-1898; 4 volumes.

ROADS AND BRIDGES [*See* **MISCELLANEOUS RECORDS**]

SCHOOL RECORDS [*See* **MISCELLANEOUS RECORDS**]

TAX AND FISCAL RECORDS
Lists of Taxables, 1842-1859; 2 volumes.
Tax Records, 1839-1917, 1927; 2 Fibredex boxes.

WILLS
Wills, 1841-1920; 6 Fibredex boxes.
Wills, Cross Index to, 1843-1905; 1 volume.
Wills, Index to, 1843-1868; 1 volume.

MICROFILM RECORDS

CORPORATIONS AND PARTNERSHIPS
Corporations, Record of, 1886-1962; 1 reel.
Partnerships, Record of, 1913-1966; 1 reel.

COURT RECORDS
County Court of Pleas and Quarter Sessions
Minutes, 1843-1867; 1 reel.
Superior Court
Equity Minutes, 1852-1866; 1 reel.
Judgments, Index to, Defendant, 1948-1968; 2 reels.
Judgments, Index to, Plaintiff, 1948-1968; 1 reel.
Minutes, 1845-1957; 12 reels.

ELECTION RECORDS

Elections, Record of, 1896-1968; 1 reel.

ESTATES RECORDS

Accounts, Record of, 1869-1968; 6 reels.
Administrators, Executors, and Guardians, Record of, 1913-1930; 1 reel.
Administrators, Record of, 1921-1968; 3 reels.
Appointment of Executors, 1870-1910; 1 reel.
Estates, Index to, 1843-1968; 1 reel.
Executors, Record of, 1930-1968; 1 reel.
Guardians, Record of, 1926-1968; 1 reel.
Indigent Children and Lunacy Funds, Record of, 1934-1953; 1 reel.
Inheritance Tax Records, 1923-1968; 1 reel.
Inventories of Estates, 1859-1867; 1 reel.
Settlements, Record of, 1872-1968; 5 reels.
Widows' Year's Allowance, Record of, 1923-1966; 1 reel.

LAND RECORDS

Deeds, Record of, 1843-1956; 66 reels.
Land Entry Books, 1843-1956; 2 reels.
Map Books, 1925-1968; 1 reel.
Map Books, Index to, 1925-1968; 1 reel.
Real Estate Conveyances, Index to, Grantee, 1842-1961; 7 reels.
Real Estate Conveyances, Index to, Grantor, 1842-1961; 7 reels.
Sales by Trustees and Mortgagees, Record of, 1921-1968; 2 reels.
Surveys, Record of, 1905-1913; 1 reel.

MARRIAGE, DIVORCE, AND VITAL STATISTICS

Births, Index to, 1914-1979; 2 reels.
Deaths and Delayed Births, Index to, 1913-1967; 2 reels.
Maiden Names of Divorced Women, 1940-1965; 1 reel.
Marriage Bonds, 1842-1868; 1 reel.
Marriage Licenses, 1868-1961; 10 reels.
Marriage Registers, 1851-1945; 2 reels.
Marriage Registers, Index to, 1851-1968; 1 reel.

MISCELLANEOUS RECORDS

Alien Registration, 1927-1942; 1 reel.
Inquisition of Lunacy, 1899-1968; 1 reel. [*See also* **ESTATES RECORDS**]
Orders and Decrees, 1869-1957; 1 reel.
Special Proceedings, 1870-1953; 8 reels.
Special Proceedings, Index to, 1870-1953, 1968-1980; 3 reels.

OFFICIALS, COUNTY

Board of County Commissioners, Minutes, 1868-1968; 5 reels.

SCHOOL RECORDS

County Board of Education, Minutes, 1873-1968; 2 reels.

TAX AND FISCAL RECORDS

Tax Lists, 1842-1859; 1 reel.

WILLS

Wills, Index to, 1843-1968; 1 reel.
Wills, Record of, 1843-1968; 4 reels.

MECKLENBURG COUNTY

Established in 1762 (effective 1763) from Anson County.

ORIGINAL RECORDS

BONDS

- Apprentice Bonds, 1871-1920; 2 volumes.
- Officials' Bonds and Records, 1779-1954; 2 Fibredex boxes.

CORPORATIONS AND PARTNERSHIPS [*See* **MISCELLANEOUS RECORDS**]

COURT RECORDS

- Circuit Criminal Court
  - Minutes, 1898; 1 volume.
- County Court of Pleas and Quarter Sessions
  - Appeal Docket, 1810-1822; 1 volume.
  - Appearance Dockets, 1824-1867; 5 volumes.
  - Execution Dockets, 1774-1861; 19 volumes.
  - Levy Docket, 1827-1830; 1 volume.
  - Minutes, 1774-1868; 12 volumes.
  - State Dockets, 1828-1868; 3 volumes.
  - Trial, Appearance, and Reference Dockets, 1774-1810; 2 volumes and 1 pamphlet.
  - Trial Dockets, 1810-1866; 7 volumes.
- Criminal Court
  - Minutes, 1885-1890; 1 volume.
- Eastern District Criminal Court
  - Minutes, 1899-1901; 1 volume.
- Inferior Court
  - Minutes, 1877-1885; 2 volumes.
- Superior Court
  - Appearance Docket, 1811-1838; 1 volume.
  - Civil Action Papers, 1784-1959, 1966; 146 Fibredex boxes. [*See also* **CRX RECORDS**]
  - Civil Action Papers Concerning Land, 1784-1959, 1961, 1965; 64 Fibredex boxes.
  - Civil Action Papers Concerning Occupational Licensing Boards, 1922-1953; 2 Fibredex boxes.
  - Criminal Action Papers, 1778-1875, 1914, 1935, 1961; 1 Fibredex box.
  - Equity Minutes, 1822-1852, 1859-1869; 2 volumes.
  - Equity Trial Dockets, 1846-1868; 2 volumes.
  - Execution Dockets, 1811-1836, 1846-1854; 4 volumes.
  - Minutes, 1811-1885; 8 volumes.
  - Receipt Docket, 1825-1828; 1 volume.
  - Recognizance Docket, 1825-1852; 1 volume.
  - Trial, Appearance, and Reference Docket, 1807-1810; 1 volume.
  - Trial Dockets, 1811-1843; 2 volumes.

ELECTION RECORDS [*See also* **CRX RECORDS**]

- Elections, Record of, 1924-1932; 1 volume.

ESTATES RECORDS

- Accounts, Record of, 1785-1966; 83 volumes.
- Administrators' Bonds, 1870-1911; 8 volumes.
- Administrators, Executors, and Guardians, Record of, 1911-1914; 1 volume.

Appointment of Administrators, Executors, and Guardians, 1906-1928; 1 volume.
Estates Records, 1762-1957; 282 Fibredex boxes.
Executors, Record of, 1958-1967; 6 volumes.
Guardians' Bonds, 1870-1911; 5 volumes.
Guardians, Record of, 1914-1967; 18 volumes.
Guardians' Records, 1779-1955; 11 Fibredex boxes.
Guardians [Veterans], Record of, 1961-1967; 1 volume.
Probate (Estates), Record of, 1868-1907; 1 volume.
Settlements, Record of, 1869-1904; 3 volumes.

LAND RECORDS

Attachments, Executions, and Liens on Land, 1855-1968; 17 Fibredex boxes.
Deeds of Sale and Miscellaneous Deeds, 1772-1938; 1 Fibredex box. [*See also* **CRX RECORDS**]
Ejectments, 1793-1954, 1977; 4 Fibredex boxes.
Foreclosures of Mortgages and Deeds of Trust, 1870-1955; 25 Fibredex boxes.
Land Condemnations, 1892-1968; 2 Fibredex boxes.
Land Entries, 1778-1855; 2 volumes.
Land Grants and Deeds, 1789-1845; 1 volume.
Land Sold for Taxes, 1893, 1896, 1931-1950; 1 Fibredex box.
Miscellaneous Land Records, 1767-1953; 2 Fibredex boxes.
Probate of Deeds, Record of, 1858-1868; 1 volume.

MARRIAGE, DIVORCE, AND VITAL STATISTICS

Divorce Records, 1846-1969; 322 Fibredex boxes.
Marriage Bonds, 1783-1868; 13 Fibredex boxes.
Marriage Register, 1868-1884; 1 volume.

MILITARY AND PENSION RECORDS [*See* **ESTATES RECORDS**]

MISCELLANEOUS RECORDS

Alien, Naturalization, and Citizenship Records, 1822, 1886-1927; 1 Fibredex box.
Alien Registration, 1927-1942; 2 volumes.
Assignees, Receivers, and Trustees, Records of, 1847-1958; 55 Fibredex boxes.
Child Custody and Support Records, 1866-1956, 1964, 1975; 3 Fibredex boxes.
Commissions to Hold Court, 1886-1937, 1951; 1 Fibredex box.
County Accounts, 1868-1884; 2 volumes.
Insolvents and Homestead and Personal Property Exemptions, 1787-1919; 1 Fibredex box.
Miscellaneous Records, 1759-1959; 5 Fibredex boxes.
Orders and Decrees, 1869-1902; 8 volumes.
Partnership Records, 1871-1955; 2 Fibredex boxes.
Promissory Notes and Personal Accounts, 1758-1897; 1 Fibredex box.
Railroad Records, 1856-1955; 33 Fibredex boxes.
Road, Bridge, and Ferry Records, 1783-1921; 1 Fibredex box.
School Records, 1798, 1863-1955; 3 Fibredex boxes.
Special Proceedings Dockets, 1869-1962; 9 volumes.
Special Proceedings Dockets, Index to, 1924-1940; 1 volume.

ROADS AND BRIDGES [*See* **MISCELLANEOUS RECORDS**]

SCHOOL RECORDS [*See* **MISCELLANEOUS RECORDS**]

TAX AND FISCAL RECORDS
List of Taxables, 1797-1824; 1 volume.

WILLS
Wills, 1749-1967; 237 Fibredex boxes.
Wills, Cross Index to, 1763-1929; 2 volumes.
Wills, Record of, 1761-1854; 9 volumes.

CRX RECORDS
Civil Action Papers, 1843-1861; 7 folders.
Deeds of Sale, 1797, 1833, 1835; 2 folders.
Election Returns, 1964; 1 folder.

MICROFILM RECORDS

BONDS
Apprentice Bonds, 1871-1920; 1 reel.
Officials' Bonds, 1889-1930; 1 reel.

CORPORATIONS AND PARTNERSHIPS
Corporations, Record of, 1884-1947; 12 reels.
Incorporations, Index to, 1884-1965; 1 reel.
Limited Partnerships, Record of, 1942-1965; 1 reel.
Partnerships and Assumed Names, Index to, 1913-1971; 1 reel.
Partnerships, Record of, 1913-1937; 1 reel.

COURT RECORDS
Circuit Criminal Court
Minutes, 1898; 1 reel.
County Court of Pleas and Quarter Sessions
Minutes, 1774-1868; 6 reels.
Criminal Court/Eastern District Criminal Court
Minutes, 1885-1901; 1 reel.
Inferior Court
Minutes, 1877-1885; 1 reel.
Superior Court
Equity Minutes, 1822-1852, 1859-1869; 2 reels.
Judgments, Index to, Defendant, 1909-1968; 7 reels.
Judgments, Index to, Plaintiff, 1909-1956; 3 reels.
Minutes, 1811-1885; 4 reels.
Minutes, Civil, 1885-1960; 42 reels.
Minutes, Criminal, 1909-1926; 2 reels.

ELECTION RECORDS
Board of Elections, Minutes, 1936-1956; 1 reel.
Elections, Record of, 1908-1932; 1 reel.

ESTATES RECORDS
Accounts, Record of, 1785-1965; 38 reels.
Administrators' Bonds, 1870-1911; 2 reels.
Administrators, Executors, and Guardians, Record of, 1911-1928; 1 reel.
Administrators, Record of, 1912-1955; 19 reels.
Estates, Index to, 1765-1965; 9 reels.
Executors and Guardians, Record of, 1868-1964; 6 reels.

Guardians' Bonds, 1870-1911; 1 reel.
Guardians, Record of, 1914-1963; 8 reels.
Guardians of World War Veterans, Record of, 1930-1961; 1 reel.
Inheritance Tax Records, 1919-1964; 5 reels.
Settlements, Record of, 1869-1965; 19 reels.

LAND RECORDS

Land Entries, 1778-1855, 1870-1937; 2 reels.
Land Grants, 1789-1848; 1 reel.
Plats, 1892, 1907-1951; 4 reels.
Real Estate Conveyances, Index to, Grantee, 1763-1955; 41 reels.
Real Estate Conveyances, Index to, Grantee: Firms and Corporations, 1919-1936, 1948-1955; 3 reels.
Real Estate Conveyances, Index to, Grantor, 1763-1955; 48 reels.
Real Estate Conveyances, Record of, 1763-1959; 773 reels.

MARRIAGE, DIVORCE, AND VITAL STATISTICS

Births, Index to, 1913-1947; 4 reels.
Deaths, Index to, 1909-1947; 2 reels.
Delayed Births, Index to, various years; 1 reel.
Maiden Names of Divorced Women, 1937-1965; 1 reel.
Marriage Bonds, 1783-1868; 4 reels.
Marriage Licenses, 1851-1962; 47 reels.
Marriage Registers, 1850-1960; 3 reels.
Marriages, Record of, Black, 1850-1867; Record of Cohabitation, 1866-1867; 1 reel.

MILITARY AND PENSION RECORDS [*See* ESTATES RECORDS]

MISCELLANEOUS RECORDS

Board of Social Services, Minutes, 1937-1954; 4 reels.
Lunacy, Record of, 1899-1953; 5 reels.
Official Reports, Record of, 1875-1887; 1 reel.
Orders and Decrees, 1869-1960; 27 reels.
Special Proceedings, 1869-1965; 6 reels.
Special Proceedings and Orders and Decrees, Index to, Defendant, 1896-1968; 2 reels.
Special Proceedings and Orders and Decrees, Index to, Plaintiff, 1896-1968; 3 reels.
Special Proceedings, Index to, 1968-1977; 2 reels.

TAX AND FISCAL RECORDS

List of Taxables, 1797-1824; 1 reel.
Tax Scrolls, 1915; 1 reel.

WILLS

Wills, Index to, Devisee, 1763-1968; 2 reels.
Wills, Index to, Devisor, 1763-1968; 2 reels.
Wills, Record of, 1763-1965; 25 reels.

MITCHELL COUNTY

Established in 1861 from Burke, Caldwell, McDowell, Watauga, and Yancey counties.
Several records believed destroyed during move into new courthouse in 1907.

ORIGINAL RECORDS

BONDS

Apprentice Bonds and Records, 1863-1904; Bastardy Bonds and Records, 1867-1906; 2 Fibredex boxes.

COURT RECORDS

County Court of Pleas and Quarter Sessions
- Minutes, 1861-1868; 1 volume.

Superior Court
- Civil Action Papers, 1862-1913; 9 Fibredex boxes.
- Civil Action Papers Concerning Land, 1869-1925; 11 Fibredex boxes.
- Criminal Action Papers, 1861-1915; 21 Fibredex boxes.
- Minutes, 1861-1910; 11 volumes.

ELECTION RECORDS

Elections, Record of, 1880-1924; 4 volumes.

ESTATES RECORDS

Administrators' Bonds, 1907-1909; 1 volume.
Appointment of Administrators, Executors, Guardians, and Masters, 1871-1909; 1 volume.
Estates Records, 1826-1946; 15 Fibredex boxes.
Guardians' Bonds, 1907-1911; 1 volume.
Guardians' Records, 1866-1926; 3 Fibredex boxes.

LAND RECORDS

Attachments, Executions, and Levies on Land, 1867-1908; 1 Fibredex box.
Deeds, 1846-1951; 2 Fibredex boxes.
Ejectments, 1862-1893; 1 Fibredex box.
Miscellaneous Deeds, 1881-1951; 1 Fibredex box.
Miscellaneous Land Records, 1789-1936; 1 Fibredex box.
Probate of Deeds, Record of, 1861-1882; 2 volumes.

MARRIAGE, DIVORCE, AND VITAL STATISTICS

Divorce Records, 1867-1915; 5 Fibredex boxes.

MISCELLANEOUS RECORDS

Alien Registration, 1927, 1940; 1 volume.
Assignees, Receivers, and Trustees, Records of, 1885-1910; 1 Fibredex box.
Board of Road Commissioners, Minutes, 1915-1926; 1 volume.
Licenses to Trades, Registry of, 1877-1902; 1 volume.
Miscellaneous Records, 1861-1935; 2 Fibredex boxes.

ROADS AND BRIDGES [*See* **MISCELLANEOUS RECORDS**]

TAX AND FISCAL RECORDS

Tax List, 1861-1868; 1 volume.
Tax Records, 1873-1911; 1 Fibredex box.

WILLS

Wills, 1823-1927; 2 Fibredex boxes.

MICROFILM RECORDS

CORPORATIONS AND PARTNERSHIPS

Corporations, Record of, 1887-1962; 1 reel.
Partnerships, Record of, 1913-1918; 1 reel.

COURT RECORDS

County Court of Pleas and Quarter Sessions
  Minutes, 1861-1868; 1 reel.
Superior Court
  Judgment Docket, Land Tax Sales, 1931-1968; 1 reel.
  Minutes, 1861-1966; 9 reels.
  Minutes, Divorce Proceedings, 1948; 1 reel.

ELECTION RECORDS

Elections, Record of, 1880-1970; 1 reel.

ESTATES RECORDS

Accounts of Indigent Orphans, 1909-1961; 1 reel.
Accounts, Record of, 1875-1968; 3 reels.
Administrators' Bonds, 1907-1909; 1 reel.
Administrators, Executors, and Guardians, Record of, 1909-1943; 1 reel.
Administrators and Executors, Index to, 1871-1968; 1 reel.
Administrators, Record of, 1919-1968; 2 reels.
Appointment and Record of Administrators, 1871-1909; 1 reel.
Dowers, Record of, 1908-1938; 1 reel.
Executors, Record of, 1943-1968; 1 reel.
Guardians' Bonds, 1907-1911; 1 reel.
Guardians, Cross Index to, 1871-1968; 1 reel.
Guardians, Record of, 1919-1968; 1 reel.
Inheritance Tax Records, 1924-1970; 1 reel.
Settlements, Record of, 1868-1969; 2 reels.

LAND RECORDS

Commissioners' Deeds, Record of, 1936-1951; 1 reel.
Deeds, Record of, 1861-1958; 57 reels.
Federal Tax Lien Index, 1944-1951, 1957-1968; 1 reel.
Land Entry Books, 1901-1950; 1 reel.
Real Estate Conveyances, Index to, Grantee, 1861-1977; 4 reels.
Real Estate Conveyances, Index to, Grantor, 1861-1977; 4 reels.
Sales by Trustees, Mortgagees, and Executors, Record of, 1923-1968; 1 reel.
Taxes for Mortgagees, Record of, 1931-1947; 1 reel.

MARRIAGE, DIVORCE, AND VITAL STATISTICS

Births, Index to, 1913-1992; 1 reel.
Deaths, Index to, 1913-1992; 1 reel.
Delayed Births, Index to, 1913-1970; 1 reel.
Divorce Proceedings [*See* **COURT RECORDS**, Superior Court]
Marriage Licenses, Index to, 1860-1937; 1 reel.
Marriage Registers, 1861-1969; 1 reel.

MISCELLANEOUS RECORDS

Appointment of Receivers, 1907-1932; 1 reel.
Clerk's Minute Docket, 1921-1951; 1 reel.
Homesteads, Record of, 1907-1939; 1 reel.
Lunacy, Record of, 1899-1964; 1 reel.
Officials' Settlements, Record of, 1910-1968; 1 reel.
Orders and Decrees, 1870-1963; 1 reel.
Special Proceedings Dockets, 1902-1968; 4 reels.
Special Proceedings, Index to, 1968-1977; 1 reel.
Special Proceedings and Orders and Decrees, Index to, 1869-1968; 1 reel.

OFFICIALS, COUNTY

Board of County Commissioners, Minutes, 1868-1965; 4 reels.

ROADS AND BRIDGES

Road Commissioners' Docket, 1915-1926; 1 reel.

SCHOOL RECORDS

County Board of Education, Minutes, 1901-1928; 1 reel.
School Deeds, Index to, 1946; 1 reel.

TAX AND FISCAL RECORDS

Tax List, 1861-1868; 1 reel.

WILLS

Wills, Cross Index to, 1887-1969; 1 reel.
Wills, Record of, 1887-1969; 2 reels.

MONTGOMERY COUNTY

Established in 1779 from Anson County.
Courthouse fire of 1835 destroyed many records.

ORIGINAL RECORDS

BONDS

Apprentice Bonds and Records, 1840-1897; 1 Fibredex box.
Bastardy Bonds and Records, 1843-1897; 1 Fibredex box.
Officials' Bonds and Records, 1837-1918; 1 volume, 2 Fibredex boxes.

COURT RECORDS

County Court of Pleas and Quarter Sessions
- Minutes, 1843-1868; 5 volumes.
- Minutes, Partial Index to, 1843-1868; 1 volume.
- Trial Dockets, 1843-1868; 2 volumes.

Superior Court
- Civil Action Papers, 1799-1940; 15 Fibredex boxes.
- Civil Action Papers Concerning County Commissioners, 1872-1904; 1 Fibredex box.
- Civil Action Papers Concerning Land, 1843-1916; 8 Fibredex boxes.
- Civil Execution Docket, 1843-1852; 1 volume.
- Criminal Action Papers, 1833-1921; 13 Fibredex boxes.
- Equity Enrolling Dockets, 1807-1827; 2 volumes.
- Minutes, 1843-1912; 9 volumes.
- Recognizance Docket, 1821-1845; 1 volume.
- State Docket, 1843-1859; 1 volume.
- State Execution Docket, 1843-1860; 1 volume.
- Trial Dockets, 1855, 1865-1868; 2 volumes.

ELECTION RECORDS

Election Records, 1779-1922; 2 Fibredex boxes.
Elections, Record of, 1878-1924; 6 volumes.

ESTATES RECORDS

Accounts, Record of, 1868-1900; 2 volumes.
Administrators' Bonds, 1870-1891; 1 volume.
Appointment of Administrators, Executors, Guardians, and Masters, 1868-1901; 1 volume.
Estates, Record of, 1843-1868; 3 volumes.
Estates Records, 1818-1970; 56 Fibredex boxes.
Guardians' Accounts, 1843-1868; 1 volume.
Guardians' Bonds, 1874-1904; 2 volumes.
Guardians' Records, 1843-1933; 5 Fibredex boxes.
Settlements, Record of, 1868-1924; 2 volumes.

LAND RECORDS

Condemnation of Land, 1877-1908; 1 Fibredex box.
Deeds of Sale, 1794-1920; 1 Fibredex box.
Ejectments, 1840-1892; 1 Fibredex box.
Land Entries, 1837-1858; 2 volumes.
Land Sales for Taxes, 1845-1870; 1 Fibredex box.

Miscellaneous Deeds, 1783-1924; 1 Fibredex box.
Miscellaneous Land Records, 1769-1922; 1 Fibredex box.
Tax Levies on Land, 1873-1880; 1 volume.

MARRIAGE, DIVORCE, AND VITAL STATISTICS

Divorce Records, 1856-1907; 1 Fibredex box.
Marriage Bonds, 1779-1868; 3 Fibredex boxes.
Marriage Certificates, Record of, 1866-1867; 1 volume.

MISCELLANEOUS RECORDS

Alien Registration, 1927, 1940; 1 volume.
Assignees, Receivers, and Trustees, Records of, 1843-1932; 1 Fibredex box.
Board of County Commissioners, Minutes, 1868; 1 volume.
County Accounts and Claims, 1844-1911; 2 volumes, 1 Fibredex box.
County Board of Education, Minutes, 1872-1883; 1 volume.
Insolvent Debtors, 1787-1920; 1 Fibredex box.
Miscellaneous Records, 1785-1922; 3 Fibredex boxes.
Orders and Decrees, 1868-1912; 3 volumes.
Railroad Records, 1891-1910; 1 Fibredex box.
Road Orders, 1843-1868; 1 volume.
Road Records, 1839-1926; 2 Fibredex boxes.
Timber Records, 1867-1907; 1 Fibredex box.
Wardens of the Poor, Minutes, 1831-1867; 1 volume.
Witness Tickets, 1844-1868; 1 Fibredex box.

OFFICIALS, COUNTY [*See* **MISCELLANEOUS RECORDS**]

ROADS AND BRIDGES [*See* **MISCELLANEOUS RECORDS**]

SCHOOL RECORDS [*See* **MISCELLANEOUS RECORDS**]

TAX AND FISCAL RECORDS

Lists of Taxables, 1843-1873; 5 volumes.
Tax Records, 1843-1890; 1 Fibredex box.

WILLS

Wills, 1785-1970; 8 Fibredex boxes.

MICROFILM RECORDS

CORPORATIONS AND PARTNERSHIPS

Corporations, Record of, 1890-1933; 1 reel.

COURT RECORDS

County Court of Pleas and Quarter Sessions
- Minutes, 1843-1868; 2 reels.
- Minutes, Partial Index to, 1843-1868; 1 reel.

Superior Court
- Equity Minutes, 1808-1824; 1 reel.
- Minutes, 1843-1964; 10 reels.

ELECTION RECORDS

Elections, Record of, 1896-1962; 2 reels.

ESTATES RECORDS

Accounts, Record of, 1847-1964; 5 reels.
Administrators' Bonds, 1874-1891; 1 reel.
Administrators, Record of, 1900-1964; 4 reels.
Amounts Paid for Indigent Children, Record of, 1913-1947; 1 reel.
Appointment of Administrators, Executors, and Guardians, 1868-1901; 1 reel.
Appointment of Executors, 1902-1946; Appointment of Guardians, 1901-1964; 1 reel.
Estates, Record of, 1842-1858; 2 reels.
Estates under $300, Record of, 1932-1958; 1 reel.
Guardians' Bonds, 1894-1904; 1 reel.
Inheritance Tax Records, 1923-1964; 1 reel.
Settlements, Record of, 1868-1964; 3 reels.

LAND RECORDS

Deeds, Record of, 1774-1807, 1838-1961; 47 reels.
Federal Tax Lien Index, 1925-1969; 1 reel.
Land Entries, 1837-1955; 1 reel.
Real Estate Conveyances, Index to, Grantee, 1838-1964; 4 reels.
Real Estate Conveyances, Index to, Grantor, 1838-1964; 4 reels.
Resales, Record of, 1923-1964; 2 reels.
Surveys, Record of, 1904-1912; 1 reel.

MARRIAGE, DIVORCE, AND VITAL STATISTICS

Delayed Births, Index to, various years; 2 reels.
Marriage Bond Abstracts, 1842-1868; 1 reel.
Marriage Bonds, 1842-1868; 1 reel.
Marriage Licenses, 1846-1964; 10 reels.
Marriage Registers, 1843-1981; 3 reels.
Vital Statistics, Index to, 1913-1981; 2 reels.

MISCELLANEOUS RECORDS

County Accounts and Claims, 1841-1870; Board of County Commissioners, Minutes, 1868-1870; 1 reel.
Orders and Decrees, 1868-1962; 7 reels.
Special Proceedings, 1869-1933; 1 reel.
Special Proceedings, Index to, 1869-1933; 1 reel.
Wardens of the Poor, Minutes, 1831-1867; 1 reel.

OFFICIALS, COUNTY [*See also* **MISCELLANEOUS RECORDS**]

Board of County Commissioners, Minutes, 1870-1931; 3 reels.

SCHOOL RECORDS

County Board of Education, Minutes, 1884-1926; 1 reel.

TAX AND FISCAL RECORDS

Tax Lists, 1873-1916; 8 reels.
Tax Scrolls, 1899-1916; 3 reels.

WILLS

Wills, Cross Index to, 1848-1964; 1 reel.
Wills, Record of, 1843-1964; 4 reels.

MOORE COUNTY

Established in 1784 from Cumberland County.
Courthouse fire of 1889 destroyed most land records and many court records.

ORIGINAL RECORDS

BONDS

Apprentice Bonds, 1890-1903; 1 volume.

COURT RECORDS

County Court of Pleas and Quarter Sessions
- Appearance Docket, 1841-1854; 1 volume.
- Execution Dockets, 1818-1867; 6 volumes.
- Minutes, 1784-1858; 7 volumes.
- Trial and Appearance Dockets, 1798-1841; 3 volumes.
- Trial Docket, 1841-1845; 1 volume.
- Trial Docket, Index to, 1785-1868; 1 volume.

Superior Court
- Appearance Dockets, 1835-1869; 2 volumes.
- Civil Action Papers, 1829-1915; Criminal Action Papers, 1883-1916; 12 Fibredex boxes.
- Civil Action Papers Concerning Land, 1874-1924; 16 Fibredex boxes.
- Equity Trial Docket, 1850-1868; 1 volume.
- Execution Dockets, 1834-1881; 4 volumes.
- Minutes, 1869-1873; 1 volume.
- Recognizance Docket, 1836-1844, 1849; 1 volume.
- State Docket, 1834-1851; 1 volume.

ELECTION RECORDS

Elections, Record of, 1878-1932; 4 volumes.

ESTATES RECORDS

Administrators' Bonds, 1864-1922; 4 volumes.
Dowers, Record of, 1889-1921; 1 volume.
Estates, Record of, 1820-1862; 6 volumes.
Estates Records, 1828-1921; 19 Fibredex boxes. [*See also* **CRX RECORDS**]
Guardians' Accounts, 1834-1857, 1889-1931; 3 volumes.
Guardians' Bonds, 1889-1929; 2 volumes.
Guardians' Records, 1847, 1870-1912; 1 Fibredex box.
Widows' Year's Support, Record of, 1889-1968; 2 volumes.

LAND RECORDS [*See also* CRX RECORDS]

Attachments, Executions, Liens, and Levies on Land, 1869-1915; 1 Fibredex box.
Deeds, 1797-1923; 1 Fibredex box.
Ejectments, 1881-1913; 1 Fibredex box.
Miscellaneous Land Records, 1798-1926; 2 Fibredex boxes.
Mortgage Deeds and Deeds of Trust, 1834-1926; 1 Fibredex box.

MARRIAGE, DIVORCE, AND VITAL STATISTICS

Divorce Records, 1887-1915; 2 Fibredex boxes.

MILITARY AND PENSION RECORDS [*See* MISCELLANEOUS RECORDS]

MISCELLANEOUS RECORDS

Applications for Pensions, List of, 1885-1888; 1 manuscript box.
Appointment of Road Overseers, 1875-1895; 1 volume.
Assignees, Receivers, and Trustees, Records of, 1869-1933; 4 Fibredex boxes.
County Accounts, 1796-1841; 1 volume.
Homestead and Personal Property Exemptions, 1864-1924; 4 Fibredex boxes.
Mining Records, 1882-1913; 1 Fibredex box.
Miscellaneous Records, 1784-1935; 5 Fibredex boxes.
Naturalization, Record of, 1887-1917; 1 volume.
Pensions, Record of, 1890-1919; 2 volumes.
Railroad Records, 1889-1915; 3 Fibredex boxes.

ROADS AND BRIDGES [*See* **MISCELLANEOUS RECORDS**]

TAX AND FISCAL RECORDS

Tax List, 1852-1860; 1 volume.

WILLS [*See also* **CRX RECORDS**]

Wills, 1831, 1859-1921; 3 Fibredex boxes.

CRX RECORDS

Estates Record, 1857; 1 folder.
Land Grant, 1789; 1 folder.
Petition to the General Assembly, 1907; 1 folder.
Treasurer's Account Book, 1889-1890; 1 folder.
Will, 1815; 1 folder.

MICROFILM RECORDS

CORPORATIONS AND PARTNERSHIPS

Corporations, Record of, 1889-1944; 2 reels.
Partnership Records, 1913-1965; 1 reel.

COURT RECORDS

County Court of Pleas and Quarter Sessions
- Minutes, 1784-1858; 3 reels.

Superior Court
- Criminal Judgment Dockets, 1887-1907; 2 reels.
- Equity Trial Docket, 1850-1868; 1 reel.
- Minutes, 1835-1956; 18 reels.
- Minutes, Index to, Defendant, 1786-1953; 4 reels.
- Minutes, Index to, Plaintiff, 1786-1953; 2 reels.

ELECTION RECORDS

Elections, Record of, 1934-1964; 1 reel.

ESTATES RECORDS

Accounts for Indigent Orphans, Record of, 1909-1959; 1 reel.
Accounts, Record of, 1868-1965; 6 reels.
Administrators' Bonds, 1880-1897, 1923-1963; 5 reels.
Administrators and Executors, Index to, 1787-1819, 1898-1916; 1 reel.
Appointment of Executors, 1868-1902; 1 reel.
Appointment of Guardians, 1932-1968; 1 reel.
Dowers and Widows' Year's Support, Record of, 1889-1964; 1 reel.

Estates Not Exceeding $300, 1950-1965; 1 reel.
Estates, Record of, 1820-1831, 1837-1851, 1856-1861; 1 reel.
Final Accounts: Administrators, Index to, 1868-1965; 1 reel.
Final Accounts: Guardians, Index to, 1868-1965; 1 reel.
Guardians' Accounts, 1888-1965; 3 reels.
Guardians' Bonds, 1890-1909; 1 reel.
Guardians, Index to, 1889-1915; 1 reel.
Guardians, Record of, 1834-1857; 1 reel.
Inheritance Tax Records, 1923-1966; 1 reel.
Settlements, Record of, 1869-1965; 6 reels.

Land Records

Deeds, Record of, 1889-1961; 124 reels.
Entry Book, 1889-1958; 1 reel.
Grants, Record of, 1787-1965; 2 reels.
Map Books, 1902-1965; Index to Maps, 1907-1965; 3 reels.
Real Estate Conveyances, Index to, Grantee, 1889-1966; 10 reels.
Real Estate Conveyances, Index to, Grantor, 1889-1966; 10 reels.
Real Estate Conveyances, Index to, Grantor and Grantee: Banks and Trustees, 1940-1966; 1 reel.
Sales and Resales of Land, Record of, 1930-1966; 3 reels.

Marriage, Divorce, and Vital Statistics

Births, Index to, 1913-1964; 2 reels.
Deaths, Index to, 1913-1973; 1 reel.
Delayed Births, Index to, 1879-1956; 1 reel.
Maiden Names of Divorced Women, 1939-1963; 1 reel.
Marriage Licenses, 1889-1961; 10 reels.
Marriage Record, 1851-1867; 1 reel.
Marriage Registers, 1889-1965; 2 reels.

Military and Pension Records

Pensions, Record of, 1885-1905; 1 reel.

Miscellaneous Records

Orders and Decrees, 1868-1951; 11 reels.
Receivers' and Assignees' Accounts, 1896-1951; 1 reel.
Special Proceedings, 1901-1920; 1 reel.
Special Proceedings, Index to, Defendant, 1869-1965; 2 reels.
Special Proceedings, Index to, Plaintiff, 1869-1965; 3 reels.

Officials, County

Board of County Commissioners, Minutes, 1889-1945; 4 reels.

Road and Bridges

Road Overseers, 1875-1895; 1 reel.

School Records

County Board of Education, Minutes, 1872-1941; 1 reel.

Tax and Fiscal Records

Tax List, 1852-1860; 1 reel.
Tax Scrolls, 1900-1940; 7 reels.

WILLS

Wills, Index to, Devisee, 1793-1965; 1 reel.
Wills, Index to, Devisor, 1793-1965; 1 reel.
Wills, Record of, 1783-1965; 12 reels.

NASH COUNTY

Established in 1777 from Edgecombe County.

ORIGINAL RECORDS

Bonds

Apprentice Bonds, 1793-1868, 1900-1918; 1 volume, 3 Fibredex boxes.
Bastardy Bonds and Records, 1779-1883; 1 volume, 3 Fibredex boxes.
Clerks' Bonds, 1807-1885; 1 Fibredex box.
Constables' Bonds, 1779-1882; 3 Fibredex boxes.
Officials' Bonds, 1778-1888; 2 volumes, 2 Fibredex boxes.

Court Records

Circuit Criminal Court/Eastern District Criminal Court
- Minutes, 1897-1901; 1 volume.

County Court of Pleas and Quarter Sessions
- Appearance Dockets, 1826-1868; 4 volumes, 1 manuscript box.
- Appearance and Trial Dockets, 1779-1826; 2 volumes, 3 manuscript boxes.
- Execution Dockets, 1782-1867; 9 volumes.
- Minutes, 1778-1868; 14 volumes.
- State Dockets, 1779-1793, 1808-1868; 4 volumes, 1 manuscript box.
- Trial Dockets, 1823-1868; 6 volumes.

Superior Court
- Civil Action Papers, 1751-1908; 75 Fibredex boxes.
- Criminal Action Papers, 1783-1897; 26 Fibredex boxes.
- Criminal Action Papers Concerning Fornication and Adultery, 1789-1871; 1 Fibredex box.
- Equity Trial Dockets, 1811-1868; 4 volumes.
- Execution Dockets, 1825-1868; 2 volumes.
- Minutes, 1807-1915; 16 volumes.
- Miscellaneous Dockets, 1779-1880; 1 Fibredex box.
- State Dockets, 1813-1853; 3 volumes.
- Trial and Appearance Dockets, 1813-1859; 3 volumes.

Election Records

Election Records, 1830-1908; 2 Fibredex boxes.
Elections, Record of, 1878-1924; 5 volumes.

Estates Records

Accounts, Record of, 1869-1915; 7 volumes.
Administrators' Bonds, 1857-1910; 5 volumes.
Division of Slaves, 1830-1861; 1 volume. [*See also* **Marriage, Divorce, and Vital Statistics**, Cohabitation, Record of, 1866]
Estates, Record of, 1818-1868; 8 volumes.
Estates Records, 1770-1909; 83 Fibredex boxes.
Guardians' Accounts, 1820-1867; 4 volumes.
Guardians' Bonds, 1857-1915; 5 volumes.
Guardians' Records, 1784-1874; 13 Fibredex boxes.
Miscellaneous Estates Records, 1779-1881; 3 Fibredex boxes.
Settlements, Record of, 1869-1915; 3 volumes.
Widows' Year's Support, Record of, 1883-1918; 1 volume.

LAND RECORDS

Deeds of Gift, 1797-1896; 2 Fibredex boxes.
Deeds of Sale, 1774-1913; 17 Fibredex boxes.
Deeds of Trust, 1794-1917; 2 Fibredex boxes.
Ejectments, 1787-1861; 1 Fibredex box.
Land Entries, 1838-1909; 1 volume.
Land Records, 1739-1911; 2 Fibredex boxes.
Leases and Bills of Sale, 1794-1911; 1 Fibredex box.
Miscellaneous Deeds and Liens on Land, 1825-1918; 1 Fibredex box.
Mortgage Deeds, 1849-1912; 2 Fibredex boxes.

MARRIAGE, DIVORCE, AND VITAL STATISTICS

Cohabitation, Record of, 1866; Division of Slaves, 1862-1865; 1 volume.
Divorce Records, 1818-1866; 1 Fibredex box.
Marriage Bonds, 1777-1868; 7 Fibredex boxes.
Marriage Certificates, Record of, 1851-1867; 1 volume.
Miscellaneous Marriage Records, 1836-1887; 1 manuscript box.

MISCELLANEOUS RECORDS

Alien Registration, 1927, 1940; 1 volume.
Board of Superintendents of Common Schools, Minutes, 1843-1864; 1 volume.
Bridge Records, 1779-1874; 2 Fibredex boxes.
County Accounts, 1778-1899; 1 volume, 3 Fibredex boxes.
Insolvent Debtors and Homestead and Personal Property Exemptions, 1829-1910; 1 Fibredex box.
Magistrates, Lists of, 1779-1861; 1 Fibredex box.
Mill Records, 1782-1875; 1 Fibredex box.
Miscellaneous Records, 1778-1909; 2 Fibredex boxes.
Naturalization Record, 1908; 1 volume.
Officials' Appointments, 1784-1914; 1 Fibredex box.
Officials' Reports, 1815-1898; 1 Fibredex box.
Powers of Attorney, 1788-1913; 1 Fibredex box.
Public Works, 1819-1884; 1 Fibredex box.
Road Records, 1768-1887; 2 Fibredex boxes.
School Records, 1844-1884; 2 Fibredex boxes.
Slave Records, 1781-1864; 2 Fibredex boxes.
Wardens of the Poor, Minutes, 1844-1869; 1 volume.

OFFICIALS, COUNTY [*See* **MISCELLANEOUS RECORDS; CRX RECORDS**]

ROADS AND BRIDGES [*See* **MISCELLANEOUS RECORDS**]

SCHOOL RECORDS [*See* **MISCELLANEOUS RECORDS**]

TAX AND FISCAL RECORDS

Tax Records, 1787-1902; 2 Fibredex boxes.

WILLS

Wills, 1778-1922; 10 Fibredex boxes.
Wills, Index to, 1779-1926; 1 volume.
Wills, Record of, 1778-1873; 4 volumes.

CRX RECORDS

Justice of the Peace Appointment, 1875; 1 folder.

MICROFILM RECORDS

BONDS

Apprentice Bonds, 1919-1931; 1 reel.

CORPORATIONS AND PARTNERSHIPS

Incorporations, Record of, 1887-1945; 1 reel.

COURT RECORDS

County Court of Pleas and Quarter Sessions
Minutes, 1778-1868; 7 reels.
Superior Court
Equity Minutes, 1811-1857, 1861-1867; 1 reel.
Minutes, 1807-1963; 17 reels.

ELECTION RECORDS

Elections, Record of, 1904, 1932-1962; 1 reel.

ESTATES RECORDS

Accounts of Indigent Orphans, 1909-1975; 1 reel.
Accounts, Record of, 1869-1964; 17 reels.
Administrators' Bonds, 1910-1933; 1 reel.
Administrators, Executors, and Guardians, Index to, 1868-1968; 2 reels.
Appointment of Administrators, 1922-1964; 5 reels.
Appointment of Administrators, Executors, and Guardians, 1868-1923; 2 reels.
Appointment of Executors, 1923-1964; 1 reel.
Appointment of Guardians, 1906-1964; 2 reels.
Division of Slaves, 1829-1861; 1 reel. [*See also* **MARRIAGE, DIVORCE, AND VITAL STATISTICS,** Cohabitation, Record of, 1866]
Estates, Record of, 1818-1868; 4 reels.
Guardians' Accounts, 1820-1867; 2 reels.
Guardians, Index to, 1868-1963; 2 reels.
Inheritance Tax Records, 1913-1964; 2 reels.
Settlements, Record of, 1869-1968; 9 reels.
Trust Fund Records, 1918-1958; 1 reel.
Widows' Year's Support, 1883-1963; 1 reel.

LAND RECORDS

Deeds, General Index to, Grantee, 1777-1963; 12 reels.
Deeds, General Index to, Grantor, 1777-1963; 12 reels.
Deeds, Record of, 1778-1964; 223 reels.
Land Entries, 1776-1794; 1 reel.
Plats, 1937-1960; 1 reel.
Sales by Mortgagees, Trustees, and Executors, Record of, 1919-1963; 2 reels.

MARRIAGE, DIVORCE, AND VITAL STATISTICS

Births, Index to, 1913-1960; 3 reels.
Cohabitation, Record of, 1866; Division of Slaves, 1862-1865; 1 reel.
Deaths, Index to, 1913-1987; 4 reels.
Delayed Births, Index to, various years; 1 reel.
Maiden Names of Divorced Women, 1940-1964; 1 reel.
Marriage Bonds, 1777-1868; 2 reels.
Marriage Registers, 1872-1964; 4 reels.
Marriages, Record of, 1851-1857; 1 reel.

MISCELLANEOUS RECORDS

Inebriety, Record of, 1940-1964; 1 reel.
Orders and Decrees, 1869-1962; 20 reels.
Orders and Decrees, Index to, Defendant, 1869-1969; 2 reels.
Orders and Decrees, Index to, Plaintiff, 1869-1969; 2 reels.

OFFICIALS, COUNTY

Board of County Commissioners, Minutes, 1868-1930; 3 reels.

SCHOOL RECORDS

Community School Register, District 22, 1878-1889; 1 reel.
County Board of Education, Minutes, 1896-1956; 1 reel.

TAX AND FISCAL RECORDS

Tax Scrolls, 1875; 1 reel.

WILLS

Unrecorded Wills, 1790-1922; 1 reel.
Wills, Index to, Devisee, 1778-1963; 3 reels.
Wills, Index to, Devisor, 1778-1963; 2 reels.
Wills, Record of, 1778-1968; 6 reels.

NEW HANOVER COUNTY

Established in 1729 from Carteret Precinct as a precinct of Bath County.
Courthouse fires have destroyed a few records through the years.

ORIGINAL RECORDS

BONDS

Apprentice Bonds and Records, 1797-1899; 2 volumes, 2 Fibredex boxes.
Bastardy Bonds and Records, 1818-1906; 1 volume, 1 Fibredex box.
Constables' Bonds, 1846-1865; 1 volume.
Inspectors' Bonds, 1870-1893; 2 volumes.
Lumber Inspectors' Bonds, 1844-1868; 2 volumes.
Naval Stores Inspectors' Bonds, 1844-1868; 2 volumes.
Naval Stores and Lumber Inspectors' Bonds, 1841-1843; 1 volume.
Officials' Bonds and Records, 1766-1908; 2 volumes, 5 Fibredex boxes.
Sheriffs' Bonds, 1841-1867; 2 volumes.
Sheriffs' and Constables' Bonds, 1857-1858; 1 volume.

CORPORATIONS AND PARTNERSHIPS [*See* MISCELLANEOUS RECORDS]

COURT RECORDS

Circuit Criminal Court/Eastern District Criminal Court
- Minutes, 1895-1901; 1 volume.

County Court of Pleas and Quarter Sessions
- Appeal Dockets, 1841-1868; 2 volumes.
- Appearance Dockets, 1801-1814, 1827-1868; 6 volumes.
- Appointments and Orders, Record of, 1774-1868; 3 volumes.
- Execution Dockets, 1758-1862; 24 volumes, 1 manuscript box.
- Magistrates' Dockets, 1832-1841; 2 volumes.
- Minutes, 1738-1868; 30 volumes.
- Recognizance Docket, 1841-1860; 1 volume.
- Reference (Trial) and Appearance Dockets, 1750-1758; 2 volumes.
- State Dockets, 1808-1814, 1844-1867; 3 volumes.
- Trial, Appearance, and Reference Dockets, 1771-1786; 2 volumes.
- Trial Dockets, 1786-1797; 7 volumes.
- Trial and Reference Dockets, 1797-1860; 17 volumes.

Criminal Court
- Minutes, 1867-1868, 1877-1884, 1888-1895; 4 volumes.

Superior Court
- Appearance Dockets, 1804-1868; 3 volumes.
- Civil Action Papers, 1758-1915; 52 Fibredex boxes.
- Civil Action Papers Concerning Land, 1848-1940, 1955; 26 Fibredex boxes.
- Criminal Action Papers, 1788-1907; 11 Fibredex boxes.
- Equity Appearance Docket, 1848-1868; 1 volume.
- Equity Execution Docket, 1853-1866; 1 volume.
- Equity Minutes, 1860-1868; 1 volume.
- Equity Trial Docket, 1848-1868; 1 volume.
- Execution Dockets, 1810-1868; 6 volumes.
- Minutes, 1806-1910; 22 volumes.

Recognizance Docket, 1806-1821; 1 volume.
State Dockets, 1824-1829, 1836-1875, 1891; 4 volumes.
Trial and Reference Dockets, 1807-1868; 7 volumes.

ELECTION RECORDS

Election Records, 1832-1919; 4 Fibredex boxes.
Elections, Record of, 1878-1928; 2 volumes.

ESTATES RECORDS

Accounts, Record of, 1868-1915; 6 volumes.
Administrators' Bonds, 1844-1918; 12 volumes.
Appointment of Administrators, Executors, Guardians, and Masters, 1868-1879; 1 volume.
Estates, Record of, 1830-1894; 7 volumes.
Estates Records, 1741-1939; 118 Fibredex boxes.
Guardians' Accounts, 1867-1918; 3 volumes.
Guardians' Bonds, 1841-1911; 6 volumes.
Guardians' Records, 1763-1934; 18 Fibredex boxes.
Inventory of Estate of John Rowan, 1782; 1 volume.
Settlements, Record of, 1869-1884; 1 volume.

LAND RECORDS

Attachments, Executions, Levies, and Liens on Land, 1847, 1868-1917; 3 Fibredex boxes.
Block Book, 1911-1922; 1 volume.
Decrees Concerning Land, 1875-1914; 1 volume.
Deeds, 1757-1945; 13 Fibredex boxes.
Deeds, General Index to, Vendee, 1729-1914; 11 volumes.
Deeds, General Index to, Vendor, 1729-1914; 11 volumes.
Deeds Proved, Lists of, 1808-1863; 1 Fibredex box.
Deeds, Record of, 1805-1810, 1813-1818; 2 volumes.
Deeds of Trust, 1846-1967; 1 Fibredex box.
Ejectments, 1784-1898; 1 Fibredex box.
Land Entry Book, 1784-1796; 1 volume.
Miscellaneous Land Records, 1748-1950; 2 Fibredex boxes.
Mortgage Deeds, 1816-1945; 3 Fibredex boxes.
Quit Claim Deeds, 1874-1945; 2 Fibredex boxes.

MARRIAGE, DIVORCE, AND VITAL STATISTICS

Cohabitation Certificates, 1866-1868; 1 manuscript box.
Cohabitation, Record of, 1866-1868; 2 volumes.
Divorce Records, 1858-1945; 10 Fibredex boxes.
Marriage Bonds, 1741-1868; 4 Fibredex boxes.
Marriage Bonds, Certificates, and Licenses, Record of, 1791-1904; 3 manuscript boxes.
Marriage Licenses, 1867-1937, 1944-1963; 63 Fibredex boxes.
Marriage Licenses, Record of, 1843-1863; 1 volume.
Marriage Registers, 1867-1943; 9 volumes.

MILITARY AND PENSION RECORDS [*See* **MISCELLANEOUS RECORDS**]

MISCELLANEOUS RECORDS

Alien Registration, 1927, 1940; 2 volumes.
Assignees, Receivers, and Trustees, Records of, 1861-1915; 14 Fibredex boxes.
Board of County Commissioners, Minutes, 1873-1878, 1887-1918; 4 volumes.

Board of Magistrates, Minutes, 1878-1894; 1 volume.
Citizenship and Naturalization Records, 1842-1908; 4 Fibredex boxes.
Claims Allowed by Committee of Finance, Registry of, 1843-1877; 1 volume.
Clerk's Minute Dockets (Special Proceedings), 1877-1904; 5 volumes.
Committee of Finance, Journal of, 1846-1868; 1 volume.
Coroners' Inquests, 1768-1880; 2 Fibredex boxes.
County Accounts and Correspondence, 1783-1898; 1 Fibredex box.
County Board of Health, Minutes, 1879-1895; 1 volume.
County Bonds, Registry of, 1877-1895; 1 volume.
County Examiner Letterbook, 1869-1874; 1 volume.
County Treasurer, Journals of, 1870-1873; 2 volumes.
County Trustee, Journal of, 1866-1868; 1 volume.
Incorporations, 1879-1906; 2 Fibredex boxes.
Insolvent Debtors and Homestead and Personal Property Exemptions, 1809-1916; 4 Fibredex boxes.
Inventories and Accounts of Assignees, Record of, 1894-1913; 1 volume.
Licenses to Trades, Registry of, 1869-1894; 2 volumes.
Miscellaneous Records, 1756-1945; 5 Fibredex boxes.
Orders and Decrees, 1869-1918; 3 volumes.
Pensions, Record of, 1926-1949; 2 volumes.
Railroad Records, 1858-1915; 8 Fibredex boxes.
Road Records, 1798-1868; 1 Fibredex box.
School Fund Journals, 1882-1913; 3 volumes.
School Records, 1841-1913; 1 Fibredex box.
Slaves and Free Persons of Color, Records of, 1786-1888; 1 Fibredex box.
Stock Marks, 1862-1917; 2 volumes.
Treasurers' Accounts with Wardens of the Poor, 1867-1868; 1 volume.
Wardens of the Poor, Minutes, 1850-1868; 1 volume.

OFFICIALS, COUNTY [*See* **MISCELLANEOUS RECORDS**]

ROADS AND BRIDGES [*See* **MISCELLANEOUS RECORDS**]

SCHOOL RECORDS [See MISCELLANEOUS RECORDS; CRX RECORDS]

TAX AND FISCAL RECORDS

Assessment for Taxes, 1847, n.d. [ca. 1874]; 2 volumes.
Lists of Taxables, 1815-1846; 5 volumes.
Tax Records, 1779-1909; 2 Fibredex boxes.

WILLS

Wills, 1732-1961; 111 Fibredex boxes.
Wills, Cross Index to, 1744-1943; 2 volumes.
Wills, Record of, 1790-1816, 1830-1848; 3 volumes.

CRX RECORDS

School Records, 1847-1849; 3 folders.

MICROFILM RECORDS

BONDS

Bastardy Bonds, 1877-1879; 1 reel.

Corporations and Partnerships

Corporations, Record of, 1885-1904; 1 reel.
Partnerships, Record of, 1969-1976; 1 reel.

Court Records

County Court of Pleas and Quarter Sessions
- Magistrates' Docket, 1832-1837; 1 reel.
- Minutes, 1738-1868; 9 reels.

Superior Court
- Equity Minutes, 1860-1868; 1 reel.
- Judgments and Special Proceedings, Index to, Defendant, 1941-1968; 6 reels.
- Judgments and Special Proceedings, Index to, Plaintiff, 1941-1968; 2 reels.
- Minutes, 1806-1939; 17 reels.
- Minutes, Criminal, 1939-1943; 1 reel.

Election Records

Elections, Record of, 1878-1960; 1 reel.

Estates RECORDS

Accounts, Record of, 1829-1832, 1835-1847, 1879-1940; 7 reels.
Administrators' Bonds, 1844-1946; 9 reels.
Administrators, Guardians, and Wards, Index to, 1843-1853; 1 reel.
Appointment of Executors, 1868-1878; 1 reel.
Division of Land and Dowers, 1800-1934; 1 reel.
Guardians' Accounts, 1904-1934; 1 reel.
Guardians' Bonds, 1856-1911; 2 reels.
Guardians, Record of, 1910-1946; 2 reels.

Land Records

Deeds, Record of, 1734-1941; 173 reels.
Foreclosure Accounts, 1924-1964; 1 reel.
Land Entries, 1778-1948; 1 reel.
Map Book Index, 1914-1964; 1 reel.
Map Books, 1914-1970; 3 reels.
Real Estate Conveyances, Index to, Grantee, 1729-1954; 12 reels.
Real Estate Conveyances, Index to, Grantor, 1729-1954; 13 reels.
Surveyors' Entry Book, 1905-1907; 1 reel.

Marriage, Divorce, and Vital Statistics

Births, Index to, 1913-1961, 1971-1974; 4 reels.
Births in Wilmington, Record of, 1903-1910; 1 reel.
Cohabitation Certificates, 1866-1867; 1 reel.
Cohabitation, Record of, 1866-1868; 1 reel.
Deaths, Index to, 1913-1961; 2 reels.
Deaths in Wilmington, Record of, 1903-1907; 1 reel.
Delayed Births, Index to, 1879-1928, various years; 2 reels.
Marriage Bonds, 1740-1868; 2 reels.
Marriage Licenses, 1867-1960; 42 reels.
Marriage Licenses Issued, Record of, 1843-1863; 1 reel.
Marriage Registers, Black, 1848-1939; 1 reel.
Marriage Registers, White, 1848-1961; 2 reels.

MISCELLANEOUS RECORDS

Homesteads, Record of, 1869-1933; 1 reel.
Orders and Decrees, 1869-1943; 3 reels.
Parties to Actions, Cross Index to, 1935, no date; 1 reel.
Special Proceedings, 1877-1964; 14 reels.

TAX AND FISCAL RECORDS

Assessment for Taxes, 1847; 1 reel.
Tax Lists, 1815-1819, 1836-1846, 1856-1900, 1905, 1910, 1915, 1925; 17 reels.

WILLS

Wills, Cross Index to, 1735-1961; 2 reels.
Wills, Record of, 1747-1961; 10 reels.

NORTHAMPTON COUNTY

Established in 1741 from Bertie County.
A few records are missing; reason unknown.

ORIGINAL RECORDS

Bonds

Apprentice Bonds and Records, 1797-1911; 1 volume, 1 Fibredex box.
Bastardy Bonds and Records, 1783-1894; 6 Fibredex boxes.
Bastardy Docket, 1876-1880; 1 volume.
Constables' Bonds, 1787-1874; 3 Fibredex boxes.
Officials' Bonds, 1787-1899; 2 Fibredex boxes.

Court Records

County Court of Pleas and Quarter Sessions
- Appearance Docket, 1860-1868; 1 volume.
- Execution Dockets, 1818-1821, 1828-1868; 6 volumes.
- Minutes, 1792-1796, 1813-1868; 14 volumes.
- State Docket, 1857-1868; 1 volume.
- Trial, Appearance, and State Dockets, 1802-1868; 10 volumes.

Eastern District Criminal Court
- Judgment Docket, 1899-1900; 1 volume.
- Minutes, 1899-1901; 1 volume.

Inferior Court
- Criminal Issues Docket, 1877-1881; 1 volume.
- Judgment Docket, 1877-1885; 1 volume.
- Minutes, 1877-1885; 1 volume.

Superior Court
- Civil Action Papers, 1771-1926; 93 Fibredex boxes.
- Civil Action Papers Concerning Land, 1784-1925; 9 Fibredex boxes.
- Civil Issues Dockets, 1868-1877, 1882-1885; 3 volumes.
- Criminal Action Papers, 1779-1878; 22 Fibredex boxes.
- Criminal Issues Docket, 1868-1884; 1 volume.
- Equity Minutes, 1807-1868; 3 volumes.
- Equity Trial and Appearance Docket, 1850-1861; 1 volume.
- Execution Dockets, 1844-1869; 2 volumes.
- Judgment Dockets, 1868-1874; 3 volumes.
- Minutes, 1818-1908; 16 volumes.
- Summons Docket, 1868-1874; 1 volume.
- Trial, Appearance, and State Dockets, 1833-1866; 2 volumes.

Election Records

Election Records, 1828-1897; 2 Fibredex boxes.
Elections, Record of, 1878-1953; 3 volumes.
Permanent Registration of Voters, 1902-1908; 1 volume.

Estates Records

Accounts, Record of, 1868-1909; 9 volumes.
Administrators' Bonds, 1868-1918; 4 volumes.
Clerk's Receipt Book (Estates), 1891-1923; 1 volume.

Estates, Record of, 1781-1868; 15 volumes.
Estates Records, 1785-1929; 229 Fibredex boxes.
Guardians' Accounts, 1781-1802, 1818-1868; 9 volumes.
Guardians' Bonds, 1868-1918; 2 volumes.
Guardians' Docket, 1821-1874; 1 volume.
Guardians' Records, 1785-1926; 53 Fibredex boxes.
Probate Court Docket, 1885-1890; 1 volume.
Probate (Estates), Record of, 1869-1874; 1 volume.
Settlements, Record of, 1869-1907; 3 volumes.

LAND RECORDS

Attachments, Executions, and Liens on Land, 1833-1873; 2 Fibredex boxes.
Deed Book 3, Index to, [1759-1766]; 1 pamphlet.
Deeds, 1743-1878; 26 Fibredex boxes.
Deeds of Gift, 1767-1866; 1 Fibredex box.
Deeds of Trust, 1798-1925; 4 Fibredex boxes.
Ejectments, 1782-1869; 2 Fibredex boxes.
Land Records, 1784-1924; 2 Fibredex boxes.
Levies on Land, 1805-1869; 2 Fibredex boxes.
Miscellaneous Deeds and Land Records, 1774-1920; 1 Fibredex box.
Mortgage Deeds, 1741-1924; 2 Fibredex boxes.

MARRIAGE, DIVORCE, AND VITAL STATISTICS

Divorce Records, 1818-1951; 3 Fibredex boxes.
Marriage Bonds, 1811-1868; 7 Fibredex boxes.

MILITARY AND PENSION RECORDS [*See* **MISCELLANEOUS RECORDS**]

MISCELLANEOUS RECORDS

Bills of Sale, 1779-1875; 2 Fibredex boxes.
Bridge Records, 1785-1867; 2 Fibredex boxes.
Boundary Agreement, 1957; 1 manuscript box.
Coroners' Reports, 1793-1905; 1 Fibredex box.
County Accounts, 1787-1879; 3 Fibredex boxes.
Court Martial Minutes, 1824-1850; 1 volume.
Magistrates, Record of, 1887-1926; 2 volumes.
Mill Records, 1786-1859; 1 Fibredex box.
Miscellaneous Records, 1774-1936; 6 Fibredex boxes.
Orders and Decrees, 1869-1876; 2 volumes.
Partnership, Record of, 1914-1967; 1 volume.
Powers of Attorney, 1740, 1808-1879; 1 Fibredex box.
Provisions Furnished Indigent Families, 1861-1865; 1 Fibredex box.
Railroad Records, 1832-1916; 4 Fibredex boxes.
Road Records, 1789-1867; 5 Fibredex boxes.
Slave Records, 1785-1867; 3 Fibredex boxes.
Special Proceedings, Cross Index to, 1877-1890; 1 volume.
Special Proceedings Docket, 1877-1894, 1903, 1906; 1 volume.
Wardens of the Poor, St. George's Parish, Minutes, 1773-1814; 1 volume.
Witness Tickets, 1806-1868; 3 Fibredex boxes.

ROADS AND BRIDGES [*See* **MISCELLANEOUS RECORDS**]

SCHOOL RECORDS [*See* **CRX RECORDS**]

TAX AND FISCAL RECORDS

Lists of Taxables, 1823-1851; 3 volumes.
Tax Records, 1784-1879; 3 Fibredex boxes.

WILLS

Wills, 1764-1950; 46 Fibredex boxes.
Wills, Record of, 1762-1791; 2 volumes.

CRX RECORDS

School Records, no date; 1 folder.

MICROFILM RECORDS

BONDS

Apprentice Bonds, 1869-1918; 1 reel.

CORPORATIONS AND PARTNERSHIPS

Corporations, Record of, 1887-1961; 1 reel.
Partnership Records, 1930-1958; 1 reel.

COURT RECORDS

County Court of Pleas and Quarter Sessions
- Minutes, 1792-1796, 1813-1868; 6 reels.

Inferior Court
- Minutes, 1877-1885; 1 reel.

Superior Court
- Equity Minutes, 1807-1834, 1857-1868; 1 reel.
- Judgments, Index to, 1868-1968; 1 reel.
- Minutes, 1818-1834, 1845-1946; 9 reels.

ELECTION RECORDS

Elections, Record of, 1880-1917, 1924-1950; 1 reel.

ESTATES RECORDS

Accounts, Record of, 1868-1961; 9 reels.
Administrators' Bonds, 1883-1918; 1 reel.
Administrators, Record of, 1911-1961; 4 reels.
Estates, Record of, 1781-1792, 1796-1868; 7 reels.
Executors, Record of, 1923-1961; 1 reel.
Guardians' Bonds, 1868-1918; 1 reel.
Guardians' and Other Fiduciaries' Accounts, 1781-1802, 1811-1825; 1 reel.
Guardians, Record of, 1908-1961; 1 reel.
Settlements, Record of, 1861-1961; 5 reels.

LAND RECORDS

Deeds and Mortgages, Index to, Grantee, 1741-1976; 8 reels.
Deeds and Mortgages, Index to, Grantor, 1741-1976; 6 reels.
Deeds, Record of, 1741-1935; 74 reels.
Plat Book, 1912-1949; 1 reel.
Resale of Land by Mortgagees and Trustees, Record of, 1921-1961; 2 reels.

Marriage, Divorce, and Vital Statistics

Births, Index to, 1913-1979; 2 reels.
Deaths, Index to, 1913-1979; 1 reel.
Delayed Births, Index to, various years; 1 reel.
Maiden Names of Divorced Women, 1946-1968; 1 reel.
Marriage Bonds, 1741-1868; 2 reels.
Marriage Licenses, 1863-1961; 9 reels.
Marriage Registers, 1851-1974; 3 reels.
Marriages, Index to, 1865-1974; 1 reel.

Miscellaneous Records

Clerk's Minute Dockets, 1924-1961; 1 reel.
Orders and Decrees, 1869-1934; 6 reels.
Special Proceedings, Cross Index to, 1869-1961; 1 reel.
Wardens of the Poor, Minutes and Accounts, 1773-1814; 1 reel.

School Records

County Board of Education, Minutes, 1872-1961; 1 reel.

Tax and Fiscal Records

Lists of Taxables, 1823-1851; 2 reels.

Wills

Wills, Cross Index to, 1760-1961; 1 reel.
Wills, Record of, 1759-1961; 5 reels.

ONSLOW COUNTY

Established in 1734 from New Hanover Precinct as a precinct of Bath County.
Storms of 1752 and 1786 destroyed many records.
Later court records are missing; reason unknown.

ORIGINAL RECORDS

BONDS

Apprentice Bonds and Records, 1757-1907; 1 Fibredex box.
Bastardy Bonds and Records, 1764-1909; 1 volume, 2 Fibredex boxes.
Officials' Bonds and Records, 1779-1913; 4 Fibredex boxes.

COURT RECORDS

County Court of Pleas and Quarter Sessions
- Appeal Docket, 1787-1790; 1 volume.
- Appearance Dockets, 1801-1868; 4 volumes.
- Crown Dockets, 1763-1774; 2 volumes.
- Execution Dockets, 1762-1868; 15 volumes.
- Minutes, 1732-1868; 20 volumes.
- State Dockets, 1795-1868; 2 volumes.
- Trial and Appeal Dockets, 1793-1800; 4 volumes.
- Trial, Appearance, and Crown Dockets, 1745-1763; 5 volumes.
- Trial and Appearance Dockets, 1763-1788; 4 volumes.
- Trial Dockets, 1827-1868; 4 volumes.

Superior Court
- Appearance Docket, 1834-1868; 1 volume.
- Civil Action Papers, 1759-1919; 72 Fibredex boxes.
- Civil Action Papers Concerning Land, 1778-1929; 7 Fibredex boxes.
- Civil Transfer Docket, 1869-1877; 1 volume.
- Criminal Action Papers, 1765-1914; 22 Fibredex boxes.
- Equity Minutes, 1839-1850; 1 volume.
- Equity Trial and Appearance Docket, 1840-1852; 1 volume.
- Execution Dockets, 1851-1868; 2 volumes.
- Minutes, 1844-1909; 8 volumes.
- Presentments Docket, 1879-1893; 1 volume.
- State Docket, 1854-1869; 1 volume.
- Trial Dockets, 1834-1869; 3 volumes.

ELECTION RECORDS

Elections, Record of, 1878-1932; 3 volumes.

ESTATES RECORDS

Accounts, Record of, 1830-1909; 5 volumes.
Administrators' Bonds, 1870-1913; 4 volumes.
Appointment of Administrators, Executors, Guardians, and Masters, 1868-1912; 1 volume.
Estates Records, 1735-1914; 83 Fibredex boxes.
Guardians' Bonds, 1857-1912; 4 volumes.
Guardians' Records, 1775-1909; 9 Fibredex boxes.
Inventories and Accounts of Sale, 1829-1862; 4 volumes.

Inventories of Estates, 1780-1785; 1 volume.
Settlements, Record of, 1869-1895; 1 volume.

LAND RECORDS
Deeds, Record of, 1740-1807; 25 volumes.
Deeds of Sale, 1751-1900; 6 Fibredex boxes.
Ejectments, 1790-1901; 1 Fibredex box.
Entry Books, 1778-1889; 7 volumes.
Land Grant Books, 1781-1794; 3 volumes.
Miscellaneous Deeds, 1790-1862; 1 Fibredex box.
Miscellaneous Land Records, 1753-1908; 1 Fibredex box.
Mortgage Deeds, 1833-1908; 1 Fibredex box.
Petitions for Partition, 1870-1909; 1 Fibredex box.

MARRIAGE, DIVORCE, AND VITAL STATISTICS [*See also* **CRX RECORDS**]
Divorce Records, 1866-1906; 1 Fibredex box.
Marriage Bonds, 1745-1868; 4 Fibredex boxes.

MILITARY AND PENSION RECORDS [*See* **MISCELLANEOUS RECORDS**]

MISCELLANEOUS RECORDS
Appointment of Road Overseers, 1827-1853; 1 volume.
Miscellaneous Records, 1732-1950; 10 Fibredex boxes.
Orders and Decrees, 1868-1926; 1 volume.
Pensions, Record of, 1911-1932; 1 volume.
Special Proceedings Docket, 1883-1926; 1 volume.

ROADS AND BRIDGES [*See* **MISCELLANEOUS RECORDS**]

TAX AND FISCAL RECORDS
Tax Records, 1774-1912; 4 Fibredex boxes.

WILLS
Wills, 1746-1968; 22 Fibredex boxes.
Wills, Cross Index to, 1829-1939; 2 volumes.
Wills and Inventories of Estates, 1774-1790; 1 volume.
Wills, Record of, 1757-1783; 1 volume.

CRX RECORDS
Marriage Records, 1851-1860; 1 folder.

MICROFILM RECORDS

BONDS
Bastardy Bonds, 1871-1878; 1 reel.

COURT RECORDS
County Court of Pleas and Quarter Sessions
Minutes, 1734-1868; 6 reels.
Superior Court
Equity Minutes, 1839-1850; 1 reel.
Judgments, Index to, 1867-1950; 1 reel.
Judgments, Index to, Defendant, 1951-1968; 1 reel.
Judgments, Index to, Plaintiff, 1951-1968; 1 reel.
Minutes, 1866-1968; 15 reels.

ELECTION RECORDS

Elections, Record of, 1878-1944; 1 reel.

ESTATES RECORDS

Accounts, Record of, 1868-1961; 3 reels.
Administrators' Bonds, 1870-1912; 2 reels.
Administrators, Record of, 1913-1944; 2 reels.
Appointment of Executors, 1869-1912; 1 reel.
Estates, Record of, 1824-1861; 2 reels.
Executors, Record of, 1928-1968; 1 reel.
Final Settlements, Record of, 1869-1961; 3 reels.
Guardians' Bonds, 1857-1912; 1 reel.

LAND RECORDS

Deeds, Record of, 1740-1945; 62 reels.
Land Entries, 1781-1955; 2 reels.
Land Grants, 1712-1839, 1877-1928; 3 reels.
Real Estate Conveyances, Index to, Grantee, 1734-1965; 8 reels.
Real Estate Conveyances, Index to, Grantor, 1734-1965; 7 reels.
Reports of Sales, 1921-1961; 1 reel.

MARRIAGE, DIVORCE, AND VITAL STATISTICS

Births, Index to, 1914-1960; 2 reels.
Deaths, Index to, 1907-1985; 2 reels.
Delayed Births, Index to, various years; 1 reel.
Marriage Bonds, 1745-1868; 1 reel.
Marriage Licenses, 1893-1961; 8 reels.
Marriage Registers, 1851-1947; 1 reel.

MILITARY AND PENSION RECORDS

Pensions, Record of, 1911-1929; 1 reel.

MISCELLANEOUS RECORDS

Homestead Returns, 1869-1922; 1 reel.
Orders and Decrees, 1868-1926; 1 reel.
Special Proceedings, 1882-1923; 3 reels.
Special Proceedings, Index to, Defendant, 1869-1968; 1 reel.
Special Proceedings, Index to, Plaintiff, 1869-1968; 1 reel.

OFFICIALS, COUNTY

Board of County Commissioners, Minutes, 1868-1924; 2 reels.

ROAD RECORDS

Road Overseers, Record of, 1827-1853; 1 reel.

TAX AND FISCAL RECORDS

Tax Lists, 1774-1790; 1 reel.

WILLS

Wills, 1790-1968; 4 reels.
Wills, Index to, Devisee, 1790-1970; 1 reel.
Wills, Index to, Devisor, 1790-1970; 1 reel.

ORANGE COUNTY

Established in 1752 from Bladen, Granville, and Johnston counties.
Many court records are missing; reason unknown.

ORIGINAL RECORDS

BONDS

- Apprentice Bonds and Records, 1780-1905; 1 volume, 3 Fibredex boxes.
- Bastardy Bonds and Records, 1782-1908; 9 Fibredex boxes.
- Constables' Bonds, 1786-1915; 3 Fibredex boxes.
- Officials' Bonds, 1782-1939; 2 volumes, 2 Fibredex boxes.
- Sheriffs' Bonds, 1782-1928; 1 Fibredex box.

COURT RECORDS [*See also* **CRX RECORDS**]

- County Court of Pleas and Quarter Sessions
  - Costs Docket, 1854-1860; 1 volume.
  - Execution Dockets, 1807-1820, 1853-1861; 1 volume, 1 manuscript box.
  - Minutes, 1752-1766, 1777-1868; 34 volumes, 1 manuscript box.
  - State Docket, 1772-1797; 1 volume.
  - Trial and Appearance Docket, 1848-1857; 1 volume.
  - Trial, Appearance, and Reference Docket, 1782-1786; 1 volume.
- Superior Court
  - Civil Action Papers, 1771-1943; 135 Fibredex boxes.
  - Civil Action Papers Concerning Land, 1778-1934; 8 Fibredex boxes.
  - Civil Issues Docket, 1923-1929; 1 volume.
  - Criminal Action Papers, 1778-1909; 78 Fibredex boxes.
  - Equity Fee Books, 1797-1843; 2 volumes.
  - Equity Minutes, 1834-1864; 2 volumes.
  - Equity Prosecution Bond Docket, 1789-1817; 1 volume.
  - Execution Docket, 1829-1839; 1 volume.
  - Judgment Dockets, 1868-1936; 6 volumes. [*See also* **LAND RECORDS**]
  - Judgments, Cross Index to, 1868-1936; 2 volumes.
  - Lien Docket, 1873-1928; 1 volume.
  - Minutes, 1807-1889; 8 volumes.

ELECTION RECORDS

- Election Records, 1783-1910; 11 Fibredex boxes.
- Elections, Record of, 1878-1922, 1938-1966; 4 volumes.
- Permanent Registration of Voters, 1902-1908; 1 volume.
- Voter Registration Book, Cole Store Precinct, 1896-1898; 1 volume.

ESTATES RECORDS

- Administrators' Bonds, 1868-1913; 7 volumes.
- Clerk's Account Books, Estates, 1868-1938; 3 volumes.
- Clerk's Account Books (Trust Funds), 1938-1968; 5 volumes.
- Equity Account Book, 1858-1868; 1 volume.
- Estates Records, 1754-1944; 135 Fibredex boxes.
- Guardians' Accounts, 1819-1910; 4 volumes.
- Guardians' Bonds, 1868-1933, 1947; 3 volumes.
- Guardians' Records, 1782-1941; 26 Fibredex boxes.

Guardians of World War Veterans, 1931-1966; 1 volume.
Inventories, Sales, and Accounts of Estates, 1756-1785, 1800-1912; 24 volumes.

LAND RECORDS [*See also* **CRX RECORDS**]
Deeds, 1755-1927; 8 Fibredex boxes.
Deeds, Index to, 1755-1869; 3 volumes, 1 manuscript box.
Deeds of Trust and Mortgage Deeds, 1797-1930; 2 Fibredex boxes.
Ejectments, 1782-1902; 4 Fibredex boxes.
Judgment Dockets, Land Tax Sales, 1929-1936; 3 volumes. [*See also* **COURT RECORDS**, Superior Court]
Judgments—Land Tax Sales, Cross Index to, 1929-1936; 1 volume.
Land Entry Book, 1830-1908; 1 volume.
Land Grant Book, 1779-1794; 1 volume.
Land Records, 1752-1940; 2 Fibredex boxes.
Levies on Land and/or Personal Property, 1784-1886; 4 Fibredex boxes.
Miscellaneous Deeds, 1764-1925; 1 Fibredex box.
Registration of Deeds, 1752-1793; 2 volumes.
Sales and Resales, Record of, 1916-1968; 7 volumes.
Tax Suit Judgment Docket, 1961-1962; 1 volume.

MARRIAGE, DIVORCE, AND VITAL STATISTICS
Applications for Marriage Licenses, Record of, 1929-1930; 1 volume.
Cohabitation Certificates, 1866-1868; 1 volume.
Divorce Records, 1824-1908; 3 Fibredex boxes.
Maiden Names of Divorced Women, 1941-1969; 1 volume.
Marriage Bonds, 1779-1868; 19 Fibredex boxes.
Marriage Certificates, Record of, 1860-1861, 1865-1867; 1 volume.

MILITARY AND PENSION RECORDS [*See* **ESTATES RECORDS; MISCELLANEOUS RECORDS**]

MISCELLANEOUS RECORDS [*See also* **CRX RECORDS**]
Account Book, County Jail, 1837-1843; 1 volume.
Account Book, County Trustee, 1834-1848, 1864-1875; 2 volumes.
Alien Registration, 1940; 1 volume.
Astray Book, 1831-1847; 1 volume.
Bills of Sale, 1778-1886; 1 Fibredex box.
Board of County Commissioners, Minutes, 1868-1936; 9 volumes.
Bridge Records, 1787-1868; 1 Fibredex box.
Coroners' Inquests, 1785-1911; 1 Fibredex box.
County Accounts, 1767-1893; 3 Fibredex boxes.
Grand Jury Presentments, 1781-1887; 1 Fibredex box.
Homestead and Personal Property Exemptions, 1821-1918; 1 Fibredex box.
Inquisition of Inebriety, 1939-1966; 1 volume.
Insolvents, 1773-1887; 8 Fibredex boxes.
Jury Records, 1772-1878; 2 Fibredex boxes.
Lunacy, Record of, 1899-1968; 5 volumes.
Magistrates, Record of, 1877-1944; 2 volumes.
Miscellaneous Records, 1768-1942; 5 Fibredex boxes.
Nurses' Certificates of Registration, 1912-1959; 1 volume.
Official Reports, Record of, 1874-1908; 1 volume.
Officials' Oaths, 1936-1966; 1 volume.
Orders and Decrees, 1868-1941; 8 volumes.

Personal Accounts, 1773-1862; 1 Fibredex box.
Physicians' and Surgeons' Certificates of Registration, 1953-1956; 1 volume.
Powers of Attorney, 1781-1909; 1 Fibredex box.
Promissory Notes, 1773-1869; 2 Fibredex boxes.
Provisions for Families of Soldiers, 1863-1865; 1 Fibredex box.
Receivers' Accounts, 1870-1938; 1 volume.
Road Records, 1786-1909; 4 Fibredex boxes.
Slave Records, 1783-1865; 1 Fibredex box.
Special Proceedings and Incorporation, Record of, 1878-1924; 1 volume.
Wardens of the Poor, Account Book, 1842-1868; 1 volume.
Wardens of the Poor, Minutes, 1832-1879; 2 volumes.

OFFICIALS, COUNTY [*See* **MISCELLANEOUS RECORDS**]

ROADS AND BRIDGES [*See* **MISCELLANEOUS RECORDS**]

TAX AND FISCAL RECORDS
Federal Direct Taxes Collected, Record of, 1866; 1 volume.
Poll Tax Register, 1902-1914; 1 volume.
Tax Lists, 1780-1801, 1817, 1827, 1915; 1 volume, 3 Fibredex boxes, 1 manuscript box.

WILLS
Wills, 1753-1968; 65 Fibredex boxes.

CRX RECORDS
Account Book, County Trustee, 1823-1834; 1 volume.
Clerk's Fee and Receipt Book, Court of Pleas and Quarter Sessions, 1858-1866; 1 volume.
Clerk's Receipt Book, Estates, 1854-1860; 1 volume.
Deed, 1771; 1 folder.
Execution Docket, Court of Pleas and Quarter Sessions, 1791-1794; 1 volume.
Minute Docket (Rough), Court of Pleas and Quarter Sessions, 1849-1850, 1859-1861; 2 volumes in manuscript boxes.
Miscellaneous Records, 1774-1915; 2 Fibredex boxes, 13 folders.

MICROFILM RECORDS

BONDS
Apprentice Bonds, 1889-1905; 1 reel.
Officials' Bonds, 1868-1939; 1 reel.

CORPORATIONS AND PARTNERSHIPS
Incorporations, Record of, 1878-1952; 1 reel.
Partnership Records, 1930-1962; 1 reel.
Partnership Records, Index to, 1930-1962; 1 reel.

COURT RECORDS
County Court of Pleas and Quarter Sessions
Minutes, 1752-1766, 1777-1800, 1805-1868; 11 reels.
Superior Court
Equity Account Book, 1833-1843; 1 reel.
Equity Minutes, 1789-1864; 2 reels.
Judgments, Index to, 1868-1955; 1 reel.
Judgments, Index to, Defendant, 1956-1968; 1 reel.
Judgments, Index to, Plaintiff, 1956-1968; 1 reel.
Minutes, 1807-1955; 10 reels.

ELECTION RECORDS

Elections, Record of, 1897-1960; 1 reel.

ESTATES RECORDS

Accounts, Record of, 1869-1949; 2 reels.
Administrators' Bonds, 1891-1913; 1 reel.
Administrators, Executors, and Guardians, Record of, 1915-1929; 1 reel.
Administrators, Record of, 1918-1962; 4 reels.
Appointment of Executors, 1870-1915; 1 reel.
Equity Account Book, 1858-1868; Clerk's Receipt Book (Estates), 1868-1938; 1 reel.
Estates, Record of, 1758-1785, 1800-1912; 11 reels.
Executors, Record of, 1929-1962; 1 reel.
Guardians' Accounts, 1819-1853, 1909-1951; 2 reels.
Guardians' Bonds, 1880-1891; 1 reel.
Guardians, Record of, 1929-1962; 1 reel.
Inheritance Tax Records, 1921-1962; 1 reel.
Inventories, Record of, 1912-1951; 1 reel.
Inventories, Sales, and Settlements of Estates, 1837-1843; 1 reel.
Settlements, Record of, 1868-1954; 4 reels.

LAND RECORDS

Deeds, Index to, Grantee, 1755-1962; 3 reels.
Deeds, Index to, Grantor, 1755-1962; 4 reels.
Deeds, Record of, 1755-1961; 112 reels.
Federal Tax Lien Index, 1928-1962; 1 reel.
Land Entry Book, 1830-1908; 1 reel.
Land Grant Book, 1779-1794; 1 reel.
Registration of Deeds, 1752-1793; 1 reel.
Sales and Resales, Record of, 1917-1962; 3 reels.

MARRIAGE, DIVORCE, AND VITAL STATISTICS

Births, Index to, 1913-1961; 1 reel.
Cohabitation Certificates, 1866-1868; 1 reel.
Deaths, Index to, 1913-1961; 1 reel.
Maiden Names of Divorced Women, 1941-1969; 1 reel.
Marriage Bond Abstracts, 1752-1868; 1 reel.
Marriage Bonds, 1752-1868; 10 reels.
Marriage Licenses, 1866-1962; 8 reels.
Marriage, Record of, 1866-1867; 1 reel.
Marriage Registers, 1851-1962; 2 reels.

MISCELLANEOUS RECORDS

Astray Book, 1831-1847; 1 reel.
Clerk's Minute Docket, 1919-1953; 1 reel.
County Trustees' Account Books, 1834-1875; 1 reel.
Jail Account Book, 1831-1847; 1 reel.
Official Reports, Record of, 1874-1908; 1 reel.
Orders and Decrees, 1868-1952; 5 reels.
Poor House Book, 1842-1868; 1 reel.
Special Proceedings, Cross Index to, 1878-1962; 1 reel.
Wardens of the Poor, 1832-1879; 2 reels.

OFFICIALS, COUNTY

Board of County Commissioners, Minutes, 1868-1962; 4 reels.

SCHOOL RECORDS

County Board of Education, Minutes, 1872-1962; 1 reel.

TAX AND FISCAL RECORDS

List of Taxables, 1780-1827; 3 reels.
Tax Lists, 1779-1783; 2 reels.

WILLS

Wills, Cross Index to, 1756-1962; 1 reel.
Wills, Record of, 1752-1946; 7 reels.

PAMLICO COUNTY

Established in 1872 from Beaufort and Craven counties.

ORIGINAL RECORDS

BONDS

Bastardy Bonds and Records, 1874-1910; .5 Fibredex box.
Officials' Bonds and Records, 1872-1928; 1.5 Fibredex boxes.

COURT RECORDS

Superior Court

Civil Action Papers, 1873-1921; 1 Fibredex box.
Civil Action Papers Concerning Land, 1872-1935; 2 Fibredex boxes.
Criminal Action Papers, 1875-1914; 1 Fibredex box.
Criminal Issues Dockets, 1872-1948; 2 volumes.
Judgment Dockets, 1873-1968; 5 volumes. [*See also* **LAND RECORDS**, Tax Suit Judgment Dockets]
Judgments, Cross Index to, 1873-1968; 3 volumes.
Minutes, 1872-1968; 7 volumes.

ELECTION RECORDS

Elections, Record of, 1926-1968; 2 volumes.
Permanent Registration of Voters, 1902-1908; 1 volume.

ESTATES RECORDS

Accounts of Indigent Orphans, Record of, 1906-1953; 1 volume.
Accounts, Record of, 1872-1968; 6 volumes.
Administrators, Executors, and Guardians, Record of, 1907-1965; 2 volumes.
Administrators, Record of, 1927-1968; 3 volumes.
Estates Records, 1872-1939; 10 Fibredex boxes.
Executors and Administrators, Cross Index to, 1872-1968; 1 volume.
Executors and Trustees under Wills, Record of, 1965-1968; 1 volume.
Guardians, Cross Index to, 1873-1968; 1 volume.
Guardians, Record of, 1942-1968; 1 volume.
Guardians' Records, 1875-1920; 1 Fibredex box.
Inheritance Tax, Record of, 1923-1969; 2 volumes.
Settlements, Record of, 1881-1968; 4 volumes.
Widows' Dowers and Year's Support, 1899-1945; 1 volume.

LAND RECORDS

Deeds and Miscellaneous Land Records, 1869-1919; 2 Fibredex boxes.
Land Sold for Taxes, Record of, 1930-1965; 4 volumes.
Sale and Resale of Land, Record of, 1921-1968; 2 volumes.
Sales by Mortgagees and Trustees, Record of, 1924-1941; 1 volume.
Tax Suit Judgment Dockets, 1939-1948, 1961; 4 volumes. [*See also* **COURT RECORDS**, Superior Court, Judgment Dockets]

MARRIAGE, DIVORCE, AND VITAL STATISTICS

Divorce Records, 1874-1915; 1 Fibredex box.
Maiden Names of Divorced Women, 1938-1966; 1 volume.

Miscellaneous Records
Accounts of Receivers, 1899-1920; 1 volume.
Assignees, Record of, 1905-1913; 1 volume.
Clerk's Minute Docket (Special Proceedings), 1933-1950; 1 volume.
Drainage Record, 1908-1937; 1 volume.
Lunacy, Record of, 1904-1948; 1 volume.
Miscellaneous Records, 1874-1937; 2 Fibredex boxes.
Official Reports, Record of, 1874-1879; 1 volume.
Partnership, Record of, 1915-1932; 1 volume.
Receivers, Record of, 1907-1908; 1 volume.
Rights of Way, Record of, 1873-1884; 1 volume.
Stock Marks, Record of, 1874-1919; 1 volume.

Wills
Wills, 1872-1967; 8 Fibredex boxes.

MICROFILM RECORDS

Corporations and Partnerships
Incorporations, Record of, 1887-1968; 1 reel.

Court Records
Superior Court
Minutes, 1872-1947; 3 reels.

Estates Records
Accounts, Inventories, and Sales of Estates, 1930-1968; 2 reels.
Accounts, Record of, 1872-1935; 1 reel.
Administrators and Executors, Cross Index to, 1872-1968; 1 reel.
Administrators, Executors, and Guardians, Record of, 1907-1948; 1 reel.
Administrators, Record of, 1927-1968; 1 reel.
Clerk's Receiver Accounts, 1901-1920; 1 reel.
Guardians, Cross Index to, 1872-1968; 1 reel.
Guardians, Record of, 1942-1968; 1 reel.
Inheritance Tax Records, 1923-1968; 1 reel.
Settlements, Record of, 1881-1968; 2 reels.
Widows' Year's Support, 1899-1945; 1 reel.

Land Records
Deeds and Mortgages, General Index to, Grantee, 1872-1968; 3 reels.
Deeds and Mortgages, General Index to, Grantor, 1872-1968; 4 reels.
Deeds, Record of, 1872-1960; 57 reels.
Land Entry Book, 1872-1961; 1 reel.
Land Registration, Record of, 1916-1967; 1 reel.
Sale of Land by Trustees and Mortgagees, Record of, 1921-1968; 1 reel.

Marriage, Divorce, and Vital Statistics
Maiden Names of Divorced Women, 1928-1966; 1 reel.
Marriage Licenses, 1872-1968; 6 reels.
Marriage Registers, 1872-1968; 1 reel.
Vital Statistics, Index to, 1913-1968; 1 reel.

Military and Pension Records
Confederate Veterans, Record of, 1889-1918; 1 reel.

MISCELLANEOUS RECORDS

Orders and Decrees, 1873-1962; 1 reel.
Special Proceedings, 1872-1954; 3 reels.

OFFICIALS, COUNTY

Board of County Commissioners, Minutes, 1872-1944; 4 reels.

SCHOOL RECORDS

County Board of Education, Minutes, 1885-1893, 1922-1968; 1 reel.

TAX AND FISCAL RECORDS

Tax Scrolls, 1920-1955; 5 reels.

WILLS

Wills, Cross Index to, 1872-1968; 1 reel.
Wills, Record of, 1872-1968; 2 reels.

PASQUOTANK COUNTY

Established by 1670 as a precinct of Albemarle County.
Many early records are missing; reason unknown.

ORIGINAL RECORDS

BONDS

Apprentice Bonds and Records, 1716-1898; 10 volumes, 2 Fibredex boxes.
Bastardy Bonds and Records, 1740-1917; 3 Fibredex boxes.
Constables' Bonds, 1737, 1785-1880; 1 volume, 2 Fibredex boxes.
Officials' Bonds, 1741-1882; 1 Fibredex box.
Ordinary Bonds, 1766-1867; 1 Fibredex box.
Sheriffs' Bonds, 1741-1882; 1 Fibredex box.

COURT RECORDS

County Court of Pleas and Quarter Sessions
Appearance Dockets, 1845-1868; 3 volumes.
Clerk's Account Book, 1790-1808; 1 volume.
Execution Dockets, 1755-1862, 1866-1868; 23 volumes.
Minutes, 1737-1868; 19 volumes.
Petition Docket, 1856-1868; 1 volume.
Reference (Trial) and Appearance Dockets, 1700, 1755-1765; 3 volumes.
State Dockets, 1785-1791, 1798-1868; 4 volumes.
Trial, Appearance, and Reference Dockets, 1765-1824; 11 volumes.
Trial, Appearance, Reference, and Petition Dockets, 1819-1857; 12 volumes.
Trial Dockets, 1856-1862, 1866-1868; 2 volumes.

Superior Court
Civil Action Papers, 1712-1925; 89 Fibredex boxes. [*See also* **CRX RECORDS**]
Civil Action Papers Concerning Land, 1756-1922; 14 Fibredex boxes.
Criminal Action Papers, 1729-1919; 13 Fibredex boxes.
Equity Execution Docket, 1824-1831; 1 volume.
Equity Minutes, 1822-1868; 2 volumes.
Equity Trial Docket, 1822-1850; 1 volume.
Execution Dockets, 1822-1868; 2 volumes.
Minutes, 1807-1861, 1866-1922; 10 volumes.
Miscellaneous Court Records, 1721-1897; 1 Fibredex box.
State Dockets, 1807-1869; 3 volumes.
Trial and Appearance Dockets, 1807-1881; 5 volumes.

ELECTION RECORDS

Elections, Record of, 1878-1920; 3 volumes.
Voter Registration Books, 1892, 1900; 15 volumes.
Voter Registration Challenge Book, no date; 1 volume

ESTATES RECORDS

Accounts, Record of, 1868-1919; 6 volumes.
Accounts of Sale of Estates, 1797-1868; 8 volumes.
Administrators' Bonds, 1798-1868, 1881-1907; 17 volumes.
Estates (Accounts and Settlements), Record of, 1795-1868; 14 volumes.
Estates Records, 1712-1931; 202 Fibredex boxes.

Fiduciary Account Book, 1808-1828; 1 volume.
Guardians' Accounts (Orphans' Court), 1757-1797; 2 volumes.
Guardians' Bonds, 1798-1896; 18 volumes.
Guardians' Records, 1719-1931; 25 Fibredex boxes.
Inventories of Estates, 1797-1854; 2 volumes.
Settlements, Record of, 1868-1920; 3 volumes.

LAND RECORDS

Attachments, Executions, Levies, and Liens on Land, 1801-1917; 2 Fibredex boxes.
Deeds, 1666-1947; 11 Fibredex boxes.
Deeds, Record of, 1700-1786; 7 volumes.
Ejectments, 1746-1901; 2 Fibredex boxes.
Land Drainage Records, 1765-1878; 1 Fibredex box.
Land Entry Books, 1778-1793, 1831-1838; 2 volumes.
Miscellaneous Deeds, 1723-1948; 6 Fibredex boxes.
Miscellaneous Land Records, 1694-1946; 2 Fibredex boxes, 1 oversized manuscript box.
Petitions to Divide and Sell Land and Reports of Sale, 1744-1904; 2 Fibredex boxes.
Probate of Deeds and Mortgages, Record of, 1903-1915; 1 volume.
Tax Levies on Land, 1874-1899; 1 volume.

MARRIAGE, DIVORCE, AND VITAL STATISTICS

Births, Deaths, Marriages, Brands, and Flesh Marks, 1691-1822; 2 volumes.
Cohabitation, Record of, 1866-1867; 1 volume.
Divorce Records, 1838-1919; 10 Fibredex boxes.
Marriage Bonds, 1741-1868; 3 Fibredex boxes.

MISCELLANEOUS RECORDS

Assignees, Receivers, and Trustees, Records of, 1801-1922; 4 Fibredex boxes.
Board of Justices of the Peace, Minutes, 1878-1882; 1 volume.
County Accounts, Buildings, and Correspondence, 1752-1896; 2 Fibredex boxes.
County Board of Education, Minutes, 1872-1885; 1 volume.
Insolvent Debtors, 1744-1877; 8 Fibredex boxes.
Justices of the Peace, Records of, 1720-1896; 1 Fibredex box.
Loyalty Oaths, 1865; 2 volumes.
Miscellaneous Records, 1703-1940; 7 Fibredex boxes. [*See also* **CRX RECORDS**]
Orders and Decrees, 1869-1911; 4 volumes.
Personal Accounts, 1730-1899; 1 Fibredex box.
Powers of Attorney, 1711-1907; 1 Fibredex box.
Promissory Notes, 1720-1920; 2 Fibredex boxes.
Railroad Records, 1875-1921; 6 Fibredex boxes.
Records Concerning Elizabeth City, 1828-1918; 5 Fibredex boxes.
Road Records, 1734-1920; 4 Fibredex boxes.
School Records, 1757-1914; 3 Fibredex boxes.
Slaves and Free Persons of Color, Records of, 1733-1892; 2 Fibredex boxes.
Wardens of the Poor, Minutes, 1807-1868; 2 volumes.

OFFICIALS, COUNTY [*See* **MISCELLANEOUS RECORDS**]

ROADS AND BRIDGES [*See* **MISCELLANEOUS RECORDS**]

SCHOOL RECORDS [*See* **MISCELLANEOUS RECORDS; CRX RECORDS**]

TAX AND FISCAL RECORDS

Miscellaneous Tax Records, 1785-1912; 2 Fibredex boxes.
Poll Tax Record, 1914-1918; 1 volume.
Tax Lists, 1735-1882; 7 volumes, 3 Fibredex boxes.

WILLS

Wills, 1709-1917; 20 Fibredex boxes.
Wills, Record of, 1752-1792; 3 volumes.

CRX RECORDS

Civil Action, 1726/7; 1 folder.
Miscellaneous Records, 1899-1955; 5 Fibredex boxes, 1 manuscript box, 1 oversized manuscript box.
School and Miscellaneous Records, 1832-1860; 6 folders.

MICROFILM RECORDS

BONDS

Apprentice Bonds, 1798-1898; 2 reels.
Apprentice Bonds for Negroes, 1842-1861; 1 reel.

CORPORATIONS AND PARTNERSHIPS

Partnerships, Record of, 1917-1960; 1 reel.

COURT RECORDS

County Court of Pleas and Quarter Sessions
- Minutes, 1737-1868; 5 reels.

Superior Court
- Civil Actions, Index to, no date, 1752-1915; 2 reels.
- Equity Minutes, 1822-1868; 1 reel.
- Judgments, Index to, Defendant, 1873-1966; 2 reels.
- Judgments, Index to, Plaintiff, 1878-1966; 3 reels.
- Minutes, 1807-1908, 1946-1957; 5 reels.

ELECTION RECORDS

Elections, Record of, 1878-1960; 1 reel.

ESTATES RECORDS

Accounts, Record of, 1868-1919; 3 reels.
Accounts of Sale of Estates, 1797-1868; 4 reels.
Administrators' Bonds, 1865-1868, 1881-1904; 1 reel.
Administrators' and Guardians' Accounts, 1803-1834; 2 reels.
Administrators, Record of, 1913-1943; 1 reel.
Executors, Record of, 1915-1960; 1 reel.
Guardians' Accounts, 1779-1866; 4 reels. [*See also* Orphans' Accounts]
Guardians' Bonds, 1798-1896; 5 reels.
Guardians, Record of, 1915-1966; 1 reel.
Inventories of Estates, 1795-1854; 1 reel.
Orphans' Accounts, 1757-1829; 2 reels. [*See also* Guardians' Accounts]
Settlements, Record of, 1868-1928, 1956-1960; 2 reels.
Widows' Year's Support, 1881-1960; 1 reel.

LAND RECORDS
Deeds, Index to, Grantee, 1700-1980; 4 reels.
Deeds, Index to, Grantor, 1700-1980; 5 reels.
Deeds, Record of, 1700-1945; 75 reels.
Land Division, Record of, 1793-1885; 1 reel.
Land Entry Books, 1778-1793, 1831-1838; 1 reel.
Map Book, 1940-1960; 1 reel.

MARRIAGE, DIVORCE, AND VITAL STATISTICS
Births, Deaths, Marriages, Brands, and Flesh Marks, 1691-1822; 1 reel.
Births, Index to, 1903-1960; 1 reel.
Cohabitation, Record of, 1866-1867; 1 reel.
Deaths, Index to, 1903-1982; 2 reels.
Deaths, Record of, 1903-1911; 1 reel.
Maiden Names of Divorced Women, 1937-1959; 1 reel.
Marriage Bonds, 1741-1868; 2 reels.
Marriage Licenses, 1867-1960; 29 reels.
Marriage Registers, 1865-1960; 3 reels.
Marriages, General Index to, 1865-1960; 4 reels.

MISCELLANEOUS RECORDS
Orders and Decrees, 1869-1915; 3 reels.
Orders and Decrees, Index to, Defendant, 1869-1960; 1 reel.
Orders and Decrees, Index to, Plaintiff, 1869-1960; 1 reel.
Wardens of the Poor, Minutes, 1807-1868; 1 reel.

OFFICIALS, COUNTY
Board of County Commissioners, Minutes, 1868-1906; 2 reels.

TAX AND FISCAL RECORDS
Tax Levies, 1874-1899; 1 reel.
Tax Lists, 1797-1897, 1905, 1915, 1925; 15 reels.

WILLS
Original Wills, 1720-1804; 3 reels.
Wills, Index to, 1766-1966; 2 reels.
Wills, Record of, 1752-1966; 7 reels.

PENDER COUNTY

Established in 1875 from New Hanover County.

ORIGINAL RECORDS

BONDS

Officials' Bonds, 1875-1886; 1 volume.

COURT RECORDS

Superior Court

Civil Action Papers, 1878-1949; 3 Fibredex boxes.

Civil Action Papers Concerning Land, 1877-1955; 15 Fibredex boxes.

ESTATES RECORDS

Administrators' Bonds, 1875-1903; 1 volume.

Dowers, Record of, 1875-1922; 1 volume.

Estates Records, 1866-1969; 16 Fibredex boxes.

Guardians' Bonds, 1875-1903; 1 volume.

Guardians' Records, 1856-1945; 2 Fibredex boxes.

LAND RECORDS

Attachments, Executions, Levies, and Liens on Land, 1870-1940; 1 Fibredex box.

Deeds, 1819-1946; 4 Fibredex boxes.

Deeds, Index to, 1875-1900; 2 volumes.

Ejectments, 1877-1941; 1 Fibredex box.

Land Grants, 1784-1954; 1 Fibredex box.

Miscellaneous Land Records, 1873-1966; 4 Fibredex boxes.

Mortgage Deeds and Deeds of Trust, 1874-1945; 2 Fibredex boxes.

MARRIAGE, DIVORCE, AND VITAL STATISTICS

Divorce Records, 1877-1950; 5 Fibredex boxes.

Marriage Registers, 1875-1936; 6 volumes.

MISCELLANEOUS RECORDS

Assignees, Receivers, and Trustees, Records of, 1882-1964; 2 Fibredex boxes.

Coroners' Inquests, 1876-1968; 9 Fibredex boxes.

Licenses to Trades, Registry of, 1875-1879; 1 volume.

Miscellaneous Records, 1856-1965; 3 Fibredex boxes.

Railroad Records, 1881-1946; 3 Fibredex boxes.

Stock Marks, 1875-1925; 2 volumes.

ROADS AND BRIDGES [*See* **MISCELLANEOUS RECORDS**]

WILLS

Wills, 1832, 1875-1969; 27 Fibredex boxes.

MICROFILM RECORDS

BONDS

Officials' Bonds, 1875-1886; 1 reel.

CORPORATIONS AND PARTNERSHIPS

Corporations and Partnerships, Index to, 1903-1982; 1 reel.

Corporations and Partnerships, Record of, 1903-1976; 2 reels.

COURT RECORDS

Superior Court

Judgments, Liens, and Special Proceedings, Index to, Defendant, 1875-1968; 3 reels.
Judgments, Liens, and Special Proceedings, Index to, Plaintiff, 1875-1968; 3 reels.
Minutes, 1875-1961; 6 reels.
Minutes, Index to, Defendant, 1875-1968; 3 reels.
Minutes, Index to, Plaintiff, 1875-1968; 1 reel.

ELECTION RECORDS

Elections, Record of, 1918-1966; 1 reel.

ESTATES RECORDS

Administrators' Bonds, 1875-1903; 1 reel.
Administrators, Executors, and Guardians, Record of, 1903-1968; 4 reels.
Amounts Paid for Indigent Children, Record of, 1913-1926; 1 reel.
Dowers, Record of, 1875-1922; 1 reel.
Executors and Guardians, Record of, 1939-1967; 1 reel.
Final Accounts, Index to, 1875-1968; 1 reel.
Final Accounts, Record of, 1875-1968; 3 reels.
Guardians' Bonds, 1875-1903; 1 reel.
Inheritance Tax Records, 1923-1959; 1 reel.
Inventories, Record of, 1875-1968; 4 reels.

LAND RECORDS

Deeds, Record of, 1875-1955; 92 reels.
Federal Tax Lien Index, 1928-1968; 2 reels.
Land Entry, Record of, 1875-1963; 1 reel.
Plat Books, 1881-1957; 1 reel.
Plats, Index to, 1920-1982; 1 reel.
Real Estate Conveyances, Index to, Grantee, 1875-1977; 8 reels.
Real Estate Conveyances, Index to, Grantor, 1875-1977; 8 reels.
Registration of Land Titles, 1916-1967; 2 reels.
Resale of Land by Trustees and Mortgagees, Record of, 1923-1968; 3 reels.

MARRIAGE, DIVORCE, AND VITAL STATISTICS

Births, Index to, 1913-1998; 2 reels.
Deaths, Index to, 1913-1999; 2 reels.
Delayed Births, Index to, various years; 1 reel.
Maiden Names of Divorced Women, 1937-1943; 1 reel.
Marriage Licenses, 1886-1968; 11 reels.
Marriage Registers, 1875-1971; 2 reels.
Marriages, Index to, 1972-1999; 1 reel.

MILITARY AND PENSION RECORDS

Confederate Pensions, Record of, 1927-1934; 1 reel.

MISCELLANEOUS RECORDS

Lunacy, Record of, 1903-1960; 1 reel.
Orders and Decrees, 1875-1947; 1 reel.
Special Proceedings, 1875-1968; 7 reels.
Special Proceedings, Cross Index to, 1875-1900; 1 reel.

School Records

County Board of Education, Minutes, 1875-1954; 3 reels.

Wills

Wills, Cross Index to, 1875-1931; 1 reel.
Wills, Index to, Devisee, 1875-1968; 1 reel.
Wills, Index to, Devisor, 1875-1968; 1 reel.
Wills, Record of, 1875-1968; 4 reels.

PERQUIMANS COUNTY

Established by 1670 as a precinct of Albemarle County.
A few of the early records are missing; reason unknown.

ORIGINAL RECORDS

BONDS

Apprentice Bonds and Records, 1737-1892; 3 volumes, 4 Fibredex boxes.
Bastardy Bonds and Records, 1756-1905; 2 volumes, 4 Fibredex boxes.
Constables' Bonds, 1777-1907; 1 Fibredex box.
Officials' Bonds, 1720-1908; 3 Fibredex boxes.

COURT RECORDS [*See also* **CRX RECORDS**]

County Court of Pleas and Quarter Sessions
- Execution Dockets, 1784-1864; 6 volumes.
- Executions Returned by Sheriff, 1842-1843; 1 volume.
- Levy Docket, 1840-1853, 1857; 1 volume.
- Minutes, 1738-1868; 11 volumes.
- Minutes (Precinct Court), 1688-1738; 3 volumes.
- State Dockets, 1835-1868; 2 volumes.
- Trial and Appearance Dockets, 1852-1862; 2 volumes.
- Trial, Appearance, and Reference Dockets, 1779-1852; 11 volumes.

Superior Court
- Civil Action Papers, 1709-1912; 53 Fibredex boxes.
- Civil Action Papers Concerning Land, 1838-1911; 4 Fibredex boxes.
- Criminal Action Papers, 1740-1905; 21 Fibredex boxes.
- Equity Enrolling Docket, 1838-1867; 1 volume.
- Equity Execution Docket, 1825-1850; 1 volume.
- Equity Minutes, 1819-1868; 2 volumes.
- Execution Dockets, 1808-1869; 3 volumes.
- Minutes, 1807-1908; 5 volumes.
- State Dockets, 1840-1868; 2 volumes.
- Trial and Appearance Dockets, 1807-1852; 2 volumes.

ELECTION RECORDS

Election Records, 1790-1868; 1 Fibredex box.
Elections, Record of, 1878-1936; 3 volumes.
Voter Registration Books, 1950-1960; 2 volumes.

ESTATES RECORDS

Accounts, Record of, 1869-1909; 3 volumes.
Administrators' Bonds, 1842-1911; 9 volumes.
Appointment of Administrators, Executors, Guardians, and Masters, 1868-1911; 1 volume.
Divisions of Estates, 1841-1861; 1 volume.
Estates (Audited Accounts), Record of, 1804-1868; 3 volumes.
Estates Records, 1714-1930; 147 Fibredex boxes.
Guardians' Accounts, 1808-1870; 4 volumes.
Guardians' Bonds, 1842-1911; 4 volumes.
Guardians' Records, 1709-1925; 21 Fibredex boxes.

Inventories and Accounts of Sale, 1806-1868; 5 volumes.
Orphans' Docket, 1806-1820; 1 volume.
Settlements, Record of, 1868-1904; 1 volume.

LAND RECORDS

Deeds, 1709-1938; 6 Fibredex boxes.
Deeds and Deeds of Trust, Grantee Index to, 1879-1893; 1 volume.
Deeds and Deeds of Trust, Grantor Index to, 1879-1893; 1 volume.
Deeds and Grants, Record of, 1780-1791; 2 volumes.
Deeds, Index to, 1814-1819; 1 pamphlet.
Deeds, Record of, 1739-1824; 10 volumes.
Deeds and Wills, Record of, 1744-1794; 3 volumes.
Ejectments, 1737-1887; 1 Fibredex box.
Land Entries, 1879-1940; .5 Fibredex box. [*See also* **MISCELLANEOUS RECORDS**, Licenses to Trades, Registry of, 1879-1882]
Land Records, 1709-1907; 2 Fibredex boxes.
Probate of Deeds, Record of, 1878-1884; 1 volume.

MARRIAGE, DIVORCE, AND VITAL STATISTICS

Births, Marriages, and Flesh Marks, 1659-1820; 2 volumes.
Divorce Records, 1824-1912; 3 Fibredex boxes.
Marriage Bonds, 1742-1868; 7 Fibredex boxes.
Marriage Bonds, Record of, 1847-1859; 3 volumes.
Marriage Licenses and Certificates, Record of, 1860-1867; 1 volume.
Marriage Registers, 1867-1940; 3 volumes.

MILITARY AND PENSION RECORDS [*See* **MISCELLANEOUS RECORDS; CRX RECORDS**]

MISCELLANEOUS RECORDS [*See also* **CRX RECORDS**]

Alien Registration, 1905, 1907; 1 volume.
Committee of Finance, Settlement of County Accounts, 1845-1872; 1 volume.
Coroners' Inquests, 1794-1892; 1 Fibredex boxes.
County Accounts, 1756-1869; 3 Fibredex boxes.
Insolvent Debtors, 1789-1861; 1 Fibredex box.
Jury Lists, 1709-1868; 1 Fibredex box.
Jury Tickets, 1791-1867; 1 Fibredex box.
Licenses to Trades, Registry of, 1869-1882; 2 volumes.
Marks and Brands, Record of, 1876-1926; 1 volume.
Miscellaneous Records, 1710-1933; 6 Fibredex boxes.
Official Reports, Record of, 1875-1927; 1 volume.
Orders and Decrees, 1868-1914; 2 volumes.
Pensions, Record of, 1907-1918; 1 volume.
Personal Accounts, 1714-1930; 3 Fibredex boxes.
Promissory Notes, 1712-1863; 1 Fibredex box.
Railroad Records, 1881-1912; 1 Fibredex box.
Road Records, 1711-1910; 5 Fibredex boxes.
Slave Records, 1759-1864; 1 Fibredex box.
Wardens of the Poor, Minutes, 1818-1874; 1 volume.

ROADS AND BRIDGES [*See* **MISCELLANEOUS RECORDS**]

Tax and Fiscal Records

Assessment of Land for Taxation, Bear Swamp Drainage District, 1918-1922; 1 volume.
Federal Direct Taxes Collected, Record of, 1866; 1 volume.
Lists of Taxables, 1742-1859; 1 volume, 5 Fibredex boxes.
Tax Receipts, 1875; 1 volume.
Tax Records, 1795-1868; 1 Fibredex box.

Wills

Wills, 1711-1909; 15 Fibredex boxes.

CRX Records

Civil Action Paper, 1821; 1 folder.
Minutes, Court of Pleas and Quarter Sessions, 1782-1784; 1 volume.
Minutes, Superior Court, 1818-1827; 1 volume.
Miscellaneous Records, 1762-1891; 1 Fibredex box.
Oath of Allegiance, 1865; 1 folder.
State Docket, Superior Court, 1808-1837; 1 volume.

MICROFILM RECORDS

Bonds

Apprentice Bonds, 1852-1890; 1 reel.

Court Records

County Court of Pleas and Quarter Sessions
- Minutes, 1688-1706, 1735-1868; 6 reels.

Superior Court
- Judgments, Index to, 1867-1874; 1 reel.
- Judgments, Index to, 1860-1966; 1 reel.
- Judgments, Index to, Defendant, 1762-1941; 1 reel.
- Judgments, Index to, Plaintiff, 1762-1941; 1 reel.
- Minutes, 1807-1915; 3 reels.

Estates Records

Accounts, Record of, 1864-1966; 4 reels.
Administrators' Bonds, 1842-1911; 1 reel.
Administrators, Executors, and Guardians, Record of, 1911-1937; 1 reel.
Administrators, Record of, 1919-1954; 1 reel.
Appointment of Administrators, Executors, and Guardians, 1868-1911; 1 reel.
Divisions of Estates, 1841-1861; 1 reel.
Executors and Guardians, Cross Index to, 1806-1966; 1 reel.
Executors and Guardians, Record of, 1939-1966; 1 reel.
Guardians' Accounts, 1808-1865; 2 reels.
Guardians' and Administrators' Accounts, 1809-1837; 1 reel.
Guardians' Bonds, 1842-1911; 1 reel.
Guardians, Cross Index to, 1806-1966; 1 reel.
Inheritance Tax Records, 1923-1970; 1 reel.
Inventories and Accounts of Sale, 1804-1864; 3 reels.
Inventories, Reports, and Accounts of Receivership, Record of, 1804-1835; 1 reel.
Orphans' Docket, 1806-1820, 1864-1870; 1 reel.
Report of Auditors (Estates), 1796-1827; 1 reel.
Settlements, Record of, 1867-1965; 4 reels.

LAND RECORDS

Deeds, Record of, 1681-1949; 39 reels.
Land Entries, 1838-1876; 1 reel.
Plat Books, 1808-1947; 1 reel.
Real Estate Conveyances, Index to, Grantee, 1681-1968; 4 reels.
Real Estate Conveyances, Index to, Grantor, 1681-1968; 4 reels.
Sale and Resale under Mortgagees and Trustees, Record of, 1924-1967; 1 reel.
Town Lot Sales, Record of, 1759-1824; 1 reel.

MARRIAGE, DIVORCE, AND VITAL STATISTICS

Births, Marriages, Deaths, and Flesh Marks, 1659-1820; 1 reel.
Delayed Births, Index to, 1882-1946; 1 reel.
Marriage Bonds, 1740-1868; 2 reels.
Marriage Bonds, Record of, 1847-1859; 1 reel.
Marriage Licenses, Record of, 1851-1867; 1 reel.
Marriage Registers, 1852-1995; 3 reels.
Marriages by Freedmen, Record of, 1866-1867; 1 reel.
Vital Statistics, Births and Deaths, Index to, 1913-1995; 1 reel.

MISCELLANEOUS RECORDS

Clerk's Minute Docket, 1923-1944; 1 reel.
Marks and Brands, Record of, 1875-1926; 1 reel.
Orders and Decrees, 1868-1921; 2 reels.
Special Proceedings, Cross Index to, 1880-1964; 1 reel.

OFFICIALS, COUNTY

Board of County Commissioners, Minutes, 1868-1902; 1 reel.

SCHOOL RECORDS

County Board of Education, Minutes, 1872-1960; 1 reel.

TAX AND FISCAL RECORDS

Tax Book, 1866; 1 reel.
Taxables, 1742-1859; 1 reel.

WILLS

Wills, 1711-1800; 2 reels.
Wills, Index to, 1761-1966; 1 reel.
Wills, Record of, 1761-1966; 4 reels.

PERSON COUNTY

Established in 1791 (effective 1792) from Caswell County.

ORIGINAL RECORDS

BONDS

Apprentice Bonds and Records, 1801-1925; 1 volume, 1 Fibredex box.
Bastardy Bonds and Records, 1793-1891; 1 Fibredex box.
Constables' Bonds and Records, 1792-1854; 1 Fibredex box.
Officials' Bonds and Records, 1792-1954; 2 volumes, 1 Fibredex box.

CENSUS RECORDS (County Copy)

Census, 1880; 2 volumes.

COURT RECORDS

County Court of Pleas and Quarter Sessions
- Execution Dockets, 1813-1825, 1838-1868; 5 volumes.
- Levy Dockets, 1795-1826, 1837; 2 volumes.
- Minutes, 1792-1868; 14 volumes.
- Rough Minutes and Dockets, 1803-1866; 1 Fibredex box.
- State Dockets, 1792-1868; 4 volumes.
- Summons Docket (Writs Issued), 1793-1807; 1 volume.
- Trial and Appearance Dockets, 1792-1814, 1824-1868; 5 volumes.
- Witness Fee Docket, 1822-1853; 1 volume.

Superior Court
- Civil Action Papers, 1813-1939; 8 Fibredex boxes.
- Civil Action Papers Concerning Board of County Commissioners, 1871-1906; 1 Fibredex box.
- Civil Action Papers Concerning Land, 1775-1948; 4 Fibredex boxes.
- Criminal Action Papers, 1815-1908; 1 Fibredex box.
- Equity Minutes, 1808-1854; 2 volumes.
- Equity Trial and Appearance Docket, 1854-1868; 1 volume.
- Equity Trial and Execution Docket, 1807-1853; 1 volume.
- Execution Dockets, 1808-1857; 3 volumes.
- Minutes, 1807-1864, 1869-1909; 8 volumes.
- State Dockets, 1808-1838, 1851-1868; 2 volumes.
- Summons Docket, 1869-1870; 1 volume.
- Trial and Appearance Dockets, 1807-1868; 3 volumes.

ELECTION RECORDS

Election Records, 1804-1918; 1 Fibredex box.

ESTATES RECORDS [*See also* **WILLS**]

Accounts, Record of, 1868-1908; 4 volumes.
Administrators' Bonds, 1870-1882, 1889-1898; 2 volumes.
Estates Records, 1775, 1776, 1784, 1791-1951; 78 Fibredex boxes.
Guardians' Accounts, 1810-1865; 4 volumes.
Guardians' Bonds, 1870-1899; 1 volume.
Guardians' Records, 1792-1949; 6 Fibredex boxes.
Settlements, Record of, 1869-1898; 1 volume.

LAND RECORDS

Deeds, 1777-1918; 4 Fibredex boxes.
Land Entry Book, 1873-1887, 1899; 1 volume.
Miscellaneous Deeds, 1774-1923; 2 Fibredex boxes.
Miscellaneous Land Records, 1775-1940; 2 Fibredex boxes.
Petitions for Partition, 1838-1918; 1 Fibredex box.
Petitions for Sale, 1856-1934; 3 Fibredex boxes.

MARRIAGE, DIVORCE, AND VITAL STATISTICS

Cohabitation, Record of, 1866; 1 volume.
Divorce Records, 1821-1939; 3 Fibredex boxes.
Marriage Bonds, 1791-1868; 10 Fibredex boxes.
Marriage Licenses, 1868-1899; 5 Fibredex boxes.

MISCELLANEOUS RECORDS

Alien Registration, 1927, 1940; 1 volume.
Appointment of Road Overseers, 1823-1868; 2 volumes.
Assignees, Receivers, and Trustees, Records of, 1842-1939; 3 Fibredex boxes.
Board of Magistrates, Minutes, 1880-1894; 1 volume.
County Accounts, 1881-1885; 2 volumes.
Licenses to Trades, Registry of, 1877-1901; 1 volume.
List of Jurors, 1893-1915; 1 volume.
Magistrates and Notaries Public, Record of, 1923-1945; 1 volume.
Magistrates, Record of, 1893-1922; 1 volume.
Miscellaneous Records, 1771-1954; 3 Fibredex boxes.
Oaths of Allegiance, 1865; 4 pamphlets.
Powers of Attorney, 1785-1900; 1 Fibredex box.
Railroad Records, 1876-1921; 3 Fibredex boxes.
Road Records, 1797-1888; 1 Fibredex box.
School Records, 1832-1930; 1 Fibredex box.
School Registers, 1887-1904; 8 volumes.
Tobacco and Snuff Manufacturer's Record, 1869-1871; 1 volume.
Wardens of the Poor, Minutes, 1792-1868; 2 volumes.

OFFICIALS, COUNTY [*See* **COURT RECORDS**, Superior Court, Civil Action Papers; **MISCELLANEOUS RECORDS**]

ROADS AND BRIDGES [*See* **MISCELLANEOUS RECORDS**]

SCHOOL RECORDS [*See* **MISCELLANEOUS RECORDS**]

TAX AND FISCAL RECORDS [*See also* **WILLS**]

List of Insolvents, 1892-1898; 1 volume.
Lists of Taxables, 1915, 1925; 3 volumes.
Schedule B Taxes, 1869-1883; 1 volume.
Tax Receipt Book, 1871; 1 volume.
Tax Records, 1792-1886; 2 Fibredex boxes.

WILLS

Wills, 1790-1943; 17 Fibredex boxes.
Wills, Inventories, Sales of Estates, and Taxables, Record of, 1792-1844; 15 volumes.

MICROFILM RECORDS

CORPORATIONS AND PARTNERSHIPS

Corporations, Record of, 1895-1966; 1 reel.
Partnership Records, 1913-1966; 1 reel.

COURT RECORDS

County Court of Pleas and Quarter Sessions
Minutes, 1792-1868; 4 reels.
Superior Court
Civil Actions, Index to, 1955-1968; 1 reel.
Criminal Actions, Index to, 1954-1968; 1 reel.
Equity Minutes, 1808-1854; 2 reels.
Judgments, Index to, 1867-1967; 2 reels.
Judgments, Index to, Defendant, 1945-1968; 1 reel.
Judgments, Index to, Plaintiff, 1945-1968; 1 reel.
Minutes, 1807-1864, 1869-1966; 9 reels.

ELECTION RECORDS

Elections, Record of, 1906-1964; 1 reel.

ESTATES RECORDS [*See also* WILLS]

Accounts, Record of, 1868-1966; 7 reels.
Administrators' Bonds, 1870-1966; 5 reels.
Appointment of Executors, 1868-1894; Record of Executors, 1925-1966; 1 reel.
Appointment of Guardians, 1899-1966; 1 reel.
Clerk's Receiver Accounts, 1894-1903; 1 reel.
Estates, Index to, 1947-1966; 1 reel.
Guardians' Accounts, 1810-1944; 1 reel.
Guardians' Bonds, 1870-1899; 1 reel.
Inheritance Tax Records, 1919-1961; 1 reel.
Settlements, Record of, 1869-1966; 5 reels.

LAND RECORDS

Deeds, Record of, 1789-1959; 56 reels.
Entry Book, 1872-1899; 1 reel.
Plat Books, 1901-1964; 2 reels.
Plats, Index to, 1842-1986; 1 reel.
Real Estate Conveyances, Index to, Grantee, 1790-1974; 4 reels.
Real Estate Conveyances, Index to, Grantee: Trustees, 1900-1974; 2 reels.
Real Estate Conveyances, Index to, Grantor, 1790-1974; 6 reels.
Resale of Land by Trustees and Mortgagees, Record of, 1920-1960; 1 reel.

MARRIAGE, DIVORCE, AND VITAL STATISTICS

Births, Index to, 1913-1979; 2 reels.
Cohabitation, Record of, 1866; 1 reel.
Deaths, Index to, 1913-1986; 1 reel.
Maiden Names of Divorced Women, 1938-1966; 1 reel.
Marriage Bonds, 1791-1868; 6 reels.
Marriage Certificates, Record of, 1851-1867; 1 reel.
Marriage Registers, 1867-1966; 1 reel.

MISCELLANEOUS RECORDS

Orders and Decrees, 1868-1962; 9 reels.
Special Proceedings, Index to, Defendant, 1954-1968; 2 reels.
Special Proceedings, Index to, Plaintiff, 1954-1966; 1 reel.
Wardens of the Poor, Minutes, 1792-1868; 1 reel.

OFFICIALS, COUNTY

Board of County Commissioners, Minutes, 1868-1947; 3 reels.

SCHOOL RECORDS

Board of Superintendents of Common Schools, Minutes, 1841-1864; County Board of Education, Minutes, 1872-1886, 1909-1953; 1 reel.

TAX AND FISCAL RECORDS [*See also* **WILLS**]

Tax Scrolls, 1876-1925; 4 reels.

WILLS

Original Wills, 1791-1900; 3 reels.
Wills, Cross Index to, 1792-1956; 1 reel.
Wills, Index to, Devisee, 1970-1986; 1 reel.
Wills, Inventories, Sales of Estates, and Taxables, 1792-1844; 7 reels.
Wills, Record of, 1847-1968; 5 reels.

PITT COUNTY

Established in 1760 (effective 1761) from Beaufort County.
Courthouse fire of 1857 destroyed most of the court records.

ORIGINAL RECORDS

BONDS

Bastardy Bonds and Records, 1858-1926; 2 Fibredex boxes.

COURT RECORDS

County Court of Pleas and Quarter Sessions
- Bench Docket (Civil and Criminal), 1858-1863, 1866; 1 volume.
- Execution Docket, 1858-1868; 1 volume.
- Minutes, 1858-1868; 4 volumes.
- Trial Dockets, 1850-1868; 3 volumes.

Inferior Court
- Minutes, 1877-1885; 1 volume.

Superior Court
- Bench Docket (Civil and Criminal), 1858-1867; 1 volume.
- Civil Action Papers, 1850-1907; 19 Fibredex boxes.
- Civil Action Papers Concerning Canals and Land Drainage, 1857-1902; 2 Fibredex boxes.
- Civil Action Papers Concerning Land, 1859-1921; 15 Fibredex boxes.
- Civil Issues Docket, Index to, 1869-1927; 2 volumes.
- Civil Issues Dockets, 1869-1935; 5 volumes.
- Criminal Action Papers, 1771, 1857-1931; 31 Fibredex boxes.
- Equity Minutes, 1858-1868; 1 volume.
- Execution Docket, 1858-1864, 1867; 1 volume.
- Judgment Dockets, 1860-1957; 40 volumes. [*See also* **LAND RECORDS**]
- Judgments, Index to, 1857-1880; 2 volumes.
- Judgments, Index to, Defendant, 1900-1969; 8 volumes.
- Minutes, 1858-1968; 50 volumes.
- State Docket, 1858-1863, 1866-1870; 1 volume.
- Trial Docket, 1858-1873; 1 volume.

ELECTION RECORDS

Elections, Record of, 1896-1903; 1 volume.

ESTATES RECORDS

- Accounts, Record of, 1868-1926; 6 volumes.
- Appointment of Trustees under Wills, 1956-1968; 1 volume.
- Dowers and Widows' Year's Support, Record of, 1858-1885; 1 volume.
- Estates Records, 1791, 1827-1947; 77 Fibredex boxes.
- Guardians' Accounts, 1858-1916; 5 volumes.
- Guardians' Records, 1858-1919, 1923; 19 Fibredex boxes.
- Inventories and Accounts of Sale, 1857-1872; 2 volumes.
- Settlements, Record of, 1858-1923; 7 volumes.
- Trustees, Record of. [*See* Appointment of Trustees under Wills]

LAND RECORDS [*See also* **COURT RECORDS**, Superior Court]

- Deeds, Deeds of Trust, and Mortgage Deeds, 1763-1892; 1 Fibredex box.
- Deeds, Record of, 1817-1818; 1 volume.

Entry Book, 1858-1941; 1 volume.
Judgment Dockets, Tax Sales, 1930-1955; 5 volumes. [*See also* **COURT RECORDS**, Superior Court]
Land Grant Books, 1779-1800; 2 volumes.
Miscellaneous Land Records, 1778-1923; 2 Fibredex boxes.
Sales and Resales, Record of, 1920-1968; 9 volumes.

MARRIAGE, DIVORCE, AND VITAL STATISTICS
Cohabitation, Record of, 1866; 1 volume.
Divorce Records, 1861, 1866, 1870-1906; 4 Fibredex boxes.
Maiden Names of Divorced Women, 1942-1968; 1 volume.
Marriage Bonds, 1826-1833; 1 folder in Fibredex box.
Marriage Registers, 1867-1875; 3 volumes.

MILITARY AND PENSION RECORDS [*See* **MISCELLANEOUS RECORDS**]

MISCELLANEOUS RECORDS
Alien Registration, 1940; 1 volume.
Appointment of Receivers, 1918-1968; 3 volumes.
Assignees, Receivers, and Trustees, Records of, 1870-1925; 2 Fibredex boxes.
Board of Justices of the Peace, Minutes, 1877-1894; 1 volume.
Clerk's Minute Docket (Special Proceedings), 1946-1968; 4 volumes.
Coroners' Inquests, 1861-1960; 14 Fibredex boxes.
Homestead and Personal Property Exemptions, 1870-1916; 1 Fibredex box.
Lunacy, Record of, 1899-1968; 6 volumes.
Miscellaneous Records, 1763-1924; 3 Fibredex boxes.
Officials' Oaths, Record of, 1945-1968; 1 volume.
Pensions, Record of, 1920-1969; 1 volume.
Railroad Records, 1893-1906; 2 Fibredex boxes.
Slaves and Free Persons of Color, Records of, 1858-1870; 1 Fibredex box.

OFFICIALS, COUNTY [*See* **MISCELLANEOUS RECORDS**]

ROADS AND BRIDGES [*See* **MISCELLANEOUS RECORDS**]

WILLS [*See also* **ESTATES RECORDS**; **CRX RECORDS**]
Wills, 1805, 1808, 1817, 1836-1930, 1938; 18 Fibredex boxes.

CRX RECORDS
Will (Robert Williams), 1838; 1 folder.

MICROFILM RECORDS

BONDS
Apprentice Bonds, 1911-1926; 1 reel.

CORPORATIONS AND PARTNERSHIPS
Corporations, Record of, 1885-1948; 2 reels.
Limited Partnerships, Record of, 1943-1962; 1 reel.
Partnerships, Index to, 1915-1963; 1 reel.

COURT RECORDS
County Court of Pleas and Quarter Sessions
Minutes, 1858-1868; 1 reel.

Inferior Court
Minutes, 1877-1885; 1 reel.
Superior Court
Equity Minutes, 1858-1868; 1 reel.
Judgments, Index to, Defendant, 1900-1968; 4 reels.
Judgments, Index to, Plaintiff, 1900-1968; 2 reels.
Minutes, 1858-1915; 10 reels.
Minutes, Civil, 1915-1968; 13 reels.
Minutes, Criminal, 1914-1968; 7 reels.

ELECTION RECORDS
Elections, Record of, 1878-1952; 1 reel.

ESTATES RECORDS
Accounts, Record of, 1868-1951; 6 reels.
Accounts and Settlements, Record of, 1858-1868; 1 reel.
Administrators, Record of, 1912-1950; 5 reels.
Appointment of Administrators, Executors, and Guardians, 1868-1916; 1 reel.
Dowers and Widows' Year's Allowance, 1858-1946; 1 reel.
Estates, Record of, 1858-1871; 1 reel.
Executors, Record of, 1916-1963; 1 reel.
Final Accounts and Administrators, Index to, 1868-1963; 2 reels.
Guardians' Accounts, 1896-1950; 3 reels.
Guardians, Record of, 1913-1950; 2 reels.
Guardians' Returns, 1858-1872; 1 reel.
Inheritance Tax Records, 1923-1963; 1 reel.
Settlements, Record of, 1868-1952; 7 reels.

LAND RECORDS
Deeds, Record of, 1762-1946; 152 reels.
Land Divisions, 1858-1936; 2 reels.
Land Grants, 1779-1941; 3 reels.
Plat Book, 1911-1953; Index to Plats, 1911-1963; 1 reel.
Real Estate Conveyances, Index to, Grantee, 1762-1963; 7 reels.
Real Estate Conveyances, Index to, Grantor, 1762-1952; 7 reels.
Sales by Trustees and Mortgagees, Record of, 1920-1938; 3 reels.

MARRIAGE, DIVORCE, AND VITAL STATISTICS
Births, Index to, 1913-1957; 2 reels.
Cohabitation Records, 1966; 1 reel.
Deaths, Index to, 1916-1961; 1 reel.
Delayed Births, Index to, various years; 1 reel.
Maiden Names of Divorced Women, 1942-1963; 1 reel.
Marriage Bonds, 1826, 1829, 1833; 1 reel.
Marriage Licenses, 1890-1961; 17 reels.
Marriage Registers, 1868-1961; 3 reels.
Marriages, Record of, 1851-1867; 1 reel.

MISCELLANEOUS RECORDS
Board of Justices of the Peace, Minutes, 1877-1894; 1 reel.
Civil Actions and Special Proceedings, General Index to, Defendant, 1869-1963; 4 reels.
Civil Actions and Special Proceedings, General Index to, Plaintiff, 1869-1963; 4 reels.
Inquisition of Lunacy, 1899-1947; 1 reel.

Orders and Decrees, 1869-1947, 1962-1963; 14 reels.
Special Proceedings Dockets, 1872-1949; 4 reels.

OFFICIALS, COUNTY

Board of County Commissioners, Index to Minutes, 1936-1950; 1 reel.
Board of County Commissioners, Minutes, 1868-1963; 8 reels.

SCHOOL RECORDS

County Board of Education, Minutes, 1885-1989; 5 reels.

WILLS

Wills, Index to, Devisee, 1858-1968; 1 reel.
Wills, Index to, Devisor, 1858-1968; 1 reel.
Wills, Record of, 1858-1963; 5 reels.

POLK COUNTY

Established in 1847 from Henderson and Rutherford counties;
act repealed in 1848. Re-established in 1855.

ORIGINAL RECORDS

BONDS

Apprentice Bonds, 1877-1912; 2 volumes.
Officials' Bonds, 1865-1866; Record of Deeds, 1862, 1865-1867; 1 volume.
Officials' Bonds, Record of, 1870-1928; 1 volume.

COURT RECORDS

County Court of Pleas and Quarter Sessions
- Execution Docket, 1855-1868; 1 volume.
- Minutes, 1847-1848, 1855-1868; 2 volumes.
- State Docket, 1855-1868; 1 volume.
- Trial and Appearance Docket, 1855-1868; 1 volume.

Superior Court
- Appearance Docket, 1856-1869; 1 volume.
- Civil Action Papers, 1852-1909; 7 Fibredex boxes.
- Civil Action Papers Concerning County Officials, 1870-1908; 1 Fibredex box.
- Civil Action Papers Concerning Land, 1853-1917; 5 Fibredex boxes.
- Civil Issues Dockets, 1869-1937; 3 volumes.
- Criminal Action Papers, 1854-1911; 21 Fibredex boxes.
- Criminal Issues Dockets, 1869-1919; 4 volumes.
- Equity Execution Docket, 1858-1868; 1 volume.
- Equity Trial and Appearance Docket, 1848, 1856-1868; 1 volume.
- Execution Dockets, 1855-1917; 5 volumes.
- Minutes, 1855-1942; 9 volumes. [*See also* **RUTHERFORD COUNTY, ESTATES RECORDS**, Guardians' Accounts, 1866-1868]
- State Docket, 1855-1868; 1 volume.
- Trial Docket, 1855-1868, 1870; 1 volume.

ELECTION RECORDS

Elections, Record of, 1878-1950; 5 volumes.
Permanent Registration of Voters, 1902-1908; 1 volume.

ESTATES RECORDS

Accounts, Record of, 1869-1947; 5 volumes.
Administrators' Bonds, 1876-1911; 1 volume.
Amounts Paid to Indigent Children, Record of, 1913-1948; 1 volume.
Appointment of Administrators, Executors, Guardians, and Masters, 1869-1918; 1 volume.
Estates Records, 1851-1956; 35 Fibredex boxes.
Executors and Administrators, Cross Index to, 1869-1939; 1 volume.
Guardians' Bonds, 1872-1911; 1 volume.
Guardians, Cross Index to, 1869-1939; 1 volume.
Guardians' Records, 1852-1915; 1 Fibredex box.
Settlements, Record of, 1869-1936; 2 volumes.

LAND RECORDS

Deeds, 1830-1925; 2 Fibredex boxes.
Deeds, General Index to, 1855-1900; 1 volume.
Deeds, Record of, 1863-1865; 1 volume. [*See also* **BONDS**, Officials' Bonds, 1865-1866]
Ejectments, 1854-1897; 1 Fibredex box.
Land Entries, 1870-1950; 1 volume.
Levies on Land for Taxes, 1887-1894; 1 volume.
Probate, Record of, 1855-1902; 3 volumes.
Sale and Resale of Land, Record of, 1923-1936; 1 volume.

MARRIAGE, DIVORCE, AND VITAL STATISTICS

Divorce Records, 1856-1909; 1 Fibredex box.
Maiden Names of Divorced Women, 1942-1968; 1 volume.
Marriage Bonds, 1855-1868; 2 Fibredex boxes.
Marriage Register, 1867-1909; 1 volume.

MILITARY AND PENSION RECORDS [*See* **MISCELLANEOUS RECORDS**]

MISCELLANEOUS RECORDS

Alien Registration, 1927, 1940, 1948; 1 volume.
Assignees, Receivers, and Trustees, Records of, 1855-1909; 1 Fibredex box.
Clerk's Minute Dockets (Special Proceedings), 1878-1931, 1947; 5 volumes.
County Accounts and Claims Allowed, Record of, 1857-1896; 1 volume.
Declaration of Intent (to Become a Citizen), 1912; 1 volume.
Licenses to Trades, Registry of, 1872-1902; 1 volume.
List of Justices of the Peace, 1888-1890; 1 volume.
Lunacy, Record of, 1907-1945; 1 volume.
Miscellaneous Records, 1856-1921; 4 Fibredex boxes.
Orders and Decrees, 1931-1949; 1 volume.
Pensions, Record of, 1911-1913; 1 volume.
Railroad Records, 1872-1909; 1 Fibredex box.
Wardens of the Poor, Minutes, 1861-1864; 1 volume.

ROADS AND BRIDGES [*See* **MISCELLANEOUS RECORDS**]

WILLS

Wills, 1855-1968; 25 Fibredex boxes.
Wills, Cross Index to, 1855-1939; 1 volume.
Wills, Record of, 1855-1867; 1 volume.

MICROFILM RECORDS

BONDS

Apprentice Bonds, 1877-1912; 1 reel.

CORPORATIONS AND PARTNERSHIPS

Corporations, Record of, 1884-1969; 1 reel.
Partnerships and Assumed Names, Record of, 1945-1969; 1 reel.

COURT RECORDS

County Court of Pleas and Quarter Sessions
Minutes, 1847-1848, 1855-1868; 1 reel.

Superior Court

Criminal Actions, General Index to, 1855-1968; 1 reel.
Judgments, Index to, Defendant, 1855-1968; 1 reel.
Judgments, Index to, Plaintiff, 1855-1968; 1 reel.
Judgments, Liens, and Lis Pendens, Index to, Defendant, 1926-1968; 1 reel.
Judgments, Liens, and Lis Pendens, Index to, Plaintiff, 1926-1968; 1 reel.
Minutes, 1847-1848, 1855-1958; 5 reels.

Election Records

Elections, Record of, 1878-1950; 1 reel.

Estates Records

Accounts, Record of, 1869-1966; 4 reels.
Administrators' Bonds, 1876-1911; 1 reel.
Administrators, Executors, and Guardians, Record of, 1911-1939; 1 reel.
Administrators, Record of, 1923-1968; 2 reels.
Amounts Paid for Indigent Children, Record of, 1913-1948; 1 reel.
Annual Accounts and Final Settlements, Index to, 1869-1968; 1 reel.
Appointment of Administrators, Executors, and Guardians, 1869-1918; 1 reel.
Estates, Administrators, Executors, and Guardians, Index to, 1868-1968; 1 reel.
Estates, Index to, 1868-1969; 1 reel.
Executors, Record of, 1939-1968; 1 reel.
Guardians' Bonds, 1872-1911; 1 reel.
Guardians, Record of, 1928-1968; 1 reel.
Inheritance Tax Records, 1923-1968; 1 reel.
Settlements, Record of, 1870-1968; 3 reels.
Trust Fund Record, 1931-1935; 1 reel.

Land Records

Deeds, Record of, 1848-1967; 29 reels.
Land Entries, 1870-1950; 1 reel.
Real Estate Conveyances, Index to, Grantee, 1855-1969; 2 reels.
Real Estate Conveyances, Index to, Grantor, 1855-1969; 2 reels.

Marriage, Divorce, and Vital Statistics

Delayed Births, Index to, 1868-1994; 1 reel.
Maiden Names of Divorced Women, 1942-1968; 1 reel.
Marriage Bonds, 1855-1868; 1 reel.
Marriage Licenses, 1868-1969; 2 reels.
Marriage Registers, 1866-1969; 1 reel.
Vital Statistics, Index to, Birth and Death, 1913-1976; 1 reel.

Military and Pension Records

Soldiers in World War I, Record of, 1917-1919; 1 reel.

Miscellaneous Records

Appointment of Receivers, 1927-1959; 1 reel.
Orders and Decrees, 1931-1949; 1 reel.
Special Proceedings, 1878-1966; 5 reels.
Special Proceedings, Index to, 1878-1968; 1 reel.

Officials, County

Board of County Commissioners, Minutes, 1871-1963; 4 reels.

SCHOOL RECORDS

County Board of Education, Minutes, 1936-1969; 1 reel.

TAX AND FISCAL RECORDS

Tax Scrolls, 1945; 1 reel.

WILLS

Wills, Index to, 1855-1968; 1 reel.
Wills, Record of, 1855-1968; 5 reels.

RANDOLPH COUNTY

Established in 1779 from Guilford County.
Many court records are missing; reason unknown.

ORIGINAL RECORDS

BONDS [*See also* **CRX RECORDS**]

Apprentice Bonds and Records, 1779-1923; 1 volume, 4 Fibredex boxes.
Bastardy Bonds and Records, 1770, 1780-1930; 1 volume, 9 Fibredex boxes.
Officials' Bonds, 1784-1953; 2 volumes, 6 Fibredex boxes.

CENSUS RECORDS (County Copy)

Census, 1880; 2 pamphlets.

CORPORATIONS AND PARTNERSHIPS [*See* **MISCELLANEOUS RECORDS**]

COURT RECORDS [*See also* **CRX RECORDS**]

County Court of Pleas and Quarter Sessions
- Clerk's Fee and Receipt Books, 1851-1867; 2 volumes.
- Execution Dockets, 1784-1868; 13 volumes.
- Levy Docket, 1820-1839; 1 volume.
- Minutes, 1794-1868; 17 volumes.
- Recognizance Dockets, 1813-1841; 3 volumes.
- State Dockets, 1783-1868; 7 volumes.
- Trial and Appearance Dockets, 1845-1868; 3 volumes.
- Trial, Appearance, and Reference Dockets, 1779-1845; 9 volumes.
- Witness Fee Docket, 1800-1809; 1 volume.

Superior Court
- Civil Action Papers, 1772-1930; 88 Fibredex boxes.
- Civil Action Papers Concerning Land, 1787-1931; 11 Fibredex boxes.
- Civil Issues Dockets, Index to, 1912-1920s; 1 volume.
- Clerk's Fee and Receipt Book, 1854-1860; 1 volume.
- Criminal Action Papers, 1780-1920; 65 Fibredex boxes.
- Equity Execution Docket, 1860-1868; 1 volume.
- Equity Minutes, 1825-1868; 3 volumes.
- Equity Trial and Appearance Dockets, 1827-1868; 3 volumes.
- Execution Dockets, 1815-1827, 1841-1868; 6 volumes.
- Federal Tax Liens, 1925-1970; 6 volumes.
- Federal Tax Liens, Index to, 1933-1969; 1 volume.
- Judgment Dockets, 1869-1970; 55 volumes. [*See also* **LAND RECORDS**, Tax Suit Judgment Dockets]
- Lien Dockets, 1878-1970; 3 volumes.
- Minutes, 1833-1970; 39 volumes.
- State Dockets, 1821-1868; 3 volumes.
- Trial and Appearance Dockets, 1853-1868; 2 volumes.
- Trial, Appearance, and Reference Dockets, 1813-1852; 4 volumes.

ELECTION RECORDS

Election Records, 1791-1902; 6 Fibredex boxes.
Elections, Record of, 1880-1936, 1944-1968; 6 volumes.
Permanent Registration of Voters, 1902-1908; 2 volumes.

ESTATES RECORDS

Accounts, Record of, 1868-1952; 20 volumes.
Administrators' Bonds, 1870-1886; 2 volumes.
Amounts Paid for Indigent Children, Record of, 1903-1971; 2 volumes.
Appointment of Administrators, Executors, Guardians, and Masters, 1868-1913; 1 volume.
Appointment of Receivers for Orphans Without Guardians, 1908-1918; 1 volume.
Estates Records, 1781-1928; 153 Fibredex boxes. [*See also* **CRX RECORDS**]
Guardians' Accounts, 1833-1868; 2 volumes.
Guardians' Bonds, 1878-1918; 5 volumes.
Guardians' Records, 1793-1928; 15 Fibredex boxes.
Probate, Record of, 1943-1946; 1 volume.
Settlements, Record of, 1869-1942; 9 volumes.
Widows' Dowers and Year's Support, 1872-1913; 2 volumes.

LAND RECORDS

Clerk's Receipt Books (Land Sales), 1923-1931; 2 volumes.
Deeds, 1788-1920; 1 Fibredex box.
Deeds of Trust, Mortgage Deeds, and Bills of Sale, 1784-1917; 1 Fibredex box.
Ejectments, 1792-1897, 1930; 3 Fibredex boxes.
Judgments, Land Tax Sales, Index to, 1930-1955; 1 volume.
Land Entries, 1802-1833; 2 volumes. [*See also* **CRX RECORDS**]
Levies on Land, 1790-1905; 5 Fibredex boxes.
Lists of Deeds and Bills of Sale Proved, 1784-1832; 1 Fibredex box.
Miscellaneous Land Records, 1782-1929; 1 Fibredex box.
Sales and Resales, Record of, 1931-1940; 1 volume.
Surveys, Record of, 1908-1926; 1 volume.
Tax Suit Judgment Dockets, 1930-1942, 1961-1962; 2 volumes. [*See also* **COURT RECORDS**, Superior Court, Judgment Dockets]

MARRIAGE, DIVORCE, AND VITAL STATISTICS

Divorce Records, 1804-1927; 4 Fibredex boxes.
Maiden Names of Divorced Women, 1944-1970; 1 volume.
Marriage Bonds, 1779-1868; 14 Fibredex boxes.

MILITARY AND PENSION RECORDS [*See* **MISCELLANEOUS RECORDS**]

MISCELLANEOUS RECORDS

Alien Registration, 1927, 1940; 1 volume.
Appointment of Commissioners of Affidavits, Record of, 1897-1907; 1 volume.
Appointment of Overseers of Roads, 1817-1833; 2 volumes.
Articles of Incorporation, 1877-1898; 1 Fibredex box.
Assignees, Receivers, and Trustees, Records of, 1843-1929; 3 Fibredex boxes.
Board of County Commissioners, Minutes, 1874-1946; 10 volumes.
Civil War Records, 1861-1865, 1870; 1 Fibredex box.
County Accounts and Claims, 1784-1887; 2 Fibredex boxes.
Disbursements Register, 1919-1922; 1 volume.
Insolvent Debtors, 1792-1878; 5 Fibredex boxes.
Jurors, Record of, 1904-1951; 4 volumes.
Jury Lists and Excuses, 1779-1869; 2 Fibredex boxes.
List of Sheriffs, Game Wardens, Railroad Policemen, and Notaries Public, 1927-1930; 1 volume.

Lunacy, Record of, 1899-1952; 3 volumes.
Magistrates, Record of. [*See* Oaths of Magistrates and Notaries Public, Record of]
Miscellaneous Records, 1781-1922; 6 Fibredex boxes. [*See also* **CRX RECORDS**]
Oaths of Magistrates and Notaries Public, Record of, 1933-1969; 2 volumes.
Official Reports, Record of, 1875-1898, 1919-1924; 3 volumes.
Orders and Decrees, 1869-1951; 18 volumes.
Partnership, Record of, 1913-1946; 1 volume.
Road Orders, 1783-1868; 13 Fibredex boxes.
Road Petitions, 1791-1868; 3 Fibredex boxes.
Road, Railroad, and Bridge Records, 1784-1898; 2 Fibredex boxes.
School Fund Account Book, 1901-1902; 1 volume.
Slaves and Free Persons of Color, Records of, 1788-1887; 2 Fibredex boxes.
Special Proceedings Dockets, 1906-1927; 3 volumes.
Stock Law Order and Account Book, 1900-1915; 1 volume.
Strays, Record of, 1800-1845; 1 volume.

OFFICIALS, COUNTY [*See also* **MISCELLANEOUS RECORDS**]

ROADS AND BRIDGES [*See also* **MISCELLANEOUS RECORDS**]

TAX AND FISCAL RECORDS
Lists of Taxables, 1784-1867; 1 volume, 4 Fibredex boxes.
Miscellaneous Tax Records, 1782-1886; 1 Fibredex box. [*See also* **CRX RECORDS**]

WILLS
Wills, 1775-1902; 14 Fibredex boxes. [*See also* **CRX RECORDS**]
Wills, Settlements, and Sales, Index to, 1794-1832; 1 manuscript box.

CRX RECORDS
Bonds, 1779-1867; 1 Fibredex box.
Criminal Action Papers, 1813-1923; 1 Fibredex box.
Estates and Miscellaneous Records, 1782-1883; 11 folders.
Estates Records, 1792-1922; 2 Fibredex boxes.
Land Entry Book, 1783-1801; 6 volumes.
Lists of Taxables, 1785-1848; 3 Fibredex boxes.
Minutes, Court of Pleas and Quarter Sessions, 1779-1782, 1787-1794; 2 volumes.
Minutes, Superior Court, 1807-1833; 2 volumes.
Miscellaneous Records, 1779-1950; 6 Fibredex boxes.
State Docket, Superior Court, 1816-1820; 1 volume.
Will, 1786; 1 folder.

MICROFILM RECORDS

BONDS
Apprentice Bonds, 1890-1923; 1 reel.

CORPORATIONS AND PARTNERSHIPS
Corporations, Record of, 1883-1955; 1 reel.

COURT RECORDS
County Court of Pleas and Quarter Sessions
Minutes, 1779-1868; 6 reels.
Superior Court
Equity Minutes, 1825-1868; 1 reel.
Judgments, Index to, Defendant, 1869-1970; 15 reels.

Judgments, Index to, Plaintiff, 1869-1970; 16 reels.
Minutes, 1807-1833, 1850-1970; 19 reels.

Election Records

Elections, Record of, 1878-1972; 1 reel.

Estates Records

Accounts for Indigent Orphans, 1904-1958; 1 reel.
Accounts, Record of, 1868-1964; 12 reels.
Administrators' Bonds, 1870-1964; 9 reels.
Administrators, Executors, and Guardians, Cross Index to, 1868-1964; 1 reel.
Administrators, Record of, 1953-1964; 2 reels.
Appointment of Executors, 1868-1913; 1 reel.
Distribution Dockets, 1885-1958; 2 reels.
Guardians' Accounts, 1812-1851; 2 reels.
Guardians' Bonds, 1885-1918; 2 reels.
Guardians, Record of, 1916-1964; 2 reels.
Guardians' Settlements, 1852-1868; 1 reel.
Inheritance Tax Records, 1923-1964; 1 reel.
Settlements, Record of, 1867-1964; 7 reels.
Widows' Year's Allowance, Record of, 1888-1964; 1 reel.

Land Records

Deeds, Record of, 1779-1963; 249 reels.
Federal Tax Lien Index, 1933; 1 reel.
Land Entries, 1794-1801, 1833-1837; 1 reel.
Real Estate Conveyances, Index to, Grantee, 1779-1964; 24 reels.
Real Estate Conveyances, Index to, Grantor, 1779-1964; 22 reels.
Resale of Land, Record of, 1931-1940; 1 reel.

Marriage, Divorce, and Vital Statistics

Births, Index to, 1913-1981; 3 reels.
Deaths, Index to, 1913-1980; 2 reels.
Delayed Births, Index to, various years; 1 reel.
Maiden Names of Divorced Women, 1945-1970; 1 reel.
Marriage Bond Abstracts, 1779-1868; 1 reel.
Marriage Bonds, 1779-1868; 10 reels.
Marriage Registers, 1851-1981; 3 reels.
Marriages, Index to, Female, 1851-1964; 1 reel.
Marriages, Index to, Male, 1851-1981; 1 reel.

Miscellaneous Records

Miscellaneous Historical Records, 1779-1838; 1 reel.
Orders and Decrees, 1869-1951; 9 reels.
Special Proceedings, 1901-1964; 3 reels.
Special Proceedings, Cross Index to, 1915-1957; 1 reel.

Officials, County

Board of County Commissioners, Minutes, 1874-1964; 3 reels.

Roads and Bridges

Appointment of Road Overseers, 1817-1833; 1 reel.

SCHOOL RECORDS

County Board of Education, Minutes, 1881-1885, 1910-1964; 1 reel.
Report of the Board of Superintendents of Common Schools, 1840-1864; 1 reel.

TAX AND FISCAL RECORDS

Tax Scrolls, 1872-1915; 17 reels.

WILLS

Wills, Cross Index to, 1773-1964; 1 reel.
Wills, Record of, 1773-1964; 9 reels.

RICHMOND COUNTY

Established in 1779 from Anson County.
A few of the court records are missing; reason unknown.

ORIGINAL RECORDS

BONDS

Apprentice Bonds and Records, 1782-1912; 1 volume, 1 Fibredex box.
Bastardy Bonds and Records, 1783-1880; 1 volume, 1 Fibredex box.
Officials' Bonds and Records, 1794-1924; 3 volumes, 2 Fibredex boxes. [*See also* **CRX RECORDS**]
Sheriffs' Bonds and Records, 1785-1912; 3 Fibredex boxes.

COURT RECORDS

County Court of Pleas and Quarter Sessions
- Allowance Dockets, 1830-1841, 1848-1868; 2 volumes.
- Execution Dockets, 1783-1863; 2 volumes, 2 manuscript boxes.
- Minutes, 1779-1797, 1800-1868; 14 volumes, 1 manuscript box.
- Recognizance Docket, 1797-1815; 1 manuscript box.
- State Dockets, 1784-1823; 2 volumes.
- Trial, Appearance, and Reference Dockets, 1785-1814; 2 manuscript boxes.
- Trial Docket, 1855-1868; 1 volume.

Superior Court
- Appearance Docket, 1831-1867; 1 volume.
- Civil Action Papers, 1772-1928; 37 Fibredex boxes.
- Civil Action Papers Concerning County Commissioners and Municipalities, 1838-1910; 1 Fibredex box.
- Civil Action Papers Concerning Land, 1773-1926; 6 Fibredex boxes.
- Civil Issues Dockets, 1869-1900; 6 volumes.
- Criminal Action Papers, 1777-1941; 31 Fibredex boxes.
- Criminal Issues Dockets, 1869-1899; 3 volumes.
- Equity Enrolling Docket, 1851-1868; 1 manuscript box.
- Equity Execution Dockets, 1830-1868; 2 volumes.
- Equity Minutes, 1829-1868; 3 volumes.
- Equity Trial Docket, 1860-1868; 1 volume.
- Execution Dockets, 1809-1824, 1845-1868; 4 volumes.
- Minutes, 1823-1913; 15 volumes.
- Miscellaneous Dockets, 1782-1934; 1 Fibredex box.
- Recognizance Docket, 1807-1834; 1 manuscript box.
- State Dockets, 1831-1868; 4 volumes.
- Trial and Appearance Docket, 1807-1823; 1 volume.
- Trial Dockets, 1831-1868; 2 volumes.

ELECTION RECORDS

Election Records, 1786-1936; 2 Fibredex boxes.
Elections, Record of, 1878-1936; 5 volumes.
Permanent Registration of Voters, 1902-1908; 1 volume.

ESTATES RECORDS

Accounts, Record of, 1869-1916; 5 volumes.
Administrators' Bonds, 1870-1911; 3 volumes.

Amounts Paid to Indigent Children, Record of, 1912-1927; 1 volume.
Appointment of Administrators, Executors, Guardians, and Masters, 1868-1915; 2 volumes.
Estates, Record of, 1778-1833, 1848-1863; 4 volumes.
Estates Records, 1772-1933; 69 Fibredex boxes.
Fiduciary Account Book, 1834; 1 volume.
Guardians' Accounts, 1858-1868; 1 volume.
Guardians' Bonds, 1870-1915; 3 volumes.
Guardians' Records, 1784-1913; 13 Fibredex boxes.
Settlements, Record of, 1869-1904; 1 volume.
Widows' Year's Allowance, Record of, 1927-1967; 1 volume.

LAND RECORDS

Deeds of Sale, 1794-1930; 7 Fibredex boxes.
Ejectments, 1786-1887; 2 Fibredex boxes.
Land Entries, 1780-1798, 1849-1890; 3 volumes.
Land Sold for Taxes, Record of, 1932-1936; 5 volumes.
Levies on Land, 1779-1894; 1 Fibredex box.
Miscellaneous Deeds, 1820-1934; 1 Fibredex box.
Miscellaneous Land Records, 1762-1931; 1 Fibredex box.
Mortgage Deeds, 1822-1926, 1936; 2 Fibredex boxes.
Petitions for Partition, 1847-1912; 1 Fibredex box.

MARRIAGE, DIVORCE, AND VITAL STATISTICS

Applicants for Marriage Licenses, Record of, 1929-1932; 1 volume.
Cohabitation Certificates, 1866-1868; 1 manuscript box.
Divorce Records, 1816-1910; 3 Fibredex boxes.
Marriage Bonds, 1791-1868; 1 Fibredex box.
Marriage Certificates, Record of, 1851-1872; 1 volume.
Marriage Registers, 1867-1937; 9 volumes.

MISCELLANEOUS RECORDS

Alien Registration, 1940, 1956; 1 volume.
Assignees, Records of, 1782-1911; 2 Fibredex boxes.
Bridge Records, 1790-1897; 1 Fibredex box.
County Accounts, 1783-1923; 2 Fibredex boxes.
Homestead and Personal Property Exemptions, Record of, 1869-1874; 1 volume.
Licenses to Trades, Registry of, 1875-1885; 1 volume.
Miscellaneous Records, 1779-1939; 5 Fibredex boxes.
Oaths of Justices of the Peace, Record of, 1891-1916; 1 volume.
Official Reports, Record of, 1875-1927; 2 volumes.
Orders and Decrees, 1869-1903; 6 volumes.
Railroad Records, 1867-1914; 3 Fibredex boxes.
Receivers and Trustees, Records of, 1784-1929; 1 Fibredex box.
Road Dockets, 1850-1866, 1877-1879; 2 volumes.
Road Records, 1778-1909; 3 Fibredex boxes.
School Records, 1839-1903; 2 Fibredex boxes.
Slave Records, 1778-1866; 2 Fibredex boxes.
Special Proceedings Docket, 1883-1916; 1 volume.

OFFICIALS, COUNTY [*See* **CRX RECORDS**]

ROADS AND BRIDGES [*See* **MISCELLANEOUS RECORDS**]

School Records [*See* **Miscellaneous Records**]

Tax and Fiscal Records

Assessment of Land and Cost Docket, 1855, 1868-1869; 1 volume.
Tax Records, 1783-1898; 1 Fibredex box.

Wills

Wills, 1779-1971; 36 Fibredex boxes.
Wills, Cross Index to, 1779-1934; 1 volume.
Wills and Inventories, Record of, 1789-1807; 1 pamphlet.
Wills, Record of, 1848-1864; 1 volume.

CRX Records

Officials' Bonds and Records, 1793-1868; 2 folders.

MICROFILM RECORDS

Corporations and Partnerships

Incorporations, Record of, 1887-1963; 2 reels.
Partnerships, Record of, 1915-1973; 1 reel.

Court Records

County Court of Pleas and Quarter Sessions
- Minutes, 1779-1797, 1800-1868; 4 reels.

Superior Court
- Equity Minutes, 1829-1868; 1 reel.
- Judgment Docket, 1967-1968; 1 reel.
- Judgments, Index to, Defendant, 1913-1968; 2 reels.
- Judgments, Index to, Plaintiff, 1913-1964; 2 reels.
- Minutes, 1823-1964; 15 reels.

Election Records

Elections, Record of, 1878-1964; 1 reel.

Estates Records

Accounts and Receivership of Minors, Record of, 1925-1953; 1 reel.
Accounts, Record of, 1869-1964; 7 reels.
Administrators, Executors, and Guardians, Index to, 1911-1964; 1 reel.
Administrators, Record of, 1911-1964; 4 reels.
Amounts Paid for Indigent Children, 1912-1927, 1955-1973; 1 reel.
Appointment of Administrators, Executors, and Guardians, 1865-1935; 1 reel.
Appointment of Executors, 1926-1968; 1 reel.
Appointment of Guardians, 1935-1968; 2 reels.
Inheritance Tax Records, 1923-1965; 1 reel.
Qualification of Trustees Under Wills, 1963; 1 reel.
Settlements, Record of, 1854-1964; 5 reels.
Widows' Year's Allowance, 1927-1967; 1 reel.

Land Records

Deeds, Record of, 1777-1962; 183 reels.
Federal Tax Lien Index, 1935-1951; 1 reel.
Land Entries, 1780-1795, 1849-1945; 1 reel.
Land Grants, 1854-1929; 1 reel.
Real Estate Conveyances, Index to, Grantee, 1784-1964; 6 reels.

Real Estate Conveyances, Index to, Grantor, 1784-1964; 7 reels.
Resale by Trustees and Mortgagees, Record of, 1921-1964; 4 reels.

MARRIAGE, DIVORCE, AND VITAL STATISTICS

Births, Index to, 1914-1972; 2 reels.
Cohabitation Certificates, 1866-1868; 1 reel.
Deaths, Index to, 1913-1967; 1 reel.
Delayed Births, Index to, various years; 1 reel.
Marriage Bonds, 1779-1868; 1 reel.
Marriage Licenses, 1870-1964; 8 reels.
Marriage Registers, 1851-1964; 2 reels.

MISCELLANEOUS RECORDS

Appointment of Receivers, 1955-1968; 1 reel.
Clerk's Minute Dockets, 1916-1960; 2 reels.
Homesteads and Exemptions, 1869-1874; 1 reel.
Orders and Decrees, 1869-1964; 12 reels.
Special Proceedings, 1883-1968; 2 reels.

OFFICIALS, COUNTY

Board of County Commissioners, Minutes, 1868-1964; 9 reels.

SCHOOL RECORDS

Board of Superintendents of Common Schools, Minutes, 1839-1840; County Board of Education, Minutes, 1877-1925; 1 reel.

TAX AND FISCAL RECORDS

Land Assessments, 1855; 1 reel.
Tax List, 1915; 1 reel.

WILLS

Wills, Cross Index to, 1779-1968; 2 reels.
Wills, Record of, 1779-1964; 5 reels.

ROBESON COUNTY

Established in 1787 from Bladen County.
Many of the court records are missing; reason unknown.

ORIGINAL RECORDS

BONDS

Apprentice Bonds and Records, 1820-1904; 1 Fibredex box.
Bastardy Bonds and Records, 1813-1911, 1935-1966; 5 Fibredex boxes.
Officials' Bonds and Records, 1795-1914; 2 Fibredex boxes.

COURT RECORDS

Circuit Criminal Court/Eastern District Criminal Court
- Minutes, 1895-1900; 1 volume.

County Court of Pleas and Quarter Sessions
- Execution Dockets, 1855-1867; 2 volumes.
- Minutes, 1797-1813, 1830-1868; 11 volumes.
- Trial Docket, 1858-1868; 1 volume.

Inferior Court
- Minutes, 1883-1885; 1 volume.

Superior Court
- Appearance Docket, 1859-1868; 1 volume.
- Civil Action Papers, 1801-1921; 33 Fibredex boxes.
- Civil Action Papers Concerning Land, 1816-1926; 28 Fibredex boxes.
- Criminal Action Papers, 1803-1966; 183 Fibredex boxes.
- Equity Execution Docket, 1850-1868; 1 volume.
- Equity Minutes, 1847-1868; 1 volume.
- Execution Dockets, 1836-1867; 3 volumes.
- Judgments, Index to, 1867-1891; 2 volumes.
- Minutes, 1844-1912; 19 volumes.
- Minutes, Criminal, 1909-1966; 19 volumes.
- Minutes, Cross Index to, 1873-1912; 7 volumes.
- Recognizance Docket, 1841-1847; 1 volume.
- State Dockets, 1841-1869; 2 volumes.
- Trial Docket, 1846-1851, 1862; 1 volume.

ELECTION RECORDS

Elections, Record of, 1910-1938; 3 volumes.

ESTATES RECORDS

Accounts, Record of, 1870-1910; 5 volumes.
Administrators' Bonds, 1880-1891, 1899-1903; 2 volumes.
Estates, Record of, 1829-1870; 7 volumes.
Estates Records, 1801-1935; 90 Fibredex boxes.
Guardians' Accounts, 1857-1902; 1 volume.
Guardians' Accounts, Cross Index to, [1857-1902]; 1 volume.
Guardians' Bonds, 1900-1902; 1 volume.
Guardians' Records, 1821-1928; 8 Fibredex boxes.
Probate (Estates) and Appointment, Record of, 1868-1936; 1 volume.
Settlements, Cross Index to, [1869-1914]; 1 volume.
Settlements, Record of, 1869-1914; 1 volume.

LAND RECORDS

Attachments, Executions, Levies, and Liens on Land, 1821-1914; 2 Fibredex boxes.
Deeds, Record of, 1792-1826; 6 volumes.
Ejectments, 1824-1900; 5 Fibredex boxes.
Miscellaneous Land Records, 1782-1926; 3 Fibredex boxes.

MARRIAGE, DIVORCE, AND VITAL STATISTICS

Divorce Records, 1841-1920; 5 Fibredex boxes.
Marriage Bonds, 1803-1868; 7 Fibredex boxes.

MILITARY AND PENSION RECORDS [*See* **MISCELLANEOUS RECORDS**]

MISCELLANEOUS RECORDS

Alien Registration, 1927; 1 volume.
Appointment of Road Overseers, 1833-1868; 1 Fibredex box.
Assignees, Receivers, and Trustees, Records of, 1877-1927; 5 Fibredex boxes.
Assignment Books, 1893-1905; 2 volumes.
Coroners' Inquests, 1857-1965; 27 Fibredex boxes.
County Accounts, Buildings, and Correspondence, 1810-1910; 1 Fibredex box.
Insolvents and Homestead and Personal Property Exemptions, 1793-1904; 2 Fibredex boxes.
Lumber, Timber, and Mills, Records Concerning, 1835-1911; 1 Fibredex box.
Miscellaneous Records, 1817-1939; 5 Fibredex boxes.
Orders and Decrees, 1869-1904; 5 volumes.
Pensions, Record of, 1908-1939; 1 volume.
Petitions for Naturalization, 1911-1913; 1 volume.
Railroad Records, 1857-1914; 7 Fibredex boxes.
Road and Bridge Records, 1833-1924; 1 Fibredex box.
Slaves and Free Persons of Color, Records Concerning, 1814-1867; 4 Fibredex boxes.

ROADS AND BRIDGES [*See* **MISCELLLANEOUS RECORDS**]

TAX AND FISCAL RECORDS

List of Taxables, 1837-1845; 1 volume.
Tax Records, 1788-1910; 2 Fibredex boxes.

WILLS

Wills, 1783-1918, 1930, 1933, 1935; 13 Fibredex boxes.

MICROFILM RECORDS

CORPORATIONS AND PARTNERSHIPS

Corporations and Partnerships, Index to, 1890-1966; 1 reel.
Corporations, Record of, 1890-1946; 2 reels.
Partnerships, Record of, 1915-1966; 1 reel.

COURT RECORDS

County Court of Pleas and Quarter Sessions
- Minutes, 1797-1868; 4 reels.

Superior Court
- Equity Minutes, 1847-1868; 1 reel.
- Judgments, Index to, Defendant, 1941-1966; 2 reels.
- Judgments, Index to, Plaintiff, 1941-1966; 2 reels.
- Minutes, 1844-1899; 6 reels.

Minutes, Civil, 1899-1960; 23 reels.
Minutes, Criminal, 1901-1955; 7 reels.
Minutes, Cross Index to, 1872-1966; 5 reels.

ELECTION RECORDS [*See also* **SCHOOL RECORDS**]

Elections, Record of, 1878-1922, 1940-1965; 1 reel.

ESTATES RECORDS

Accounts, Record of, 1870-1961; 17 reels.
Administrators, Executors, Justices of the Peace, and Notaries, Record of, 1869-1936; 1 reel.
Administrators, Record of, 1907-1966; 8 reels.
Amounts Paid for Indigent Children, Record of, 1912-1966; 1 reel.
Estates, Record of, 1829-1870; 3 reels.
Executors, Record of, 1911-1966; 3 reels.
Guardians, Record of, 1907-1966; 4 reels.
Inheritance Tax Records, 1923-1958; 1 reel.
Qualification of Trustees under Wills, 1962-1965; 1 reel.
Settlements, Cross Index to, 1869-1914; 1 reel.
Settlements, Record of, 1869-1914; 1 reel.

LAND RECORDS

Deeds, Record of, 1787-1960; 161 reels.
Entry Takers' Book, 1854-1945; 1 reel.
Federal Tax Lien Index, 1928-1969; 1 reel.
Land Grants, Record of, 1788-1797; 1 reel.
Land Sold for Taxes, Record of, 1925; 1 reel.
Real Estate Conveyances, Index to, Grantee, 1787-1966; 12 reels.
Real Estate Conveyances, Index to, Grantor, 1787-1966; 10 reels.
Registration of Land Titles, 1914-1923; 1 reel.
Resale of Land, Record of, 1931-1966; 3 reels.

MARRIAGE, DIVORCE, AND VITAL STATISTICS

Births, Index to, 1913-1965; 3 reels.
Deaths, Index to, 1911-1963; 1 reel.
Delayed Births, Index to, various years; 1 reel.
Maiden Names of Divorced Women, 1940-1968; 1 reel.
Marriage Bonds, 1786-1868; 7 reels.
Marriage and Cohabitation, Record of, 1850-1866; 1 reel.
Marriage Registers, 1867-1966; 7 reels.
Marriages, Index to, 1787-1973; 3 reels.

MISCELLANEOUS RECORDS

Homestead Allotments, Record of, 1919-1961; 1 reel.
Orders and Decrees, 1869-1960; 27 reels.
Special Proceedings Dockets, 1868-1951; 6 reels.
Special Proceedings, Index to, Defendant, 1868-1966; 1 reel.
Special Proceedings, Index to, Plaintiff, 1868-1966; 1 reel.

OFFICIALS, COUNTY

Board of County Commissioners, Minutes, 1868-1936; 9 reels.

SCHOOL RECORDS

Boundaries of School Districts and Record of Elections, 1904-1927; 1 reel.
County Board of Education, Minutes, 1885-1911; 1 reel.

TAX AND FISCAL RECORDS

List of Taxables, 1837-1845; 1 reel.

WILLS

Original Wills, 1783-1851; 2 reels.
Wills, Cross Index to, 1787-1966; 2 reels.
Wills, Record of, 1787-1966; 10 reels.

ROCKINGHAM COUNTY

Established in 1785 from Guilford County.
A few of the court records are missing; reason unknown.

ORIGINAL RECORDS

BONDS

- Apprentice Bonds, 1871-1919; 2 volumes.
- Bastardy Bonds, 1873-1878; 1 volume.
- Officials' Bonds and Records, 1803-1925; 1 Fibredex box.

COURT RECORDS

- County Court of Pleas and Quarter Sessions
  - Execution Dockets, 1788-1868; 13 volumes.
  - Minutes, 1786-1868; 17 volumes.
  - State Dockets, 1800-1868; 6 volumes.
  - Trial and Appearance Dockets, 1786-1861; 10 volumes.
- General County Court
  - Judgments, Index to, 1926-1927; 1 volume.
  - Minutes, 1925-1927; 1 volume.
- Inferior Court
  - Minutes, 1878-1880; 1 volume.
- Recorder's Court
  - Minutes, 1909-1970; 33 volumes.
- Superior Court
  - Civil Action Papers, 1804-1923; 14 Fibredex boxes.
  - Civil Action Papers Concerning Land, 1827-1928; 5 Fibredex boxes.
  - Civil Actions, Index to, ca. 1920-1950; 1 volume.
  - Clerk's Minute Docket, Proceedings Supplemental to Execution, 1907; 1 volume.
  - Criminal Action Papers, 1807-1925; 8 Fibredex boxes.
  - Equity Bills of Cost, 1860-1874; 1 volume.
  - Equity Minutes, 1807-1868; 4 volumes.
  - Equity Proceeding, 1822-1828; 1 volume.
  - Equity Trial and Appearance Dockets, 1807-1868; 3 volumes.
  - Execution Dockets, 1814-1868; 5 volumes.
  - Judgment Dockets, 1869-1957; 13 volumes.
  - Judgments, Index to, 1867-1877; 1 volume.
  - Judgments, Index to, 1869-1970; 11 volumes.
  - Minutes, 1807-1970; 44 volumes.
  - Recognizance Docket, 1811-1845; 1 volume.
  - State Docket, 1809-1821; 1 volume.
  - Trial and Appearance Dockets, 1807-1850; 2 volumes.
  - Trial Docket, 1850-1870; 1 volume.

ELECTION RECORDS

- Elections, Record of, 1878-1968; 7 volumes.

ESTATES RECORDS

- Accounts of Indigent Orphans, 1908-1936; 1 volume.
- Accounts, Record of, 1868-1970; 41 volumes.
- Administration and Guardianship, Ledger of Letters of, 1927-1942; 1 volume.

Administrators' Bonds, 1870-1880, 1909-1935; 4 volumes.
Administrators, Executors, and Guardians, Accounts of, 1930-1942; 2 volumes.
Administrators, Executors, and Guardians, Index to Accounts of, 1930-1942; 1 volume.
Administrators, Record of, 1926-1970; 7 volumes.
Appointment of Executors, 1868-1895; 1 volume.
Appointment of Executors and Administrators, 1896-1919; 1 volume.
Appointments, Record of, 1919-1970; 3 volumes.
Estate Book of William Pannill, 1875-1893; 1 volume.
Estates Not Exceeding $300, 1929-1937; 1 volume.
Estates, Record of, 1829-1868; 9 volumes.
Estates Records, 1780-1926; 58 Fibredex boxes.
Executors and Administrators, Cross Index to, 1868-1939; 2 volumes.
Executors, Record of, 1931-1970; 5 volumes.
Guardians' Accounts, 1855-1868; 1 volume.
Guardians' Bonds, 1872-1893, 1906-1937; 4 volumes.
Guardians, Cross Index to, 1869-1943; 1 volume.
Guardians' Records, 1807-1925; 6 Fibredex boxes.
Guardians of World War Veterans, 1930-1938; 1 volume.
Inheritance Tax Record, 1923-1970; 5 volumes.
Renunciations and Dissents from Wills, Record of, 1964-1970; 1 volume.
Settlements, Record of, 1817-1970; 34 volumes.

LAND RECORDS

Attachments, Executions, Liens, and Levies on Land, 1806-1924; 4 Fibredex boxes.
Deeds of Gift, 1797-1895; 1 Fibredex box.
Deeds of Mortgage, 1821-1913; 1 Fibredex box.
Deeds of Sale, 1786-1899; 18 Fibredex boxes.
Deeds of Trust, 1808-1914; 3 Fibredex boxes.
Deeds of Warranty and Quit Claim, 1788-1913; 1 Fibredex box.
Ejectments, 1808-1909; 1 Fibredex box.
Miscellaneous Land Records, 1789-1926; 1 Fibredex box.
Processioners' Record, 1836-1842; 1 volume.
Sales and Resales, Record of, 1918-1970; 4 volumes.

MARRIAGE, DIVORCE, AND VITAL STATISTICS

Divorce Records, 1824-1921; 2 Fibredex boxes.
Maiden Names of Divorced Women, 1937-1970; 1 volume.
Marriage Bonds, 1785-1868; 9 Fibredex boxes.
Marriage Certificates, Record of, 1851-1867; 1 volume.
Marriages, Index to, 1790-1868; 1 volume.
Miscellaneous Marriage Records, 1812-1925; 1 Fibredex box.

MILITARY AND PENSION RECORDS [*See* **ESTATES RECORDS**]

MISCELLANEOUS RECORDS

Alien Registration, 1927-1940; 1 volume.
Appointment of Road Overseers, Record of, 1811-1829; 1 volume.
Assignees, Receivers, and Trustees, Records of, 1861-1925; 9 Fibredex boxes.
Board of Superintendents of Common Schools, Minutes, 1841-1864; 1 volume.
Homestead Records, 1871-1927; 1 Fibredex box.
Jury Lists and Tickets, 1819-1851; 1 Fibredex box.

Lunacy, Record of, 1899-1970; 5 volumes.
Miscellaneous Business Records, 1852-1925; 1 Fibredex box.
Miscellaneous Records, 1786-1925; 2 Fibredex boxes. [*See also* **CRX RECORDS**]
Orders and Decrees, 1887-1969; 40 volumes.
Pensions, Record of, 1940-1970; 2 volumes.
Powers of Attorney, 1784-1923; 1 Fibredex box.
Professional Registration, Certificates of, 1886-1967; 3 volumes.
Railroad Records, 1867-1901; 3 Fibredex boxes.
Receivers' Accounts, 1902-1937; 1 volume.
Receivers, Record of, 1920-1925, 1959-1965; 2 volumes.
Road and Bridge Records, 1822-1899; 1 Fibredex box.
Slaves and Free Persons of Color, Records of, 1795-1867; 2 Fibredex boxes.

ROADS AND BRIDGES [*See* **MISCELLANEOUS RECORDS**]

SCHOOL RECORDS [*See* **MISCELLANEOUS RECORDS**]

TAX AND FISCAL RECORDS
Miscellaneous Tax Records, 1857-1899; 2 Fibredex boxes.

WILLS
Wills, 1772-1925, 1936, 1938; 24 Fibredex boxes.
Wills, Record of, 1804-1931; 7 volumes.

CRX RECORDS
Miscellaneous Records, 1793-1910; 28 folders.

MICROFILM RECORDS

BONDS
Apprentice Bonds, 1871-1919; 1 reel.
Bastardy Bonds, 1873-1878; 1 reel.

CORPORATIONS AND PARTNERSHIPS
Corporations, Record of, 1884-1967; 4 reels.
Partnership, Record of, 1913-1972; 1 reel.

COURT RECORDS
County Court of Pleas and Quarter Sessions
    Minutes, 1786-1868; 5 reels.
Superior Court
    Equity Minutes, 1807-1868; 1 reel.
    Judgments, Index to, Defendant, 1921-1970; 2 reels.
    Judgments, Index to, Plaintiff, 1921-1970; 2 reels.
    Minutes, 1807-1970; 22 reels.

ELECTION RECORDS
Elections, Record of, 1878-1968; 2 reels.

ESTATES RECORDS
Accounts for Indigent Orphans, 1908-1937; 1 reel.
Accounts, Record of, 1868-1966; 15 reels.
Administrators' Bonds, 1870-1880; 1 reel.
Administrators, Record of, 1926-1954; 2 reels.
Appointment of Administrators, Executors, and Guardians, 1895-1962; 3 reels.

Appointment of Guardians and Trustees under Wills, 1962-1970; 1 reel.
Estates Not Exceeding $300, 1929-1937; 1 reel.
Estates, Record of, 1829-1868; 3 reels.
Executors, Record of, 1931-1954; 1 reel.
Guardians' Bonds, 1872-1919; 1 reel.
Guardians and Trustees, Index to, 1868-1970; 1 reel.
Guardians and Trustees under Wills, Appointment of, 1962-1970; 1 reel.
Inheritance Tax Records, 1922-1965; 2 reels.
Renunciations, Record of, 1964-1970; 1 reel.
Settlements, Record of, 1817-1965; 12 reels.

LAND RECORDS

Deeds, Record of, 1785-1957; 103 reels.
Federal Tax Liens, Index to, 1929-1965; 1 reel.
Foreclosures Under Deeds of Trust, Record of, 1924-1965; 1 reel.
Land Entries, Record of, 1904-1929; 1 reel.
Processioners' Book. [*See* **MARRIAGE, DIVORCE, AND VITAL STATISTICS**, Marriages, Record of, 1836-1842]
Real Estate Conveyances, Index to, Grantee, 1785-1962; 9 reels.
Real Estate Conveyances, Index to, Grantor, 1785-1962; 10 reels.
Resales by Mortgagees and Trustees, Record of, 1919-1923; 1 reel.
Sales by Mortgagees, Trustees, and Executors, Record of, 1918-1923; 1 reel.

MARRIAGE, DIVORCE, AND VITAL STATISTICS

Births, Index to, 1913-1978; 3 reels.
Deaths, Index to, 1913-1978; 2 reels.
Delayed Births, Index to, various years; 1 reel.
Maiden Names of Divorced Women, 1937-1970; 1 reel.
Marriage Bonds, 1785-1868; 9 reels.
Marriage Licenses, Bonds, and Certificates, Index to, 1790-1868; 1 reel.
Marriage Registers, 1867-1972; 6 reels.
Marriages, Record of, 1851-1867; 1 reel.
Marriages, Record of, 1865-1867; Processioners' Book, 1836-1842; 1 reel.

MISCELLANEOUS RECORDS

Lunacy, Record of, 1899-1952; 1 reel.
Orders and Decrees, 1869-1952; 8 reels.
Receivers' Accounts, Record of, 1902-1957; 1 reel.
Special Proceedings, Index to, Defendant, 1869-1969; 1 reel.
Special Proceedings, Index to, Plaintiff, 1869-1969; 1 reel.

OFFICIALS, COUNTY

Board of County Commissioners, Minutes, 1870-1979, 1984-1986; 6 reels.
County Board of Health, Minutes, 1911-1925, 1946-1965; 1 reel.

ROADS AND BRIDGES

Overseers of Roads, 1811-1829; 1 reel.

SCHOOL RECORDS

Board of Superintendents of Common Schools, Minutes, 1841-1864; 1 reel.
County Board of Education, Minutes, 1877-1885, 1909-1965; 1 reel.

TAX AND FISCAL RECORDS

Tax Lists, 1887, 1888, 1890, 1899, 1904, 1912, 1915; 3 reels.

WILLS

Wills, Cross Index to, 1804-1965; 1 reel.
Wills, Record of, 1785-1966; 7 reels.

ROWAN COUNTY

Established in 1753 from Anson County.
A few records were destroyed by Federal troops in 1865.

ORIGINAL RECORDS

BONDS [*See also* **CRX RECORDS**]

- Apprentice Bonds and Records, 1777-1904; 1 volume, 1 Fibredex box.
- Bastardy Bonds and Records, 1757-1925; 2 volumes, 2 Fibredex boxes.
- Officials' Bonds and Records, 1768-1900; 1 Fibredex box.

CENSUS RECORDS [*See* **CRX RECORDS**]

CORPORATIONS AND PARTNERSHIPS [*See* **MISCELLANEOUS RECORDS**]

COURT RECORDS [*See also* **CRX RECORDS**]

- County Court of Pleas and Quarter Sessions
  - Appearance Dockets, 1809-1868; 5 volumes.
  - Argument and Petition Docket, 1807-1832; 1 volume.
  - Clerk's Receipt Book, 1811-1826; 1 volume.
  - Execution Dockets, 1761-1833, 1845-1868; 11 volumes.
  - Minutes, 1753-1868; 24 volumes.
  - Minutes, Probate Court, 1819-1822; 1 volume.
  - Recognizance Docket, 1811-1818; 1 volume.
  - Reference Dockets, 1814-1849; 2 volumes.
  - Rough Minutes, 1767-1859; 2 Fibredex boxes.
  - State Dockets, 1791-1818, 1830-1868; 4 volumes.
  - Trial, Appearance, and Reference Dockets, 1753-1810; 9 volumes.
  - Trial Dockets, 1810-1868; 8 volumes.
- Inferior Court
  - Criminal Issues Docket, 1877-1885; 1 volume.
  - Judgment Docket, 1877-1885; 1 volume.
  - Minutes, 1877-1885; 2 volumes.
- Superior Court
  - Appearance and Reference Docket, 1808-1835; 1 volume.
  - Appearance Dockets, 1835-1869; 2 volumes.
  - Civil Action Papers, 1755-1915; 5 Fibredex boxes.
  - Civil Action Papers Concerning Land, 1758-1912; 6 Fibredex boxes.
  - Clerk's Cashbook, 1876-1901; 1 volume.
  - Clerk's Fee Book, 1932-1935; 1 volume.
  - Clerk's Receipt Book, 1823-1838; 1 volume.
  - Criminal Action Papers, 1756-1913; 6 Fibredex boxes.
  - Equity Enrolling Dockets, 1805-1806, 1820-1844; 5 volumes.
  - Equity Minutes, 1818-1864; 3 volumes.
  - Equity Trial and Appearance Dockets, 1806-1868; 2 volumes, 1 pamphlet.
  - Execution Dockets, 1809-1869; 6 volumes.
  - Minutes, 1811-1904, 1909-1910; 22 volumes.
  - Recognizance Docket, 1823-1827; 1 volume.
  - Reference Docket, 1820-1838; 1 volume.

State Dockets, 1821-1869; 3 volumes.
Trial Dockets, 1807-1869; 5 volumes.

ELECTION RECORDS [*See also* **CRX RECORDS**]
Election Records, 1796-1944; 3 Fibredex boxes.
Elections, Record of, 1878-1932; 3 volumes.

ESTATES RECORDS [*See also* **CRX RECORDS**]
Accounts, Record of, 1869-1928; 7 volumes.
Administrators' Bonds, 1870-1930; 12 volumes.
Appointment of Administrators, Executors, Guardians, and Masters, 1868-1879; 1 volume.
Clerk's Receiver Accounts, 1902-1919; 1 volume.
Division of Estates, 1807-1868; 2 volumes.
Estates Records, 1753-1929; 166 Fibredex boxes.
Fiduciary Account Book (Estate of Daniel Cress), 1823; 1 volume.
Guardians' Accounts, 1849-1860; 1 volume.
Guardians' Bonds, 1870-1883, 1893-1952; 8 volumes.
Guardians' Records, 1769-1928; 10 Fibredex boxes.
Inventories and Accounts of Sale, 1849-1864; 4 volumes.
Probate (Estates), Record of, 1868-1896; 1 volume.
Settlements, Record of, 1849-1903; 7 volumes.

LAND RECORDS [*See also* **CRX RECORDS**]
Deeds, Index to, Grantee, 1753-1921; 4 volumes.
Deeds, Index to, Grantor, 1753-1921; 5 volumes.
Deeds and Land Records, 1753-1881; 1 Fibredex box.
Ejectments, 1791-1881; 1 Fibredex box.
Miscellaneous Land Records, 1753-1921; 1 Fibredex box.
Probate of Deeds and Mortgages, Record of, 1884-1885; 1 volume.
Processioners' Returns, 1803-1824, 1879-1893; 2 volumes.

MARRIAGE, DIVORCE, AND VITAL STATISTICS [*See also* **CRX RECORDS**]
Divorce Records, 1805-1900; 4 Fibredex boxes.
Marriage Bonds, 1758-1868; 23 Fibredex boxes.
Register of Marriage Bonds, 1758-1866; 1 volume.

MILITARY AND PENSION RECORDS [*See* **MISCELLANEOUS RECORDS; CRX RECORDS**]

MISCELLANEOUS RECORDS [*See also* **CRX RECORDS**]
Alien and Naturalization Records, 1823-1915; 1 Fibredex box.
Alien Registration, 1927, 1940; 1 volume.
Appointment of Road Overseers, Record of, 1824-1831; 1 volume.
Corporation Records, 1871-1903; 1 Fibredex box.
County Claims Allowed, 1805-1836; 1 volume.
County Trustees' Account Book, 1805-1826; 1 volume.
Farmers Educational and Co-operative Union of America, Minutes, 1915-1929; 1 volume.
Jurors, Record of, 1905-1914; 1 volume.
Jury Lists, 1779-1913; 1 Fibredex box.
Justices of the Peace, Records of, 1778-1924; 1 volume, 1 Fibredex box.
Military Records, 1781-1919; 2 Fibredex boxes.
Mining Records, 1833-1909; 2 Fibredex boxes.

Miscellaneous Records, 1740-1940; 4 Fibredex boxes.
Miscellaneous School Records, 1812-1906; 1 Fibredex box.
Orders and Decrees, 1896-1911; 1 volume.
Persons Convicted and Sentenced to Chain Gang and Jail, 1908-1909; 1 volume.
Petitions for Naturalization, 1910-1914; 1 volume.
Railroad Records, 1855-1915; 1 Fibredex box.
Road Records and Reports, 1757-1913; 2 Fibredex boxes.
School Census Records, 1848-1904; 3 Fibredex boxes.
Special Proceedings Docket, 1873-1909; 1 volume.
Treasurers' Account of General Fund, 1918-1920; 1 volume.
Treasurer's Account of Public School Fund, 1918-1919; 1 volume.
Treasurers' Account of Township Road Fund, 1919-1920; 1 volume.
Wardens of the Poor, 1771-1871; 1 Fibredex box.
Wardens of the Poor, Minutes, 1818-1865; 2 volumes.

OFFICIALS, COUNTY [*See* **MISCELLANEOUS RECORDS; CRX RECORDS**]

ROADS AND BRIDGES [*See* **MISCELLANEOUS RECORDS; CRX RECORDS**]

SCHOOL RECORDS [*See* **MISCELLANEOUS RECORDS; CRX RECORDS**]

TAX AND FISCAL RECORDS [*See also* **CRX RECORDS**]
Lists of Taxables, 1802-1849; 4 volumes.
Tax Records, 1758-1910; 5 Fibredex boxes.

WILLS [*See also* **CRX RECORDS**]
Wills, 1743-1971; 111 Fibredex boxes.
Wills, Cross Index to, 1761-1953; 3 volumes.

CRX RECORDS
Accounts, 1822-1824; 2 folders.
Apprentice Bonds and Records, 1784-1888; 1 Fibredex box.
Bastardy Records, 1808-1888; 1 Fibredex box, 5 folders.
Bridge Bond, 1855; 1 folder.
Civil Action Papers, 1753-1907; 12 Fibredex boxes, 8 folders.
County Accounts, 1783-1881; 1 Fibredex box.
Criminal Action Papers, 1771-1909; 9 Fibredex boxes, 2 folders.
Election Records, 1806-1934; 5 Fibredex boxes, 2 folders.
Estates Records, 1760-1893; 10 Fibredex boxes, 7 folders.
Guardians' Records, 1784-1880; 2 Fibredex boxes, 1 folder.
Insolvent Debtors, 1830-1875; 1 Fibredex box.
Land Records, 1765-1909; 2 Fibredex boxes, 11 folders.
Marriage Records, 1800, 1855; 1 folder.
Military Records, 1862-1865; 2 folders.
Miscellaneous Records, 1763-1940; 4 Fibredex boxes, 25 folders.
Officials' Bonds and Records, 1787-1855; 1 Fibredex box.
Receivers' Records, 1841-1907; 5 Fibredex boxes.
Road Records, 1784-1891; 1 Fibredex box, 3 folders.
School Records, 1847-1907; 10 Fibredex boxes.
Slave Records, 1779-1866; 1 Fibredex box, 1 folder.
State Census, 1787; 1 folder.
Tax Records, 1758-1894; 1 Fibredex box, 34 folders.
Wills, 1785, 1820; 2 folders.

MICROFILM RECORDS

BONDS

Commissioners' Bonds, 1937-1944; 1 reel.

CENSUS RECORDS (County Copy)

Census, 1860; 1 reel.

CORPORATIONS AND PARTNERSHIPS

Corporations, Index to, 1960-1962; 1 reel.
Corporations, Record of, 1904-1959; 3 reels.
Partnership Records, 1923-1973; 1 reel.

COURT RECORDS

County Court of Pleas and Quarter Sessions
- Abstracts of Minutes, 1753-1795; 1 reel.
- Abstracts of Minutes, Index to, 1753-1795; 1 reel.
- Minutes, 1753-1868; 7 reels.
- Minutes, Probate Court, 1819-1822; 1 reel.

Superior Court
- Clerk's Receipt Book, 1823-1861; 1 reel.
- Criminal Actions, Index to, 1923-1970; 1 reel.
- Equity Minutes, 1815-1820; 1 reel.
- Judgments, Index to, 1862-1937; 3 reels.
- Judgments, Index to, Defendant, 1938-1970; 2 reels.
- Judgments, Index to, Plaintiff, 1938-1970; 2 reels.
- Minutes, 1820-1871, 1904-1942; 10 reels.

ELECTION RECORDS

Elections, Record of, 1880-1948; 2 reels.

ESTATES RECORDS

Accounts, Record of, 1908-1959; 9 reels.
Administrators' Bonds, 1823-1830, 1903-1959; 3 reels.
Administrators, Record of, 1879-1959; 7 reels.
Appointment of Administrators, Executors, and Guardians, 1879; 1 reel.
Appointment of Administrators, and Guardians, 1889-1909; 1 reel.
Division of Estates, 1807-1868. [*See* **LAND RECORDS**, Processioners' Returns, 1803-1824]
Estates, Index to, 1952-1962; 1 reel.
Executors, Record of, 1926-1934; 1 reel.
Guardians' Bonds, 1764-1830, 1911-1918; 5 reels.
Guardians, Record of, 1909-1959; 4 reels.
Qualification of Trustees under Wills, Record of, 1933-1956; 1 reel.
Settlements, Record of, 1902-1959; 10 reels.

LAND RECORDS

Deeds, Record of, 1753-1962; 207 reels.
Federal Tax Lien Index, 1925-1962; 1 reel.
Land Entries, 1778-1925; 1 reel.
Processioners' Returns, 1803-1824; Division of Estates, 1807-1868; 1 reel.
Real Estate Conveyances, Index to, Grantee, 1753-1962; 18 reels.
Real Estate Conveyances, Index to, Grantor, 1753-1962; 18 reels.
Sales by Mortgagees, Trustees, and Executors, Record of, 1915-1959; 3 reels.

Marriage, Divorce, and Vital Statistics

Births, Index to, 1913-1972; 3 reels.
Cohabitation, Record of, 1866; 1 reel.
Deaths, Index to, 1913-1972; 2 reels.
Maiden Names of Divorced Women, 1937-1963; 1 reel.
Marriage Bond Abstracts, 1753-1868; 2 reels.
Marriage Bonds, 1753-1868; 6 reels.
Marriage Records, 1759-1867; 2 reels.
Marriage Registers, 1895-1962; 2 reels.

Military and Pension Records

Roster of Soldiers in the War of 1812, Index to, no date; 1 reel.

Miscellaneous Records

Alien Registration, 1927-1940; 1 reel.
Lunacy, Record of, 1957-1970; 1 reel.
Miscellaneous Historical Records, various dates; 1 reel.
Orders and Decrees, 1911-1959; 3 reels.
Special Proceedings, 1879-1906, 1911-1959; 17 reels.
Special Proceedings, Index to, Defendant, 1938-1970; 1 reel.
Special Proceedings, Index to, Plaintiff, 1938-1970; 1 reel.
Wardens of the Poor, 1818-1865, 1878-1908; 1 reel.

Officials, County

Board of County Commissioners, Minutes, 1872-1958; 5 reels.

Roads and Bridges

Road Overseers, Record of, 1824-1831; 1 reel.

School Records

Board of Superintendents of Common Schools, Minutes, 1847-1865; 1 reel.
County Board of Education, Minutes, 1877-1962; 2 reels.

Tax and Fiscal Records

Land Valuation, 1868; 1 reel.
Tax Lists, 1802-1895; 4 reels.
Tax Scrolls, 1874-1892; 3 reels.
Taxes Levied to Defray Convention Expense, 1868; 1 reel.

Wills

Wills, Cross Index to, 1761-1959; 1 reel.
Wills, Record of, 1762-1959; 8 reels.

RUTHERFORD COUNTY

Established in 1779 from Tryon County.
Courthouse fire of 1907 destroyed many court records.

ORIGINAL RECORDS

BONDS

Apprentice Bonds, 1872-1919; 2 volumes.
Bastardy Bonds, 1872-1878; 1 volume.
Officials' Bonds, 1880-1920; 1 Fibredex box.

COURT RECORDS

County Court of Pleas and Quarter Sessions

- Appearance Dockets, 1786-1792, 1843-1868; 1 volume, 1 manuscript box.
- Execution Dockets, 1796-1868; 8 volumes.
- Levy Docket, 1844-1862; 1 volume.
- Minutes, 1779-1868; 18 volumes, 1 manuscript box.
- State Dockets, 1783-1793, 1800-1868; 4 volumes, 1 manuscript box.
- Trial and Appearance Dockets, 1792-1843; 6 volumes, 2 manuscript boxes.
- Trial Dockets, 1785-1792, 1843-1868; 3 volumes, 2 manuscript boxes.

Superior Court

- Appearance Docket, 1855-1870; 1 volume.
- Civil Action Papers, 1783-1940; 23 Fibredex boxes.
- Civil Action Papers Concerning Land, 1870-1938; 20 Fibredex boxes.
- Civil Action Papers Concerning Mines, 1894-1917; 2 Fibredex boxes.
- Criminal Action Papers, 1868-1946; 8 Fibredex boxes.
- Equity Execution Docket, 1843-1868; 1 volume.
- Equity Minutes (Orders and Decrees), 1839-1868; 1 volume.
- Equity Trial and Appearance Docket, 1839-1868; 1 volume.
- Execution Dockets, 1843-1860; 2 volumes.
- Minutes, 1807-1911; 12 volumes.
- State Dockets, 1808-1821, 1831-1868; 4 volumes.
- Trial and Appearance Dockets, 1807-1859; 7 volumes.
- Trial Docket, 1860-1868; 1 volume.

ELECTION RECORDS [*See also* **CRX RECORDS**]

Elections, Record of, 1878-1917; 2 volumes.

ESTATES RECORDS

Administrators' Bonds, 1871-1896; 2 volumes.
Estates, Record of, 1831-1868; 6 volumes.
Estates Records, 1802-1968; 109 Fibredex boxes.
Guardians' Accounts, 1824-1868; 4 volumes.
Guardians' Bonds, 1872-1911; 3 volumes.
Guardians' Records, 1851-1968; 24 Fibredex boxes.

LAND RECORDS

Attachments, Executions, Liens, and Levies on Land, 1858-1940; 1 Fibredex box.
Deeds, 1794-1934; 3 Fibredex boxes.
Deeds, Index to, [1776-1853]; 1 volume.
Deeds, Record of, 1776-1810, 1817-1829; 20 volumes.
Land Entries, 1778-1898; 8 volumes. [*See also* **CRX RECORDS**]

Miscellaneous Land Records, 1768-1940; 2 Fibredex boxes.
Tax Levies on Land, 1896-1965; 6 Fibredex boxes.

MARRIAGE, DIVORCE, AND VITAL STATISTICS
Divorce Records, 1870-1940; 10 Fibredex boxes.
Marriage Bonds, 1774-1868; 11 Fibredex boxes.

MILITARY AND PENSION RECORDS [*See* **MISCELLANEOUS RECORDS**]

MISCELLANEOUS RECORDS
Alien Registration, 1940; 1 volume.
Assignees, Trustees, and Receivers, Records of, 1888-1956; 5 Fibredex boxes.
County Accounts, Claims, and Correspondence, 1814, 1901-1938; 1 Fibredex box.
Homestead and Personal Property Exemptions, 1869-1934; 1 Fibredex box.
Inmate Register, County Home, 1914-1961; 1 volume.
Military Records, 1854-1937; 1 Fibredex box.
Miscellaneous Records, 1784-1950; 4 Fibredex boxes.
Railroad Records, 1876-1930; 6 Fibredex boxes.
Road Dockets, 1803-1868; 3 volumes.
School Records, 1880-1948; 1 Fibredex box.

ROADS AND BRIDGES [*See* **MISCELLANEOUS RECORDS**]

SCHOOL RECORDS [*See* **MISCELLANEOUS RECORDS**]

WILLS
Wills, 1784-1968; 41 Fibredex boxes.

CRX RECORDS
Land Entry Book, 1898-1949; 1 volume.
Voter Registration Books, 1930-1940; 4 volumes in 1 manuscript box.

MICROFILM RECORDS

BONDS
Apprentice Bonds, 1872-1919; 1 reel.
Bastardy Bonds, 1872-1878; 1 reel.

CORPORATIONS AND PARTNERSHIPS
Assumed Business Names, 1960-1977; 1 reel.
Corporations, Record of, 1887-1944; 1 reel.
Partnership Records, 1908-1977; 2 reels.

COURT RECORDS
County Court of Pleas and Quarter Sessions
Minutes, 1779-1868; 5 reels.
Superior Court
Equity Minutes, 1839-1868; 1 reel.
Minutes, 1807-1939; 11 reels.
Minutes, Civil, 1939-1964; 3 reels.
Minutes, Criminal, 1939-1964; General Index to Criminal Minutes, 1939-1964; 2 reels.

ELECTION RECORDS
Elections, Record of, 1878-1964; 1 reel.

ESTATES RECORDS
Accounts, Record of, 1868-1964; 7 reels.
Administrators' Bonds, 1871-1896; 1 reel.
Administrators, Record of, 1896-1963; 5 reels.
Appointment of Executors, 1868-1964; 1 reel.
Appointment of Receivers, Trustees, and Executors, Record of, 1922-1934; 1 reel.
Estates, Record of, 1831-1868; 2 reels.
Final Accounts, Index to, 1835-1964; 1 reel.
Guardians' Accounts, 1824-1868; 1 reel.
Guardians' Bonds, 1872-1911; 1 reel.
Guardians, Record of, 1911-1964; 2 reels.
Inheritance Tax Records, 1922-1964; 1 reel.
Settlements, Record of, 1868-1964; 5 reels.
Widows' Year's Allowance, Record of, 1884-1964; 1 reel.

LAND RECORDS
Deeds, Record of, 1779-1965; 104 reels.
Deeds of Trust, 1894-1910; 4 reels.
Federal Tax Lien Index, 1926-1949; 1 reel.
Land Entries, Record of, 1804-1949; 2 reels.
Real Estate Conveyances, Index to, Grantee, 1779-1965; 10 reels.
Real Estate Conveyances, Index to, Grantor, 1779-1965; 10 reels.
Sales by Mortgagees, Record of, 1921-1926; 1 reel.

MARRIAGE, DIVORCE, AND VITAL STATISTICS
Births, Index to, 1914-1976; 2 reels.
Deaths, Index to, 1914-1976; 1 reel.
Delayed Births, Index to, various years; 1 reel.
Maiden Names of Divorced Women, 1937-1964; 1 reel.
Marriage Bonds, 1779-1868; 7 reels.
Marriage Registers, 1851-1976; 3 reels.

MISCELLANEOUS RECORDS
Special Proceedings, 1868-1950; 10 reels.
Special Proceedings, Index to, 1968-1977; 1 reel.
Special Proceedings, Index to, Defendant, 1868-1964; 2 reels.
Special Proceedings, Index to, Plaintiff, 1868-1964; 2 reels.

OFFICIALS, COUNTY
Board of County Commissioners, Minutes, 1868-1944; 7 reels.

ROAD RECORDS
Road Overseers, 1803-1868; 1 reel.

SCHOOL RECORDS
County Board of Education, Minutes, 1880-1922; 1 reel.

WILLS
Wills, Cross Index to, 1782-1964; 1 reel.
Wills, Record of, 1782-1964; 6 reels.

SAMPSON COUNTY

Established in 1784 from Duplin County.
Early court records are missing; losses may have been caused by Federal sympathizers in 1865 and clerk's office fire of 1921.

ORIGINAL RECORDS

BONDS

Bastardy Bonds and Records, 1835-1924; 2 Fibredex boxes.

COURT RECORDS

County Court
- Criminal Minutes, 1957-1968; 5 volumes.

County Court of Pleas and Quarter Sessions
- Appearance Dockets, 1821-1842, 1853-1868; 4 volumes.
- Execution Dockets, 1800-1868; 4 volumes.
- Minutes, 1794-1868; 15 volumes.
- Recognizance Docket, 1800-1806. [*See* **CRX RECORDS**]
- State Dockets, 1806-1868; 7 volumes.
- Trial and Appearance Dockets, 1784-1791, 1808-1814; 2 volumes.
- Trial Dockets, 1820-1868; 7 volumes.

Inferior Court
- Minutes, 1881-1885; 1 volume.

Recorder's Court
- Minutes, 1952-1957; 2 volumes.

Superior Court
- Appearance Docket, 1858-1868; 1 volume.
- Civil Action Papers, 1790-1924; 20 Fibredex boxes.
- Civil Action Papers Concerning Land, 1791-1932; 13 Fibredex boxes.
- Civil Actions, Index to, [1868-1877]; 1 volume.
- Civil Issues Dockets, 1892-1925; 7 volumes.
- Civil Issues Docket, Cross Index to, n.d.; 1 volume.
- Clerk's Minute Docket, 1925-1931; 1 volume.
- Criminal Action Papers, 1823-1934; 26 Fibredex boxes.
- Criminal Issues Dockets, 1868-1968; 9 volumes.
- Equity Execution Dockets, 1823-1868; 2 volumes.
- Equity Minutes, 1807-1868; 2 volumes.
- Equity Trial Dockets, 1816-1862; 2 volumes.
- Execution Dockets, 1819-1832, 1858-1869; 2 volumes.
- Judgment Dockets, 1868-1946; 42 volumes.
- Judgments, Index to, [1868-1877]; 1 volume.
- Minutes, 1814-1968; 36 volumes.
- State Dockets, 1832-1868; 3 volumes.
- Trial and Appearance Docket, 1809-1831; 1 volume.
- Trial Dockets, 1845-1869; 2 volumes.

ELECTION RECORDS

Elections, Record of, 1878-1926; 3 volumes.
Permanent Voter Registration, 1902-1908; 1 volume.

ESTATES RECORDS

Accounts, Record of, 1868-1968; 24 volumes.
Administrators' Bonds, 1854-1908; 4 volumes.
Amounts Paid for Indigent Children, Record of, 1930, 1937; 1 volume.
Estates, Record of, 1830-1849, 1855-1868; 8 volumes.
Estates Records, 1784-1923; 74 Fibredex boxes.
Inheritance Tax Records, 1924-1969; 5 volumes.
Guardians' Bonds, 1854-1914; 3 volumes.
Guardians, Record of, 1914-1968; 5 volumes.
Guardians' Records, 1803-1918, 1929; 6 Fibredex boxes.
Settlements, Record of, 1869-1934, 1940-1946; 7 volumes.

LAND RECORDS

Attachments, Executions, Liens, and Levies on Land, 1825-1920; 3 Fibredex boxes.
Land Divisions, 1811-1927; 1 volume.
Miscellaneous Land Records, 1810-1928; 1 Fibredex box.
Surveys, Record of, 1895-1911; 1 volume.

MARRIAGE, DIVORCE, AND VITAL STATISTICS

Cohabitation, Record of. [*See* **CRX RECORDS**]
Divorce Records, 1869-1921; 4 Fibredex boxes.
Maiden Names of Divorced Women, 1939-1971; 1 volume.

MISCELLANEOUS RECORDS

Alien Registration, 1927, 1940; 1 volume.
Appointment of Road Overseers, Record of, 1829-1868; 3 volumes.
Assignees, Trustees, and Receivers, Records of, 1856-1927; 5 Fibredex boxes.
County Claims Allowed, 1828-1852; 1 volume.
Homestead and Personal Property Exemptions, 1869-1923; 2 Fibredex boxes.
Inquisition of Inebriates, 1940-1963; 2 volumes.
Lunacy, Record of, 1900-1968; 5 volumes.
Miscellaneous Records, 1798-1928; 4 Fibredex boxes. [*See also* **CRX RECORDS**]
Petitions for Naturalization, 1911-1914; 1 volume.
Railroad Records, 1869-1921; 4 Fibredex boxes.
Special Proceedings, 1867-1906; 23 Fibredex boxes.
Wardens of the Poor, Minutes, 1785-1824; 1 volume.

ROADS AND BRIDGES [*See* **MISCELLANEOUS RECORDS**]

TAX AND FISCAL RECORDS

Miscellaneous Tax Records, 1789-1922; 1 Fibredex box.

WILLS

Wills, 1778-1953; 20 Fibredex boxes. [*See also* **CRX RECORDS**]

CRX RECORDS

Cohabitation, Record of, 1866; 1 volume.
Miscellaneous Records, 1799-1837; 2 folders.
Recognizance Docket, Court of Pleas and Quarter Sessions, 1800-1806; 1 volume.
Wills, 1812, 1852; 2 folders.

MICROFILM RECORDS

COURT RECORDS

County Court of Pleas and Quarter Sessions
    Minutes, 1794-1868; 5 reels.
Superior Court
    Judgments, Index to, Defendant, 1909-1968; 3 reels.
    Judgments, Index to, Plaintiff, 1909-1968; 3 reels.
    Minutes, 1814-1944; 12 reels.

ELECTION RECORDS

Elections, Record of, 1920-1964; 1 reel.

ESTATES RECORDS

Accounts, Record of, 1868-1958; 10 reels.
Administrators' Bonds, 1908-1950; 5 reels.
Amounts Paid for Indigent Children, 1930, 1937; 1 reel.
Annual and Final Accounts, Index to, 1924-1937; 1 reel.
Divisions and Sales of Estates, Cross Index to, 1848-1927; 1 reel.
Estates, Guardians, Administrators, and Executors, Index to, 1925-1965; 1 reel.
Estates, Index to, various dates; 1 reel.
Estates, Record of, 1830-1849, 1855-1868; 3 reels.
Guardians' Bonds, 1907-1965; 3 reels.
Guardians, Cross Index to, 1854-1965; 1 reel.
Inheritance Tax Records, 1924-1965; 1 reel.
Settlements, Record of, 1869-1961; 7 reels.

LAND RECORDS

Deeds, Record of, 1752-1958; 302 reels.
Land Divisions, 1811-1927; 1 reel.
Land Grants, 1770-1814; 2 reels.
Land Grants and Entries, 1789-1874; 1 reel.
Real Estate Conveyances, Cross Index to, 1754-1940; 15 reels.
Real Estate Conveyances, Index to, Grantee, 1941-1965; 7 reels.
Real Estate Conveyances, Index to, Grantee: Trustees, 1962-1965; 1 reel.
Real Estate Conveyances, Index to, Grantor, 1941-1965; 7 reels.
Resale, Record of, 1922-1957; 5 reels.
Surveys, Record of, 1895-1911; 1 reel.

MARRIAGE, DIVORCE, AND VITAL STATISTICS

Births, Index to, 1913-1964; 2 reels.
Deaths, Index to, 1913-1964; 1 reel.
Delayed Births, Index to, various years; 1 reel.
Maiden Names of Divorced Women, 1939-1964; 1 reel.
Marriage Registers, 1867-1968; 2 reels..

MISCELLANEOUS RECORDS

Miscellaneous Orders and Decrees, and Appointment of Notaries Public and Railroad Policemen, 1913-1961; 1 reel.
Orders and Decrees, 1867-1956; 18 reels.
Special Proceedings, 1868-1950; 2 reels.
Special Proceedings, Index to, Defendant, 1867-1965; 1 reel.

Special Proceedings, Index to, Plaintiff, 1867-1965; 1 reel.
Wardens of the Poor, Minutes, 1785-1824; 1 reel.

OFFICIALS, COUNTY

Board of County Commissioners, Minutes, 1868-1943; 5 reels.

SCHOOL RECORDS

County Board of Education, Minutes, 1895-1965; 1 reel.

TAX AND FISCAL RECORDS

Tax Lists, 1877-1893; 3 reels.

WILLS

Wills, Index to, 1820-1965; 2 reels.
Wills Not Probated, Record of, 1782-1964; 1 reel.
Wills, Record of, 1821-1965; 8 reels.

SCOTLAND COUNTY

Established in 1899 from Richmond County.

ORIGINAL RECORDS

COURT RECORDS

Superior Court

- Civil Action Papers, 1887-1955; 29 Fibredex boxes.
- Civil Action Papers Concerning Land, 1893-1951; 12 Fibredex boxes.
- Criminal Action Papers, 1891-1952; 9 Fibredex boxes.
- Criminal Judgment Docket, 1912-1913; 1 volume.
- Judgment Dockets, 1902-1966; 27 volumes. [*See also* **LAND RECORDS**]
- Minutes, 1959-1966; 3 volumes.

ELECTION RECORDS

Election Book (Abstract of Votes), 1904-1924; 1 volume.
Elections, Record of, 1940-1956; 1 volume.

ESTATES RECORDS

Accounts of Indigent Orphans, 1913-1942; 1 volume.
Accounts, Record of, 1901-1966; 7 volumes.
Administrators, Executors, and Guardians, Record of, 1913-1935; 2 volumes.
Administrators, Record of, 1930-1966; 4 volumes.
Appointment of Guardians and Administrators, Record of, 1901-1912; 1 volume.
Estates Records, 1887-1951; 44 Fibredex boxes.
Executors and Guardians, Record of, 1935-1953; 1 volume.
Executors, Guardians, and Trustees, Record of, 1953-1965; 1 volume.
Executors, Record of, 1964-1966; 1 volume.
Guardians' Records, 1901-1951; 10 Fibredex boxes.
Guardians and Trustees, Record of, 1965-1966; 1 volume.
Inheritance Tax Records, 1923-1966; 2 volumes.
Probate, Record of, 1926; 1 volume.
Receivers, Record of, 1928-1930, 1934; 1 volume.
Settlements, Record of, 1901-1966; 10 volumes.

LAND RECORDS

Deeds, 1903-1940; 1 Fibredex box.
Federal Tax Lien Index, 1924-1962; 1 volume.
Judgment Docket, Land Tax Sales, 1930-1943; 1 volume. [*See also* **COURT RECORDS**, Superior Court]
Land Sales for Taxes, 1923-1949; 2 Fibredex boxes.
Miscellaneous Land Records, 1901-1955; 1 Fibredex box.
Petitions for Partition of Land, 1906-1943; 2 Fibredex boxes.
Petitions for Sale of Land, 1901-1948; 1 Fibredex box.
Sale of Land by Trustee and Mortgagee, Record of, 1916-1967; 2 volumes.

MARRIAGE, DIVORCE, AND VITAL STATISTICS

Divorce Records, 1901-1948; 11 Fibredex boxes.
Maiden Names of Divorced Women, 1939-1966; 1 volume.
Marriage and Family Records, 1901-1951; 1 Fibredex box.

MISCELLANEOUS RECORDS

Alien Registration, 1927-1938; 1 volume.
Assignees, Receivers, and Trustees, Records of, 1901-1951; 5 Fibredex boxes.
Assignments, Record of, 1904-1918; 1 volume.
Coroners' Inquests, 1902-1946; 5 Fibredex boxes.
Miscellaneous Records, 1901-1955; 2 Fibredex boxes.
Officials' Oaths, Record of, 1934-1965; 1 volume.
Orders and Decrees, 1901-1966; 19 volumes.
Petitions for Naturalization, 1911-1912; 1 volume.
Railroad Records, 1901-1939; 4 Fibredex boxes.
Special Proceedings, 1900-1968; 3 volumes.

ROADS AND BRIDGES [*See* **MISCELLANEOUS RECORDS**]

WILLS

Wills, 1893, 1896, 1900-1937; 6 Fibredex boxes.

MICROFILM RECORDS

COURT RECORDS

Superior Court
  Minutes, 1901-1959; 4 reels.

ELECTION RECORDS

Elections, Record of, 1904-1968; 1 reel.

ESTATES RECORDS

Accounts for Indigent Orphans, Record of, 1913-1941; 1 reel.
Accounts, Record of, 1901-1966; 4 reels.
Administrators, Executors, and Guardians, Record of, 1913-1935; 1 reel.
Administrators, Record of, 1930-1966; 4 reels.
Appointment of Administrators and Guardians, 1901-1913; 1 reel.
Estates, Index to, 1966-1970; 1 reel.
Executors and Guardians, Record of, 1935-1965; 1 reel.
Executors, Record of, 1963-1966; 1 reel.
Guardians and Trustees, Record of, 1965-1966; 1 reel.
Inheritance Tax Records, 1920-1966; 2 reels.
Orphans' Trust Fund, 1943-1965; 1 reel.
Receivers of Estates, Record of, 1928-1930, 1934; 1 reel.
Settlements, Record of, 1901-1966; 5 reels.

LAND RECORDS

Deeds and Mortgages, Index to, Grantee, 1900-1970; 3 reels.
Deeds and Mortgages, Index to, Grantor, 1900-1970; 5 reels.
Deeds, Record of, 1900-1962; 32 reels.
Grants, Index to, 1900-1950; 1 reel.
Grants, Record of, 1900-1950; 1 reel.
Land Entry Books, 1900-1955; 1 reel.
Resale of Land by Trustees and Mortgagees, Record of, 1916-1967; 1 reel.

MARRIAGE, DIVORCE, AND VITAL STATISTICS

Delayed Births, Index to, various years; 1 reel.
Maiden Names of Divorced Women, 1939-1966; 1 reel.

Marriage Licenses, 1900-1970; 4 reels.
Marriage Registers, 1900-1970; 1 reel.
Miscellaneous and Foreign Marriage and Birth Records, various dates; 1 reel.
Vital Statistics, Index to, 1913-1970; 3 reels.

MISCELLANEOUS RECORDS

Assignments, Record of, 1904-1918; 1 reel.
Clerk's Minute Dockets, 1907-1931; 1 reel.
Funeral Register, 1904-1914; 1 reel.
Orders and Decrees, 1901-1966; 10 reels.
Special Proceedings, 1900-1966; 2 reels.
Special Proceedings, Index to, 1900-1970; 1 reel.

OFFICIALS, COUNTY [*See also* **ROADS AND BRIDGES**]

Board of County Commissioners, Minutes, 1900-1970; 4 reels.

ROADS AND BRIDGES

County Board of Public Roads, Minutes, 1904-1905; 1 reel.

TAX AND FISCAL RECORDS

Tax Scrolls, 1905, 1915, 1925, 1935, 1945, 1955, 1965; 2 reels.

WILLS

Wills, Index to, 1899-1966; 1 reel.
Wills, Record of, 1898-1966; 3 reels.

STANLY COUNTY

Established in 1841 from Montgomery County.
A few early court records are missing; reason unknown.

ORIGINAL RECORDS

Bonds

Apprentice Bonds, 1872-1938; 2 volumes.
Bastardy Bonds and Records, 1843-1923; 1 volume, 1 Fibredex box.
Officials' Bonds, 1848-1918; 2 volumes, 2 Fibredex boxes.

Court Records

County Court of Pleas and Quarter Sessions
- Appearance Docket, 1862-1868; 1 volume.
- Appearance (and Trial) Docket, 1841-1861; 1 volume.
- Execution Dockets, 1841-1868; 4 volumes.
- Minutes, 1841-1868; 5 volumes.
- Trial Dockets, 1846-1868; 3 volumes.

Recorder's Court
- Minutes, 1915-1925; 1 volume.

Superior Court
- Appearance Dockets, 1841-1883; 2 volumes.
- Civil Action Papers, 1842-1917; 12 Fibredex boxes.
- Civil Action Papers Concerning Land, 1845-1941; 5 Fibredex boxes.
- Civil Issues Dockets, 1870-1968; 5 volumes.
- Criminal Action Papers, 1841-1925; 18 Fibredex boxes.
- Criminal Cost Dockets, 1875-1907; 2 volumes.
- Criminal Issues Dockets, 1869-1894, 1899-1930; 3 volumes.
- Equity Execution Docket, 1849-1869; 1 volume.
- Equity Minutes, 1841-1868; 1 volume.
- Equity Trial and Appearance Docket, 1841-1868; 1 volume.
- Execution Docket, 1842-1854; 1 volume.
- Judgment Dockets, 1867-1949; 7 volumes. [*See also* **Land Records**, Tax Suit Judgment Dockets]
- Judgments, Index to, 1867-1877; 1 volume.
- Minutes, 1841-1968; 32 volumes.
- State Docket, 1856-1868; 1 volume.
- Trial Docket, 1868-1869; 1 volume.

Election Records

Elections, Record of, 1878-1922; 4 volumes.
Permanent Registration of Voters, 1902-1908; 1 volume.

Estates Records

Accounts, Record of, 1868-1968; 18 volumes.
Administrators' Bonds, 1870-1917; 4 volumes.
Administrators, Executors, and Guardians, Cross Index to, 1868-1903; 1 volume.
Administrators, Record of, 1899-1916; 1 volume.
Appointment of Administrators, Executors, and Guardians, 1868-1903; 1 volume.

Clerk's Receipt Books (Estates), Record of, 1905-1935; 2 volumes.
Clerk's Receiver Accounts, 1908-1927; 1 volume.
Estates, Record of, 1842-1869; 2 volumes.
Estates Records, 1820, 1839-1952; 49 Fibredex boxes.
Guardians' Accounts and Returns, 1841-1870; 1 volume.
Guardians' Bonds, 1887-1923; 3 volumes.
Guardians, Record of, 1924-1936; 1 volume.
Guardians' Records, 1841-1941; 6 Fibredex boxes.
Guardians of World War Veterans, 1930-1938; 1 volume.
Settlements, Record of, 1868-1928; 4 volumes.

LAND RECORDS [*See also* **COURT RECORDS**, Superior Court]
Attachments, Executions, Liens, and Levies on Land, 1841-1927; 2 Fibredex boxes.
Deeds, 1857-1968; 6 Fibredex boxes.
Deeds, Index to, [1841-1877]; 1 volume.
Deeds, Record of, 1841-1847, 1854-1870; 3 volumes.
Ejectments, 1840-1866; 1 Fibredex box.
Land Entry Book, 1841-1932; 1 volume.
Land Sold for Taxes, Record of, 1936-1943; 2 volumes.
Miscellaneous Land Records, 1844-1963; 1 Fibredex box.
Sales of Land, Record of, 1875-1899; 1 volume.
Tax Suit Judgment Docket, 1958-1959; 1 volume. [*See also* **COURT RECORDS**, Superior Court, Judgment Dockets]

MARRIAGE, DIVORCE, AND VITAL STATISTICS
Divorce Records, 1854-1920; 2 Fibredex boxes.
Maiden Names of Divorced Women, 1946-1968; 1 volume.
Marriage Licenses Issued, Record of, 1859-1905; 2 volumes.
Marriages, Record of, 1850-1867; 1 volume.

MILITARY AND PENSION RECORDS [*See* **ESTATES RECORDS**]

MISCELLANEOUS RECORDS
Alien Registration, 1927, 1959; 2 volumes.
Appointment of Road Overseers, Record of, 1841-1860; 1 volume.
Assignees, Trustees, and Receivers, Records of, 1855-1913; 1 Fibredex box.
Clerk's Minute Dockets (Special Proceedings), 1869-1905; 2 volumes.
Common School Registers, 1858-1863; 2 volumes.
County Accounts, 1841-1882; 1 volume.
County Claims Allowed, 1842-1861; 1 volume.
County School Account Book, 1894-1905; 1 volume.
Ledger, Bank of Oakboro, Oakboro, 1931-1935; 1 volume.
Ledger, Peoples Bank & Trust, Richfield, 1911-1917; 1 volume.
Licenses to Trades, Registry of, 1874-1904; 1 volume.
Loyalty Oaths, 1865; 2 volumes.
Lunacy, Record of, 1899-1968; 4 volumes.
Magistrates, Record of, 1896-1936; 1 volume.
Miscellaneous Records, 1841-1965; 4 Fibredex boxes.
Orders and Decrees, 1868-1887; 1 volume.
Petitions for Naturalization, 1921-1928; 1 volume.
Railroad Records, 1891-1917; 2 Fibredex boxes.
Report of the County Superintendent of Public Instruction, 1882-1891; 1 volume.

Road Records, 1842-1921; 1 Fibredex box.
School Fund Ledgers, 1910-1920; 3 volumes.
Slaves and Free Persons of Color, Records of, 183_, 1843-1868; 1 Fibredex box.
Wardens of the Poor, Minutes, 1849-1873; 2 volumes.

ROADS AND BRIDGES [*See* **MISCELLANEOUS RECORDS**]

SCHOOL RECORDS [*See* **MISCELLANEOUS RECORDS**]

TAX AND FISCAL RECORDS
Lists of Taxables, 1840-1869; 3 volumes.
Miscellaneous Tax Records, 1857-1912; 1 Fibredex box.
Poll Tax Record, 1912-1918; 1 volume.

WILLS
Wills, 1839-1927; 3 Fibredex boxes.

MICROFILM RECORDS

BONDS
Apprentice Bonds, 1872-1938; 1 reel.

CORPORATIONS AND PARTNERSHIPS
Corporations, Record of, 1906-1948; 1 reel.

COURT RECORDS
County Court of Pleas and Quarter Sessions
Minutes, 1841-1868; 2 reels.
Superior Court
Equity Minutes, 1841-1868; 1 reel.
Judgments, Index to, Defendant, 1920-1968; 2 reels.
Judgments, Index to, Plaintiff, 1920-1968; 2 reels.
Minutes, 1841-1955; 12 reels.

ELECTION RECORDS
Elections, Record of, 1878-1922, 1928-1964; 2 reels.

ESTATES RECORDS
Accounts of Receivers of Estates, 1910-1927; 1 reel.
Accounts, Record of, 1868-1968; 9 reels.
Administrators' Bonds, 1870-1917; 1 reel.
Administrators and Executors, Cross Index to, 1868-1903; 1 reel.
Administrators, Executors, and Guardians, Index to, 1915-1968; 1 reel.
Administrators, Record of, 1899-1968; 6 reels.
Appointment of Administrators, Executors, and Guardians, 1914-1920; 1 reel.
Clerk's Record of Monies Received for Payment to Minors, 1905-1921; 1 reel.
Estates, Record of, 1841-1869; 1 reel.
Executors, Record of, 1931-1967; 1 reel.
Guardians' Accounts and Returns, 1841-1870; 1 reel.
Guardians' Bonds, 1887-1912; 1 reel.
Guardians' Oaths and Bonds, Record of, 1930-1938, 1967-1968; 1 reel.
Guardians, Record of, 1924-1967; 2 reels.
Inheritance Tax Records, 1923-1947; 1 reel.
Settlements, Record of, 1841-1967; 10 reels.

Land Records
Deeds, Index to, Grantee, 1841-1955; 7 reels.
Deeds, Index to, Grantor, 1841-1955; 6 reels.
Deeds, Record of, 1841-1955; 89 reels.
Land Entry Books, 1841-1939; 1 reel.
Resale of Land by Trustees and Mortgagees, Record of, 1920-1967; 2 reels.

Marriage, Divorce, and Vital Statistics
Births and Delayed Births, Index to, 1913-1993; 3 reels.
Deaths, Index to, 1913-1993; 2 reels.
Maiden Names of Divorced Women, 1945-1968; 1 reel.
Marriage Licenses, 1867-1967; 24 reels.
Marriage Registers, 1867-1968; 3 reels.
Marriages Performed by Ministers and Justices of the Peace, Record of, 1850-1867; 1 reel.

Miscellaneous Records
Orders and Decrees, 1868-1950; 9 reels.
Special Proceedings, 1899-1961; 2 reels.
Special Proceedings, Index to, Defendant, 1840-1967; 1 reel.
Special Proceedings, Index to, Plaintiff, 1840-1967; 1 reel.

Officials, County
Board of County Commissioners, Minutes, 1868-1933; 3 reels.

Roads and Bridges
Road Overseers, 1841-1860; 1 reel.

School Records
County Board of Education, Minutes, 1885-1961; 1 reel.

Tax and Fiscal Records
Tax Lists, 1841-1869; 1 reel.
Tax Scrolls, 1872-1900, 1905, 1915; 6 reels.

Wills
Wills, Cross Index to, 1841-1967; 1 reel.
Wills, Record of, 1841-1968; 5 reels.

STOKES COUNTY

Established in 1789 from Surry County.
A few court records are missing; reason unknown.

ORIGINAL RECORDS

BONDS

Apprentice Bonds and Records, 1790-1909; 5 Fibredex boxes. [*See also* **CRX RECORDS**]
Apprentices and Masters, Record of, 1790-1817; 1 volume.
Bastardy Bonds and Records, 1790-1932; 6 Fibredex boxes.
Officials' Bonds and Records, 1790-1932; 8 Fibredex boxes.
Tavern Bonds, 1795-1818; 1 Fibredex box.

COURT RECORDS

County Court of Pleas and Quarter Sessions
- Appearance Dockets, 1804-1868; 8 volumes.
- Clerk's Fee Docket, 1790-1811; 1 volume.
- Clerk's Receipt Book, 1859-1861; 1 volume.
- Execution Dockets, 1790-1858; 18 volumes.
- Minutes, 1790-1843, 1847-1868; 19 volumes.
- Recognizance Dockets, 1824-1867; 5 volumes.
- State Dockets, 1790-1868; 12 volumes.
- Trial, Appearance, and Reference Dockets, 1790-1804; 2 volumes, 1 manuscript box.
- Trial Dockets, 1848-1868; 2 volumes.
- Trial and Reference Dockets, 1804-1847; 9 volumes.

General County Court
- Minutes, 1953-1970; 7 volumes.

Inferior Court
- Minutes, 1878-1885; 1 volume.

Superior Court
- Appearance Dockets, 1807-1834, 1855-1868; 2 volumes.
- Civil Action Papers, 1782-1942; 69 Fibredex boxes. [*See also* **FORSYTH COUNTY, MISCELLANEOUS RECORDS**]
- Civil Action Papers Concerning Land, 1791-1942; 16 Fibredex boxes.
- Civil Issues Dockets, 1868-1970; 6 volumes.
- Clerk's Account Book, 1905-1918; 1 volume.
- Clerk's Fee and Receipt Book, 1808-1828; 1 volume.
- Criminal Action Papers, 1790-1944; 17 Fibredex boxes.
- Equity Fee and Receipt Book, 1857-1871; 1 volume.
- Equity Minutes, 1849-1868; 1 volume.
- Equity Trial and Appearance Docket, 1849-1868; 1 volume.
- Execution Dockets, 1815-1869, 1888-1899; 4 volumes, 1 manuscript box.
- Judgment Dockets, 1889-1950; 7 volumes. [*See also* **LAND RECORDS**, Tax Suit Judgment Dockets]
- Minutes, 1807-1846, 1878-1970; 16 volumes.
- Recognizance Dockets, 1816-1858; 4 volumes.
- State Dockets, 1807-1815, 1835-1869; 3 volumes, 1 manuscript box.
- Summons Dockets, 1869-1970; 4 volumes.
- Trial and Reference Dockets, 1807-1857; 5 volumes.

Election Records

Election Records, 1790-1932; 7 Fibredex boxes.

Estates Records [*See also* **FORSYTH COUNTY, Miscellaneous Records**]

Administrators' Bonds, 1886-1908; 2 volumes.
Administrators, Record of, 1790-1817; 1 volume.
Clerk's Receipt Book (Estates), 1886-1902; 1 volume.
Estates, Record of, 1790-1849, 1861-1869; 15 volumes.
Estates Records, 1753-1941; 118 Fibredex boxes. [*See also* **CRX Records**]
Guardians' Bonds, 1872-1894; 1 volume.
Guardians' Records, 1790-1933; 6 Fibredex boxes.
Inheritance Tax, Record of, 1920-1925, 1928-1982; 5 volumes.
Orphans' Docket, 1790-1821; 1 volume.
Settlements, Record of, 1869-1912; 2 volumes.

Land Records

Attachments, Executions, Levies, and Liens on Land, Personal Property, and Slaves, 1790-1934; 27 Fibredex boxes.
Clerk's Deed Book (Land Sold for Taxes), 1813-1816; 1 volume.
Deeds, 1760-1929; 1 Fibredex box.
Ejectments, 1791-1915, 1936; 3 Fibredex boxes.
Land Entries, 1790-1798, 1809-1926; 3 volumes.
Land Grants and Entries, 1779-1924; 1 Fibredex box.
Land Sold for Taxes, 1828, 1927-1941; 7 Fibredex boxes.
Miscellaneous Land Records, 1784-1932; 1 Fibredex box.
Petitions for Partition and to Sell Land, 1861, 1873-1911, 1935; 1 Fibredex box.
Probate, Record of, 1959-1970; 3 volumes.
Sales of Land under Deeds of Trust, 1916-1925; 1 volume.
Tax Suit Judgment Dockets, 1932-1935, 1939-1966; 2 volumes. [*See also* **Court Records**, Superior Court, Judgment Dockets]

Marriage, Divorce, and Vital Statistics

Cohabitation and Negro Marriages, Record of, 1866-1873; 1 volume.
Divorce Records, 1816-1941; 8 Fibredex boxes.
Maiden Names of Divorced Women, 1937-1974; 1 volume.
Marriage Bonds, 1790-1868; 13 Fibredex boxes.
Marriage Certificates, Record of, 1851-1873; 2 volumes.
Marriage Licenses, Index to, 1868-1869; 1 volume.
Marriage Registers, 1873-1909; 2 volumes.

Military and Pension Records [*See* **Miscellaneous Records**]

Miscellaneous Records

Appointment of Road Overseers, Record of, 1806-1867; 4 volumes.
Assignees, Receivers, and Trustees, Records of, 1896-1942; 3 Fibredex boxes.
Bills of Sale, Powers of Attorney, and Bonds, Record of, 1801-1841; 1 volume.
Board of County Commissioners, Minutes, 1871-1909; 4 volumes.
Board of Road Commissioners of Quaker Gap Township, Minutes, 1919-1921; 1 volume.
Coroners' Inquests, 1805-1916; 1 Fibredex box.
County Board of Education, Minutes and Accounts of School Fund, 1872-1903; 2 volumes.
County Claims, 1790-1868; 4 volumes, 7 Fibredex boxes.

County Claims Allowed, 1822-1844, 1866, 1910-1927; 3 volumes.
County Trustee Account Books, 1811-1868; 3 volumes.
Grand Jury Records and Presentments, 1790-1915; 1 Fibredex box.
Inquisition of Lunacy, 1899-1971; 4 volumes.
Insolvent Debtors and Homestead and Personal Property Exemptions, 1790-1931; 2 Fibredex boxes.
Jury Records, 1790-1868; 1 Fibredex box.
Lunacy, Record of, Index to, 1899-1971; 1 volume.
Lunacy Records, 1794-1931; 2 Fibredex boxes.
Marks, Brands, and Strays, 1789-1861; 1 volume, 1 Fibredex box.
Military and Pension Records, 1779-1913; 1 Fibredex box.
Miscellaneous Records, 1781-1932; 4 Fibredex boxes. [*See also* **CRX RECORDS**]
Personal Accounts, 1791-1864; 1 Fibredex box.
Railroad Records, 1887-1934; 1 Fibredex box.
Returns of Fees, Fines, and Forfeitures, 1810-1851, 1879-1927; 4 volumes.
Road and Bridge Records, 1790-1943; 1 volume, 10 Fibredex boxes.
School Records, 1840-1939; 6 Fibredex boxes.
Slave Records, 1806-1860; 1 Fibredex box.

OFFICIALS, COUNTY [*See* **MISCELLANEOUS RECORDS**]

ROADS AND BRIDGES [*See* **MISCELLANEOUS RECORDS**]

SCHOOL RECORDS [*See* **MISCELLANEOUS RECORDS**]

TAX AND FISCAL RECORDS
Assessment of Real Property for Taxation, 1799; 1 volume.
Lists of Taxables, 1790-1863; 9 volumes.
Merchants' Purchase Returns, 1873-1899; 3 Fibredex boxes.
Tax Records, 1790-1927; 10 Fibredex boxes.
Tax Scrolls, 1929, 1931; 2 volumes.

WILLS
Wills, 1775-1967; 49 Fibredex boxes.

CRX RECORDS
Apprentice Bond, 1827; 1 folder.
Estates Record (Phillip Howard), 1837; 1 folder.
Miscellaneous Records, 1792-1796; 2 folders.

MICROFILM RECORDS

BONDS
Apprentice Bonds, 1790-1817; 1 reel.

CORPORATIONS AND PARTNERSHIPS
Corporations, Record of, 1887-1965; 1 reel.
Partnership Records, 1968-1969; 1 reel.

COURT RECORDS
County Court of Pleas and Quarter Sessions
Minutes, 1790-1868; 5 reels.

Superior Court

Civil Actions, Index to, Defendant, 1869-1970; 1 reel.
Civil Actions, Index to, Plaintiff, 1869-1970; 1 reel.
Minutes, 1807-1846, 1878-1970; 8 reels.

ELECTION RECORDS

Elections, Record of, 1926-1964; 1 reel.

ESTATES RECORDS

Accounts, Record of, 1914-1965; 4 reels.
Administrators, Index to, 1790-1817; 1 reel.
Administrators, Record of, 1919-1965; 2 reels.
Appointment of Administrators, Executors, and Guardians, 1868-1935; 1 reel.
Clerk's Receipt Books (Estates), 1930-1970; 2 reels.
Estates Not Exceeding $300, 1932-1959; 1 reel.
Estates, Record of, 1790-1849, 1861-1869; 5 reels.
Executors, Record of, 1936-1970; 2 reels.
Final Accounts, Index to, 1869-1970; 3 reels.
Inheritance Tax Records, 1931-1971; 1 reel.
Settlements, Record of, 1846-1857, 1869-1960; 3 reels.

LAND RECORDS

Deeds, Record of, 1788-1960; 94 reels.
Real Estate Conveyances, Index to, Grantee, 1787-1962; 4 reels.
Real Estate Conveyances, Index to, Grantor, 1787-1962; 4 reels.

MARRIAGE, DIVORCE, AND VITAL STATISTICS

Births, Index to, 1913-1994; 2 reels.
Deaths, Index to, 1913-1995; 1 reel.
Delayed Births, Index to, various years; 1 reel.
Maiden Names of Divorced Women, 1937-1965; 1 reel.
Marriage Bond Abstracts, 1790-1868; 1 reel.
Marriage Bonds, 1790-1868; 10 reels.
Marriage Licenses, 1839-1961; 9 reels.
Marriage Registers, 1851-1955; 3 reels.
Marriages, Index to, 1956-1965; 1 reel.

MISCELLANEOUS RECORDS

Orders and Decrees, 1869-1970; 11 reels.

OFFICIALS, COUNTY

Board of County Commissioners, Minutes, 1871-1943; 4 reels.

TAX AND FISCAL RECORDS

Lists of Taxables, 1790-1863; 3 reels.
Property Valuations, 1799; 1 reel.
Tax Lists, 1933, 1945; 2 reels.

WILLS

Wills, Index to, Devisee, 1790-1970; 1 reel.
Wills, Index to, Devisor, 1790-1970; 1 reel.
Wills, Record of, 1790-1965; 4 reels.

SURRY COUNTY

Established in 1770 (effective 1771) from Rowan County.

ORIGINAL RECORDS

BONDS

Apprentice Bonds and Records, 1779-1921; 1 Fibredex box.
Bastardy Bonds and Records, 1782-1928; 1 Fibredex box.
Officials' Bonds and Records, 1777-1968; 2 volumes, 1 Fibredex box.

COURT RECORDS

County Court of Pleas and Quarter Sessions
- Appearance Dockets, 1811-1868; 5 volumes.
- Execution Dockets, 1772-1857; 14 volumes.
- Minutes, 1774-1867; 22 volumes, 6 manuscript boxes.
- Prosecution Bond Docket, 1788-1801; 1 volume.
- State Dockets, 1786-1796, 1808-1855; 6 volumes.
- Trial, Appearance, and Reference Dockets, 1774-1805; 6 volumes.
- Trial Docket, 1861-1868; 1 volume.
- Trial and Reference Dockets, 1811-1827, 1836-1861; 7 volumes.

Superior Court
- Appearance Dockets, 1807-1867; 2 volumes.
- Civil Action Papers, 1770-1929; 16 Fibredex boxes. [*See also* **CRX RECORDS**]
- Civil Action Papers Concerning Land, 1778-1928; 7 Fibredex boxes.
- Civil Issues Dockets, 1953-1970; 3 volumes.
- Criminal Action Papers, 1770-1928; 21 Fibredex boxes.
- Criminal Issues Dockets, 1869-1934; 8 volumes.
- Criminal Judgment Dockets, 1903-1916, 1937-1947; 2 volumes.
- Equity Minutes, 1855-1867; 1 volume.
- Equity Trial Dockets, 1819-1867; 2 volumes.
- Execution Dockets, 1808-1844; 2 volumes.
- Minutes, 1807-1863, 1866-1941; 25 volumes.
- Miscellaneous Dockets, 1806-1872; 1 manuscript box.
- Recognizance Dockets, 1815-1841; 2 volumes.
- State Dockets, 1807-1848; 4 volumes.
- Trial and Reference Dockets, 1807-1867; 3 volumes, 1 manuscript box.
- Witness Docket, 1827-1839; 1 volume.

ELECTION RECORDS

Elections, Record of, 1878-1920; 4 volumes.
Permanent Registration of Voters, 1902-1908; 2 volumes.
Poll Books, 1878-1894, 1916-1950; 4 manuscript boxes.
Voter Registration Books, 1896-1950; 3 manuscript boxes.

ESTATES RECORDS

Accounts of Indigent Orphans, 1907-1939; 2 volumes.
Accounts, Record of, 1868-1970; 30 volumes.
Administrators' Bonds, 1876-1915; 1 volume, 2 manuscript boxes.
Administrators, Record of, 1915-1970; 10 volumes.
Estates, Record of, 1784-1868; 10 volumes.
Estates Records, 1771-1943; 75 Fibredex boxes.

Guardians' Bonds, 1879-1903; 1 volume, 1 manuscript box.
Guardians, Record of, 1903-1970; 5 volumes.
Guardians' Records, 1784-1935; 5 Fibredex boxes.
Probate (Estates), Record of, 1868-1902, 1918; 1 volume.
Settlements, Record of, 1868-1942; 6 volumes.

LAND RECORDS

Deeds, 1774-1902; 5 Fibredex boxes. [*See also* **CRX RECORDS**]
Deeds, Record of, 1774-1780; 1 volume.
Deeds of Trust, 1791-1910; 2 Fibredex boxes.
Ejectments, 1798-1905; 1 Fibredex box.
Land Entries, 1778-1875; 4 volumes.
Land Grants, 1782-1877; 1 Fibredex box.
Levies, Executions, and Attachments, 1772-1930; 3 Fibredex boxes.
Miscellaneous Land Records, 1778-1922; 1 Fibredex box.
Processioners, Record of, 1795-1851; 1 volume.

MARRIAGE, DIVORCE, AND VITAL STATISTICS

Divorce Records, 1826-1927; 2 Fibredex boxes.
Maiden Names of Divorced Women, 1939-1970; 1 volume.
Marriage Bonds, 1778-1868; 13 Fibredex boxes.
Marriage Certificates, Record of, 1853-1867; 1 volume.
Marriage Licenses, 1868-1899; 7 Fibredex boxes.
Marriage Registers, 1867-1940; 8 volumes.

MISCELLANEOUS RECORDS

Alien Registration, 1927, 1940; 1 volume.
Appointment of Road Overseers, 1807-1869; 4 volumes.
Assignments, Record of, 1894-1897; 1 volume.
Board of County Commissioners, Minutes, 1881-1884; 1 Fibredex box.
Clerk's Minute Dockets (Special Proceedings), 1869-1874, 1877-1908; 3 volumes.
Declaration of Intent (to Become a Citizen), 1911-1925; 1 volume.
Insolvent Debtors and Homestead and Personal Property Exemptions, 1784-1911; 2 Fibredex boxes.
Lunacy, Record of, 1899-1970; 2 volumes.
Magistrates and Notaries Public, Record of, 1907-1930; 1 volume.
Miscellaneous Records, 1771-1928; 6 Fibredex boxes. [*See also* **CRX RECORDS**]
Orders and Decrees, 1868-1914; 2 volumes.
Orders and Decrees in re Liquidation of Bank of Mt. Airy, 1934-1937; 1 volume.
Petitions for Naturalization, 1910-1928; 1 volume.
Road Records, 1772-1931; 2 Fibredex boxes.
Special Proceedings, Cross Index to, no date; 2 volumes.
Trustees, Record of, 1897-1901; 1 volume.
Wardens of the Poor, Minutes, 1852-1877; 1 volume.

OFFICIALS, COUNTY [*See* **MISCELLANEOUS RECORDS**]

ROADS AND BRIDGES [*See* **MISCELLANEOUS RECORDS**]

TAX AND FISCAL RECORDS [*See also* **CRX RECORDS**]

Lists of Taxables, 1815-1866; 5 volumes.
Tax Records, 1775-1888; 6 Fibredex boxes.

WILLS

Wills, 1770-1970; 38 Fibredex boxes.
Wills, Cross Index to, 1772-1934; 1 volume.
Wills, Record of, 1789-1901; 7 volumes.

CRX RECORDS

Civil Action, 1828; 1 folder.
Deed, 1803; 1 folder.
List of Taxable Property, 1812; 1 folder.
Miscellaneous Records, 1774-1869; 1 Fibredex box, 15 folders.

MICROFILM RECORDS

CORPORATIONS AND PARTNERSHIPS

Corporations, Record of, 1886-1953; 2 reels.

COURT RECORDS

County Court of Pleas and Quarter Sessions
- Minutes, 1779-1867; 4 reels.
- Prosecution Bond Docket, 1788-1801; 1 reel.

Superior Court
- Criminal Actions, Index to, 1944-1970; 1 reel.
- Equity Minutes, 1855-1867; 1 reel.
- Judgments, Liens, and Lis Pendens, Index to, Defendant, 1920-1970; 2 reels.
- Judgments, Liens, and Lis Pendens, Index to, Plaintiff, 1920-1970; 1 reel.
- Minutes, 1807-1849, 1870-1970; 25 reels.

ELECTION RECORDS

Elections, Record of, 1878-1920; 1 reel.

ESTATES RECORDS

Accounts of Indigent Orphans, 1907-1937; 1 reel.
Accounts, Record of, 1868-1959; 8 reels.
Administrators' Bonds, 1876-1958; 5 reels.
Estates, Record of, 1792-1868; 3 reels.
Guardians' Bonds, 1879-1963; 3 reels.
Inheritance Tax Records, 1923-1963; 1 reel.
Inventories, Accounts, and Settlements, Index to, 1868-1970; 1 reel.
Petitions for Dower and Partition of Land, Record of, 1830-1874; 1 reel.
Settlements, Record of, 1869-1963; 6 reels.

LAND RECORDS

Contracts, Agreements, and Assignments, Record of, 1925-1931; 1 reel.
Deeds, Record of, 1771-1941; 37 reels.
Federal Tax Lien Index, 1928-1963; 1 reel.
Land Entries, 1778-1795, 1817-1883; 2 reels.
Land Title Proceedings, 1935; 1 reel.
Plat Books, 1920-1959; 2 reels.
Processioners' Book, 1801-1877; 1 reel.
Real Estate Conveyances, Cross Index to, 1771-1879; 1 reel.
Real Estate Conveyances, Index to, Grantee, 1878-1957; 5 reels.
Real Estate Conveyances, Index to, Grantor, 1878-1957; 5 reels.
Resale of Land Sold by Mortgagees and Trustees, 1924-1944; 1 reel.

MARRIAGE, DIVORCE, AND VITAL STATISTICS

Births, Index to, 1913-1994; 2 reels.
Deaths, Index to, 1909-1994; 2 reels.
Delayed Births, Index to, various years; 1 reel.
Maiden Names of Divorced Women, 1939-1963; 1 reel.
Marriage Bonds, 1780-1868; 5 reels.
Marriage Licenses, 1868-1961; 11 reels.
Marriage Registers, 1853-1940; 3 reels.
Marriage Registers, Index to, 1853-1977; 2 reels.

MISCELLANEOUS RECORDS

Assignees and Trustees, Record of, 1894-1897, 1901-1906; 1 reel.
Lunacy Records, 1899-1961; 2 reels.
Orders and Decrees, 1868-1970; 8 reels.
Receivers, Record of, 1894-1906; 1 reel.
Special Proceedings, 1877-1970; 3 reels.
Special Proceedings Judgments, 1915-1963; 1 reel.
Special Proceedings, Orders and Decrees, and Special Proceedings Judgments, Index to, Defendant, 1868-1970; 1 reel.
Special Proceedings, Orders and Decrees, and Special Proceedings Judgments, Index to, Plaintiff, 1868-1970; 1 reel.

OFFICIALS, COUNTY

Board of County Commissioners, Minutes, 1869-1951; 4 reels.
County Board of Health, Minutes, 1944-1963; 1 reel.
County Board of Social Services, Minutes, 1937-1963; 1 reel.

ROADS AND BRIDGES

Appointment of Road Overseers, 1833-1858; 1 reel.

SCHOOL RECORDS

County Board of Education, Minutes, 1941-1963; 1 reel.

TAX AND FISCAL RECORDS

List of Taxables and Sheriffs' Accounts, 1789-1795; 1 reel.
Tax Lists, 1815-1866; 2 reels.

WILLS

Wills, Index to, Devisee, 1771-1970; 1 reel.
Wills, Index to, Devisor, 1771-1970; 1 reel.
Wills, Record of, 1771-1963; 7 reels.

SWAIN COUNTY

Established in 1871 from Jackson and Macon counties.
Courthouse fire of 1879 destroyed many records.

ORIGINAL RECORDS

BONDS

Apprentice Bonds, 1873-1918; 2 volumes.
Bastardy Bonds, 1871-1880; 1 volume.

COURT RECORDS

Superior Court
Minutes, 1871-1907; 7 volumes.

ELECTION RECORDS

Elections, Record of, 1878-1912; 2 volumes.

ESTATES RECORDS

Administrators' Bonds, 1873-1908; 1 volume.
Estates Records, 1818-1956; 4 Fibredex boxes.
Guardians' Bonds, 1871-1910; 1 volume.
Guardians' Records, 1889-1954; 2 Fibredex boxes.

LAND RECORDS

Deeds, Cross Index to, 1872-1913; 5 volumes.
Deeds and Grants, Record of, 1872-1878; 2 volumes.
Land Entries, 1871-1944; 1 volume.
Probate of Deeds, 1885-1891; 1 volume.

MISCELLANEOUS RECORDS

Citizenship Records, 1894; 1 manuscript box.
Strays, Record of, 1885-1937; 1 volume.

MICROFILM RECORDS

BONDS

Apprentice Bonds, 1873-1918; 1 reel.

CORPORATIONS AND PARTNERSHIPS

Incorporations, Record of, 1884-1970; 1 reel.
Partnerships, Record of, 1913-1915; 1 reel.

COURT RECORDS

Superior Court
Judgments, Index to, 1872-1966; 1 reel.
Minutes, 1871-1949; 8 reels.

ELECTION RECORDS

Elections, Record of, 1878-1968; 1 reel.

ESTATES RECORDS

Accounts, Record of, 1877-1970; 2 reels.
Administrators' Bonds, 1873-1908; 1 reel.
Administrators, Executors, and Guardians, Record of, 1908-1927; 1 reel.
Administrators, Record of, 1919-1966; 1 reel.

Guardians' Bonds, 1871-1910; 1 reel.
Guardians, Record of, 1925-1966; 1 reel.
Inheritance Tax Records, 1925-1967; 1 reel.
Settlements, Record of, 1920-1937; 1 reel.

LAND RECORDS

Deeds, Index to, Grantee, 1872-1970; 5 reels.
Deeds, Index to, Grantor, 1872-1970; 4 reels.
Deeds, Record of, 1872-1958; 39 reels.
Grants, Cross Index to, 1872-1917; 1 reel.
Land Entry Books, 1872-1944; 1 reel.
Land Sales Book, 1931-1932; 1 reel.
Right-of-Way Easements, 1953-1961; 1 reel.
Sales by Mortgagees, Trustees, and Executors, Record of, 1921-1966; 1 reel.
State Highway Commission Right-of-Way Plans, 1968; 1 reel.
Surveys, Record of, 1905-1924; 1 reel.
Tax Suit Judgment Docket, 1932-1933; 1 reel.
Taxes for Mortgagees, Record of, 1931-1932; 1 reel.

MARRIAGE, DIVORCE, AND VITAL STATISTICS

Delayed Births, Index to, various years; 1 reel.
Maiden Names of Divorced Women, 1940-1966; 1 reel.
Marriage Registers, 1871-1959; 2 reels.

MISCELLANEOUS RECORDS

Clerk's Minute Docket, 1908-1909; 1 reel.
Lunacy, Record of, 1909-1917; 1 reel.
Orders and Decrees, 1873-1908; 1 reel.
Special Proceedings, 1883-1966; 3 reels.
Special Proceedings, Cross Index to, 1913-1966; 1 reel.

OFFICIALS, COUNTY

Board of County Commissioners, Minutes, 1871-1970; 5 reels.

SCHOOL RECORDS

County Board of Education, Minutes, 1908-1970; 2 reels.

TAX AND FISCAL RECORDS

Tax List, 1915; 1 reel.

WILLS

Wills, Cross Index to, 1873-1966; 1 reel.
Wills, Record of, 1873-1966; 1 reel.

TRANSYLVANIA COUNTY

Established in 1861 from Henderson and Jackson counties.

ORIGINAL RECORDS

BONDS

Apprentice Bonds, 1879-1906; 1 volume.
Bastardy Bonds, 1879-1880; 1 volume.
Officials' Bonds. [*See* **CRX RECORDS**]

COURT RECORDS

County Court of Pleas and Quarter Sessions
- Minutes, 1861-1868; 1 volume.
- State Docket, 1861-1868; 1 volume.
- Trial and Appearance Docket, 1861-1868; 1 volume.

Superior Court
- Civil Action Papers, 1850-1932; 1 Fibredex box.
- Civil Action Papers Concerning Land, 1862-1932; 3 Fibredex boxes.
- Criminal Action Papers, 1862-1921; 1 Fibredex box.
- Equity Minutes, 1864-1867; 1 volume.
- Minutes, 1867-1910; 8 volumes.
- State Docket, 1862-1867; 1 volume.

ELECTION RECORDS

Elections, Record of, 1874-1926; 3 volumes.
Voter Registration Books, 1902-1934; 17 volumes.

ESTATES RECORDS

Administrators' Bonds, 1876-1916; 2 volumes.
Estates, Record of, 1861-1916, 1931; 2 volumes.
Estates Records, 1810-1951; 20 Fibredex boxes.
Guardians' Bonds, 1876-1917; 2 volumes.
Guardians, Record of, 1863-1918; 3 volumes.
Guardians' Records, 1852-1925; 11 Fibredex boxes.
Probate (Estates), Record of, 1875-1899; 1 volume.
Settlements, Record of, 1880-1936; 2 volumes.

LAND RECORDS

Attachments, Executions, Levies, and Liens on Land, 1863-1931; 3 Fibredex boxes.
Deeds, 1827-1923; 2 Fibredex boxes.
Deeds, Record of, 1861-1885; 4 volumes.
Land Entry Books, 1865-1883, 1888-1917; 2 volumes.
Miscellaneous Land Records, 1854-1925; 2 Fibredex boxes.
Probate of Chattel Mortgages and Mortgage Deeds, Record of, 1882-1889; 1 volume.
Probate of Deeds, Record of, 1861-1889; 2 volumes.

MARRIAGE, DIVORCE, AND VITAL STATISTICS

Divorce Records, 1866-1921; 2 Fibredex boxes.
Marriage Bonds, 1861-1868; 8 folders in Fibredex box.
Marriage Registers, 1872-1934; 2 volumes.
Marriages, Record of, 1861-1872; 1 volume.

MISCELLANEOUS RECORDS

Miscellaneous Records, 1864-1926; 3 Fibredex boxes.
Official Reports, Record of, 1879-1912; 1 volume.
Railroad Records, 1900-1918; 1 Fibredex box.
School Records, 1881-1927; 1 Fibredex box.

ROADS AND BRIDGES [*See* **MISCELLANEOUS RECORDS**]

SCHOOL RECORDS [*See* **MISCELLANEOUS RECORDS**]

WILLS

Wills, 1838-1926; 2 Fibredex boxes.
Wills, Cross Index to, 1879-1949; 1 volume.

CRX RECORDS

Officials' Bonds, 1875-1877; 1 folder.

MICROFILM RECORDS

BONDS

Apprentice Bonds, 1879-1906; 1 reel.
Bastardy Bonds, 1879-1880; 1 reel.

CORPORATIONS AND PARTNERSHIPS

Corporations, Record of, 1903-1945; 1 reel.
Partnerships, Record of, 1913-1970; 1 reel.

COURT RECORDS

County Court of Pleas and Quarter Sessions
- Minutes, 1861-1868; 1 reel.

General County Court
- Minutes, 1913-1932; 1 reel.

Superior Court
- Equity Minutes, 1864-1867; 1 reel.
- Minutes, 1867-1950; 9 reels.
- Minutes, General Index to, Defendant, 1920-1968; 2 reels.
- Minutes, General Index to, Plaintiff, 1920-1950; 1 reel.

ELECTION RECORDS

Elections, Record of, 1874-1904, 1938-1968; 2 reels.

ESTATES RECORDS

Accounts and Probate Matters, Record of, 1875-1899; 1 reel.
Accounts, Record of, 1861-1968; 4 reels.
Administrators' Bonds, 1876-1916; 1 reel.
Administrators and Executors, Cross Index to, 1862-1968; 1 reel.
Administrators, Executors, and Guardians, Record of, 1916-1941; 1 reel.
Administrators, Record of, 1929-1968; 2 reels.
Amounts Paid for Indigent Children, Record of, 1916-1964; 1 reel.
Estates, Index to, 1960-1970; 1 reel.
Estates, Record of, 1861-1888; 1 reel.
Executors, Record of, 1941-1968; 1 reel.
Guardians' Bonds, 1876-1917; 1 reel.
Guardians, Cross Index to, 1866-1968; 1 reel.
Guardians, Record of, 1863-1968; 2 reels.

Inheritance Tax Records, 1923-1968; 1 reel.
Settlements, Record of, 1880-1968; 3 reels.

LAND RECORDS

Deeds, General Index to, Grantee, 1861-1970; 13 reels.
Deeds, General Index to, Grantor, 1861-1970; 14 reels.
Deeds, Record of, 1861-1958; 53 reels.
Land Entry Books, 1865-1959; 1 reel.
Sales and Resales, Record of, 1921-1968; 2 reels.
Surveys, Record of, 1906-1959; 1 reel.
Tax Suit Judgment Dockets, 1929-1948, 1962-1969; 2 reels.

MARRIAGE, DIVORCE, AND VITAL STATISTICS

Births, Index to, 1913-1969; 1 reel.
Deaths, Index to, 1913-1969; 1 reel
Maiden Names of Divorced Women, 1954-1968; 1 reel.
Marriage Bonds, 1861-1865; 1 reel.
Marriage Licenses, 1901-1970; 3 reels.
Marriage Registers, 1861-1970; 1 reel.

MISCELLANEOUS RECORDS

Orders and Decrees, 1878-1966; 1 reel.
Special Proceedings, 1884-1956; 6 reels.
Special Proceedings, Cross Index to, 1884-1968; 1 reel.

OFFICIALS, COUNTY

Board of County Commissioners, Minutes, 1868-1970; Court of Pleas and Quarter Sessions, Minutes, 1861-1868 (copy); 5 reels.

TAX AND FISCAL RECORDS

Tax Scrolls, 1876, 1877, 1889, 1897, 1905; 1 reel.

WILLS

Wills, Cross Index to, 1879-1968; 1 reel.
Wills, Record of, 1879-1968; 3 reels.

TRYON COUNTY

Established in 1768 (effective 1769) from Mecklenburg County.
Divided into Lincoln and Rutherford counties in 1779.

ORIGINAL RECORDS

COURT RECORDS [*See also* **CRX RECORDS**]

County Court of Pleas and Quarter Sessions

Minutes, 1769-1779; 2 volumes.

LAND RECORDS

Deeds, Record of, 1769-1779; 7 volumes. [*See also* **CRX RECORDS**]

MISCELLANEOUS RECORDS

Miscellaneous Records, 1765-1783; 1 manuscript box.

CRX RECORDS

Deeds, Record of, 1769; 1 volume.

Trial, Appearance, and Reference Docket, Court of Pleas and Quarter Sessions, 1772-1778; 1 volume.

MICROFILM RECORDS

COURT RECORDS

County Court of Pleas and Quarter Sessions

Minutes, 1769-1782; 1 reel.

Trial, Appearance, and Reference Docket, 1772-1778; 1 reel.

LAND RECORDS

Deeds, Record of, 1769-1779; 2 reels.

MISCELLANEOUS RECORDS

Miscellaneous Records, 1765-1788; 1 reel.

TYRRELL COUNTY

Established in 1729 from Bertie, Chowan, Currituck, and Pasquotank precincts as a precinct of Albemarle County. A few of the early records are missing; reason unknown.

ORIGINAL RECORDS

BONDS

Apprentice Bonds and Records, 1742, 1782-1906; 1 volume, 2 Fibredex boxes.
Bastardy Bonds and Records, 1735-1922; 3 Fibredex boxes.
Officials' Bonds, 1743-1899, 1908, 1910; 3 Fibredex boxes.

COURT RECORDS

County Court of Pleas and Quarter Sessions
- Appearance Dockets, 1852-1868; 2 volumes.
- Clerk's Recording Docket, 1756-1762; 1 volume.
- Execution Dockets, 1756-1866; 9 volumes, 1 manuscript box.
- Levy Docket, 1838-1844; 1 volume.
- Minutes, 1735-1834, 1841-1868; 17 volumes, 1 manuscript box.
- State Dockets, 1762-1828, 1856-1859; 1 manuscript box.
- Trial and Appearance Dockets, 1798-1855; 7 volumes, 1 manuscript box.
- Trial, Appearance, and Reference Dockets, 1754-1798; 2 manuscript boxes.
- Trial Dockets, 1855-1868; 2 volumes, 1 manuscript box.

Superior Court
- Bench Docket, 1816-1840; 1 volume.
- Civil Action Papers, 1736-1926; 36 Fibredex boxes.
- Civil Action Papers Concerning Land, 1794-1925, 1929; 8 Fibredex boxes.
- Civil and Criminal Action Papers Concerning County Officials, 1798-1922; 1 Fibredex box.
- Criminal Action Papers, 1739-1918; 22 Fibredex boxes.
- Equity Minutes, 1852-1859, 1866-1868; 1 volume.
- Execution Dockets, 1808-1862, 1867, 1869; 2 volumes.
- Executions, 1782-1915, 1924; 23 Fibredex boxes.
- Minutes, 1807-1883; 4 volumes, 1 manuscript box.
- State Dockets, 1815-1864, 1867-1869, 1874-1895, 1899-1905; 3 volumes.
- Trial and Appearance Dockets, 1816-1864; 2 volumes.

ELECTION RECORDS

Elections, Record of, 1878-1968; 5 volumes.

ESTATES RECORDS

Administrators' Bonds, 1904-1924; 1 volume.
Appointment of Administrators, Executors, Guardians, and Masters, 1868-1878; 1 manuscript box.
Estates, Record of, 1802-1869; 4 volumes.
Estates Records, 1738-1935, 1947-1960, 1968; 58 Fibredex boxes. [*See also* **CRX RECORDS**]
Fiduciary Account Book, 1758-1775; Account Book of Dr. J. H. Ellis, 1819-1828; 1 volume.
Guardians' Bonds, 1859-1868; 1 manuscript box.
Guardians' Records, 1754-1925, 1944-1954; 3 Fibredex boxes.

LAND RECORDS [*See also* **CRX RECORDS**]

Deeds and Miscellaneous Deeds, 1744-1911, 1924; 1 Fibredex box.
Deeds, Record of, 1736-1819; 12 volumes.
Ejectments, 1786-1921; 3 Fibredex boxes.
Land Entry Books, 1778-1796, 1887-1924; 1 volume, 1 manuscript box.
Miscellaneous Land Records, 1755-1923, 1941, 1981; 2 Fibredex boxes.
Petitions for Partition and Sale of Land, 1810-1952; 2 Fibredex boxes.
Processioners' Records, 1748, 1800-1921; 2 Fibredex boxes.

MARRIAGE, DIVORCE, AND VITAL STATISTICS

Divorce Records, 1815-1925, 1954; 2 Fibredex boxes.
Marriage Bonds, 1742-1868; 6 Fibredex boxes.

MILITARY AND PENSION RECORDS [*See* **MISCELLANEOUS RECORDS**]

MISCELLANEOUS RECORDS

Canal and Drainage Records, 1805-1927; 1 Fibredex box.
Confederate Veterans Association, Minutes, 1889-1917; 1 volume.
Insolvent Debtors and Homestead and Personal Property Exemptions, 1821-1928; 2 Fibredex boxes.
Justices of the Peace, Records of, 1812-1912; 1 Fibredex box.
Miscellaneous Records, 1735, 1756-1975; 3 Fibredex boxes. [*See also* **CRX RECORDS**]
Railroad Records, 1886-1923; 1 Fibredex box.
Road Records, 1786-1929; 3 Fibredex boxes.
Slaves and Free Persons of Color, Records of, 1793-1868; 2 Fibredex boxes.
Stock Marks, Record of, 1763-1819; 1 pamphlet.
Strays, Record of, 1918, 1923; School Records, 1893; 1 volume.

ROADS AND BRIDGES [*See* **MISCELLANEOUS RECORDS**]

TAX AND FISCAL RECORDS

Tax Records, 1782-1929; 1 Fibredex box.

WILLS

Wills, 1744-1925; 6 Fibredex boxes.

CRX RECORDS

Deeds, 1759; 1 folder.
Estates Record, 1910; 1 folder.
Miscellaneous Records, 1764-1937; 10 folders.

MICROFILM RECORDS

COURT RECORDS

County Court of Pleas and Quarter Sessions
    Minutes, 1735-1868; 4 reels.
Superior Court
    Equity Minutes, 1852-1868; 1 reel.
    Judgments, Index to, Defendant, 1869-1968; 1 reel.
    Judgments, Index to, Plaintiff, 1869-1968; 1 reel.
    Minutes, 1807-1968; 5 reels.

ELECTION RECORDS

Elections, Record of, 1880-1968; 3 reels.

ESTATES RECORDS

Accounts, Record of, 1868-1961; 2 reels.
Administrators' Bonds, 1904-1924; 1 reel.
Administrators and Executors, Cross Index to, 1940-1968; 1 reel.
Administrators, Executors, and Guardians, Record of, 1915-1967; 1 reel.
Administrators, Record of, 1929-1961; 1 reel.
Appointment of Administrators, Executors, Guardians, and Masters, 1868-1889; 1 reel.
Appointment of Executors, 1868-1878; 1 reel.
Dowers, Record of, 1939; 1 reel.
Estates, Record of, 1802-1868; 3 reels.
Guardians' Bonds, 1859-1868; 1 reel.
Guardians, Cross Index to, 1906-1916; 1 reel.
Ormond, Wyriott, Estate Records and Miscellaneous Accounts, 1758-1828; 1 reel.
Settlements, Record of, 1867-1968; 2 reels.

LAND RECORDS

Deeds, Record of, 1736-1959; 52 reels.
Grants, Record of, 1779-1780; 1 reel.
Land Entries, 1887-1924; 1 reel.
Map Book, 1911-1975; 1 reel.
Real Estate Conveyances, Index to, Grantee, 1729-1960; 2 reels.
Real Estate Conveyances, Index to, Grantor, 1729-1960; 2 reels.
Registration of Land Titles, 1918-1960; 1 reel.
Resale of Land by Mortgagees and Trustees, Record of, 1932-1956; 1 reel.

MARRIAGE, DIVORCE, AND VITAL STATISTICS

Delayed Births, Index to, various years; 1 reel.
Marriage Bond Abstracts, 1741-1868; 1 reel.
Marriage Bonds, 1741-1868; 3 reels.
Marriage Records, 1851-1868; 1 reel.
Marriage Registers, 1877-1975; 2 reels.
Vital Statistics, Index to, 1913-1961; 1 reel.

MILITARY AND PENSION RECORDS

Confederate Veterans Association, Minutes, 1889-1917; 1 reel.

MISCELLANEOUS RECORDS

Clerk's Minute Docket, 1925-1929; 1 reel.
Inquisition of Lunacy, Record of, 1900-1914; 1 reel.
Orders and Decrees, 1868-1961; 2 reels.
Special Proceedings, 1907-1968; 4 reels.
Special Proceedings, Cross Index to, 1907-1968; 1 reel.

OFFICIALS, COUNTY

Board of County Commissioners, Minutes, 1878-1981; 5 reels.
County Board of Social Services, Minutes, 1937-1986; 2 reels.
County Planning Board, Minutes, 1970-1986; 1 reel.

SCHOOL RECORDS

County Board of Education, Minutes, 1911-1975; 2 reels.

TAX AND FISCAL RECORDS

Lists of Taxables, 1782, 1850; 1 reel.
Tax Lists, 1877-1899, 1901, 1915; 2 reels.

WILLS

Wills, Cross Index to, 1750-1968; 1 reel.
Wills, Record of, 1750-1961; 2 reels.

UNION COUNTY

Established in 1842 from Anson and Mecklenburg counties.
A few of the court records are missing; reason unknown.

ORIGINAL RECORDS

BONDS

Apprentice Bonds, 1871-1910; 1 manuscript box.
Bastardy Bonds, 1871-1882; 1 volume.

COURT RECORDS

County Court of Pleas and Quarter Sessions
- Appearance Docket, 1843-1868; 1 volume.
- Execution Dockets, 1843-1868; 7 volumes.
- Minutes, 1843-1868; 5 volumes.
- State Dockets, 1843-1868; 2 volumes.
- Trial Dockets, 1843-1868; 3 volumes.

Justice's Court
- Judgment Docket, 1876-1894; 1 volume.

Recorder's Court
- Judgment Dockets, 1907-1922; 5 volumes.
- Minutes, 1909-1922; 3 volumes.

Superior Court
- Appearance Docket, 1844-1870; 1 volume.
- Civil Action Papers, 1843-1969; 40 Fibredex boxes.
- Civil Action Papers Concerning Land, 1853-1968; 23 Fibredex boxes.
- Civil Action Papers Concerning Mines, 1844-1967; 3 Fibredex boxes.
- Civil Issues Dockets, 1879-1968; 5 volumes.
- Criminal Action Papers, 1844-1965; 1 Fibredex box.
- Criminal Issues Dockets, 1869-1968; 11 volumes.
- Equity Execution Docket, 1847-1868; 1 volume.
- Equity Minutes, 1843-1868; 1 volume.
- Equity Trial Docket, 1844-1868; 1 volume.
- Execution Dockets, 1844-1862, 1868-1870; 5 volumes.
- Judgment Dockets, 1888-1951; 16 volumes. [*See also* **LAND RECORDS**, Tax Suit Judgment Docket]
- Judgments, Cross Index to, 1868-1923; 4 volumes.
- Minutes, 1844-1969; 38 volumes.
- State Docket, 1844-1869; 1 volume.
- Summons Docket, 1870-1912; 1 volume.
- Trial Dockets, 1844-1878; 2 volumes.

ELECTION RECORDS

Elections, Record of, 1878-1900, 1924-1968; 4 volumes.
Permanent Roll of Registered Voters, 1902; 1 volume.

ESTATES RECORDS

Accounts, Record of, 1868-1969; 22 volumes.
Administrators' Bonds, 1871-1909; 6 volumes.
Administrators and Executors, Record of, 1908-1940; 6 volumes.
Administrators, Record of, 1871-1880, 1936-1968; 7 volumes.

Amounts Paid to Indigent Children, Record of, 1926-1953; 1 volume.
Appointment of Administrators, Executors, Masters, and Guardians, 1868-1896, 1907; 1 volume.
Estates, Index to Record of, [1855-1870]; 1 volume.
Estates, Record of, 1843-1870; 7 volumes.
Estates Records, 1818-1969; 236 Fibredex boxes.
Executors and Administrators, Cross Index to, 1871-1916; 1 volume.
Executors, Record of, 1940-1968; 3 volumes.
Guardians' Bonds, 1871-1910; 3 volumes.
Guardians, Record of, 1908-1968; 4 volumes.
Guardians' Records, 1846-1968; 38 Fibredex boxes.
Guardians and Wards, Cross Index to, 1871-1915; 1 volume.
Inheritance Tax Records, 1923-1972; 4 volumes.
Settlements, Record of, 1869-1970; 20 volumes.

LAND RECORDS

Attachments, Executions, Liens, and Levies on Land, 1844-1968; 5 Fibredex boxes.
Ejectments, 1848-1965; 1 Fibredex box.
Land Sold for Taxes, Record of, 1936; 1 volume.
Miscellaneous Land Records, 1796-1964; 1 Fibredex box.
Partitions and Sales of Land, 1869-1969; 6 Fibredex boxes.
Probate, Record of, 1852-1881; 2 volumes.
Sale and Resale of Land, Record of, 1916-1942; 5 volumes.
Tax Suit Judgment Docket, 1935-1936; 1 volume. [*See also* **COURT RECORDS**, Superior Court, Judgment Dockets]

MARRIAGE, DIVORCE, AND VITAL STATISTICS

Divorce Records, 1865-1968; 46 Fibredex boxes.

MILITARY AND PENSION RECORDS [*See* **MISCELLANEOUS RECORDS**]

MISCELLANEOUS RECORDS

Alien Registration Record, 1927, 1940; 1 volume.
Assignees, Trustees, and Receivers, Records of, 1883-1974; 6 Fibredex boxes.
Committee of Finance, Settlement of County Accounts, 1850-1873; 1 volume.
Confederate and World War I Veterans, Register of, 1903, 1933; 1 volume.
Confederate Pension Records, 1921-1970; 1 volume.
Declaration of Intent (to Become a Citizen), Record of, 1915-1928; 1 volume.
Lunacy, Record of, 1899-1968; 5 volumes.
Miscellaneous Records, 1844-1967; 3 Fibredex boxes.
Orders and Decrees, 1870-1948; 17 volumes.
Partnership Records, 1914-1960; 1 volume.
Petitions for Naturalization, 1914-1928; 1 volume.
Railroad Records, 1875-1968; 6 Fibredex boxes.
Receivers, Record of, 1927-1941; 1 volume.
Road and Bridge Records, 1848-1959; 1 Fibredex box.
Road Docket, 1849-1868, 1877-1879; 1 volume.
School Records, 1896-1959; 1 Fibredex box.
Special Proceedings Docket, 1887-1918; 1 volume.
Special Proceedings and Ex Parte, Judgment Dockets, 1927-1968; 2 volumes.

Special Proceedings and Ex Parte, Minutes, 1917-1968; 5 volumes.
Wardens of the Poor, Minutes and Accounts, 1858-1881; 1 volume.

ROADS AND BRIDGES [*See* **MISCELLANEOUS RECORDS**]

SCHOOL RECORDS [*See* **MISCELLANEOUS RECORDS**]

TAX AND FISCAL RECORDS
Lists of Taxables, 1842-1853; 2 volumes.

WILLS
Wills, 1837-1968, 1977, 1978; 56 Fibredex boxes.
Wills, Cross Index to, 1843-1932; 1 volume.
Wills, Record of, 1843-1968; 12 volumes.

MICROFILM RECORDS

BONDS
Apprentice Bonds, 1871-1882; 1 reel.
Officials' Bonds, 1872-1892; 1 reel.

CORPORATIONS AND PARTNERSHIPS
Corporations, Record of, 1885-1971; 4 reels.
Limited Partnerships, Record of, 1944-1974; 1 reel.
Partnerships and Assumed Names, Record of, 1913-1947; 1 reel.

COURT RECORDS
County Court of Pleas and Quarter Sessions
Minutes, 1843-1868; 3 reels.
Superior Court
Civil Actions, Index to, 1932-1961; 1 reel.
Equity Minutes, 1843-1865; 1 reel.
Judgments, Index to, Defendant, 1917-1968; 2 reels.
Judgments, Index to, Plaintiff, 1917-1968; 2 reels.
Minutes, 1858-1863, 1895-1961; 15 reels.

ELECTION RECORDS
Elections, Record of, 1878-1968; 2 reels.
Permanent Registration of Voters, 1902-1908; 1 reel.

ESTATES RECORDS
Accounts, Record of, 1868-1967; 11 reels.
Accounts and Sales of Estates, 1916-1962; 3 reels.
Administrators' Bonds, 1871-1909; 2 reels.
Administrators, Executors, and Guardians, Record of, 1908-1968; 10 reels.
Administrators and Executors, Cross Index to, 1872-1914; 1 reel.
Amounts Paid for Indigent Children, Record of, 1926-1953; 1 reel.
Appointment of Executors, 1868-1907; 1 reel.
Estates, Record of, 1841-1876; 4 reels.
Executors and Guardians, Record of, 1940-1968; 2 reels.
Guardians' Bonds, 1871-1910; 1 reel.
Guardians, Record of, 1908-1968; 3 reels.
Inheritance Tax Records, 1923-1972; 3 reels.
Settlements, Record of, 1867-1970; 13 reels.

LAND RECORDS

Deeds, Index to, Grantee, 1842-1972; 6 reels.
Deeds, Index to, Grantor, 1842-1972; 6 reels.
Deeds, Record of, 1843-1958; 97 reels.
Land Sold for Taxes, Record of, 1930-1934; 2 reels.
Plats, Index to, 1891-1982; 1 reel.

MARRIAGE, DIVORCE, AND VITAL STATISTICS

Births, Index to, 1913-1971; 3 reels.
Deaths, Index to, 1913-1981; 2 reels.
Delayed Births, Index to, various years; 1 reel.
Maiden Names of Divorced Women, 1938-1968; 1 reel.
Marriage Bonds and Certificates, 1843-1871; 2 reels.
Marriage Licenses, 1873-1967; 12 reels.
Marriage Registers, 1843-1938; 2 reels.
Marriage Registers, Index to, 1843-1965; 4 reels.

MILITARY AND PENSION RECORDS

Register of Confederate Soldiers of Monroe, 1903-1933; 1 reel.
Roster of Confederate and Revolutionary Soldiers, 1958; 1 reel.

MISCELLANEOUS RECORDS

Alien Registration Records, 1924-1940; 1 reel.
Board of Trustees of Monroe Township, Minutes, 1878-1901; 1 reel.
Lunacy, Record of, 1899-1946; 1 reel.
Naturalization, Record of, 1914-1928; 1 reel.
Orders and Decrees, 1881-1957; 12 reels.
Reports of Receivers, 1927-1931; 1 reel.
Special Proceedings Costs Docket, 1938-1968; 1 reel.
Special Proceedings Dockets, 1887-1969; 5 reels.
Special Proceedings Files, Index to, 1869-1968; 2 reels.
Special Proceedings, Index to, 1927-1960; 4 reels.
Wardens of the Poor, Minutes, 1851-1881; 1 reel.

OFFICIALS, COUNTY

Board of County Commissioners, Minutes, 1868-1955; 4 reels.

ROADS AND BRIDGES

Commissioners' Road Docket, 1869-1905; 1 reel.
Road Overseers, Record of, 1849-1868; 1 reel.

SCHOOL RECORDS

County Board of Education, Minutes, 1885-1967; 2 reels.

TAX AND FISCAL RECORDS

County Board of Equalization and Review, Minutes, 1968-1982; 2 reels.
Tax Lists, 1842-1869; 1 reel.

WILLS

Wills, Cross Index to, 1842-1968; 1 reel.
Wills, Record of, 1842-1968; 7 reels.

VANCE COUNTY

Established in 1881 from Franklin, Granville, and Warren counties.

ORIGINAL RECORDS

BONDS

Officials' Bonds, Record of, 1881-1925; 1 volume.

LAND RECORDS

Deeds, Cross Index to, 1849-1934; 5 volumes.

TAX AND FISCAL RECORDS

Tax Records, 1882-1884; 1 manuscript box.

MICROFILM RECORDS

BONDS

Apprentice Bonds, 1882-1922; 1 reel.

CORPORATIONS AND PARTNERSHIPS

Corporations, Record of, 1888-1948; 1 reel.

COURT RECORDS

Superior Court

Minutes, 1881-1963; 14 reels.

ELECTION RECORDS

Elections, Record of, 1884-1966; 1 reel.

ESTATES RECORDS

Accounts, Record of, 1881-1968; 11 reels.
Administrators' Bonds, 1906-1913, 1922-1925; 1 reel.
Administrators and Executors, Record of, 1925-1929; 1 reel.
Administrators, Record of, 1930-1968; 4 reels.
Estates, Index to, 1968-1969; 1 reel.
Guardians' Bonds, 1926-1938; 1 reel.
Guardians, Record of, 1938-1968; 1 reel.
Inheritance Tax Records, 1923-1958, 1968-1969; 1 reel.
Qualification of Trustees under Wills, 1960-1968; 1 reel.
Settlements, Record of, 1883-1968; 6 reels.

LAND RECORDS

Deeds, Record of, 1881-1963; 42 reels.
Deeds of Trust, Record of, 1882-1893; 2 reels.
Real Estate Conveyances, Index to, Grantee, 1881-1969; 2 reels.
Real Estate Conveyances, Index to, Grantor, 1881-1969; 4 reels.
Resale, Record of, 1925-1969; 2 reels.
Surveys, Record of, 1886-1907; 1 reel.

MARRIAGE, DIVORCE, AND VITAL STATISTICS

Delayed Births, Index to, various years; 1 reel.
Maiden Names of Divorced Women, 1937-1968; 1 reel.
Marriage Licenses, 1897, 1902, 1911-1968; 9 reels.
Marriage Register, Index to, 1963-1969; 1 reel.

Marriage Registers, 1881-1962; 1 reel.
Vital Statistics, Index to, 1913-1968; 2 reels.

MISCELLANEOUS RECORDS

Orders and Decrees, 1881-1953; 8 reels.
Special Proceedings, Index to, Defendant, 1881-1969; 1 reel.
Special Proceedings, Index to, Plaintiff, 1881-1969; 1 reel.

OFFICIALS, COUNTY

Board of County Commissioners, Minutes, 1883-1955; 4 reels.

SCHOOL RECORDS

County Board of Education, Minutes, 1899-1967; 1 reel.

TAX AND FISCAL RECORDS

Tax Scrolls, 1883-1899, 1903, 1925, 1935, 1945, 1955, 1956, 1965; 7 reels.

WILLS

Wills, Cross Index to, 1903-1969; 1 reel.
Wills, Record of, 1881-1968; 5 reels.

WAKE COUNTY

Established in 1771 from Cumberland, Johnston, and Orange counties.
A few early court records are missing; reason unknown.
Several deed books were destroyed in register's office fire in 1832.

ORIGINAL RECORDS

BONDS

- Apprentice Bonds and Records, 1770-1903; 1 Fibredex box.
- Bastardy Bonds and Records, 1772-1937; 2 volumes, 2 Fibredex boxes.
- Constables' Bonds, 1787-1867; 1 Fibredex box.
- Officials' Bonds, 1878-1898; 2 volumes.

CENSUS RECORDS (County Copy)

- Census, 1880; 6 volumes.

COURT RECORDS [*See also* **CRX RECORDS**]

- County Court of Pleas and Quarter Sessions
  - Appearance Dockets, 1783-1818, 1838-1868; 6 volumes.
  - Execution Dockets, 1772-1830, 1840-1868; 13 volumes.
  - Levy Dockets, 1805-1819; 2 volumes.
  - Minutes, 1777-1868; 24 volumes.
  - Recognizance Docket, 1820-1837; 1 volume.
  - Reference Docket, 1799-1832; 1 volume.
  - Scire Facias Docket, 1799-1813; 1 volume.
  - State Dockets, 1771-1868; 7 volumes.
  - Trial Dockets, 1778-1868; 9 volumes.
- Criminal Court
  - Criminal Issues Docket, 1877-1879; 1 volume.
  - Judgment Docket, 1877-1879; 1 volume.
  - Judgments, Index to, 1877-1878; 1 volume.
  - Minutes, 1877-1879; 2 volumes.
- Superior Court
  - Appearance Dockets, 1835-1869; 2 volumes.
  - Civil Action Papers, 1770-1942; 92 Fibredex boxes.
  - Civil Action Papers Concerning Land, 1773-1947; 55 Fibredex boxes.
  - Civil Issues Dockets, 1868-1886, 1943-1945; 2 volumes.
  - Clerk's Fee Book, 1889-1912; 1 volume.
  - Clerk's Minute Dockets, 1921-1968; 11 volumes.
  - Clerk's Record of Fines and Penalties, 1879-1898; 1 volume.
  - Costs Dockets (Criminal), 1839-1844, 1902-1903; 3 volumes.
  - Criminal Action Papers, 1771-1946; 3 Fibredex boxes.
  - Criminal Issues Dockets, 1869-1933; 21 volumes.
  - Equity Appearance Dockets, 1818-1868; 3 volumes.
  - Equity Execution Dockets, 1820-1868; 2 volumes.
  - Equity Minutes, 1818-1836, 1851-1868; 2 volumes.
  - Equity Trial Dockets, 1818-1866; 3 volumes.
  - Execution Dockets, 1808-1871; 6 volumes.
  - Judgment Dockets, 1868-1905; 9 volumes. [*See also* **LAND RECORDS**, Tax Suit Judgment Dockets]
  - Judgments and Special Proceedings, Index to, 1918-1922; 1 volume.

Minutes, 1818-1942; 58 volumes.
Minutes, Civil, 1942-1968; 22 volumes.
Minutes, Criminal, 1942-1968; 18 volumes.
Minutes, Divorces, 1947-1950; 1 volume.
Minutes of Resident Judge (Special Terms), 1933-1940, 1952-1966; 3 volumes.
Minutes (Rough), 1859-1866, 1915-1930; 10 volumes.
Special Civil Order Docket, 1884; 1 volume.
State Dockets, 1814-1868; 4 volumes.
Summons Dockets, 1868-1913; 7 volumes.
Trial, Appearance, and Reference Dockets, 1814-1824; 2 volumes.
Trial Docket, 1864-1868; 1 volume.
Trial and Reference Dockets, 1825-1863; 3 volumes.

ELECTION RECORDS

Election Records, 1790-1938; 5 Fibredex boxes.
Elections, Record of, 1896-1928; 5 volumes.
Permanent Registration of Voters, 1904-1906; 1 volume.

ESTATES RECORDS [*See also* **WILLS**]

Accounts, Record of, 1868-1942; 14 volumes.
Administrators' Bonds, 1868-1892; 3 volumes.
Administrators' Bonds and Appointments, 1892-1911; 5 volumes.
Administrators, Executors, and Guardians, Record of, 1892-1943; 13 volumes.
Administrators' and Guardians' Accounts, Index to, no date; 1 volume.
Amounts Paid for Indigent Orphans, Record of, 1899-1918, 1921-1942; 3 volumes.
Appointment of Administrators, Executors, Guardians, and Masters, 1868-1893; 2 volumes.
Appointment of Administrators and Executors, Record of, 1858-1891; 3 volumes.
Clerk's Receiver Accounts, 1913-1929; 2 volumes.
Estates Records, 1771-1952, 1962, 1968; 383 Fibredex boxes.
Executors and Administrators, Index to, 1858-1934; 2 volumes.
Guardians' Accounts, 1878-1939; 12 volumes.
Guardians' Bonds, 1868-1892; 3 volumes.
Guardians' Dockets, 1817-1818, 1822-1828; 2 volumes.
Guardians, Index to, 1858-1934; 1 volume.
Guardians, Record of, 1892-1910; 2 volumes.
Guardians' Records, 1772-1948; 44 Fibredex boxes.
Inventories and Accounts of Sale, 1878-1940; 8 volumes.
Minutes, Probate Court, 1878-1883; 3 volumes.
Minutes, Probate Court, Index to, 1878-1880; 1 volume.
Settlements, Record of, 1868-1940; 17 volumes.
Widows' Year's Support, Record of, 1878-1967; 3 volumes.

LAND RECORDS

Attachments, Executions, Levies, and Liens on Land, 1806, 1814, 1841-1942; 7 Fibredex boxes.
Clerk's Minutes—Tax Sales, 1932-1968; 8 volumes.
Condemnation Proceedings for Land, 1891-1940; 3 Fibredex boxes.
Deeds, 1774-1940; 2 Fibredex boxes.
Deeds of Trust, 1824-1940; 1 Fibredex box.
Ejectments, 1789-1937; 2 Fibredex boxes.
Land Divisions, 1820-1854, 1871-1937; 1 volume, 1 Fibredex box.

Land Entries, 1778-1846; 1 volume.
Liens and Lis Pendens, Record of, 1948-1962; 2 volumes.
Liens and Mortgages, Index to, 1934; 1 volume.
Miscellaneous Land Records, 1800-1939; 1 Fibredex box.
Mortgage Deeds, 1859-1935; 2 Fibredex boxes.
Sale and Resale of Land, Record of, 1924-1940; 9 volumes.
Sales by Mortgagees and Trustees, Record of, 1916-1935; 3 volumes.
Tax Suit Judgment Docket, Index to, 1929-1937; 1 volume.
Tax Suit Judgment Dockets, 1878-1887, 1929-1962; 15 volumes. [*See also* **COURT RECORDS**, Superior Court, Judgment Dockets]

MARRIAGE, DIVORCE, AND VITAL STATISTICS

Cohabitation, Record of, 1866; 1 volume.
Death Certificates, 1900-1909; 9 volumes.
Divorce Records, 1831-1952; 56 Fibredex boxes. [*See also* **COURT RECORDS**, Superior Court, Minutes]
Marriage Bonds, 1790-1865; 21 Fibredex boxes.
Marriage Licenses, 1852-1930; 87 Fibredex boxes.
Marriage Registers, 1868-1901; 3 volumes.
Marriages, Record of, 1851-1857, 1862-1866; 1 volume.

MILITARY AND PENSION RECORDS [*See* **MISCELLANEOUS RECORDS**]

MISCELLANEOUS RECORDS

Alien Registration, 1927, 1940; 1 volume.
Architects' Certificates of Registration, 1915-1967; 2 volumes.
Assignees, Receivers, and Trustees, Records of, 1867-1959; 43 Fibredex boxes.
Assignments, Record of, 1894-1921; 3 volumes.
Board of County Commissioners, Minutes, 1869-1910; 6 volumes.
Board of Directors of County Workhouse, Minutes, 1866-1874; 1 volume.
Chiropractors' Certificates of Registration, 1917-1956; 1 volume.
Commissions from Governors to hold Court, 1929, 1938-1940; 1 Fibredex box.
County Accounts, 1890-1894; 1 volume.
County Board of Education, Minutes, 1872-1885; 1 volume.
County Home Accounts, 1911-1915; 1 volume.
Dentists' Certificates of Registration, 1947-1960; 1 volume.
Fraternal Organizations, 1895-1940; 3 Fibredex boxes.
General County Accounts, 1911-1915; 2 volumes.
Grand Jury Reports, 1826-1949; 1 Fibredex box.
Homestead and Personal Property Exemptions, 1869-1945; 1 volume, 9 Fibredex boxes.
Insolvent Debtors, 1800-1868; 3 Fibredex boxes.
Jury Tickets, 1927-1931, 1939; 5 volumes.
Licenses to Trades, Registry of, 1876-1877; 1 volume.
Lists of Empaneled Jurors, 1895-1911; 2 volumes.
Lists of Jurors, 1893-1929; 2 volumes.
Magistrates' Settlements (Fines, Penalties, and Forfeitures), Record of, 1874-1877; 1 volume.
Miscellaneous Records, 1772-1952; 6 Fibredex boxes.
Naturalization Records, 1821-1908, 1937; 1 Fibredex box.
Nurses' Certificates of Registration, 1946-1953; 1 volume.
Oaths of Notaries Public, 1907-1929; 2 volumes.
Opticians' Certificates of Registration, 1952-1966; 2 volumes.
Optometrists' Certificates of Registration, 1950-1965; 1 volume.

Orders and Decrees, 1875-1936; 26 volumes.
Osteopaths' Certificates of Registration, 1931-1947; 1 volume.
Partnership, Record of, 1913-1945; 1 volume.
Personal Accounts, 1770-1913; 3 Fibredex boxes.
Physicians' and Surgeons' Certificates of Registration, 1939-1967; 5 volumes.
Railroad Records, 1837-1940; 34 Fibredex boxes.
Receivers' Accounts, 1895-1918; 1 volume.
Receivers, Record of, 1937-1949; 1 volume.
Road Records, 1800-1938; 2 Fibredex boxes.
Roster of Wake County Confederate Soldiers Association, 1886-1914; 1 volume.
School Census, Raleigh Township, 1897-1910; 7 volumes.
School Records, 1856-1939; 4 Fibredex boxes.
Southern Bell Telephone & Telegraph Co. Rate Hearings, 1932-1934; 2 Fibredex boxes.
Special Proceedings Dockets, 1870-1941; 14 volumes.

OFFICIALS, COUNTY [*See* **MISCELLANEOUS RECORDS**]

ROADS AND BRIDGES [*See* **MISCELLANEOUS RECORDS**]

SCHOOL RECORDS [*See* **MISCELLANEOUS RECORDS; CRX RECORDS**]

TAX AND FISCAL RECORDS
Federal Direct Taxes Collected, Record of, 1865; 1 volume.
Lists of Persons Paying Poll Taxes, 1904-1917; 6 volumes.
Tax Lists, 1781-1867; 11 volumes, 2 Fibredex boxes.
Tax Records, 1870-1939; 4 Fibredex boxes.

WILLS
Wills, 1771-1966; 119 Fibredex boxes.
Wills, Cross Index to, 1774-1935; 2 volumes.
Wills, General Index to, 1771-1952; 2 volumes.
Wills, Inventories, and Estates, Record of, 1771-1782; 1 volume.

CRX RECORDS
Civil and Criminal Action Papers, 1857; 3 folders.
Minutes, Court of Pleas and Quarter Sessions, 1771-1776; 1 volume.
School Records, Cary High School, 1907-1926; 1 Fibredex box.

MICROFILM RECORDS

CORPORATIONS AND PARTNERSHIPS
Corporations, Record of, 1883-1913; 1 reel.

COURT RECORDS
County Court of Pleas and Quarter Sessions
Minutes, 1771-1868; 10 reels.
Superior Court
Civil Actions, Index to, Plaintiff, 1960-1968; 1 reel.
Criminal Judgment Docket, 1950-1955; 2 reels.
Equity Minutes, 1818-1866; 1 reel.
Judgment Docket, 1952-1954; 1 reel.
Judgments, Index to, Defendant, 1921-1968; 7 reels.
Judgments, Index to, Plaintiff, 1921-1968; 6 reels.
Minutes, 1818-1944; 33 reels.
Minutes, Criminal, 1949-1957; 2 reels.

ELECTION RECORDS

Election Returns, 1886; Abstracts of Congressional and Judicial Elections; 1 reel.

ESTATES RECORDS [*See also* **WILLS**]

Dowers, Index to, 1804-1946; 1 reel.
Dowers, Record of, 1868-1953; 1 reel.
Estates, Record of, 1868-1888; 2 reels.
Final Accounts with Administrators, Executors, and Collectors, Record of, 1933-1939, 1946-1952; 2 reels.
Final Settlements, Record of, 1883-1946; 8 reels.
Guardians, Index to, 1858-1932; 1 reel.
Inventories of Executors and Administrators, 1891-1940; 3 reels.

LAND RECORDS

Deeds, Record of, 1785-1936; 229 reels.
Divisions of Land, General Index to, 1792-1940; 1 reel.
Land Divisions, Record of, 1820-1854; 1 reel.
Maps and Plats, 1885, 1911; 1 reel.
Partition of Land, Record of, 1879-1966; 3 reels.
Real Estate Conveyances, Index to, Grantee, 1785-1958; 13 reels.
Real Estate Conveyances, Index to, Grantee: Firms and Corporations, 1771-1971; 7 reels.
Real Estate Conveyances, Index to, Grantor, 1785-1958; 15 reels.
Real Estate Conveyances, Index to, Grantor: Firms and Corporations, 1771-1971; 8 reels.
Sales and Resales by Mortgagees and Trustees, Record of, 1934-1936; 1 reel.

MARRIAGE, DIVORCE, AND VITAL STATISTICS

Cohabitation, Record of, 1866; 1 reel.
Death Certificates, 1900-1909; 4 reels.
Divorces, Minutes, 1947-1966; 2 reels.
Maiden Names of Divorced Women, 1938-1968; 1 reel.
Marriage Bonds, 1770-1868; 5 reels.
Marriage Licenses, 1851-1990; 63 reels.
Marriage Registers, 1839-1967; 18 reels.

MISCELLANEOUS RECORDS

Orders and Decrees, 1878-1965; 22 reels.
Special Proceedings, 1879-1968; 9 reels.
Special Proceedings, Index to, 1879-1968; 7 reels.
Wardens of the Poor, Record of, 1846-1872; 1 reel.

OFFICIALS, COUNTY

Board of County Commissioners, Minutes, 1868-1935; 6 reels.

SCHOOL RECORDS

County Board of Education, Minutes, 1873-1959; 3 reels.

TAX AND FISCAL RECORDS

Lists of Taxables, 1781-1817; 1 reel.
Tax Lists, 1809-1904, 1925, 1934; 14 reels.

WILLS

Wills, Index to, Devisee, 1771-1967; 2 reels.
Wills, Index to, Devisor, 1771-1968; 1 reel.
Wills, Inventories, and Settlements of Estates, Record of, 1771-1868; 16 reels.
Wills, Record of, 1868-1966; 20 reels.

WARREN COUNTY

Established in 1779 from Bute County.
Some court records are missing; reason unknown.

ORIGINAL RECORDS

BONDS

Apprentice Bonds and Records, 1779-1912; 2 Fibredex boxes.
Bastardy Bonds and Records, 1779-1912; 2 Fibredex boxes.
Officials' Bonds, 1779, 1790-1871; 3 Fibredex boxes.
Tavern Bonds, 1800-1859; 1 Fibredex box.

COURT RECORDS [*See also* **CRX RECORDS**]

Circuit Criminal Court/Eastern District Criminal Court
- Minutes, 1895-1901; 1 volume.

County Court of Pleas and Quarter Sessions
- Appearance Dockets, 1834-1868; 2 volumes.
- Execution Dockets, 1793-1868; 5 volumes.
- Judgment Dockets, 1787-1813; 2 volumes.
- Minutes, 1780-1813, 1823-1868; 20 volumes.
- Prosecution Bond Docket, 1826-1834; 1 volume.
- State Docket, 1851-1857; 1 volume.
- Trial and Appearance Dockets, 1807-1825; 3 volumes.
- Trial, Appearance, and State Dockets, 1794-1807; 7 volumes.
- Trial Dockets, 1827-1868; 3 volumes.

Inferior Court
- Minutes, 1877-1895; 1 volume.

Superior Court
- Appearance Docket, 1823-1867; 1 volume.
- Civil Action Papers, 1779-1928; 17 Fibredex boxes.
- Civil Action Papers Concerning Land, 1869-1917, 1926, 1930; 6 Fibredex boxes.
- Criminal Action Papers, 1783-1942; 17 Fibredex boxes. [*See also* **TAX AND FISCAL RECORDS**]
- Equity Minutes, 1819-1868; 3 volumes.
- Execution Docket, 1807-1839; 1 volume.
- Executions, 1785-1928; 2 Fibredex boxes.
- Minutes, 1822-1931; 12 volumes.
- State Docket, 1857-1868; 1 volume.
- Trial Dockets, 1823-1868; 2 volumes.

ELECTION RECORDS

Election Records, 1821-1878, 1911; 2 Fibredex boxes.
Elections, Record of, 1878-1933; 4 volumes.

ESTATES RECORDS [*See also* **CRX RECORDS**]

Accounts, Record of, 1868-1925; 4 volumes.
Estates Records, 1772-1940; 79 Fibredex boxes.
Guardians, Record of, 1770-1795; 1 volume (contains Bute County Record of Guardians).
Guardians' Records, 1787-1934; 9 Fibredex boxes.
Settlements, Record of, 1879-1930; 2 volumes.

LAND RECORDS [*See also* **CRX RECORDS**]

Deeds, 1790-1971; 2 Fibredex boxes.
Miscellaneous Deeds, 1784-1986; 2 Fibredex boxes.
Miscellaneous Land Records, 1778-1964; 4 Fibredex boxes.

MARRIAGE, DIVORCE, AND VITAL STATISTICS

Divorce Records, 1874-1918, 1927; 3 Fibredex boxes.
Marriage Bonds, 1779-1868; 9 Fibredex boxes.
Marriage Certificates, Record of, 1851-1867; 1 volume.

MILITARY AND PENSION RECORDS [*See* **MISCELLANEOUS RECORDS**]

MISCELLANEOUS RECORDS

Alien Registration, 1940; 1 volume.
Appointment of Road Overseers, Record of, 1805-1815, 1848-1866; 3 volumes.
Assignees, Receivers, and Trustees, Records of, 1874-1936; 1 Fibredex box.
Board of Superintendents of Common Schools, Minutes, 1853-1860; 1 volume.
Bridge Records, 1800-1887, 1924; 1 Fibredex box.
Common School Registers, 1858-1864, 1882-1884; 12 volumes.
Coroners' Inquests, 1800-1848, 1902-1967; 2 Fibredex boxes.
County Accounts, 1779-1921; 2 Fibredex boxes.
County Buildings, 1818-1965; 1 Fibredex box.
County Claims Allowed, 1806-1814; 1 volume.
Court Martial Proceedings, 1791-1815; 1 volume.
Insolvent Debtors and Homestead and Personal Property Exemptions, 1799-1931, 1935; 1 Fibredex box.
Jury Lists and Tickets, 1818-1907; 1 Fibredex box
Miscellaneous Records, 1769-1963; 4 Fibredex boxes. [*See also* **CRX RECORDS**]
Pension Records, 1817-1941; 1 Fibredex box.
Petitions for Naturalization, 1906-1914, 1957; 1 volume.
Railroad Records, 1836-1925; 2 Fibredex boxes.
Road Records, 1792-1921; 2 Fibredex boxes.
Slaves and Free Persons of Color, Records of, 1779-1870; 1 Fibredex box.

ROADS AND BRIDGES [*See* **MISCELLANEOUS RECORDS**]

SCHOOL RECORDS [*See* **MISCELLANEOUS RECORDS; CRX RECORDS**]

TAX AND FISCAL RECORDS [*See also* **CRX RECORDS**]

Criminal Actions Concerning Taxation, 1875-1925; 2 Fibredex boxes.
Federal Direct Taxes Collected, Record of, 1866; 1 volume.
Lists of Taxables, 1781-1801, 1824-1828, 1866-1878; 4 volumes, 2 Fibredex boxes.
Merchants' Purchase Returns, 1901-1904; 1 Fibredex box.
Miscellaneous Tax Records, 1780-1935; 1 Fibredex box.
Tax Abstracts, 1822-1864, 1897-1915; 1 Fibredex box.

WILLS

Wills, 1779-1931; 23 Fibredex boxes.

CRX RECORDS

Board of Superintendents of Common Schools, Minutes, 1857-1864; 1 volume.
Civil Action Papers, 1779-1893; 15 Fibredex boxes.
County School Fund Apportionment Record, 1904-1905; 1 volume.
Criminal Action Papers, 1779-1902; 3 Fibredex boxes.

Criminal Action Papers and Land Records, 1779-1897; 1 Fibredex box.
Equity Docket, Superior Court, 1805-1833; 1 volume.
Equity Fee Books, 1793-1866; 2 volumes.
Estates and Miscellaneous Records, 1853-1866; 51 folders.
Estates Records, 1765-1894; 7 Fibredex boxes, 1 folder.
Guardians' Records, 1784-1875; 1 Fibredex box.
Land Records, 1791-1894; 1 Fibredex box.
Minutes, Court of Pleas and Quarter Sessions, 1826; 1 volume.
Minutes, Superior Court, 1807-1821; 1 volume.
Miscellaneous Records, 1779-1935; 4 Fibredex boxes.
Tax Lists, 1851; 1 folder.

MICROFILM RECORDS

CORPORATIONS AND PARTNERSHIPS

Assumed Business Names, Index to, 1936-1964; 1 reel.
Corporations, Record of, 1892-1964; 1 reel.
Partnership Records, 1913-1964; 1 reel.

COURT RECORDS

County Court of Pleas and Quarter Sessions
- Minutes, 1777-1813, 1823-1868; 6 reels.
- Minutes (Rough), 1801-1805; 1 reel.

Superior Court
- Equity Minutes, 1819-1838, 1855-1868; 1 reel.
- Judgment Dockets, 1894-1925; 1 reel.
- Judgments, Index to, Defendant, 1904-1968; 1 reel.
- Judgments, Index to, Plaintiff, 1904-1968; 1 reel.
- Minutes, 1822-1964; 7 reels.
- Minutes, Criminal, Index to, 1823-1968; 1 reel.

ELECTION RECORDS

Elections, Record of, 1880-1964; 1 reel.

ESTATES RECORDS

Accounts, Record of, 1868-1964; 5 reels.
Administrators, Cross Index to, 1866-1965; 1 reel.
Administrators and Executors, Cross Index to, 1927-1936; 1 reel.
Administrators and Guardians, Record of, 1905-1906; 1 reel.
Administrators, Record of, 1912-1964; 3 reels.
Division of Estates, 1820-1821; 1 reel.
Executors, Record of, 1919-1964; 1 reel.
Guardians, Cross Index to, 1926-1936; 1 reel.
Guardians, Record of, 1926-1964; 1 reel.
Inheritance Tax Records, 1923-1964; 1 reel.
Settlements, Record of, 1878-1964; 3 reels.

LAND RECORDS

Deeds, Record of, 1764-1958; 96 reels.
Federal Tax Lien Index, 1926-1964; 1 reel.
Land Sold for Taxes, Record of, 1931; County Tax Lien, 1933-1934; 1 reel.
Map Book, 1913-1954; 1 reel.
Real Estate Conveyances, Cross Index to, 1764-1918; 1 reel.

Real Estate Conveyances, General Index to, 1918-1925; 1 reel.
Real Estate Conveyances, Index to, Grantee, 1860-1964; 3 reels.
Real Estate Conveyances, Index to, Grantor, 1860-1964; 4 reels.
Resale of Land, Record of, 1941-1964; 1 reel.

MARRIAGE, DIVORCE, AND VITAL STATISTICS

Births, Index to, 1914-1991; 1 reel.
Cohabitation Records, 1866; 1 reel.
Deaths, Index to, 1914-1991; 1 reel.
Delayed Births, Index to, various years; 1 reel.
Maiden Names of Divorced Women, 1937-1968; 1 reel.
Marriage Bond Abstracts, 1779-1868; 1 reel.
Marriage Bonds, 1779-1868; 4 reels.
Marriage Licenses, 1861-1964; 13 reels.
Marriage Registers, 1851-1978; 4 reels.

MISCELLANEOUS RECORDS

Assignments, Record of, 1898-1939; 1 reel.
Orders and Decrees, 1877-1955; 8 reels.
Special Proceedings, 1918-1947; 1 reel.
Special Proceedings, Index to, 1870-1965; 2 reels.

OFFICIALS, COUNTY

Minutes, Board of County Commissioners, 1868-1879, 1907-1965; 2 reels.
Minutes, County Board of Health, 1946-1964; 2 reels.

SCHOOL RECORDS

Minutes, Board of Superintendents of Common Schools, 1853-1858; 1 reel.
Minutes, County Board of Education, 1872-1964; 1 reel.

TAX AND FISCAL RECORDS

Tax Lists, 1779-1808; 1 reel.

WILLS

Wills, Accounts, Inventories, and Settlements, Record of, 1764-1863; 16 reels.
Wills, Index to, Devisee, 1763-1968; 1 reel.
Wills, Index to, Devisor, 1763-1968; 1 reel.
Wills, Record of, 1863-1964; 3 reels.

WASHINGTON COUNTY

Established in 1799 from Tyrrell County.
Courthouse destroyed in Federal bombardment of 1862.
Courthouse fires of 1869, 1873, and 1881, along with the destruction of 1862, destroyed most of the court records and many of the land records.

ORIGINAL RECORDS

COURT RECORDS

Superior Court

- Civil Action Papers, 1815-1930; 3 Fibredex boxes.
- Civil Action Papers Concerning Land, 1876-1932; 4 Fibredex boxes.
- Criminal Action Papers, 1855, 1873-1918; 7 Fibredex boxes.
- Minutes, 1822-1921; 9 volumes.

ELECTION RECORDS

Elections, Record of, 1878-1952; 2 volumes.
Voter Registration Books, 1940-1948; 13 volumes in 2 Fibredex boxes.

ESTATES RECORDS

Estates Records, 1795-1959; 13 Fibredex boxes.
Guardians' Records, 1870-1941; 6 Fibredex boxes.

LAND RECORDS

Deeds, 1830-1931; 1 Fibredex box.
Deeds, Record of, 1800-1801; 1 volume.
Deeds of Trust and Mortgage Deeds, 1878-1928; 1 Fibredex box.
Land Records, 1856-1944; 1 Fibredex box.

MARRIAGE, DIVORCE, AND VITAL STATISTICS

Divorce Records, 1851, 1873-1903; 1 Fibredex box.
Freedmen's Marriages, Record of, 1866-1872; 1 volume.

MISCELLANEOUS RECORDS

Licenses to Trades, Registry of, 1883-1902; 1 volume.
Miscellaneous Records, 1867-1933; 2 Fibredex boxes.
Stock Marks, Record of, 1869-1930; 1 volume.

WILLS

Wills, 1856-1964; 5 Fibredex boxes.

MICROFILM RECORDS

CORPORATIONS AND PARTNERSHIPS

Corporations, Record of, 1932-1986; 2 reels.
Partnership Records, 1917-1975; 1 reel.

COURT RECORDS

Superior Court

- Minutes, 1822-1959; 8 reels.

ESTATES RECORDS

Accounts of Administrators, Executors, and Guardians, Record of, 1873-1951; 2 reels.
Administrators, Executors, and Guardians, Record of, 1911-1929; 1 reel.

Administrators, Record of, 1919-1967; 2 reels.
Executors, Record of, 1944-1967; 1 reel.
Guardians, Record of, 1929-1967; 1 reel.
Inheritance Tax Records, 1935-1967; 1 reel.
Settlements, Record of, 1873-1950; 2 reels.

LAND RECORDS

Deeds, Record of, 1800-1960; 62 reels.
Real Estate Conveyances, Index to, Grantee, 1779-1967; 2 reels.
Real Estate Conveyances, Index to, Grantor, 1779-1967; 2 reels.
Registration of Land Titles, 1915-1962; 7 reels.
Resale of Land by Trustees and Mortgagees, Record of, 1919-1967; 2 reels.

MARRIAGE, DIVORCE, AND VITAL STATISTICS

Births, Index to, 1912-1985; 1 reel.
Deaths, Index to, 1912-1986; 1 reel.
Maiden Names of Divorced Women, 1944-1967; 1 reel.
Marriage Registers, 1885-1986; 3 reels.
Marriages, Record of, 1851-1884; 1 reel.

MISCELLANEOUS RECORDS

Orders and Decrees, 1873-1964; 1 reel.
Special Proceedings, Cross Index to, 1909-1967; 1 reel.
Special Proceedings Dockets, 1873-1954; 2 reels.

OFFICIALS, COUNTY

Board of County Commissioners, Minutes, 1868-1950; 3 reels.

SCHOOL RECORDS

Board of Superintendents of Common Schools, Minutes, 1841-1862; County Board of Education, Minutes, 1872-1926; 1 reel.

WILLS

Wills, Cross Index to, 1873-1967; 1 reel.
Wills, Record of, 1873-1967; 2 reels.

WATAUGA COUNTY

Established in 1849 from Ashe, Caldwell, Wilkes, and Yancey counties.
Courthouse fire of 1873 destroyed all of the land records
and most of the court records.

ORIGINAL RECORDS

Bonds

Apprentice Bonds, 1874-1906; 2 volumes.
Apprentice Bonds, 1899-1900; Bastardy Bonds, 1874-1935; 1 Fibredex box.
Bastardy Bonds, 1873-1878; 1 volume.
Officials' Bonds, 1873-1958; 3 Fibredex boxes.

Court Records

Superior Court
- Civil Action Papers, 1873-1953; 12 Fibredex boxes.
- Civil Action Papers Concerning Land, 1874-1948; 21 Fibredex boxes.
- Criminal Action Papers, 1873-1962; 10 Fibredex boxes. [*See also* **CRX RECORDS**]
- Minutes, 1873-1924; 9 volumes.

Election Records

Elections, Record of, 1878-1938; 3 volumes.

Estates Records

Accounts, Record of, 1873-1914; 2 volumes.
Administrators' Bonds, 1873-1911; 2 volumes.
Appointment of Administrators, Executors, Guardians, and Masters, 1873-1926; 1 volume.
Estates Records, 1858-1948; 40 Fibredex boxes.
Guardians' Bonds, 1888-1910; 1 volume.
Guardians' Records, 1873-1955; 7 Fibredex boxes.
Settlements, Record of, 1873-1925; 1 volume.

Land Records

Attachments, Executions, Levies, and Liens on Land, 1876-1947; 1 Fibredex box.
Deeds, 1858-1976; 12 Fibredex boxes.
Deeds, Cross Index to, 1873-1949; 10 volumes.
Deeds of Trust, 1882-1976; 4 Fibredex boxes.
Ejectments (Summary Proceedings), 1915-1947; 1 Fibredex box.
Land Sold for Taxes, Record of, 1935-1938; 1 volume.
Miscellaneous Land Records, 1830-1962; 1 Fibredex box.
Mortgage Deeds, 1877-1957; 1 Fibredex box.
Probate, Record of, 1873-1885; 1 volume.
Tax Levies on Land, 1874-1939; 1 Fibredex box.

Marriage, Divorce, and Vital Statistics

Divorce Records, 1874-1948; 13 Fibredex boxes.
Marriage Licenses, 1873-1894; 1 Fibredex box.
Marriage Registers, 1873-1954; 3 volumes.

Miscellaneous Records

Alien Registration, 1940; 1 volume.
Assignees, Receivers, and Trustees, Records of, 1911-1936; 2 Fibredex boxes.

Board of County Commissioners, Minutes, 1913-1921; 2 volumes.
County Treasurer Reports, Record of, 1911-1931; 1 volume.
Directors of Peoples Bank and Trust Co., Boone, Minutes, 1929-1934; 1 volume.
Homestead and Personal Property Exemptions, 1874-1933; 1 Fibredex box.
Miscellaneous Records, 1858-1974; 3 Fibredex boxes.
Road and Bridge Records, 1867-1946; 5 Fibredex boxes.
Sheriff's Road Fund Account Book, 1925-1926; 1 volume.
School Census, 1869-1896; 2 Fibredex boxes.
School Vouchers and Miscellaneous School Records, 1870-1936; 3 Fibredex boxes.

OFFICIALS, COUNTY [*See* **MISCELLANEOUS RECORDS; CRX RECORDS**]

ROADS AND BRIDGES [*See* **MISCELLANEOUS RECORDS; CRX RECORDS**]

SCHOOL RECORDS [*See* **MISCELLANEOUS RECORDS**]

TAX AND FISCAL RECORDS

Miscellaneous Tax Records, 1873-1936; 1 Fibredex box.
Tax Collections and Land Sales, Sheriff's Record of, 1929-1931; 1 volume.

WILLS

Wills, 1859, 1872-1947; 7 Fibredex boxes.

CRX RECORDS

Board of Road Commissioners, Minutes, 1918-1921; 1 volume.
Criminal Action Papers, 1904; 2 folders.

MICROFILM RECORDS

BONDS

Apprentice Bonds, 1874-1906; 1 reel.

CORPORATIONS AND PARTNERSHIPS

Corporations, Record of, 1889-1969; 1 reel.

COURT RECORDS

Superior Court
Minutes, 1873-1959; 8 reels.

ELECTION RECORDS

Elections, Record of, 1878-1968; 1 reel.

ESTATES RECORDS

Accounts, Record of, 1873-1968; 4 reels.
Administrators' Bonds, 1873-1911; 1 reel.
Administrators and Executors, Index to, 1873-1968; 1 reel.
Administrators, Record of, 1911-1968; 2 reels.
Appointment of Administrators and Guardians, 1873-1926; 1 reel.
Executors, Record of, 1925-1968; 1 reel.
Guardians, Index to, 1873-1968; 1 reel.
Guardians, Record of, 1911-1968; 1 reel.
Inheritance Tax Records, 1920-1969; 1 reel.
Settlements, Record of, 1873-1968; 3 reels.
Trust Funds and Accounts for Indigent Children, 1915-1968; 1 reel.

LAND RECORDS

Deeds, Record of, 1870-1958; 53 reels.
Plat Books, 1922-1967; 1 reel.
Real Estate Conveyances, Index to, Grantee, 1872-1969; 5 reels.
Real Estate Conveyances, Index to, Grantor, 1872-1969; 5 reels.
Resale of Land, Record of, 1922-1968; 1 reel.
Surveys, Record of, 1904-1953; 1 reel.

MARRIAGE, DIVORCE, AND VITAL STATISTICS

Births, Index to, 1914-1969; 2 reels.
Deaths, Index to, 1914-1968; 1 reel.
Marriage Registers, 1873-1969; 2 reels.

MISCELLANEOUS RECORDS

Assignees and Receivers, Record of, 1910-1920; 1 reel.
Orders and Decrees, 1872-1967; 6 reels.
Orders and Decrees, Cross Index to, 1873-1968; 1 reel.
Special Proceedings Docket, 1902-1921; 1 reel.
Special Proceedings, Index to, 1968-1980; 1 reel.

OFFICIALS, COUNTY

Board of County Commissioners, Minutes, 1873-1938; 4 reels.

TAX AND FISCAL RECORDS

Tax Lists, 1913-1942; 14 reels.
Tax Scrolls, 1888-1940; 5 reels.

WILLS

Wills, Cross Index to, 1873-1969; 1 reel.
Wills, Record of, 1873-1968; 2 reels.

WAYNE COUNTY

Established in 1779 from Dobbs County.
A few early court records are missing; reason unknown.

ORIGINAL RECORDS

BONDS

- Apprentice Bonds and Records, 1800-1917; 3 volumes, 5 Fibredex boxes.
- Bastardy Bonds and Records, 1786-1879, 1889; Constables' Bonds, 1862-1865; 2 volumes, 5 Fibredex boxes.
- Officials' Bonds and Records, 1786-1925; 7 volumes, 6 Fibredex boxes.
- Tax Collectors' Bonds, 1892-1894; 1 volume.

CORPORATIONS AND PARTNERSHIPS [*See* **ESTATES RECORDS**]

COURT RECORDS

- County Court of Pleas and Quarter Sessions
  - Appearance Docket, 1857-1868; 1 volume.
  - Execution Dockets, 1802-1868; 9 volumes.
  - Minutes, 1787-1794, 1823-1867; 11 volumes. [*See also* **CRX RECORDS**]
  - State Dockets, 1785-1802, 1811-1868; 5 volumes.
  - Trial and Appearance Docket, 1820-1822; 1 volume.
  - Trial Dockets, 1823-1841, 1855-1868; 4 volumes.
- Inferior Court
  - Minutes, 1877-1885; 1 volume.
- Superior Court
  - Civil Action Papers, 1782-1924; 76 Fibredex boxes.
  - Civil Action Papers Concerning Land, 1785-1930; 13 Fibredex boxes.
  - Civil Issues Dockets, 1869-1876, 1885-1892, 1896-1901; 4 volumes.
  - Criminal Action Papers, 1785-1929; 39 Fibredex boxes.
  - Criminal Issues Dockets, 1868-1876, 1887-1930; 7 volumes.
  - Equity Execution Docket, 1858-1868; 1 volume.
  - Equity Minutes, 1839-1843, 1851-1868; 3 volumes.
  - Equity Trial and Appearance Dockets, 1807-1861; 3 volumes.
  - Minutes, 1807-1968; 48 volumes.
  - State Dockets, 1834-1843, 1856-1871; 2 volumes.
  - Trial and Appearance Dockets, 1807-1832; 2 volumes.
- Wayne County Court
  - Minutes, 1913-1922; 2 volumes.

ELECTION RECORDS

- Election Records, 1792-1913; 2 Fibredex boxes.
- Elections, Record of, 1878-1966; 6 volumes.
- Permanent Registration of Voters, 1902-1908; 1 volume.

ESTATES RECORDS [*See also* **CRX RECORDS**]

- Accounts Filed, Index to, 1907-1920; 1 volume.
- Accounts, Record of, 1869-1953; 18 volumes.
- Administrators' Bonds, 1861-1896; 6 volumes.

Administrators, Executors, and Guardians, Record of, 1874-1882; 1 volume.
Administrators, Record of, 1897-1940; 9 volumes.
Appointment of Administrators, Executors, Guardians, and Masters, 1868-1903; 1 volume.
Appointment of Administrators, Executors, and Guardians, Record of, 1940-1957; 9 volumes.
Estates, Record of, 1782-1868; 21 volumes.
Estates Records, 1782-1937; 173 Fibredex boxes.
Executors and Administrators, Cross Index to, 1903-1919; 1 volume.
Executors and Guardians, Record of, 1899-1916; 2 volumes.
Executors, Record of, 1914-1940; 3 volumes.
Guardians' Bonds, 1824-1900; 9 volumes.
Guardians, Cross Index to, 1903-1919; 1 volume.
Guardians, Record of, 1916-1941; 3 volumes.
Guardians' Records, 1787-1937; 19 Fibredex boxes.
Inheritance Tax, Record of, 1923-1968; 4 volumes.
Probate Court, Minutes, 1869-1890; Record of Corporations, 1884-1900; Record of Notaries Public, 1914-1924; 1 volume.
Settlements, Record of, 1878-1953; 11 volumes.

LAND RECORDS [*See also* **CRX RECORDS**]
Commissioners' and Trustees' Accounts of Sale, 1926-1968; 3 volumes.
Deeds, 1785-1920; 4 Fibredex boxes.
Ejectments, 1788-1874, 1935; 3 Fibredex boxes.
Land Divisions, Cross Index to, 1785-1939; 1 volume.
Land Divisions and Sales of Land, 1814-1930; 1 Fibredex box.
Levies on Land, 1788-1889; 9 Fibredex boxes.
Miscellaneous Land Records, 1790-1927; 1 Fibredex box.
Sale and Resale of Land, Record of, 1921-1930, 1935-1960; 4 volumes.
Tax Suit Judgment Dockets, 1931-1969; 5 volumes.

MARRIAGE, DIVORCE, AND VITAL STATISTICS
Divorce Records, 1822-1930; 7 Fibredex boxes.
Maiden Names of Divorced Women, 1939-1969; 1 volume.
Marriage Bonds, 1790-1859; 2 folders in Fibredex box.
Marriage Licenses, 1851-1861, 1863; 2 volumes.

MISCELLANEOUS RECORDS
Alien Registration, 1927, 1933, 1935, 1940, 1954; 1 volume.
Appointment of Road Overseers, 1857-1879; 1 volume.
Assignees, Receivers, and Trustees, Records of, 1875-1935; 1 Fibredex box.
Bridge Records, 1793-1886; 1 Fibredex box.
Corporations, Record of, 1884-1900. [*See* **ESTATES RECORDS**, Probate Court, Minutes, 1869-1890]
County Accounts and Court Orders, 1785-1868; 3 Fibredex boxes.
County Highway Commission, Minutes, 1915-1931; 2 volumes.
Declaration of Intent (to Become a Citizen), 1908, 1910; 1 volume.
Drainage Record, 1911-1934; 1 volume.
Goldsboro Township Board of Trustees, Minutes, 1869-1877; 1 volume.
Homestead and Personal Property Exemptions, 1849, 1867-1933; 1.5 Fibredex boxes.
Inebriates, Record of, 1942-1965; 1 volume.
Insolvent Debtors, 1800-1863; 2.5 Fibredex boxes.

Jury Lists, 1797-1867; 1 Fibredex box.
Licenses to Trades, Registry of, 1884-1903; 1 volume.
Lunacy, Record of, 1899-1969; 6 volumes.
Miscellaneous Records, 1788-1936; 5 Fibredex boxes.
Notaries Public, Record of, 1914-1924. [*See* **ESTATES RECORDS**, Probate Court, Minutes, 1869-1890]
Official Reports, Record of, 1875-1919; 2 volumes.
Officials' Oaths, Record of, 1938-1968; 1 volume.
Orders and Decrees, 1869-1954; 22 volumes.
Railroad Records, 1837-1912; 3 Fibredex boxes.
Receivers, Record of, 1929-1964; 2 volumes.
Road Records, 1791-1914; 4 Fibredex boxes.
School Fund Ledger, 1884-1885; 1 volume.
Slaves and Free Persons of Color, Records of, 1783-1869; 4 Fibredex boxes.
Special Proceedings Dockets, 1884-1939; 3 volumes.
Special Proceedings Judgment Docket, 1938-1952; 1 volume.
Wardens of the Poor, Minutes and Accounts, 1819-1841; 1 volume.

ROADS AND BRIDGES [*See* **MISCELLANEOUS RECORDS**]

SCHOOL RECORDS [*See* **MISCELLANEOUS RECORDS**]

TAX AND FISCAL RECORDS [*See also* **BONDS; CRX RECORDS**]
Tax Collections, Record of, 1935-1936; 2 volumes.
Tax Levies under the Stock Law of 1885, 1885-1886; 1 volume.
Tax Records, 1780-1920; 2 Fibredex boxes.
Schedule "B" Tax Lists, 1896-1899; 3 volumes.

WILLS
Wills, 1776-1927; 18 Fibredex boxes.
Wills, Cross Index to, 1782-1939; 2 volumes.

CRX RECORDS
Deed, 1874; 1 folder.
Estates Records, 1788-1852; 7 folders.
Guardians' Bonds, 1857-1867; 1 volume.
Land Entry Book, 1780-1796, 1852-1903; 1 volume.
Minutes, Court of Pleas and Quarter Sessions, 1820-1823; 1 volume.
Tax Book, 1833-1867; 1 volume.

MICROFILM RECORDS

BONDS
Apprentice Bonds, 1861-1889; 1 reel.
Constables' and Bastardy Bonds, 1861-1878, 1889; 1 reel.

CORPORATIONS AND PARTNERSHIPS
Corporations, Record of, 1869-1965; 3 reels.
Partnership Records, 1914-1965; Limited Partnerships, 1945-1965; 1 reel.

COURT RECORDS
County Court of Pleas and Quarter Sessions
Minutes, 1787-1794, 1823-1868; 4 reels.

Inferior Court
- Minutes, 1877-1885; 1 reel.

Superior Court
- Civil Actions, Index to, Plaintiff, n.d.; 1 reel.
- Criminal Actions, Index to, 1913-1968; 3 reels.
- Equity Minutes, 1819-1868; 1 reel.
- Judgments, Index to, 1911-1968; 11 reels.
- Minutes, 1826-1942; 13 reels.

ELECTION RECORDS

Elections, Record of, 1932-1964; 1 reel.

ESTATES RECORDS

Accounts, Index to, 1907-1920; 1 reel.
Accounts, Record of, 1869-1953; 9 reels.
Administrators' Bonds, 1861-1892; 1 reel.
Administrators and Executors, Cross Index to, 1903-1919; 1 reel.
Administrators, Record of, 1897-1940; 5 reels.
Appointment of Administrators and Guardians, Record of, 1940-1957; 5 reels.
Appointment of Executors, 1869-1903; 1 reel.
Divisions and Dowers, 1867-1950; 4 reels.
Estates, General Index to: Decedents and Minors, 1788-1965; 1 reel.
Estates, General Index to: Executors, Administrators, Guardians, and Trustees, 1820-1965; 1 reel.
Estates Records, 1782-1805; 1 reel.
Executors and Guardians, Record of, 1899-1914; 1 reel.
Executors, Record of, 1914-1940; 1 reel.
Final Accounts, Index to, 1877-1936; 1 reel.
Guardians' Bonds, 1824-1878; 1 reel.
Guardians, Cross Index to, 1903-1919; 1 reel.
Guardians, Record of, 1916-1941; 1 reel.
Inheritance Tax Collections, 1914-1965; 2 reels.
Receivers of Estates, Record and Index of, 1937-1964; 1 reel.
Settlements, Record of, 1878-1953; 5 reels.

LAND RECORDS

Deeds, Record of, 1779-1958; 242 reels.
Federal Tax Lien Index, 1928-1969; 1 reel.
Grants, Record of, 1826-1892; 1 reel.
Land Divisions, Cross Index to, 1786-1938; 1 reel.
Plat Books and Index to Plats, 1847-1965; 4 reels.
Processioners' Record, 1819-1820; 1 reel.
Real Estate Conveyances, Index to, Grantee, 1780-1963; 11 reels.
Real Estate Conveyances, Index to, Grantor, 1780-1963; 10 reels.
Resale under Trustees and Mortgagees, Record of, 1921-1965; 5 reels.
Trustees' and Commissioners' Accounts of Land Sales, 1926-1965; 1 reel.

MARRIAGE, DIVORCE, AND VITAL STATISTICS

Births, Index to, 1913-1986; 6 reels.
Certificates of Marriage, 1851-1868; 1 reel.

Deaths, Index to, 1913-1987; 3 reels.
Delayed Births, Index to, various years; 1 reel.
Maiden Names of Divorced Women, 1939-1968; 1 reel.
Marriage Bonds, 1814-1868; 1 reel.
Marriage Licenses, 1877-1964; 20 reels.
Marriage Registers, 1861-1961; 4 reels.

MISCELLANEOUS RECORDS

Inebriates, Record of, 1942-1965; 1 reel.
Lunacy, Record of, 1899-1965; 2 reels.
Orders and Decrees, 1869-1948; 10 reels.
Special Proceedings, 1884-1952; 1 reel.
Special Proceedings, Index to, Defendant, 1884-1965; 1 reel.
Special Proceedings, Index to, Plaintiff, 1884-1965; 1 reel.

OFFICIALS, COUNTY

Board of County Commissioners, Minutes, 1868-1950; 5 reels.
County Board of Health, Minutes, 1930-1965; 1 reel.

SCHOOL RECORDS

County Board of Education, Minutes, 1921-1965; 1 reel.

TAX AND FISCAL RECORDS

Tax Lists, 1882-1883, 1891-1900, 1905; 4 reels.

WILLS

Wills, Accounts, Inventories, and Sales of Estates, Record of, 1782-1868; 8 reels.
Wills, Index to, Devisee, 1782-1968; 1 reel.
Wills, Index to, Devisor, 1782-1968; 1 reel.
Wills, Record of, 1868-1957; 5 reels.

WILKES COUNTY

Established in 1777 (effective 1778) from Surry County and the District of Washington.
A few early records are missing; reason unknown.

ORIGINAL RECORDS

Bonds

Apprentice Bonds and Records, 1778-1916; 2 volumes, 1 Fibredex box.
Bastardy Bonds and Records, 1773-1911; 1 volume, 5 Fibredex boxes.
Officials' Bonds and Records, 1777-1914; 5 Fibredex boxes.

Court Records

County Court of Pleas and Quarter Sessions
- Appearance Docket, 1840-1853; 1 volume.
- Execution Dockets, 1837-1868; 2 volumes.
- Minutes, 1778-1868; 11 volumes, 3 manuscript boxes.
- Miscellaneous Dockets, 1778-1859; 1 manuscript box.
- State Docket, 1778-1792; 1 manuscript box.
- Trial and Appearance Docket, 1824-1827; 1 volume.
- Trial Docket, 1837-1859; 1 volume.
- Witness Dockets, 1807-1837; 2 volumes.

Superior Court
- Appearance Docket, 1823-1846; 1 volume.
- Civil Action Papers, 1771-1936; 58 Fibredex boxes.
- Civil Action Papers Concerning Land, 1778-1928; 19 Fibredex boxes.
- Criminal Action Papers, 1761, 1778-1945; 62 Fibredex boxes.
- Criminal Issues Dockets, 1873, 1879-1884; 3 volumes.
- Equity Enrolling Dockets, 1813-1857; 2 volumes.
- Equity Execution Docket, 1814-1861; Equity Appearance Docket, 1815-1830; 1 manuscript box.
- Equity Minutes, 1819-1860; 1 manuscript box.
- Execution Dockets, 1807-1860; 6 volumes.
- Judgment Dockets, 1868-1877; 2 volumes.
- Minutes, 1807-1931; 30 volumes, 2 manuscript boxes, 1 Fibredex box.
- Miscellaneous Dockets, 1807-1855; 1 Fibredex box.
- Recognizance Docket, 1812-1832; 1 volume.
- State Dockets, 1807-1822, 1837-1866; 3 volumes.
- Trial and Appearance Docket, 1807-1822; 1 volume.
- Trial Docket, 1822-1844; 1 volume.
- Witness Docket, 1824-1833; 1 volume.

Election Records

Elections, Record of, 1904-1922; 2 volumes.

Estates Records [*See also* **Wills**]

Accounts, Record of, 1868-1939; 6 volumes.
Administrators' Bonds, 1890-1919; 2 volumes.
Administrators, Executors, and Guardians, Record of, 1915-1941; 5 volumes.
Amounts Paid to Indigent Children, Record of, 1913-1935; 1 volume.
Appointment of Administrators, Executors, and Guardians, 1903-1915; 1 volume.

Appointment of Administrators, Executors, Guardians, and Masters, 1868-1903; 1 volume.
Estates Records, 1777-1945; 49 Fibredex boxes.
Guardians' Bonds, 1910-1921; 1 volume.
Guardians' Records, 1780-1939; 4 Fibredex boxes.
Settlements, Record of, 1805-1834, 1869-1944; 5 volumes.
Widows' Year's Allowance, Record of, 1871-1970; 2 volumes.

LAND RECORDS

Deeds, 1741-1944; 4 Fibredex boxes.
Deeds and Grants, Record of, 1779-1796; 3 volumes.
Deeds, Record of, 1789-1851; 11 volumes.
Ejectments, 1799-1907; 2 Fibredex boxes.
Land Entries, 1783-1851; 5 volumes, 2 manuscript boxes.
List of Land Entries, 1808-1828; 1 volume.
Miscellaneous Land Records, 1778-1925; 2 Fibredex boxes.
Petitions for Partition and Sale of Land, 1892-1912, 1932; 1 Fibredex box.
Processioners' Record, 1883-1884; 1 volume.
Sale of Land for Taxes, Record of, 1870-1887; 1 volume.

MARRIAGE, DIVORCE, AND VITAL STATISTICS

Divorce Records, 1820-1912; 5 Fibredex boxes.
Marriage Bonds, 1778-1868; 12 Fibredex boxes.
Marriage and Family Records, 1788-1912; 1 Fibredex box.

MILITARY AND PENSION RECORDS [*See* **MISCELLANEOUS RECORDS**]

MISCELLANEOUS RECORDS

Alien Registration, 1940; 1 volume.
Assignees, Receivers, and Trustees, Records of, 1872-1915; 1 Fibredex box.
Clerk's Minute Dockets (Special Proceedings), 1884-1941; 8 volumes.
County Accounts, 1773-1903; 1 Fibredex box.
Good Roads Commission, Minutes, 1924-1931; 1 volume.
Homestead Records, 1871-1917; 1 Fibredex box.
Insolvents' Records, 1780-1896; 1 Fibredex box.
Jurors, Record of, 1893-1906; 1 volume.
Justices of the Peace, Record of, 1877-1898; 1 volume.
Lunacy, Record of, 1899-1937; 2 volumes.
Miscellaneous Records, 1775-1946; 5 Fibredex boxes.
Orders and Decrees, 1869-1935, 1938; 2 volumes.
Pension Records, 1814-1927; 1 Fibredex box.
Pensions, Record of, no date; 1 volume.
Physicians' Certificates of Registration, 1889-1988; 1 manuscript box.
Road Dockets, 1822-1833, 1850-1856; 2 volumes.
Road Records, 1776-1911; 4 Fibredex boxes.
School Records, 1840-1904; 4 Fibredex boxes.
Special Proceedings, Cross Index to, 1880-1933; 1 volume.
Special Proceedings Dockets, 1880-1941; 3 volumes.
Strays, Record of, 1822-1839; 1 volume.

ROADS AND BRIDGES [*See* **MISCELLANEOUS RECORDS**]

SCHOOL RECORDS [*See* **MISCELLANEOUS RECORDS**]

Tax and Fiscal Records

Tax Lists, 1778-1888; 4 Fibredex boxes.
Tax Records, 1781-1908; 1 Fibredex box.

Wills

Wills, 1778-1970; 37 Fibredex boxes.
Wills, Bonds, Inventories, and Bills of Sale, Record of, 1778-1799; 2 volumes.

MICROFILM RECORDS

Bonds

Bastardy Bonds, 1871-1883; 1 reel.

Corporations and Partnerships

Corporations, Record of, 1891-1970; 2 reels.
Partnerships, Record of, 1914-1964; 1 reel.

Court Records

County Court of Pleas and Quarter Sessions
- Minutes, 1778-1868; 3 reels.

Superior Court
- Criminal Issues Docket (Solicitor), 1879-1883; 1 reel.
- Equity Enrolling Dockets, 1813-1857; 1 reel.
- Equity Minutes, 1819-1860; 1 reel.
- Judgments, Index to, Defendant, 1924-1970; 2 reels.
- Judgments, Index to, Plaintiff, 1924-1970; 2 reels.
- Minutes, 1807-1945; 19 reels.

Election Records

Elections, Record of, 1904-1922, 1938-1954; 1 reel.

Estates Records

Accounts of Indigent Orphans, 1913-1935; 1 reel.
Accounts, Record of, 1868-1963; 5 reels.
Administrators' Bonds, 1890-1919; 1 reel.
Administrators, Guardians, and Executors, Cross Index to, 1869-1943; 1 reel.
Appointment of Administrators, Executors, and Guardians, 1868-1964; 7 reels.
Guardians' Bonds, 1910-1921; 1 reel.
Inheritance Tax Records, 1919-1923, 1963-1964; 1 reel.
Settlements, Record of, 1805-1834, 1869-1960; 5 reels.
Widows' Annual Allowance, 1871-1963; 1 reel.

Land Records

Deeds and Bonds, Record of, 1784-1854; 1 reel.
Deeds, Record of, 1779-1964; 214 reels.
Land Entries, Record of, 1783-1962; 5 reels.
Real Estate Conveyances, Index to, Grantee, 1779-1964; 15 reels.
Real Estate Conveyances, Index to, Grantor, 1779-1980; 15 reels.
Surveys, Record of, 1906-1931; 1 reel.

Marriage, Divorce, and Vital Statistics

Births, Index to, 1913-1994; 2 reels.
Deaths, Index to, 1913-1994; 1 reel.

Delayed Births, Index to, various years; 1 reel.
Maiden Names of Divorced Women, 1945-1962; 1 reel.
Marriage Bonds, 1778-1868; 5 reels.
Marriage Registers, 1870-1965; 2 reels.

MISCELLANEOUS RECORDS

Orders and Decrees, 1869-1938; 1 reel.
Special Proceedings, 1880-1964; 2 reels.
Special Proceedings, Index to, 1970-1980; 1 reel.

OFFICIALS, COUNTY

Board of County Commissioners, Minutes, 1868-1964; 6 reels.

SCHOOL RECORDS

Board of Superintendents of Common Schools, Minutes, 1841-1853; 1 reel.
County Board of Education, Minutes, 1885-1963; 4 reels.

TAX AND FISCAL RECORDS

Tax Lists, 1778-1823, 1904; 2 reels.

WILLS

Wills, Cross Index to, 1780-1948; 1 reel.
Wills, Inventories, and Sales of Estates, Record of, 1779-1852; 1 reel.
Wills, Record of, 1778-1963; 7 reels.

WILSON COUNTY

Established in 1855 from Edgecombe, Johnston, Nash, and Wayne counties.
A few early court records are missing; reason unknown.

ORIGINAL RECORDS

BONDS

Apprentice Bonds, 1869-1919; 2 volumes.
Bastardy Bonds and Records, 1855-1908; 3 Fibredex boxes.
Constables' Bonds, 1857-1868; 1 volume.
Officials' Bonds and Records, 1855-1958; 1 volume, 1 Fibredex box.

COURT RECORDS

Circuit Criminal Court/Eastern District Criminal Court
- Minutes, 1897-1901; 1 volume.

County Court of Pleas and Quarter Sessions
- Execution Dockets, 1855-1868; 3 volumes.
- Minutes, 1855-1868; 1 volume.
- State Docket, 1855-1868; 1 volume.
- Trial and Appearance Docket, 1855-1867; 1 volume.

Inferior Court
- Minutes, 1877-1885; 1 volume.

Superior Court
- Civil Action Papers, 1850-1922; 64 Fibredex boxes.
- Civil Action Papers Concerning Land, 1854-1916; 5 Fibredex boxes.
- Criminal Action Papers, 1855-1919; 52 Fibredex boxes.
- Equity Minutes, 1855-1866; 2 volumes.
- Equity Trial Docket, 1861-1868; 1 volume.
- Minutes, 1855-1914; 9 volumes.
- Trial and Appearance Docket, 1855-1868; 1 volume.

ELECTION RECORDS

Elections, Record of, 1878-1936; 4 volumes.

ESTATES RECORDS

Accounts (Branch Banking and Trust Co.), Record of, 1933-1968; 12 volumes.
Accounts, Record of, 1868-1968; 24 volumes.
Administrators' Bonds, 1882-1896; 3 volumes.
Administrators, Executors, and Guardians, Cross Index to, 1897-1925; 1 volume.
Dowers and Land Partitions and Sales, Index to, [1855-1937]; 1 volume.
Estates Records, 1854-1959; 65 Fibredex boxes.
Guardians' Accounts, 1855-1868; 1 volume.
Guardians' Bonds, 1869-1939; 5 volumes.
Guardians' Records, 1855-1915; 19 Fibredex boxes.
Inventories and Accounts of Sale, 1855-1868; 3 volumes.
Land Divisions, Dowers, and Widows' Year's Support, Record of, 1855-1868, 1879, 1914-1915; 1 volume.
Settlements (Branch Banking and Trust Co.), Record of, 1936-1968; 2 volumes.
Settlements, Record of, 1868-1968; 18 volumes.

LAND RECORDS [*See also* **COURT RECORDS**, Superior Court]
Chattel Mortgages, 1858-1889; 1 Fibredex box.
Deeds of Release, 1861-1962; 1 Fibredex box.
Deeds of Sale, 1836-1962; 10 Fibredex boxes.
Deeds of Trust, 1848-1961; 1 Fibredex box.
Miscellaneous Deeds, 1850-1963; 2 Fibredex boxes.
Miscellaneous Land Records, 1856-1962; 4 Fibredex boxes.
Mortgage Deeds, 1855-1955; 5 Fibredex boxes.

MARRIAGE, DIVORCE, AND VITAL STATISTICS
Divorce Records, 1859-1912; 5 Fibredex boxes.
Indexed Registers of Marriage, 1855-1903; 2 volumes.
Maiden Names of Divorced Women, 1937-1969; 1 volume.
Marriage Records, 1874-1957; 1 Fibredex box.

MISCELLANEOUS RECORDS
Adultery Records, 1855-1915; 2 Fibredex boxes.
Alien Registration, 1924-1944; 1 volume.
Assignees, Receivers, and Trustees, Records of, 1855-1958; 8 Fibredex boxes.
Board of County Commissioners, Road Orders, 1898-1914; 1 volume.
Board of Directors of Farmers' Banking and Trust Company, Minutes, 1920-1927; 1 volume.
Coroners' Inquests, 1859-1915; 2 Fibredex boxes.
Homestead Records, 1867-1930; 1 Fibredex box.
Miscellaneous Records, 1786-1961; 3 Fibredex boxes.
Officials' Oaths, 1868-1924; 1 volume.
Orders and Decrees, 1868-1904; 1 volume.
Petitions for Naturalization, 1909-1910; 1 volume.
Powers of Attorney, 1859-1961; 1 Fibredex box.
Road Docket, 1855-1858; 1 volume.
Road Records, 1856-1911; 2 Fibredex boxes.
Slave Records, 1855-1864; 1 Fibredex box.
Special Proceedings, Cross Index to, [1868-1927]; 1 volume.
Tobacco Board of Trade of the City of Wilson, Minutes, 1904-1922; 1 volume.

OFFICIALS, COUNTY [*See* **MISCELLANEOUS RECORDS**]

ROADS AND BRIDGES [*See* **MISCELLANEOUS RECORDS**]

TAX AND FISCAL RECORDS
Tax Records, 1858-1935; 1 Fibredex box.
Tax Scrolls, 1915, 1920, 1921; 3 volumes.

WILLS
Wills, 1840-1925; 7 Fibredex boxes.
Wills, Cross Index to, 1857-1926; 1 volume.

MICROFILM RECORDS

CORPORATIONS AND PARTNERSHIPS
Corporations, Record of, 1869-1951; 2 reels.
Incorporations, Index to, 1915-1976; 1 reel.
Partnership, Record of, 1924-1944; 1 reel.

COURT RECORDS

Circuit Criminal Court/Eastern District Criminal Court
- Minutes, 1897-1901; 1 reel.

County Court of Pleas and Quarter Sessions
- Minutes, 1855-1868; 1 reel.

General County Court
- Judgment Dockets, Criminal, 1913-1935; 2 reels.
- Minutes, 1913-1951; 3 reels.

Inferior Court
- Minutes, 1877-1885; 1 reel.

Superior Court
- Civil Actions, Index to, 1868-1968; 2 reels.
- Civil Judgments, Index to, 1915-1968; 4 reels.
- Criminal Judgments, Index to, 1916-1968; 1 reel.
- Judgment Dockets, 1867-1920; 3 reels.
- Judgment Dockets, Criminal, 1868-1924; 2 reels.
- Judgments, Index to, 1867-1926; 1 reel.
- Minutes, 1855-1868, 1886-1954; 7 reels.
- Trial and Appearance Docket, 1855-1868; 1 reel.

ELECTION RECORDS

Elections, Record of, 1878-1968; 1 reel.

ESTATES RECORDS

Accounts, Record of, 1868-1924; 6 reels.
Administrators' Bonds, 1869-1897, 1908-1916; 2 reels.
Administrators, Executors, and Guardians, Record of, 1897-1909; 1 reel.
Administrators, Record of, 1917-1926; 2 reels.
Appointment of Administrators and Executors, Index to, 1900-1968; 1 reel.
Appointment of Guardians, Index to, 1900-1960; 1 reel.
Division of Land, Record of Dowers, and Widows' Year's Support, 1855-1923; 1 reel.
Executors, Record of, 1912-1960; 2 reels.
Guardians' Bonds, 1855-1885; 2 reels.
Guardians, Record of, 1908-1919; 1 reel.
Settlements, Record of, 1868-1923; 2 reels.

LAND RECORDS

Deeds and Mortgages, Index to, Grantee, 1855-1946; 5 reels.
Deeds and Mortgages, Index to, Grantor, 1855-1945; 3 reels.
Deeds, Record of, 1855-1942; 54 reels.
Land Divisions, 1906-1960; 2 reels.
Plat Books, 1914-1960; 1 reel.
Plats, Index to, 1906-1960; 1 reel.

MARRIAGE, DIVORCE, AND VITAL STATISTICS

Births, Index to, 1913-1958; 2 reels.
Cohabitation, Record of, 1866; 1 reel.
Deaths, Index to, 1913-1976; 2 reels.
Delayed Births, Index to, various years; 1 reel.

Maiden Names of Divorced Women, 1937-1960; 1 reel.
Marriage Licenses, 1864-1957; 15 reels.
Marriage Registers, 1867-1954; 2 reels.
Marriages, Record of, 1855-1866; 1 reel.

MISCELLANEOUS RECORDS

Alien Registration Record, 1924, 1927, 1940, 1944; 1 reel.
Lunacy Dockets, 1899-1917, 1956-1960; 1 reel.
Orders and Decrees, 1868-1920; 3 reels.
Orders and Decrees, Index to, Defendant, 1897-1968; 2 reels.
Orders and Decrees, Index to, Plaintiff, 1897-1968; 2 reels.
Petitions for Naturalization, 1902-1911; 1 reel.
Special Proceedings, 1868-1917, 1934-1960; 5 reels.
Special Proceedings, Index to, Defendant, 1868-1960; 1 reel.
Special Proceedings, Index to, Plaintiff, 1868-1960; 1 reel.

OFFICIALS, COUNTY

Board of County Commissioners, Minutes, 1868-1954; 7 reels.
Public Library Board of Trustees, Minutes, 1938-1975; 1 reel.

SCHOOL RECORDS

County Board of Education, Minutes, 1885-1976; 3 reels.

TAX AND FISCAL RECORDS

Tax Scrolls, 1915, 1920-1921; 1 reel.

WILLS

Wills, Index to, 1855-1971; 1 reel.
Wills, Record of, 1855-1960; 6 reels.

YADKIN COUNTY

Established in 1850 from Surry County.

ORIGINAL RECORDS

BONDS

Apprentice Bonds and Records, 1850-1937; 2 volumes, 1 Fibredex box.
Bastardy Bonds and Records, 1851-1934; 2 volumes, 4 Fibredex boxes.
Officials' Bonds, 1851-1902; 1 Fibredex box.

COURT RECORDS

County Court of Pleas and Quarter Sessions
- Appearance Docket, 1851-1868; 1 volume.
- Execution Dockets, 1852-1868; 2 volumes.
- Minutes, 1851-1868; 2 volumes.
- State Docket, 1851-1868; 1 volume.
- Trial Docket, 1851-1868; 1 volume.

Inferior Court
- Minutes, 1877-1886; 1 volume.

Superior Court
- Civil Action Papers, 1845-1940; 19 Fibredex boxes.
- Civil Action Papers Concerning Land, 1846-1934; 9 Fibredex boxes.
- Criminal Action Papers, 1851-1926; 12 Fibredex boxes.
- Equity Minutes, 1851-1868; 1 volume.
- Minutes, 1851-1898; 6 volumes.
- Miscellaneous Letters, Court Papers, and Documents, 1852-1878; 1 manuscript box.

ELECTION RECORDS

Election Records, 1852-1881; 4 Fibredex boxes.
Elections, Record of, 1878-1932; 4 volumes.

ESTATES RECORDS

Accounts, Record of, 1868-1903; 4 volumes.
Administrators' Bonds, 1868-1917; 5 volumes.
Appointment of Administrators, Executors, Guardians, and Masters, 1868-1905; 1 volume.
Estates, Record of, 1851-1871; 2 volumes.
Estates Records, 1850-1920; 54 Fibredex boxes.
Guardians' Accounts, 1856-1868; 1 volume.
Guardians' Bonds, 1868-1913; 3 volumes.
Guardians' Records, 1851-1927; 4 Fibredex boxes.
Settlements, Record of, 1872-1912; 2 volumes.

LAND RECORDS

Deeds, 1793-1951; 4 Fibredex boxes.
Deeds, Cross Index to, 1850-1945; 3 volumes.
Deeds of Trust, 1842-1951; 1 Fibredex box.
Miscellaneous Land Records, 1851-1953; 1 Fibredex box.
Probate, Record of, 1874-1885; 1 volume.

MARRIAGE, DIVORCE, AND VITAL STATISTICS

Divorce Records, 1851-1931; 2 Fibredex boxes.
Marriage Bonds, 1850-1868; 4 Fibredex boxes.

MISCELLANEOUS RECORDS

County Accounts, 1843-1879; 1 Fibredex box.
Homestead and Personal Property Exemptions, 1860-1958; 1 Fibredex box.
Insolvent Debtors, 1851-1874; 1 Fibredex box.
Miscellaneous Records, 1843-1952; 2 Fibredex boxes. [*See also* **CRX RECORDS**]
Paupers' Book, 1885-1888; 1 volume.
Road Records, 1839-1922; 3 Fibredex boxes.
School Records, 1853-1878; 1 Fibredex box.

ROADS AND BRIDGES [*See* **MISCELLANEOUS RECORDS**]

SCHOOL RECORDS [*See* **MISCELLANEOUS RECORDS**]

WILLS

Wills, 1836-1942; 7 Fibredex boxes.

CRX RECORDS

Miscellaneous Records, 1853-1884; 16 folders.

MICROFILM RECORDS

BONDS

Apprentice Bonds, 1870-1939; 1 reel.

CORPORATIONS AND PARTNERSHIPS

Corporations, Record of, 1891-1969; 1 reel.

COURT RECORDS

County Court of Pleas and Quarter Sessions
- Minutes, 1851-1868; 1 reel.

Superior Court
- Equity Minutes, 1851-1868; 1 reel.
- Minutes, 1851-1961; 7 reels.

ELECTION RECORDS

Elections, Record of, 1878-1968; 2 reels.

ESTATES RECORDS

Accounts, Record of, 1856-1880, 1888-1970; 5 reels.
Administrators' Bonds, 1868-1917; 1 reel.
Administrators and Executors, Record of, 1915-1949; 2 reels.
Administrators, Record of, 1949-1969; 2 reels.
Appointment of Administrators, Executors, and Guardians, 1868-1905; 1 reel.
Estates, Index to, 1911-1947; 1 reel.
Executors, Record of, 1940-1969; 1 reel.
Guardians' Bonds, 1868-1913; 1 reel.
Guardians, Record of, 1911-1969; 1 reel.
Indigent Children, Record of, 1946-1969; 1 reel.
Inheritance Tax Records, 1923-1969; 1 reel.
Inventories of Estates, 1851-1888; 1 reel.
Settlements, Record of, 1872-1971; 6 reels.

LAND RECORDS

Deeds, Record of, 1851-1963; 52 reels.
Federal Tax Lien Index, 1925-1969; 1 reel.
Land Entries, 1852-1940; 1 reel.
Plats, Index to, 1911-1969; 1 reel.
Real Estate Conveyances, Index to, Grantee, 1850-1969; 4 reels.
Real Estate Conveyances, Index to, Grantor, 1850-1969; 3 reels.
Resale of Land by Trustees and Mortgagees, Record of, 1923-1969; 1 reel.

MARRIAGE, DIVORCE, AND VITAL STATISTICS

Births, Index to, 1914-1995; 2 reels.
Deaths, Index to, 1914-1993; 2 reels.
Marriage Bonds, 1850-1868; 4 reels.
Marriage Licenses, 1867-1969; 11 reels.
Marriage Registers, 1851-1969; 1 reel.

MISCELLANEOUS RECORDS

Lunacy Docket, 1944-1969; 1 reel.
Orders and Decrees, 1871-1955; 5 reels.
Orders and Decrees and Special Proceedings, Index to, 1940-1969; 1 reel.
Special Proceedings, Cross Index to, 1871-1943; 1 reel.

OFFICIALS, COUNTY

Board of County Commissioners, Minutes, 1868-1942; 4 reels.

TAX AND FISCAL RECORDS

Tax Register, 1851-1862; 1 reel.
Tax Scrolls, 1925, 1935, 1945, 1955, 1965; 3 reels.

WILLS

Wills, Cross Index to, 1851-1957; 2 reels.
Wills, Record of, 1851-1969; 3 reels.

YANCEY COUNTY

Established in 1833 from Buncombe and Burke counties.
Many early court records are missing; reason unknown.

ORIGINAL RECORDS

BONDS

Apprentice Bonds, 1874-1912; 1 volume.
Apprentice Bonds, 1893, 1909; Bastardy Bonds, 1866-1914; Officials' Bonds, 1872-1891; 1 Fibredex box.
Bastardy Bonds, 1875-1879; 1 volume.

COURT RECORDS

County Court of Pleas and Quarter Sessions
- Execution Dockets, 1835-1848, 1855-1859; 5 volumes.
- Minutes, 1834-1868; 4 volumes.
- State Dockets, 1834-1861; 2 volumes.
- Trial and Appearance Dockets, 1834-1861; 3 volumes.

Superior Court
- Civil Action Papers, 1861-1914; 7 Fibredex boxes.
- Civil Action Papers Concerning Land, 1867-1923; 8 Fibredex boxes.
- Criminal Action Papers, 1865-1920; 12 Fibredex boxes.
- Equity Execution and Trial Docket, 1845-1863; 1 volume.
- Equity Minutes, 1845-1868; 2 volumes.
- Execution Dockets, 1835-1849; 3 volumes.
- Minutes, 1834-1913; 12 volumes.
- State Docket, 1835-1855; 1 volume.
- Trial and Appearance Docket, 1855-1868; 1 volume.

ELECTION RECORDS

Elections, Record of, 1878-1933; 3 volumes.

ESTATES RECORDS

Accounts, Record of, 1870-1917; 1 volume.
Administrators' Bonds, 1870-1900; 1 volume.
Administrators, Executors, and Guardians, Record of, 1901-1928; 1 volume.
Appointment of Administrators, Executors, Guardians, and Masters, 1870-1904; 1 volume.
Estates Records, 1853-1915; 31 Fibredex boxes.
Guardians' Bonds, 1872-1902; 1 volume.
Guardians' Records, 1874-1921; 2 Fibredex boxes.

LAND RECORDS

Attachments, Executions, Liens, and Levies on Land and Personal Property, 1866-1915; 1 Fibredex box.
Deeds and Miscellaneous Land Records, 1847-1915; 1 Fibredex box.
Probate, Record of, 1834-1871; 3 volumes.

MARRIAGE, DIVORCE, AND VITAL STATISTICS [*See also* CRX RECORDS]

Divorce Records, 1866-1914; 8 Fibredex boxes.

Miscellaneous Records

Alien Registration, 1940; 1 volume.
Assignees, Receivers, and Trustees, Records of, 1887-1916; 1 Fibredex box.
Bridge Records, 1899, 1903; Road Records, 1867-1915; 1 Fibredex box.
Miscellaneous Records, 1854-1915; 2 Fibredex boxes.
Orders and Decrees, 1869-1909; 2 volumes.
Railroad Records, 1877-1918; 6 Fibredex boxes.

Roads and Bridges [*See* **Miscellaneous Records**]

Wills

Wills, 1885-1909; 1 Fibredex box.
Wills, Record of, 1857-1869; 1 volume.

CRX Records

Marriage Licenses, 1870, 1883; 1 folder.

MICROFILM RECORDS

Corporations and Partnerships

Partnerships and Corporations, Record of, 1908-1967; 1 reel.

Court Records

County Court of Pleas and Quarter Sessions
- Minutes, 1834-1868; 2 reels.

Superior Court
- Equity Minutes, 1866-1868; 1 reel.
- Judgment Docket, 1902-1914; 1 reel.
- Minutes, 1866-1956; 10 reels.

Election Records

Elections, Record of, 1878-1966; 1 reel.

Estates Records

Accounts, Record of, 1870-1967; 4 reels.
Administrators, Executors, and Guardians, Record of, 1909-1961; 1 reel.
Administrators and Guardians, Record of, 1922-1934; 1 reel.
Administrators, Record of, 1934-1967; 1 reel.
Appointment of Administrators, Executors, and Guardians, 1870-1928; 1 reel.
Guardians, Record of, 1956-1967; 1 reel.
Inheritance Tax Records, 1923-1967; 1 reel.
Settlements, Record of, 1870-1923; 1 reel.
Settlements, Wills, Inventories, and Accounts, Record of, 1855-1869; 1 reel.

Land Records

Deeds, Cross Index to, 1831-1944; 3 reels.
Deeds, Leases, and Options, Index to, Grantee, 1944-1967; 1 reel.
Deeds, Leases, and Options, Index to, Grantor, 1944-1967; 1 reel.
Deeds, Record of, 1831-1958; 55 reels.
Land Entries, 1851-1946; 1 reel.
Probate, Record of, 1834-1846; 1 reel.
Resale of Land, Record of, 1923-1967; 1 reel.
Surveys, Record of, 1909-1933; 1 reel.

MARRIAGE, DIVORCE, AND VITAL STATISTICS

Births, Index to, 1913-1986; 2 reels.
Deaths, Index to, 1913-1986; 1 reel.
Delayed Births, Index to, 1873-1949; 1 reel.
Maiden Names of Divorced Women, 1941-1967; 1 reel.
Marriage Certificates, Record of, 1851-1879; 1 reel.
Marriage Licenses, 1870-1967; 8 reels.
Marriage Register, 1851-1967; 1 reel.

MISCELLANEOUS RECORDS

Orders and Decrees, 1869-1952; 3 reels.
Special Proceedings, 1919-1952; 3 reels.
Special Proceedings, Cross Index to, 1919-1967; 1 reel.

OFFICIALS, COUNTY

Board of County Commissioners, Minutes, 1870-1967; 7 reels.
Board of County Commissioners, Minutes, Index to, 1965-1967; 1 reel.

SCHOOL RECORDS

Board of Superintendents of Common Schools, Minutes, 1842-1868; 1 reel.
County Board of Education, Minutes, 1885-1953; 1 reel.

TAX AND FISCAL RECORDS

Tax Scrolls, 1936, 1945, 1955, 1965; 2 reels.

WILLS [*See also* **ESTATES RECORDS**]

Wills, Record of, 1838-1967; 2 reels.

GLOSSARY

[Editor's note: The definitions and explanations herein are taken from the North Carolina Administrative Office of the Courts and the State Archives' Local Records Manual. The record series descriptions were meticulously prepared by Kenrick N. Simpson in 2001. The North Carolina Genealogical Society graciously allowed the use of *North Carolina Research*, edited by Helen F. M. Leary and Maurice Stirewalt (Raleigh, N.C.: The North Carolina Genealogical Society, 1980) in compiling this glossary.]

Account: A detailed written statement of receipts and payments; any right to payment for goods or services; a form of action at common law whereby a person to whom or on whose behalf a fiduciary was bound to render an account but who failed or refused to do so.

Account of Sale: An account of property disposed of at an estate sale, generally listing the items sold, the prices paid, and frequently the names of purchasers.

Accounts and Final Settlements. *See* Record of Estates/Accounts

Accounts of Indigent Children/Orphans: Receipts signed for funds less than $300 (after 1949, less than $500) belonging to orphans without guardians and expended by the clerk for their benefit. Also includes accounts of clerk in his capacity as receiver of estates of orphans without guardians.

Action: A suit brought in a court by which one party prosecutes another for the enforcement or protection of a right, the redress or prevention of a wrong, or the punishment of a public offense. In common law and equity procedures "action" pertains to the forms at law, "suit" pertains to the forms in equity.

Administration: The management and settling of the estate of an intestate under the supervision of the court.

Administrator's Accounts. *See* Record of Estates/Accounts

Administrators' Bonds: Bonds by which an administrator obliged himself to execute faithfully his duties upon penalty of payment of a specified sum of money, usually twice the estimated value of the estate. Blank-form bonds show names of intestate, administrator, and bondsman; date and amount of bond; and clerk's certificate of acceptance of bond. Loose bonds are filed in Estates Records. After 1919, see Appointment and Record of Administrators. Arranged chronologically.

Affidavit: A written and signed statement of facts, sworn under oath or affirmation.

Alien: A resident of a country who is not native born and has not been granted citizenship.

Alien, Naturalization, and Citizenship Records: Records of aliens residing in a county, showing name, age, nationality, address, and previous address of each, together with names and addresses of five persons who know each alien. Records relating to the naturalization of foreign-born citizens, in which the clerk of superior court acted as federal agent. May include Declaration of Intent to Become a Citizen, Petitions for Naturalization, and/or Alien Registration.

Alien Registration. *See* Alien, Naturalization, and Citizenship Records

Amounts Paid to Indigent Children/Orphans, Record of. *See* Accounts of Indigent Children/Orphans

Annual Accounts, Record of. *See* Record of Estates/Accounts

Appeal: To carry a legal matter to an appellate court from a trial court in order to right an injustice or error of the lower court.

Appeal Docket, Court of Pleas and Quarter Sessions: Record of cases appealed to the Superior Court.

Appeal Docket, Superior Court: Record of cases appealed to the Supreme Court.

Appearance Docket, Court of Pleas and Quarter Sessions: Record of issuance of writs, summonses, and subpoenas to bring defendants and witnesses to the next term of court. Also records appearances of appeals from magistrates' courts and of proceedings by petition (sometimes recorded in separate Petitions Dockets). Prior to 1820, appearance dockets were often kept in same volume with trial dockets. Columnar arrangement shows number of case and name or initials of attorneys; names of parties; form of action; disposition of writ; and any rule or action taken by court at term, including confessed judgments.

Appearance Docket, Superior Court: Record of issuance of writs, summonses, and subpoenas to bring defendants and witnesses to the next term of court. List of civil cases to appear for any other purpose than jury trial, usually for preliminary pleading shows name of parties, nature of action, and a summary of pleading or proceedings had. Later appearance dockets usually were merely lists of persons bonded or otherwise held to appear before court in criminal matters, including persons on probation and material witnesses. This record series ended in 1868. Also records appearances of appeals from lower courts and of proceedings by petition (sometimes recorded in separate Petitions Dockets). After 1868, the functions of the appearance docket were continued with some modifications in the Summons Docket. Columnar arrangement shows number of case and name or initials of attorneys; names of parties; form of action; disposition of writ; and any rule or action taken by court at term, including confessed judgments.

Appellate Court: A court having jurisdiction of appeal and review.

Appointment and Record of Administrators: Post-1868 record of appointment and qualification of administrators of estates. After 1919, includes oath and bond of administrators. Series also includes volumes (1868–ca. 1915) entitled Appointment of Administrators, Executors, Guardians, and Masters; in some counties, these are entitled Record of Probate (Estates) or Minutes, Probate Court. May also include an index to administrators.

Appointment and Record of Executors: Post-1868 record of qualification of executors. Prior to ca. 1915, executors were included in a volume entitled Appointment of Administrators, Executors, Guardians, and Masters. In some counties, see also Record of Probate (Estates).

Appointment and Record of Guardians: Record of appointment of guardians, giving name of ward, name and address of guardian, and date of issue of letter of guardianship. Usually also includes guardian's bonds. Post-1868 record of appointment and qualification of guardians. After 1919, includes oaths and bonds of guardians. Prior to ca. 1915, guardians were included in a volume entitled Appointment of Administrators, Executors, Guardians, and Masters; in some counties, these are entitled Record of Probate (Estates) or Minutes, Probate Court. May also include an index to guardians and wards.

Appointment of Administrators, Executors, Guardians, and Masters. *See* Appointment of Guardians, Record of; Appointment and Record of Administrators; Appointment and Record of Executors; Appointment and Record of Guardians

Appointment of Guardians, Record of. *See* Appointment and Record of Guardians

Apprentice: A person (usually a minor) bound to serve a master in return for life's necessities and instruction in some trade or occupation.

Apprentice Bonds and Records: Contracts of apprenticeship usually filled in on printed forms, showing name of master and apprentice, trade to be taught, details of contract, amount of master's bond, and name of sureties. May include petitions for apprenticeship, petitions for "freedom dues" upon the completion of an apprenticeship, and civil and criminal actions concerning masters or wards. Arranged chronologically.

Assessment of Land for Taxation, Record of. *See* Miscellaneous Tax Records

Assignee: A person to whom an assignment is made by an assignor.

Assignees, Accounts of. *See* Records and Accounts of Receivers and Trustees of Estates; Records of Assignees, Receivers, and Trustees

Assignment: A transfer in writing of all or any part of an interest in property.

Assumed Business Names, Corporations, and Partnerships: Lists of persons or unincorporated firms doing business under a title that does not reveal the identity of the owner(s), showing the name of the business and of the owner(s). Records concerning corporations and partnerships. May include Record of Incorporation and Record of Partnerships (or Record of Assumed Business Names).

Astray. *See* Estray

Attachment: Seizing or taking into custody persons or property by legal process in order to satisfy a court judgment.

Bastard: A person whose parents were not married to one another at the time of his birth. Such a person was commonly known by his mother's surname and was prohibited from inheriting property unless legitimated by his father.

Bastardy Bonds and Records: Usually on printed forms, posted by putative fathers of illegitimate children to insure that the child is supported without public expense. Gives name of father and his bondsman, as well as that of the mother and child and the amount of the bond posted. May include presentments against and examinations of unwed mothers and mothers-to-be, warrants to bring the putative fathers to court, and receipts for payments made on behalf of bastard children. Arranged chronologically.

Bill: Written statement, declaration, or complaint; in equity, the initial pleading of the plaintiff or petitioner.

Bill of Sale: A written contract by which personal property, usually of considerable value, is conveyed from one person to another.

Birth, Death, and Vital Records: Include record of births and deaths, county copies of death certificates, and indexes to vital statistics.

Board of County Commissioners, Minutes of the. *See* Minutes of the Board of County Commissioners

Board of Education, Minutes of the County: *See* Minutes of the County Board of Education

Board of Health, Minutes of the County. *See* Minutes of the County Board of Health

Bond: A document by which a person, called the principal, obligates himself to fulfill certain conditions under penalty of payment of a stated sum of money.

Brand. *See* Flesh Mark

Case: A general term for an action, cause, or suit; a question contested before a court of justice; a statement of facts drawn up in writing for submission to a court or judge.

Cause: A suit, litigation, or action in a court of justice; the grounds for such suit, etc.

Census: An official count of the people in a given area.

Census Records: (county copies) Include census years 1850, 1860, and 1870 for most counties.

Certificates of Registration of Professionals. *See* Merchant and Professional Licenses and Registration Books

Chattels: Moveable or personal property, including both animate and inanimate forms.

Circuit Criminal Courts. *See* Minute Dockets, Other Courts

Citizenship Records. *See* Alien, Naturalization, and Citizenship Records

Civil: Relating to private rights of individuals.

Civil Action: An action brought to enforce or protect private rights or redress private wrongs.

Civil Action Papers: Civil case files from magistrates' courts, Court of Pleas and Quarter Sessions, Superior Court, and, in some counties, other inferior courts. In most counties, also contains executions issued supplementary to civil judgments. Civil actions concerning land are filed separately. Other sub-groupings may include actions concerning county officials, the Board of County Commissioners, occupational licensing boards, canals, mines, and timber. Arranged chronologically.

Civil Issues Docket, Superior Court: Trial docket for civil cases, including name of parties, history of cases carried forward from Summons Docket, and note of proceeding had at trial. *See also* Trial Docket, Superior Court

Clerk: The preparer and keeper of certain records; in early usage, a minister of the Church of England.

Cohabitation: A living together as man and wife.

Cohabitation Bonds and Records: Official county records of the registration of the legalized marital status of slaves emancipated at the end of the Civil War.

Committee of Finance, Minutes of the. *See* County Accounts and Claims

Common law: The body of governmental principles and judicial theory and actions based on ancient usages and customs, or on judgments of the courts affirming such usages. North Carolina was a common-law state until 1868 when the forms of common law were abandoned.

Constable: A minor county official who kept the peace in his district, served legal papers, summoned persons to list taxes, and performed other similar duties.

Contract: A legally binding agreement between two or more persons that creates an obligation to do or not to do a specified thing; the writing that contains such an agreement.

Conveyance: A document transferring title to property.

Coroner: A county official charged with the investigation of unusual deaths, who also performed the duties of sheriff on occasion.

Coroners' Records: Records of coroners' inquests. May also include record of coroners. Arranged chronologically.

Corporation: A group of persons organized as prescribed by law into a legal entity; such an entity is treated by the law as an individual person. *See* Assumed Business Names, Corporations, and Partnerships

County Accounts and Claims: Include accounts and claims against the county for services rendered. May include County Claims Allowed; Settlement of County Accounts with the Committee of Finance (or County Trustee); Minutes of the Committee of Finance; Treasurer's Account Book; and Record of Official Reports, a compilation of financial reports from the sheriff, treasurer, clerk of superior court, and register of deeds to the board of county commissioners (1875–). Claims against the county are arranged chronologically.

County Board of Education, Minutes of the: *See* Minutes of the County Board of Education

County Board of Health, Minutes of the. *See* Minutes of the County Board of Health

County Boundaries: Records concerning boundary agreements or disputes between two or more counties.

County Claims Allowed. *See* County Accounts and Claims

County Commissioners, Board of, Minutes of the. *See* Minutes of the Board of County Commissioners

County Courts. *See* Pleas and Quarter Sessions, Courts of

Court: Collectively, the persons duly authorized and assembled to administer justice. In the past, a court often exercised governmental as well as judicial powers.

Court Martial: A court composed of military officers and convened for the transaction of business pertinent to a military unit or the trial of offenders who are under jurisdiction of the military.

Court Records. *See* Miscellaneous Court Records

Criminal Action: An action prosecuted by the State against a party charged with a public offense.

Criminal Action Papers: Criminal case files from magistrates' courts, Court of Pleas and Quarter Sessions, Superior Court and, in some counties, other inferior courts. In most counties, also includes executions issued supplementary to criminal actions. Arranged chronologically.

Criminal Court. *See* Minute Dockets, Other Courts

Criminal Issues Docket, Superior Court: Lists of criminal actions and key information about them. *See also* State Docket, Superior Court

(Cross) Index to Deeds: Superseded volumes of indexes, usually cross referenced to grantee and grantor.

(Cross) Index to Wills: Alphabetical index by testator and testate of "Record of Wills." Prior to court reform, this was known as the "Cross – Index to Wills." Since court reform, this has been known as the "Index to Devisee." This is an alphabetical list of devisees by last name. It provides the estate name, file number, and docket number.

Crown Docket. *See* State (or Crown) Docket, Court of Pleas and Quarter Sessions

Declaration: In common law, the first pleading in an action, containing the plaintiff's statement and demand for relief.

Declaration of Intent to Become a Citizen. *See* Alien, Naturalization, and Citizenship Records

Decree: A decision or sentence by the court.

Deed(s): Written sealed agreements by which real property or an interest therein is transferred from one party to another in exchange for a specified sum called the consideration. The seller is generally called the grantor, the buyer the grantee. Include record of deeds and original handwritten deeds left in the courthouse after being deposited with the clerk for probate and recording. The loose deeds may be segregated into various types, such as deeds of sale, deeds of gift, deeds of trust, mortgage deeds, and quitclaim (or release) deeds. In many counties, all but the deeds of sale are boxed together as miscellaneous deeds. Deeds of sale are arranged alphabetically by the surname of the grantee; other deeds are arranged chronologically.

Deed of Gift: A deed executed and delivered without consideration.

Deed of Trust: A conditional transfer of property ownership to a trustee as a means of securing a debt or the performance of a condition. A deed of trust can generally be recognized by the mention of three parties, rather than two, in the opening phrases of the deed.

Delayed Births: The recording of births that occurred before 1913, using census data or family Bibles as proof of age. A delayed birth certificate was filed.

Devise: To give real property by will; the property so willed.

Devisee, Index to. *See* (Cross) Index to Wills

Devisor: A person who conveys real property by will.

Disinterment/Reinterment Permits: County copies (1953–1987) of permits to disinter bodies, transport them across county lines, and rebury them.

Division: The procedure of allotting real or personal property to those entitled to it; the document recording such a division. *See also* Partition

Divorce Records: Records of divorced women arranged in alphabetical order by the name of their former husband. Denote maiden name of divorcee and date of notice of intention to resume maiden name. Include divorce actions taken from Civil Action Papers. Also, beginning in 1937, includes a volume listing Maiden Names of Divorced Women. Arranged alphabetically.

Docket: A brief formal record of all the important acts done in a court in the conduct of each case; a list or calendar of cases set to be tried at a specific term of court.

Dower: That portion of a man's real property which was set aside by law for the support of his widow and the nurture of any minor children born of the marriage; the estate in a portion of her husband's real property to which a wife had a right by virtue of her marriage.

Dowers and Partition Proceedings. *See* Record of Dowers and Widows' Year's Support

Dowers and Widows' Year's Support, Record of. *See* Record of Dowers and Widows' Year's Support

Ear Mark. *See* Flesh Mark

Eastern District Criminal Courts. *See* Minute Dockets, Other Courts

Education, Minutes of the County Board of: *See* Minutes of the County Board of Education

Ejectment(s): A form of action at common law brought to recover real property and win damages for its unlawful retention, but whose real purpose was to prove true ownership of the land in dispute. Ejectment was an artificial form under common law devised to try title to land. After 1868, when common law forms were abolished under the new state constitution, ejectment cases were tried as a summary proceeding (without a jury). Arranged chronologically.

Election Records: Include election returns, Permanent Registration of Voters (grandfather clause registrations, 1902–1908), poll books, and minutes of the county board of elections. May also include civil and criminal actions concerning elections. Arranged chronologically.

Entry, Land: The initial step in the process of acquiring a grant (patent) of land from the state, Crown, or Lords Proprietors. *See also* Land Entries

Equity: A legal system that existed concurrently with common law, under which a person could seek relief for an injury not covered by the established forms of common law or when following those forms would produce disproportionate hardship. Equity matters were decided on what was "fair and just" in the dealings of one person with another based on the facts of each particular case, rather than on the requirements of common-law pleadings.

Equity Enrolling Docket, Superior Court of Law and Equity: Record of complaints, petitions, and answers filed in suits in equity.

Equity Execution Docket, Superior Court of Law and Equity: Record of money due to successful litigants in actions at equity, fines and court costs; the type of recovery writ issued; and the execution of writ and satisfaction of judgment.

Equity Minute Docket, Superior Court of Law and Equity: Minutes of the Superior Court of Law and Equity (1806–1868).

Equity Trial (and Appearance) Docket, Superior Court of Law and Equity: Record of equity actions expected to come to trial during a given term. Brings forward information from appearance docket and also shows pleadings of defendant, prior ruling by court, judgment, and final orders.

Estate(s): Real property formerly owned by a decedent. The owner may determine the disposition of the property even in the event of his death and that such property can be inherited by his heirs if he dies intestate.

Estates, Sales of, Record of. *See* Record of Sales of Estates

Estates Records: May include appointments and renunciations of executors and administrators; administrators' and guardians' bonds; inventories; accounts of sale; annual accounts; final settlements; civil actions and executions involving administrators, executors, and guardians; and actions in equity or special proceedings involving property of an estate. If the father of wards can be determined from guardians' papers, they are filed with the estate of the deceased rather than with the guardians' records. Arranged alphabetically by name of decedent. *See also* Miscellaneous Estates Records

Estray: A stray; an animal roaming at large without immediate evidence of someone's management. *See also* Marks, Brands, and Strays

Execute: To complete; to sign as "the testator executes his will." To carry out the terms of, as "an executor executes the terms of the will."

Execution: The process of carrying some act to its completion; a process for enforcing the court's judgments and decrees, usually by seizing and selling the lands, goods, or chattels of the debtor.

Execution Docket, Court of Pleas and Quarter Sessions: Record of money due to successful litigant, fines and court costs; the type of recovery writ issued; and the execution of writ and satisfaction of judgment.

Execution Docket, Superior Court: Record of money due to successful litigants, fines and court costs; the type of writ issued to recover same; and the execution of writ and satisfaction of judgment. List of cases executions have been issued returnable to given term of court. Shows names of parties to action; nature of action; amount of judgment; bill of costs, itemized; type of writ issued; and sheriff's return. After 1868, in most counties this information was recorded in Judgment Dockets, although some continued to use separate Execution Dockets.

Executions: Writs issued by magistrates and the clerks of Court of Pleas and Quarter Sessions and Superior Court for the recovery of judgments, fines, penalties, and court costs. In most counties, these records are filed with the civil and criminal action papers or in the series of attachments, executions, liens, and levies on land in the Miscellaneous Land Records. They are filed as a separate series in Hyde and Tyrrell counties. *See* Land Records

Federal Direct Taxes Collected, Record of. *See* Miscellaneous Tax Records

Fiduciary: Having the characteristics of a trustee; a person or institution managing money or property for another.

Final Account: The financial statement presented by a fiduciary at the conclusion of his trust.

Finance, Minutes of the Committee of. *See* County Accounts and Claims

Flesh Mark: Livestock mark denoting the animal's owner—commonly cuts, slits, or holes made in one or both ears, sometimes accompanied by a brand, a mark burned into the animal's hide. *See also* Marks, Brands, and Strays

Foreclosure: Taking away or ending all rights of a mortgagor in the property covered by the mortgage; a sale of mortgaged property.

General County Court. *See* Minute Dockets, Other Courts

Grand Jury: A jury including more than twelve people. In common law grand juries consisted of between twelve and twenty-three men. Grand juries are sworn to act as bodies of inquiry in criminal matters; they do not decide the guilt of a criminal defendant, but rather whether he will be tried for an offense. Under the North Carolina county court system prior to 1868, grand juries also oversaw the maintenance and repair of public buildings.

Grant: To sell; to confer or give. The transfer of public land to private persons by a "grant of patent" for the land. The document acknowledging the transfer is called a land grant. *See* Land Grants

Grantee: The buyer or donee of land conveyed by deed. A recipient of a land grant.

Grantor: The seller or donor of land conveyed by deed.

Guardian: One who has the legal authority and duty to care for the person or the property (or both) of an individual who, because of age, insufficient understanding, or lack of self-control, is considered by law or court action to be incapable of managing his or her own affairs. *See also* Next Friend.

Guardians' Accounts: In most counties, these have been filed with the Guardians' Records. Arranged chronologically. *See also* Record of Estates/Accounts

Guardians' Bonds: Blank-form bonds of guardians, showing names of ward and guardian, date and amount of bond, name of surety, and clerk's certificate of approval of bond. Loose bonds are filed in either the Estates Records (by decedent) or the Guardians' Records (by ward). After 1919, see Appointment and Record of Guardians. Arranged chronologically.

Guardians' Dockets: Brief summary list of guardians' accounts filed, showing names of guardian and ward, date of filing, amount carried over from last account, total amounts received and disbursed, and balance carried forward. Includes dockets from Orphan's Court (days set aside in the Court of Pleas and Quarter Sessions for the handling of matters relating to guardians and wards), guardians' summons dockets, and guardians' scire facias dockets.

Guardians' Records: Papers may include appointments, oaths, and bonds of guardians; annual accounts; final settlements; civil actions and executions involving guardians; and actions in equity or special proceedings involving the property of a ward's estate. These records also include indigent wards for whom the clerk of superior court served as receiver. If the father of the wards can be determined from the papers, they are filed with the estate of the deceased rather than with the guardians' records. Arranged alphabetically by surname of wards.

Health, County Board of, Minutes of the. *See* Minutes of the County Board of Health

Homestead: Part of a person's property that is deemed necessary for his livelihood and therefore protected by law from the claims of creditors.

Incompetent: A person considered by law to be incapable of managing his own affairs; incompetents included minors, idiots, the insane, the imprisoned, and even married women.

Incorporation, Record of. *See* Assumed Business Names, Corporations, and Partnerships

Indenture: A mutual agreement in writing. Originally each party to an indenture received an exact copy of the agreement, the copies being made on a single sheet of paper and cut in two along a wavy (indented) line. By extension, indenture meant a deed or an agreement of apprenticeship. *See* Apprentice Bonds and Records

Index to Deeds. *See* (Cross) Index to Deeds

Index to Wills. *See* (Cross) Index to Wills

Indigent Children, Record of. *See* Accounts of Indigent Children/Orphans

Inebriates, Record of. *See* Lunacy Records

Inebriety Docket. *See* Lunacy Records

Inferior Court. *See* Minute Dockets, Other Courts

Inheritance Tax Records: Twentieth-century record of settlement of tax assessed on estates worth more than $2,000 provided to the clerk of superior court by the State Commissioner of Revenue. Statements include names of deceased and administrator or executor, approximate valuation of estate, and heirs or devisees. Loose papers concerning inheritance tax are filed in Estates Records.

Inquest: An investigation conducted by a coroner, sometimes with the aid of a jury, into the cause of a sudden or unnatural death. A formal inquiry into any matter by a jury.

Inquisition of Incompetence, Record of. *See* Lunacy Records

Inquisition of Lunacy, Record of. *See* Lunacy Records

Insolvent: A person who is unable to pay debts or taxes.

Insolvent Debtors and Homestead and Personal Property Exemptions: Records relating to insolvent debtors (1773–1868) and homestead and personal property exemptions (1868–). Records include applications of debtors, oaths, notices to creditors, property schedules of insolvents, and reports of committees to lay off homesteads exempted from forced sales. May also include homestead returns.

Inventories and Accounts of Assignees, Record of. *See* Records and Accounts of Receivers and Trustees of Estates

Inventories of Estates: Detailed inventories of property of deceased persons filed by administrators and executors upon assuming administration of estates. Record of initial inventories of estates filed by administrators and executors; before 1868, may also include accounts of sale. May be recorded in Record of Estates/Accounts. *See also* Estates Records

Inventory: A list of property; a list of the property, usually excluding land, belonging to a decedent.

Journals and Ledgers of County Officials: Include account books of county officials, except those of clerks of court, county treasurer, county trustee, and committee of finance.

Judgment: The decision of a court; sentence passed by the court.

Judgment Docket, Superior Court: *See* Execution Docket, Superior Court. In many counties, the information formerly recorded in trial dockets (i.e., the actual "judgment" of the court in the case) was recorded in the judgment dockets.

Judicial Hospitalizations, Inebriety and Lunacy, Record of. *See* Lunacy Records

Juror: One of a number of persons sworn to deliver a verdict as a body; a member of a jury. At common law, jurymen were required to be freeholders, to be unrelated to either of the parties to the cause by blood or certain other relationships, and to live within the jurisdictional limits of the courts. Jurymen who sat on special juries called to hear slave cases were further required to be slave owners.

Jury: A body of persons sworn to give a true answer, or verdict, upon some matter brought to court. Such a verdict is based on the facts submitted to them by the parties to the case and the instructions on points of law as given them by the judge.

Jury Lists and Tickets: Include jury lists and tickets, arranged chronologically.

Jury Ticket: A statement of money due a juror for his service.

Justices of the Peace, Records of. *See* Records of Magistrates and Justices of the Peace

Land Divisions, Partitions, and Surveys: Include records concerning divisions of land between tenants in common and the processioning of boundary lines between contentious neighbors. Volumes may include Record of Surveys and Record of Processions. Loose papers may include petitions for partition or sale of land (culled from actions at equity and, after 1868, special proceedings) and processioners' records.

Land Entries: Include land entry books and boxes of loose entries. *See also* Entry, Land

Land Grants: Include Record of Grants and boxes of loose grants. *See* Patent

Land Records. *See* Miscellaneous Land Records

Land Sales for Taxes: Include volumes and boxes concerning the sale of land for nonpayment of taxes. Volumes may include Tax Levies on Land, Tax Suit Judgment Dockets, and Sheriffs' Deed Books. Papers from tax suits that resulted in the sale of land are arranged chronologically.

Ledger: A book of accounts.

Levy: To assess; to collect; to seize. A tax.

License: Legal authorization; a document granting formal authority to a person for some stated purpose; to grant such authority.

Lien: A claim, charge, or encumbrance on real or personal property for payment of some debt.

Lunacy, Record of. *See* Lunacy Records

Lunacy Docket. *See* Lunacy Records

Lunacy Records: A detailed record of hearings for commitment of insane and inebriates. Includes name of alleged lunatic, oaths of parties testifying to his lunacy, and copies of clerk's order of commitment and of superintendent of State Hospital's order of release. Records of lunacy inquisitions may include appointment of guardians to oversee the property of the unfit. After 1899, the clerk was required to keep lunacy matters in a distinct volume, entitled Record of Inquisition of Lunacy or Lunacy Docket. From 1868 to 1899, lunacy proceedings were recorded in the Orders and Decrees and Special Proceedings. Arranged chronologically.

Maiden Names of Divorced Women. *See* Divorce Records

Magistrate: A public civil officer invested with judicial and/or executive powers.

Magistrates, Records of. *See* Records of Magistrates and Justices of the Peace

Mark. *See* Flesh Mark

Marks, Brands, and Strays: Records relating to the registration of marks and brands on livestock, and to the recovery of lost animals. *See also* Estray; Flesh Mark

Marriage Bonds: Documents by which a prospective groom obligated himself to pay a stated sum if impediments to the marriage were subsequently discovered to exist.

Marriage Bonds and Certificates: Marriage bonds (used between 1741 and 1868) are statements of intent to marry that were attested by the prospective groom before the clerk of court in the bride's county of residence. Typically, one or more bondsmen signed as security for the forfeiture of the penal sum (originally 50 pounds, increased to 500 pounds in 1778, and to one thousand dollars in the nineteenth century) should the marriage not occur or prove to be illegal. Most marriage bonds give the names of the groom, bride, bondsmen and witnesses, the county in which filed, and the date. If accompanied by a marriage certificate, the information may also include the date of marriage, the name of the person performing the rites, and, towards the end of the period, the names of parents. The more than 170,000 marriage bonds in the Archives have been abstracted. Volumes of abstracts are available for each county from which bonds have been received. There is also a statewide index, arranged by both grooms and brides, available on microfiche. Arranged alphabetically by groom.

Marriage Certificate: A document completed by a minister or magistrate as evidence that he has performed a marriage; in North Carolina it is commonly printed as part of a marriage license.

Marriage Licenses: Documents giving a man and woman official permission to marry each other, or for a minister or magistrate to perform such a marriage. Includes licenses, applications for licenses, and record of licenses issued used after 1868. Licenses prior to 1868 are filed with the marriage bonds. May also include lists of marriage bonds and licenses. Arranged alphabetically by groom.

Marriage Records. *See* Miscellaneous Marriage Records

Marriage Register(s): A record of marriages performed within a given jurisdiction. Include record of marriage certificates (generally 1851–1867) and marriage registers.

Merchant and Professional Licenses and Registration Books: Certificates of registration of professionals practicing in a county, showing name and address and date of issue. Include registry of licenses to trades, a listing of merchants and other tradesmen subject to a license tax (Schedule "B"), and stub books of professional licenses for doctors, dentists, nurses, optometrists, chiropractors, and architects.

Military Records: Includes records relating to military service and militia activities. May include record of courts martial, minutes of Confederate veterans' associations, and rosters of soldiers from a particular county who served in the Civil War or World War I.

Militia: A body of citizens enrolled under local jurisdiction as a military force for periodic instruction, discipline, and drill but not called into active service except in emergencies.

Minor: A person under legal age, sometimes called "infant."

Minute Docket, Court of Pleas and Quarter Sessions: County courts of pleas and quarter sessions evolved from precinct courts in 1738. The courts were composed of three or more justices of the peace and sat four times each year. The functions of county courts may be categorized into three distinct areas: judicial, probate, and administrative. The courts exercised both civil and criminal jurisdiction, original and appellate (from magistrates' courts). Probate responsibilities included acknowledgment and probate of deeds; probate of wills; appointment and qualification of administrators, executors, and guardians, binding of apprentices; and inquisitions of lunacy. The court also served as the governing body of the county, responsible for the appointment and qualification of local officials, levying of local taxes, expenditure of public funds, granting of licenses (tavern keepers, ferry operators, and peddlers), registration of stock marks, paternity inquisitions, and emancipation and manumission of slaves. Courts of pleas and quarter sessions were abolished by the Constitution of 1868. The judicial functions devolved to county superior courts and justices of the peace courts; the probate function was vested in the clerk of superior court; and administrative responsibilities were inherited by the newly created boards of county commissioners.

Minute Docket, Superior Court: Superior courts were established in each county in 1806, replacing the district superior courts that had functioned since 1778. These courts were clothed with original and appellate civil and criminal jurisdiction, as well as actions in equity. Criminal jurisdiction extended to serious felonies, such as murder, rape, larceny, house breaking, assault and battery, riot, forgery, and the like; civil jurisdiction extended to suits involving $100 or more (after 1868, $200 or more). Extra-judicial matters assigned to superior court included legitimization of bastards, emancipation and manumission of slaves, registration of aliens, and hearing of grand jury presentments and reports. County superior court sat twice each year, spring and fall terms, with six judges riding circuit. Each county had separate clerks for law and for equity. The minute dockets record the daily transactions of the court, generally giving judgments in civil and criminal actions. They also reflect the internal workings of the court, recording the appointment and qualification of clerks, the summoning and impaneling of juries, and the hearing of grand jury reports.

Minute Dockets, Other Courts: Includes minute dockets from various inferior courts which were operational at times between the court reforms of 1868 and 1965, such as Criminal Court (in Craven, Mecklenburg, New Hanover, and Wake counties), Inferior Court (1877–1885), Circuit Criminal Courts (reconstituted as Eastern/Western District Criminal Courts, 1895–1901), Recorder's Court (1900–1970), and General County Court (1923–1970).

Minutes: An authoritative written summary of official proceedings.

Minutes, Probate Court. *See* Appointment and Record of Administrators; Appointment and Record of Guardians

Minutes of the Board of County Commissioners: Minutes of the board of county commissioners, the county administrative body after 1868.

Minutes of the Committee of Finance. *See* County Accounts and Claims

Minutes of the County Board of Education: Minutes of the county boards of education (1868–) and their predecessors, the boards of superintendents of common schools.

Minutes of the County Board of Health: Minutes of the county boards of health, created by statute in 1893.

Miscellaneous Court Records: Includes miscellaneous court records and dockets from both Court of Pleas and Quarter Sessions and Superior Court.

Miscellaneous Estates Records: May include records of probate of estates, including minutes of Probate Court (1868–1883); clerks' account and receipt books concerning estates; volumes concerning divisions of land and slaves of estates; account books of individual fiduciaries; and indexes. *See also* Estates Records

Miscellaneous Land Records: Contains records from other series of land records of insufficient quantity to make a full box. May also include condemnation proceedings; foreclosures; attachments, executions, liens, and levies on land; and records relating to the probate of deeds. Many titles may be specific to one or two counties.

Miscellaneous Marriage Records: May include indexes to marriages and miscellaneous marriage and family records. *See also* Marriage Bonds and Certificates; Marriage Licenses; Marriage Registers

Miscellaneous Records: Include records from other series, except land records, of insufficient quantity to make a full box. May also include records of slaves and free persons of color; bills of sale; promissory notes; canal and drainage records; shipping and fishing records; mill records; mining records; timber records; powers of attorney; grand jury records; witness tickets. Many titles may be specific to only one or two counties.

Miscellaneous Tax Records: Records relating to taxation. May include tax lists, civil and criminal actions concerning taxation, lists of insolvent taxpayers, tax receipts, and merchants' purchase returns. May also include Record of Federal Direct Taxes Collected, Poll Tax Register, Record of Assessment of Land for Taxation, and Schedule "B" Taxes.

Mortgage: A limited conveyance of property to secure a debt, upon condition that the conveyance is void if the debt is discharged.

Mortgagee: A person to whom property is mortgaged.

Mortgagor: A person who mortgages property.

Naturalization: The process by which a person, not native born, becomes a citizen.

Naturalization Records. *See* Alien, Naturalization, and Citizenship Records

Next Friend: One acting in a court in behalf of a minor orphan, married woman, or other incompetent without being a regularly appointed guardian.

Nol. Pros.: Not prosecuted; not prosecuted further.

Oath(s): A pledge made under an immediate, expressed sense of responsibility to God for the truth of a statement or intention to discharge some duty faithfully. Include loyalty oaths of ex-Confederates and oaths of county officials.

Official Reports, Record of. *See* County Accounts and Claims

Officials' Bonds (and Records): Bonds of various county officials. In some counties, there are sufficient quantities to make up separate boxes of constables, sheriffs, or clerks bonds. May also include record or register of officials' bonds. Some counties also include appointments, oaths, resignations, and civil and criminal actions involving county officials; in others, these are filed among the miscellaneous records. Arranged alphabetically by office, then chronologically.

Orders and Decrees and Special Proceedings: Include volumes created in the hearing of special proceedings before the clerk: special proceedings (summons) docket, clerk's minute docket, orders and decrees, and (cross) indexes. Special proceedings case files were usually appraised and distributed among other series, especially estates and guardians' records, land divisions, partitions and surveys, miscellaneous land records, and miscellaneous records. In Forsyth, Gaston, and Sampson counties, the files were kept in their original sequence and are included in this series. *See also* Special Proceeding

Ordinary: A judicial officer or court with power over wills, administration, guardianship, and other probate matters. A public house where meals were provided at a fixed price and that frequently served as the social center of a community. *See also* Tavern, since the terms were often used interchangeably.

Orphan: A child whose father and mother are dead; formerly a child whose father was dead but whose mother may have been living.

Orphan's Court. *See* Guardians' Dockets

Other Bonds: Includes tavern (ordinary) bonds and miscellaneous bonds.

Other Dockets, Court of Pleas and Quarter Sessions: May include levy docket; costs docket; allowance docket; clerk's account, fee, and receipt books; prosecution bond docket; witness fee docket; writs docket; and petition docket.

Other Dockets, Other Courts: Includes criminal issues dockets, judgment dockets, execution dockets, clerk's minute dockets, costs dockets, and half fee dockets from various inferior courts.

Other Dockets, Superior Court: Include costs or fee dockets; motion dockets; transfer dockets; clerk's account, fee, or receipt books; presentment dockets; and clerks' minute dockets (not special proceedings). Other titles may be specific to one or two counties. Other miscellaneous dockets specific to one or two counties are also included.

Overseer: A minor county official in charge of some area of responsibility, frequently the local roads.

Owelty: The amount paid or secured by one owner to another to equalize a partition of property in kind.

Partition: A division of real property between co-owners or co-inheritors, either by physical division among the parties or by court-ordered sale and division of proceeds. *See also* Division

Partnership(s): A contract by which two or more persons join together in business with the understanding that they will share proportionately in its profits and losses. *See* Assumed Business Names, Corporations, and Partnerships

Patent: An instrument whereby a government conferred some right or privilege; especially, a document by which the government transferred vacant land to a private person; often called a land grant.

Pauper: A person so poor that he must be supported at public expense.

Pension Records: Include records concerning the issuance of pensions for Confederate service. The clerk of superior court served as chairman of the county pension board and maintained the records of application and examination of prospective pensioners, and of payment and receipt of pensions.

Permanent Registration of Voters. *See* Election Records

Personal Accounts: Include personal and merchants' accounts. The majority of these records were probably submitted in court as evidence in civil actions for debt, but became separated from the case files. Arranged chronologically.

Petition: A formal written request by an individual to some governmental authority for action on some matter.

Petitions Dockets. *See* Appearance Docket(s)

Petitions for Naturalization. *See* Alien, Naturalization, and Citizenship Records

Plaintiff: The person who commences an action or suit; the injured party who seeks redress of a wrong or protection of a right.

Plat: An officially prepared map of a parcel of land drawn to an identified scale and used to describe the land in recorded transfers of title.

Plea: A written statement in support of his cause made to the court by a party to a suit or action.

Pleas: A designation for a court having jurisdiction over civil matters.

Pleas and Quarter Sessions, Courts of: County courts that met four times a year and had jurisdiction over minor civil actions (Pleas) and criminal matters not punishable by loss of life or limb (Quarter Sessions), and also had administrative jurisdiction over such things as public roads, bridges, mills, licensing of ordinaries, and oversight of tax collection. The county court system, under this and other names, existed in North Carolina from 1670 to 1868.

Poll: Head; an individual person; a person liable for payment of a head (poll) tax, as opposed to property or income taxes.

Poll List: A list of persons voting in a given place in a given election.

Poll Tax: A head tax.

Poll Tax Register. *See* Miscellaneous Tax Records

Power of Attorney: Authorization to act for another outside a court of law. A power of attorney carries the power to act in general or only in a specific matter.

Presentment: A statement of any offense or unlawful state of affairs made by a grand jury from their own knowledge or observation.

Probate: Court procedure for proving the authenticity and validity of a will or deed; by extension, the term has come to include all matters and procedures connected with estates.

Probate Court, Minutes. *See* Appointment and Record of Administrators; Appointment and Record of Guardians

Probate (Estates), Record of. *See* Appointment and Record of Administrators; Appointment and Record of Executors; Appointment and Record of Guardians

Proceeding: Generally, the form and manner in which the court conducts its business. Any step taken in conducting litigation(s). Any action, hearing, investigation, inquest, or inquiry conducted by an agency or person authorized by law.

Processioning: Determining the boundaries of land by physically walking them in company with an authorized "processioner" and the owners of adjoining land.

Processions, Record of. *See* Land Divisions, Partitions, and Surveys

Prosecution: A court proceeding to determine the guilt or innocence of a person charged with a crime. The pursuit of a court action to its conclusion.

Quarter Sessions: Designates a court that meets four times a year to hear minor criminal cases.

Quitclaim Deed: A deed by which one person releases to another whatever title or interest he has or may have in property, without any guarantee that such title is valid; most commonly associated with land divisions and estate settlements.

Real Property: Land and anything permanently attached to it (such as buildings, fences, and trees).

Receiver: A person entrusted to hold property subject to litigation while a suit is pending. A trustee appointed by the court to hold the property of an insolvent pending sale and settlement of debts. In criminal law, one who receives stolen goods.

Receivers of Estates, Record of. *See* Records and Accounts of Receivers and Trustees of Estates; Records of Assignees, Receivers, and Trustees

Recognizance: An obligation, entered into before a court or magistrate, to perform or refrain from performing some act (such as appearing in court or keeping the peace) on penalty of payment of a specified sum to a specified party.

Recognizance Docket, Court of Pleas and Quarter Sessions: Record of persons expected and required to appear at term in criminal prosecutions.

Recognizance Docket, Superior Court: Record of persons expected and required to appear at term in criminal prosecutions.

Record of Assessment of Land for Taxation. *See* Assessment of Land for Taxation, Record of

Record of Assumed Business Names. *See* Assumed Business Names, Corporations, and Partnerships

Record of Dowers and Widows' Year's Support: Copies of reports of commissioners appointed to partition estates and allot widow's dower. Volumes relating to the apportionment of widows' dower rights in the real property of her deceased husband, and the allocation of a sufficiency of provisions to enable her to support herself and family during the first year after his death, while the estate was being settled. Papers concerning dower and widows' year's support are filed in the estates records under the name of the deceased husband. *See also* Year's Allowance; Year's Provisions

Record of Estates/Accounts: Copies of annual accounts filed with the clerk by guardians, administrators, executors, and other fiduciaries. Usually includes disbursements, inventories, accounts of sales of estates, and other special accounts. Prior to 1868, this series includes inventories, accounts and final settlements of estates, and guardians' accounts. After 1868, the series in most counties contains only inventories, accounts of sales, and annual accounts of administrators and executors. *See also* Guardians' Accounts; Inventories of Estates

Record of Federal Direct Taxes Collected. *See* Miscellaneous Tax Records

Record of Grants. *See* Land Grants

Record of Incorporation. *See* Assumed Business Names, Corporations, and Partnerships

Record of Inquisition of Lunacy. *See* Lunacy Records

Record of Inventories and Accounts of Assignees. *See* Records and Accounts of Receivers and Trustees of Estates

Record of Official Reports. *See* County Accounts and Claims

Record of Partnerships. *See* Assumed Business Names, Corporations, and Partnerships

Record of Probate (Estates). *See* Appointment and Record of Administrators; Appointment and Record of Executors; Appointment and Record of Guardians

Record of Processions. *See* Land Divisions, Partitions, and Surveys

Record of Receivers of Estates. *See* Records and Accounts of Receivers and Trustees of Estates

Record of Sale and Resale of Land: Twentieth-century record of land sold under foreclosure by trustees and mortgagees. Case papers from foreclosure actions may be filed in some counties as civil actions concerning land or as miscellaneous land records.

Record of Sales of Estates: These are accounts of the sale at public auction of personal property of deceased persons, listing each article sold and the amount received. Record of sales by administrators and executors of estates. Often included in record of estates/accounts or in inventories and accounts of sales.

Record of Settlements: Volumes of settlements or final accounts submitted by administrators and executors after the complete distribution of the assets of an estate.

Record of Surveys. *See* Land Divisions, Partitions, and Surveys

Record of Wills. *See* Wills

Recorder's Court. *See* Minute Dockets, Other Courts

Records and Accounts of Receivers and Trustees of Estates: Includes volumes of Record of Receivers of Estates, and Record of Inventories and Accounts of Assignees.

Records of Assignees, Receivers, and Trustees: Include records concerning assignees, receivers, and trustees appointed to settle the financial affairs of bankrupt individuals and businesses. In some counties, the records are merged into one chronological series; in others, the records of the three types of agents have been separated. Also includes accounts of assignees, receivers, and trustees.

Records of Magistrates and Justices of the Peace: Records concerning the appointment, election, qualification, and resignation of justices of the peace. May include the minutes of the Board of Magistrates, record of magistrates (1893–), and record of oaths.

Records of the Wardens of the Poor: Include records concerning the care of the poor and infirm, a function of the county before assumed by the State Board of Charities and Public Welfare in 1917. In colonial times, care for the poor was an ecclesiastical responsibility; records from this period may be found in vestry minutes. From 1777 to 1868, maintenance of the unfortunate was entrusted to the Wardens of the Poor; after 1868, the Board of County Commissioners assumed the responsibility. May include vestry minutes, minutes and accounts of the Wardens of the Poor, accounts and registers of the county home, and accounts of outside poor (impoverished persons living at home rather than in the county home).

Reference: A recommendation from one person to another (either specified or "to whom it may concern") concerning a third person. The court action whereby a cause is sent to a referee.

Reference Docket, Court of Pleas and Quarter Sessions: May serve one of three purposes: 1) to track suits not concluded on appearance docket but not yet ready to come to trial (usage rare after 1778); 2) to record causes referred to referee at law returnable during term, showing decisions of referees; or 3) to show civil cases referred to the present term for trial, in essence, a trial docket. Usually recorded in the same volume with trial and/or appearance dockets.

Reference Docket, Superior Court: Record of causes referred to referee at law returnable during term, showing decisions of referees.

Registration: An official recording.

Report: An official's information given to the court as a result of investigating a matter about which he had no first-hand knowledge.

Return: A written statement made to the court as to the facts concerning something done or observed by an official, as opposed to a report. The bringing back to the court of a writ, notice, process, or other instrument by the sheriff, constable, or like official.

Road Records: Include records concerning appointment of road overseers, reports on condition of roads, and petitions for new roads. May also include criminal actions concerning negligence of overseers and claims against the county for services on the roads. Records concerning bridges and railroads are also included in this series, usually as separate sub-series. May also include minutes of the county highway or good roads commission.

Sale and Resale of Land, Record of. *See* Record of Sale and Resale of Land

Sales of Estates, Record of. *See* Record of Sales of Estates

Schedule "B" Taxes. *See* Miscellaneous Tax Records

School Records: Include school census records, school registers, school fund account books, vouchers of teachers, and miscellaneous school records.

Scire Facias: "You make known"; a writ or a proceeding whereby one party to a matter of record is compelled to show cause why the other party to the matter should not have the advantage to which he is entitled by that record, or, in some cases, why that record should not be annulled.

Scire Facias Docket. *See* Guardians' Dockets

Settlement: An agreement between or among contesting parties. Closing; the conclusion of a transaction involving real property. The final disposition of an estate by a fiduciary.

Settlement of County Accounts with the Committee of Finance (or County Trustee). *See* County Accounts and Claims

Settlements, Record of. *See* Record of Settlements

Sheriff: A major county official; the chief executive and administrative officer, charged with keeping the peace, carrying out court orders, summoning juries, and the like.

Sheriffs' Deed Books. *See* Land Sales for Taxes

Special Proceeding: A broad term covering any proceeding at law that is neither a civil action nor a criminal action; the category includes many proceedings pertaining to estates and real property. *See also* Orders and Decrees and Special Proceedings

State (or Crown) Docket, Court of Pleas and Quarter Sessions: Criminal docket tracking appearance and trial of state prosecutions. During the colonial period, known as Crown Docket.

State Docket, Superior Court: Criminal docket tracking appearance and trial of state prosecutions. After 1868, known as Criminal Issues Docket. *See also* Criminal Issues Docket, Superior Court

Stock Mark. *See* Flesh Mark

Stray. *See* Estray

Subpoena: A writ commanding witnesses to appear in court under penalty of law. The process commanding a defendant in equity to appear and answer.

Suit: In equity, a proceeding by which a person sought the redress of a private injury or wrong for which there was no remedy at common law. After 1868 in North Carolina, when proceedings at law and in equity were merged, "suit" came to include any civil action brought by plaintiff against defendant.

Summons: A citation to appear in court addressed to a person named as defendant in an action and served (delivered) by a sheriff, marshal, etc.

Summons Dockets. *See* Appearance Docket(s); Civil Issues Docket, Superior Court; Guardians' Dockets

Survey: A determination of boundaries of a tract of land; the process of measuring the land boundaries.

Surveyor: A person (often a county official) who views land, makes scientific determination of its boundaries, and submits a written, verbal, and visual report of his findings.

Surveys, Record of. *See* Land Divisions, Partitions, and Surveys

Tavern: A public house or taproom where wine was retailed. *See also* Ordinary, since the terms were often used interchangeably.

Tax: A payment due to public authority, levied to meet the regular expenses of government and for special purposes as defined by law; to impose a levy.

Tax Levies on Land. *See* Land Sales for Taxes

Tax Records. *See* Miscellaneous Tax Records

Tax Scrolls: Tax rolls prepared by individual list takers, from which the official tax list is compiled.

Tax Suit Judgment Dockets. *See* Land Sales for Taxes

Taxable: Liable to taxation; a person so liable.

Taxables, Lists of: Tax lists, chronologically arranged.

Testate: A person who died having made a valid will; the state of having died leaving a valid will.

Testator: One who disposes of property by will.

Torrens Act: An act for registering title to land under the Torrens system, according to which the government guarantees properly registered title, simplifying transfers and making title insurance unnecessary. Modeled in 1858 by Sir Robert Torrens, after a method for recording ownership interest in ships.

Treasurer's Account Book. *See* County Accounts and Claims

Trial and Reference Docket, Court of Pleas and Quarter Sessions. *See* Trial Docket, Court of Pleas and Quarter Sessions

Trial and Reference Docket, Superior Court: Usually filed with trial dockets.

Trial Docket, Court of Pleas and Quarter Sessions: Record of civil causes expected to come to trial during term. Brings forward information from appearance docket and also shows pleadings of defendant, prior ruling by court, verdict, judgment, and final orders. In most counties prior to 1820, appearance, trial, and reference dockets were maintained in one civil docket at the convenience of the clerk. These combined dockets are generally included in this series. With the proliferation of cases after 1820, most clerks began keeping the various civil dockets in separate volumes.

Trial Docket, Superior Court: Record of civil causes expected to come to trial during term. Brings forward information from appearance docket and also shows name of parties, nature of action, pleadings of defendant, prior ruling by court, concluding verdict, judgment, and final orders. In most counties prior to 1820, appearance, trial, and reference dockets were maintained in one civil docket at the convenience of the clerk. These combined dockets are generally included in this series. With the proliferation of cases after 1820, most clerks began keeping the various civil dockets in separate volumes. This record series ended in 1868 so after that date this information was recorded in civil issues dockets. *See also* Civil Issues Docket, Superior Court

Trustee(s). *See* County Accounts and Claims; Records and Accounts of Receivers and Trustees of Estates; Records of Assignees, Receivers, and Trustees

Vestry: The laymen elected or appointed to act as trustees to oversee the property and assets of a parish. Colonial Anglican vestries also had some governmental powers and duties such as the processioning of land and care of the poor, indigent, and orphaned.

Vital Statistics: The records of birth and death in the form of certificates. These were not recorded prior to 1913.

Ward: A person under the care of a guardian.

Warden. *See* Guardian

Wardens of the Poor, Records of. *See* Records of the Wardens of the Poor

Western District Criminal Courts. *See* Minute Dockets, Other Courts

Widows' Dowers, Petitions for. *See* Record of Dowers and Widows' Year's Support

Will: The formal statement of a person's wishes regarding disposition of his property after his death. Such a statement is commonly made in a writing that it signed, sealed, declared, and witnessed.

Wills: Include record of wills and original wills. Many of the older record of wills may also record estates matters (inventories, accounts of sale, and final settlements) and deeds. Arranged alphabetically by decedent.

Wills, Record of. *See* Wills

Witness: One who is present and personally sees or hears a thing. A person called upon to establish the truth or authenticity of something under oath or by affirmation.

Witness Ticket: A statement of sums due a witness for his appearance in court.

Writ: An order issuing from a court requiring a specific act, or giving authority to have it done.

Year's Allowance; Year's Provisions: Foodstuffs and necessities allowed to a widow, upon her petition, for the support of herself and family for the year following her husband's death intestate. The year's provisions were based on an estimate by commissioners appointed by the court for that purpose, and were allotted to the widow out of her husband's goods and chattels prior to any other disbursal of his estate. *See also* Record of Dowers and Widows' Year's Support

Year's Support, Widow's. *See* Record of Dowers and Widows' Year's Support

INDEX

D

E

F

G

H

I

J